Manual of
Soil and Water
Conservation Practices

Manual of
Soil and Water
Conservation Practices

Gurmel Singh
C Venkataramanan
G Sastry
BP Joshi

Oxford & IBH Publishing Co. Pvt. Ltd.
New Delhi
(A Unit of CBS Publishers & Distributors Pvt Ltd *)*

CBSPD

CBS Publishers & Distributors Pvt Ltd

New Delhi • Bengaluru • Chennai • Kochi • Kolkata • Lucknow • Mumbai
Hyderabad • Jharkhand • Nagpur • Patna • Pune • Uttarakhand

Manual of
**Soil and Water
Conservation Practices**

ISBN-13: 978-81-204-0552-3
ISBN-10: 81-204-0552-8

© 1990, Gurmel Singh, C Venkataramanan, G Sastry, PB Joshi

CBS Reprint: 2017, 2019, 2023

OXFORD & IBH
New Delhi
(A Unit of CBS Publishers & Distributors Pvt Ltd)

Published by **Satish Kumar Jain** and produced by **Varun Jain** for
CBS Publishers & Distributors Pvt Ltd
4819/XI Prahlad Street, 24 Ansari Road, Daryaganj, New Delhi 110 002, India
Ph: 011-23289259, 23266861   Website: www.cbspd.com
                                    e-mail: delhi@cbspd.com

Corporate Office: 204 FIE, Industrial Area, Patparganj, Delhi 110 092, India
Ph: 011-4934 4934   Fax: 011-4934 4935   e-mail: publishing@cbspd.com;
                                    publicity@cbspd.com

Branches

- **Bengaluru:** Seema House 2975, 17th Cross, KR Road, Banasankari 2nd Stage, Bengaluru 560 070, Karnataka, India
  Ph: +91-80-26771678/79   Fax: +91-80-26771680   e-mail: bangalore@cbspd.com
- **Chennai:** 7, Subbaraya Street, Shenoy Nagar, Chennai 600 030, Tamil Nadu, India
  Ph: +91-44-26680620, 26681266   Fax: +91-44-42032115   e-mail: chennai@cbspd.com
- **Kochi:** 42/1325, 1326, Power House Road, Opp KSEB, Power House, Ernakulum Kochi 682 018, Kerala, India
  Ph: +91-484-4059061-65,67   e-mail: kochi@cbspd.com
- **Kolkata:** 147, Hind Ceramics Compound, 1st Floor, Nilgunj Road, Belghoria, Kolkata-700056, West Bengal, India
  Ph: +033-25633055, 033-25633056   e-mail: kolkata@cbspd.com
- **Lucknow:** Basement, Khushnuma Complex, 7 Meerabai Marg (Behind Jawahar Bhawan), Lucknow-226001, UP, India
  Ph : 91-522-4000032   e-mail: tiwari.lucknow@cbspd.com
- **Mumbai:** PWD Shed, Gala no 25/26, Ramchandra Bhatt Marg, Next to JJ Hospital Gate no. 2, Opp. Union Bank of India Noorbaug, Mumbai-400009, Maharashtra, India
  Ph: 022-66661880/89   e-mail: mumbai@cbspd.com

Representatives

- Hyderabad   0-9885175004   • Jharkhand   0-9811541605   • Nagpur   0-9421945513
- Patna   0-9334159340   • Pune   0-9923910676   • Uttarakhand 0-9716462459

Printed at   Chaman Enterprises, Daryaganj, New Delhi, India

Preface

The Manual is prepared to provide the present and prospective Soil and Water Conservationists with information to plan and implement the Soil & Water Conservation Programmes on Watershed basis efficiently. It is designed primarily for planners, executers, designers and post-graduate students of Universities. The Manual provides formally specifications, charts and drawings that can be used as a reference in planning and applying soil and water conservation practices on watershed basis in the field. The material on subject matter are set forth in such a manner and order, as to enable them to better understand and follow to a reasonable degree of uniformity, their approach to the problems of soil and water conservation and management.

In the revised Manual, Statistics on Land use, extent of soil erosion problems, achievement in terms of physical targets, etc., have been updated till Seventh Five Year Plan. More numericals with solution have been introduced. Topics like Agro-climatic zones, sediment retention structures, prediction models for runoff and soil loss agricultural drainage and Soil Conservation technology have been added to give more impetus to developmental aspects of soil and water conservation.

Suggestions for further improvement are welcome.

GURMEL SINGH
VENKATARAMANAN, C.
SASTRY, G.
JOSHI, B.P.

Preface

The Manual is prepared to provide the present and prospective Soil and Water Conservationists with information to plan and implement the Soil & Water Conservation Programmes on Watershed basis efficiently. It is designed primarily for planners, executers, designers and post graduate students of Universities. The Manual provides formally specifications, charts and drawings that can be used as a reference in planning and applying soil and water conservation practices on watershed basis in the field. The material on subject matter are set forth in such a happier and order, as to enable them to better understand and follow to a reasonable degree of uniformity their approach to the problems of soil and water conservation and management.

In the revised Manual, Statistics on Land use, extent of soil erosion problems, achievement in terms of physical targets, etc. have been updated till Seventh Five Year Plan. More numericals with solution have been introduced. Topics like Agro-climatic zones, sediment retention structures, prediction models for runoff and soil loss, agricultural drainage and Soil Conservation technology have been added to give more impetus to developmental aspects of soil and water conservation.

Suggestions for further improvement are welcome.

GURMEL SINGH
VENKATARAMANAN C.
SASTRY G.
JOSHI, B.P.

Contents

Contents

1

Problems of Soil Erosion and Achievements in India

1.1 Problems

Soil-water-plant resources are nature's gift to mankind. Overgrazing, deforestation, faulty cultivation (Plate 1 to 3), shifting cultivation and carelessly built roads in the catchment areas, have led to devastating effects downstream. These include gullying and floods leading to destruction of farm lands and villages; drop in flow during the dry season and consequent loss of crops; and siltation of reservoirs and canals. The problem has been further aggravated due to high rate of population growth—both, human and livestock, resulting in indiscriminate exploitation of natural resources, for meeting the ever-increasing demand for food, fodder, fuel, fibre and fertilizers. Thus continuous degradation of production base and imbalance in land-water-plant, human-animal systems is leading to ecological imbalance and economic insecurity, through severe soil erosion, both by water and wind and threat to the quality of our life and cultivation.

Even though no systematic survey for ascertaining the extent of various problem areas in the country has so far been conducted, it is estimated (Das, 1985) that out of a total reported geographical area of 329 m ha, about 167 m ha (about 51% of total) are affected by serious water and wind erosion, erosion due to shifting cultivation and erosion of culturable wastelands (Table 1.1).

The forms of soil erosion by water are sheet erosion (4–10 tonne/ha/year in red soil, 17–43 tonne/ha/year in black soil and 4–14 tonne/ha/year in alluvial soils), gully erosion (about 33 tonne/ha/year in ravine regions), hill side erosion (more than 80 tonne/ha/year in landslide, mine spoil areas, etc.), and stream bank erosion. (Plate 4 to 7).

In a recent analysis of annual soil erosion rates in India (Dhurva and Ram Babu, 1983), it was estimated that about 5334 m tonne (16.35 tonne/ha) of soil is detached annually due to agriculture and associated activities alone. The country's rivers carry about 2052 million tonnes (6.26 tonne/ha) of this, nearly 1572 m tonne (29% of the total eroded soil) are carried away by the rivers into the sea every year and 480 m tonne (10% of the total eroded) are being deposited in various reservoirs, resulting in the loss of 1 to 2% of the storage capacity.

The estimated 167 m ha of total problem are includes about 127 m ha, subject to serious soil erosion and 40 m ha degraded through gully and ravines, shifting cultivation, water-logging, salinity, alkalinity, shifting of river courses, desert area, etc. (Tables 1.2, 1.3 and 1.4).

1.2 Achievements

India can be counted among the foremost nations in the third world to have taken note of these serious problems of soil erosion and land degradation, with the beginning of the planned development in India in 1951.

Table 1.1 *Distribution of problem areas due to soil erosion under
various land utilization classes and different types of land degradations*
(Das, 1985)

| Soil erosion in land utilization classes | With 1981–82 data | | Remarks |
	Total area	Problem area	
1.0 Cultivated land			
1.1 Rainfed non-paddy	77.88	77.88	Rainfed Non-paddy-Net sown
			(Net irrigated + Upland paddy)
1.2 Current fallows	13.48	3.37	
1.3 Fallows other than current fallows	9.56	4.78	
1.4 Permanent pastures grazing land	12.01	4.16	
1.5 Misc. tree crops and groves	3.62	0.72	
1.6 Cultivable wasteland	16.41	8.29	
Sub-total of 1.0	132.96	99.20	
2.0 Forest Land			
2.1 Reserve forest	39.01	3.90	
2.2 Protected forest	23.21	9.28	
2.3 Unclassed forest	12.63	6.31	
Sub-total of 2.0	74.85	19.49	
3.0 Area not available for agriculture and not under forest			
3.1 Non-agricultural use	19.51	3.90	
3.2 Barren and unculturable	20.22	4.03	
Sub-total of 3.0	39.73	7.93	
4.0 Degraded lands			
4.1 Gullies and Ravines	3.98	3.98	Table lands not included
4.2 Shifting cultivation	4.36	4.36	With increased figure from Orissa mainly
4.3 Water logged area	8.53	8.53	Includes area sub. to surface flooding as RBA*
4.4 Alkali soils	3.58	3.58	3.88 lakh ha increase for U. P., Punjab, & Haryana
4.5 Saline soil	4.04	4.04	Some report incomplete—55 lakh ha is as per
4.6 Coastal sandy areas	1.47	1.47	Anon. 1984. As per NCA such area ranges from
4.7 Riverain lands and torrents	2.73	2.73	5 to 8 m ha and av. is 6.5 m ha
			Figures from H. P., Assam & Sikkim not available
4.8 Desert	22.25	11.77	According to Report of NCA, 32 m ha are subject to wind erosion including 23.49 m ha of desert in Rajasthan, Haryana, & Gujarat. Latest figure for Rajasthan is less
Sub-total of 4.0	50.94	40.46	
Grand total of 1.0 to 4.0	298.48	167.08	

* Rashtriya Barh Ayog

Table 1.2 *Categories of degraded land in India*

Degraded land category	(Area-m ha)
Rainfed non-paddy areas	77.88
Other cultivable land including permanent pastures and cultivable wastelands	21.32
Forest land including protected and unclassified forest	19.49
Area not available for cultivation	7.93
Special problems such as gullied, ravines, alkali and saline lands, etc.	40.46
Total	167.08

Table 1.3 *State wise distribution of estimated affected area by soil erosion under various land utilization classes (Das, 1985)*

Sl. No.	State/U.T.	Total cultivable land	Forest lands	Permanent pastures and grazing grounds	Non-cultivable Barren lands	Non-agril. uses	Total for the State	Remarks
1.	Andhra Pradesh	9.095	1.148	0.367	0.454	0.438	11.502	Total cultivable lands
2.	Assam	0.770	0.883	0.074	0.308	0.182	2.217	include rainfed non-
3.	Bihar	2.634	1.021	0.056	0.202	0.347	4.260	paddy current fallow,
4.	Gujarat	8.410	0.484	0.336	0.500	0.216	9.946	fallow other than
5.	Haryana	1.440	0.056	0.010	0.014	0.071	1.591	current fallow miscel-
6.	Himachal Pradesh	0.585	0.839	0.442	0.024	0.024	1.914	laneous, tree crops &
7.	Jammu & Kashmir	0.510	0.210	0.048	0.055	0.060	0.883	groves and cultivable
8.	Karnataka	9.314	0.764	0.526	0.169	0.216	10.989	wastelands. The
9.	Kerala	1.503	0.180	0.002	0.017	0.055	1.757	problem area of the
10.	Madhya Pradesh	14.145	4.100	0.451	0.469	0.445	19.610	above lands has
11.	Maharashtra	16.412	1.592	0.633	0.346	0.198	19.181	been estimated to
12.	Manipur	0.005	0.080	—	0.284	0.005	0.374	be 25, 50, 20 and
13.	Meghalaya	0.479	0.289	0.007	0.046	0.017	0.838	50% of total
14.	Nagaland	0.271	0.128	—	—	0.006	0.405	area, respectively.
15.	Orissa	2.368	1.807	0.224	0.053	0.126	4.578	The problem area has
16.	Punjab	0.809	0.093	0.002	0.018	0.085	1.007	been estimated to
17.	Rajasthan	17.213	1.061	0.734	0.592	0.302	19.902	be 10% of reserved
18.	Sikkim	0.166	0.045	0.041	0.041	0.010	0.303	forests, 40%
19.	Tamil Nadu	2.707	0.398	0.066	0.116	0.353	3.640	protected, 50% of
20.	Tripura	0.021	0.122	—	0.024	—	0.167	unclassed forests,
21.	Uttar Pradesh	5.093	1.212	0.119	0.222	0.464	7.110	20% of barren
22.	West Bengal	0.479	0.269	0.002	0.024	0.259	1.033	total lands, and
23.	Arunachal Pradesh	0.131	2.286	0.020	0.004	0.003	2.444	20% of total
24.	Mizoram	0.243	0.134	0.002	0.040	0.002	0.421	non-agricultural
25.	Andaman & Nicobar	0.032	0.225	0.002	—	—	0.259	use lands.
26.	Chandigarh	—	—	—	—	0.001	0.001	
27.	Delhi	0.062	0.001	—	0.004	0.007	0.074	
28.	Goa, Daman, Diu	0.128	0.065	—	0.003	0.004	0.200	
29.	Pondicherry	0.001	—	—	—	0.002	0.003	
30.	Dadra, Nagar Haveli	0.010	0.002	—	—	—	0.012	
	Total	95.030	19.494	4.164	4.029	3.898	126.620	

Till 1987–88 both under state (29.34 m ha) and central (2.74 m ha) sectors, about 32.08 m ha of agricultural and non-agricultural lands have been treated, by various soil conservation measures and under special programmes at an expenditure of about Rs.1739 crores. (Table 1.5)

Table 1.4 *State wise distribution of estimated area under special problems of degradation (Das, 1985)*

(Area-m ha)

Sl. No.	States/U.T.	Gully and Ravine	Shifting cultivation	Water logged NCA	Water logged RBA by surface flooding	Alkali soils	Saline including coastal saline sandy area	Riverain lands Diara/ Khader Chaur	Riverain lands Torrents/ Chos, Khad	Desert	Total for States
1.	Andhra Pradesh	—	0.150	0.339	—	0.064	0.176	—	—	—	0.729
2.	Assam	0.193*	0.139	—	0.450	—	—	NA	—	—	0.792
3.	Bihar	0.600	0.081	0.117	0.590	0.004	—	0.900	—	—	2.292
4.	Gujarat	0.400	—	0.484	—	0.942++	0.100	0.010	—	0.704	2.640
5.	Haryana	**	—	0.620	—	0.450	0.076	0.025	NA	1.400	2.571
6.	Himachal Pradesh	*	—	—	—	—	—	NA	NA	—	—
7.	Jammu & Kashmir	—	—	0.010	—	—	—	—	—	—	0.010
8.	Karnataka	—	—	0.010	—	0.076	0.328	—	—	—	0.414
9.	Kerala	—	—	0.061	—	—	0.117	—	—	—	0.178
10.	Madhya Pradesh	0.683	0.125	0.057	—	0.164	0.078	—	—	—	1.107
11.	Maharashtra	0.020	NA	0.111	—	0.059	0.475	—	—	—	0.665
12.	Manipur	—	0.360	—	—	—	—	—	—	—	0.360
13.	Meghalaya	—	0.265	—	—	—	—	—	—	—	0.265
14.	Nagaland	—	0.077	—	—	—	—	—	—	—	0.077
15.	Orissa	0.113	2.648	0.060	—	—	0.404	—	—	—	3.225
16.	Punjab	0.120**	—	1.090	—	0.718	—@	0.045	0.250	—	2.223
17.	Rajasthan	0.452	—	0.348	—	++	1.000	—	—	9.692	11.492
18.	Sikkim	—	—	—	—	—	—	—	NA	—	—
19.	Tamil Nadu	0.060	NA	0.018	—	0.004	0.100	—	—	—	0.182
20.	Tripura	—	0.112	—	—	—	—	—	—	—	0.112
21.	Uttar Pradesh	1.230	—	0.810	1.170	1.100	0.195	1.500	NA	—	6.005
22.	West Bengal	0.104	—	1.850	0.330	—	0.986	NA	NA	—	3.270
23.	Arunachal Pradesh	—	0.210	—	—	—	—	—	—	—	0.210
24.	Mizoram	—	0.189	—	—	—	—	—	—	—	0.189
25.	Delhi	-	—	0.001	—	—	—	—	—	—	0.001
	Total	3.975	4.356	5.986	2.540	3.581	5.500 (4.035 +1.465)	2.480	0.250	11.796	40.464

* Combined figure for Himalayan foot hills in Assam and Himachal Pradesh

** Figure for united Punjab including Haryana

++ Includes the areas of arid Rajasthan and Gujarat

@ Includes saline areas of arid Rajasthan and Runn of Kutch

1.3 Programme

With a view to checking soil erosion, soil and moisture conservation programmes were launched both under state as well as central sectors during the Five Year Plans.

COMPONENTS OF SOIL AND WATER CONSERVATION

The main components of soil and water conservation on different types of lands and various programmes have been as under:

(a) *Agricultural lands*: Bunding, terracing, land sloping, levelling, contour

Table 1.5 *State wise total problem areas, areas treated and balance yet to be treated (Das, 1985)*

SI. No.	States/U.T.	Total problem area		Total problem area	Area treated till 1987–88	Balance to be treated
		Due to soil erosion	Land degradation			
1.	Andhra Pradesh	11.502	0.729	12.231	0.927	11.304
2.	Assam	2.217	0.782	2.999	0.191	2.808
3.	Bihar	4.260	2.292	6.552	1.285	5.267
4.	Gujarat	9.946	2.640	12.586	2.381	10.205
5.	Haryana	1.591	2.571	4.162	0.497	3.665
6.	Himachal Pradesh	1.914	—	1.914	0.276	1.638
7.	Jammu & Kashmir	0.883	0.010	0.893	0.222	0.671
8.	Karnataka	10.989	0.414	11.403	3.260	8.143
9.	Kerala	1.757	0.178	1.935	0.434	1.501
10.	Madhya Pradesh	19.610	1.107	20.717	4.102	16.615
11.	Maharashtra	19.181	0.665	19.846	10.125	9.721
12.	Manipur	0.374	0.360	0.734	0.099	0.635
13.	Meghalaya	0.837	0.265	1.102	0.102	1.000
14.	Nagaland	0.405	0.077	0.482	0.088	0.394
15.	Orissa	4.578	3.225	7.803	0.724	7.079
16.	Punjab	1.007	2.223	3.230	0.630	2.600
17.	Rajasthan	19.902	11.492	31.394	1.628	29.766
18.	Sikkim	0.303	—	0.303	0.109	0.194
19.	Tamil Nadu	3.640	0.182	3.822	1.244	2.578
20.	Tripura	0.167	0.112	0.279	0.122	0.157
21.	Uttar Pradesh	7.110	6.005	13.115	3.148	9.967
22.	West Bengal	1.033	3.270	4.303	0.344	3.959
23.	Arunachal Pradesh	2.444	0.210	2.654	0.008	2.646
24.	Goa	0.200	—	0.200	0.027	0.173
25.	Mizoram	0.421	0.189	0.610	0.005	0.605
Union Territories						
26.	A & N Islands	0.259	—	0.259		
27.	Chandigarh	0.001	—	0.001		
28.	Dadra, Nagar Haveli	0.012	—	0.012	0.096**	0.254**
29.	Delhi	0.074	0.001	0.075		
30.	Daman, Diu	—	—	—		
31.	Lakshadweep	—	—	—		
32.	Pondicherry	0.003	—	0.003		
		126.620	38.999	165.619	32.074	133.545
			1.465*	1.465*		1.465
			40.464	167.084	-	135.010

* Coastal sandy not reported statewise.   ** Total for SI No. 26 to 32

cultivation and planting, water escapes and outlets for removal of excess water, follow up with improved crop technology (to be carried out through extension services).

(b) *Non-agricultural lands*: Closures, afforestation, raising of utility trees, plantations, grasslands development, contour trenching, stone walls, etc.

(c) *Engineering measures*: Engineering measures like water harvesting and silt detention structures, treating gullies, stream banks, landslides and slips, mine spoils, etc., in both agricultural and non-agricultural lands.

(d) *Reclamation/restoration of degraded lands*: Particularly alkali soils, ravines, shifting cultivation areas, coastal saline lands, sand dune stabilization, etc.

SOIL AND WATER CONSERVATION PROGRAMMES
The following soil and water conservation programmes are being carried out by the central as well as the state governments under central/centrally sponsored foreign aided programmes during the Seventh Five Year Plan.

(a) *Soil conservation in catchment of river valley project (RVP)*

Year of start: Third Five Year Plan.
Objective: Treating the catchment areas for reducing silt production rate and subsequent siltation of the costly reservoir, thereby increasing their useful life. The scheme also helps to improve the productivity of the catchments by checking land erosion.

(b) *Integrated Watershed Management in the Catchments of Flood Prone Rivers (FPR).*

Year of start: Fourth Five Year Plan.
Objective: Mitigate flood hazards, improve productivity of catchment area.
Area of operation: Catchments of eight flood prone rivers in the Gangetic Basin namely Ajoy, Gomti, Punpun, Roopnarain, Sahibi, Sone, Upper Ganga and Upper Yamuna. The total area of these eight catchments is 16.7 m ha and covers parts of the states of Bihar, Haryana, Himachal Pradesh, Madhya Pradesh, Rajasthan, Uttar Pradesh, West Bengal and the union territory of Delhi.
Programme: Integrated watershed management in priority watersheds covering all types of land.
Achievement: The area treated up to 1987–88 is 0.28 m ha, out of an estimated 7 m ha of priority area (4%), with an expenditure of nearly Rs. 66 crores.

(c) *Drought Prone Area Programme (DPAP)*

Year of start: 1970–71
Objective: Integrated area development programme for restoration of ecological balance and optimum utilization of land, water, livestock and human resources, to mitigate the effects of drought.
Area of operation: The scheme operates in 615 blocks of 91 districts in 13 states. The total area covered by the programme is about 53.6 m ha (19% of geographical area of the concerned states). The population covered is 70.75 m.
Programme: Soil and moisture conservation including proper land use practices, water harvesting, afforestation, development of pastures and fodder resources are the major activities.
Achievement: Up to 1987–88, an area of about 2.1 m ha has been treated with soil and moisture conservation, 1.2 m ha has been covered under forestry and pasture development and irrigation potential has been created for nearly 0.8 m ha. The total investment up to 1987–88 has been about Rs.934 crores.

(d) Desert Development Programme (DDP)

Year of start: 1977–78

Objective: Mitigating the effect of drought in the desert areas, control desertification, restore ecological balance and raise the productivity of land, water, livestock and human resources.

Area of operation: 131 blocks of 21 districts in five states covering both hot and cold arid areas. The states covered are Rajasthan, Haryana, Gujarat (hot arid region), Jammu and Kashmir, Himachal Pradesh (cold arid region). The total area covered by the programme is about 36.2 m ha and the population covered is about 15 m.

Programme: Mostly sectoral programmes of different line departments. Afforestation, sand dune stabilisation, shelter belt plantation, grassland development, water resource development, soil and moisture conservation and development of livestock resources are the main activities.

Achievement: Up to 1987–88 the achievements are 1.37 lakh ha covered under forestry and pasture development, 0.67 lakh ha treated with soil and moisture conservation and irrigation potential created for nearly 0. 22 lakh ha. The total expenditure is about Rs.197 crores.

(e) National Watershed Development Programme for Rainfed Agriculture (NWDPRA)

Year of start: 1986–87

Objective: To conserve and upgrade both crop lands and culturable wastelands on watershed basis; to stabilize and increase crop yields from rainfed farming; to augment the fruit, fodder and fuel resources through appropriate alternate landuse systems; to develop and disseminate technologies for proper soil and moisture conservation.

Area of operation: The programme is being implemented in the unirrigated arable lands mostly falling in the rainfall range 500–1125 mm and also above. The programme covers 99 districts in 16 states. The districts having more than 30% area under irrigation are generally excluded.

Programme: The main components of the programme are as follows:

(i) Land and moisture management including scientifically tuned cropping system, dryland horticulture, fodder production and farm forestry.

(ii) Contingency seed and planting material stocking.

(iii) Training, seminars, study tours for staff and farmers within the state/ regional/ national level.

(iv) Adoptive research trials on different crops in small and marginal farmers fields.

(v) Procurement, fabrication and supply of survey equipment and prototype implements.

(vi) Preparation of field manuals publicity materials.

The pattern of expenditure per ha is Rs.1000 on land and water development, Rs.1000 on crop production technology and Rs. 500 for staff, contingencies, etc.

Achievement: Up to 1987–88, 1.13 lakh ha has been covered with a total expenditure of Rs.13.38 crores.

(f) *Soil, Water and Tree Conservation in the Himalayas (Operation Soil Watch)*

Year of start: 1980–81

Objectives: To provide stability to the fragile and vulnerable Himalayan eco-system through engineering as well as vegetative methods of soil and water conservation. The scheme aims at giving integrated production treatments to selected catchments/watersheds mostly within the reserved and other forest lands.

Area of operation: The programme is continuing in the Himalayan ranges covering parts of 14 states, viz. Jammu and Kashmir, Punjab, Haryana, Himachal Pradesh, Uttar Pradesh, West Bengal, Sikkim, Assam, Arunachal Pradesh, Nagaland, Meghalaya, Manipur, Mizoram and Tripura.

Programme: The main components are afforestation, pasture development, stabilization of slips, gullies, torrents and terracing of critically eroding agricultural lands.

Achievement: Up to 1987–88 a total of about 2.3 lakh ha have been covered with a total expenditure of about Rs. 61.7 crores.

(g) *Operational Research Projects on Integrated Watershed Management (ICAR)*

Year of start: 1983–84

Objectives: To develop a programme with peoples' participation for arresting the deterioration of our environment and building up permanent assets in the form of water, sustainable vegetation and improved productivity of our cropped land.

Area of operation: As many as 47 watersheds (17 with CSWCRTI, Dehradun and 30 with CRIDA, Hyderabad) spread over 16 states, viz. Andhra Pradesh (4), Bihar (2), Gujarat (3), Haryana (6), Madhya Pradesh (5), Maharashtra (5), Orissa (2), Punjab (1), Himachal Pradesh (1), Jammu and Kashmir (1), Karnataka (5), Kerala (1), Rajasthan (3), Tamil Nadu (2), Uttar Pradesh (9) and West Bengal (2), covering a total area of 35,739 na.

Programme: Integrated management of natural resources, viz. soil, water, plant, man and animal for optimizing production of food, fodder, fuel, fibre, etc., on watershed basis was implemented by the state government, in which ORP is located, on the basis of the master plans prepared for the watersheds by CSWCRTI, Dehradun and CRIDA, Hyderabad. Funds for the programme was provided by the Ministry of Agriculture and Rural Development, Government of India and under the technical guidance of the ICAR.

Achievement: In most of the model watersheds, small-scale water resource system surface as well as underground have been created. Significant increases in water storage and recycling of the stored water were accomplished in most of the watershed, resulting in increased crop yields. *In situ* moisture conservation practices, such as contour cultivation, mulching, flat-on-grade and ridging systems, preformed bed-furrow system, off-season tillage, etc., have been implemented in the farmers field in the watershed. Even in the year of a severe drought in the country in 1987, the efforts of watershed management have minimized the severity of hardships in the watershed (Dhruva Narayana *et al.*, 1987).

(h) *Reclamation of Alkali Soils (Usar) in the State of Haryana, Punjab and Uttar Pradesh*

Year of start: The new programme was initiated in Punjab during 1985–86 and in Haryana and Uttar Pradesh during 1986–87.

Objectives: Reclamation of alkali soils and saline soils.

Area of operation: To cover large areas of alkali soils and saline soils in an area of about 7 m ha (alkalinity 4.5 m ha and salinity 2.5 m ha) covering the state of Punjab, Haryana and Uttar Pradesh.

Programme: Treating alkali soils with gypsum.

Achievement: A total of about 3.75 lakh ha have been reclaimed in the state of Punjab, Haryana and Uttar Pradesh.

i) *Ravine Reclamation in the Dacoit Prone Areas of Uttar Pradesh, Madhya Pradesh and Rajasthan to accelerate their Development*

Year of start: 1980

Objectives: To check further spread of ravines into the adjoining productive table lands, improve the production of crops, fodder, fuel and other biomass, thereby improving the socio-economic conditions of the local people.

Area of operation: The scheme is in operation in 28 districts in the states of Uttar Pradesh (12), Madhya Pradesh (11), and Rajasthan (5).

Programme: The main components of the programme are peripheral bunding to check the spread of ravines, land development within 200 m along the peripheral bunds, afforestation of medium and deep ravines through manual planting and aerial seeding and reclamation of shallow ravines for cultivation with provision of irrigation.

Achievement: Till the end of the Seventh Plan, it is expected that an area of about 46,000 ha will be treated with an investment of Rs. 42.1 crores.

(j) *Control of Shifting Cultivation*

Year of start: 1986–87

Objectives: Restoring ecological balance in hilly areas and improving socio-economic conditions.

Area of operation: The programme is in operation in nine states (seven states of North Eastern Region, Andhra Pradesh and Orissa).

Programme: Settling nearly 25,000 Jhumia families on agricultural and plantation lands.

Achievement: About 2500 families have been settled over 5000 ha at a cost of about Rs. 2.17 crores.

(k) *World Bank Himalayan Watershed Project (Uttar Pradesh)*

Year of start: Seven years from 1983.

Objectives: Minimise deterioration of ecosystem. Improve productivity of all land uses.

Area of operation: Two watersheds in Garhwal and Kumaon regions of Uttar Pradesh covering 3.12 lakh ha.

Programme: Integrated watershed development.

World Bank Project on Watershed Development in Rainfed Area

Period of operation: Seven years from 1984.

Objectives: Develop technology for increasing crop and forage, fuelwood and timber yields in selected rainfed areas.

Area of operation: As much as 25,000 ha each in the states of Andhra Pradesh, Karnataka, Madhya Pradesh and Maharashtra.
Programme: Integrated development.

(m) *World Bank aided Kandi Development Project*

Period of operation: The Sixth and Seventh Plans
Objectives: Development of land, water and forest resource of Kandi area.
Area of operation: Kandi area in Punjab
Programme: Integrated development

(n) *Indo-EEC Watershed Management Project (Gujarat)*

Period of operation: Two and a half years from 1986.
Objectives: To increase agricultural production, fodder, fuel and help small and marginal farmers in tribal areas.
Area of operation: As many as 89 watersheds in 14 districts to cover about 50,900 ha in Gujarat state.
Programme: Integrated development

(o) *Indo-EEC integrated Watershed Management in Ravinous areas of Chambal and Uttar Pradesh*
Period of operation: Six years from 1987.
Objectives: To improve production of ravinous areas for agriculture, forests, to control ravines extension, to improve economic condition.
Area of operation: Parts of Agra and Etawah districts of Uttar Pradesh, covering 57,000 ha.
Programme: Integrated development

During the Eighth Five Year Plan (1990–91 to 1994–95), a total area of 14.565 m ha is likely to be treated, consisting of 11.425 m ha of agricultural land and 3.14 m ha of non-agricultural lands at a total cost of Rs.4,203.50 crores as compared to the Seventh Plan target of 7.5 m ha at an outlay of Rs. 826.27 crores.

During the Eighth Plan, additional biomass production is estimated to be of the order of

(i) 5 m tonnes of food grains, pulses, oilseeds;

(ii) 15 million cu m of biomass/annum from non-arable lands.

A total of 840 million man days of employment is expected to be generated with the above soil conservation plan.

The strategy for agricultural development during the Eighth Five Year Plan (FYP) is to achieve the national objectives of self-reliance, food security, generation of employment and improvement of the socio-economic condition of the small farmers. Realising the importance of land and water as life supporting resources, the important components of strategy should cover massive land development, reclamation of degraded lands and development of optional land use for different farming systems and other land uses as per the nature, capabilities, problems and potentials of the land and water resources in different physiographic-cum-agroclimatic regions and sub-regions of the country.

Soil and water conservation meaning proper land and water management on sustained basis, improving the productivity of these resources and stemming the deterioration assumes an important place in implementing the Eighth FYP strategy, so as to lead to sustained development and upward looking stable economy and it is more so, in the face of ever rising human animal population and increasing diversified competing demands on land and water.

1.4 National Land Resource Regions

Classification of land into land resource regions and areas is useful for determining the national soil and water conservation needs, for organising research and also for correlating the technical guides between the political divisions (states). This classification also helps in utilizing the research experience of one place to other places of similar soil climatic and topographic conditions. The CSWCRTI, Dehradun, therefore, prepared a land resource region and areas map of India, based on the available information on soil, forest areas, forest types, rainfall, land use and elevation of India (Gupta et al., 1970).

The country has been divided into 20 land resource regions (A, B, C, . . ., T) based on vegetation, soil and rainfall. All the islands of the country have been grouped into one region (Table 1.6). Region N (black soil region) has the largest area (67 m ha) followed by O region (eastern red soil region—57 m ha).

Table 1.6 *Areas of land resource regions*

	Area	Land (Area-m ha)
A)	Northern Himalayas snow clad region	11.600
B)	Northern Himalayas alpine grass and meadow region	9.825
C)	Northern Himalayas forest region	13.175
D)	Punjab-Haryana alluvial plain region	10.125
E)	Upper Gangetic alluvial plain region	20.000
F)	Lower Gangetic alluvial plain region	14.550
G)	North-Eastern Himalaya alpine grass and meadow region	1.600
H)	North Eastern forest region	16.100
I)	Assam valley region	8.850
J)	Rajasthan desert region	19.100
K)	Runn of Kutch region	4.050
L)	Gujarat alluvial plain region	6.275
M)	Mixed yellow, red and black soil region	11.575
N)	Black soil region	67.350
O)	Eastern red soil region	57.350
P)	Gangetic delta region	2.525
Q)	Western coastal region	6.100
R)	Southern red soil region	34.775
S)	Eastern coastal region	9.350
T)	Andaman, Nicobar and other islands	0.800
	Total for the country	325.675

Twenty land resource regions have been sub-divided into 186 land resource areas (1, 2, 3, . . ., 186). mostly based on the land use, e.g. forest, irrigated or unirrigated land. Unirrigated agricultural lands have been sub-divided into different land resource areas, depending upon rainfall and soil type. The rainfall zones of 0 to 10, 10 to 40, 40 to 80, 80 to 200 and 200 to 400 cm have been used and named as arid, semi-arid, sub-humid, humid, and per-humid, respectively.

Land resource area No. 137 in land resource region O (Eastern red soil region) is maximum (21 m ha). With this broad grouping of land resource region and areas, it is essential that land resource unit maps are prepared on large scale on state maps, using the detailed data available with the states. This will help to take into account the many details of local significance, which had to be omitted in the preparation of the National Land Resource Regions and Areas Map.

Recently (Das, 1977) the above land resource regions have been regrouped into ten soil conservation regions. The extent of area, rainfall and major problems are briefly discussed in Table 1.7.

Planning Commission (Khanna, 1989) has initiated Planning process of the Eighth Five Year Plan for the 15 agro-climatic regions, based on the criteria of homogeneity in agro-characteristics such as rainfall, temperature, soil, topography, cropping and farming systems and water resources.

Agro-Climatic Region (ACR)

(a) *Western Himalayan Region*

Area of operation: Sub-zones of Jammu and Kashmir, Himachal Pradesh and Uttar Pradesh Hills.

Characteristics: Skeletal soils of cold region of podsolic soils, mountain meadow soils and hilly brown soils, steep slopy lands, silt loam soils, prone erosion hazards and landslides and slips are quite common.

Thrust area	Strategy
Water conservation and use	Integrated watershed development programme including forestry, horticulture, commercial crops and fodder for animals
Land use planning	Using land as per its capability. Up to 30% slopes—suitable for agriculture on terraces. 30–50% slope—Horticulture and silvi-pastoral programme. Above 50% slope—Forestry
Crop diversification	High value and low value crops, such as pomology, olericulture, floriculture, medicinal and aromatic plants and tea
Post harvest technology	Storage and cold storage, transport, marketing and processing
Irrigation management	Water harvesting techniques, water saving devices such as drip, mist formation and sprinkler

Table 1.7 *Statement showing distribution of different soil conservation problems in various soil conservation regions of India*

Sl. No.	Soil conservation region	Area (m ha)	Rainfall (mm)	Important areas	Problems
1	2	3	4	5	6
1.	North Himalayan (excluding cold desert areas)	25.53	500–2500	Snow clad mountains, temperate, arid, semi-arid and sub-humid areas of J & K, hill areas and H. P. (Kundi areas)	Soil erosion along hill slopes, landslides, torrent management of ravine lands siltation of reservoirs, over grazing and deforestation
2.	North-Eastern Himalayas	17.70	1500–2500	North-eastern hills of Sikkim, Arunachal Pradesh, Meghalaya, Manipur, Mizoram, Assam, Nagaland, Tripura and West Bengal	Shifting cultivation, landslides, torrents and gullies, problem of riverine lands, siltation of reservoirs and stream beds
3.	Indo-Gangetic Alluvium soils	50.90	700–1000	Punjab, Haryana, North-Eastern Rajasthan, U. P., and Bihar plains, Chambal command in Rajasthan, command areas in Gujarat	Sheet erosion, ravines, floods, stream bank erosion, ravine lands, saline alkaline lands, water logging and riverine lands, prolonged dry spells and failure of rains, shortage of fuel and fodder
4.	Assam Valley and Gangetic delta	11.18	1500–2500	Plains of Assam, Tripura, North Bengal and Gangetic deltas, areas of West Bengal	Gully erosion, stream bank erosion, waterlogging, coastal salinity
5.	Desertic area	23.85	150–500	Western-Central Rajasthan, contiguous areas of Haryana and Gujarat, Runn of Kutch	Shifting sand dunes, wind erosion, extreme moisture stress and drought, overgrazing, improper land management
6.	Mixed Red, black and yellow soils	11.57	600–700	Districts of Pali, Bhilwara, Ajmer, Chittorgarh, Udaipur, Jhalawar and Southern U. P. (including Bundelkhand area) and Northern M. P.	Ravine, shortage of moisture, recurring drought, problem of drainage, overgrazing, improper crop technology, siltation of reservoirs and tanks
7.	Black soils (excluding shallow, medium and deep black soils)	67.45	Outer part 600–750–1000 inner 500–600	South-Eastern Rajasthan, part of Western Madhya Pradesh, large tracts of Maharashtra, Andhra Pradesh, Karnataka and small parts of Tamil Nadu	Sheet erosion, acute water shortage, recurring droughts, ill-drained soils and improper technology for agriculture and fodder, i.e., siltation of reservoirs, ground water recharge
8.	Eastern Red soils	57.45	1000–1500	Bulk of West Bengal, Bihar, Orissa and Eastern Madhya Pradesh including Chotanagpur and Chattisgarh area, part of Andhra Pradesh	Problem of sheet erosion, gullies, acute water shortage, recurring drought, heavy grazing and improper technology for crop husbandry and land management, siltation of reservoir and tanks

Table 1.7   *(Contd.)*

2	3	4	5	6
Southern red soils	34.77	Around 750 in Kerala up to 2500	Bulk of Kerala, Tamil Nadu hills and plains, Karnataka, Andhra Pradesh and part of Maharashtra	Problem of sheet eros or, gullies acute water shortage, recurring drought, lack of fodder and fuel, improper crop husbandry, siltation of reservoir and tanks, ground water recharge
D. East-West coasts	19.20	East-Coast about 1000 and rest heavy rain-fall	East and West Coast from Orissa to Saurashtra	Problem of coastal salinity, soil erosion, coastal sand dunes, wind erosion and flooding of cultivated lands by sea water or rain water.

Livestock management	Integrated approach to breeding, feeding and adequate health cover
Public finance	Credit support strengthening and simplified procedure

(b) *Eastern Himalayan Region*

Area of operation: Sikkim and Darjeeling Hills, Arunachal Pradesh, Meghalaya, Nagaland, Manipur, Tripura, Mizoram, Assam and Jalpaiguri and Cooch Behar districts of West Bengal.

Characteristics: High rainfall—high forest cover-shifting cultivation *(Jhum)*, practised in nearly one-third of the cultivated area, has caused denudation and degradation of soils with the resultant heavy runoff, massive soil erosion and floods in the lower reaches and basins.

Thrust area	*Strategy*
Soil and water conservation	Integrated watershed development programme
Improvement of farming system	Legislation and people's awareness about the ill effects of shifting cultivation
	Integrated farming system

(c) *Lower Gangetic Plains*

Area of operation: The West Bengal-Lower Gangetic plains region consisting of four sub-regions, namely Basind plains, central alluvial plains, alluvial coastal plains and rarh plains.

Characteristics: Frequent floods destroy standing crops in Basins and Central Plains:—Poor water management and drainage systems—Inadequate water harvesting techniques—Lack of well knit marine fisheries programmes

Thrust area	*Strategy*
Minor irrigation development	Supplemental irrigation, increase ground water exploitation

| Crop productivity improvement | Increase productivity in crops |
| Livestock, poultry and fisheries development | Integrated approach to breeding, feeding and adequate health cover, as well as development of marine fisheries. |

(d) Middle Gangetic Plains

Area of operation: As many as 12 districts of eastern Uttar Pradesh and 27 districts of Bihar plains.

Characteristics: An area of 16 m ha with a high population of 85 m; high rainfall with a cropping intensity of 142%. In Bihar plains, flood prone areas amount to about 1.7 m ha and problem area of diara lands account for 1.0 m ha.

Thrust area	Strategy
Crop productivity improvement	Increase rice productivity
Poultry, dairy and inland fisheries	Integrated approach to breeding, feeding and adequate health cover.

(e) Upper Gangetic Plains

Area of operation: As many as 32 districts of Uttar Pradesh (sub-zones of central, north-west and south-west)

Characteristics: This area has 131% irrigation intensity, 144% cropping intensity with 9 lakh ha problem soils.

Thrust area	Strategy
Crop productivity improvement	Increase rice productivity
Crop diversification	Increase area under fruits and vegetables
Processing and marketing	Agro-based industries
Dairy improvement	Breeding, feeding and adequate health cover.

(f) Trans-Gangetic Plains

Area of operation: Punjab, Haryana, union territory of Delhi and Chandigarh and Sriganga district of Rajasthan.

Characteristics: Highest net sown area, irrigated area, least poverty level, high cropping intensity, high ground water utilization.

Thrust area	Strategy
Water management soil correction	Maximise production per unit of land and water reclamation of salt affected lands
Crop diversification	Introduction of pulses, increased area under fodder, fruits and vegetables
Livestock management	Integrated breeding, feeding and management
Processing and marketing	Agro-based industries

(g) *Eastern Plateau and Hills*

Area of operation: (i) Sub-region of Wainganga, Madhya Pradesh eastern hills and Orissa inland; (ii) Orissa northern and Madhya Pradesh eastern hills and plateau; (iii) Chotanagpur north and eastern hills and plateau; (iv) Chotanagpur south and West Bengal hills and plateau; and (v) Chattisgarh and south-western Orissa hills.

Characteristics: Rainfall is high and soils are shallow and medium in depth. Topography is undulating with a slope of 1 to 10%. Tank irrigation and tubewell irrigation are adopted.

Thrust area	Strategy
Water conservation and use	Integrated watershed development programme, rain water harvesting and management
Minor irrigation development	Supplementary irrigation and increased ground water exploitation
Crop productivity improvement	Increase rice productivity
Horticulture development	Marketing and processing facilities
Soil correction	Reclamation of acidic soils by application of lime
Animal husbandry, fisheries, poultry duck farming development	Breeding, feeding and development
Rehabilitation of degraded land	Rehabilitation of peripheral forests on a large scale

(h) *Central Plateau and Hills*

Area of operation: As many as 46 districts of Madhya Pradesh, Uttar Pradesh and Rajasthan.

Characteristics: Ravine and hill topography. One-third of the land is not available for cultivation. Irrigation and intensity of cropping are low. The literacy percentage is low and the poverty percentage is high; 75% of the area is rainfed.

Thrust area	Strategy
Soil and water conservation	Integrated watershed development programme
Crop productivity improvement	Low value cereal crops to be substituted by high value ones
Minor irrigation development	Increase ground water exploitation
Crop diversification	Increase area under fruits and vegetable crops
Ravine area development	Reclamation of ravine land
Improvement of cattle productivity	Breeding and supply of better quality fodder

(i) *Western Plateau and Hills*
Area of operation: Major part of Maharashtra, parts of Madhya Pradesh and one district of Rajasthan.
Characteristics: Annual average rainfall is 904 mm. Net sown area is around 65%, forests occupy 11%, irrigated area by canal system is 12.4%. *jowar* and cotton are the major crops of the area—50% of the country's *jowar* production and one-fifth of the countries cotton production is from this region. This zone is well known for oranges, grapes and bananas. The area under fruit crop is 0.1 m ha.

Thrust area	Strategy
Minor irrigation development	Supplemental irrigation and increase ground water exploitation
Soil and water conservation	Integrated watershed development programme, rain water harvesting and management
Improvement of cattle productivity	Breeding and feeding

(j) *Southern Plateau and Hills*
Area of operation: As many as 35 districts of semi-arid zone of Andhra Pradesh, Karnataka and Tamil Nadu.
Characteristics: Rainfed farming comprises 81% of the area, cropping intensity is 111%, low value cereals and minor millets predominate in the cropping system.

Thrust area	Strategy
Minor irrigation development	Increase ground water exploitation
Crop diversification	Increase area under crops requiring low moisture
Horticulture development	Develop each year 0.5 m ha under mango, *ber*, pomegranate, citrus and guava
Improvement of cattle productivity	Breeding and feeding

(k) *East Coast Plains and Hills*
Area of operation: Orissa coastal, north coastal Andhra Pradesh and Ganjam, south coastal Andhra, north coastal Tamil Nadu, Thanjavur and south coastal Tamil-Nadu.
Characteristics: This zone accounts for 20% of all India production of rice and 17% of the total groundnut output. Alkaline and saline lands are found in the coastal areas and covers 4.9 lakh ha. Waterlogging is quite common.

Thrust area	Strategy
Fisheries	Development of fisheries
Soil and water conservation	Integrated watershed development programme
Water management	Maximise production per unit of land and water
Management of paddy lands	Integrated irrigation-cum-drainage system

Fisheries	Improvement of marine and brackish water fisheries and aquaculture
Improvement of farming system	Shifting cultivation to be replaced by an integrated horticulture-agricultural programme
Improvement of cattle productivity	Breeding and feeding

(l) *West Coast Plains and Ghats*

Area of operation: West coast covering parts of Tamil Nadu, Kerala, Karnataka, Maharashtra and Goa.

Characteristics: Important zone for plantation crop and spices. Literacy is the highest in Kerala and so is unemployment.

Thrust area	*Strategy*
Rain water management	Conserve rain water
Minor irrigation development	Increase ground water exploitation
Crop diversification	Increase area under fruits and vegetables
Fisheries development	Strengthen marine and inland fisheries
Soil correction	Reclamation of *Pokhali* lands

(m) *Gujarat Plains and Hills*

Area of operation: As many as 19 districts of Gujarat classified into seven sub-zones.

Characteristics: The zone is arid with low rainfall in most parts and only 22.5% of the area irrigated through wells and tubewells. As much as 50% of the cultivated area is occupied by food crops, rendering it a deficit zone. It is an important oilseed zone. Cropping intensity is 114%. About 60% of the area is considered drought prone and 78% of farming is rainfed.

Thrust area	*Strategy*
Water conservation and use	Integrated watershed development programme, rain water harvesting and management, development of water grid
Dryland farming	Evolve suitable technology for dryland farming
Water management	Maximise production per unit of land and water, check overdrawal of groundwater
Wasteland development	Develop agroforestry and arid horticulture

(n) *Western Dry Region*

Area of operation: As many as 9 districts of Rajasthan

Characteristics: This area is characterized by hot sandy desert, erratic rainfall, high evaporation, no perennial river and scanty vegetation. Ground water is deep and often brackish. Famine and drought are common features. Land-man ratio is high (1.73 ha/person). Average annual rainfall is only 395 mm, forest area is only

1.2%, land under pasture is also low (4.3%). The net irrigated area is only 6.3% of net sown area (44.4%), cropping intensity is just 105%. *Bajra*, *guar* and *moth* are the lead crops in *Kharif* and wheat and gram in *Rabi*—density of livestock is 1.08 animal/ha and 1.56 animal per person.

Thrust area	*Strategy*
Desert land development	Develop silvipastoral and energy plantation, sand dune stabilization
Water conservation and use	Integrated watershed development programme. *in situ* moisture conservation on practices

(o) *Island Region*

Area of operation: It comprises island territories of the Andaman and Nicobar Islands and Lakshadweep.

Characteristics: Rainfall is 3000 mm, spread over 8 to 9 months. Largely it is a forest zone with undulating areas leading to heavy loss of soil due to runoff. Half the cropped area is under coconut. It has a high literacy rate and low poverty level.

Thrust area	*Strategy*
Crop improvement	Maximise production for unit of land
Water management	Integrated watershed development programme, rainwater harvesting and management
Fisheries	Development of fisheries

2

Prerequisites for Soil and Water Conservation Measures

Soil conservation is by itself the proper land husbandry, which would preserve the land and its fertility on a sustained basis and at the same time promote better agriculture, increase yields and achieve maximum benefits from such land. Such land husbandry should be based upon proper classification of land utilization and balanced allotment of lands for the different purposes, for which various local conditions are suitable. In planning reorganization of a farm for efficiently controlling soil erosion, conserving moisture and improving the productivity of soil, the characteristics of the following factors and the mechanics of erosion by water and wind are to be assessed:

— Physiography (size, shape, relief and drainage)
— Soil properties (soil series and soil phases, physical, chemical and biological properties, hydrologic soil groups, soil moisture regime)
— Vegetative cover
— Land use practices
— Nature and distribution of rainfall
— Prediction of peak runoff rate
— Floods/droughts and
— Socio-economic factors

Since we cannot alter the climate and the inherent soil properties, we can do something to modify the other factors of topography and vegetation to reduce soil and water losses. And we can minimize the effects of climate and improve/maintain the properties of soil in such a way that erosion is controlled and moisture conserved, thereby resulting in improved production in the yield of agricultural, annual and perennial crops.

2.1 Physiography

SIZE
Both, runoff volumes and rates increase as watershed size increases. However, both rate and volume per unit of watershed area decrease as the area increases.

The size namely, area of watershed, is an important parameter in determining the peak rate of runoff. Computation of peak rate of runoff is essential for designing erosion control structures and channels to carry maximum runoff.

SHAPE
Long and narrow watersheds are likely to have longer times of concentration resulting in lower runoff rates than more compact watersheds of the same size. Use of

shape factor of a watershed in computation of peak rate of runoff (Cook's method) is described in the succeeding paragraph (peak rate of runoff).

RELIEF (H)

It is the elevation difference between any reference point on the basin with respect to outlet elevation. This is necessary for computing time of concentration, to compute the pump sizes required to lift water and deliver at any required point for supplemental irrigation, etc.

MEAN ELEVATION

The mean elevation (reduced to mean sea level) is necessary to plan developmental programmes, Ex.-cropping practices, afforestation and horticultural plantation, utilization of different sources of energy, etc.

LAND SLOPE

Slope has major implications for land use. The speed and extent of runoff depend on slope of the land. The greater the slope, the greater the velocity of flow of the runoff water. According to law of falling bodies, velocity varies as a square root of the vertical drop. Hence if the land slope is increased four times, the velocity of water flowing on the slope is doubled.

If the velocity is doubled, the energy and consequently the erosive or cutting capacity is increased four times. Thus the erosive capacity of runoff varies in direct proportion with the slope of a land on which the runoff occurs. Also, if the velocity is doubled, the quantity of material that can be carried is increased about 32 times and the size of the particles that can be transported by pushing or rolling is increased by about 64 times.

Land slope cannot be directly changed but can be modified in its effect on runoff by the use of transverse channels or terraces or by bunding along contours. By these methods, long slopes are divided into a series of short units, thus minimizing the velocity and the resulting runoff.

The land slope in per cent can be determined from a topographic map by the following formula:

$$S = \frac{MN}{A} \times 100 \qquad \qquad \ldots (2.1)$$

where, M = total length of all contours within a watershed (m);
N = contour interval (m); and A = area of watershed (m²).

The degree of slope sets limits on land use for annual crops, plantation and even on land reclamation, depending on soil depth, stoniness, etc. Hence, degree of slope and length of slope are important.

DRAINAGE

Factors affecting drainage of an area are required to assess the susceptibility to erosion, runoff pattern, sedimentation and locating erosion control structures and erosion thereof.

High drainage density affects runoff pattern, in that a high drainage density affects surface water rapidly decreasing the lag-time and increasing the peak of hydrograph.

$$\text{Drainage density} = \frac{\text{Total length of all streams (km)}}{\text{Catchment area (km}^2)}$$

DRAINAGE PATTERN

Drainage map of an area may serve as a beneficial precursor for the understanding and the preparation of an erosion assessment map, so necessary in the Watershed Management Programme.

Drainage pattern of an area refers to the design of the stream courses and their tributaries. It is influenced by the slope of the land, lithology and structure. The distribution and attitude of the rock systems and their arrangements also control the drainage pattern. A study of drainage pattern and drainage texture is helpful in the interpretation of geomorphic features and understanding land form evolution.

Fine drainage texture (Fig. 2.1) of dendritic pattern indicates that the rock formations are impervious and the permeability is low. Soils formed in such areas are deep, heavy and slowly permeable. They are subject to severe erosion hazards forming gullies at several places.

Drainage of medium texture (Fig. 2.1) is observed in rock formations characterised by fractures and joints. Permeability is moderate. The soils are moderately deep, medium in texture and moderately permeable. Usually drainage patterns of radial, braided and pinnate types are observed.

In drainage patterns of rectangular and angulate, normally coarse drainage texture is associated. Hydraulic conductivity is high. The soils are generally shallow and coarse in texture. Erosion hazards may be mostly due to steep slopes.

In general, coarser the drainage texture, higher is the conductivity. Also finer the drainage texture, heavier is the soil type.

Erosion hazards are relatively less in areas where trellis, annular, rectangular and annular drainage patterns are observed due to previous and resistant nature of the rock strata. Areas covered by drainage patterns and braided are subject to moderate to severe erosion hazards. In the areas where dendritic drainage pattern is observed, the erosion hazards are severe to very severe.

Drainage patterns can act as guidelines, to locate vulnerable areas requiring different kinds and degree of soil conservation measures.

2.2 Soils

SOIL SERIES

Soil series gives information about the nature of soil and the different soil forming processes taking place in a region, indicating the fertility status of the soil.

In studying about the soil properties, texture of the soil, soil depth, depth and occurrence of hard pans/*kankar* pans, etc., stoniness, permeability and soil reaction (soil acidity and alkalinity) are to be determined.

A large number of Indian soil series have been examined and based on the findings, India has been divided into four hydrological soil group zones—A to D. In arriving at these groups, four major characteristics of soil namely, effective depth (depth of soil readily penetrated by plant roots), average clay content in the whole profile depth, infiltration and permeability were taken into consideration. These groups are defined as:

HYDROLOGIC SOIL GROUP—A (LOW RUNOFF POTENTIAL)

Soils having high infiltration rates even when thoroughly wetted and consisting chiefly of deep, well to excessively drained sands and gravels. These soils have a high rate of water transmission.

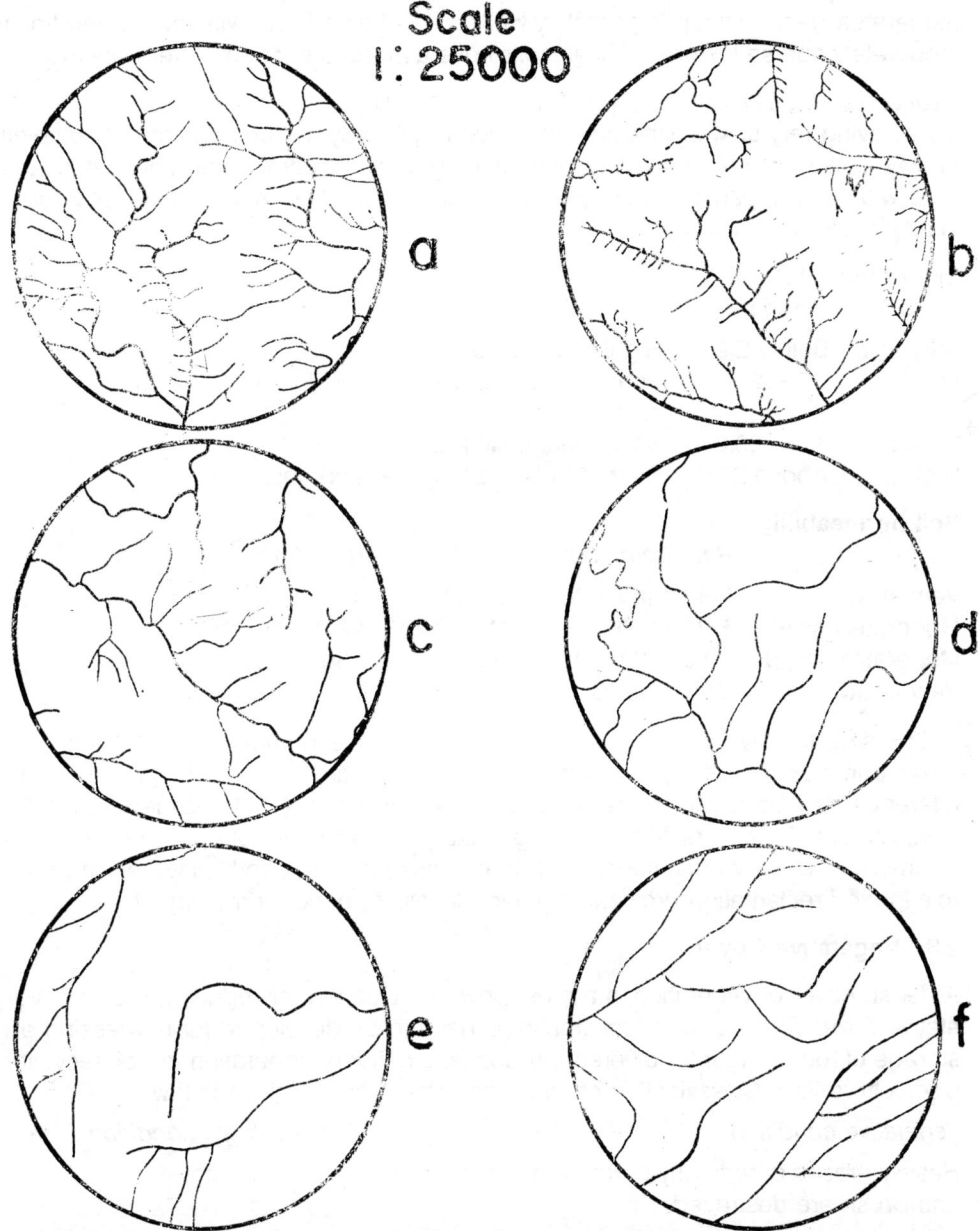

Fig. 2.1 (a) Fine drainage texture on Cuddapah shale; (b) fine drainage texture on Gondwana shale; (c) medium drainage texture on granite gniess; (d) medium drainage texture on quartzite; (e) coarse drainage texture on Cuddapah sandstone; (f) coarse drainage texture on Gondwana sand stone.

HYDROLOGIC SOIL GROUP—B (MODERATELY LOW RUNOFF POTENTIAL)

Soils having moderate infiltration rates when thoroughly wetted and consisting chiefly of moderately deep to deep, moderately well to well-drained soils with fine to moderately coarse textures. These soils have a moderate rate of water transmission.

HYDROLOGIC SOIL GROUP—C (MODERATELY HIGH RUNOFF POTENTIAL)

Soils having slow infiltration rates when thoroughly wetted, and consisting chiefly of moderately deep to deep, moderately well to well-drained soils with moderately fine to moderately coarse textures. These soils have a moderate rate of water transmission.

HYDROLOGIC SOIL GROUP—D (HIGH RUNOFF POTENTIAL)

Soils having very slow infiltration rates when thoroughly wetted and consisting chiefly of clay soils with a high swelling potential, soils with a permanent high water table, soils with a clay pan or clay layer at or near the surface and shallow soils cover nearly impervious material.

Infiltration rates

Class	mm/hour	Remarks
Very low	Below 2.5	Highly clayey soils
Low	2.5–12.5	Shallow soils, clay soils, soils low in organic matter
Medium	12.5–25.0	Sandy loam, silt loam
High	Above 25.0	Deep sands, well aggregated soils.

Soil permeability

	Rate (mm/hour)		Rate (mm/hour)
Very slow	Less than 1 30	Slow	1.31–5.00
Moderately slow	5.01–20.00	Moderate	20.01–50.00
Moderately rapid	50.01–130.00	Rapid	130.01–250.00
Very rapid	Over 250.00		

By using the hydrologic groups with run off curve numbers for hydrologic soil cover complex, runoff from a watershed could be arrived at. For further details, reference may be made to the Hand Book of Hydrology (1972), issued by the Soil Conservation Division of Ministry of Agriculture, Government of India, New Delhi.

Among the above-mentioned soil characteristics, soil depth plays an important role in land reclamation projects, e.g. land levelling, bench terracing, etc.

2.3 Vegetative Cover

A dense cover of vegetation is a most powerful weapon for reducing erosion. Vegetative cover vis-a-vis runoff relationships have to be developed for harnessing and storage of runoff water for different purposes, e.g. flood moderation, runoff recycling, pisciculture, etc. Classification of forest and tree crops is given below:

Vegetative condition	Hydrologic condition
Heavily grazed or regularly burnt. Litter, small trees and brush are destroyed.	Poor
Grazed but not burnt. There may be some litter but these woods are not protected.	Fair
Protected from grazing. Litter and shrubs cover the soils.	Good

2.4 Present Land Use and Practices

A record of present land use and practices followed by the farmers in a region is essential for further planning and reorganization of land use according to its land use capability classification, to get sustained production.

2.5 Rainfall

AVERAGE DEPTH OF RAINFALL OVER AN AREA

For any storm, the rainfall over a large area will not be the same. If sufficient number of rain gauges are located spread over the entire area, each rain gauge will record certain depth of rainfall. To calculate the average rainfall for the entire area, three methods are available. These are: (1) arithmetic mean, (2) Thiessen method, and (3) isohyetal method.

ARITHMETIC MEAN

As the name indicates, in this method, the average rainfall is obtained by dividing the sum of the depths recorded at all stations in the area by the number of stations. This method gives reasonably accurate results, provided the rain gauges are distributed all over the area and at the same time the rainfall varies in a regular manner. This is not the usual case and as such more accurate methods as described below should be adopted.

Thiessen Method

In this method, location of the rain gauges is plotted on a map of the area and the stations are connected by means of straight lines. Perpendicular bisectors are constructed on each of the lines, such that each of the rain gauge station is enclosed in a certain area (Fig. 2.2). For example, station C is enclosed by the polygon $O_1 O_2 O_7 O_6$.

If $P_1, P_2, P_3, \ldots$ are the amounts of rainfall recorded in each of the rain gauges and $A_1, A_2, A_3, \ldots$ are the areas of the polygons enclosing them, the average rainfall P, over the given area A is given by

$$P = \frac{P_1A_1 + P_2A_2 + P_3A_3 + \cdots}{A_1 + A_2 + A_3 + \cdots} \qquad \ldots (2.2)$$

Isohyetal Method

In this method, after plotting the location of the rain gauge stations and the amounts of rainfall at each of the stations, isohyetals (lines of equal rainfall) are drawn by interpolation (Fig. 2.3). The area between the successive isohyetals is determined. Planimeter is an instrument which can be conveniently used for measuring the areas of such irregular figures. The same formula as used in the Thiessen's method is used, where $A_1, A_2, \ldots$ now represent the areas between two successive isohyetals and $P_1, P_2, \ldots$ represents the average rainfall of the area.

The Thiessen's method and the isohyetal method give more accurate information than the simple arithmetic mean. Data from rain gauge stations slightly beyond the area under consideration can be used in both these methods.

Example 1—Calculate the equivalent depth of rainfall for the basin for a storm whose recorded depths are shown in Fig. 2.2.
Solution

(i) By arithmetic mean the equivalent depth of rainfall (P) is given by

$$P = \frac{5.5 + 4.5 + 5.4 + 4.0 + 5.75}{5} = 5.03 \text{ cm}$$

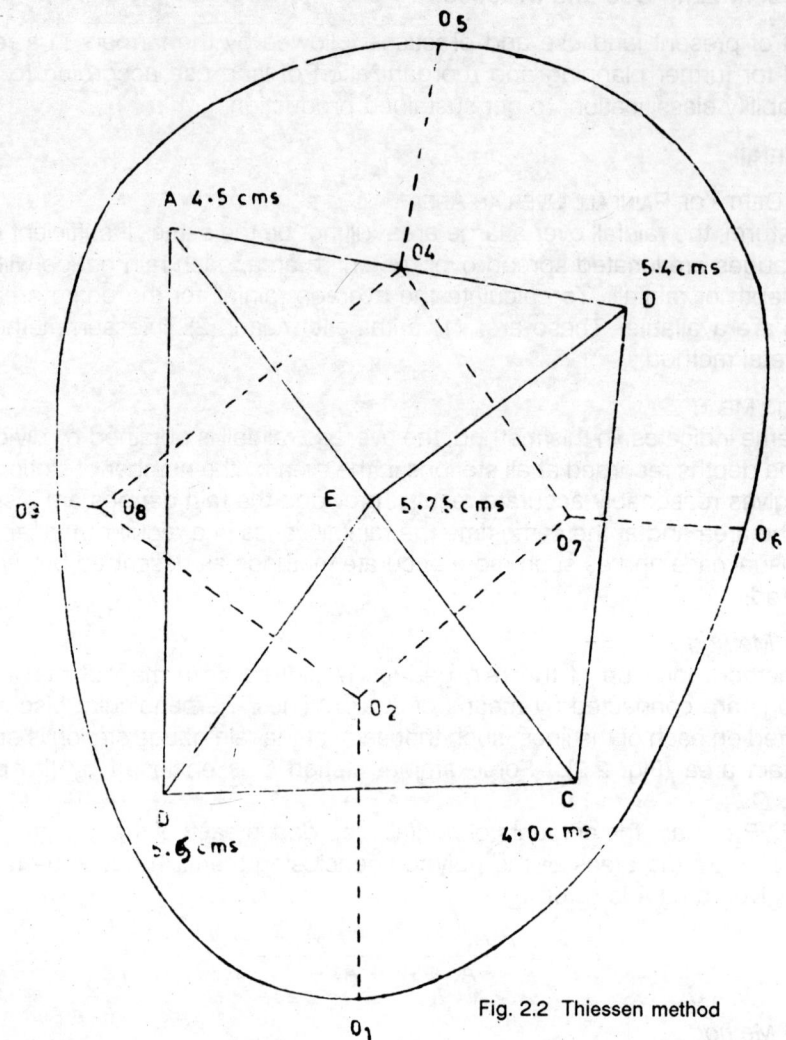

Fig. 2.2 Thiessen method

(ii) By Thiessen polygonal network

Considering the area of each of the polygons in which the rain gauges are situated,

$$P = \frac{(5.5 \times 16) + (4.5 \times 18) + (5.4 \times 18) + (4.0 \times 20) + (5.75 \times 18)}{16 + 18 + 18 + 20 + 18} = 5.0 \text{ cm}$$

(iii) By isohyetal method

Isohyetal	Rainfall between isohyetals (cm)	Area
< 4	3.5	12
4	4.25	17
4.5	4.75	21
5.0	5.25	23
5.5	5.625	17
		90

$$P = \frac{(12 \times 3.5) + (17 \times 4.25) + (21 \times 4.75) + (23 \times 5.25) + (17 \times 5.625)}{12 + 17 + 21 + 23 + 17}$$

$$= 4.78 \text{ cm}$$

Rainfall intensity-duration-return period equations and nomographs on regional basis are required in the country for design of soil conservation, runoff disposal structures and for planning flood control projects. Automatic recording raingauge charts are analysed for total rainfall, intensities for various time intervals and maximum intensities for specific time intervals.

The above rainfall characteristics for 42 stations were analysed (Ram Babu et al, 1979) and intensity-duration-return period equations and nomographs have been developed. With the help of these equations and/or nomographs, the intensity for any desired duration (or frequency) may be determined. The general form of the intensity-duration-return period relationship is

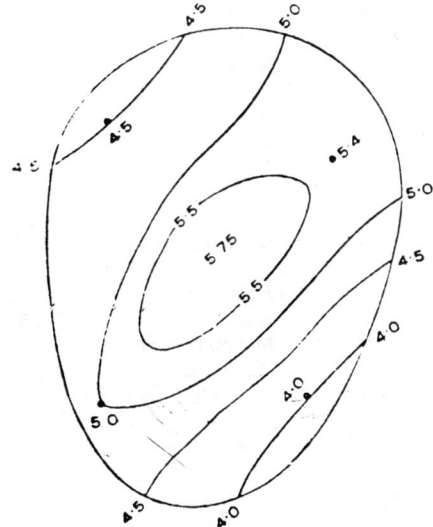

Fig. 2.3 Isohyetal Method

$$I = \frac{K \, T^a}{(t + b)^n} \qquad \qquad \ldots (2.3)$$

where, I = intensity (cm/hr);
T = return period (years); and
t = storm duration (hours).

Step 1: For finding out intensity of any particular place, select the values for K, a, b and n against corresponding places, which are provided in Table 2.1.

Step 2: The Return period (T in Eq. 2.3) can be selected from Table 2.2 for the structures under consideration.

Step 3: The parameter, t (duration, hr) the time of concentration of a watershed which can be computed by using the following equations:

$$t = 0.01947 \, K^{0.77}$$

where, $K = \sqrt{\dfrac{L^3}{H}}$ $\ldots (2.4)$

Table 2.1   *Intensity-duration-return period relationships, India*

Zone	Station	K	a	b	n
Northern zone	Agra	4.911	0.1667	0.25	0.6293
	Allahabad	8.570	0.1692	0.50	1.0190
	Amristar	14.41	0.1304	1.40	1.2963
	Dehradun	6.00	0.22	0.50	0.8000
	Jaipur	6.219	0.1026	0.50	1.1172
	Jodhpur	4.098	0.1677	0.50	1.0369
	Lucknow	6.074	0.1813	0.50	1.0331
	New Delhi	5.208	0.1574	0.50	1.1072
	Srinagar	1.503	0.2730	0.25	1.0636
	Northern zone	5.914	0.1623	0.50	1.0127
Central zone	Bagra-tawa	8.5704	0.2214	1.25	0.9331
	Bhopal	6.9296	0.1892	0.50	0.8767
	Indore	6.9280	0.1394	0.50	1.0651
	Jabalpur	11.379	0.1746	1.25	1.1206
	Jagdalpur	4.7065	0.1084	0.25	0.9902
	Nagpur	11.45	0.1560	1.25	1.0324
	Punasa	4.7011	0.2608	0.50	0.8653
	Raipur	4.683	0.1389	0.15	0.9284
	Thikri	6.088	0.1747	1.00	0.8587
	Central zone	7.4645	0.1712	0.75	0.9599
Western zone	Aurangabad	6.081	0.1459	0.50	1.0923
	Bhuj	3.823	0.1919	0.25	0.9902
	Mahabaleswar	3.483	0.1267	0.00	0.4853
	Nandurbar	4.254	0.2070	0.25	0.7704
	Vengurla	6.863	0.1670	0.75	0.8683
	Veraval	7.787	0.2087	0.50	0.8908
	Western zone	3.974	0.1647	0.15	0.7327
Eastern zone	Agarthala	8.097	0.1177	0.50	0.8191
	Dumdum	5.940	0.1150	0.15	0.9241
	Gauhati	7.206	0.1557	0.75	0.9401
	Gaya	7.176	0.1483	0.50	0.9459
	Imphal	4.939	0.1340	0.50	0.9719
	Jamshedpur	6.930	0.1307	0.50	9.8737
	Jharsuguda	8.596	0.1392	0.75	0.8740
	North Lakhimpur	14.070	0.1256	1.25	1.0730
	Sagar Island	16.524	0.1402	1.50	0.9635
	Shillong	6.728	0.1502	0.75	0.9575
	Eastern zone	6.933	0.1353	0.50	0.8801
Southern zone	Bangalore	6.275	0.1262	0.50	1.1280
	Hyderabad	5.250	0.1354	0.50	1.0295
	Kodaikanal	5.914	0.1711	0.50	1.0086
	Madras	6.126	0.1664	0.50	0.8027
	Mangalore	6.744	0.1395	0.50	0.9374
	Tiruchirapalli	7.135	0.1638	0.50	0.9624
	Trivandrum	6.762	0.1536	0.50	0.8158
	Visakhapatnam	6.646	0.1692	0.50	0.9963
	Southern zone	6.311	0.1523	0.50	0.9465

t = time of concentration (min.);
L = maximum length of travel in metre; and

$H=$ difference in elevation between most remote point and outlet in metre.

$$t\text{ (hrs)} = \frac{\text{distance from the most remote point to the outlet of the area (m)}}{\text{average velocity (m/sec)} \times 3600}$$

Table 2.2 *Recommended maximum runoff frequencies for various types of structures*

Type of structures	Frequency, year
Storage and diversion dams having permanent spillways	50–100
Earthfill dams-storage having natural spillways	25–50
Stock water dams	25
Small permanent masonry gully control structures	10–15
Terrace outlets and vegetated waterways	10
Field diversions	15

The average velocity of flow of water can be chosen from Table 2.3 in determining the time of concentration (t) under conditions where the main waterways are broad and flat and not gullied to any great extent.

2.6 Prediction of Design Peak Runoff Rate

Runoff is that portion of rainfall which moves down to the stream, channel, river or ocean as surface or subsurface flow. If the farmer can intelligently harvest the runoff from his field (one of the nature's gift), store it in a pond and recycle it for life saving or supplemental irrigation to crop(s), it will be possible to maximise the crop production and thus obtain good returns.

Table 2.3 *Recommended average velocities for use in determining time of concentration (t)*

Average slope (%) of the channel extending from the farthest point of the watershed to the outlet	Velocity (m/sec)
1–2	0.6
2–4	0.9
4–6	1.2
6–10	1.5

In soil and water conservation measures, the design of hydrologic structures, quantitative estimates of runoff rates, volumes and distribution are to be worked out. Structures and channels are planned to carry maximum runoff, which can be expected in a specified recurrence interval. Recommended peak runoff frequencies for various types of structures are given in Table 2.2.

There are three main methods commonly used in arriving at the peak rate of runoff; (a) Rational Method, (b) Cook's Method and (c) Hydrologic Soil-cover Complex Method. The following basic assumptions are made in deriving the above methods:

—Rainfall occurs at uniform intensity for a duration at least equal to the time of concentration of the watershed.

—Rainfall occurs on a uniform intensity over the entire watershed.

RATIONAL METHOD

This method is the oldest, simplest and possibly the most-consistent one in its ability to adjust with the new concepts and developments in evaluating a watershed condition. The method is expressed by an equation

$$Q = \frac{CIA}{360} \qquad \qquad \dots (2.5)$$

where, Q = design peak runoff rate in cubic metre/sec;

    C = runoff coefficient;

    I = intensity of rain in mm/hour for the design recurrence interval and for duration equal to the time of concentration (t) of the watershed;

    A = watershed area in ha.

Values for the runoff coefficient (C) can be obtained from Table 2.4.

Table 2.4   *Values of C in Rational formula*

Vegetative cover and slope	Soil texture		
	Sandy loam	Clay and silt loam	Stiff clay
I. Cultivated land			
0–5%	0.3	0.5	0.6
5–10%	0.4	0.6	0.7
10–30%	0.52	0.72	0.82
II. Pasture land			
0–5%	0.10	0.30	0.40
5–10%	0.16	0.36	0.55
10–30%	0.22	0.42	0.60
III. Forest land			
0–5%	0.10	0.30	0.40
5–10%	0.25	0.35	0.50
10–30%	0.30	0.50	0.60

Example 2—Estimate peak rate of runoff of 25 years frequency for a 25 ha watershed in medium black soil (clay) having 15, 5, and 5 ha under cultivation, forest and grassland, respectively. The watershed has general slope of 2.5%. The area is located somewhere in Central zone. The maximum length of run is approximately 2500 m and the elevation of the highest and outlet points is 250 m and 200 m, respectively.
Solution
Coefficient of runoff (C in Rational Formula—refer Table 2.4)
Against clay soils and 0.5% slope

                     C value

Cultivated land   0.5
Pasture land   0.3
Forest land   0.3

Weighted value of C for entire watershed

$$= \frac{15 \times 0.5 + 5 \times 0.3 + 5 \times 0.3}{15 + 5 + 5}$$

On simplification $C = 0.42$

The time of concentration (t) of the watershed is given by $t = 0.1947\ (K)^{0.77}$

where, $K = \sqrt{\dfrac{L^3}{H}}$

Maximum length of run = 2500 m

Relief = 250–200 = 50 m

$$K = \sqrt{\frac{L^3}{H}} = \sqrt{\frac{2500 \times 2500 \times 2500}{50}}$$

$$= 17,677$$

Substituting value of K in the formula

$$t = 0.01947\ (K)^{0.77}$$

$$= 0.01947\ (17677)^{0.77}$$

$$t = 36 \text{ minutes or } (36/60) \text{ hour.}$$

The intensity (I) of rainfall for a recurrence interval (T) of 25 years (for constructing a farm pond with suitable spillway) is obtained from

$$I = \frac{KT^a}{(t + b)^n}$$

The values of K, a, b and n can be obtained from Table 2.1 (values taken against Central zone)
$K = 7.4645$, $a = 0.1712$, $b = 0.75$ and $n = 0.9599$

Recurrence interval (T) given as 25 years, time of concentration (t) worked out as $\dfrac{36}{60}$ hour.

Substituting in the equation

$$I = \frac{KT^a}{(t + b)^n}$$

$$= \frac{7,4645(25)^{0.1712}}{\left[\dfrac{36}{60} + 0.75\right]^{0.9599}}$$

$$= 9.71 \text{ cm/hour}$$

or 97 mm/hour

Substituting value of $C = 0.42$, $I = 97$ mm/hour and $A = 25$ ha in the Rational Formula

$$Q = \frac{CIA}{360}$$

$$= \frac{0.42 \times 97 \times 25}{360} = 2.82 \text{ cumecs}$$

Peak rate of runoff = 2.82 cumec.

COOK'S METHOD

This method is considered most suitable for watersheds up to about 400 ha as encountered in executing soil conservation measures. By this method, the runoff characteristics of a watershed are examined under the four categories of relief, soil infiltration, vegetal cover and surface storage. Approximate weightage for these can be obtained from Table 2.5. Runoff curves presented in Fig. 2.4 are then entered with the drainage area and the $\sum W$, and a value of peak runoff for 10 year return period is obtained. This peak runoff value is modified by multiplying it with the rainfall factor (R obtained from Fig. 2.5), frequency factor for various zones (F from Fig. 2.6) and shape factor (S_f from Table 2.6).

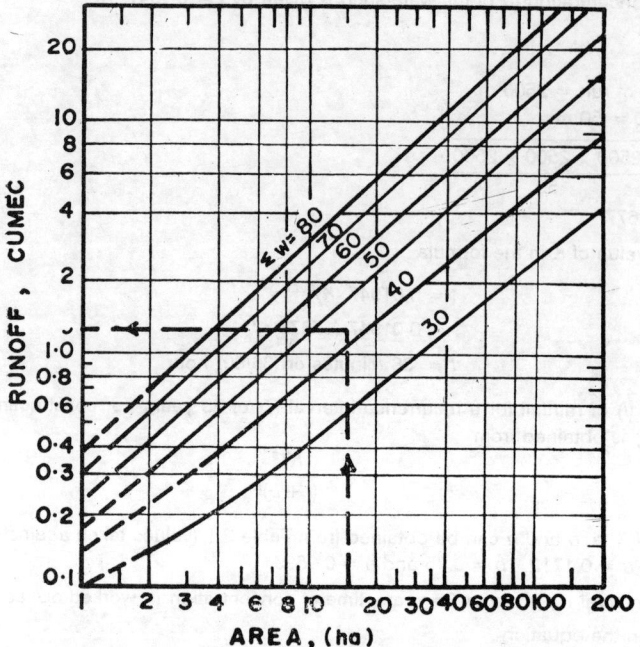

Fig. 2.4 Drainage area versus runoff for 10 year return period

Example 3—Estimate peak rate of runoff for 25 year frequency from 10 ha cultivated (1% slope, 0.75 cm/hour infiltration capacity, vegetal cover less than 10% under good cover, low well defined small drainage ways) and 5 ha of grassland (2% slopes, infiltration rate 1.8 cm/hour, vegetal cover excellent, 90% under permanent good cover, low well-defined drainage ways). The area is located at 75° longitude and 20° latitude.

Solution

Setp 1: Estimation of $\sum W$ from Table 2.5.

	Agricultural land	Grassland
Relief	2	4
Soil infiltration	15	11
Vegetal cover	15	5
Surface drainage	15	15
	$\sum W = 47$	$\sum W = 35$

Weighted $\sum W = \dfrac{47 \times 10 + 35 \times 5}{15} = 43$.

Step 2: Runoff curves presented in Fig. 2.4 are then entered with drainage area (15 ha) and the $\sum W$ (43) and a value of 1.31 cumecs of peak runoff for a 10 year return period is obtained.

Step 3: Rainfall factor R for the area at 75° longitude, 20° latitude = 1.2 (From Fig. 2.5).

Step 4: Frequency factor F for the area is 1.3 at 75° longitude, 20° latitude for 25 years (from Fig. 2.6).

Table 2.5 *Runoff producing characteristics for the determination of summation W*

Designation of watershed characteristics	Runoff producing characteristics			
	Extreme	High	Normal	Low
Relief	(40) to (30) Steep rugged terrain with average slopes generally above 30%	(30) to (20) Hilly, with average slopes of 10% to 30%	(23) to (10) Rolling, with average slopes of 5% to 10%	(10) to (0) Relatively flat land; with average slopes of 0% to 5%
Soil infiltration	(20) No effective soil cover, either rock or thin soil mantle of negligible infiltration capacity, less than 0.25 cm/hour	(15) Slow to take up water; clay or other soil of low infiltration capacity, 0.25 to 0.75 cm/hour	(10) Normal; deep permeable soils, 0.75 to 2 cm/hour	(5) High; sand, loamy sand and other loose open soil, over 2 cm/hour
Vegetal cover	(20) No effective plant cover bare or very sparse cover	(15) Poor to fair; clean cultivated crops or less than 10% of drainage area under good cover	(10) Fair to good; about 50% of drainage area in good grass land, woodland or equivalent cover; not more than 50% of area in clean cultivated crops	(5) Good to excellent; about 90% of drainage area in good land, woodland grass land of or equivalent cover
Surface storage	(20) Negligible; surface depressions few and shallow drainage ways steep and small, no ponds or marshes	(15) Low; well-defined system of small drainage ways; no ponds or marshes	(10) Normal; considerable surface depression storage; drainage system similar to that of typical prairie lands, lakes, ponds and marshes less than 2% of drainage area	(5) High; surface depression storage high; drainage system not sharply defined, large flood-plain storage or a large number of lakes; ponds and marshes

(Source: USDA Soil Conservation Service, 'Engineering Handbook' for work unit staff (Texas), 1929).

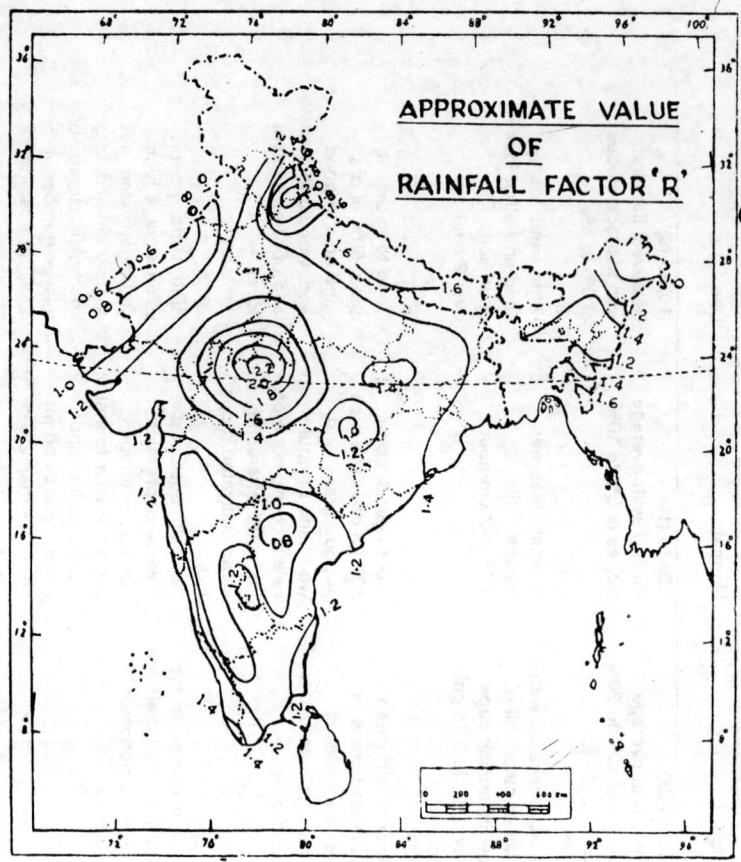

Fig. 2.5 Rainfall factor 'R'

Step 5: Shape factor for the area is 0.88 (from Table 2.6).

Step 6: Peak rate of runoff (Q_{25}) = 1.8 cumec.

Table 2.6 *Shape factors*

Ratio of Length to width	Watershed area, ha				
	20	40	80	200	240
1	1.00	1.00	1.00	1.00	1.00
1.5	0.92	0.92	0.91	0.90	0.90
2	0.88	0.87	0.86	0.84	0.83
2.5	0.85	0.84	0.82	0.80	0.78
3	0.81	0.80	0.78	0.76	0.74
4	0.76	0.75	0.73	0.71	0.69
5	0.74	0.72	0.70	0.68	0.66
6	0.72	0.70	0.68	0.66	0.64
7	0.70	0.68	0.66	0.64	0.62
8	0.68	0.66	0.64	0.61	0.59

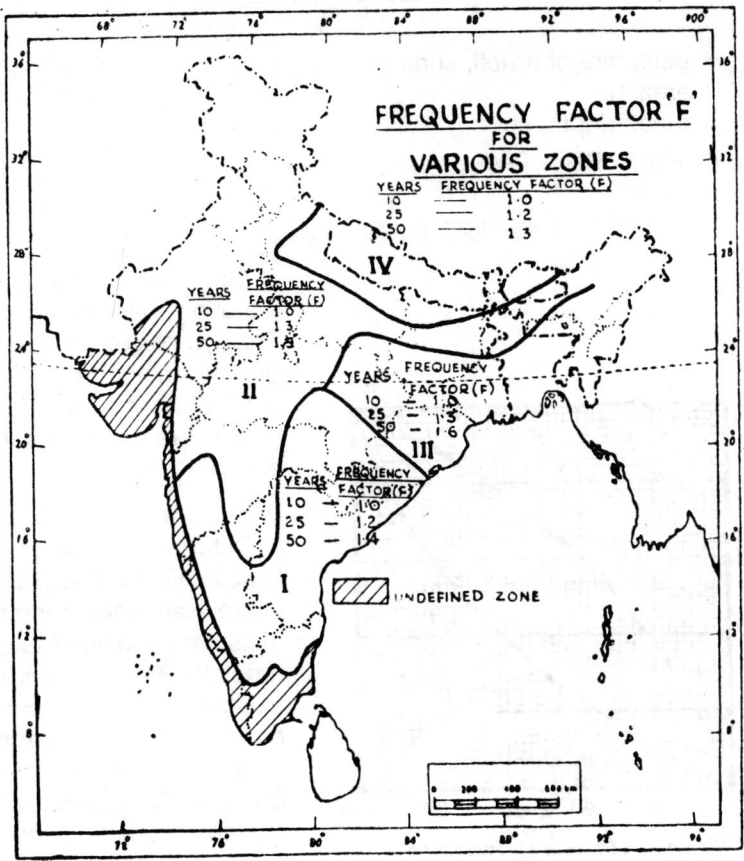

Fig. 2.6 Frequency factor 'F' for various zones

Cook's Method are used by Tamil Nadu State
Against the drainage area read peak runoff for 50 year return period (Appendix A-1) for a rainfall factor of 1.0. Multiply this runoff figure by the rainfall factor (R) for the area concerned as obtained from Fig. 2.5. This will give expected runoff from a storm of 50 years frequency. For a storm of 25 and 10 year frequency, multiply expected runoff by 0.83 and 0.71, respectively. The obtained runoff figures are then multiplied by applicable shape factor (Table 2.6).

HYDROLOGIC SOIL COVER COMPLEX NUMBER METHOD
The method developed by Ogrosky and Mockus (1957) determining peak rate of runoff for small watersheds by synthesizing information about flow characteristics, physiographic factors and soil cover data. Soils have been divided into four groups according to their hydrologic properties and characteristics.

Various steps involved in estimation of peak rate of runoff by this method are detailed later. Ogrosky and Mockus (1957) suggested the use of 6 hour rainfall for the design frequency for small watersheds which are within purview of soil conservation. This method involves conversion of rainfall to runoff depth and the peak rate of runoff is obtained by the following relationship

$$q_{peak} = \frac{0.0208 \times A \times Q_d}{T_p} \qquad \ldots (2.6)$$

where, q_{peak} = peak rate of runoff, cumec;

     A = area, ha

     Q_d = runoff depth, cm

     T_p = time to peak, hour

        = $0.6\, T_c + \sqrt{T_c}$

     T_c = time of concentration, hour

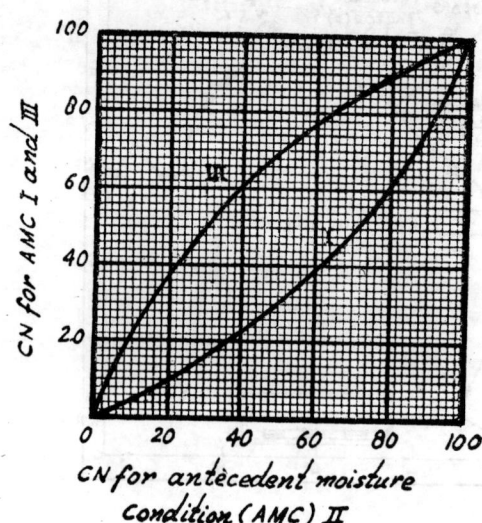

Fig. 2.7   Conversion of curve number (CN) from antecedent moisture condition (AMC) II to I and III

Graphical solution of the above equation has been developed. The hydrologic soil cover complex number method can be used for estimation of water yield as well as peak rate of runoff from areas above 50 ha.

Procedure

Determine the weighted hydrologic curve number (Table 2.7) for entire watershed for antecedent moisture condition (AMC) II. If the runoff for AMC I or III are to be estimated the antecedent moisture conditions can be determined approximately by using the criteria given in Table 2.8. Figure 2.7 may then be used to obtain corresponding curve number (CN) values.

—Determine the 6 hour rainfall from Fig. 2.8 to 2.10 for the desired frequency.

—Determine T_c (from Fig. 2.8 using maximum length of run and the fall) and corresponding T_p (Fig. 2.12).

—Obtain Q peak (cumec) by entering Fig. 2.13 from rainfall (mm) to curve number, turn left horizontally to area (ha), turn vertically down to T_p and finally turn right horizontally to read Q peak (cumec).

Example 4—Find the maximum rate of runoff 50 years recurrence interval for antecedent moisture condition III from a watershed with 40 ha of row crop cultivated good terraced land, 10 ha of good pasture land and 20 ha of fair wood land. The watershed is situated at 30° N latitude and 76° E longitude. The soil is of hydrologic soil group, C. The maximum length of run, the elevation of the highest point and outlet point elevation are 2200, 780 and 700 m, respectively. In between there are sudden drops totalling to 20 m.

Solution

Weighted curve number, CN (Table 2.7)

$$= \frac{78 \times 40 + 74 \times 10 + 73 \times 20}{70} = 76$$

Converted weighted CN, 76 for antecedent moisture condition III (Fig. 2.7) = 89
The 6-hour 50 year frequency rainfall for the location is 150 mm (from Fig. 2.11)

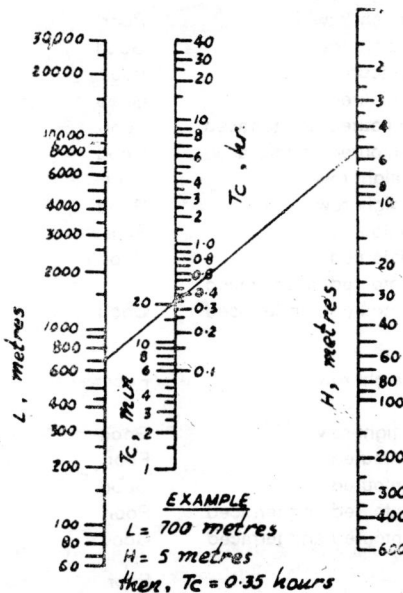

Fig. 2.8 Nomograph for estimating time of concentration, T_c

Net fall (excluding sudden drops) = 780 − (700 + 20) = 60 m

T_c = (from Fig. 2.8) = 0.48 hour
T_p = (from Fig. 2.12) = 1 hour

Peak rate of runoff (Q peak) from Fig. 2.13 = 17.5 cumec.

Example 5—Find the maximum runoff for 50 years, recurrence interval for antecedent moisture condition III from a watershed with 40 ha of row crop cultivated good terraced land, and 10 ha of good pasture land. The watershed is situated at 30° N latitude and 70° E longitude. The soil is of hydrologic soil group C. The time of concentration of the watershed = 0.48 hrs.

Solution: Using Table 2.7 the curve numbers for the terraced land is 78 and for the good pasture land is 74.

Weighted curve number for the entire watershed

$$= \frac{78 \times 40 + 74 \times 10}{50} = 77.2$$

Converted Weighted CN for AMC-III (Fig. 2.7) = 88
6 hour, 50 year frequency rainfall for the given location from figure 2.11 = 150 mm

$$\text{Recharge capacity } S \text{ from } CN = \frac{2540}{25.4 + S}$$

$$88 = \frac{2540}{25.4 + S}$$

Or

$$S = 3.46 \text{ cm}$$

$$\text{Runoff } Q = \frac{(15 - 0.2 \times 3.46)^2}{15 + 0.8 \times 3.46}$$

$$= 11.52 \text{ cm}$$

Table 2.7 *Runoff curve numbers for hydrologic soil cover complex (for watershed condition II and $I_a = 0.2S$)*

Land use cover	Treatment or practice	Hydrologic condition	Hydrologic soil group[*] A	B	C	D
Fallow	Straight row	—	77	86	91	94
Row crops	Straight row	Poor	72	81	88	91
	Straight row	Good	67	78	85	89
	Contoured	Poor	70	79	84	88
	Contoured	Good	65	75	82	86
	Contoured and terraced	Poor	66	74	80	82
	Contoured and terraced	Good	62	71	78	81
Small grain	Straight row	Poor	65	76	84	88
	Straight row	Good	63	75	83	87
	Contoured	Poor	63	74	82	85
	Contoured	Good	61	73	81	84
	Contoured and terraced	Poor	61	72	79	82
	Contoured and terraced	Good	59	70	78	81
Closed seeded legumes[1] or rotation meadow	Straight row	Poor	66	77	85	89
	Straight row	Good	58	72	81	85
	Contoured	Poor	64	75	83	85
	Contoured	Good	55	69	78	83
	Contoured and terraced	Poor	63	73	80	83
	Contoured and terraced	Good	51	67	76	80
Pasture or range		Poor	68	79	86	89
		Fair	49	69	79	84
		Good	39	61	74	80
	Contoured	Poor	47	67	81	88
	Contoured	Fair	25	59	75	83
	Contoured	Good	6	35	70	79
Meadow (permanent)		Good	30	58	71	78
Woodlands (farm woodlots)		Poor	45	66	77	83
		Fair	36	60	73	79
		Good	25	55	70	77
Farmsteads			59	74	82	86
Roads (dirt)			72	82	87	89
Roads (hard surface[2])			77	84	90	92

1. Close-drilled or broadcast
2. Including right of way

*Hydrologic soil group is obtained from (Fig. 1.2)

Table 2.8 *Rainfall limits for estimating antecedent moisture conditions*

Antecedent moisture condition	5 days total antecedent rainfall, cm Dormant season	Growing season
I	Less than 1.25	Less than 3.5
II	1.25 to 2.75	3.5 to 5.25
III	Over 2.75	Over 5.25

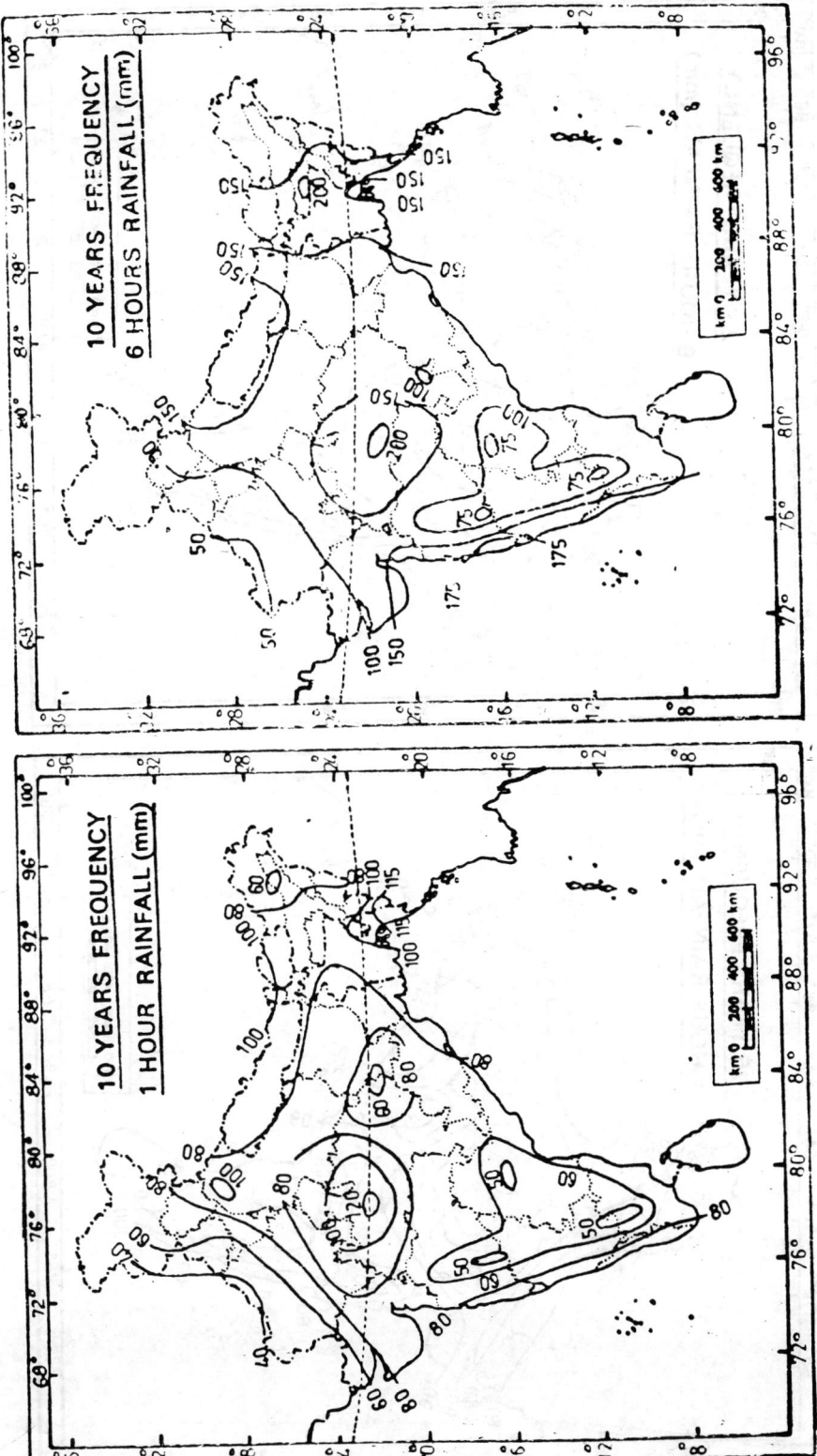

Fig. 2.9 Maps showing rainfall characteristics for runoff calculations

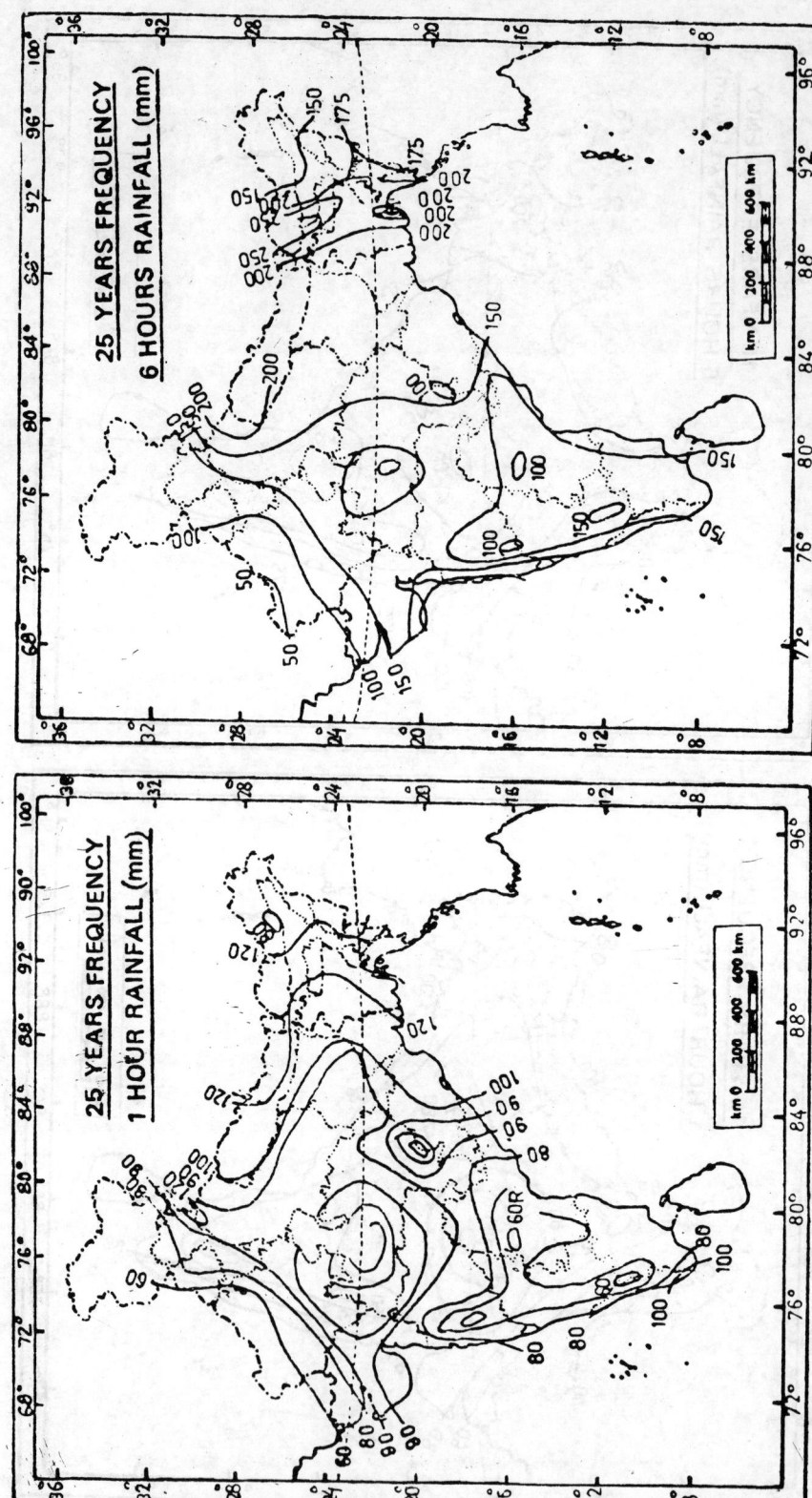

Fig. 2.10 25 years frequency 1 hour and 6 hours rainfall

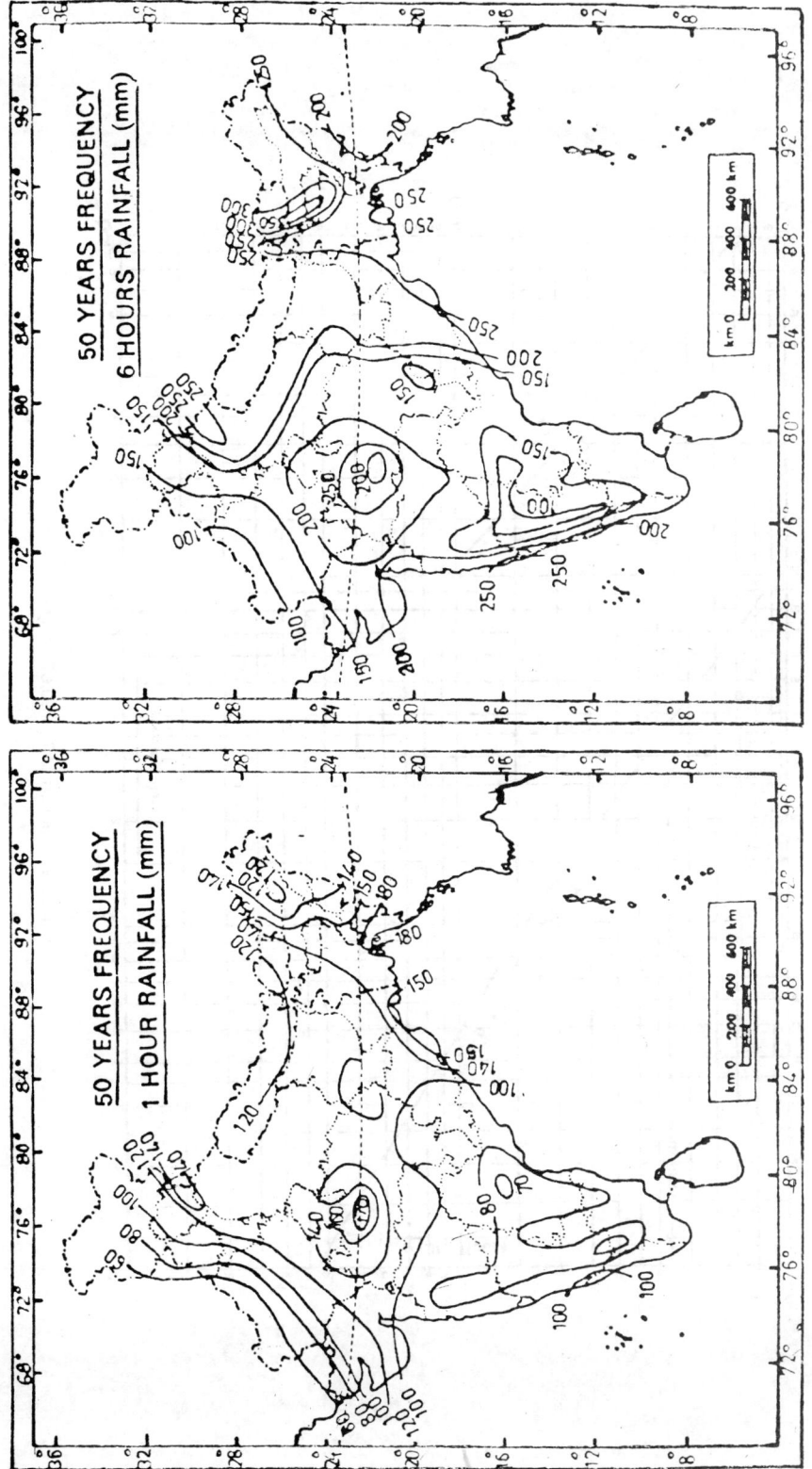

Fig 2.11 50 years frequency 1 hour and 6 hours rainfall

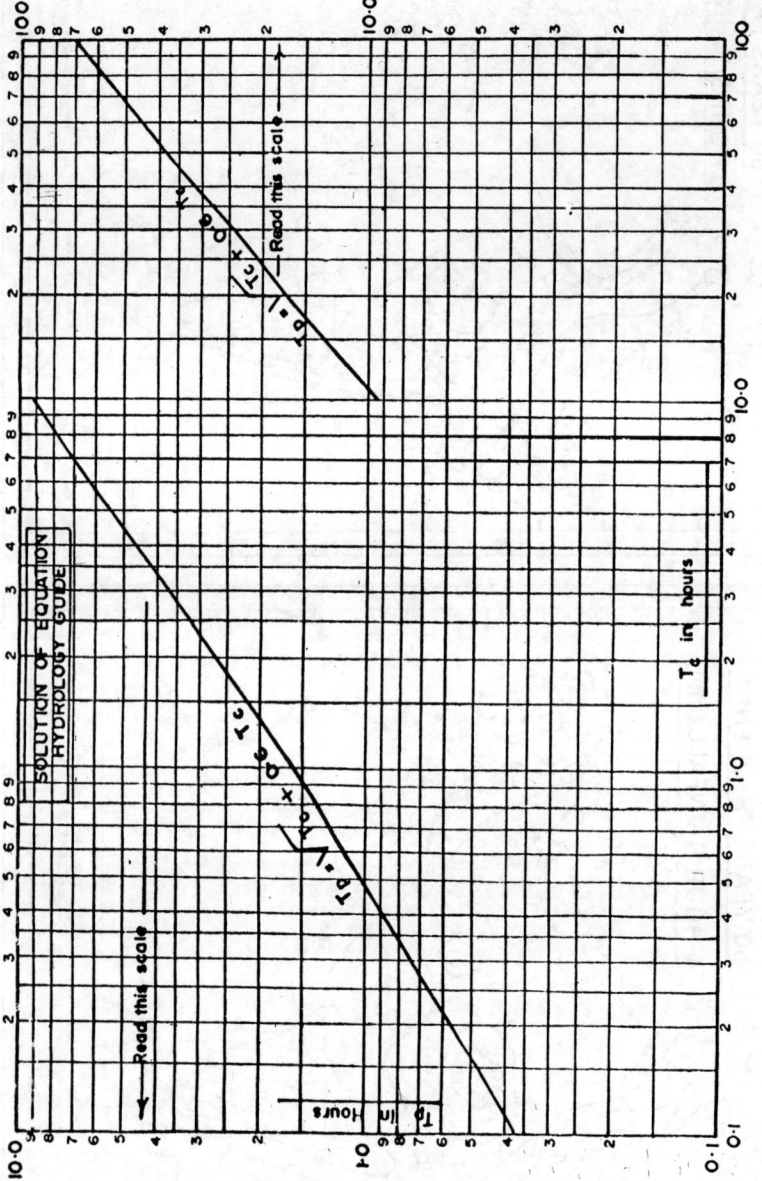

Fig. 2.12 Solution of $T_p = 0.6T_c + \sqrt{T_c}$

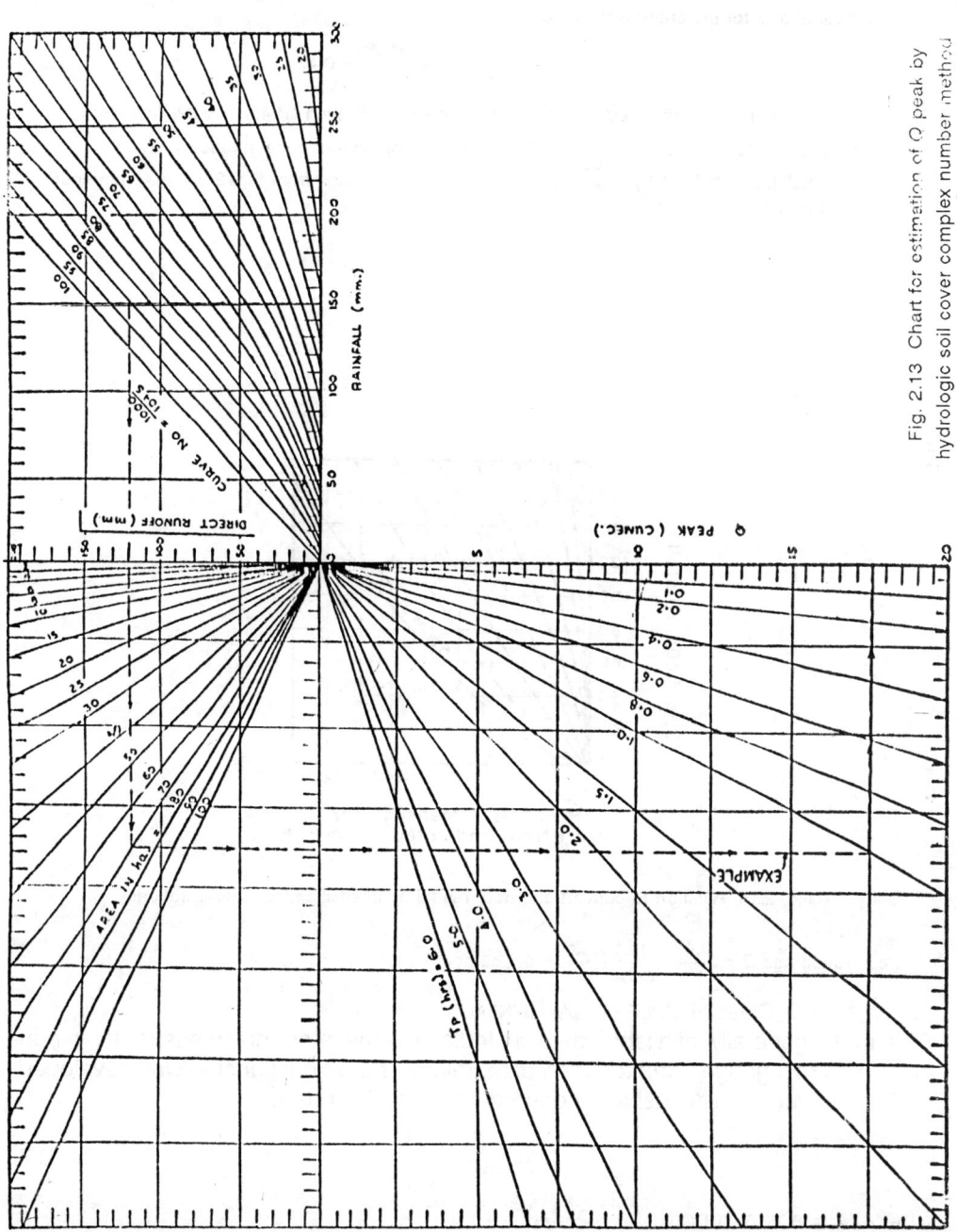

Fig. 2.13 Chart for estimation of Q peak by hydrologic soil cover complex number method

Example 6—Estimate the peak rate of runoff for a 10 year frequency from a watershed of 25 ha, having 15 ha under cultivation ($C = 0.5$), 5 ha under forests ($C = 0.4$) and 5 ha under grass cover ($C = 0.45$). There is fall of 5 m in a distance of 700 m. The distance from the remotest point in the watershed to the outlet is 700 m.

Solution

Weighted value of C for the entire watershed

$$= \frac{15 \times 0.5 + 5 \times 0.4 + 5 \times 0.45}{25} = 0.47$$

Time of concentration (t_c) is obtained from the formula given by Kirpich (1940) $= 0.02L^{0.77}S^{-0.385}$

Substituting $L = 700$ m and $S = \dfrac{5}{700}$ in the above equation time of concentration = 21 min.

1 hour rainfall intensity for 10 years frequency at the given location from Fig. 2.9 = 100 mm/hour.

Intensity for 21 minutes rainfall, using Fig. 2.14 = 175 mm/hour

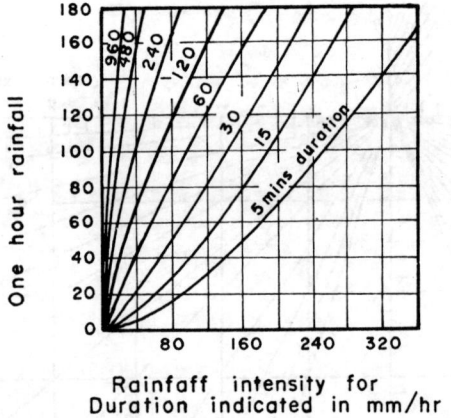

Fig. 2.14 Relation to convert one hour rainfall to intensities for other durations

Peak runoff rate $Q = \dfrac{0.47 \times 17.5 \times 25}{360} = 5.7$ cumec.

ESTIMATION OF DIRECT RUNOFF FROM RAINFALL

The most generally available data in India are the amounts measured by non-recording rain gauges and for such data, rainfall–runoff relationship was developed.

Rainfall–runoff relationship, in general form, is given as:

$$Q = \frac{(P - I_a)^2}{(P - I_a) + S} \qquad \ldots (2.7)$$

where, Q = actual runoff

$\quad P$ = the rainfall

$\quad S$ = potential maximum retention and

$\quad I_a$ = initial abstraction during the period between the beginning of rainfall and runoff in equivalent depth over the catchment.

CONDITION OF REGION

Black soils region AMC-II and III $I_a = 0.1\,S$
Black soils region AMC-I $I_a = 0.3\,S$
All other regions $I_a = 0.3\,S$

To show the rainfall–runoff relationship graphically, S values are transformed into curve number (CN) by the following equation

$$CN = \frac{25400}{254 + S} \qquad \qquad \dots (2.8)$$

Using the above, equations developed are

$$Q = \frac{(P - 0.3S)^2}{(P + 0.7S)} \qquad \qquad \dots (2.9)$$

$$Q = \frac{(P - 0.1S)^2}{(P + 0.9S)} \qquad \qquad \dots (2.10)$$

Equation (2.9) is applicable to all soil regions of India except the black soil areas referred to hydrologic soil groups.

Equation (2.10) applies to the black soil region. This equation should be used with the assumption that the cracks which are typical of these soils when dry, have been filled. Therefore, the equation should be used where the AMC would fall into groups II and III. When AMC I needs to be analyzed, use Eq. 2.9.

Solution of above equation is presented in Figs. 2.15 and 2.16.

Example 7—Given a 8.122 ha farm with an average slope 0.9%. The watershed is under cultivated straight row crop and falls under the hydrologic soil grouping B. 2-year rainfall of 24 hours duration is 95.25 mm. Compute runoff depth.

Step 1: CN for given land use and hydrologic soil group B is 86 (Table 2.7).

Step 2: To find Q, enter Fig. 2.15
       Q is 56.5 mm for the watershed.

Example 8—A watershed of 7.5 km^2 area has an average slope of 1.5%. The watershed is under 55% of weeds, 20% of good napier grass, 10% of open forest and 15% of paddy crops. It falls under the hydrologic soil grouping C and 2-year rainfall of 24-hours duration is 76.2 mm. Compute runoff depth.

Step 1: Enter Table 2.7 to get CN for different land use and hydrologic soil group C.

	% of area	CN	Number times
	per cent		
Weeds	55	85	4675
Napier grass	20	74	1480
Open forest	10	60	600
Paddy crop	15	95	1425
Total	100		8180

Weighted number $= \dfrac{8180}{100} = 81.8$

Round off to 82

Step 2: To find Q, enter Fig. 2.15

(Solution of runoff equation, $Q = \dfrac{(P - 0.3S)^2}{(P + 0.7S)}$

       Q is 31 mm.

Example 9—Given a 80 ha farm with an average slope of 1%. The farm is under cultivated straight row crop and falls under the hydrologic soil grouping $B - 6\%$ $C - 80\%$, and $D - 14\%$. 2-year rainfall of 24 hour duration for the farm is 115 mm. Compute runoff depth.

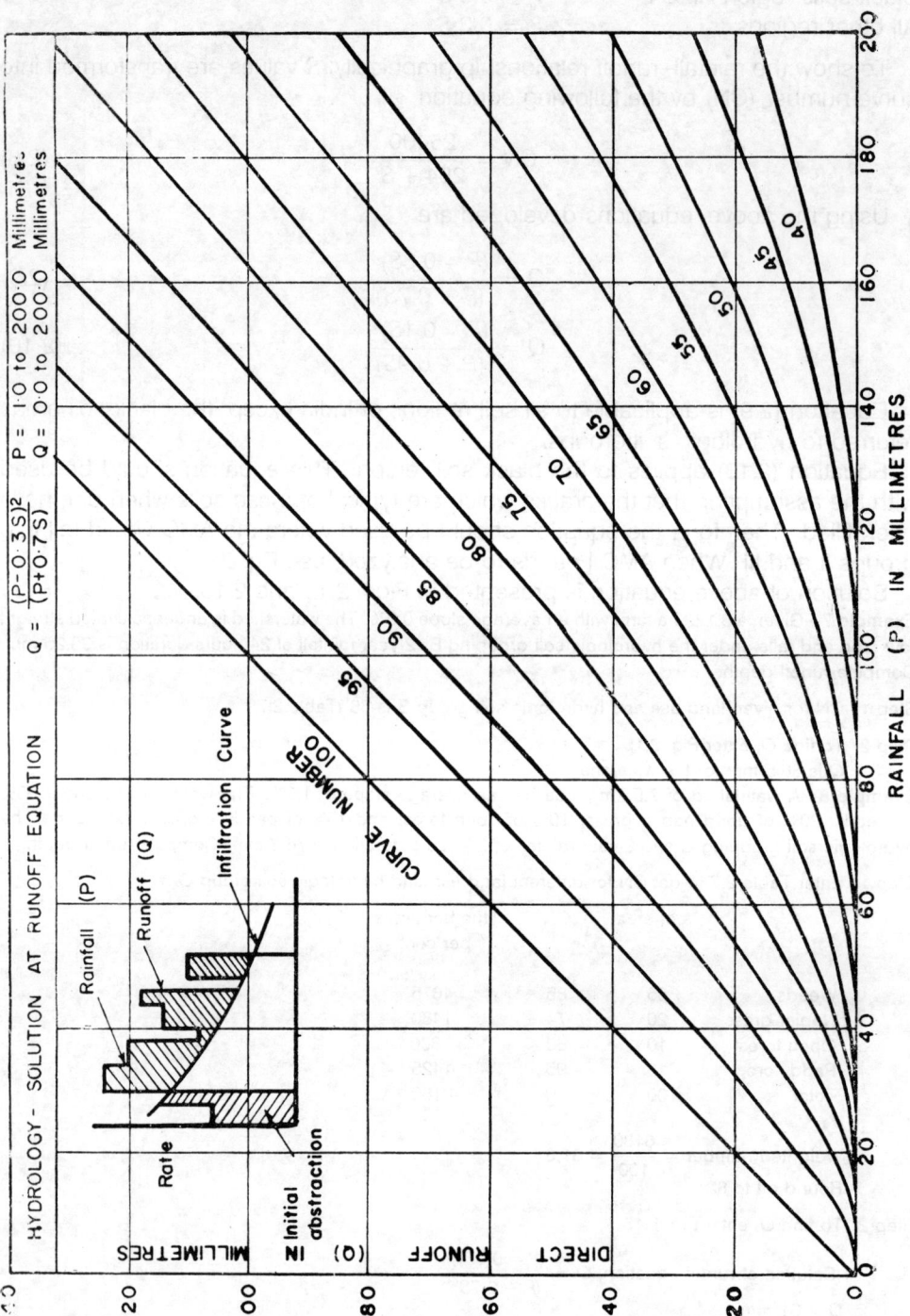

Fig. 2.15 Estimation of direct runoff

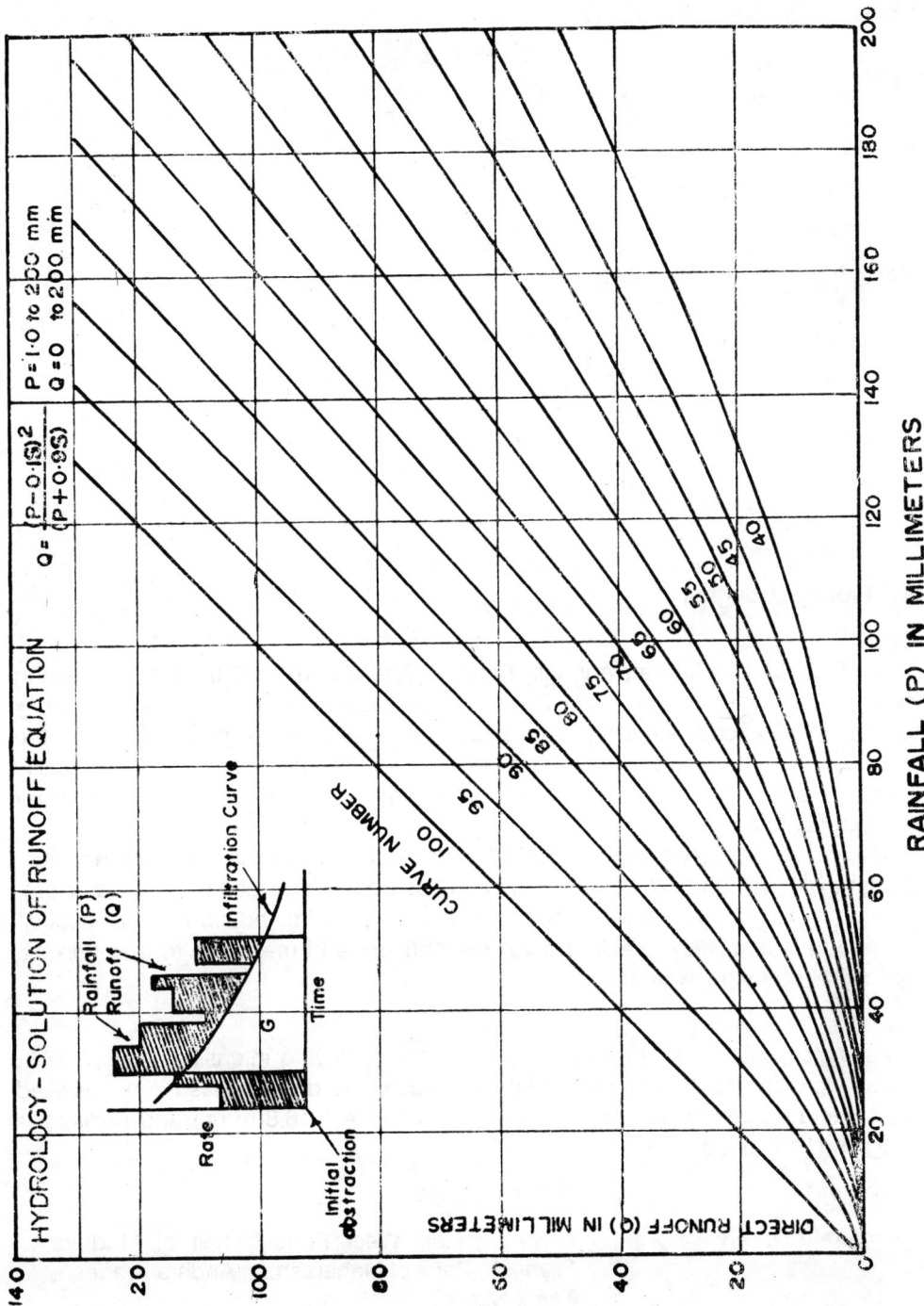

Fig. 2.16 Estimation of direct runoff

Step 1: Enter Table 2.7, to compute CN for different hydrologic soil groupings:

Hydrologic soil grouping	% of area	Curve number	Number times per cent
B	6	86	516
C	80	90	7,200
D	14	93	1,302
Total	100		9,018

$$\text{Weighted number} = \frac{9018}{100} = 90.18$$

Rounding off to 90.

Step 2: To find out Q, enter Fig. 2.16

Hydrologic soil grouping	% of area	Q	Q times per cent
B & C	86	84.5	7,267
D	14	89.5	1,253
Total	100		8,520

$$\text{Weighted number} = \frac{8520}{100}$$

$$Q = 85.2 \text{ mm}$$

2.7 Floods/Droughts

Floods

In India about 9.0 m ha gets annually flooded (Anonymous, 1988) (Plate 8) causing damages to crops, property and lives. It is necessary to examine the frequency distribution and flood occurrences over the years vis-a-vis the probability of entire basin/watershed getting fully saturated. It is also necessary to examine the feasibility of intense storm falling over the entire catchment and thus leading to historically unmanageable floods.

The answer to moderate the flood lies in blending the techniques of land management with soil and water conservation measures, afforestation, head water erosion control works, downstream engineering works for immediate flood protection to reduce the cumulative peak and volume of flood, and measures to maintain the capacity of drainage system.

Droughts

An estimated 260 m ha are subject to droughts of varying intensities (Das, 1977). By climatic crop growth indices (CCGI), area subject to drought has been classified into moderate (7.62 m ha), large (4.70 m ha), severe (116.8 m ha) and disastrous droughts (19.7 m ha).

Droughts	*States affected*
Moderate	Orissa, Bihar, West Bengal, half of Madhya Pradesh, Parts of Maharashtra, Andhra Pradesh, Tamil Nadu.
Large	Uttar Pradesh, Central Madhya Pradesh, Maharashtra, Punjab and Haryana.

Severe	Karnataka, Tamil Nadu, greater parts of Uttar Pradesh, and Madhya Pradesh and small north-western parts of Maharashtra.
Disastrous	Western Rajasthan, with a small pocket in Karnataka centering district of Bellary.

2.8 Socio-Economic Factors

The success of soil conservation or land reclamation project depends upon socio-economic factors of the particular region. Sociological impact studies should be done in three successive phases:

— an analysis of the human milieu and of sociological and organizational structures;

— a definition of norms, standards and ways and means for altering this milieu for immediate application; and

— a critical analysis of changes in the original situation effected

Analysis of the Human Milieu or Society
The appraisal of the traditional sociological milieu should be based on a series of surveys. As a rule, such studies must be based on available documentation supplemented by field surveys conducted by psycho-sociologists.

Demographic and Sociological Features
The total population of the area, population structure (sex, age, ethnic groups, locations or occupations, etc.) and future trends, in the light on the one hand, of natural changes, and on the other hand, in anticipation of either spontaneous or organized population shifts or migrations;

— data on community life (clans, lineage, families); social stratification, the lines of authority and political organization existing in village communities, their composition (groupings relationships, age groups, social status and political role of members) occupations and economic activities, their functioning (exercise of authority, relations between members) and their spatial distribution (definition of village lands).

Land Tenure Structure

— definition of levels of land holdings (by tribes, class, individuals) and manner of land tenure (as property, or use rights);

— methods of acquisition, transmittal and alienation of land titles or rights;

— authorities on land tenure affairs and settlement of land disputes;

— relation between land rights and social, political and religious systems;

— farming practices (farming directly by holder, land leasing, share-cropping, etc.).

Farm Structure

— size of farms and main features (area, number of farm workers, capital);

— organization of work (division of labour on farms, collective farming and individual farming);

— traditional crops, cultivation techniques and stockraising systems.

Attitudes and Behaviour

— reactions of farmers to schemes or action projects launched or planned;

— their understanding of and views on, social and economic progress (scale of values, expression of needs, etc.).

Demographic research on the migratory movements of people may involve problems of habitat, authority and the social life of people with different backgrounds. Solution to these problems must be sought in advance in order to avoid conflicts between ethnic groups or between new immigrant and settled land owners.

As regards land tenure, erosion control projects definitely increases land values. This may entail contradictory claims or may encourage speculation. Thus, before a project has started it is important to delimit the precise boundaries of the land area to be developed and to determine land titles and rights. The next step is to consolidate small plots and redistribute them, with due regard to the extent possible of well-founded rights and titles. Evicted land-owners should be compensated according to law. Contracts should be made with new tenants. They should establish the conditions of land use, the manner of transmission of land rights, maintenance costs and financial charges.

This offers the advantage of granting the people on the land only, the rights of exclusive use. Provision should be made to withdraw these rights in case the land-owner fails to comply with the contract.

Studies of human society, especially those of social structure and of the behaviour patterns of farmers should make it possible to decide what type of farming should be promoted and what type of organization (village groupings, collective farms) would be desirable.

2.9 Critical Analysis After Treatment of Land with Soil Conservation Measures

It is necessary that after the land has been treated with soil and water conservation measures, to make an analysis of its social and psychological impact to:

— measure results of the transformation of the human milieu (e.g., the settlement of nomads, the modernization of the farming system, etc.);

— asses the efficacy of the new organizational structures;

— find out the opinion of the people involved and find ways of improving their collaboration.

This information gathered can be used to redress negative aspects and eliminate any maladjustment due to traditional social behaviour or organizational structure.

The achievements of any soil conservation project cannot be expressed in static figures, once and for all, but must be the basis for continuing dialectics; further action being decided on the basis of progress made.

3

Erosion Control Structures for Agricultural Lands

The conservation treatments meant to reduce or prevent sheet erosion while achieving the desired moisture conservation and/or runoff disposal range from narrow-based terracing (contour bunding) to bench terracing.

The important principles to be kept in view while planning measures for proper conservation and utilization of water are:

— increasing the time of concentration and thereby allowing more runoff water to be absorbed and held in the soil profile;

— intercepting a long slope into several short ones, so as to maintain less than a critical velocity for the runoff water; and

— protection against damage owing to excessive runoff.

Terracing (bunding) is by far the most effective and widely practiced field measure for controlling or preventing erosion in different soil conservation regions. Terracing has also been adopted in different ways to meet varied physiographic and climatic conditions. In a general way, it can be defined as series of mechanical barriers across the land slope to break the slope length and also to reduce the slope degree wherever necessary.

DIFFERENT TYPES OF BUNDS

— Bunds constructed along contours or with permissible deviations from contours are called *contour bunds*.

— Bunds constructed at extreme ends of the contour bund, running along the slope are called *side bunds*.

— Bunds constructed along the slope in between two side bunds in order to prevent concentration of water along one side and to break the length of contour bund into convenient bits are called *lateral bunds*.

— Bunds constructed between two contour bunds so as to limit a horizontal spacing to the maximum required are called *supplemental bunds*.

— Bunds constructed along margins of the watershed, road margins, river or stream margins, gully margins and the like are called *marginal bunds*.

3.1 Contour Bunding (Narrow Base Terracing)

FUNCTION

For rolling (slopes less than about 6%) and flatter lands, with scanty or erratic rainfall contour bunding is practiced to intercept the runoff flowing down the slope by an embankment whose ends may be closed or open to conserve moisture as well as reduce soil erosion. For better moisture conservation, on large areas as well as control of soil erosion, it is necessary that land treatment between the bunds g. partial levelling, contour cultivation offers better protection as well as moisture conditions favourable for higher production. It is also necessary in contour bunding system to remove excessive runoff resulting from high intensity storms, surplussing arrangements being provided wherever necessary.

SOILS SUITABLE FOR BUNDING

Contour bunding (Plate 9) can be adopted on all types of relatively permeable soils (e.g. alluvial, red, laterite, brown soil, shallow and medium black soils) except the clayey or deep black cotton soils.

SPECIFICATION OF CONTOUR BUNDING

For planning contour bunding for any area, the planners need information on (a) how far these bunds should be installed, (b) what should be the deviation freedom to go higher and lower than the contour bund elevation for getting better alignment in undulating part of the land, and (c) what should be the cross-section of the bund.

SPACING OF CONTOUR BUND

The main criterion for spacing of bunds is to intercept the water before it attains the erosive velocity. This will depend on many factors, the most important of them being slope, soil, rainfall, cropping programme and conservation practices adopted.

Some have proposed use of universal soil loss equation (USLE) for recommending the spacing in between the bunds and this should be used as far as possible. But the information on many of the important parameters for USLE in the country are yet to be established. Hence following formulae are used in determining in spacing:

RAMSER'S FORMULA

C.E. Ramser has established a general equation based on field observations and experiments for sub-humid areas and soils with good infiltration rates as given below:

$$VI = 0.3 \left[\frac{S}{3} + 2 \right] \qquad \qquad \ldots (3.1)$$

where, VI = vertical Interval in m between two consecutive bunds; and
S = degree of slope in per cent.

In the above general formula, no consideration was given to any other factor other than slope. In order to take other factors into account, the following was suggested:

Adjustment for soil infiltration and permeability

As much as 25% extra spacing can be provided above the mean VI in soils having high infiltration and permeability. Good follow-on conservation practices are adopted, which include contour farming and frequent use of legume in rotation. A decrease in spacing (15%) can be done where soils are of low rates of infiltration or permeability, particularly when used with unfavourable cropping conditions.

Adjustment for rainfall

Rainfall is the major factor to account for soil erosion and therefore, the mean vertical interval is needed to be increased with decrease in rainfall. Rainfall intensity and its erosive power is more important than the annual rainfall.

USDA FORMULA

$$VI = \left[2 + \frac{S}{4} \right] \times 0.3 \qquad \qquad \ldots (3.2)$$

where, VI is in metres.

As per the formula, the bunds would be nearer than in the case of Ramser's formula and consequently, the moisture status of the inter-terraced area would be better than in the case of bund spacing by Ramser's formula.

COX'S* FORMULA

$$Cox's\ formula\ is\ given\ by\ VI = (XS + Y)0.3 \qquad \dots(3.3)$$

where, X—rainfall factor; Y—infiltration and crop cover factor; S—slope percentage; and VI—Vertical interval (m).

The values of X and Y are presented in Tables 3.1 and 3.2.

Table 3.1   Values of X, the rainfall factor

Rainfall	Value of X	Remarks (annual rainfall, cm)
Scanty	0.8	64
Moderate	0.6	64-90
Heavy	0.4	Over 90

Table 3.2   Values of Y, the infiltration and crop cover factor

Intake rate	Crop cover during erosive period of rains	Value of Y
Below average (e.g, black soils)	Low coverage	1.0
Average or above	Good coverage	2.0
One of the above factors favourable and the other unfavourable.		1.5

The above formula takes into consideration the factors such as rainfall, infiltration rate and crop cover during erosive period of rains.

LIMITS OF DEVIATION

Vertical spacing by any method can be increased by 10% or by 15 cm to provide better location, alignment or to avoid any obstacle. In case a small strip is left in between the last bund and field boundary, the vertical fall may be distributed in all the bunds, rather than in only last bund. For example, if contour bunds are constructed at 0.8 m, and the fall left between boundary and last bund is 0.4 m, in that case rather than making the last bund at 1.2 m fall or even at 0.8 m thereby dividing the field in uneven segments, the 0.4 m can be distributed equally in each terrace (Fig. 3.1).

GRADE

The contour bunds are made on same elevation, i.e., on contour and therefore, the grade is zero. But in the field, having undulations, the alignment of contour bunding cannot be laid on exact contour. Some deviations, in such cases, will have to be made. These deviations, causes uneven impounding of water, which results in lesser storage capacity of bund as well as increases the potential danger of breach. It is

---

*M.P. Cox, Water Management Specialist, USAID, Bangalore.

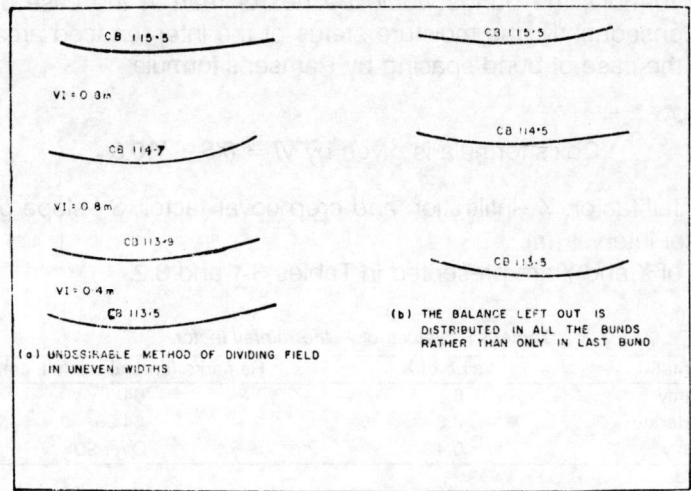

Fig. 3.1 Limits of deviation of vertical interval

always desirable to remove these local ridges and depressions by levelling prior to alignment of contour bunding.

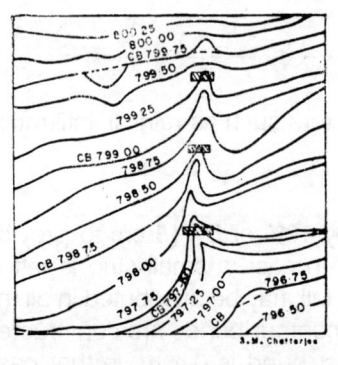

----- DISTANCE TO CROSS THE NARROW RIDGE

Fig. 3.2 Check dams in bunding

As contour bunding is recommended for semi-arid areas only, where intensive farming is not feasible without irrigation, 'levelling' to remove local depressions and ridges is not possible due to cost factor. Then, there is no other alternative than to allow some deviations for better alignment of bunds and these are to be levelled in regular farming operations in due course of time. The limits of deviation are prescribed as 10 cm on higher elevation side and 20 cm for crossing the depressions. These deviations are permitted only for crossing the narrow ridges and depressions, and should not be used in case of wide ridge or depression, forming a part of the topography.

The narrow gullies, 1 to 1.5 m deep, which start within the area proposed to be bunded are usually crossed by contour bunds (using larger cross-section in the gully—minimum 60 cm top width and preferably 3:1 upstream and 2:1 downstream). If felt essential, one or two earthen gully checks may be put in between the bunds also, to safe guard against breaches (Fig. 3.2). This (blocking of gullies by earthen bunds) is possible, because contour bunding is done in low rainfall areas and soils are permeable. The runoff, water which is a potential source of gully formation, is eliminated by bunding in case the gully start from the bunded area itself.

CROSS-SECTION

The cross-section of bund (Fig. 3.3) defines the height and top and bottom width. The shape of the bund is trapezoidal and the size of the bund is calculated as

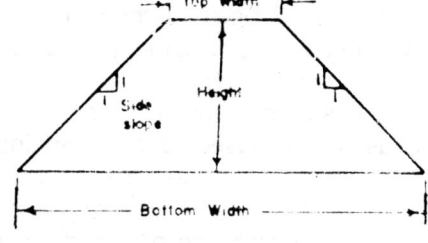

Cross-sectional area

$$= \frac{\text{Base width} + \text{Top width}}{2} \times \text{height}$$

BUND HEIGHT

The governing factors of bund height are

— depth of water to be impounded (F.S.L.)

— design depth of flow over the weir (H.F.L. over the sill)

Fig. 3.3 Cross-section of bund

— freeboard

— dependance on landowners, for the maintenance also necessitates slightly greater height than the minimum worked out.

Depth of water standing against the bund largely depends upon rainfall factor. Rainfall factor R can be obtained from (Fig. 2.3) for the region and peak rate of runoff expected for the applicable area calculated using Cook's Method, considering arbitrary depth of impounding of 30 cm against the bund taking the 10 cm of total rainfall in 24 hours duration in regions, where contour bunding works are carried out on an extensive scale.

— rate of infiltration of soils (lesser the rate more is the depth of water impounded). The soils with very poor infiltration rate, e.g. clayey soils may not be contour bunded.

— Vertical interval (more the vertical interval, more the depth of water impounded).

HEIGHT OF THE BUND

With 30 cm depth of impounding

This is the usual practice in many states. The depth of impounding is designed as 30 cm; 30 cm is provided as depth flow over the outlet and 20 cm is provided as freeboard. This makes the overall height of 80 cm. (Fig. 3.4). With top width of 0.50 m and bottom width of 2.0 m, side slope works out to 1:1 (approx). The cross-section works out to be 1 sq m. In Maharashtra state, the cross-section of bund is varied for different kinds of soil to take into account the side slope requirements and settlement. But considering the practical aspect and that the contour bunding has

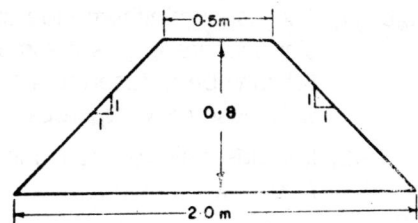

Fig. 3.4 A typical cross-section of contour bund

to be in low rainfall area with permeable soils, the cross-section of 1 sq m is suitable for contour bunding.

Some of the states tried to reduce the size to less than 1 sq m, because the depth of impounding or depth of flow over the outlet is less than 30 cm. But contour bund cross-section depends as much on the expected maintenance of design. Field experience has shown that bunding of cross-section less than 1 sq m, does not last for a long period. With the type of maintenance, farmers usually have, and because long-term loans are given for execution of bunding project, it is desirable that bunding should at least exist till the loans are recovered or farmers realise the importance of bunding and carry out maintenance. Therefore, the bund of cross-section less than 1 sq m is not desirable.

In case tractor farming is done and proper maintenance is possible, it is desirable to use broad-based contour bunding. Broad-based contour bunding has advantage of causing no hindrance to farming and the entire area remains under crop production. In fact contour bunding wastes more than 6% of the area from cultivation. For recommendation of broad-based bunding, tractor farming has been specially mentioned, because by routine ploughing operation, the cross-section of bund can be constantly built up to compensate for the soil loss due to farming. Secondly, contour bunding in tractor farmed area, cause considerable hindrance in farming, in transportation of equipment from one terraced field to another.

The broad-based bund should have settled height of more than 30 cm (preferably 50 cm) measured from natural ground surface. The convenience in farming increases with a decrease in side slope. The side slope of 5:1 is the steepest and 8:1 is preferable. But of course lesser the side slope more will be the earthwork and cost per hectare. The cross-section with different heights and side slopes is given in Table 3.3. A triangular section is assumed, and under cultivation the shape will become parabolic. Proper field operations and maintenance broaden the base and decrease the side slope.

Table 3.3 *Cross-sectional area in sq m of broad-based contour bunding with different heights and side slopes*

Height of bund/ side slope (m)	4:1	5:1	6:1	7:1	8:1
0.30	0.36	0.45	0.54	0.63	0.72
0.40	0.64	0.80	0.96	1.12	1.28
0.50	1.00	1.25	1.50	1.75	2.00

Note: (1) The usual minimum side slope recommended is 5:1.. In case of steeper slope where bunds are made nearer, the upper limit of steeper slope of 5:1 may be reduced to 4:1, but in that case the bunds have to be seeded with close growing crops.

(2) It is desirable to use minimum cross-section of 1 sq m by increasing the height or side slope.

Contour bund to store runoff from 24 hour rain storm of a given frequency
Though a design of cross-section of contour bund with arbitrary depth of impounding of 30 cm is usually adopted, it should be based so as to store runoff expected from the individual bunded area. Even otherwise, it may be desirable to know the storage capacity of contour bund with 0.30 m depth of impounding. Considering these, the basic of calculation of storage capacity requirement is given below:

Referring to Fig. 3.5, the runoff volume from one metre wide strip will be equal to

$$Q_v = \frac{R_e}{100} \times HI$$

where, Q_v = runoff volume (cu m);

R_e = 24 hours rainfall excess (cm); and

HI = horizontal interval in between bunds (m)

Rainfall excess (R_e) can be estimated by using hydrologic soil cover complex number method.

$$HI = \frac{V.I.}{Slope\ (\%)} \times 100$$

(Calculation for V.I. has been dealt with in previous paras).

The storage capacity of bund assuming it to be a triangle, is given by following the equation (neglecting the minor effect of side slope of bund).

$$Q_c = \frac{W_s \times h}{2}$$

where, Q_c = capacity of contour bund, one metre long;

W_s = water spread length behind bund (m); and

h = depth of impounding (m) near the bund.

By equating,
$$Q_v = Q_c$$

We get
$$\frac{W_s \times h}{2} = \frac{R_e}{100} \times HI$$

or,
$$h = \frac{R_e}{50} \times \frac{HI}{W_s}$$

As HI and W_s are parallel they will divide VI into the same ratio $\left[\dfrac{HI}{W_s} = \dfrac{VI}{h}\right]$ by geometry. Substituting this value in the equation above, we have:

$$h = \frac{R_e}{50} \times \frac{VI}{h}$$

or
$$h = \sqrt{\frac{R_e \times V}{50}} \qquad \ldots (3.4)$$

Using this equation, the height of impounding required for 10 years frequency (or say any other frequency) can be obtained, which will not cause any spill over.

To the depth of impounding (h), add depth of flow over the waste weir and a freeboard of 25%. Depth of flow of 0.3 m is considered over the waste weir. Once the height is fixed, then using the minimum top width of 0.5 m and side slopes of 1:1, the cross-section of contour bund can be obtained. For broad-based bund, the cross section can be designed as explained in the preceding paragraph.

PLANNING CONTOUR BUNDING

Alignment

For the purpose of alignment of contour bunding, the area shall be divided into independent blocks of lands of a convenient size, where the soil conservation works can be executed in units of say about 25–50 ha. Selection of an independent block is necessary, so that the selected block will not be affected by the runoff from adjoining blocks, even if those blocks are left untreated. To select such a

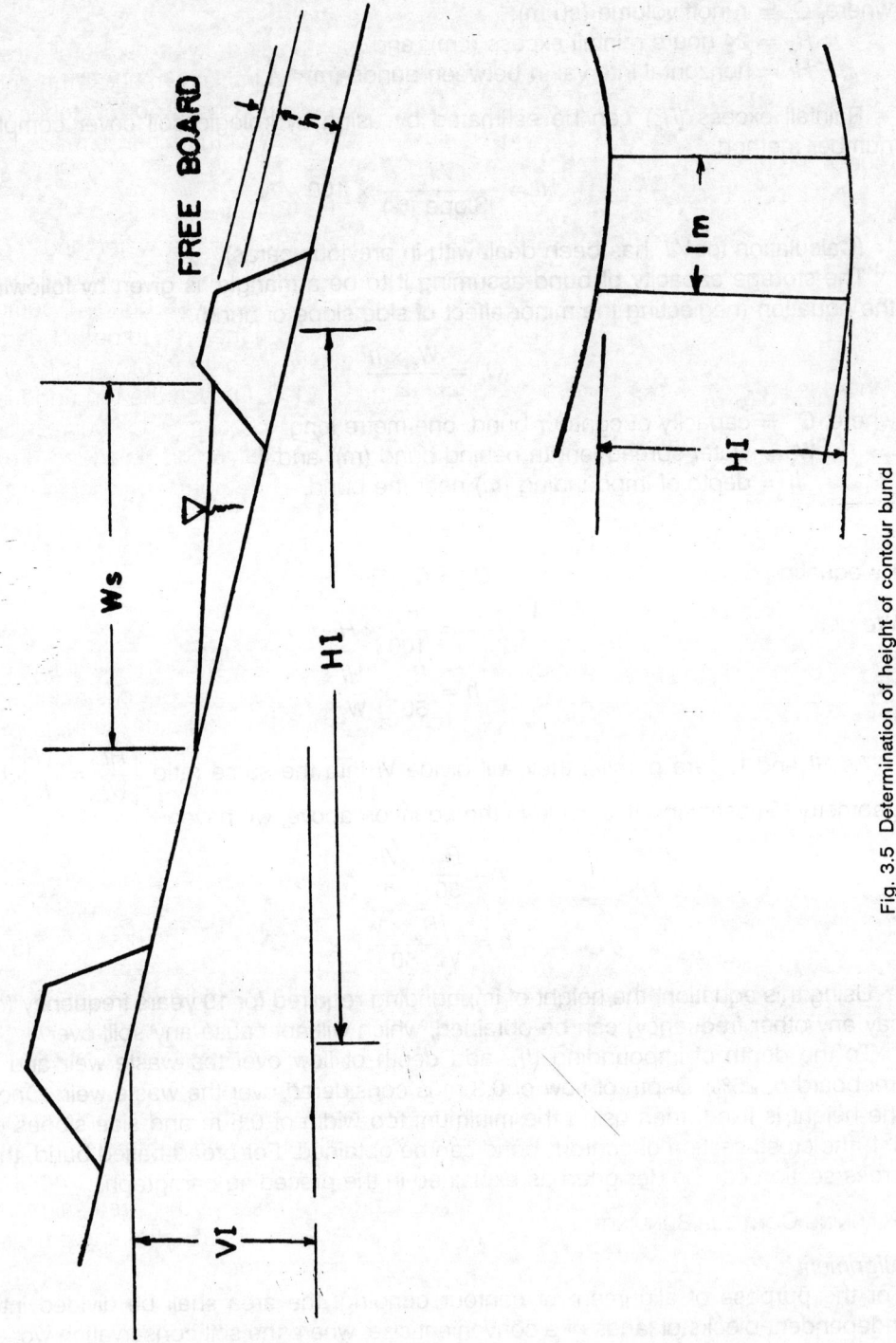

Fig. 3.5 Determination of height of contour bund

block (catchment), it is necessary to reconnoitre the area with a village map with all identifiable landmarks noted therein and mark the boundary of the catchment in the village maps as accurately as we can judge by the eye.

Having selected the blocks, a detailed map of each block drawn to scale of 1 cm = 16 m with all the boundaries of individual fields, subdivisions, etc., marked thereon is prepared. This will be a consolidated map of field measurement book sketches of all fields suited within a block. Then a topographical survey of the block is made by either of the methods, viz. direct contour or grid.

DIRECT CONTOUR

The planning and construction should be started from top of the watershed, i.e. from the highest point. At some places due to non-agricultural area at top or due to non-cooperation of the land owner situated above the area to be bunded, some provision will have to be made to divert the water away from the area to be bunded.

The rod reading by use of dumpy level or any other type of tripod level is taken on the highest point. To this, the vertical interval is added, in case the top ridge is parallel to the bund. In case highest elevation stations are not on the ridge but results in triangular catchment of the top bund, 1.5 times the vertical interval is added. For example, the reading on highest point is 0.20 m in case the ridge is parallel to first bund. In case of triangular catchment area of top bund, the bund will be constructed on ground elevation with staff reading 1.50 + 0.20 = 1.70 m. Once the staff reading on which bund has to be constructed is determined, the staff man moves up and down the slope, till the level has the desired staff reading.

The rod man marks it by pegs or small flags and moves about 20 m approximately on contour and shows again the staff. The staff is moved up and down till level man signals the correct location. Following similar procedure, the entire bund is marked. If the ends are hooked up, the ends of hooked up bund (called side bunds) are marked by deducting the height of hooking up from contour bund elevation. For example, the hooking up is done to 60 cm and contour bund staff reading is 1.20, the staff reading at which side bund will terminate, will be 1.20 − 0.60 = 0.60 m.

The next bund is aligned by adding up the one V.I. (vertical interval) to the ground reading of previous contour bund and the same is adopted until it is not possible to take reading from same setting of the instrument. In that case, the instrument is shifted and back sight on last contour bund alignment is taken and to this, new staff reading, the V.I is added. For illustration, the first bund is marked at 1.20, and V.I is 1.0 m, the next bund is marked at 2.20 m and 3.20 m. If the levelling rod is 4.0 m long, the instrument will be required to be shifted. After setting the instrument, if the back sight on the last bund is 0.40, the next bund will be aligned at 1.40, 2.40 and so on (Fig. 3.6).

Thus, contour lines are plotted for any vertical interval, by the direct contouring method. Contour lines for different vertical intervals are determined depending upon the slope of land. The topography of any block seldom contains uniform slopes. Therefore, V.I. to be chosen for the layout of contour bunds is the predominant slope of land encountered in each part of the block. The determination of vertical interval for contour line will conform to the vertical interval of the contour bund to be constructed in the area.

However, in between the contour lines directly plotted for field survey, shorter contour lines may be plotted by interpolation, using a proportional divider. Contour lines so plotted are considered accurate enough for the purpose of laying out contour bunds with deviations of strict contour, for taking the side and lateral bunds up to

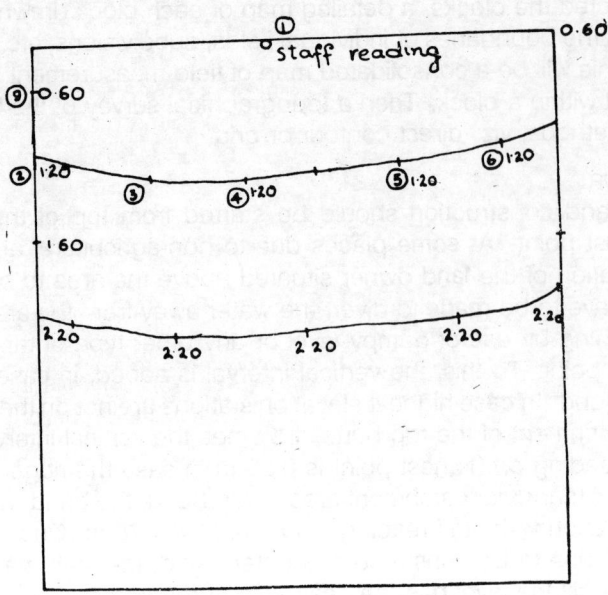

Fig. 3.6 Alignment of contour bund

the predetermined levels above the contour and for laying out supplemental bunds to be approximately parallel to the contour.

Alignment of contour bunds in the plan or block map

After plotting the contour lines in the manner detailed as above, decide maximum vertical intervals at which contour bund have to be formed. The V.I.'s in the contour bunds are decided upon to suit the slope on which the major portion of block lies, where the ridge in a block ends into a point (resulting in a triangular block) and is not a ridge line, then the first contour bund will be formed at 1.5 times V.I. chosen, since the area that will be drained up to the first bund will be only in the form of a triangle and not a rectangle, as it would be, if the ridge is a line running parallel to the first contour. Subsequent contour bunds will be formed at chosen vertical intervals below the first contour bund.

As a first step in the alignment of contour bunds, the slope of the block with the ridge point/line is duly considered. The reduced levels at which the first contour bund is to be formed is to be decided and contour bund will follow the contour line plotted on this reduced level. The alignment of contour bund should generally follow the contour line without any deviation to be of maximum utility.

In case of undulating land resulting in zig-zag contour bund alignment for crossing narrow ridge or depression, same deviations have to be made within limits (10 cm on higher side and 20 cm on lower side). As explained earlier, such deviations should be kept to the minimum and all attempts are required to be made to cut high points and fill low points in due course of time.

Layout of contour bund in the field

If it is warranted the alignment of bund can be deviated from the contour without exceeding the permissible limit, so that the bund crosses the field boundary at a wider angle than 45°. When the alignment of bund causes a narrow strip of land at one end of field and if the permissible deviations would be exceeded by shifting the bund to avoid the narrow strip of land, either the V.I. of the bund should be altered or the bund should be shifted up stream, so that the width of strip of land below would be wider. In the later case, an additional bund along the field margin would become necessary to conserve moisture above the marginal bund.

At either end of the contour bunds, side bunds will have to be aligned to run along the slope of the field up to 0.3 m above contour. These side bunds enable stagnation of water up to 0.3 m depth along the contour and make available the water to percolate down the soil profile, to be available for the crops over a long period.

Where the length of contour bund exceeds 300m, bunds along the slopes in between side bunds are necessary, in order to prevent concentration of water along one end and the break the length of contour bund into convenient bits. These bunds are called lateral bunds. They will prevent the accumulation of runoff in any one end of the contour bund and consequent breach at that end. Where a waste weir may break the length of contour bund and may facilitate draining of excess water from the block above, lateral bunds may not be necessary, unless the uninterrupted length of bund from the waste weir to any side bund is more than 300 m.

Where the horizontal interval between two consecutive bunds is more than permissible limits, supplemental bunds are formed in between two such contour bunds for the portion of the strip exceeding the maximum prescribed limit. These supplemental bunds are aligned almost parallel to the contour or across the general slope of the land. They are provided with side bunds to facilitate conservation of moisture in the strip of the land above.

The top level of the bunds should be maintained the same in the contour bund, side bund, lateral bund and supplemental bund (Fig. 3.7). Marginal bunds which are constructed along the field boundaries or road, stream, river or gully margins may have uniform cross-sections and the top level need not be maintained the same.

While aligning the contour, supplemental or marginal bunds, great care may be taken to avoid strips of land less than 30 m in width, as such narrow strips will cause inconvenience to agricultural operations.

Staking the bund alignment

The bund alignment as proposed in the plan approved by competent authority is transferred to the ground, starting from top of the catchment. The staking of the central line of the proposed bund is done by using a levelling instrument.

After setting the instrument, back sight is taken on the nearest bench mark to determine the height of the instrument. The difference between the height of the instrument and the first proposed ground elevation of the contour bund, is the staff reading on which the contour bund is to be marked. For example CB 58.60 is to be aligned, the bench mark elevation is 59.80 and back sight is 0.50. The HI=59.80+0.50=60.30 m. The staff reading for CB 58.60 will have to be 60.30 − 58.60=1.70 m. The rod man moves up and down on one side of field till level man gets the rod reading of 1.70 m. After that he moves 20 m along the contour and again moves up and down till the rod reading is 1.70 m. Same procedure is adopted to align the entire contour bund. The bund will terminate at points where ground staff reading is 1.70 − 0.60=1.10 m (in case 0.60 is the height to which it is hooked).

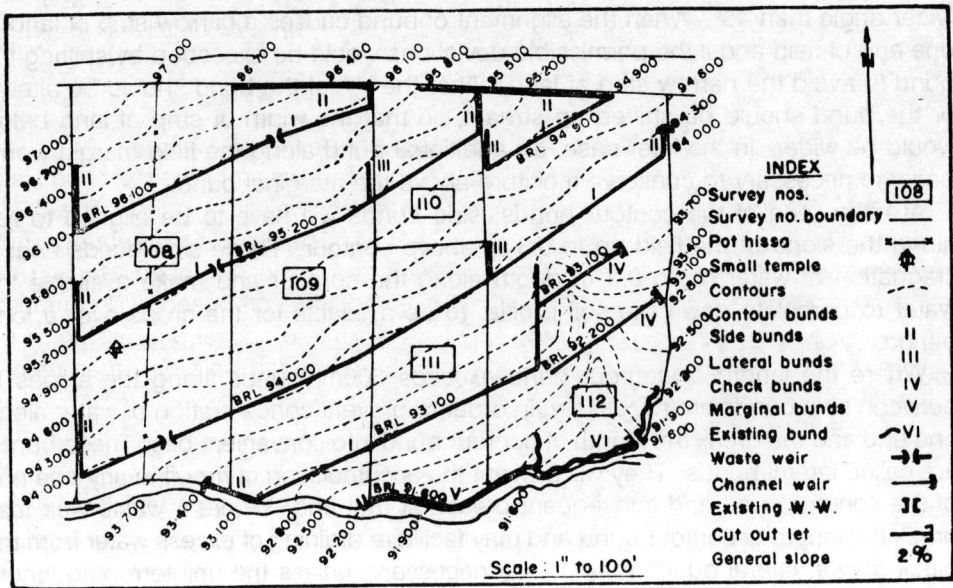

INDEX

Survey nos.	108
Survey no. boundary	———
Pot hissa	×—×——×
Small temple	⌖
Contours	----
Contour bunds	I
Side bunds	II
Lateral bunds	III
Check bunds	IV
Marginal bunds	V
Existing bund	VI
Waste weir	
Channel weir	
Existing W.W.	
Cut out let	
General slope	2%

Scale : I" to 100'

Fig. 3.7   Contour map indicating different kinds of bunds and structures for surplussing (soil: red sandy loam)

After staking one bund, the surveyor should walk along the proposed alignment and look out sharp bends in the layout and move some of the stakes if necessary to ease the sharp turns and bends. Such adjustments should be limited to not more than the permissible deviation of 20 cm from strict contour. The bottom width of contour bund is then marked with half the width on either side of the centre line, i.e. if the bottom width of bund is 2.0 m, the top of the bund will be 1.0 m on either side of this alignment or staking of the bund. This is usually done by a wooden marker, which is just a horizontal pole having two pegs driven at 2m intervals with a centre peg mid-way between them. This marker is dragged along the centre of the bund line. Thus bottom width of the bund line is staked.

Construction

Bunds are constructed out of the earth excavated from borrow pits 2.5 m wide and 0.3 m deep cut at a distance of 3 m from the toe of the proposed bunds. Invariably, these borrow pits are taken U/S side of the bund, so that they can be easily ploughed down during cultural operation or filled by whatever soil moved down during the rains. The width of borrow pits can be varied (keeping the depth constant) to the required quantity of earthwork needed, in case a bund alignment has to be deviated.

Normally the bunds are constructed with the help of manual labour. However, it can be done by using implements such as earth drag (*kehi*) drawn by bullocks in medium deep soils.

3.2   Surplussing Arrangements

In order to protect the contour bund from breaching and the standing crop from damage, masonry outlet structures which can drain away excess water, are constructed. The structures are also constructed in the lowest spaces in a holding where, due to the deviation of the contour bund to conform field boundary, the stagnation of water occurs in excess of 0.3 m and therefore, has to be drained away rapidly. The need for masonry outlets, their location in the bunds and their design are of paramount importance in the soil conservation work.

WASTEWEIRS

Need

Wherever the block that will drain into a proposed masonry weir exceeds about 3.75 ha, there is need for construction of masonry weir in a bund. The 3.75 ha mentioned above is only the area of land that will actually drain into the proposed weir and not the entire area of the sub-block above the proposed weir. In other words, the block for which soil conservation works are proposed, will comprise of several small drainage basins, each of which drain into a local depression. If each such basin exceeds 3.75 ha in extent above the proposed weir, only then there will be need for construction of an outlet.

Location

Usually the masonry weirs are located in a contour, supplemental or marginal bund, where such a bund crosses a depression. Once a masonry waste weir is provided in a contour bund, all the bunds situated below should be provided with outlets of one kind or the other along the depression of water course. Generally waste weirs are located at depressions with the crest of their body walls constructed at 0.3 m above the contour. Successive masonry waste weirs are not to be constructed in a straight line, but have to be constructed in a staggered manner, so that they will not cause gullying of the field in between the waste weirs.

The different types of outlets used commonly are as given below:

Clear overfall stone weir

A clear overfall weir (Fig. 3.8) should be provided along the contour bund ordinarily with its crest wall top 0.30 m above the contour. Thus height of 0.30 m is suitable for crops like *jowar, bajra*, etc., which are ordinarily grown as a seasonal crops in the scarcity areas.

It comprises of a masonry wall of a designed length constructed at a suitable place in the bund and the two ends of the bunds properly pitched.

A channel weir

A channel weir (Fig. 3.9) is provided at one end of the bund to prevent the nose of the bund getting breached and the fill of the channel weir is kept 0.30 m above the contour level of the bund. It also comprises of a stone wall underground with one end of the bund pitched. Stone work for these walls may be of dry rubble or *khandki*.

A cut outlet

It is a channel weir and is cut as an ordinary channel about 1.75 m away from the end of the bund with its fill kept 0.30 m above contour level. It has an approach and a tail channel to give runoff water proper entrance to and exit from the weir proper. Usually such cut outlets are proposed only in hard material.

A pipe outlet

A pipe outlet (Fig. 3.10) comprises of a pipe discharging surplus water. The design consists of a hume pipe of required diameter with one well on the upstream. A 15 cm ϕ pipe is suitable for 4 ha catchment, 22.5 cm ϕ pipe up to 6 ha and 30 cm ϕ pipe can work up to 10 ha. A well-consists of 0.45 m ϕ hume pipe for 15 cm ϕ outlet

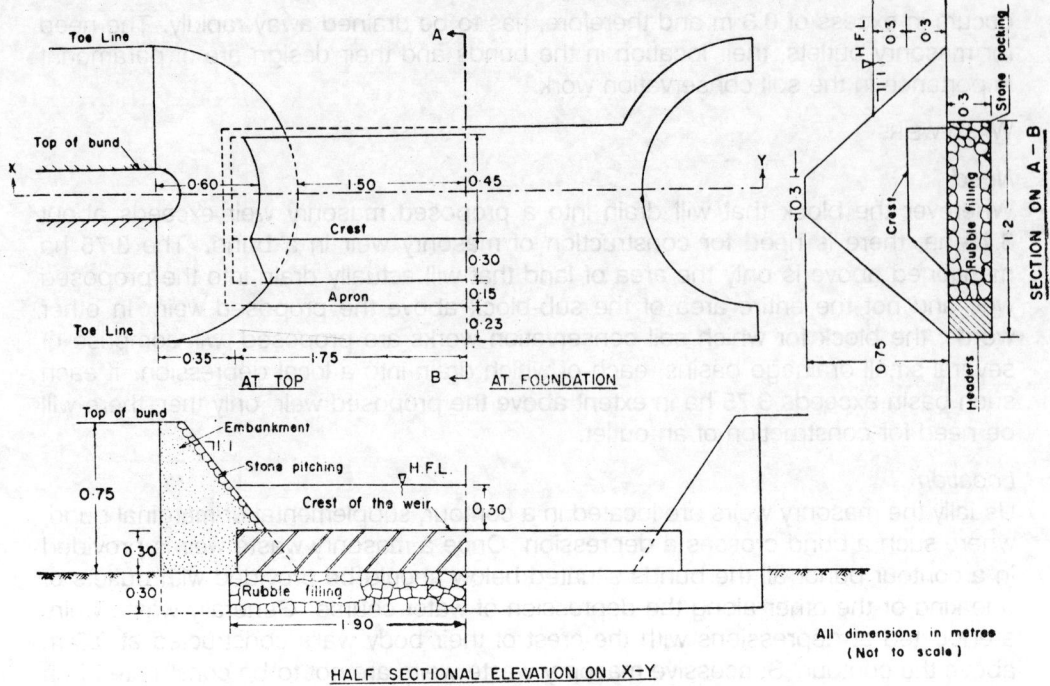

Fig. 3.8 Clear overfall stone-weir

and 0.60 m φ for 22.5 cm and 30 cm φ outlets. The well top is kept 0.30 m above contour level. While designing waste weirs, peak rate of runoff may be computed.

Ramp-cum-waste weirs
During the period when scarcity works are in progress, it is not formally possible to construct outlets immediately. Therefore, what are called, Ramp-cum-waste weirs are constructed. These are of a temporary nature. A ramp-cum-waste weir (Fig. 3.11) consists simply of an earthen bund with its top 22.5 cm above the contour level and having a slope of 1:10 like a ramp, both on the upstream and on the downstream side of the bund. When permanent waste weirs are constructed, they will be situated at the site of these ramp-cum-waste weirs. Ramp-cum-waste weirs should be pitched with grass wherever conditions of rainfall are favourable. Ramp-cum-waste weirs are also constructed as normal waste weirs, in parts of Khandesh and Gujarat.

The grass outlet is similar to the Ramp-cum-waste weirs, with the earthwork thoroughly grass-pitched.

Design of surplussing structures
The minimum length of outlet should be provided, as calculated by the formula for a rectangular weir,

$$Q = 1.7LH^{3/2} \qquad \ldots (3.5)$$

where, Q = peak rate of runoff, cumecs expected from the catchment area of bund itself and of upper bund if draining into the same (cumulative catchment); and H = 0.3 m

(Q can be computed by using any one of the three methods described earlier).

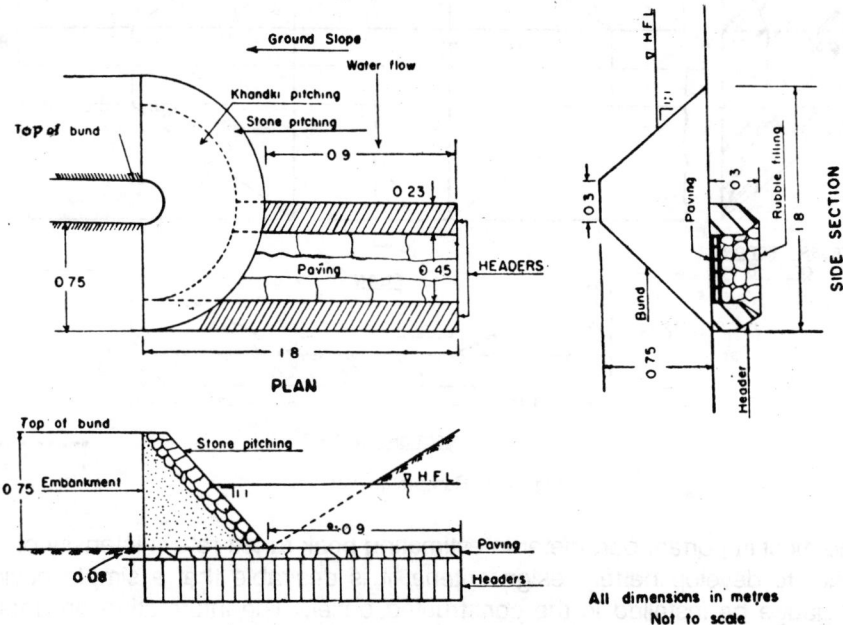

Fig. 3.9 A channel weir

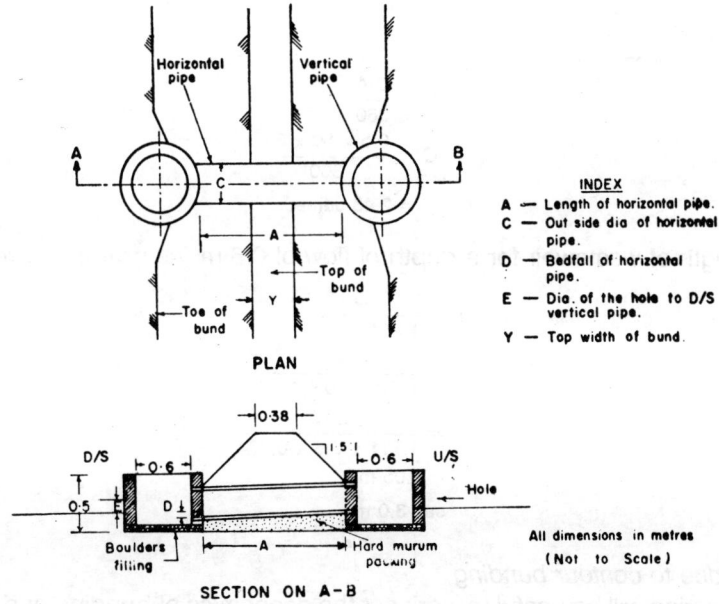

INDEX

A — Length of horizontal pipe.
C — Out side dia of horizontal pipe.
D — Bedfall of horizontal pipe.
E — Dia. of the hole to D/S vertical pipe.
Y — Top width of bund.

All dimensions in metres
(Not to Scale)

Fig. 3.10 A pipe outlet

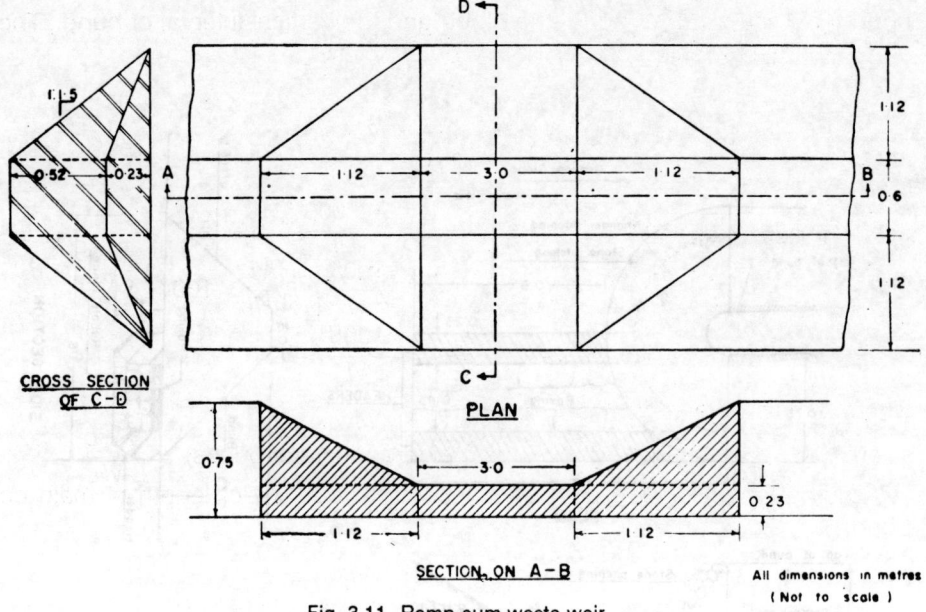

CROSS SECTION
OF C-D

PLAN

SECTION ON A-B

Fig. 3.11 Ramp-cum-waste weir

All dimensions in metres
(Not to scale)

The most important parameter in estimating peak runoff rate is intensity of rainfall. In order to develop better design criteria, it is desirable that a simple device like crest gauge be installed in the constructed outlet. The information on depth and frequency of flow will be very useful in determining the proper design peak.

Example 10—Design a wasteweir from the following data:

Cumulative catchment area	= 35 ha
HFL over the crest	= 0.6 m
Intensity of rainfall	= 50 mm/hr

Solution

Assume a coefficient of runoff = 0.5

The peak rate of runoff,

$$Q = \frac{CIA}{360}$$

$$Q = \frac{0.5 \times 50 \times 35}{360}$$

$$= 2.43 \text{ cumec}$$

The length of wasteweir for a depth of flow of 0.6 m (as given) is given by

$$L = \frac{Q}{1.711 \times h^{3/2}}$$

$$= \frac{2.43}{1.711 \times (0.6)^{3/2}}$$

$$= \frac{2.43}{1.711 \times 0.6 \times 0.774}$$

$$= 3.05 \text{ m}$$

or   say 3.0 m

Area lost due to contour bunding

This information will be useful to work out the economics of bunding and to ascertain the net yield of crops after bunding. The actual area occupied by bunds depends upon the base width of bund, the slope and the vertical interval of bund. The area occupied by the main bund alone will be as follows.

Let HI = Horizontal interval;
VI = Vertical interval; and
S = Prevailing land slope in per cent.

$$\text{Length of contour bund per ha} = \frac{10,000}{HI}$$

$$= \frac{100S}{VI} \left[\because \frac{VI}{HI} \times 100 = S \right]$$

$$\text{Area lost (sq m) due to bunding/ha} = \frac{100S}{VI} \times b$$

where, b = base width of contour bund

% area lost due to bunding (excluding side and lateral bunds) $= \dfrac{S \times b}{VI}$

Assume length of side and lateral bunds to be 30% of length of main contour bund.

$$\therefore \text{Total length of bund/ha} = 1.3 \times \frac{10,000}{HI}$$

$$\text{Total area lost due to bunding/ha} = 1.3 \times \frac{100S}{VI}$$

(including side and lateral bunds)
[Note: Bunds can be used for growing grasses or crops like castor and thus compensate for area lost.]

Number of outlets—Let K be the critical length of bunds and L be the length of main bund per ha. Assuming that the outlet receives water from both sides,

$$\text{Number of outlets required per ha} = \frac{L}{2K} \qquad \ldots (3.6)$$

Computation of earthwork for bunding—The earthwork for bunding includes main contour bund and side and lateral bunds. The area of cross section of side and lateral bunds is equal to main contour bund. The total length of bund per ha

$$= 1.3 \times \frac{100S}{VI}$$

Area of cross section of bund

$$= \frac{\text{Top width} + \text{bottom width}}{2} \times \text{Height of bund}$$

$$\text{Total earthwork/ha} = \frac{1.3 \times 100 \times S}{VI} \times \text{Area of cross section of bund} \qquad \ldots (3.7a)$$

In areas where bunds are already existing, the dimensions may be examined and necessary earthwork may be computed by multiplying length of existing bund and additional quantity required (required section minus existing section).

Ramps, if needed, their earthwork may be computed by multiplying number of ramps and quantity estimated per ramp.

Maintenance of bunds and outlets
After the works in a contour bunding project are completed, due to lack of maintenance, much of the benefits due to conservation practices are lost and in certain

cases degradation may bring more damages. The neglect of a single individual bund would endanger the whole system of the works down below.

It is, therefore, of paramount importance that the following works are attended to before the onset of rains.

— plugging of all breaches firmly;

— filling up of all sags in bunds and restoration to proper height and section;

— plugging all rat holes and fox holes, etc.;

— repairing all damaged outlets;

— growing grasses and trees on bunds to strengthen the bunds and providing fodder for cattle;

— general level in between bunds to be done to ensure greater productivity from lands; and

— In case of unprecedented rainfall (which was perhaps not accounted for in designs), large scale damage occurs to bunds and outlets are examined in detail, for which special estimates are formulated for execution and attended to in time.

PRACTICES ADOPTED IN DIFFERENT INDIAN STATES

Karnataka

Soil suitable for bunding

For the purpose of bunding, soils are generally classified on their depths except for some red soils, where the presence of sand, gravel or clay is taken into consideration.

Table 3.4   *Classification of soils suitable for bunding*

Class	Soil depth, cm	Remarks
Very shallow	Less than 7.5	
Shallow	7.5 to 22.5	
Medium	22.5 to 45	
Medium deep	45 to 90	
Alluvial deep	45 to 90	Alluvial strata having 30% or less clay
Deep (heavy clay) black soils	over 90	
Red soils mixed with (a) sandy loam or clay, (b) gravel		

Bunds in shallow, medium and medium deep-black soils are quite suitable for bunding. In deep-black soils, contour bunds has not been recommended. In very shallow soils (less than 7.5 cm) contour bunding is also not recommended.

It is further recommended that the above figures be considered as ceiling figures and one may adopt narrower intervals so long as no interference with cultivation and traditional boundaries of holdings is caused.

Base width

The bund base width has been fixed depending upon the infiltration rates of different soils, viz. soils with above average infiltration rates (gravelly to shallow soils), soils with average infiltration rates (medium soils), soils of low and very low infiltration

Table 3.5 *Spacing adapted by the Department of Agriculture, Karnataka state*

Slope, %	VI, m	Approximate horizontal distance, m
0–1	1.0	107
1–1.5	1.22	97
1.5–2	1.37	76
2–3	1.52	61
3–4	1.68	52
4–5	1.82	40
5–6	2.0	36

rates (medium deep soil and black soils of Naragund and Navalgund of Dharwar district). (Table 3.8)

Top width

Top widths range from 0.3 to 0.6 m (Table 3.8)

Side slopes—Side slopes for various soils are presented in Table 3.6

Table 3.6 *Side slopes for various soils*

Soils	Side slopes	Angle with ground
Gravelly and very shallow	1:1	45°
Shallow soils	1.3:1	37° – 34°
Sandy and sandy loam	1.5:1	33° – 41°
Medium soils	1.5:1, 2:1	
Medium deep and black soils	1.5:1 downstream	
	5:1 upstream	

Bund section at deviated points

As the contour bunds cross deviated points within permissible lines, the changed dimension of height and base width have to be considered for calculation. As the bund top level is maintained, the height of bund gets reduced or increased, while crossing a ridge or a gully by the amount of deviation on the ridge or gully, respectively. This reduction or increase in the height leads to proportionate reduction or increase in the base width. (Tables 3.7 and 3.8).

Table 3.7 *Bund section at deviated points*

Deviation (m)	Dimension (m)			Side slope	Bund section (m^2)
	Top	Base	Height		
nil	0.45	1.95	0.75	1:1	0.90
(Bund on contour)					
0.15	0.45	1.65	0.6	1:1	0.63
(cn ridge)					
0.30	0.45	2.55	1.05	1:1	1.58
(in gully)					

Shrinkage of bunds

The shrinkage is minimum in gravelly or sandy soils and maximum in clayey soils. For medium soils, it is around 13 to 20%.

Bund section:

Table 3.8 *Recommended bund sections and diversion in Karnataka State*

Particulars of soils	Top width (m)	Base width (m)	Height (m)	Side slopes Horizontal:Vertical		Area of cross Section m²	Remarks
Gravelly soils	0.30	1.2	0.6	0.75:1		0.45	
	0.30	1.5	0.6	1:1		0.54	
Red soils mixed with	0.30	2.1	0.6	1.5:1		0.72	
sandy loam or clay							
Very shallow soils	0.45	1.95	0.75	1:1		0.90	Soils 7.5 cm or less overlying murrum or kankar
Shallow soils	0.45	2.4	0.75	1.3:1		1.06	
Medium soils	0.60	3.3	0.68	2:1		1.31	
	0.53	3.0	0.83	1.5:1		1.44	
Medium deep soils	0.30	4.43	0.75	1.5:1 (downstream)	4:1 (upstream)	1.77	Full soil 0.45–0.6m
Black soils of Naragund and Navalgund areas of Dharwar district	0.30	5.18	0.75	1.5:1 (downstream)	5:1 (upstream)	2.05	Full soil 0.45–0.6m

Special precautions to be adapted for medium deep soils and black soils of Naragund and Navalgund areas of Dharwar district:

— Levelling of inter-bunded area;

— Ploughing a strip of land against the bund on the upstream before monsoon starts; and

— Planting grass, glyricidra, etc., on bunds.

Side bunds

In respect of all side bunds, the side bund ends are higher than the bunds contour by 0.6 m.

Borrow pits

For ease of taking measurements, checking and payments of the following standard sizes of borrow pits are adapted.

New construction —3.125 m × 3.125 m × 0.3 m(100ft^3)
6.25 m × 3.125 m × 0.3 m(200ft^3)
4.68 m × 3.125 m × 0.3 m(150ft^3)
3.90 m × 2.5 m × 0.3 m(100ft^3)
7.81 m × 2.5 m × 0.3 m(200ft^3)

Subsequent — 3.125 m × 1.56 m × 0.3 m(50ft^3)

construction 6.25 m × 1.56 m × 0.3 m(100ft^3)
3.90 m × 1.56 m × 0.3 m(75ft^3)

Selection of the pit size

The pit size should be so chosen (out of the standard sizes prescribed) that the berm between consecutive pits (on a contour bund) would be the minimum possible.

Formula for calculating spacing between borrow pits

The berm between the consecutive pits for a contour bund depends upon bund section and size of pit adapted. The berm can be calculated by the formula:
Berm between consecutive pits

$$= \frac{\text{Pit Quantity}}{\text{Bund section}} - \text{Length of pit parallel to bund line}$$

Example 11— Bund section = 1.44 m^2; Pit quantity = 5.66 m^3
Length of pit parallel to bund = 3.125 m

Berm between pits $= \dfrac{5.66}{1.44} - 3.125 = 0.80$ m

Location of borrow pits: Borrow pits are lined out as below:

Soils	Location
Shallow and medium soils	On the upstream side of the bund
Medium deep soils	On the downstream side of the bund
Gully crossings	Ridge portion flanking in the gully
Ridge crossing	Crests of ridges

Berm between the toe of bund and borrow pit line

A minimum of 3.125 m berm between the bund toe and pit is adapted to facilitate cultivation of that area and use of any farm machinery such as seed-drills, etc.

Ramps

Earthen ramps are provided for passage of carts, cattle and implements from field to field.

Type requirement of earthwork depends upon the width of ramps, height of bunds, soil type and slope given on either sides (Fig. 3.12). The convenient slopes are 5:1 or 6:1.

Orissa

Specification of bunds

CROSS SECTION OF A RAMP

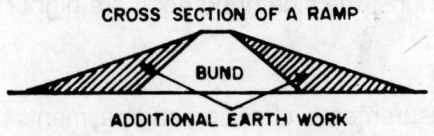

ADDITIONAL EARTH WORK

Fig. 3.12 Cross-section of Ramp

Table 3.9 *Specification of bunds constructed in land reclamation*

Type of soil	Top width, m	Bottom width, m	Side slopes	Height, m	Section m²
Heavy	0.30	2.18	1.5:1	0.6	0.744
Light	0.30	2.00	1.25:1	0.6	0.70
Irrigated soils	0.30	1.56	1:1	0.6	0.558

Experience of bunding in early plan periods by spacing the bunds according to thumb rule $VI = \dfrac{S}{2} + 3$ and $VI = \dfrac{S}{2} + 2$ did not show encouraging results. At many a situations cross bunds were put, along the slope to arrest the runoff with a view to facilitate paddy cultivation.

With above experience it was recommended to have bund spacings and size of plots by utilizing an arbitrarily fixed formula from $VI = \dfrac{S}{6} + 2$. The bunds were also given grades from 0.1 to 0.5 per cent. The details of specification are dealt with under graded bunding.

Tamil Nadu

Soils suitable for bunding

Contour bunding is adopted in all soils and is beneficial in the red and brown soil regions of Tamil Nadu, particularly in areas receiving low and erratic rainfall. Contour bunding is not adopted in the clayey and black cotton soils.

Table 3.10 *Specification for various slope groups*

Slope of land, %	Cross-section m²	Vertical interval, m	Horizontal interval, m		Length of bund per ha m
0–2	0.72	0.9	78	whichever is less	134 to 224
2–3	0.72	1.2	62.5	whichever is less	168 to 253
3–6	0.72	1.8	62.5	whichever is less	168 to 336
6–10	0.72	3.0	47.0	whichever is less	224 to 336

The dimensions of contour bund shall be:

Top width   = 0.45 m
Bottom width   = 2.0 m
Height   = 0.6 m
Side slopes   = 1.25:1

Side bunds

At either end of the contour bunds, side bund will have to be aligned along the slope of the field up to 0.3 m above the contour.

Lateral bunds

When the length of contour bund exceeds 300 m, lateral bunds along the slope are provided. It is taken up to 0.3 m above the contour from the main bund.

Borrow pits

Borrow pits of size 2.45 m and 0.3 m depth situated at a distance of 3.0 m from the toe of the bund are in vogue. They are generally dug on the upstream side of bund.

Side slopes

For red soils, side slope of 1.25: 1 is adopted.

Maharashtra (Ref. Gadkary, 1966)

Suitability

Contour bunding is adapted on lands with slopes above 0.5% up to 6% in scarcity zone in cultivable areas, having well-drained soils and high rainfall zone with soil formed from mixed rocks and in slopes up to 6% in transition zone with red to reddish brown soil.

Spacing of bunds

Table 3.11   *Spacing of bunds*

Slope, %	Vertical interval, m	Approximate horizontal distance, m
0–1	1.0	106
1–1.5	1.2	98
1.5–2	1.4	76
2–3	1.5	60
3–4	1.7	52
4–5	1.85	40
5–6	2.00	36

Bund section

The following bund sections are recommended to be adopted for bunds designed in the scarcity areas of Maharashtra state (Gadkary, 1954).

Borrow pits

Borrow pits are dug on the upstream side in case of shallow and medium soils and on the downstream side in case of deep soils. In either case a berm of 3.5 m is left beyond the base width line of the bund and beyond the berm, the required borrow pits are taken. Usually these borrow pits are of standard sizes for easy computation checking and payment. Knowing the quantity of earthwork required for a given length of bund, the number of borrow pits required are lined leaving suitable widths of berms between two borrow pits.

Gujarat

Contour bunding is adopted in dry areas up to 6% slopes.

Table 3.12 *Bund section*

Soil type	Top width, m	Bottom width, m	Side slopes	Height, m	Section, m²
Full murrum c. soil layer up to 7.5 cm	0.45	2.0	1:1	0.75	0.929
Soil layer from 7.5 cm to 22 cm	0.45	2.6	1.25:1	0.82	1.277
Full soil or soil layer from 22 cm to 45 cm	0.52	3.0	1.5:1	0.82	1.50
Full soil 45 cm to 90 cm	0.60	4.2	2:1	0.90	2.22

Table 3.13 *Bund section*

Type of soil	Top width, m	Bottom width, m	Side slopes	Height, m	Cross-section m²
Shallow soils (7.5 cm and less of soils overlying *murrum* or *kankar*)	0.3	2.14	1.5:1	0.60	0.74
Medium soils (7.5 cm to 22.5 cm layer of soil over *murrum* or *kankar*)	0.3	2.13	1.2:1	0.76	0.93
Medium black soils (22.5 cm to 0.9 m layer of soil overlying *murrum* or *kankar*)	0.3	2.6	1.5:1	0.75	1.11
Deep soils	0.6	2.9	1.5:1	0.75	1.34

Location of borrow pits
These are generally excavated on the upstream side of bund leaving a berm of 3.0 m for upstream toe of the bund.

Design of surplussing structures
In Gujarat and Khandesh, ramp-cum-waste weirs are adopted. These are provided at even 60 m along the main bund.

For channel type weirs, add 25% extra length over the lengths shown in Table 3.14.

Uttar Pradesh
Contour bunds are recommended on gentler slopes (slopes up to 6%) and in areas

Table 3.14   *Crest length versus cumulative area*

Area of cumulative catchment for which provision has to be made for surplus runoff, ha	4.85	6.0	7.28	8.5	9.7	11.0	12.1	13.75
Length of the crest, m	1.22	1.52	1.83	2.13	2.44	2.74	3.0	3.35
Area of cumulative catchment for which provision has to be made for surplus runoff, ha	15.78	17.8	19.4	21.4	23.0			
Length of the crest, m	3.66	3.96	4.27	4.57	4.88			

where average annual rainfall does not exceed 75–100 cm. Contour bunds, may be used for water spreading on gentle cultivated slopes, where soil depth and permeability are favourable. Wherever a contour bund is adopted for water spreading, the land should not have a slope more than 1.5%, preferably less than 1%. This may have to be done by performing levelling operation in the field. The contributing area should not be less than, nor more than eight times the area on which the water is to be spread. Provision should be made for surplussing arrangements.

Table 3.15   *Dimension of contour bunds*

Field slope, (%)	Vertical interval (m)	Horizontal interval (m)	Height (m)	Top width (m)
1.0	0.46	46	0.53	0.30
1.5	0.53	36	0.61	0.46
2.0	0.61	30	0.68	0.46
2.5	0.68	27	0.76	0.46
3.0	0.76	25	0.84	0.46
3.5	0.84	24	0.91	0.46
4.0	0.91	23	0.91	0.46
4.5	1.00	22	0.91	0.46
5.0	1.06	21	0.91	0.46
5.5	1.14	20	0.91	0.46
6.0	1.22	20	0.91	0.46

Side slopes
Clayey soils–1:1; sandy soils–2:1; loamy soils (clay loam, loam and sandy loam)–1.5:1.

Note: While constructing a bund settlement allowance to the extent of 10% in the height of the bund should be made to get desired compacted height. For getting a compacted height of the bund as h (m), the bund should actually be made 1.1 times h.

—Good grass sod on the bund is essential to maintain its shape

Kerala
Contour bunding (with dry rubble, gravels or laterite; pitched walls are constructed and earthen bunds where enough stones, rubble, etc., are not available) on lands having slope up to 15% with a vertical interval of 1.5–2.0 m are adopted.

Madhya Pradesh

Adaptability
Contour bunding is adapted in the open wheat fields of Malwa and Satpura plateau of Narmada valley and Gird region.

Specification
Bunds 0.6–0.9 m in height with 0.3 m top width, 1.52–2.1 m bottom width are suitable for wheat areas. Necessary surplus arrangements like waste weirs, spillways and water courses are provided to dispose off rainfall excess.

Andhra Pradesh
Contour bunding is adapted in low rainfall areas (Rayalaseema, Mehboobnagar and Nalgonda districts) with an average annual rainfall below 760 mm.

Section of bund
The average slope of the areas bunded is 1%. The bunds are designed for a maximum rainfall of 15 cm for a duration of 24 hour, which is rarely exceeded. The dimensions of the bund are —bottom width 4 m; top width 0.6 m; height 0.75 m; area 1.725 m²; side slopes 2:1; vertical interval 0.9 m; and horizontal interval 100 m.

While generally aiming at following the contour, the bund alignments have been eased to avoid creation of uncultivable pockets and sharp bends.

Borrow pits
Wide and shallow borrow pits not exceeding 15 cm in depth were located on either side of the bund 3.5 m away from the toe. As the borrow pits were shallow and wide, they were ploughed, obliterated and cultivated after the formation of bunds.

The grasses, namely *Cenchrus ciliaris, Iseilema laxum* and *Panicum antidotale*; waste weirs with dry stones with suitable dimensions for disposal of excess water at suitable locations are recommended.

Punjab
Contour bunds having a cross-sectional area 0.72 m² is adapted in the foothill region. Provision for surplussing arrangements are made.

General
Contour bunding is also adapted in the states of Assam, Bihar, Rajasthan.

Recommendation of Central Soil and Water Conservation Research and Training Institute, Dehradun
The CSWCRTI, Research Centre, Vasad (Gujarat) recommended contour bunds with an average cross-section of 0.9 to 1.3 m² spaced at 0.9 to 1.20 m vertical interval in Gujarat ravine lands, with slopes up to 6%.

As an alternative to the borrow pits in case of bunds, a shallow or elliptical channel with 6 m top width and 0.3 m depth has been found to be very useful in cultivation and early filling up of depression.

For slopes from 6–12% and sandy loam type of soil, contour bunds with 1.3 sq. m cross-section at VI of 1.8 to 3.6 m has been recommended.

In the ravines of Gujarat, *Dichanthium annulatum, Amphilophis glabra and Andro-pogon ischemum*, stabilized earthen bunds. It was also observed that lands directly under bunds could provide net annual income of Rs.385 per ha (1968 rates) from the sale of grasses.

3.3 Graded Bunding

Definition
Graded bunds (Plate 10) or graded terraces or channel terraces are laid along a pre-determined longitudinal grade instead of along contour.

Function
Graded bunds consist of constructing wide and relatively shallow channels across the slope very near the contour ridges and at critical intervals. These terraces act primarily as drainage channels for inducing and regulating the excess runoff water and draining the same with a mild and non-erosive velocity. The purpose of graded bunding is 'to make runoff water to trickle rather than to rush out'.

Suitability for graded bunding
It is adapted in areas where annual rainfall exceeds 80 cm and particularly in clayey soils even with lesser rainfall.

Factors to be considered
The first item to be considered in making preliminary field plans is the location of the most desirable terrace outlets. Secondly as a safety factor, a terrace system consisting of short terraces and several outlets located in natural water courses is to be preferred, to a system having long terraces and one outlet. In graded bunding, straightened natural waterways have advantages as terrace outlets. Where vegetation alone is not able to provide protection to conduct concentrated water down the slope, construction of structures may be done, especially in the following locations:

— sudden drops at the channel alignments;

— too great velocities to be borne by grass cover; and

— establishment of good grass cover is not possible.

SPECIFICATION OF GRADED BUNDING
Specifications of graded bunding include vertical interval, grade of channel and cross-section.

Vertical Interval
The vertical interval and horizontal spacing at which the graded bunds are to be formed, will be the same as that of contour bunds (refer to earlier description under contour bunding). However, up to 25% extra can be provided for the soils having high rates of infiltration and permeability and good cropping programme and conservation farming practices like contour cultivation. In case of low infiltration and low permeable soils, without proper cropping programme, the spacing may be needed to be reduced by 15% from the mean estimated.

Grade
In general, a grade of 0.2 to 0.4% is provided depending on the soil type. In permeable soils, the grade may vary from 0% at upper end to 0.5% at the outlet end. In

case of impervious soils, it may be started with 0.2% at upper end and increase to 0.4% at the outlet.

It is customary to change the grades at intervals of 100 to 150 m. Thus a 400 m long terrace may have zero per cent grade for first 100 m, 0.1% in second 100 m, 0.2% in third 100 m and 0.3% in the last 100 m. Where proper maintenance of grassed outlet and terraces is not anticipated, it is advisable for short terraces of 100–200 m going up to 400 m as maximum and more outlets. As regards selection between uniform grade or variable grade, the choice depends on which one will provide better alignment. For short terraces, uniform grade may be given and for large terraces, the variable grade may be considered.

Cross-section

The main requirements of satisfactory cross-section are—ample channel capacity and the channel side slopes need to be flat enough to permit farming operations without causing damage to cross-section.

Usually the channel depth of a settled terrace from bottom of terrace to the top of ridge should be at least 0.45 m. Usually terraces are made a minimum of 1 sq m in cross-section, as the design is not only based on hydrologic and hydraulic considerations, but also on condition that these may not be eliminated by faulty farming operations.

The capacity of channel of the terrace depends on cross-section and velocity. The velocity is dependent on grade in addition to other factors. The velocity which will develop in the channel, is estimated by calculating the area of cross-section, hydraulic radius (refer for detailed computation under "grassed waterway" in subsequent chapters), using the appropriate roughness coefficient (usually 0.04) and grade in metre per metre.

The velocity should not be more than the non-erosive velocity for bare soil, which is 0.50 m for sandy soils and 0.60 to 0.75 m in clayey soils. Tables 3.16 and 3.17 give the estimation of the capacity of channels with cross-sections of 1, 1.25 and 1.50 m². It may be observed that normally 1 m² will be sufficient, because by having 300 m (200 is preferable for reasons described earlier) as length, and the horizontal spacing normally not more than 50 m, rainfall will make catchment area of 15,000 sq m = 1.5 ha. With

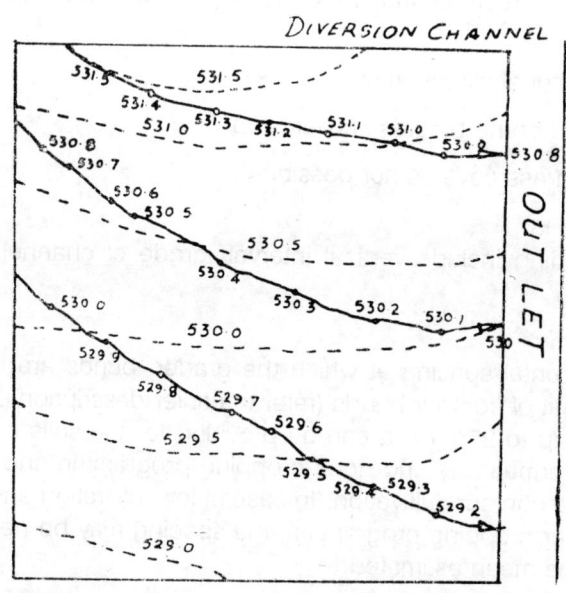

Fig. 3.13 Planning graded bunding on contour map

rainfall intensity of 150 mm per hour and 0.6 value of runoff coefficient, the peak rate of runoff will be $\left(\dfrac{1}{360}\right) \times 0.60 \times 150 \times 1.5 = 0.37$ m³/sec. The cross-section of 1 sq m is sufficient to carry this peak rate of runoff. Larger cross-section may be needed only in places where length of terrace exceeds the above mentioned value, or catchment area is more.

Table 3.16 *Details of channel cross-section and their capacity*

Channel dimensions (Parabolic)		C.S. area (m²)	Hydraulic radius (R) (m)	Slope %	Velocity (m/sec)**	Capacity (m³/sec)	Maximum catchment area (ha)
Top width (m)	Depth (m)	$A = \dfrac{2}{3}Td$	$P = T + \dfrac{8\,d^2}{3\,T}$				
5	0.22	0.75	0.15	0.1	0.22	0.17	0.68
				0.2	0.31	0.24	0.96
				0.3	0.38	0.29	1.16
				0.4	0.46	0.33	1.32
				0.5	0.50	0.37	1.98
5	0.30	1.00	0.20	0.1	0.27	0.27	1.08
				0.2	0.38	0.38	1.52
				0.3	0.47	0.47	1.88
				0.4	0.54	0.54	2.16
				0.5	0.60	0.60	2.40
6	0.31	*1.25	0.21	0.1	0.28	0.35	1.40
				0.2	0.39	0.49	1.76
				0.3	0.48	0.60	2.40
				0.4	0.56	0.70	2.80
				0.5	0.62	0.78	3.12
6	0.375	1.50	0.25	0.1	0.31	0.47	1.88
				0.2	0.44	0.67	2.68
				0.3	0.54	0.81	3.24
				0.4	0.63	0.94	3.76
				0.5	0.70	1.05	4.20

* This is worked out by rational formula with rainfall intensity of 150 mm/hour and 0.60 as runoff coefficient.

** Velocity more than 0.50 m/sec in sandy soils and 0.65 m/sec in erosion resisting soils is not safe.

PLANNING GRADED BUNDING

Planning of graded bunding can be done on similar lines as explained for the contour bunding. These can be directly aligned in the field or can be first planned on the contour map and then on the field. Use of direct alignment is possible after some experience. Both methods are described briefly with the assumption that prior to this procedure, planning and layout of the contour bunding has been well understood.

The first step in planning graded bunding is to decide the location of grassed waterway (outlet). The top catchment is diverted by construction of diversion in case bunding is not done from top catchment.

Based on vertical interval (which will be taken for first terrace as 1.5 times the *VI* if highest elevation is a point and not a ridge parallel to the terrace), the outlet elevation of the first graded is bund determined by deducting this from highest

Table 3.17 *Dimensions of bunds for different cross-sections*

Shape					
Parabolic		Trapezoidal			
					Cross-section (m²)
	Depth (m)	Top width (m)	Bottom width (m)	Height (m)	
3.25	0.35	0.5	2.25	0.55	0.75
3.75	0.40	0.5	2.00	0.80	1.00
3.75	0.50	0.5	2.60	0.80	1.25
4.50	0.50	0.5	3.50	0.80	1.50

elevation. Suppose *VI* is 0.8 m, and the highest elevation is 531.6 m, the outlet elevation of first bund will be 531.6 – 0.8 = 530.8 m (Fig. 3.13).

To provide proper grade, the distance along the contour is measured 20 or 25 m by steps and the elevation of the alignment is also raised proportionately. Suppose grade 0.4% is given, in 25 m, the elevation of 530.8 m, will be raised to 530.9 m, in each next 25 m it will be raised to 531.0, 531.1, 531.2 m, and so on. In case variable grade is given, the same procedure will by adopted except the rise in level will be proportionate to the grade. As explained earlier, some people prefer to give double the grade in the last 20 m (specially in clay soils).

The outlet elevation of second terrace is determined by deducting the *VI* from the outlet elevation of the first terrace. As in the example, the next terrace will be at 530.8 – 0.8 = 530.0 m, next one at 530.0 – 0.8 = 529.2 m and so on.

The alignment of second and subsequent terrace is done on similar lines, as explained above for first terrace. In case alignment on the map or in the field is seen to be irregular, minor adjustments may be needed to bring the alignment to the reasonably practical limits. The grade in terrace can also be modified within the limits of permissible grade to improve the alignment.

For transferring the plan to the field, the terrace lay out is marked by setting the levelling instrument at higher elevation than the highest elevation of the terrace to be marked. The *HI* (height of instrument) is obtained by taking B.S. (back sight) on the bench mark. Deduction of elevation desired from *HI* gives the required staff reading. The rod man moves along the outlet till the desired staff reading of first terrace outlet is found. After staking it, the rod man moves across the slope about 25 m (distance usually measured by steps) and moves the staff up and down the slope keeping approximately the previous marked station as centre and 25 metre as radius. The rod readings have to be reduced by proportionate rise in the elevation. For example, if the rod reading at the previous station was 3.80 and the terrace grade is 0.4%, on every 25 m distance towards further end from outlet, the rod reading will be 3.70, 3.60, 3.50 and so on. In case grade is 0.2%, then for each 25 m, the rod reading will be reduced by 0.05. In that case, for next 25 m, rod readings have to be 3.75, 3.70, 3.65 and 3.60, etc.

If the line aligned on the ground is too irregular, minor adjustments may be done. In these adjustments, the limits should be kept only 15 cm up or down, followed by cutting or filling to avoid stagnation of water.

The marked line represents the centre line of the channel of the graded bunding. The rest of the points of the terrace are then marked with the help of a tape. These points are then joined by a bullock or tractor plow. The desired cross-section is made at an interval of 25 m or 50 m and then the workers are asked to join them by construction from both ends.

CONSTRUCTION OF GRADED BUNDING

Construction of graded bunding can be done by many methods. It can be done by manual labour, by bullock-drawn scraper, tractor plows, grade terracer pulled by wheel tractor, bulldozer, motor grade, etc. Construction by manual labour is simple but is possible in places where plenty of labour is available. For use of bullock-drawn scraper, the channel is ploughed by mould board plow. In Maharashtra, usually four to six pairs of bullocks draw a 35 cm plough, which almost does loosening job as tractor plow. After loosening the earth, each bullock pair works independently with a scraper. The earth is scraped crosswise and dumped on the bund. If required, the loosening of earth is again done by plow. The basic principle is that, a scraper does most efficient work when soil is loose and loosening of soil is easier by an equipment like a plow.

Use of blade terracer is slightly more efficient than only plow. In this case also, the soil is rolled and thrown some distance, till the desired cross-section is made. But use of wheel tractor has a limitation. Experience has shown that if tractor driver is not well-trained, the wheels will spin if the blade is lowered too much, or the blade will carry only small quantity of soil. The tractor also has a tendency to 'turn' with the blade at an angle. As such, use of such implements, for commercial purposes is not recommended.

Use of bulldozer and motor grader, if available, is very efficient. The output is very high. But these equipments are not easily available and the initial cost is high. In case the work is not in large-scale, where required mechanics and spare parts can be maintained, use of machinery for bunding as compared to the manual labour or bullocks is limited.

The output of each machine depends on many factors. The main factors are texture and moisture contents of soil at the time of construction. Table 3.18 gives approximate expected output from some machinery.

MAINTENANCE OF GRADED BUNDING DURING FIRST YEAR

The graded bunds should be inspected after every heavy storm. The places of depression in the channels, undue settlement in the bund, excessive grade in the channel causing scouring and rill formations and excessive inter-bund erosion should be noted and eliminated by levelling, cutting or filling as the case may be.

Table 3.18   *Output by various equipments for terrace construction*

Type of equipment	m/hour	hour/km length
Mould board plow	40–60	16–25
Disk tiller	55–60	16–18
Whirl wind	55–65	15–18
Motor petrol grader	60–70	15–16
Bulldozer	60–70	15–16
Elevating grader (small)	60–70	15–16
Elevating grader (large)	65–85	12–15

(Converted from USDA Handbook No.57).

For maintenance, the dead furrow should always be in the centre of channel and back furrow at the top of the ridge (for broad-based graded bunding). Proper farming practices not only protect the cross-section from being reduced, but even help in constant build-up and easing the side slopes. In any case perpendicular crossing of the bund with plough or planks should be avoided. The contour bund may be planted with suitable grasses or vegetation. Many of the research centres have found that the area under bund can be economically utilized for many purposes. But again due to excessive uncontrolled grazing these have limitations for wide field use.

As discussed earlier, grassed waterway is an important part of the graded bunding programme. Proper inspection and timely correction measures in grassed waterway are essential. Most of the graded bunding in India have failed due to failure of the grassed waterway.

In many countries, underground pipelines have been used for disposal of water. These pipe lines are not designed to take care of peak rates of runoff, but are designed, (to some extent using the drainage coefficient) to remove certain depth of water from the contributing watershed within 24 hour and the bunds are made to have adequate capacity to store the excess water temporarily. In India, though technically feasible, this technique has not been used, due to economic limitation.

PRACTICES ADOPTED IN DIFFERENT INDIAN STATES

Andhra Pradesh
Graded bunding is adopted on lands up to 10% slope in Telengana and South Coastal Andhra with average annual rainfall of 700-960 mm.

Himachal Pradesh
Graded bunding is adopted on lands with slopes from 0 to 10% in valley areas of low hill zones. A longitudinal grade of 1 in 120 is maintained. Soil is excavated on the lower side of the bund.

Madhya Pradesh
In parts of Bhopal region (central part of the state), parts of Malwa region, Bundelkhand and Vindhya Pradesh, graded bunding is adopted and a grade ranging from 0.1 to 0.4% is adapted. Necessary surplussing arrangement like provision of wasteweir, etc., are made.

Maharashtra
Graded bunding is adopted in the following zones:
  — graded bunding with gully plugging for cultivable areas having slopes and 0.5% in transition zone with greyish black soil;
  — graded bunding in cultivable areas having ill-drained soils with slopes above 0.5% in scarcity zone and high rainfall zone with soil formed from mixed rocks.
  — graded bunding with nala draining in cultivable areas, with slopes above 0.5% in assured rainfall zone, with mainly Kharif crops and in moderate to moderately high rainfall zone, with soils formed from trap.

Karnataka
Graded bunds are adopted in areas with heavy rainfall above 80 cm per annum. Suitable grades adopted for graded bunding are as follows:

Soil	Gradient, per cent
Clayey	0.1 to 0.2
Mixed soils (medium silt loams, etc.)	0.3 to 4.4
Sandy soils	0.5

If the length of bund is more, smaller grade should be provided, initially increasing further down within the limitations. For example, if a 375 m long graded bund is to be constructed in medium silt loams, the grades to be adopted may be:

> First 125 m (from ridge) —0.2% grade;
> Second 125 m —0.3% grade and
> last 125 m —0.4% grade.

Bund section

By and large a 0.54 m² section bund (base with —1.5 m, top width —0.3 m and height —0.6 m) would be adequate. A pit size of 1.8 m × 6 m × 0.3 m with negligible berm between pits would suit the bund section.

Waterway

The permissible velocities of 0.9–1.5 and 1.8–2.4 m/sec are adopted in the design of waterways sodded with common legumes and good grasses, respectively. Providing grasses which could be used for grassed waterways are *Cynodon plectostachyum* (giant star grass), *Cynodon dactylon* (Bermuda grass), *Dichantium annulatum* (Marvel), *Cenchrus ciliaris* (Arjan) and *Urochloa mosambicansis*.

Orissa

The Vertical Interval has been arrived at by using an arbitrarily fixed formula

$$VI = \left[\frac{S}{6} + 2\right] \times 0.3 \qquad \ldots (3.7)$$

Slope(%)	VI (m)	HI (m)	Approximate area (ha)
1	0.6	67	0.24
2	0.7	35	0.12
3	0.75	25	0.08
4	0.82	20	0.08
5	0.85	17	0.08

Grades varying from 0.1% to 0.5% are adopted. When a variable grade more than 0.5% is adopted, masonry wasteweirs at convenient points are provided.

Tamil Nadu

For the condition of the topography, soil and rainfall distribution in Tamil Nadu, the longitudinal grade of 25 cm per 100 m length of bund is considered as adequate. The vertical interval and horizontal spacing at which the graded bunds are to be formed will be the same as that of contour bunds.

Graded bunds are not in vogue in most parts of Tamil Nadu, since almost all the areas in the plains are receiving an annual total rainfall less than 115 cm. These bunds as per the state government may be found useful in parts of Kanyakumari and Nilgiri districts and on the foothills of other districts, where rainfed cultivation is restored to

Recommendation of Central Soil and Water Conservation Research and Training Institute, Dehradun

At the Central Soil and Water Conservation Research and Training Institute, Research Centre, Kota (Rajasthan) in the table lands of ravines, which have clay loam to clay soils, graded bunds were found to be suitable in the region up to 4% slope. The graded bunds have 0.7 to 1.0 sq m cross-section and 0.1 to 0.5% grade.

A single diversion on marginal bund with 2.5 m² cross-section with 0.1 to 0.2% grade was found to be suitable for separating ravine areas from table agricultural lands.

At the CSWCRTI, Research Centre, Bellary (Karnataka), graded bunding in deep-black cotton soils with 0.87 m² cross-section, 0.6 m *VI* side slopes of channel section being 10:1, side slope of ridge bund being 2:1 and variable grade from 0.1 to 0.3% was found to be adoptable.

As an alternative to contour bunding and graded bunding, a new erosion control measure namely, conservation ditching consisting of trapezoidal ditches laid on contour at the usual vertical intervals were tried at the Research Farm successfully. However, adaptation of this measure is subject to further trials on field scale.

The conservation ditches (Plate 11) serve the dual purpose of a terrace and storage structure at individual field level. The stored water being available at low heads can be conveniently recycled by using low lift devices. *Dichanthium annulatum* grass need to be established on ditch side slopes and *jowar* stalk stubbles may be established on the upstream side to check rapid siltation of the ditch. Details of contour ditching (Fig. 3.14) are given below:

Top width = 4.58 m; Bottom width = 0.61 m; Depth = 0.61 m;
Side slopes: Upstream = 5:1 and downstream = 1.5:1

The ICRISAT (Hyderabad) on black soils, envisages two furrows and a metre wide ridge in between, planned within small watershed of 2–3 ha. The broad-based ridges of the ICRISAT method are put on a mild gradient of about 0.3% leading into a grassed waterway, which in turn leads into a farm pond, from where water is utilized not only for downstream areas, but more often recycled to donor watershed by pumping. The method is dependent upon a tool-bar implemented frame, which would cost Rs.4,000 plus additional Rs.3,000 for a few implements to be hitched to the frame. This method also needs trial on a field scale, before extending to the farmer's field.

The Central Soil and Water Conservation Research and Training Institute, Dehra-Dun (Uttar Pradesh) recommended, that in Doon Valley, on 2–4% slope, graded bunding with a vertical interval of $0.3\left(\dfrac{S}{2}+3\right)$ m, 0.45 m top width, 0.55 m height and side slopes of 1.5:1 may be adopted. A channel grade of 0.4% to 0.6% can be adopted safely.

3.4 Broad-base Terraces

Broad-base terraces (Plate 13) are also called as ridge terrace or broad-base bunds. This kind or terrace consists of a channel with a ridge on its lower side, whose function is to drain surface runoff or to absorb runoff. Thus these are drainage and absorption terraces.

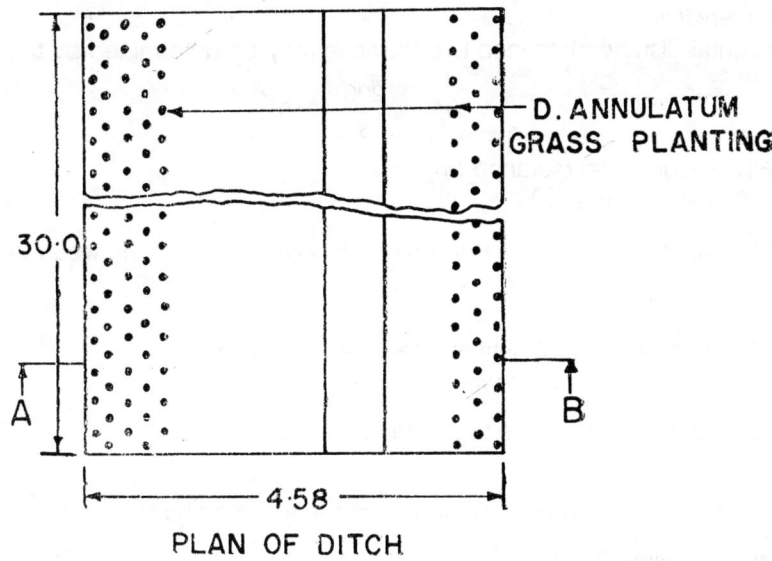

PLAN OF DITCH

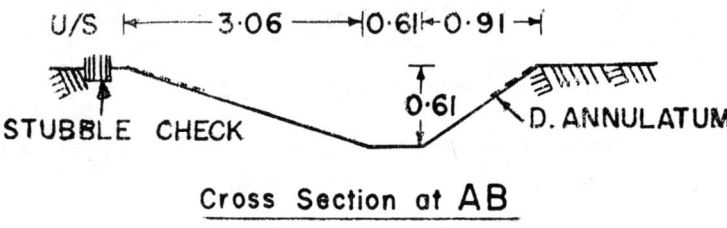

Cross Section at AB

Fig. 3.14 Details of conservation ditching (Note: Figure not scale and dimension in metres)

Suitability

These terraces are constructed on lands up to 10% land slope only. Drainage terraces are constructed on areas where:

— the slope is 3–10%;
— the permeability is slow;
— the field is dissected by gullies or depressions; and
— contour cultivation is insufficient to control surface runoff and soil erosion.

Absorption terraces are suited to areas where:

— rainfall is low and rainfall intensities are not excessive;
— the slope is less than 6%; and
— infiltration and permeability are high.

The absorption terrace differs from drainage terrace in being level along its length, and in having a longer cross-section. The channel and ridge side slopes should be 1:6 to 1:8. Ridge width on the upper side should be not less than 4 m, in case use of machinery is contemplated. The ridge should be 0.45 m higher than the channel.

DESIGN OF BROAD-BASE TERRACE

Terrace Interval
The horizontal distance between two terraces may be determined by the formula,

$$HD = \frac{200}{S} + 10 \qquad \qquad \dots (3.3)$$

where, HD = Horizontal distance (m); and
$\quad\quad S$ = land slope (%).

This formula can be used to determine the vertical interval between terraces.

$$VI = 2 + \frac{S}{10}$$

where, VI = Vertical interval between terraces (m); and
$\quad\quad S$ = slope per cent between terraces.

A 20 per cent variation in vertical Interval is permissible.

Terrace length per ha
The length per ha depends on the slope and the adjusted horizontal interval between the terraces. Following the formula $HD = \dfrac{200}{S} + 10$ and dividing 10,000 sq m by HD, length of terrace per ha is obtained.

Example 12—Length of terrace per ha on an average slope of 4%.

$$HD = \frac{200}{S} + 10$$

$$= \frac{200}{4} + 10 = 60 \text{ m}$$

$$\text{Length of terrace per ha} = \frac{10,000}{60}$$

$$= 167 \text{ m (approx.)}$$

Channel capacity—The channel capacity is calculated using rational formula,

$$Q = \frac{CIA}{360}$$

where, Q = peak rate of runoff for the cumulative terraced area, cumec.
(Detailed working of above method may be referred in the earlier chapter).
The channel capacity can be calculated using the formula:
$Q_c = A \times V$
where, Q_c = capacity of channel (m³/sec); and
$\quad\quad V$ = velocity of flow in the channel (m/sec).

Example 13—C = Coefficient of runoff for a terraced area = 0.4

I = Intensity of rainfall (mm/hr)
$\quad$ = 100 mm/hr (10 year frequency)

A = 2.5 ha

$$Q = \frac{CIA}{360} = \frac{0.4 \times 100 \times 2.5}{360}$$

$$= 0.27 \text{ cumec.}$$

Assuming the channel cross-section of 1.0 m² and a permissible velocity, 0.3 m/sec

$$Q_c = AV = 1 \times 0.3 = 0.3 \text{ cumec.}$$

Hence a channel having a cross-section area of 1.0 m² is adequate. Details for bottom width, depth and side slopes, etc., can be worked out.

PRACTICES ADOPTED IN DIFFERENT INDIAN STATES

Karnataka

The broad-based bunds are constructed in black soils by excavating soils either from both sides or from upstream side only. Such bunds are constructed on strict contour at a few places with the provision of wasteweirs to avoid stagnation of rain water.

The black soils where broad-base bunds are adopted are characterized by high clay content, low infiltration rates and low organic matter.

Specifications

Base widths of 4.75–7.5 m bund heights of 0.45–0.6 m and side slopes of 5:1 or 6:1 and with 0.1% to 0.2% channel grades are adopted. Possible bund sections are as given below:

Table 3.19 Bund section

Top width (m)	Base width (m)	Height (m)	Side slopes Hor. : Vert.	Section (m²)
0.3	4.85	0.45	5:1	1.15
0.3	6.40	0.60	5:1	1.98
0.3	5.60	0.45	6:1	1.35
0.3	7.60	0.60	6:1	2.34

Waterways

Grass species suited to grassed waterways in black soil would be *Dichanthium annulatum* and *Cenchrus ciliaris*.

Madhya Pradesh

Broad-base terraces were found successful on several mechanized farms of the states, viz. Bitul, Sagar and Hoshangabad. The broad-base terraces of 0.9 m height and with suitable recommendations of widths were adopted.

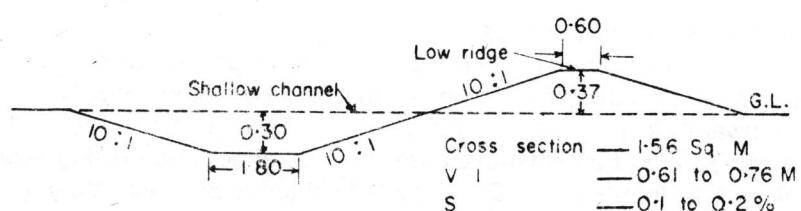

Fig. 3.15 Details of broad-based terraces-Bellary

Central Soil & Water Conservation Research & Training Instt. Dehradun

At the CSWCRTI, Research Centre, Bellary (Karnataka), broad-base terraces (Fig. 3.15) were found successful in deep black soils of semi-arid regions in lands of 1-2 per cent slope. Following are the specifications:

Vertical interval   = 0.6 m,   Area of cross-section   = 1.56 m²,
Channel section
    Bottom width = 1.83 m,   Depth = 0.305 m,   Side slopes = 10:1
    Channel grade   = 0.1 to 0.2%
Bund section
    Top width = 0.61 m;   Height slopes = 0.366 m,   Side slopes = 10:1

3.5   Bench Terracing

Bench terracing (Plate 14) is one of the most popular mechanical soil conservation practices adopted by farmers of India and other countries for ages. On sloping and undulating lands, intensive farming can be only adopted with bench terracing. It consists of construction of step-like fields along contours by half cutting and half filling. Original slope is converted into level fields and thus all hazards of erosion are eliminated. All the manure and fertilizers applied are retained in the field. In slopping irrigated land, bench terracing helps in proper water management.

TYPE OF BENCH TERRACES AND THEIR ADAPTABILITY
The bench terraces are of four types (Fig. 3.16).

Level Bench Terrace
Paddy fields require uniform impounding of water. Level bench terraces are used for the same. Contrary to usual concept that bench terraces are to be adapted on slopes steeper than 6 to 7%, level bench terraces are required in paddy growing areas on slope as mild as 1%, to facilitate uniform impounding. Sometimes this type of terraces and referred as table top, or paddy terraces, conveying the sense that such bench is as level as top of the table.

Inwardly Sloping Bench Terraces
Crops like potato are extremely susceptible to waterlogging. In that case the benches are made with inward slope to drain off excess water as quickly as possible. These are especially suited for steep slopes, it is essential to keep the excess runoff to-wards hill (original ground) rather than on fill slopes. These inwardly sloping bench terraces have a drain on inner side, which has grade along its length to convey the excess water to one side, from where it is disposed-off by well stabilised vegetated waterway. These are widely used in Nilgiri hills of Tamil Nadu state as well as on steep Himalayan slope in Himachal Pradesh and North-Eastern hill regions.

Outwardly Slopping Bench Terraces
Farmers many a times carry out the levelling process in phases, doing part of the job every year. As such outwardly sloping bench is usually a step towards construction of level or inwardly sloping bench terraces. In places of low rainfall or Shallow soils, the outwardly sloping bench terraces are used to reduce the existing steep slope to mild slope (say from 8% to 4%). In this type of terraces constructed on soils not having good permeability, provision of graded channel at lower end has to be kept, to safely dispose off surplus water to some water way. In very permeable soils a strong bund with spillway arrangement may take care for most of the rainfall events, while during heavy rainfall storm, the excess water may flow from one terrace to another. Attempt is usually made to dispose-off this to some waterway at an earliest possible spot.

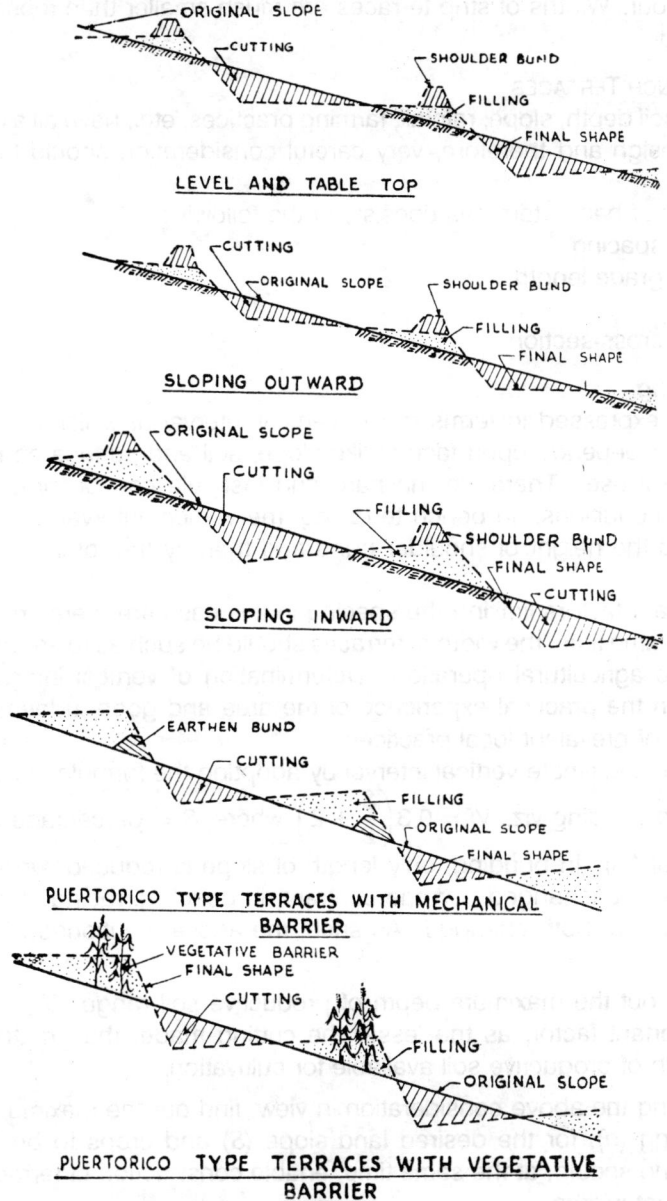

Fig. 3.16 Types of bench terraces

Puertorican or California Type of Terraces

In case of puertorican type of terrace (Plate 15), the soil is excavated little by little during every ploughing and gradually developing benches by pushing the soil downhill against a vegetative or mechanical barrier laid along contour. The terrace is developed gradually over years, by natural leveling. It is necessary that mechanical or vegetative barrier across the land at suitable interval has to be established.

Strip Terrace

This type of terraces are constructed in districts of Kangra and Kulu for growing fruit trees on contour. Widths of strip terraces are much smaller than those adopted for growing paddy.

DESIGN OF BENCH TERRACES

Condition of soil depth, slope, rainfall, farming practices, etc., have all a direct bearing on terrace design and therefore, very careful consideration should be given to all these factors.

The design of bench terraces consists of the following:
—Terrace spacing
—Terrace grade length;
and
—Terrace cross-section

Terrace spacing

It is normally expressed in terms of the vertical interval at which the terraces are constructed. It depends upon factors like slope, soil and surface condition, grade and agricultural use. Therefore, no hard and fast rule can be prescribed in this regard for all conditions. In bench terracing, the vertical interval affects the depth of cutting and the height of shoulder bund and thereby the total height of vertical drops.

The important factors limiting the spacing in this case are therefore, the soil and slope. At the same time, the width of terraces should be such as to enable convenient and economic agricultural operation. Determination of vertical interval, therefore, depends upon the practical experience of the area and good judgement with due consideration of prevalent local practices.

Many workers estimate vertical interval by adopting the formula, as used for contour or graded bunding viz., $VI = 0.3\left(\dfrac{S}{2} + 2\right)$ where, S = percentage of slope, VI = vertical interval (m). In bunding, only length of slope is reduced, while the degree of slope remains unchanged. On the contrary, in bench terracing, the degree and length of slope are both changed. As such, the above mentioned formula should not be used.

Step 1: Find out the maximum depth of productive soil range (D). This is a very important factor, as the lesser the cutting made, the greater will be the depth of productive soil available for cultivation.

Step 2: Having the above consideration in view, find out the maximum admissible cutting (d), for the desired land slope (S) and crops to be grown. This cutting should, at the same time, enable construction of terraces with convenient widths.

Step 3: Having fixed depth of cutting, the width of terrace (W), can be computed for a given slope (S) by the formula $W = \dfrac{200d}{S}$, where, W and d are in meters and S in per cent. (Refer subsequent section for derivation).

Step 4: For a batter of 1:1 riser, the vertical interval (VI) can be computed by the formula

$$VI = \frac{WS}{100 - S} \quad \text{and for a batter of 0.5 : 1 for risers} \quad \ldots (3.9)$$

$$VI = \frac{2WS}{200 - S} \quad \ldots (3.10)$$

For a given slope greater the *VI*, greater would be the width and for a given *VI*, higher the slope, smaller the width of terrace.

Terrace gradient

In high rainfall areas, for the quick disposal of the excess water, a suitable gradient has to be provided for newly laid out terraces.

Step 1: To estimate the peak rate of runoff (cumecs) from the bench terraces, rational formula $Q = \dfrac{CIA}{360}$ is used.

Step 2: The area drained, *A* (ha) can be calculated by the formula, $A = \dfrac{L \times W}{10000}$

where, *L* = length of terrace (m); and
W = average width of terrace (m)

Step 3: Permissible velocity of flow (*V*) for different soils is presented under grassed waterways chapter.

Step 4: Compute approximate area of cross-section of the channel using the formula $Q = A, V$, where *V* is the permissible velocity as obtained under step 3 and *Q* = peak rate of runoff.

Step 5: Compute hydraulic radius (*R*) for the cross-section obtained as in Step 4. For more details, see under grassed waterways chapter.

Step 6: Compute the grade of the terrace/channel using the Manning's Formula,

$$V = \frac{1}{n}R^{2/3}S^{1/2}.$$

where, *V* = permissible velocity (Step 3);
R = hydraulic radius (m) (Step 5):
n = Coefficient of rugosity or roughness coefficient
(refer tables under grassed waterway chapter)

Step 7: The grade of the terrace/channel obtained under Step 6, may be rounded-off for convenience of layout.

Step 8: For the rounding of grade (*S*), recalculate the velocity of flow for the section under consideration (if needed cross-section is to be adjusted) and verify whether the obtained velocity is less than the velocity as assumed under Step 3.

Terrace cross-section

The construction of bench terrace is such that the earthwork excavated from the upper half is deposited over the lower slope. As such, the deposited portion forms an embankment, and therefore, care should be taken to secure this well on the slope, by providing suitable key trenches and clearing the surface of all vegetation. Precaution should also be taken to provide suitable batter in cutting and embankment, so that the embankment may be well- seated on this slope. The height of the embankment rould be increased sufficiently to provide for shrinkage of soils, so that the ultimate slope after consolidation, confirms to the specification.

The cross-section of the shoulder bunds along outer edge of terrace should also be suitably designed to be stable against slipping and overtopping.

Alignment of terraces

While aligning bench terraces on slopes, the tillage convenience and field boundaries are of primary consideration. The alignment should be so made that the minimum convenient width of terrace is always available for cultivation. So also proper adjustment and necessary deviation can be made near the field boundary, In order to avoid inconvenient width of terrace strips at the field boundary.

All sharp and convenient curves should be conveniently eased out, deviating if necessary from the contour. Acute bends and straight junction should also be avoided as far as possible (Fig. 3.17).

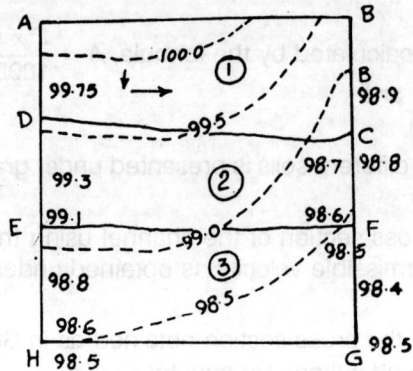

(i) When alignment is not followed on contour, earthwork will be heavy. Levelling in lengthwise direction is needed

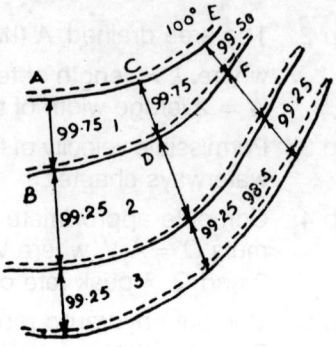

(ii) Cross-wise levelling only is needed, when alignment is followed along contours

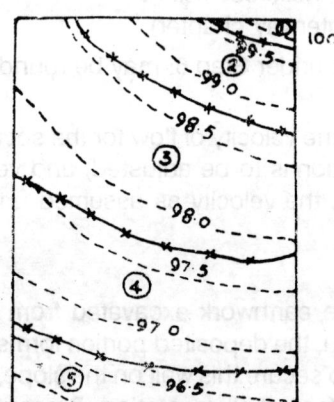

Fig. 3.17 Alignment of terraces
(iii) Inwardly sloping bench terrace have longitudinal and inward grade

Terrace execution

The contour lines were actually marked on the site by the method of direct contouring and with due reference to these lines, the alignment of terraces as per plan was staked out. The alignment was carefully examined with all consideration to the local conditions that existed at the site, like depressions, sharp turns, fields, boundaries and the like and were then finalized making deviation wherever necessary.

When the alignment has been finalized, the seat of embankment was prepared, ploughed and cleared of all vegetation and roots; and wherever necessary, key trenches were excavated. The excavation was then commenced approximately at the middle upwards and excavated earth was gradually pushed towards the lower slope until the desired level was obtained. The required gradient was then marked with dumpy level and the final scraping and levelling were attended to.

In case tractor bulldozer is used, the dozer blade may be tilted to provide grade inwards and worked along a smooth curve, pushing the soil excavated from the upper half towards the lower one. After the rough levelling was over, the end of terraces were levelled with manual labour. Proper gradients were marked with a dumpy level and the final scraping with the bulldozer was attended to carefully.

The sectioning of shoulder bunds to the required size and trimming the side slopes to proper batter had to be done with manual labour. Grass may be planted on batter for protection.

Usually the construction is taken up from top to bottom. But in case it is desired to keep the top soil on top, then levelling is needed to be done from the bottom. After levelling of first terrace, the top soil of higher adjoining aligned bench terrace is pushed on to the constructed terrace.

Then the levelling of the terrace from where top soil is borrowed is done, followed by pushing of top soil from land above to the lower terrace. Thus all terraces will have top soil of adjoining above terrace and only last top terrace will be without top soil. But this involves additional earthwork. For example, if 25 cm thick soil is scraped off, the additional earthwork per ha will be $10000 \times \dfrac{1}{4} = 2500$ m³. This may be a must, in some shallow soils having unfertile sub-soil, while in other case, it may be cheaper to do post reclamation works to build up the fertility of bench terrace constructed area.

Computation of width of terrace and earthwork for bench terracing
The width (*w*) of terrace can be computed for a given depth of soil (*d*) as follows:

$$\frac{\left(\dfrac{VI}{2}\right)}{\left(\dfrac{VI}{2}\right)+\left(\dfrac{W}{2}\right)} = \frac{d}{\left(\dfrac{W}{2}\right)}$$

$$\frac{VI}{VI + W} = \frac{2d}{W}$$

or
$$\frac{2d}{W} = \frac{S}{100}$$

Thus
$$W = \frac{200d}{S} \qquad \ldots (3.11)$$

The earthwork per ha is computed by using the formula

$$E \text{ (Earthwork per ha)} = \frac{100}{8}W.S. \qquad \ldots (3.12)$$

where, *W* = width of terrace (m); and
S = land slope (%)
Area available for cultivation
= 100(100 − *nS*)
where, *n* = batter slope (%); and
S = land slope (%).
Area lost due to benching = 100 *n.S.*
Percentage of area lost in benching = *n.S.*

Batter area to be sodded = $100\sqrt{1 + n^2}$
$$\ldots (3.13)$$

No. of terrace outlets/ha = $\dfrac{L}{2K}$ ... (3.14)

where, *L* = total length of terrace/ha; and
K = critical length of terrace.

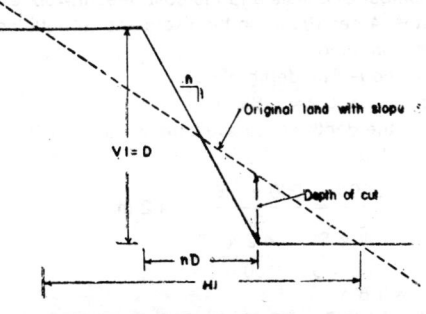

Fig. 3.18 Terrace cross-section

Cost of bench terracing

The actual cost of bench terracing depends upon conditions of soil and sub-soil; land surface including vegetation cover on it, undulation, depression, mounds, etc.; slope of the area; specification of bench terraces and deviation in its alignment and terrace outlets.

The principal item that affects cost of bench terracing/ha is the total quantity of earthwork involved and rate and the manner as to how it is executed (manual labour or bulldozer, etc.).

Example 14: On a 20% hill slope, it is proposed to construct bench terraces. If the vertical interval is 2 m, calculate (i) length per hectare, (ii) earthwork, and (iii) area lost for vertical cut. The cut should be equal to fill, when the terrace cuts are vertical.

Solution—

$$W = \frac{100.D}{S} = \frac{100 \times 2}{20} = 10 \text{ m}$$

$$\text{Length per hectare} = \frac{10,000}{10} = 1000 \text{ m}$$

Since it is vertical cut, no area is lost for cultivation, except the area for shoulder bund.

When the batter slope 1:1

Using

$$W = \frac{D(100 - S)}{S}$$

$$= \frac{2(100 - 20)}{20}$$

$$= 8 \text{ m}$$

Length per hectare

$$= \frac{10,000}{8 + 1 + 1}$$

$$= 1000 \text{ m}$$

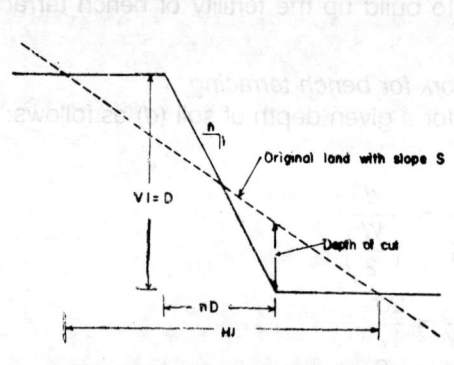

Fig. 3.19 Depth of cut in a terrace

Earthwork per hectare

$$= \frac{1}{2} \times 4 \times 1 \times 1000$$

$$= 2000 \text{ m}^3$$

Example 15: In an area of one ha lying in a hilly region, bench terracing has been proposed to bring the land under cultivation. The land has a general slope of 30%. The average depth of soil as observed by an auger is about 0.9 m. The crops to be grown after benching require at least a soil depth of 0.25 m. Risers to be laid on 1:1 gradient and will be planted with local varieties of grasses. The critical length of terrace is approximately equal to 100 m. Work out (a) cost of bench terracing only at Rs.2 per m³ (b) compute the number of outlets and the cost of earthwork excavation for the vertical drains; (c) cost of grass plantation at Rs.4 per 100 m on the risers and (d) total cost of bench terracing outlets. Mode of execution is mostly manual labour.

*Solution—*The depth of cut

$d = 0.7 \times 0.9 = 0.63$ m

Still the depth of soil available = 0.27 m which is higher than 0.25 m as indicated. Bench width (*W*) to be adopted

$$W = \frac{200d}{S} = \frac{200 \times 0.63}{30} = 4.2 \text{ m}$$

$$VI = \frac{W \times S}{100 - S} = \frac{4.2 \times 30}{100 - 30}$$

$$= 1.8 \text{ m}$$

$HI = W + VI = 4.2 + 1.8 = 6.0$ m

Earthwork involved/ha $= \frac{100}{8} \times W \times S$

$$= \frac{100}{8} \times 4.2 \times 30 = 1575 \text{ m}^3$$

$$\text{Cost of earthwork at Rs.2 per m}^3 = 1575 \times 2 = \text{Rs.3150} \qquad \text{Ans.(1)}$$

The critical length of terrace (K) = 100 m

$$L = \text{length of terrace/ha} \quad = \frac{10000}{HI}$$

$$= \frac{10000}{6} = 1666 \text{ m}$$

Number of outlets (assuming surplus water drained from both sides)

$$= \frac{L}{2K} = \frac{1666}{2 \times 100} = 8 \text{ (approx.)}$$

Approximate length of vertical drain/ha (outlet)

$$I = N \times HI$$

where N = number of outlets/ha; and

HI = horizontal interval

$$I = 8 \times 6 = 48 \text{ m}$$

The cross-section of disposal drain:

Bottom width	= 0.3 m
Top width	= 1.05 m
Height	= 0.38 m

$$\text{Area of cross-section of disposal drain} = \frac{0.3 + 1.05}{2} \times 0.38 = 0.256 \text{ m}^2$$

The earthwork involved in vertical disposal drains

$$= 48 \times 0.256 = 12.3 \text{ m}^3$$

Cost of earthwork at Rs.2

$$= 12.3 \times 2 = \text{Rs.24.60}$$

or say Rs.25.00 Ans.(2)

Cost of sodding   = Rs.4 per 100 m length

$$\text{Total cost of sodding/ha} \quad = \frac{4}{100} \times \frac{10000}{HI}$$

$$= \frac{4}{100} \times \frac{10000}{6.0} = \frac{400}{6}$$

$$= \text{Rs.66.66/ha or } \textbf{Rs.67} \qquad \text{Ans.(3)}$$

Total cost of bench terracing, outlet including sodding

$$= (1) + (2) + (3)$$
$$= 3150 + 25 + 67$$
$$= \text{Rs.3242}$$
$$\text{or } \textbf{Rs.3240.00} \text{ per ha} \qquad \text{Ans.(4)}$$

Bench terraces with stone walls

The construction of bench terraces with stone walls is justified where stone can be found in adequate quantities close to the site, and potential productivity of the land justifies the expense. However, where there are many surface stones, cultivation may be restricted.

Bench terraces with stone walls can be used for annual crops and perennial tree plantations. The latter are likely to produce the highest return on the investment, except in cases of special high value annual crops. Furthermore, tree crops require less cultivation.

All remarks regarding the use of natural features in designing terraces already dealt, apply to terraces with stone walls.

Determining the interval between bench terraces of level cross-section

The horizontal distance is a function of:

—the height of the retaining wall; and

—the slope of the land.

This can be expressed as

$$HI = \frac{100 \times H}{S}$$

where, HI = horizontal distance (m);
H = height of retaining wall (m); and
S = slope, (m/100m).

Fig. 3.20 Bench terrace constructed by
excavation of fill

Fig. 3.21 Bench terrace constructed by fill

This formula applies only to those bench terraces constructed by building a retaining wall and filling it with soil brought in from outside (Fig. 3.20). This method, however, is expensive and is only used when there is insufficient soil depth on site to be reclaimed. Usually, bench terraces of level cross-section are constructed by moving soil from the upper part down to the lower part (Fig. 3.21).

This can be expressed as

$$HI = \frac{(H_1 + H_2)}{S} \times 100 \qquad \dots (3.15)$$

where, HI = horizontal distance (m);
H_1 = depth of excavation in upper part of terrace (m);
H_2 = height of fill in lower part of terrace (m); and
S = slope (m/100 m).

This method, though cheaper than the previous one, is still fairly expensive. Level bench terraces have many advantages, but suffer from the following drawbacks:

— They are narrow and implements cannot be easily used on them;

— Many high retaining walls are needed, thus steeply raising the cost of reclamation on the one hand, and on the other hand, making access to the benches more difficult; and

— Where the soil is initially shallow, the terrace, after its construction, has relatively deep soil on its lower part, while on the upper part, the soil is often too shallow for the plant's requirements.

Determining the interval according to the presumed stable slope
The disadvantages mentioned above may be largely overcome by designing bench terraces on the principle of the stable slope (Fig. 3.22). This design is especially useful in the case of rotation crops, where an artificial stable slope of 3-8% can be maintained by using a reversible plough or disk, as already strongly recommended.

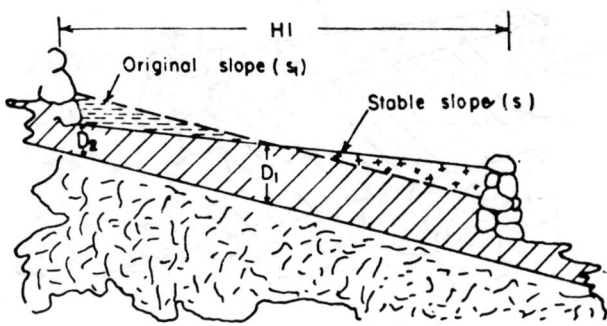

Fig. 3.22 Bench terrace constructed on the principle of the stable slope

The stable slope changes for different soils. Local observations and experience should be noted and applied. It should be possible to reach fairly exact conclusions from reviewing the condition of a given cultivated soil and comparing its stability against erosion seen on different slopes. The terrace interval can be calculated as follows:

$$HI = \frac{2(D_1 - D_2)}{S_1 - S_2} \qquad \ldots (3.16)$$

where, HI = horizontal distance (m);

D_1 = present depth of soil on the area (m);

D_2 = minimum soil depth required by the crops (m)*;

S_1 = present slope (m/m); and

S_2 = presumed stable slope (natural or artificial) (m/m).

The stable slope may be achieved in two ways:

— by transporting the soil from the upper part of the terrace to its lower part with earth moving equipment; and

— by leaving it to be done by cultivation and nature, over a period of years.

When the area is being reclaimed for orchards, it may sometimes be worthwhile to sub-bench the individual rows before planting.

With rotation crops, it is advisable to let nature and cultivation do the job of benching. The cost is thereby reduced and it is easier to build up and maintain soil fertility.

The retaining wall

The wall is constructed (Fig. 3.23) from stones collected on the spot. As a rule, close and low retaining walls are preferable to high walls set far apart.

The height of a stone retaining wall is given by:

$$H = (H_1 + X_1) + (H_2 + X_2)$$

where, H = height of wall;

H_1 = depth of soil, presumed to be lost by creep, at the foot of the wall;

---

* With rotation crops this depth is that of the upper part of the terrace, at the foot of the retaining wall. In the case of orchards, the depth is that of the root zone of the trees in the uppermost row of the terrace.

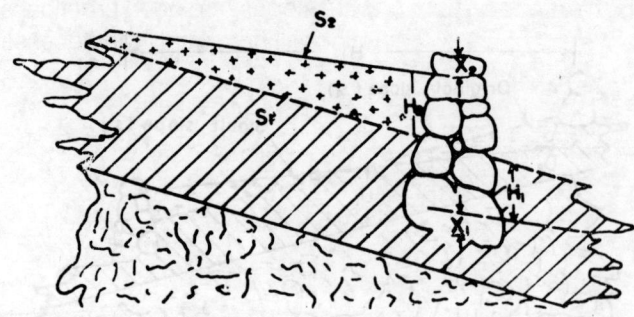

Fig. 3.23 Stone retaining wall

H_2 = depth of soil presumed to be deposited near the wall;

X_1 = safety factor (usually 30 cm); and

X_2 = safety factor (usually 10 cm).

The formula is readily understood when it is considered that the wall on its lower side must be sunk into the ground by an amount equal to the depth of soil, which is expected to be removed by creep (plus the 20 cm safety factor), and on its upper side must rise above the ground surface by an amount equal to the depth of deposition expected (plus the 10 cm safety factor).

Drainage of gravitational water

It may be frequently observed, following rainfall, how water percolating through the retaining wall wets the terrace below it. In order to drain this water, furrows are opened at the foot of every retaining wall (Fig. 3.24). These furrows need not have a large capacity, since they only conduct small quantities of water, but they need a continuous longitudinal grade. For this reason, it is important to grade the strip along which this furrow is to run.

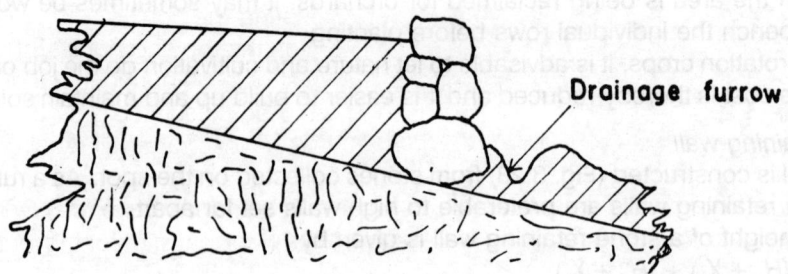

Drainage furrow

Fig. 3.24 The drainage furrow

Disposal of runoff water

In many countries a common practice is to divert the runoff from the cultivation furrows and retaining walls into deep, narrow, ditches made of stone, concrete or earth, which run straight down the slope or diagonally down it. Since such ditches cannot be crossed by machinery, they cannot be used in areas where cultivation is mechanized. On the other hand, wide, shallow, vegetated waterways, crossable by machinery, which are effective on moderate slopes, are not a practical proposition on slopes exceeding 15%, since the vegetation will not supply the necessary protection. There are two possible solutions:

Combining vegetated waterways with drop structures of stone of other material

The drop structures in the waterway are an extension of the retaining walls (Fig. 3.25). Their height is lower than that of the wall and is determined by the amount of flow in the waterway.   Where the retaining walls are set far apart, it may be necessary to construct additional drops in the waterway.   The area of the waterway itself is sown or planted with perennial grasses for complete protection.

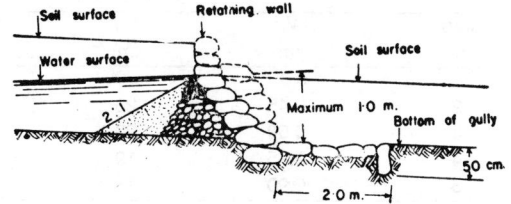

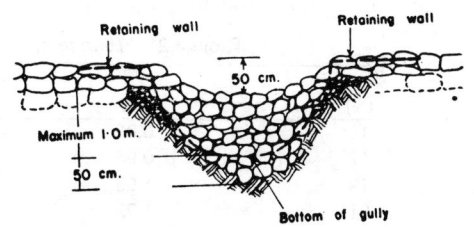

Fig. 3.25 Drop structure

Paving the waterways with stone

Paving the waterway with stone is rather costly, but the method has the particular advantage that the waterway can then be used as a field track. The provision of tracks on steep areas is a substantial fraction of the total cost of reclamation, so that combining the waterway with the field track is a promising solution.

Cost of Construction

The cost of constructing stone walls is high. It is possible to give standard costs per ha, because in each location and for each crop different requirements prevail. However, a few indications can be given for estimating the cost.

Stone walls should have a width of about 0.3 m on the top and not less than 0.8 m at the bottom, if they are 1 m high. At least, 0.3 m should be buried in the ground as a safe foundation. This depth of foundation has to be calculated after the removal of soil for the fill in the lower terrace. A length of 1 m of terrace will require 0.55 m^3 of stones.

Building of stone terraces is a specialized job requiring experience. One skilled labourer should be able to use 1 m^3 of stone (including excavation of the foundation) per day.

PRACTICES ADOPTED IN DIFFERENT INDIAN STATES

Andhra Pradesh

Suitability

Bench terracing and stone terracing are adopted in Telengana and coastal Andhra Pradesh regions, where average annual rainfall is above 76 cm and slope of the land varies up to 15%. Bench terracing is also adopted for conversion of sloping dry areas into wet, when irrigation facilities are available, as in the case of areas under irrigation projects and in high rainfall regions, where better cropping can be adopted with flat terraces.

Terrace spacing
Generally in most of the areas, an average width of not less than 12 m and *VI* not exceeding 1.2 m are adopted. (Table 3.20 and 3.21)

Table 3.20   *Terrace spacings for different slopes*

Slope (m)	V.I (m)	H.I (m)	Slope (%)	V.I (m)	H.I (m)
1	0.3	30	6	1.05	17
2	0.45	23	7	1.20	17
3	0.60	20	8	1.20	15
4	0.75	19	9	1.20	13
5	0.90	18	10	1.20	12

Table 3.21   *Terrace spacings for steep slopes*

Slope (%)	V.I (m)	Slope (%)	V.I (m)
15	0.82	25	1.50
17	0.95	27	1.12
19	1.05	29	1.25
21	1.22	31	1.35
23	1.35	33	1.50

From observation and experience in Machkund basin, 7 to 8 m is fixed as the minimum and economic width for carrying out agricultural operations. In Machkund basin, slopes of 4 to 10% are generally developed into bench terraces. For a slope of 4 to 6%, 6 to 8% and 8 to 10%, vertical intervals of 0.3 m to 0.38 m, 0.45 m and 0.7 m are adapted. Vertical intervals should not be more than what has been recommended above. (Table 3.20 and 3.21)

Width of terraces in red soils and black soils (converted dry lands for irrigation)
Dry lands are developed for irrigation either for wet or for irrigation of dry crops. For irrigated dry condition, the plots are fairly big with a gentle grade of easy flow of water. The grade given in black soils is up to 0.2% and in red soils up to 0.5%.

The following formula is adopted for determining the width of terrace (Table 3.22) for developing the lands for irrigated dry crops:

Red Soils—$W = \dfrac{42.6}{\sqrt{S}}$; **Black Soils** $= \dfrac{64}{\sqrt{S}}$

where, W = width of terrace (m); and S = land slope (%).

For wet cultivating, the land should fairly levelled to allow water to stand, the plots being smaller in size. Width of the terrace (Table 3.23) can be obtained by using the formula

$$W = \frac{21}{\sqrt{S}}$$

where, W = width of terrace (m); and S = land slope (%).

Table 3.22   *Width of terrace in red and black soils*

Slope (%)	Width (m)	
	Red Soils	Black Soils
0–1	42.6	64
1–1.5	36.5	55
1.5–2	30.0	46
2–3	24.0	36.5

Table 3.23   *Terrace width for wet cultivation*

Slope (%)	Width of terrace (m)	Slope (%)	Width of terrace (m)
0.5	30	1.50	18
0.75	24	2.00	15
1.00	21	3.00	12

Terrace gradient

A longitudinal gradient of 0.75% is adopted in heavy rainfall and highly sloping areas. The inner edge of the terraces should be lower than the outer edges in the gradient of about 0.5%.

This above grade should be provided, making due allowance for shrinkage. Normally 0.10 m/m depth of filling is assumed for shrinkage. Keeping this shrinkage also into consideration, the difference in levels of terraces between outer edge and inner edge of the terrace—DL (m) can be worked out (Table 3.24) by the formula.

$$DL = \left[\frac{D}{2} \times 0.10\right] + (0.005 \times W) \qquad \ldots (3.17)$$

where, D = Vertical drop (m);

W = Width of terrace (m);

0.1 and 0.005 are shrinkage and longitudinal factors.

Table 3.24   *Values of DL for terracing in normal areas*

D	W	DL	D	W	DL
0.3	30	0.15	0.9	18	0.12
0.45	23	0.13	1.2	17	0.12
0.60	20	0.13	1.2	15	0.10
0.75	19	0.13	1.2	12	0.10

Under Machkund conditions, for bench terracing, inward gradient of 1 in 50 and a longitudinal gradient of 1 in 200 is adopted.

Terrace length

The length of terrace is restricted to a maximum about 105 m.

Terrace cross-section

The construction of bench terraces is done by half cut and half fill method. A shoulder bund is provided along the outer edge of the terrace for holding the required amount of water and to conserved moisture and soil.

Shoulder bunds
Shoulder bund is usually 0.3 m high with bottom width of 0.75 m and side slopes of 1:1.

In dry lands which are converted into irrigated lands, bunds of 0.405 m² cross-section (0.3 m top width, 1.5 m base width and 0.45 m high) are constructed.

Batter
A batter of 1:1 is generally provided and a batter of 0.5:1 is adopted in Machkund basin.

Protection to the risers of the terraces is done either by establishing grasses or by providing stone pitching or revetment, depending upon the availability of material. The grasses which are suitable for this purpose are *Paspalum dilatatum, Bromus catharticus, Eragrostis curvula*, local available grasses can also be used. In the Machkund basin, *Koppiri* grass, a local variety is found to be useful for the purpose.

Alignment of terraces
While aligning, deviation should be as far as possible kept at minimum and should not be more than 0.3 m, while crossing depressions and in very exceptional cases up to a maximum of 0.6 m.

Earthwork excavation (Table 3.25)

Table 3.25 *Details of earthwork required for bench terracing (a sample estimate form)*

Sl.No of plot	Average VI (m)	Average HI (m)	Length of terrace, L (m)	Section of soil cut (sq m) $\frac{VI \times HI}{8}$	Shoulder bund with 0.135 m² section
1	2	3	4	5	6

	Quantity of earthwork involved		
For bench terracing (m³) Col.5 x Col.4	For shoulder bunds (m³) 0.135 x Col.4	Total earth Work (m³) Cols.(7+8)	Remarks
7	8	9	10

Terrace outlet and their location
The main drainage lines are natural outlets already existing in the field and are taken advantage of for draining out the excess water from the terrace. While utilizing the natural drainage lines, care is taken to see that the natural water courses are widened, deepened and protected with grasses and other materials in such a way, that the excess water from the terrace is safely drained without causing further erosion in the natural drainage lines.

When natural drainage lines are not available, suitable other outlets are to be constructed. For this purpose, the following methods are adopted:

Vertical drains with drop pits
Depending upon the area to be drained, suitable vertical drains with drop pits are provided at suitable intervals. The runoff from the terrace drains in vertical drains, and is safely conveyed to the bottom of the valley. The drains and drop pits should be suitably protected with grasses and locally available materials. The drop pits

intercept the flow of water as well as act as silt traps. It is necessary to clear the silt accumulated in the drop pit periodically, by spreading on the nearest bench.

Wasteweirs

In some cases, overflow type wasteweirs with crest wall flush with the ground is constructed. Minimum length of crest wall should be 0.6 m and maximum of 3.25 m. (Table 3.26)

Table 3.26   *Length of crest wall for different cumulative areas (for an intensity of 75 mm/hr rainfall and overflow of 0.45 m depth of water)*

Cumulative area (ha)	Length of crest wall (m)	Cumulative area (m)	Length of crest wall (m)
1.62	0.6	4.86	1.8
2.42	0.9	5.67	2.1
3.24	1.2	7.28	2.7
4.05	1.5	8.10	3.0

Provision of diversion drains

It will be necessary to divert the runoff water from the upper catchment above an area proposed to be bench terraced by constructing diversion drain of the required cross-section along the upper boundary of the block. Diversion drains of cross-section varying from 0.36 to 1.0 sq m depending upon the area to be drained, are to be provided. (Table 3.27)

Table 3.27   *Cross-section of diversion drains*

Catchment (ha)	Section of drain			
	Top width (m)	Bottom width (m)	Depth (m)	Cross-section m²
Up to 4.0	0.91	0.30	0.6	0.36
4.0 to 6.1	1.21	0.60	0.6	0.54
6.1 to 8.1	1.52	0.91	0.6	0.73
8.1 to 10.1	1.83	1.21	0.6	0.91
10.1 to 12.1	2.13	1.52	0.6	1.10

A grade of 0.5 to 1.0 per cent as bed slope is provided depending upon the soil conditions and terrain. Stone checks to a minimum width of 0.3 m and sodding of 0.6 to 0.9 m width should also be provided at regular intervals in the bed. Spreading type of grasses are recommended at vulnerable points and sudden drops.

Maintenance

— The terraces should be carefully watched, particularly in the rainy season and damage, if any, should be got repaired as early as possible.

— Top levels of shoulder bunds should be maintained, so that no overtopping takes place.

— In the initial years, it may be necessary to use organic manures/green manuring practices and also fertilizers, which will aid in building up the fertility of soil.

Conversion of dry areas into wet areas

In slopy dry areas, where irrigation facilities are merely provided under project areas like Tungabhadra and Nagarjuna Sagar, conversion of these drylands into level type terraced lands will help in growing paddy and other irrigated crops.

Tamil Nadu

Suitability

Bench terracing is adopted in high rainfall hilly areas of Nilgiris and Kodaikanal on land slopes between 16.66 to 13.33 per cent with a soil depth more than 0.75 m and in red loamy soils (lateritic).

Table top bench terrace is suitable for areas receiving medium rainfall, evenly distributed with highly permeable deep soils. The terraces are provided with a small shoulder bund (of about 0.2–0.30 m), 0.45–0.6 m wide at bottom, so as to avoid overtopping during high intensity rainfall.

Bench terracing sloping outward is suitable and effective in low rainfall areas with permeable soil and medium soil depth. It would be advantageous to raise stiff stemmed and tall growing trees or perennial vegetation along risers, so that they may also act as effective wash tops in case of overtopping. The outward slopes may be such that it can be protected from soil erosion by constructing shoulder bund high enough to impound the expected runoff.

Bench terrace sloping inwards is suitable in heavy rainfall regions and not less permeable soils. The inward grade may be from 2.5 to 8% and the longitudinal gradient may be from 0.33 to 0.75% according to local needs. It is advisable to construct shoulder bunds of about 0.2–0.3 m height and 0.45–0.6 m bottom width.

In puertorican type of terraces, where vegetative barrier is used, spacing of Guatemala grass (Tripsacum laxum) 30 cm from plant-to-plant and 15 cm row-to-row is recommended. If earthen bund is used as a barrier, it should have at least a cross-section of 0.40 sq m.

Terrace spacing

In the Nilgiris, the depth of production soil ranges up to a maximum of 0.9 m only, the minimum width of terrace may be assumed as 4.5 m for slopes between 15 and 25% and 3.0 m for slopes between 25 and 33%, which is the maximum limit for slope group recommended for agricultural crops.

Terrace gradient

For Nilgiris and Kodaikanal conditions, an inward slope of 1 in 40 and a longitudinal grade of 1 in 120 are provided, taking into consideration the red loamy soil prevalent in the area and the intensity of rainfall received in the locality.

Terrace length

The length of terrace has been restricted to a maximum of about 105 m and a uniform gradient is adopted.

Terrace cross-section

The cross-section of the shoulder bund along the outer edges of terraces should be suitably designed to be stable against slipping and overtopping. A shoulder bund having 1:1 side slope, height of about 0.3 m and bottom width of 0.75 m has also been suggested.

Table 3.23 *Vertical interval, width, length of terrace per ha of bench terrace recommended for Nilgiris*

Slope (%)	VI (m)*	Width of benches (m)	Length of bench terrace (m/ha)	Area lost due to terracing (%)
15	0.81		1825	16.2
17	0.93		1780	18.3
19	1.00		1735	20.4
21	1.20	4.5	1682	22.9
23	1.30		1632	25.0
25	1.50		1582	27.2
27	1.10		2302	29.5
29	1.20	3.0	2225	31.9
31	1.30		2152	31.4
33	1.5		2080	36.2

*VI can be kept constant if needed. Further it can be less than what has been indicated in the table above but not greater.

Batter

Generally, a 1:1 front batter is allowed. A 0.5:1 batter is given where the soils are loose and where the soils are stable, excavation is done almost vertically.

Experience in bench terracing in Nilgiris has shown that the batter can be effectively protected by establishing soil binding grasses like *Eragrostis curvula, Paspalum dilatatum, Bromus catharticus*, and *Dactylis glomerata, Phalaris tuberosa, Pennisetum purpureum, Festuca* spp. etc.

Alignment of terraces

While aligning, deviations should be kept at minimum as far as possible, and should be more than 0.3 m while crossing depressions or gullies, and in very exceptional cases up to a maximum of 0.6 m.

Terrace outlets and location

Where the length of the bench terrace exceeds 120 m, it is intercepted by a vertical disposal drain into which the runoff from bench terrace will flow down. Such vertical disposal drains with drop pits are provided at suitable intervals, by aligning the vertical disposal drain to follow the configuration of the bench terrace itself, i.e. in a series of stepped platform, used with drop pits provided just below the vertical drops. The cross-sectional area of the vertical disposal drain is designed to carry the runoff that needs to be disposed off from the terraces at non-erosive velocity.

The vertical disposal drains are so located that they are generally in the folds c hills or along the valley lines, so that they would lend themselves to face drainage of runoff from the terraces on either side. Such disposal drains located along the folds or the valleys will also be more stable to carry the cumulative runoff from the terraces. The bed and sides or the disposal drains and drop pits are vegetated with suitable grasses like carpet grass (*Axonopus cinicinus*) St. Angustine grass, etc., or pave the bottom and sides of these drains with dry stones.

Provisions of diversion drains

When the length of bench terrace exceeds 120 m, it is intercepted by a vertical disposal drain with drop pits, into which the runoff from bench terrace will flow down The vertical disposal drains are aligned to follow the configuration of the bench terrace, i.e. in a series of stepped platforms and with drop pits provided just below the vertical drops. Grass species such as carpet grass-*Axonopus cinicinus*, and St. Angustine grass, etc. are planted along the diversion and disposal drain.

Assam
Terracing is practised in gently sloping lands and hilly areas.

Gujarat
Terracing is adopted in hilly areas and slopes more than 6% with sufficient soil depth.

Himachal Pradesh
Other than valley areas of low hill zones with slopes ranging from 10 to 40%, inward sloping bench terraces are constructed. A vertical interval of 0.6–1.8 m (depending upon soil depth and slope) inward gradient of 1 in 15 to 1 in 20 and longitudinal gradient is provided to the bench terrace. Cut and fill method is adopted for construction. Provision of suitable outlets for disposal of excess water is also made.

Kerala
Terracing with dry rubbles or gravels or laterite pitched walls are constructed. Vertical intervals of 3 m and 5 m are adopted for land sloping up to 35% and greater than 35% respectively.

Madhya Pradesh
In the River Valley Projects of Chambal and Maha Nadi, bench terracing is adopted.

Maharashtra
Terracing is done in *Verkas* land up to 10% slope in transition zone with red to reddish brown soil and moderate to moderately high rainfall zone with soils formed from trap.

Nagaland
In sloping and hilly areas, bench terracing is adopted.

Orissa
Stone terracing and bench terracing are adopted in hilly areas, where there is pressure on land and soil depth is adequate. Stone terraces are constructed in areas where stones are available in plenty. The formation of the stone terraces help in removing the stones from the fields, which otherwise hinder agricultural operations. Stone terraces are constructed in the Machkund basin.

Spacing
Suitable spacing can be adopted depending upon the local conditions, like slope of the land and depth of soil.

Table 3.29   *Terrace spacing*

Slope (%)	HI (m)	Slope (%)	HI (m)
6	30	10	12–15
7	24–30	12	9–12
8	18–24	15 and	6–9
9	15–18	above	

Size
The cross section may be 0.36 to 0.45 m² , depending upon the depth of foundation. With the increasing of slope beyond 10%, it is advisable to give a foundation of

0.30 m instead of 0.15 m.

Alignment

The terraces should be given a longitudinal gradient of 0.2–0.3 m for 100 m towards the outlet. Grades can be varied to provide alignment of terraces as nearly parallel as topography will permit. Stone terraces should be straight as far as possible. Local depressions (15–22 cm deep) should be crossed straight in the alignment and whenever required, a neat curve may be adopted. The last stone terrace should coincide with the field boundary or be along with the alignment of a diversion at the beginning of the wider slopes down below.

Construction

A line of pegs is laid out on the proposed line. A shallow trench of 0.9 m width and 0.15 or 0.3 m depth as the case may be, is dug on the lower side of the line. The soil from the trench is put on the upper side of the pegs to form a narrow ridge, so that the percolation of runoff from the field through the stone terraces is avoided.

Stones should then be collected and packed directly into the foundation and in the super structure to form the terrace. The random rubbles should be inter-locked at least 7.5 cm in the joints and the sharp edges should be exposed outside, so that proper shape of the bund is obtained. Measurements may be taken directly after construction of bunds.

A deduction of 12½% may be made on the total measurement to give allowance for voids, but care should be taken to watch the work in progress, so that packing of stones is done properly.

Surplussing arrangement and maintenance

All the stone terraces should lead to natural outlets available, or to an artificially formed waterway. The ridge formed on the upstream side of the stone terraces should be carefully maintained and vegetation may be established on these ridges. *Fatropha*, *Vitex* or *Erithrina* spp. may be used for planting on the ridges.

Rajasthan

In the catchment area of the Chambal river valley project, bench terracing is adopted.

Uttar Pradesh

Suitability

Bench terraces have been recommended in the Himalayan region up to 33% slope. The hills have bench terraces constructed even on higher slopes from time immemorial.

Vertical Interval

It is constructed by cut and fill method and taking care to see that a minimum of 0.3 m depth of soil is left for cultivation after forming the bench. In case of lands having 33% slope, a VI of 2.4 m is provided. However, efforts are made to keep the riser not more than 1.8 m. If the slope of the riser is earthen, it could be as steep as 0.5:1 and if the riser is of rock, it is built nearly vertical. The slope of the riser may be planted to deep rooted grass. In case terrace strip is used for paddy cultivation, stone riser should positively be constructed.

Terrace gradient

Bench terraces sloping inwards (simple percolation type as named by the state Government) with an inward gradient of 3.0 to 3 5%, and longitudinal gradient of 0.3

to 0.5 per cent is given.

Outlet
An outlet for each terrace is provided at the end of longitudinal slope. The outlet is placed usually at the inner edge, with crest level being about 15 cm higher than the ground level, at the inner edge of the terrace. At times, the outlet may have to be provided in the outer edge in the 15 cm outer bund. In such a case, the crest of the outlet is kept about 5 cm above the ground level at the outer edge. The outlet may be of the following types:

— Stone lined vertical drop outlet with a small pit filled with loose stones;

— A 0.6 to 0.9 m long slate stone may be half embedded in the bund on the periphery and half length is kept projecting to make the water fall clear of the toe of the riser. In this case also, a small pit filled with loose stones is provided.

— A dry stone stepped drop structure may be built in case discharges and drops are more and it is to be disposed off in some drain.

Diversion drains
Diversion drains with drop pits are provided to carry excess runoff expected from catchment above as well as from terrace.

Punjab
Bench terracing is adopted in the foothill regions of the state.

3.6   Diversion Drains

As a rule, soil conservation measures are implemented on a whole catchment or watershed. In case a part of a catchment only is proposed to be protected with soil conservation measures (erosion control structures are constructed) and the area to be protected is situated below an unprotected area, the runoff from the unprotected or upper area will cause damage to the area proposed to be protected. To overcome this, a diversion drain is usually excavated to intercept the runoff from the area situated above and to conduct it safely to outlet. The diversion drain will follow the boundary of the area to be protected with soil conservation measures. If there is difference between the land along the boundary of the subcatchment as existing on the field and the bed grade to be provided along the proposed alignment of the diversion drain, then the problem is solved by providing bed stabilizers, which will permit the designed bed grade to be given for diversion drain. These bed stabilizers will be in the form of masonry drops at intervals, wherever the actual slope of the land exceeds the designed bed grade of the drain. In order to make provision for masonry checks or drops in the estimates and to determine where they are necessary, the existing slope of land along the proposed alignment of the diversion drain should be determined by taking levels at intervals of about 30 m, or wherever there is abrupt change of slope along the proposed alignment. The length of the diversion drain is measured on map. The area, slope of the land and its land use are to be noted in the plan in the field itself. To compute the quantity of runoff anticipated from the area, the diversion drain has to be planned, aligned, designed and executed right from the top of the catchment to be protected, until the runoff from the above catchment is safely conducted into natural streams or valleys.

The diversion drains should be aligned on non-erosive grades. It must also be protected from silting. A narrow and deep ditch does not get silted up as rapidly as a broad and shallow ditch of the same cross-sectional area and is, therefore, self maintaining.

DESIGN

Step 1. Mark the unprotected area and calculate its total area.

Step 2. For small water disposal works like diversion drains, the runoff which such ditches are expected to hold and carry is calculated by rational formula,

$$Q = \frac{CIA}{360}$$

Step 3. The cross-sectional area of the diversion ditch is designed to carry the calculated runoff (as in Step 2) at a non-erosive velocity 0.6 m/sec from most soils using the formula, $Q = A.V$ where Q is anticipated runoff.

Step 4. The non-erosive grade for the diversion ditch is calculated using Manning's Formula $V = \frac{R^{2/3}S^{1/2}}{n}$, where V is permissible velocity (m/sec) (for detailed calculations, please refer to chapters on Grassed Waterways). If excavation of diversion ditches is found difficult due to prevailing field conditions, a diversion bund capable of carrying the anticipated runoff behind it can be formed along the lower boundary of the area proposed to be protected.

CONSTRUCTION

The diversion drain or bund should be formed before the erosion control structures and constructed in the area situated below. The soil excavated from two diversion ditches shall be deposited on the lower side of the drain, leaving a berm of 0.3 m and sectioned in a trapezoidal shape with side slopes not stepper than 1:1. This spoil bank itself will serve as a freeboard for the diversion ditch and therefore, there will be no need to provide any freeboard in arriving at the depth of diversion depth.

The outlet end of the diversion ditch should be taken to the existing or stabilized safe outlets, so as to conduct the runoff properly without causing erosion. In order to protect the bed and sides of the diversion drain from scour and erosion, suitable spreading type of grasses should be planted.

3.7 Land Levelling and Grading

Land levelling or grading is the process of preparing or modifying (i.e. reshaping) the land surface to a planned grade to provide a suitable surface. Land levelling usually requires cutting of high areas and raising of low spots, in order to remove the surface irregularities and unevenness to make a plane surface. It makes suitable field surface to control the flow of water, to check soil erosion and provide better surface drainage.

FACTORS GOVERNING LAND LEVELLING

The type and amount of levelling required depends on the following factors:

Soil characteristics

The depth of soil governs the depth of cut. Excessive cut will expose the strata that is not desirable for cultivation. The soil properties like infiltration and permeability are also considered while deciding the length of irrigation runs and its economic feasibility.

Topography

The amount and cost of levelling depends on the prevailing land slope and the designed slope or grade. If the land is very steep and undulating and the soils are shallow, it may not be possible to shape the surface to the required grades and moreover it may not be economically feasible.

Cropping pattern
The kind of crops to be grown and the basis for selecting the irrigation method and the resulting land levelling criteria. Commercial crops may justify high levelling cost, whereas other crops may warrant a much smaller investment.

Method of irrigation
The different methods of irrigation have their own limitations regarding permissible slope and the area of field or plot. The level border and check basin methods are the most restrictive of all the methods.

Rainfall characteristics
Rainfall characteristics are important to determine the maximum and minimum allowable grades for a field.

Other considerations
Subdivision of the field for levelling is based on natural topographical boundaries to be considered in the initial plan. The desires of farmers regarding design standards of the job, are also to be considered.

Preparatory steps
Land levelling is probably the most intensive practice that is applied to agricultural lands and much expense can be saved by careful investigation and planning.

Land clearing (i.e. removing for trash and vegetation) should be done with heavy earth moving equipments like bulldozers or other appropriate machinery.

Prior to levelling design, the land development programme must be planned so that the location of field boundaries, irrigation water supply system, drains and farm roads are fixed. The levelling plan for an individual field must provide for furnishing burrow to or for absorbing the excavated earth from these adjacent features.

A topographical map of the farm area is necessary tool for planning field layout, water conveyance system and field drains. A topographic survey may be made by any of the conventional methods. Normally the method of grid survey is adopted for land levelling design. The area should be first cleared for vegetation and the surface prepared. A grid system established over the field and stakes are set at the grid points. The usual grid spacing is 25 m × 25 m, but other spacing as 30 m × 30 m, 20 m × 20 m and 15 m × 15 m are sometimes used, depending upon the nature of ground and precision required. However, in soil conservation works for example, renovation of bench terraces, etc. (i.e. making the benches table top), the grid spacings may be kept even 5 m × 5 m or less, depending upon the size (width) of benches. Stakes are also driven at places, where the high or low spots occur in between grid spacing. For convenience in identification, the row lines are lettered and the column lines numbered.

After staking, levels are run for all the grid corners, water lines, road, etc., with reference to a permanent bench mark established in the field.

Based on the collected data, contour map is drawn. The recommended contour intervals for land slopes in the range 0–1, 1–2, 2–5 and 5–10 per cent are 6–15, 15–30, 30–60 and 60–150 cm, respectively.

Layout

Laying out fields into workable size compartment is very important. The fields are laid out as nearly rectangular as possible. Sharp turns in field boundaries should be avoided as far as possible, in order to facilitate the use of modern equipment. The division of area into plots according to its contour and soils into parcels of land is an important step in layout. Subdivision of fields depend on ownership boundaries also. In most cases, the contour map of the area indicates the most advantageous way to sub-divide the land for grading (Fig. 3.26). Some examples are illustrated below:

— An abrupt major difference in contour interval implies sharp change in slope. Separation of fields may be desirable along a line of slope change.

— Sharp bends in otherwise nearly straight contours indicate the change in direction of slope.

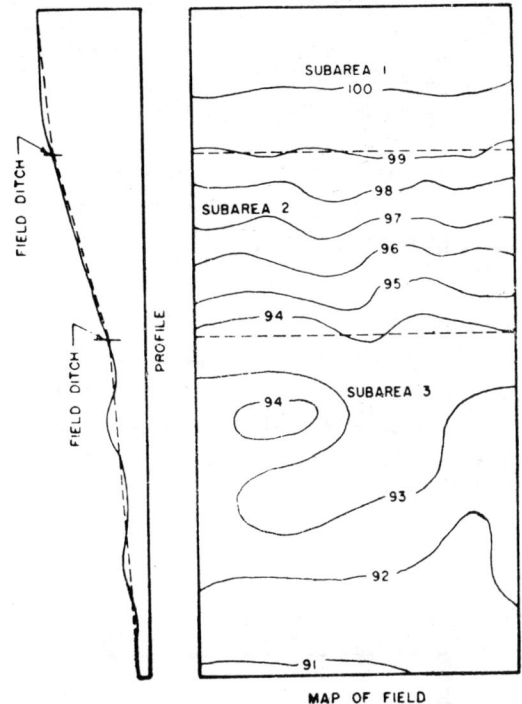

Fig. 3.26 Field subdivision for levelling

— Contour lines either too close or far apart may imply that the average slope is either too steep or too flat to be satisfactory for the land use intended and that it must be graded to a lesser or greater slope. In such cases, the lengths of fields are kept to the minimum required for efficient irrigation, so as to reduce the amount of cuts and fills required.

— Great irregularity in spacing and direction of contours may show that the topography is non-uniform to the extent that it fails to show where a separation into fields can be made advantageously.

— Irregular and/or closely spaced contours indicate that the cost of levelling may be prohibitive. Such areas may be planned for irrigation with sprinkler or drip methods.

The length of plots depends on the maximum allowable length of run for the irrigation method selected (Table 3.30). Alternatively, the field length may be limited by ownership boundaries.

Table 3.30 *Length (m) of run for different soil types*

Soil type	Length of run for border strip/furrow
Sandy and sandy loam soils	60 to 120
Medium loam soils	100 to 180
Clay loam and clay soils	150 to 300

AND LEVELLING DESIGN

The design of land levelling or grading involves the determination of level at each grid corner, up to which the land surface is to be raised or lowered. There are four basic methods of land levelling mentioned as below:

—the plane method;
—the profile method;
—the plan-inspection method; and
—the contour-adjustment method.

Each of these has some advantages and disadvantages, but when properly used, all will provide satisfactory results. Out of these the plane method is most commonly used.

The Plane Method

The plane method is so called, because the resulting land surface has a uniform down-field slope and a uniform cross slope or a table top surface. Thus, the land surface after levelling becomes a true plane surface. It is a very useful method for developing the fields where it is feasible to grade the field to a true plane.

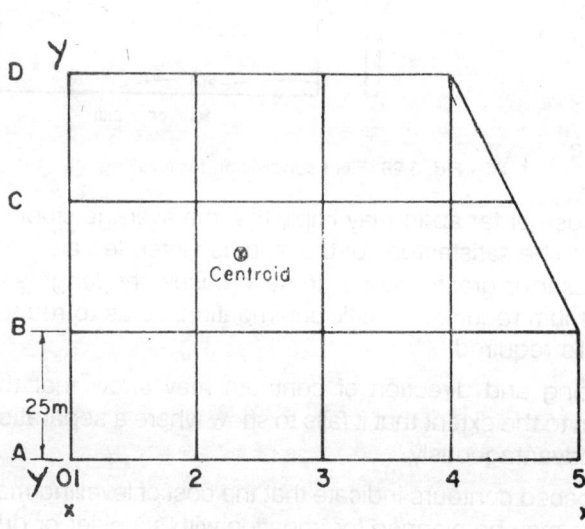

Fig. 3.27 Location of centroid

Step for design procedure
— Determine centroid of the field.   Considering each sub-division as a separate field, find out the centroid. The intersection point of the diagonals is the centroid for a rectangular field and the intersection of lines drawn from its corner to the mid-point of the opposite sides of the triangle is the centroid of a triangular field. But the centroid of an irregular field cannot be directly located. In such cases, the area is divided into triangles and rectangles and the centroid is computed by taking moments about two reference lines at right angles to each other.

— Sub-divide the entire field into sub-fields depending upon the topography, so that each subdivision can be economically developed to a plane surface.

But for simplicity in calculation, the centroid can be located with sufficient accuracy by assuming that each stake in the field represents the same area. Figure 3.27 and the calculation given below illustrate the procedure of locating centroid.

Example 16: Figure 3.27 shows the position of the stakes of a grid survey (at 25 m x 25 m grid spacing). Two reference lines XX and YY are as shown in the figure. The Number of stakes in each line multiplied by the distances from the reference XX are shown below in the tabular form.

Line	Distance	No. of stakes	Product
A	0	5	0
B	25	5	125
C	50	4	200
D	75	4	300
Total:		18	625

The distance of the centroid from the reference line $XX = \dfrac{625}{18} = 34.72$ m.

Similarly, the centroid from another reference line YY is computed as 44.44 m. With the two dimensions, centroid is located at 44.44, 34.72.

— Determine the average elevation of the field. Considering each sub-division as a separate field find out the average elevation by adding the elevations of all the grid points in the field and dividing the sum by the number of points. The plane passing through the centroid at this elevation will produce equal volumes of cut and fill.

— Compute the slope of the plane of best fit. This computation is not necessary, if the slope of the land which can be ascertained from the contour is more than the safe slope to be adopted, as per the soil conditions, omit this and assume the slope as per the soil condition.

Table 3.31   *Recommended safe limits of slope for various type of soil*

Type of soil	Slope percentage in the direction of irrigation
Heavy (clay soils)	0.10–0.40
Medium (loam soils)	0.20–0.40
Light (sandy soils)	0.25–0.65

— Determine the elevation of the plane at the centroid, giving allowance for the shrinkage and borrow or waste. Any plane passing through the centroid at the average elevation will produce equal volume of excavation of filling. However, the experience in land grading has shown that the larger volume of cut than fill must be allowed, to obtain balance earthwork. When earth is excavated, its compactness is loosened and hence the soil increases in volume. This increase is known as Swell. When the same excavated earth is placed in a fill and compacted, its volume decreases. This reference to the original volume is known as Shrinkage. It differs according to the type of soil. The reasons are:

— As the bulk of materials moved are top soil with a high organic content and relatively low bulk density, their volume is considerably reduced on compaction.

— The cut areas are subjected to considerable compaction by earth moving equipment and hence the excavated earth volume is less than the calculated volume.

The shrinkage may be expressed as:

$$\frac{Cut}{Fill} \text{ ratio} = \frac{C}{F} = \frac{10}{8.80} = 1.25$$

i.e. one cubic metre of excavation is required to fill 0.80 cubic metre of fill; or

$$\text{shrinkage factor} = \frac{1.0 - 0.80}{0.80} = 0.25 \text{ or } 25\%$$

Cut-fill ratio usually varies from 1.15 to 1.60. It may be as low as 1.1 and as much as 2.0 for heavy or light textured soils and deep or shallow cuts and fills.

It may be conveniently assumed in the plane method of levelling, that the whole field surface will be lowered by a certain amount due to compaction by the earth moving equipment. The depth of lowering of elevation may range from 0.003 to 0.01 m for very compact soil and 0.015 to 0.065 m for loose soils. It may be noted that a small change in elevation will produce a considerable change in cut-fill ratio.

If the borrow is to be taken from the field to construct roads, fill ditches, etc., the elevation of centroid may be further lowered by the required depth of lowering for borrow (i.e. by dividing the volume of borrow by the area of the field). Similarly, if some excavated earth from channels, etc., is to be utilised for filling, the elevation can be raised.

— Compute the formation levels, cuts and fills with the elevation of the centroid known and the downfield slope and cross slope selected, compute the formation or proposed level (the elevation which the point should attain after land levelling operation) of each grid point. If the land surface is to be made table top (i.e. without any slope in any direction), the proposed level at each grid point will be the same as that of the centroid.

The desired cut or fill at each grid point may be computed from a comparison of the original and the proposed elevations. When the proposed elevation is less than the original elevation of the ground, the difference indicates the depth of cut, otherwise the fill. Usually, the cut and fills are shown by the − ive and +ive signs. The cuts and fills are marked to the nearest centimetre.

Calculation of centroid

Figure 3.28 shows the level at all stakes of a grid survey (30 m square) map of a field. The reference lines XX and YY are drawn.

From the reference line XX, the number of stakes in each line multiplied by number of stakes are as given below:

Line	Distance, stakes	No. of stakes	Product
A	1	9	9
B	2	9	18
C	3	9	27
D	4	9	36
E	5	9	45
F	6	9	54
G	7	9	63
Total		63	252

$$\text{The distance of centroid of XX - line} = \frac{252}{63}$$
$$= 4 \text{ stakes}$$
$$= 4 \times 30$$
$$= 120 \text{ m}$$

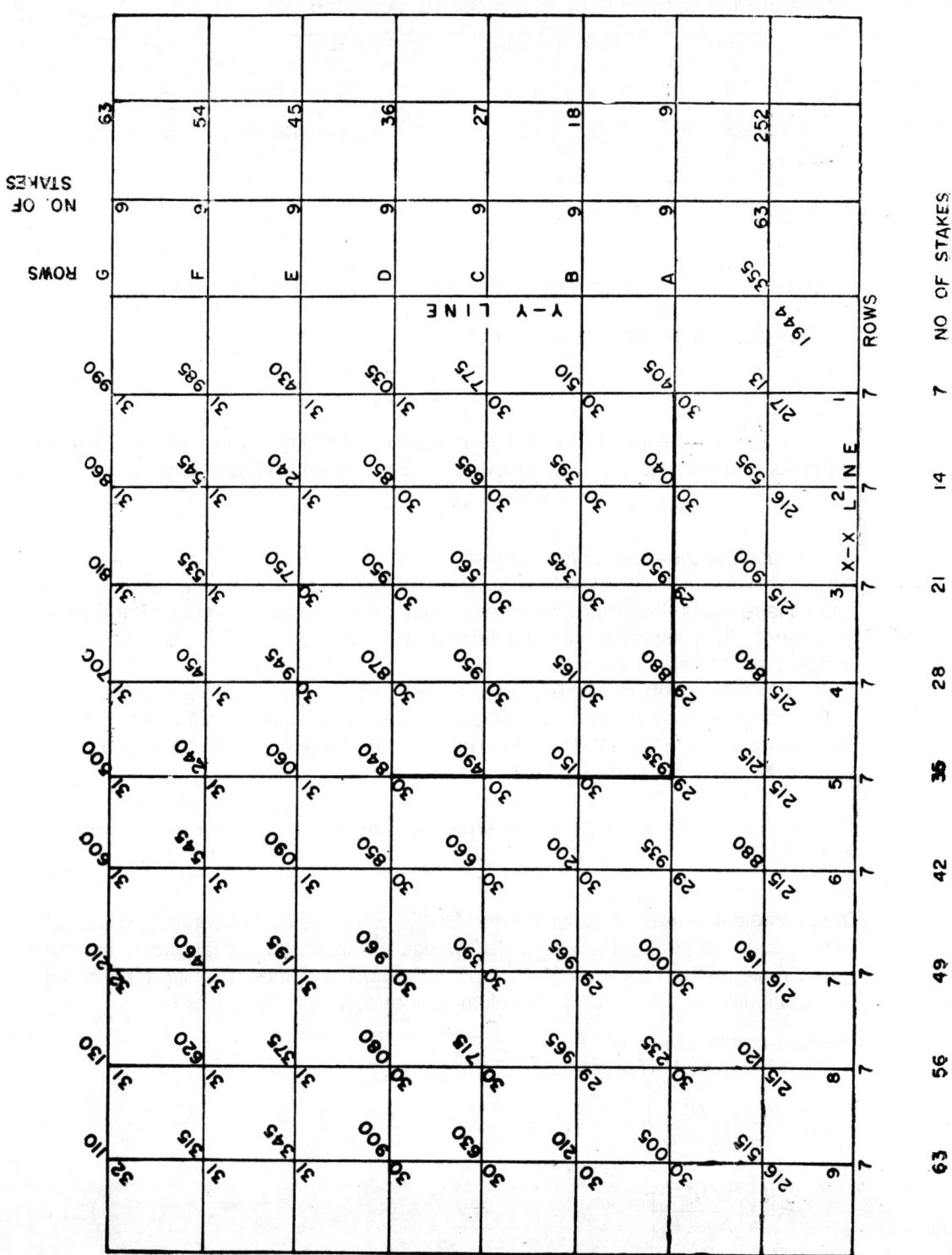

Fig. 3.28 Calculation of centroid

Similarly, the centroid from YY-line can be calculated.

Line	Distance, stakes	No. of stakes	Product
M	1	7	7
N	2	7	14
O	3	7	21
P	4	7	28
Q	5	7	35
R	6	7	42
S	7	7	49
T	8	7	56
U	9	7	63
Total		63	315

$$\text{The distance of centroid from YY line} = \frac{315}{63}$$
$$= 5 \text{ stake distances}$$
$$= 5 \times 30 = 150 \text{ m}$$

The sum of all the levels divided by the number of stakes gives average elevation of the field. In this case, sum of all levels = 1946.555 and number of stakes = 63.

$$\text{Average elevation} = \frac{1946.55}{63} = 30.900 \text{ m}$$

The elevation of the plane at the centroid
When the plane method of levelling is used, it is convenient to assume that the whole field surface will be lowered by a certain amount due to compaction by earthmoving equipment. This lowering can vary from as little as 0.005 m to 0.10 m from very compact soil to very loose soil.

For the field given in the example, the elevation of centroid works out to be 30.880 m. It is now desired to provide a slope of 0.2 per cent in the XX direction and no slope in the YY direction. The computed levels of each point and cut-fill ratio works out to be 1.03 (Fig. 3.29).

In order to provide factor for compaction, etc., the cut-fill ratio should be about 1.25. Hence, the elevation of centroid may be lowered and another trial carried out till a cut-fill ratio of 1.25 is obtained.

Earthwork volumes
The prismoidal formula is considered to be the exact method of computing the volume of earthwork in land levelling. As the use of this formula is laborious, another approximate method know as the four-point method, is commonly used for computing sufficiently accurate earthwork volumes. It requires relatively less time.

The Four-point Method
The four-point method is based on the formulae:

$$V_c = \frac{L^2}{4}\left[\frac{H_c^2}{H_c + H_f}\right] \qquad \qquad \dots (3.18)$$

and

$$V_f = \frac{L^2}{4}\left[\frac{H_f^2}{H_c + H_f}\right] \qquad \qquad \dots (3.19)$$

where, V_c = volume of cut (m³);

V_f = volume of fill (m³);

A_c = sum of cuts on four corners of the grid square (m) and
A_f = sum of fills on four corners of the grid square (m)

Row	30.640	30.700	30.760	30.820	30.880	30.940	31.000	31.060	31.120
1	32.110 (1.47)	31.130 (0.43)	32.210 (1.45)	31.600 (0.78)	31.500 (0.62)	31.700 (0.76)	31.810 (0.81)	31.860 (0.80)	31.990 (0.87)
2	31.315 (0.675)	31.620 (0.92)	31.460 (0.70)	31.545 (0.725)	31.240 (0.36)	31.430 (0.49)	31.535 (0.535)	31.545 (0.485)	31.985 (0.865)
3	31.345 (0.705)	31.375 (0.675)	31.195 (0.435)	31.090 (0.27)	31.060 (0.18)	30.845 (−0.095)	30.750 (−0.25)	31.240 (0.18)	31.430 (0.31)
4	30.900 (0.26)	30.080 (−0.62)	30.960 (0.20)	30.850 (0.03)	30.840 (−0.04)	30.870 (−0.07)	30.950 (−0.05)	30.830 (−0.23)	31.035 (−0.085)
5	30.630 (−0.01)	30.685 (−0.015)	30.390 (−0.37)	30.660 (−0.16)	30.490 (−0.39)	30.950 (0.01)	30.560 (−0.44)	30.685 (−0.375)	30.775 (−0.345)
6	30.210 (−0.43)	30.235 (−0.465)	29.965 (−0.795)	30.200 (−0.62)	30.150 (−0.73)	30.165 (−0.775)	30.345 (−0.655)	30.395 (−0.665)	30.510 (−0.61)
7	30.005 (−0.635)	30.000 (−0.70)	30.000 (−0.76)	29.935 (−0.885)	29.935 (−0.945)	29.880 (−1.06)	29.950 (−1.05)	30.040 (−1.02)	30.405 (−0.715)

	Cut (+)	Fill (−)
1.	7.990	0.0
2.	5.755	0.0
3.	2.755	0.345
4.	0.490	1.095
5.	0.01	1.782
6.	0.0	5.725
7.	0.0	7.535
	17.000	16.482

Cut-Fill Ratio $= \dfrac{17}{16.482} = 1.031$

Fig. 3.29 Calculation for cut-fill ratio for land grading

L = grid spacing (m);

H_c = sum of cuts on four corners of the grid square (m); and

H_f = sum of fills on four corners of the grid square (m)

Using the above formula, volume of cut and fill in each grid square can be calculated and the totals for the field obtained.

Example 17: Let the cuts and fills be as shown in the Figure 3.30 for a 20 m square grid.

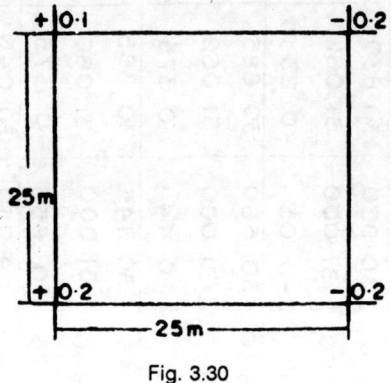

Fig. 3.30

$H_c = 0.2 + 0.2 = 0.4$ m

$H_f = 0.1 + 0.2 = 0.3$ m

$$V_c = \frac{20^2}{4} \left[\frac{(0.4)^2}{0.4 + 0.3} \right] = 22.85 \text{ m}^3$$

$$V_f = \frac{20^2}{4} = \frac{(0.3)^2}{0.4 + 0.3} = 12.85 \text{ m}^3$$

For computing the volumes in other than square grids, the same formula is used with necessary adjustments. (Fig. 3.31)

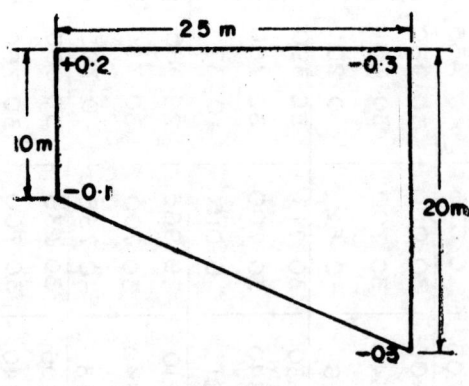

Fig. 3.31

$V_c = 0.3 + 0.4 + 0.1 = 0.8$ m

$V_f = 0.2$ m

$$\text{Grid area} = \frac{20 + 10}{2} \times 25 = 375 \text{ m}^2$$

Replacing L^2 in the original formula by this grid area:

$$V_c = \frac{375}{4} \times \frac{0.8 \times 0.8}{0.8 + 0.2} = 60 \text{ m}^3$$

$$V_f = \frac{375}{4} \times \frac{0.2 \times 0.2}{0.8 + 0.2} = 3.75 \text{ m}^3$$

For a triangular area having sides L_1 and L_2, replace L^2 by $L_1 \times L_2$, and multiply the result by 2/3. In this case, the sum of cuts and fills will be the sum for three corners of the area (Fig. 3.32).

Example 18:

$H_c = 0.4$

$H_f = 0.2$

$$V_c = \frac{2}{3} \left[\frac{25 \times 10}{4} \times \frac{0.4 \times 0.4}{0.4 + 0.2} \right] = 11.11 \text{ m}^3$$

$$V_f = \frac{2}{3} \left[\frac{25 \times 10}{4} \times \frac{0.2 \times 0.2}{0.4 + 0.2} \right] = 2.93 \text{ m}^3$$

It may be noted that normally the payment is made only for the earthwork in cutting.

Example 19:

The topographic survey of a field gave the following elevations (in metres) at grid points. Grid spacing is 20 m.

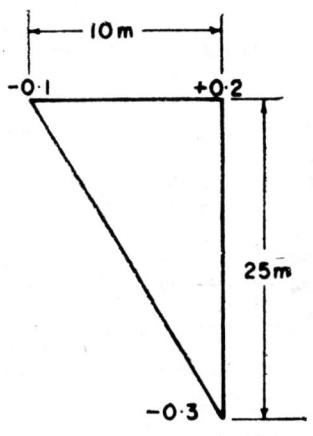

Fig. 3.32

	1	2	3	4	5	6
A	10.65	10.43	10.07	9.68	9.67
B	10.47	10.42	9.95	9.84	9.75
C	10.32	10.08	9.92	9.65	9.48
D	9.89	9.48	9.67	9.41	9.13

Calculate the elevation of the centroid of the field. It is proposed to reshape the land into a table-top surface. Calculate the cut or fill at the grid points. The soil is compact.

Solution—

Total number of solutions	= 20
Sum of elevations of 20 stations	= 197.965 m
Average elevation of the field	$= \dfrac{197.965}{20}$
	= 9.898 m.

If the elevation of centroid is treated as the calculated average elevation, it would produce equal volume of cut and fill. But cut should be more, in order to allow for settlement as already discussed.

Assuming that the level is to be lowered by 0.010 m for shrinkage, the proposed elevation at centroid. $= 9.898 - 0.010 = 9.888$ m

Now, assuming this is the final elevation at all the grid points, subtract the elevation of corresponding grid points from this proposed elevation of the centroid to compute cut/fill.

At grid point A_1 : $9.888 - 10.65 = -0.762$ m (−ive sign indicates the cut)

At grid point D_2 : $9.888 - 9.48 = 0.408$ (fill)

The cuts and fills at the different grid points are calculated in the same way, which are tabulated below:

	1	2	3	4	5
A	−0.762	−0.542	−0.182	+0.208	+0.213
B	−0.582	−0.532	−0.062	+0.048	+0.133
C	−0.432	−0.192	−0.032	+0.238	+0.403
D	−0.002	+0.408	+0.218	+0.478	+0.753

For the given example, earthwork volume are computed by four-point method and tabulated in the following form:

Sub-area	$\dfrac{H_c}{(m)}$	$\dfrac{H_f}{(m)}$	$\dfrac{H_c^2}{H_c + H_f}$ (m)	$\dfrac{H_f^2}{H_c + H_f}$ (m)	$\dfrac{V_c}{(m^3)}$	$\dfrac{V_f}{(m^3)}$
Area of square 20 × 20 = 400 m²						
AB 12	2.418	—	2.418	—	241.80	—
BC 12	1.738	—	1.738	—	173.80	—
CD 12	0.626	0.408	0.3796	0.161	37.96	16.10
AB 23	1.318	—	1.318	—	131.80	—
BC 23	0.818	—	0.818	—	81.80	—
CD 23	0.224	0.626	0.059	0.461	5.90	46.10
AB 34	0.244	0.256	0.1191	0.1311	11.91	13.11
BC 34	0.094	0.286	0.0233	0.2153	2.33	21.53
CD 34	0.032	0.934	0.011	0.9031	0.11	90.31
AB 45	—	0.612	—	0.612	—	61.20
BC 45	—	0.832	—	0.832	—	83.20
CD 45	—	1.882	—	1.882	—	188.20
Total					687.41	519.75

$$\frac{V_c}{V_f} = \frac{587.41}{519.75} = 1.32$$

Cut–fill ratio = 1.32
Earthwork volume = 687.41 m³

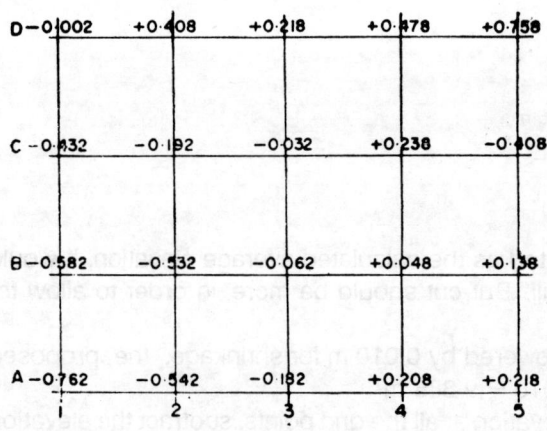

D−0.002   +0.408   +0.218   +0.478   +0.758

C −0.432   −0.192   −0.032   +0.238   −0.408

B−0.582   −0.532   −0.062   +0.048   +0.138

A −0.762   −0.542   −0.192   +0.208   +0.218

    1   2   3   4   5

Fig. 3.33 Cut and fill at different grid points

Construction

After the design is complete, the cut and fill stakes for construction purpose are driven to guide the operator. The desired cuts and fills are marked on the grid stakes (Fig. 3.33).

Land levelling is accomplished with tractor drawn and bullock drawn scrapers. Sometimes for heavy levelling works, bulldozers are used. Tractors used are both crawler or rubber tyred wheel type. The crawler tractor is frequently employed when heavy earth movement is involved. The variety of scrapers range from the terracer blade to heavy carrier type scrapers. While planning the job, following points must be considered:

— The time available for completing the job is an important factor to be considered, while deciding about the type of machines, etc. If the time is limited, use of heavy earth-moving equipment is advantageous, otherwise smaller machines and manual labour can be employed.

— The skill of operator.

— The haul distance should be kept to the minimum possible. For long hauls, rubber tyred units are usually the best.

In maintaining minimum haul distance, the selection should be made in such a way that the area of cut are as close as possible to fill area. For this, a map showing the cut-and-fill areas is prepared to plan the construction work. Care should be taken not to disturb the grid stakes, while performing the operations. To start with, first cut and fill strip of one scraper width adjacent to the stake line and bring it to the proposed level. Then the intermediate portions are scrapped and filled accordingly. The level of the surface is checked often with reference to the stakes. The grade between the stakes should be uniform. Where the depth of fill is more than 15 cm, it is necessary to build them in layers of 10, 15 cm deep, to avoid excessive settling. Under some soil conditions, it may be specified that the top soil from an area must be stockpiled, the cuts over excavated and the top soil replaced. The fill areas, too, must be stripped, the fills partly made with the material available, and the top soil replaced. Since this involves moving some earth twice, it is an expensive procedure and should be carefully justified.

When this operation is essential, first stockpile the top soil from one lane on an area requiring little cut or fill. The cuts and fills in this lane should be then be computed and the top soil from the adjacent lane stripped and used for dressing the surface of the first lane. Then progressively across the field, move the top soil to the adjacent lane, as the levelling is completed until the last lane is dressed with the top soil stockpiled from the first lane.

After the earth moving has been completed, the land surface is smoothened with a float or land plane to remove minor irregularities. This operation is carried out a number of times, first at the 45° angle to the grid lines and then at right angles to the first operation. Finally, the operation is carried out in the direction of irrigation.

Maintenance

The regular maintenance of a levelled field is a must to preserve its surface. Improper use of tillage implements should be avoided. Although annual scraping is not usually required, irrigated fields should be smoothened with a float or plane prior to sowing as a regular practice.

3.8 Grassed Waterways

Grassed waterways (Plate 16) and outlets are natural or constructed waterways shaped to required dimensions and vegetated for safe disposal of runoff from a field, diversion terrace or other structures.

The grass lined waterway is one of the basic conservation practices. Waterways subject to constant or prolonged flows require special supplemental treatment, such as grade control structures, stone center or subsurface drainage capable of carrying such flows. After establishment, protective vegetative cover must be maintained.

Vegetated outlets and waterways are used for the following purposes:

— as outlets for diversions and terraces;

— as outlets for surface and subsurface drainage systems on sloping land;

— to dispose-off water collected by road ditches or discharged through culverts; and

— to rehabilitate natural drains carrying concentration of runoff.

The waterway or outlet may be protected by using a combination of the following steps:

— Construct the waterway in advance of any other channel that will discharge into it, and divert the flow during the period of stabilization.

— Establish and maintain the vegetative cover.

Shape

Grassed waterways may be built to three general shapes—parabolic, trapezoidal or V-shaped. Parabolic waterways are the most common. The successful vegetated waterway is dependent on good conservation treatment on its watershed, which reduce the peak rate of runoff and the volume of runoff to be carried by the waterway.

Profile and cross-section

The original ground surface should be surveyed for longitudinal and cross-section in detail, to permit dividing the waterway into reaches of approximately uniform slope and shape.

Design

In designing a grassed waterway, care should be taken to see that its size is sufficient to carry all the runoff water from the contributing catchment and the gradient is such that the runoff will flow with non-erosive velocities.

Design data

The following information is required for designing a waterway:

— Watershed area (ha) together with soil characteristics, cover and topography. This information is needed to estimate peak rate of runoff.

— Grade of the proposed waterway (in per cent slope). This is fixed considering the outlet elevation.

— Vegetal cover adopting to site condition (for selecting roughness coefficient).

— Erodibility of the soil in the waterway (the information is necessary for protecting the waterway till the vegetation or grass gets established).

— permissible velocity for the condition encountered.

— Allowance for space that will be occupied by vegetative lining.

— Free-board.

Non-erosive velocity of flow

The non-erosive velocity of flow depends usually on site conditions. However, following velocities of flow can be considered safely for design purposes.

— a velocity of 0.9 m/sec should be maximum where only a sparse cover can be established or maintained;

— a velocity of 0.9 to 1.2 m/sec should be used where vegetation is to be established by seeding;

— velocity of 1.2 to 1.5 m/sec should be used only in areas where dense, vigorous sod is established quickly;

— a velocity of 1.5 to 1.8 m/sec may be used on well-established sod of excellent quality; and

— velocity of 1.8 to 2.1 m/sec may be used on well-established quality and conditions under which the flow cannot be handled at lower velocity. Also special maintenance measures are needed.

For situations where waterways are without vegetation, following values of critical velocity may be used (critical velocity is the velocity of water flowing in the channel, such that no silting or scouring takes place).

Nature of soil	Critical velocity (m/sec)	Nature of soil	Critical velocity (m/sec)
Earth	0.3–0.6	Boulders	1.5–1.8
Ordinary *murrum*	0.6–0.9	Soft rock	1.8–2.4
Hard *murrum*	1.2	Hard rock	More than 3.0

Cross-section

The area of cross-section (A), wetted perimeter (P) and top width (T) of trapezoidal section can be obtained by using the formula:

Trapezoidal (Fig. 3.34)

$A = bd + Zd^2$ and
$P = b + 2d\sqrt{1 + Z^2}$
$T = b + 2dZ$

where, b = bottom width;

d = depth of channel; and

Z = side slope.

In area of cross-section (A), wetted perimeter (P) and top (T) of parabolic and triangular sections can be obtained, by using the following formulae:

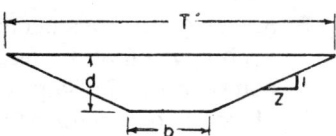

Fig. 3.34 Trapezoidal cross-section

Parabolic (Fig 3.35)

$$A = \frac{2}{3}Td$$

and $P = T + \dfrac{8}{3} \times \dfrac{d^2}{T}$

T = Top width

Triangular (Fig. 3.36)

$A = Zd^2$

$P = 2d\sqrt{1 + Z^2}$

$T = 2dZ$

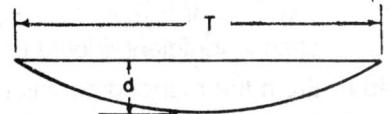

Fig. 3.35 Parabolic cross-section

The wetted perimeter (P) in the above equations is the length of line of inter-section of the plane of the cross-section with the wetted surface of the channel.

The hydraulic radius (R) is the ratio which is obtained by dividing area of cross-section (A) by the wetted perimeter (P). This is necessary to determine (R) to compute the velocity of flow of water in the channel using Manning's formula.

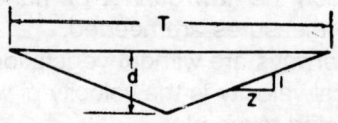

Fig. 3.36 Triangular cross-section

STEPS FOR DESIGN

Step 1. The area drained, A (ha) may be obtained from the contour maps.

Step 2. Estimate the peak rate of runoff (cumecs) for the area to be drained using the rational formula.

$$Q = \frac{CIA}{360}$$

Step 3. Permissible velocity of flow, V (m/sec) in the vegetated and non-vegetated waterways can be obtained as discussed earlier.

Step 4. Compute approximate area of cross-section of the channel using the formula, Q = A.V., where V = the permissible velocity as obtained under Step 3 and Q = peak rate of runoff.

Step 5. Knowing the cross-section from Step 4, determine the channel dimension in such a way that the area of cross-section equals the area of cross-section computed as in Step 4. (Use of different formulae given to compute area of cross-section for different shaped channels).

Step 6. Compute hydraulic radius (R) from the cross-section obtained in Step 5.

Step 7. Compute the grade of the channel using the Manning's formula,

$$V = \frac{1}{n}R^{2/3}S^{1/2}$$

where, V= permissible velocity (m/sec) (Step 3),
R= hydraulic radius (m)
n= roughness coefficient (refer Tables 3.32 and 3.33)

Step 8. The channel gradient obtained under Step 7 may be rounded for convenience of layout. The outlet elevation obtained by-computing with this channel gradient should coincide with field outlet elevation.

Step 9. From the rounded off value of grade (S), we calculate the velocity of flow for the section under consideration. If needed, cross-section is to be adjusted (by adopting the channel dimensions) and it is to be verified whether the computed velocity is approximately equal or less than the velocity as assumed under Step 3.

Example 20: Determine the dimensions of a grassed waterway for stability and capacity, with a trapezoidal cross-section using the following data:
Peak rate of runoff = 3.5 cumec
Grade = 0.3 per cent
Vegetative cover = Blue grass
n = 0.045

Table 3.32 *Values of Manning's roughness co-efficient, n. To be used with Manning's formula*

Surface	Best	Good	Fair	Bad
Uncoated cost iron pipe	0.012	0.013 .	0.014	0.015
Coated cast iron pipe	0.011	0.012*	0.013*	
Commercial wrought iron pipe, black	0.012	0.013	0.014*	0.015
Commercial wrought iron pipe, galvanized	0.013	0.014	0.015	0.017
Smooth brass and glass pipe	0.009	0.010	0.011	0.013
Riveted and spiral steel pipe	0.013	0.015*	0.017*	
Vitrified sewer pipe	0.010	0.013*	0.015	0.017
	0.011			
Common clay drainage till	0.011	0.012*	0.014*	0.017
Glazed brick work	0.011	0.012	0.013*	0.015
Brick in cement mortar, brick sewers	0.012	0.013	0.015*	0.017
Neat cement surfaces	0.010	0.011	0.012	0.013
Cement mortar surfaces	0.011	0.012	0.013*	0.015
Concrete pipe	0.012	0.013	0.015*	0.016
Concrete lined channels	0.012	0.014*	0.016*	0.018
Cement rubble surface	0.025	0.030	0.033	0.035
Dry rubble surface	0.025	0.030	0.033	0.035
Semi-circle metal flumes, smooth	0.011	0.012	0.013	0.015
Semi-circle metal flumes, corrugated	0.0225	0.025	0.0275	0.030

Canals and ditches

Earth, straight and uniform	0.017	0.020	0.0225*	0.025
Rock cuts, smooth and uniform	0.025	0.030	0.033*	0.035
Rock cuts, jagged and irregular	0.035	0.040	0.045	
Winding sluggish canals	0.0225	0.025*	0.0275	0.030
Dredged earth channels	0.025	0.0275*	0.030	0.033
Canals with rough stony beds,				
weeds on earth banks	0.025	0.030	0.035*	0.040
Earth bottom, rubble sides	0.028	0.030*	0.033*	0.035

Natural Stream Channels

Clean, straight, bank, full stage,				
no rifts or deep pools	0.025	0.0275	0.030	0.033
Same as above but some weeds and stones	0.030	0.033	0.035	0.040

*Values commonly used in designing.

Soil moderately erodible
Side slope, $Z = 2$.
Solution
Assume $B = 2m$
Area of cross-section,

$A = BD + ZD^2$
Wetted perimeter,
$P = 2D\sqrt{1 + Z^2}$
$A = 2 \times 1 + 2 \times 1^2 = 4 \text{ m}^2$
$P = 2 + 2 \times 1\sqrt{1 + 2^2}$
$\quad = 2 + 4.47 = 6.47 \text{ m}$
Hydraulic radius
$R = \dfrac{A}{P} = \dfrac{4}{6.47} = 0.62 \text{ m}$
Using the Nomograph (Fig. 3.37)
    Velocity of flow in the channel section is approximately equal to 0.9 m/sec
    $Q = A \times V = 4.0 \times 0.9 = 3.6 \text{ cumec}$
Hence, the design can be accepted.

Table 3.33   *Values of n for pipes, to be used with the Manning's formula*

Kind of pipe	Variation		Use in designs	
	From	To	From	To
Clean uncoated cast iron pipe	0.011	0.015	0.013	0.015
Clean coated cast iron pipe	0.010	0.014	0.012	0.014
Dirty or tuberculated cast iron pipe	0.015	0.035		
Riveted steel pipe	0.013	0.017	0.015	0.017
Lockbar and welded pipe	0.010	0.013	0.012	0.013
Galvanized iron pipe	0.012	0.017	0.015	0.017
Brass and glass pipe	0.009	0.013		
Wood stave pipe	0.010	0.014		
Wood stave pipe small diameter			0.011	0.012
Wood stave pipe, large diameter			0.012	0.013
Concrete pipe	0.010	0.017		
Concrete pipe with rough joints			0.016	0.017
Concrete pipe, 'dry mix' rough forms			0.015	0.016
Concrete pipe, 'wet mix' steel forms			0.012	0.014
Concrete pipe, very smooth			0.011	0.012
Vitrified sewer pipe	0.010	0.017	0.013	0.015
Common clay drainage tile	0.011	0.017	0.012	0.014

Source: *Handbook of Hydraulics*, King, McGraw-Hill Book Company, INC (Fourth edition) (1954) pages 6.12)

Example 21: Design a grassed waterway of parabolic shape to carry a flow of 2.6 m³/s, down a slope of 3 per cent. The waterway has a good stand of grass and a velocity of 1.75 m/s can be allowed. Assume the value of *n* in Manning's formula as 0.04.
Solution
Using $Q = AV$, for a velocity of 1.75 m/s, a cross-section of 2.6/1.75 = 1.5 m² is needed.

Assuming, $t = 4$ m, $d = 60$ cm

$$A = 2/3\ t.d. = 2/3 \times 4 \times 0.6 = 1.6\ m^2$$

$$P = t + \frac{8d^2}{3t} = 4 + \frac{8.062}{3 \times 4} = 4.24\ m$$

$$R = \frac{A}{P} = \frac{1.6}{4.24} = 0.377$$

$$V = \frac{R^{2/3}S^{1/2}}{n}$$

$$= \frac{(0.377)^{2/3} \times (0.03)^{1/2}}{0.04} = \frac{0.522 \times 0.173}{0.04} = 2.26\ m/s.$$

The velocity exceeds the permissible limit. Assuming a revised value of $t = 6$ m and $d = 0.4$ m,

$$A = \frac{2}{3} \times 6 \times 0.4 = 1.6\ m^2$$

$$P = 6 + \frac{8 \times 0.4^2}{3 \times 6} = 6.45,$$

$$R = \frac{1.6}{6.45} = 0.248$$

$$V = \frac{(0.248)^{2/3} \times (0.03)^{1/2}}{0.04} = 1.70.\ m/s.$$

The velocity is within permissible limits.

$$Q = 1.6 \times 1.7 = 2.72\ m^3/s$$

Hence satisfactory. A suitable freeboard to the depth is to be given in the final dimensions.

Example 22: Design a parabolic shaped grassed waterway to carry a peak flow of 3.0 m³/sec down a slope of 4.0%. An excellent stand of dub grass is maintained in the waterway.

Manning's Coefficient $n = 0.04$
Initially assume a top width $T = 4.0$ m (Fig. 3.38)
Depth of flow $d = 0.60$

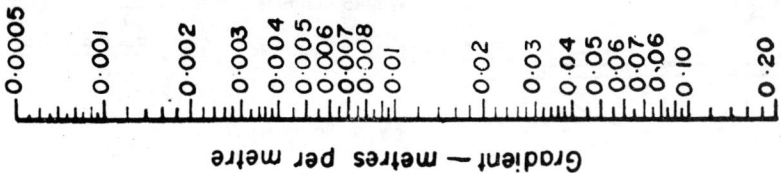

Gradient — metres per metre

Velocity — metres per second

Pivot line

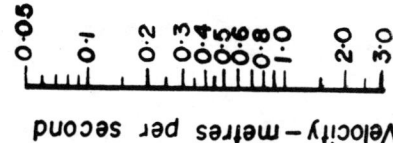

Roughness coefficient 'n'

Hydraulic radius 'R' — metres

Fig. 3.37 A nomographic solution of Manning's formula

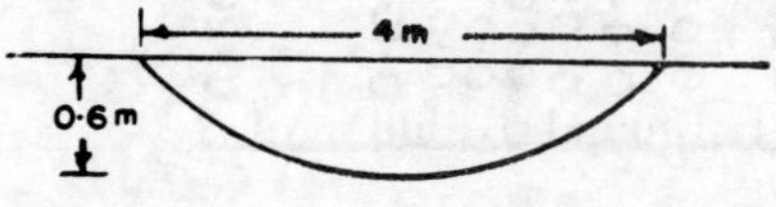

Now the area of cross-section

$$= \frac{2}{3} Td = \frac{2}{3} \times 4 \times 0.60 = 1.6 \text{ m}^2$$

Wetted perimeter, $P = T + \dfrac{8d^2}{3T}$

$$= 4 + \frac{8 \times 0.6 \times 0.6}{3 \times 4}$$

$$= 4.24 \text{ m}$$

Hydraulic radius, $R = \dfrac{a}{p} = \dfrac{1.6}{4.24}$

$$= 0.377 \text{ m}$$

Using the Nomograph, $V = 2.57$ m/s.

$Q = A \times V = 1.6 \times 2.6 = 4.16$ cumec

Fig. 3.38

The section is much higher in size. Therefore, assuming that $T = 4.15$ m and depth of flow as 0.475 m and adopting the above method, $Q = 3.007$ cumec. This is satisfactory.

DESIGN OF A DIVERSION CHANNEL

A case is met wherein an area to be improved by contour bunding receives runoff from an outside catchment. It is necessary to devise a diversion channel before undertaking contour bunding project.

Design Example 23:

Outside catchment = 15 ha
Slope = 8%
Coefficient of runoff may be assumed as 0.75
Intensity of rainfall = 25 mm/hr
Assume a coefficient of roughness = 0.05
Peak rate of runoff,

$$Q = \frac{CIA}{360} = \frac{0.75 \times 25 \times 15}{360} = 0.78 \text{ cumec}$$

Solution-Design of diversion drain

First trial —Assume $b = 2$, $d = 0.3$ m, $Z = 2$
Area of cross-section $= b + Zd^2$

$$= 2 \times 0.3 + 2 \times 0.3^2 = 0.78 \text{ m}^2$$

Wetted perimeter $= b + 2d\sqrt{1 + Z^2}$

$$= 2 + 2 \times 0.3\sqrt{1 + 2^2} = 3.338 \text{ m}$$

Hydraulic radius, $R = \dfrac{0.78}{3.338} = 0.233$ m

$V = \dfrac{1}{n} \cdot R^{2/3} \cdot S^{1/2} = \dfrac{1}{0.05} \times (0.233)^{2/3} \times (0.08)^{1/2} = 2.12$ m/s

$Q = A \times V = 0.78 \times 2.12 = 1.65$ cumec

The requirement being 0.78 cumec, the size of diversion drain is very big. Hence, the dimensions can be lowered.

2nd trial—$b = 0.6$ m; $d = 0.3$ m $Z = 2$

Area of cross-section of flow, $A = bd + Zd^2$

$$= 0.6 \times 0.3 + 2 \times 0.3 \times 0.3 = 0.36 \text{ m}^2$$

Wetted perimeter, $P = b + 2d\sqrt{1 + Z^2} = 0.6 + 2 \times 0.3\sqrt{1 + 4} = 1.94$ m

Hydraulic radius, $R = \dfrac{A}{P} = \dfrac{0.36}{1.94} = 0.185$ m

Manning's formula, $V = \dfrac{1}{n} \cdot R^{2/3} \cdot S^{1/2} = \dfrac{1}{0.05} = (0.185)^{2/3} \times (0.08)^{1/2} = 1.05$ m/s

$Q = A.V = 0.78 \times 1.05 = 0.81$ cumec

This is satisfactory. Here channel dimensions of bottom width of 0.6m and depth 0.3 m with side slopes of 2:1 can be adopted.

Plate 1.   Deforestation.

Plate 2.   Overgrazing.

Plate 3.   Faulty cultivation.

Plate 4. Sheet erosion in black soil results in soil loss 17-43 t/ha/year.

Plate 5. Rill erosion on agricultural lands.

Plate 6. Gully erosion in ravine region results in about 33 t/ha/year of soil loss.

Plate 7.   Stream bank erosion.

Plate 8.   Floods.

Plate 9. Contour bunding (Narrow base terracing).

Plate 10. Graded bunding.

Plate 11. Broad base terraces.

Plate 12. Conservation ditching.

Plate 13. Recycling stored water in the ditches.

Plate 14.   Bench terracing in Himalayas in India.

Plate 15.   Puertorican or California type of terraces in
the Nilgiris hills in India.

4

Water Resource Development and Moderation of Floods

In India, about 77% of the cultivable area depends upon *in situ* rainfall contributing about 46% of the national agricultural production. Food production from such areas can be stabilized if life saving irrigation or supplemental irrigation is given to the crops, in addition to other inputs. In case of high rainfall areas, dry spells even within the monsoon period are not uncommon, resulting in fluctuation of crop production. Moreover, in such areas, occurrence of high intensity rainfall events may result in floods. In the above circumstances, to mitigate drought and at the same time, moderate floods and develop water resources for the region, it would be wise to harvest the runoff water, which otherwise goes as waste, store it and recycle it for stabilizing agricultural production. Storing of such harvested runoff water can be accomplished in the following ways, depending on the various requirements and physical features of topography:

— Small earthen embankments (Plate 17) can be built to catch surface runoff, where topography permits;

— Dug-out farm ponds; and

— Embankment-cum-dug out farm ponds.

4.1 Small Earthen Embankments

SELECTION OF SITE

The selection of a suitable pond site should begin with preliminary studies of possible sites. From an economic view point, a pond should be located where the largest storage volume can be obtained with the least amount of earth fill. This condition will generally occur at a site where the valley is narrow, side slopes are relatively steep and slope of the valley floor will permit a large deep basin. Such sites tend to minimize the area of shallow water.

Except where the pond is to be used for wild life, large areas of shallow water should be avoided due to excessive evaporation losses and the growth of noxious aquatic plants. Where water must be used for irrigation, ponds should be located as close to the point of use as is possible.

Pollution of farm pond water should be avoided from drainage, from farmsteads, sewage lines and mine dumps. Where this cannot be done successfully, it is recommended that water from such areas should be diverted from farm pond.

FOUNDATIONS

The most satisfactory foundation is one, that consists of, or is underlain at a shallow depth by a thick layer of relatively impervious consolidated material. Such foundations cause no stability problems. It is sufficient to remove the top soil and scarify or disk the area to provide a bond with the material in the dam.

Where the impervious layer is overlain by pervious material, a compacted clay cut off, extending from the surface of the ground into the impervious layer, is required to prevent possible failure by piping and to prevent excessive seepage.

Where the foundation consists of highly pervious sand or sand gravel mixture and any impervious clay layer is very deep; a detailed investigation should be made and corrective measures will be required to prevent excessive seepage and possible failure.

A foundation consisting of or underlain by a highly plastic clay of unconsolidated material requires a very careful investigation and design, in order to obtain stability.

Water impounded on bed rock foundations seldom gives cause for concern, unless the rock contains fissures or crevices through which water may escape at an excessive rate. Whenever a rock is encountered, a careful investigation is necessary.

FOUNDATION CUT-OFFS

Where the foundation consists of pervious materials at or near the surface with rock or impervious materials at a greater depth, seepage through the pervious layer should be reduced to prevent piping and excessive losses. Usually a cut-off joining the impervious stratum in the foundation with the base of dam is needed.

A trench is cut parallel to the centre line of the dam to a depth that extends well into the impervious layer. The trench is extended into and carried up the abutments of the dam as far as pervious material exists, that might allow seepage under the embankment. The trench should have a bottom width of not less than 1.2 m, but adequate to allow use of equipment necessary to obtain proper compaction. Its sides should not be steeper than 1:1. The trench should be filled with successive thin layers of relatively impervious material, each layer being thoroughly compacted at near optimum moisture conditions, before the succeeding layer is placed. Any water collected in the trench should be removed before back fill operations are started.

BORROWPIT

It is advisable to take advantage of earth removed to fill in providing additional capacity for water storage. Where conditions are satisfactory, the borrow pit should be located immediately upstream from the toe of the embankment, to increase depth and capacity of pond. A minimum of 0.6 m of impervious should be best over any pervious strata, if present. Borrow pits located outside the pond area should be selected, so as to destroy the minimum of land and be dressed up at the conclusion of work.

EARTH FILL

Earth fill material should be impervious and have enough body to be stable under the loads imposed. A sandy clay soil is most desirable. If there is a variation in the fill material that is available, the more impervious material should be placed in the upstream two-third and that which is more pervious be used on the downstream one-third. Earth fill material should be free from sod, roots, brush and other deleterious material. The fill material should be spread in layers not exceeding 0.2 m thickness.

LAYOUT AND DESIGN OF EARTHEN EMBANKMENT

Steps in layout and design of earthen embankments are given below:

1. General Data Required

(a) Location map

    (i) Location of project

    (ii) Existing location of roads and other important public utilities

    (iii) Stream gauging sampling stations and meteorological observations, etc.

(b) Hydrologic data

    (i) Stream flow records including volumes and rates

    (ii) Water requirements including conveyance losses, seepage, percolation, evaporation losses, and wild life, etc.

    (iii) Flood studies, including inflow design floods and floods to be expected during construction stage

    (iv) Sedimentation including sediment measurement, etc.

    (v) Data on ground water table in the vicinity of dam site

(c) Climatic data

    (i) Monthly temperatures and rainfall and storm intensities

    (ii) Evaporation rates

    (iii) Maximum, minimum, and mean temperatures

    (iv) Wind directions and velocities

(d) Geologic data

    (i) Geological report comprising of formations, exposed gravel, deposits of permeable nature contributing to serious reservoir leakage

    (ii) Geological cross-sections where necessary

2. Reservoir Data

(a) Reservoir map

    (i) Topography

    (ii) Horizontal and vertical controls, preferably a triangulation survey system

    (iii) Ownership boundaries and names of owners

(b) Road and public utility surveys

    (i) Construction of public utilities, such as road, etc.

(c) Miscellaneous data

    (i) Estimate of probable life of reservoir, that is considering loss of capacity due to silting

    (ii) Tabulation of areas to be cleared, with estimated cost

    (iii) Description of lands adjacent to the proposed reservoir for public use, recreation, or other purposes

    (iv) Discussion of limitations to reservoir fluctuations

3. Data for Dams

(a) Dam site map

    (i) Topography of dam site

    (ii) Horizontal and vertical controls, preferably by a triangulation system

    (iii) Coordinate system grid

    (iv) Location of rock outcrops and apparent geological features

    (v) Location of existing works at the site

    (vi) Location of drill holes, test pits, and other foundation explorations

(b) Foundations explorations

    (i) Sufficient drill holes, auger holes, and/or test pits to determine character and depth of overburden for feasibility and specifications designs

    (ii) Description and logs of exploration

    (iii) Sufficient explorations to determine character of bedrock of impervious foundation strata for feasibility and specifications designs

(c) Materials explorations

    (i) Location and description of character of proposed material to be used in the construction of the dam, including earth, sand-gravel for aggregate and embankment, and rock for rockfill and riprap

    (ii) Map of borrow areas, showing location of test holes made for feasibility and specifications designs

    (iii) Logs of explorations

    (iv) Representative samples of materials in borrow areas

(d) Tailwater data

    (i) Stage–discharge curves for streams, if available

    (ii) Cross-sections of streams, with dated water surface elevations above and below dam

    (iii) Tailwater and backwater curves for stated high-water marks.

(e) Local conditions controlling design of the dam

    (i) Capacities and elevations of required outlets as determined by local conditions

(f) Local conditions affecting construction

    (i) Estimated cost for sufficient data for preparation of estimates for transportation facilities

    (ii) Requirements for water supply and sanitation facilities

DESIGN

Embankment Top Width
Normally the top width of the embankment is fixed by the equation:

$$W = \frac{Z}{5} + 3 \qquad \qquad ..(4.1)$$

where, W = width of crest, m; and
       Z = height of embankment above the stream bed, m.

    Where the top of the embankment is to be used for a roadway, the top width should be provided for a shoulder on each side of the travelled way to prevent raveling. The top width in such cases should not be less than 4.5 m.

Table 4.1 *Recommended top widths for earthen embankments*

Height of dam, m	Top width, m
Under 4	3.25
4 to 6	3.50
6 to 8	3.75

Embankment Side Slopes

The side slopes of a dam depend primarily on the stability of the material in the embankment. The greater the stability of the fill material, the steeper can be the side slopes. The more unstable materials require flatter side slopes.

Table 4.2 *Recommended side slopes for earthen embankments*

Soil classification	Slope (Horizontal to vertical)	
	Upstream	Downstream
Well-graded gravels, sand, gravel mixtures little or no fines	Pervious and hence not suitable	
Clayey gravels, silty gravels, gravel sand clay mixtures and gravel sand silt mixtures	2.5:1	2:1
Sandy clays, silty clays, lean clays, inorganic silts and clays	3:1	2.5:1
Inorganic clays of high plasticity and inorganic silts	3.5:1	2.5:1

Free Board

Free board is the added height of the dam, provided as a safety factor to prevent waves or runoff from storms greater than the design frequency for over-topping the embankment. It is the vertical distance between the elevation of the high flood level, after all settlement has taken place. Normally 15 per cent is adopted as free board.

Allowance for Settlement

Settlement includes the consolidation of the fill materials and the consolidation of the foundation materials due to the self-weight of fill material and the increased moisture caused by the storage of water.

Settlement or consolidation depends on the character of the materials in the dam and foundation, and on the methods and speed of construction. The design height of earth dams should be increased by an amount equal to 5% of design height.

Earthwork Computation

To estimate the borrow required should include the dam, allowance for settlement, backfill for the cutoff trench, backfill for the existing stream channels and the holes in the foundation area, etc. The common methods of estimating the volume of earthfill is the 'sum of end area' method. With the fill heights, side slopes and top width established, the end area of the cross-section at each station along the centre line is used for computation of earth work.

Computation of Storage Capacity

The storage in an earthen embankment can be roughly calculated from the formula:

$$\text{Storage (ha-m)} = 0.4 \, DA \qquad \qquad \dots (4.2)$$

where, D = maximum depth of water (m); and
A = area of water spread at wasteweir (ha).

For large embankments, water spread contours shall have to be surveyed and the storage calculated as under:

$$\text{Capacity between two contours} = \left[\frac{\text{Distance between two contours}}{2}\right] \times \left[\text{sum of areas of the contour}\right]$$

Storage at intermediate contours can be calculated, if the water spread areas are known or by the principle that the square roots of water spread areas are proportional to their depths above bed level.

Definitions

(a) *Stone pitching*
It is a protection provided to the upstream sloping face of the dam. This protection extends from the natural ground surface to about 1 m above the H.F.L. as shown in Fig. 4.1.

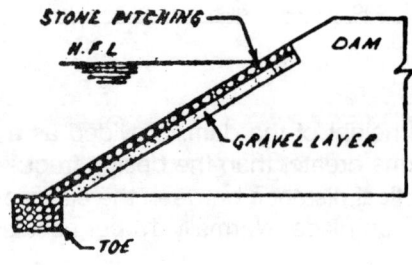

Fig. 4.1 Stone pitching

Stone pitching bears the burnt of water pressure and protects the upstream slope. It is constructed with stones firmly packed and embedded on the slope. The stones are laid perpendicular to the sloping face.

The thickness of pitching varies from 0.3 to 0.6 m. The pitching is laid over a layer of *murrum* of gravel of 15 cm thickness.

(b) *Riprap*
It is also a protection provided to the sloping faces upstream and downstream of the dam to protect the slopes from waves, men, cattle, rains, etc.

(c) *Blanket*
It is a layer of impervious material laid at the natural ground level on the upstream side. It increases the path of percolation to reduce seepage pressure.

(d) *Corewall*
It is a centrally provided fairly impervious wall in the dam. It checks the flow of water in the section of the dam. Generally the core wall extends from the ground level up to High Flood Level (H.F.L). The core wall may be constructed of various materials, namely:
(i) Puddle clay (ii) Masonry (iii) Concrete

(e) Saturation gradient

When the water is impounded on the upstream side of the dam, there is a head of water equal to the height of water stored. Under this head, water seeps in and percolates through the body of the dam. As this percolation water proceeds towards downstream, it loses head enroute.

Naturally, the head of water goes on decreasing towards the downstream end and till it meets the base at some point. Thus the saturation line is the line of demarcation between saturated soil and unsaturated soil in the dam section (Fig. 4.2).

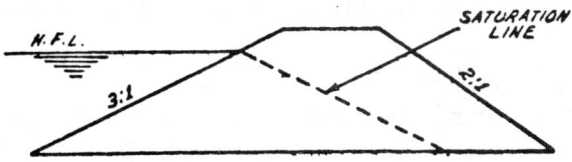

Fig. 4.2 Saturation line in an embankment

The slope of the saturation line is called the saturation gradient.

For stability of the dam, it is essential that the saturation line should meet the base within the dam section.

(f) Cut-off

It is a fairly impervious barrier provided at the foundation in the centre of the base of an earth dam. There is flow of water in the foundation under pressure. The cut-off tries to check this flow of water and increases the path of percolation. It generally extends up to the impervious rock bed if it is near or goes sufficiently below in the foundation.

(g) Filter

When the saturation line goes beyond the limits of the dam or when it meets the downstream sloping face, a layer of graded coarse material is provided in the dam section on downstream side at the base, as shown in Fig. 4.3.

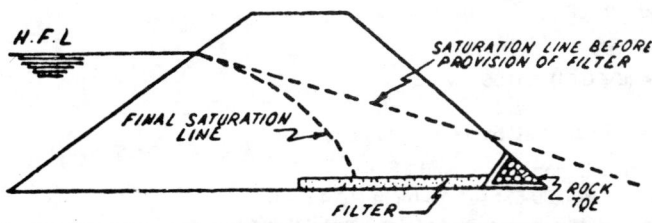

Fig. 4.3 Filter in an earth dam

As the filter attracts the flow of water, the saturation line is brought within the limits of the dam.

(h) Sod

It is a grass turf maintained on the downstream sloping face of a dam to protect it from heavy rainfall, etc. If the downstream face is left unprotected, gullies may be formed.

(i) Optimum moisture content

Even compacted soil contains water and air in small pores. Naturally, its density also depends on the percentage of volume of the moisture content and the air in small pores. Optimum moisture content is that percentage of moisture in the soil, which gives maximum dry density when compacted with this percentage of moisture. If moisture content is increased or decreased, then the dry density of compacted soil reduces. To achieve the maximum weight for stabilizing earth dam under its own weight, it is very essential to consolidate the embankment with optimum moisture content.

(j) Phreatic line in an earth dam

It is already mentioned that the saturation line is the line of demarcation between saturated and unsaturated zones in the earth dam. Similarly, Phreatic line is the line which joins the points in the dam section, at which pressure is equal to the atmospheric pressure.

(k) Breaching section in an earth dam

Overtopping of an earth dam by flood water causes failure of the dam by washout. Hence every precaution is taken to avoid overtopping. To achieve this object, a natural saddle on the periphery of the reservoir is selected. In the saddle, an ordinary retaining wall is constructed. The top of the retaining wall is kept about 1 metre lower than the top of the dam. However, the top of the retaining wall is higher than Full Reservoir Level (F.R.L.). When the water level in the reservoir rises dangerously, the flood water breaches the periphery at this section. To carry out the flow safely, good channel is provided below the section. Thus the flood water finds its way out of the reservoir without damaging the main dam. If a natural saddle is not available, the breaching section can be constructed artificially at a suitable site away from the earth dam.

Example 24—Design a pond to provide water for 200 steers, for irrigating a 0.2 ha (0.5 ac) garden, and for a family of six persons. A suitable site for the dam has a drainage area of 27 ha (67 ac), and the estimated design peak runoff for a 25 year return period storm is 2.12 m³/s (75 cfs).

Seepage and evaporation losses from the pond are estimated as 60 per cent of the storage capacity.

Solution:

From Table 4.3 the annual water requirements are:

200 steers (200× 0.002)	0.40 ha-m	
Irrigation (0.2× 0.45)	0.09	
Household use (6× 0.01)	0.06	
	———	
Total	0.55 ha-m (4.46 ac-ft)	

Storage requirements allowing 57 per cent losses
    = 0.55× 100/(100-57) = 1.28 ha-m (10.4 ac-ft)

About six acres of drainage area are required for each ac-ft of storage. Required watershed size is 10.2× 6/2.47 = 25.2 ha (62.2 ac), which is adequate. From a contour map of the reservoir area and a field investigation of the soils, a dam site was selected as shown in Fig. 4.4. By measuring the area within each contour line with a planimeter, the water-level height was determined (see Table 4.5). The area

Table 4.3 *Water requirements for farm uses*

Type of use	Average use in		
	Gallons* per day	ac-ft per year	ha-m per year
Household, all purposes, per person	50–100	0.08	0.01
Fire protection	–	0.23	0.03
Dry cow or steer,	9–18	0.015	0.002 to
Milk cow, 450 kg (1000 lb) including milkhouse and barn sanitation	18–40	0.032	0.004
Horse or mule	8–12	0.011	0.0014
Turkeys per 100 head	10–15	0.014	0.0017
Chickens per 100 head	6–9	0.008	0.001
Swine per 45 kg (100 lb)	1–1.5	0.002	0.0002
Sheep per 45 kg (100 lb)	1–1.5	0.002	0.0002
Orchard sparing, per year of tree age per application	1		
Irrigation (humid regions) per season		1–1.5ft	0.3–0.45m
Irrigation (arid regions) per season		1–5ft	0.3–1.5m

* For air temperatures of 50 and 90° F, respectively

Source: Midwest Plan Service (1968).

was measured to the centre line of the dam. This procedure is sufficiently accurate because most of the soil in the dam is usually taken from the reservoir area. (An approximate volume may be obtained by multiplying the water-surface area by 0.4 times the maximum water depth). Storage at this site could be increased by raising the water level or by moving the dam further downstream. If by so doing, sufficient storage could not be obtained, another site would have to be selected.

By interpolation between contours at elevations of 91 and 92 m, 1.28 ha-m of storage is available at an elevation of 91.8 m, which is the normal water surface. The following specifications are determined:

- Crest elevation of mechanical spillway   91.8 m
- Flood storage depth (minimum)   0.3 m

     Flood spillway elevation   92.1 m

From Fig. 4.4 measure the water surface fetch, 200 m.

- Substituting in Hawksley's formula $h = 0.014 (Df)^{1/2}$ where h = height of wave in meters from trough to crest and Df = fetch or exposure in meters, $h = 0.014(200)^{1/2} = 0.2$– m wave height

- Assuming frost depth of 0.15 m, net freeboard = 0.2 + 0.15 =   0.35
- Flow depth in flood spillway (assumed) =   0.3

     Elevation of top of dam (settled height) =   92.75 m

— Allowance for settlement at station 0 + 22 10% × (92.75 – 89.00) = 0.38 m (1.2 ft)

— Top width of dam from Equation $W = 0.4 H + 1$ $W = 0.4 (92.75 – 89.00) 1 = 2.5$ m (8.2 ft)

— Select side slopes of 3:1 upstream and 2:1 downstream.

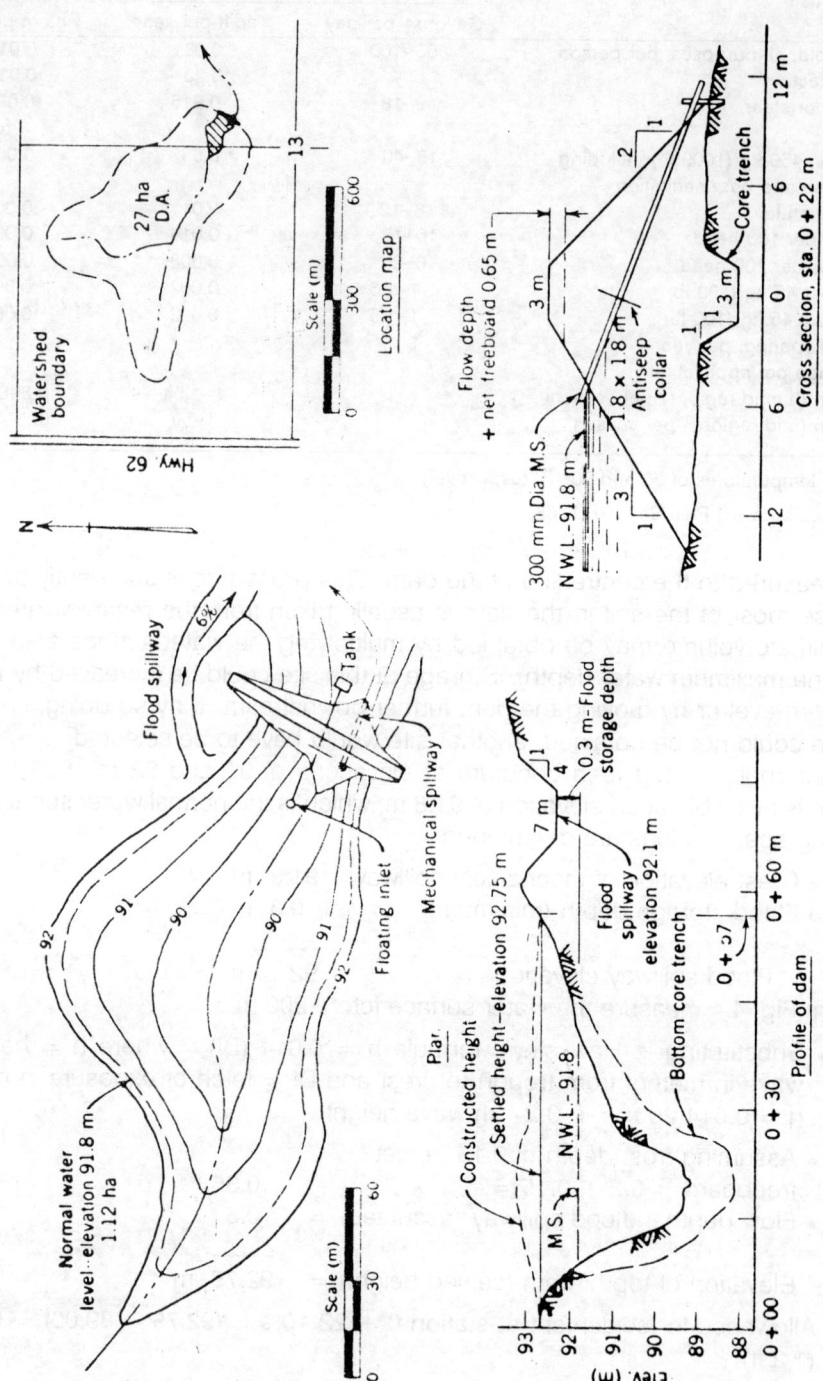

Fig. 4.4 Farm pond plan and layout for Example 24

Table 4.4   *Mechanical spillway pipe diameters for farm ponds (Schwab et al 1981)*

Peak runoff rate for 25 years return period (m³/s)	Water surface area at normal water level in hectares				
	0.2	0.4	0.8	1.2	2.0
0.5 or less	200 mm	150 mm	150 mm	–	–
0.5 to 1.0	200	200	150	150 mm	–
1.0 to 1.5	250	250	200	200	150 mm
1.5 to 2.0	250	250	250	250	200
2.0 to 2.5	–	300	300	300	250

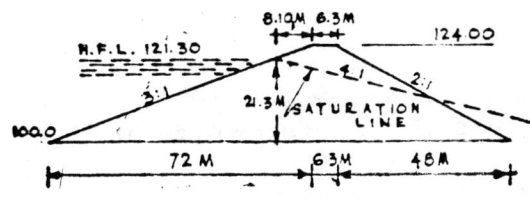

Fig. 4.5   Problem

— From Table 4.4, read 300 mm mechanical spillway diameter for 2.12 m³/s and 1.12 ha water surface.

— Antiseep collar for estimated 15 m pipe length and 10 per cent increase in creep distance required one 1.8×1.8 m collar or two 1×1 m collars.

— Livestock water pipe, select 32 mm (1.25 inches) diameter steel pipe approximately 30 m (100 ft) in length.

— Volume of fill in dam and in core trench is computed in Table 4.6 from fill height measured from profile in Fig. 4.4.

Table 4.5   *Volume of pond-water storage**

Contour elevation (m)	Area within contour line to Center line of Dam (ha)	Av. area (ha)	Contour interval (m)	Volume of storage (ha–m)
89.5	0.05			
90	0.25	0.15	0.5	0.08
91	0.64	0.45	1.0	0.45
92	1.24	0.94	1.0	0.94
			Total	1.47 (11.9 ac-ft)

To elevation 91.8, storage is 1.47 – (0.94 × 0.2/1) = 1.28 ha-m and water surface area = 1.24 – 0.2(1.24 – 0.64) = 1.12 ha (2.8 ac).

* The number of contour lines is reduced to simplify computations.

Table 4.6   *Volume of Earth Dam**

Station along Center line (m)	Height of dam (m)	Cross sectional Area** (m²)	Av. cross sectional area (m²)	Length of section (m)	Volume of section (m³)
0 + 00	0	0			
0 + 08	0.9	4.28	2.14	8	17.12
0 + 15	3.6	41.40	22.84	7	159.88
0 + 22	3.8	45.60	43.50	7	304.50
0 + 27	1.7	11.48	28.54	5	142.70
0 + 37	1.0	5.00	8.24	10	82.40
0 + 57	0	0	2.50	20	50.00

Total fill   756.60

Core trench volume, av. depth 1 m, av. width 4 m, and length 40 m.   160.00

Total fill and core trench   916.60 m³ (1199 yd³)

* Computed for dam in Fig. 4.4 and example given below
** Cross sectional area = $2.5 h^2 + 2.5 h$, where h is the dam height

— Flood spillway width at control section
$q = CLh^{3/2}$
where, $C = 1.67$
    $L = 2.12/(1.67 \times 0.3^{3/2}) = 7.3$ m (24 ft)

— Flood spillway below dam with 6 per cent slope, maximum velocity of 1.5 m/s (5 fps), and 4:1 side slopes for trapezoidal vegetated water will require a bottom width of about 10.7 m (35 ft).

Example 25—Design an earth dam with the following data:

    Reduced Level (R.L.) of natural surface at site = 100.00
    Reduced Level of F.R L.   = 118.30
    Reduced Level of H.F.L.   = 121.30
    Slope of saturation line 4:1
    Assume other data.

Solution:
Height of water up to H.F.L. = 21.30 m
Assuming fetch of wave as 25 km

Height of waves $= 0.384 \times \sqrt{F} + 0.763 - 0.271 \sqrt[4]{F}$
                $= 0.384 \times 5 + 0.763 - 0.271 \times 2.24$
                $= 2.082$

Taking free board as 2.70 m
Height of the dam = 21.30 + 2,70 = 24.00 m
Top width of dam $= \dfrac{24}{5} + 1.5 = 6.3$ m
Upstream slope may be adopted as 3:1
Downstream slope may be adopted as 2:1
∴ Section will be as shown in Fig. 4.5

Actual length required for saturation line to be in the dam = 21.3 × 4 = 85.2 m horizontal distance from *A*.

Length available for saturation line in the body of the dam = 8.10 + 6.30 + 48 = 62.40 m.

Hence it is clear that the saturation line meets the downstream face, which makes the section unstable. Hence the section has to be modified.

After modification, the following section (Fig. 4.6) can be adopted as final section for the given data.

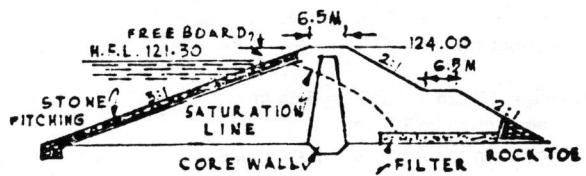

Fig. 4.6 Problem

Example 26—An earth dam has the following dimensions:

  (i)   base width   75 m

 (ii)   top width   3 m

(iii)   depth of water   12 m

(iv)   free board   3 m

 (v)   depth of previous foundation   30 m

(vi)   coefficient of permeability   3 cm/min.

       of foundation material

It is proposed to reduce seepage through the foundation by 80 per cent of original value.

Compute the size of an impervious upstream blanket required. Neglect seepage through blanket.

Solution:

Seepage loss through the foundation is given by Darcy's equation

$$Q = K i a$$

$$= K \cdot \frac{h}{B} \cdot d \qquad \qquad \dots (1)$$

where Q is seepage loss through the foundation per metre length of the dam.

Assuming length of upstream blanket to be L m, seepage loss is say Q_1

$$\therefore Q_1 = K \cdot \frac{h}{(B + L)} \cdot d$$

It is given that $Q_1 = 0.2Q$

$$\therefore 0.2Q = K \cdot \frac{h}{(B + L)} \cdot d$$

$$\text{or } Q = K \cdot h \cdot d \cdot \frac{1}{0.2(B + L)} \qquad \qquad \dots (2)$$

Equating Eqs. (1) and (2)

$$\frac{1}{B} = \frac{1}{0.2(B + L)}$$

or $0.8 B = 0.2 L$

$\therefore L = 4 B$

   $= 4 \times 75 = 300$ m

It will be enough to take 2 m thickness of the blanket.

DESIGN OF AN EARTH DAM

Example 27:

Design an earthen embankment with the following data:

RL of natural surface	= 100.00 m
RL of HFL	= 106.25 m
Slope of saturation line	= 4:1
Assume a fetch of about 1.0 km	

Solution:

Height of water up to HFL = 106.25 − 100.00 = 6.25 m

Height of waves assuming fetch to be 1.0 km

$= 0.384\sqrt{F} + 0.763 - 0.271(F)^{1/4}$, where F = fetch (km)

Substituting $F = 1$ km

Height ∕ waves = 0.384 + 0.763 − 0.271 = 0.876 m

Free board (assumed) $= \dfrac{15}{100} \times 6.25 = 0.93$ m or say 1.0 m

Since the free board is higher than height of waves, this value can be adopted.

Height of dam = 6.25 + 1.0 = 7.25

Consolidation (5%) $= \dfrac{5}{100} \times 7.25$

Gross height of dam = 1.05 × 7.25 = 7.65 m

Top width of dam $= \dfrac{H}{5} + 1.5 = \dfrac{7.65}{5} + 1.5 = 3.03$ or say 3.0 m

Adopt upstream and downstream slopes of 3:1 and 2:1, respectively. The length available for saturation line or phreatic line = 22.50 m. With above specifications, the saturation line meets the downstream face, which makes the section unstable (Fig. 4.7). Hence the section has to be modified.

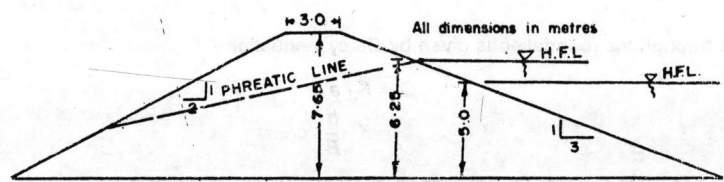

Fig. 4.7 Section of embankment showing phreatic line meeting down stream face causing unstability

By adopting downstream slope as 2.5:1 and providing a berm of 3.0 m, the section will be safe (Fig. 4.8). However, to ensure future safety, a stone filter may be provided.

Example 28: An earthen embankment with a top width of 2.0 m is proposed for construction across a valley, whose fill heights at every 10 m are presented below. The section has side slopes of 2 horizontal to 1 vertical. A core trench having 0.75 m depth, bottom width of 1.75 m and side slopes of 1:1 is also under consideration. Calculate the earthwork needed for embankment. The fill heights at 10 m interval is presented in Fig. 4.9.

Solution —The areas of cross-section at every 10 m interval may be computed in the first instance.

$A = BD + nD^2$

where, $B = 2$ m and $n = 2$ (Fig. 4.10)

Therefore, $A = 2D + 2D^2 = 2(D + D^2)$

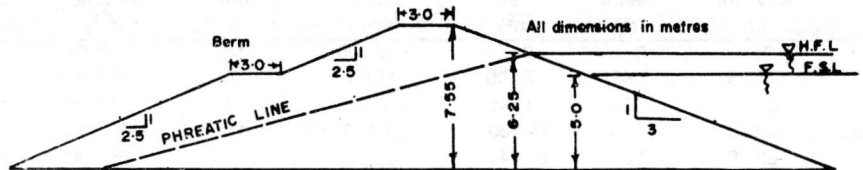

Fig. 4.8 Safe modified embankment section with phreatic line meet the base

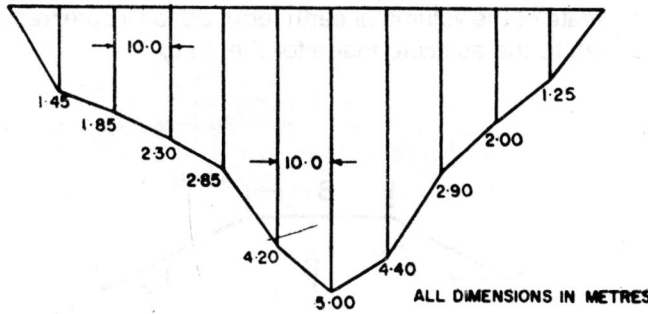

Fig. 4.9 Fill heights across the valley

D	D^2	$(D + D^2)$	Area of cross section $= 2(D + D^2)$
1.45	2.1025	3.5525	7.105
1.85	3.4225	5.2725	10.545
2.30	5.2900	7.5900	15.180
2.85	8.1225	10.9725	21.945
4.2	17.6400	21.8400	43.680
5.0	25.0000	30.0000	60.000
4.4	19.3600	23.7600	47.520
2.9	8.4100	11.3100	22.620
2.0	4.0000	6.0000	12.000
1.25	1.5625	2.8125	5.625

Using the principle of 'Sum of end areas' method, the earth work needed can be computed. The sample calculations are presented below:

Station	Ground elevation (m)	Fill height (m)	End area (m²)	Sum of end areas (m²)	Distance (m)	Double volume (m³)	Volume (m³)
0+00	35	0	0	7.105	10	71.05	35.50
0+10	33.55	1.45	7.105	17.65	10	176.50	88.25
0+20	33.15	1.85	10.545	25.725	10	257.25	128.62
0+30	32.70	2.30	15.180	37.120	10	371.20	185.60
0+40	32.15	2.85	21.940	65.62	10	656.20	328.1
0+50	30.80	4.20	43.68	103.68	10	1036.80	518.4
0+60	30.00	5.00	60.00	107.52	10	1075.20	537.6
0+70	30.60	4.4	47.52	70.14	10	701.40	350.7
0+80	32.10	2.9	22.62	34.62	10	346.20	173.1
0+90	33.00	2.0	12.00	17.62	10	176.20	88.1
1+00	33.75	1.25	5.62	5.62	10	56.20	28.1
1+10	35.00	0	0				
						Total:	2462.09

The above computation shows only the volume of earthwork required to complete dam itself. An estimate of the volume of earth required to fill core trench, etc., should be made and added to the estimate made for the dam.

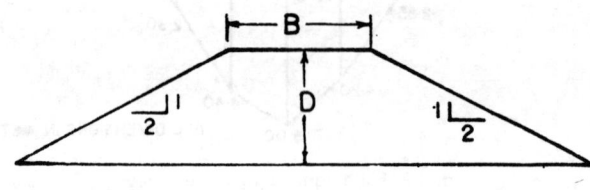

Fig. 4.10 Solution

Average depth = 0.75 m
Bottom width = 1.75 m
Side slopes   = 1:1
Length   = 110 m

   Area of cross-section

$Z = 1.75 \times 0.75 + 2 \times 0.75 \times 0.75$
$\quad = 1.3125 + 1.125 = 2.4375 \text{ m}^2$

Volume of backfill = 2.4375×110
$\qquad\qquad\qquad = 268 \text{ m}^3$
Total earthwork needed for dam, works out to be
   $268 + 2462 = 2730 \text{ m}^3$

4.2   Drought Farm Pond

Where the topography does not lend itself to embankments construction, dugout or excavated ponds can be constructed in a relatively flat terrain. Since dugout ponds can be constructed to expose a minimum water surface area in proportion to volume, they are advantageous where evaporation losses are high and water is scarce.

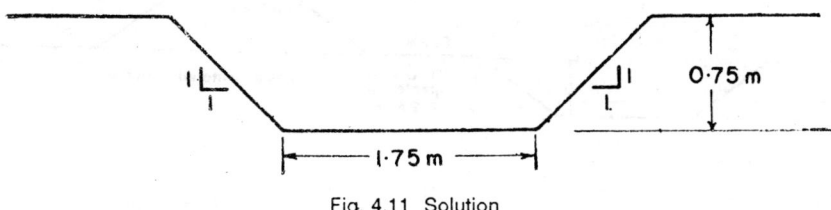

Fig. 4.11 Solution

SELECTION OF SITE

Some of the important physical features that must be considered in locating dugout sites are the watershed characteristics, silting possibilities, topography and soil type.

The watershed must be capable of furnishing the annual runoff sufficient to fill the dugout. Diversion ditches are often used in adding supplemental drainages. The low point of a natural depression is often a good location for a dugout pond. Location with favourable discharge condition should be selected.

The soil type at the site should be thoroughly investigated to determine the permeability of the soil that will form the bottom and sites of the dugout, as well as to avoid cutting in very hard stuff. In case the seepage rates of farm ponds are excessive, suitable lining may have to be resorted to (ex. puddling and compacting to the optimum bulk density, bitumen spray, etc.). Soils underlain by limestone containing crevices, sinks or channels should be avoided.

At location, where the water table rise within a few metres of the ground surface, dugouts can be constructed to intercept the water adjusting the depth to the fluctuations expected. Location of this type may furnish supplies all the year round.

Planning

Excavated ponds may be constructed to almost any shape desired; however, a rectangular shape is usually convenient.

The size of the pond depends on the extent of area draining into the pond, the extent of area that could be put under pond and its surrounding bund of excavated soil, the amount of money considered appropriate to invest, the nature and amount of rainfall, soil type and expected runoff into the pond.

The length and width of an excavated pond will not ordinarily be limited, except that the type and size of the excavating equipment, if used, may become a factor for consideration.

The side slopes of a dugout pond should not be steeper than the natural angle of repose of the material being excavated. In most cases, the side slopes should be flatter than 1:1.

DISPOSAL OF EXCAVATED MATERIAL

Proper disposal with prolong useful life of the pond, improve its appearance and facilitate its maintenance and establishment of vegetation. The excavated material should be placed in a manner, that its weight will not endanger the stability of the pond, side slopes and the rainfall will not wash the material back into the pond. A berm with a width equal to depth of pond may be adapted (Fig. 4.12).

Construction

The pond site and waste areas should first be cleared of all vegetation. The limb of excavation and soil placement areas should be demarcated and excavated by

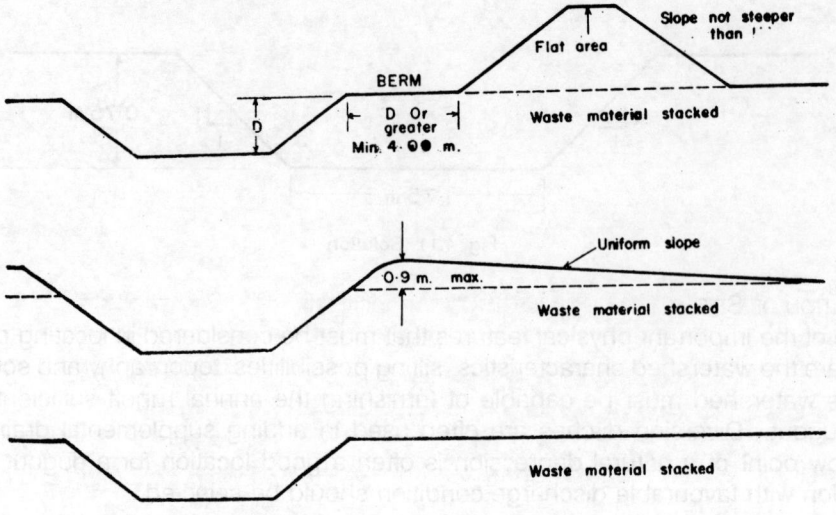

Fig. 4.12 Disposal of excavated material

step method using manual labour. Excavation and the placement of the excavated material are the principal items of work required in the construction of this type of pond.

ESTIMATION OF VOLUME OF A POND

The volume of excavation required can be estimated with sufficient accuracy by use of Prismoidal Formula

$$V = \frac{A + 4B + C}{6} \times D \qquad \qquad \dots (4.3)$$

where, V = volume of excavation (m³);

   A = area of excavation at the ground surface (m²);

   B = area of excavation at the mid-depth point ($\frac{1}{2}D$) (m²);

   C = area of the excavation at the bottom of pond (m²); and

   D = average depth of the pond (m).

Example 29—Compute the volume of excavation required to construct an excavated pond with an average depth (D) of 4.0 m, a bottom width (W) of 12 m, and a bottom length (L) of 30 m. The side slopes adopted are 2:1.

   Solution—The volume of excavation required

$$V = \frac{A + 4B + C}{6} \times D$$

Top length = 30 + (4 × 2)2 = 46 m

Top width = 12 + (4 × 2)2 = 28 m

   A = 46 m × 28 m = 1288 m²

Mid-length = 30 + (2 × 2)2 = 38 m²

Mid-width = 12 + (2 × 2)2 = 20 m²

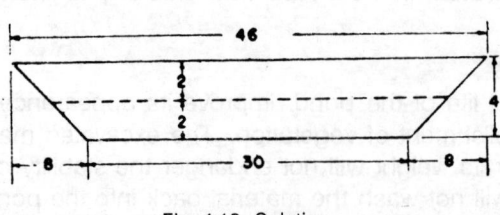

Fig. 4.13 Solution

$4B = (38 \text{ m} \times 20 \text{ m}) \times 4 = 3040 \text{ m}^2$

$C = 12 \text{ m} \times 30 \text{ m} = 360 \text{ m}^2$

$A + 4B + C = 4688 \text{ m}^2$

$\therefore V = \dfrac{4688}{6} \times 4 = 3124 \text{ m}^3 \text{ or } 0.3124 \text{ ha} - \text{m}$

PRACTICES ADAPTED IN DIFFERENT INDIAN STATES

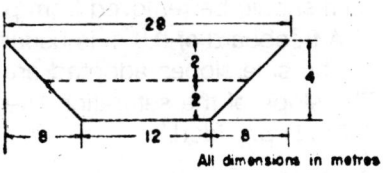

Fig. 4.14 Solution

Karnataka

Suitability

Farm ponds are constructed in deep-black soils (clayey), where storage is easy owing to very low rate of seepage loss. In light and medium soils, lined ponds are located in low lands. Seepage from unlined ponds in calcium aggregated soils can be reduced by treatment with sodium carbonate without causing compaction.

Size

By and large, impounding one ha-cm of water per ha of runoff contributing catchment is roughly the guiding factor. Sizes from 21 m × 21 m to 36 m × 36 m with 2.4 m to 4.6 m depth are generally adopted and the side slopes given are 1.5:1.

Minimizing of evaporation losses

Evaporation losses (20 to 33%) could be reduced by having deeper ponds.

Construction

For the ease of excavation, a step-like cross-section (each step representing rectangular cross-section) is usually adopted (Fig. 4.15)

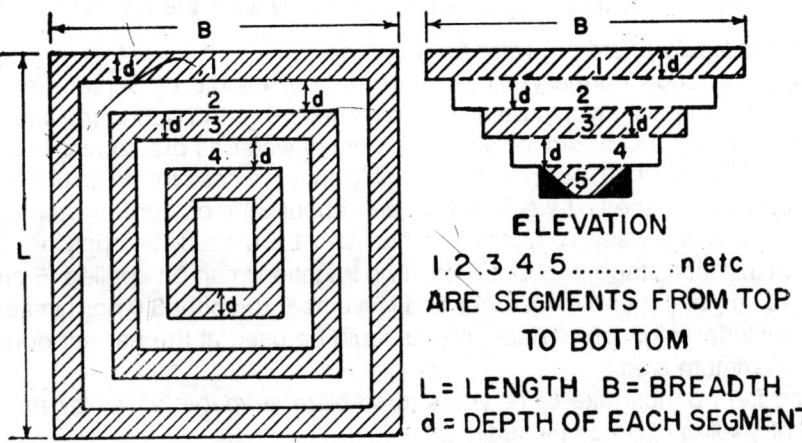

ELEVATION

1.2.3.4.5..........n etc

ARE SEGMENTS FROM TOP

TO BOTTOM

L = LENGTH B = BREADTH

d = DEPTH OF EACH SEGMENT

Fig. 4.15 Excavation of dugout from pond

Provision of spillways

At the entrance of runoff into the farm pond, a masonry chute spillway cement pointed (cement:sand = 1:3) is adopted.

Tamil Nadu

In the construction of earthen embankments, the ground should be dug up or ploughed along the length of the ploughed bund to form a good joint for the new earth to be laid over it. If the foundation is soft rock, trenches 0.9 m in width and 0.6 m in depth should be dug at 1.8 m intervals along cross-section. Earth for the dam should be removed from projections in the gully bank above the dam.

A freeboard of 0.9 m is usually provided for the spillways.

The side slopes adopted are 1.5:1 in the upstream and 2:1 in the downstream. The slope of the saturation line is assumed to be 1 in 4. A minimum top width of 1.2 m is provided.

Central Soil and Water Conservation Research & Training Institute, Dehra Dun

Suitability

Results of research investigations conducted by the Institute have revealed that in Doon Valley, in the sub-montaneous lower hill regions of Himalayas located in a high rainfall zone, on an average runoff of 16% of monsoon rainfall can be expected from agricultural treated watersheds. Thus one farm pond of capacity of about 2.0 ha-m is suggested for a catchment of 10–12 ha (Fig. 4.16). The above suggested capacity of farm pond is after taking consideration of losses due to seepage and evaporation.

Soils

The above suggestion is applicable to regions having similar agro-climatic conditions and soils of alluvial nature derived from sand stones and shales and have silty clay loam texture.

Planning

The watershed area was treated with a series of graded bunding at suitable intervals. The runoff from these individual terraces is led to the grassed waterway, which ultimately feeds the farm pond. The outflow from the farm pond is discharged into the grassed waterways downstream, which ultimately joins the natural stream.

Period of availability of stored water for recycling

South-west monsoon normally withdraws by about middle of September. About 50% of storage capacity would be available in the farm pond during the last week of October and it can be utilized for applying 5 cm of water as pre-sowing irrigation to about 10 ha of area at 80% of conveyance efficiency. In case the moisture condition is favourable during the last week of October, about 30% of stored water would be available in the last week of November and can be utilized for applying 5 cm at crown root initiation stage to about 6 ha. Two irrigations can be applied (5 cm each, i.e. total 10 cm) at the end of October and November to about 3.0 ha. Limited water thus available for irrigation of *Rabi* crops should be used at the earliest opportunity to cover maximum area.

Unlined farm ponds take 8–10 years to stabilize seepage losses by the natural process of sealing of pores by sediment.

Central Soil and Water Conservation Research & Training Institute, Research Centre Bellary

Suitability

Results of research conducted by the Research Centre, Bellary (Karnataka) have revealed that under semi-arid deep black soils, with an average annual rainfall of about 508 mm, runoff of about 10 per cent of rainfall can be expected from agricultural watersheds. Thus one farm pond of 50 ha-cm capacity is recommended for about 10 ha watershed area. The quality of harvested and stored runoff water in the farm pond was observed to be of good quality, both for human consumption as well as for irrigation as compared to the water in the adjoining wells or Tungabhadra river water.

Recycling

Water harvested and stored in the farm pond can be recycled in periods of moisture efficiency over an area equivalent to 40% of the watershed giving two protective irrigations of 5 cm each. Seepage losses in the deep-black soils are negligible. Annual evaporation losses is roughly equivalent to 60% of open pan evaporation.

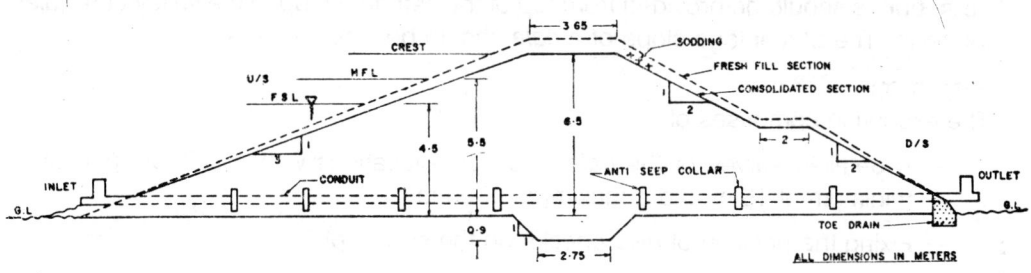

Fig. 4.16 Salient features of farm pond   Fig. 4.16(a) Section of embankment

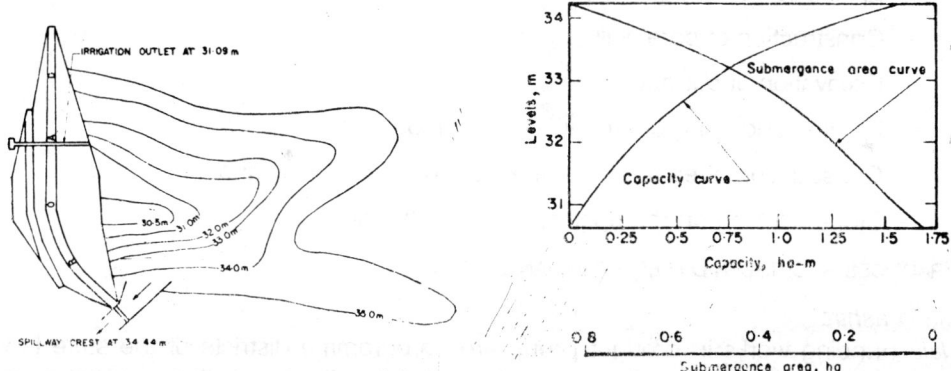

Fig. 4.16(b) Contour map of farm pond

Fig. 4.16(c) Capacity-submergence area contour level relationship.(below)

4.3 Nala Bunding

Nala bunding work consists of constructing bunds of suitable dimensions across the nala or gullies to hold the maximum runoff water to create flooding of the upstream area temporarily for some days or weeks, with surplussing arrangements at suitable intervals to drain the water. Wherever necessary, the number of such bunds depends upon the slope of the gully and the quantity of runoff expected to flow. The temporary storage of runoff against these bunds carries deposition of silt carried and the water is drained off in a controlled manner. The impounding of water facilitates the percolation of water with the deeper layers of soil profile, which otherwise will flow with intense velocity, causing erosion silting the natural drainage courses, lakes and reservoirs. The water released from the bunds will be free from silt and velocity to erode. Before it can acquire erosive velocity, it will meet the next bund below in the catchment. The basin at the upstream side of the bund will be enriched by the silt deposited progressively and the general level will be raised. Construction of such bunds facilitates reclamation of gullied lands and also recharge of ground water, which in turn increases availability of underground water for irrigation, increasing command area.

LOCATION
In semi-arid and arid regions with low annual rainfall having relatively permeable soils, bunds should be provided from top of the catchment up to the valley at regular intervals. The percentage slope of a *nala* should be less than 3.5.

EXECUTION
The execution comprises of:

— A detailed survey of the *nala* at suitable locations with a suitable grid of a minimum of 15 m and a maximum of 90 m

— Fixing the position of *nala* checks on the survey plan

— Preparing a detailed estimate

— Laying out foundation after fixing the different points such as FSL and HFL and cut outlets

— Excavation of a required puddle trench

— Construction of core wall

— Excavation of cut out

— Digging and filling of embankment portion

— Construction of earthen embankment over core wall, and

— Stone pitching on the upstream side of the bund.

PRACTICES ADOPTED IN DIFFERENT INDIAN STATES

Maharashtra
Nala bunding works in drought prone area programme districts of the state have been carried out. *Nala* bunding is adopted in black soil region with an annual rainfall less than 750 mm. The catchment upstream of the structure should be between 80 and 500 ha. The percentage of *nala* should not be more than 3%. There should be sufficient number of wells in the percolation zone of *nala*.

For easy calculation on the design of bund, detailed tables have been prepared by the Department of State Soil Conservation, to facilitate easy preparation of plans and estimates.

Karnataka
Nala bunding works are carried out in the state (Fig. 4.17). Small gullies are plugged by stone plugs with height usually not exceeding 1.2 m, slope—upstream (nearly vertical) and downstream—1:4, foundation—0.6 m in hard ground and flanks—taken about 1.2 m inside the natural ground on both sides to prevent flood water out flanking the structure.

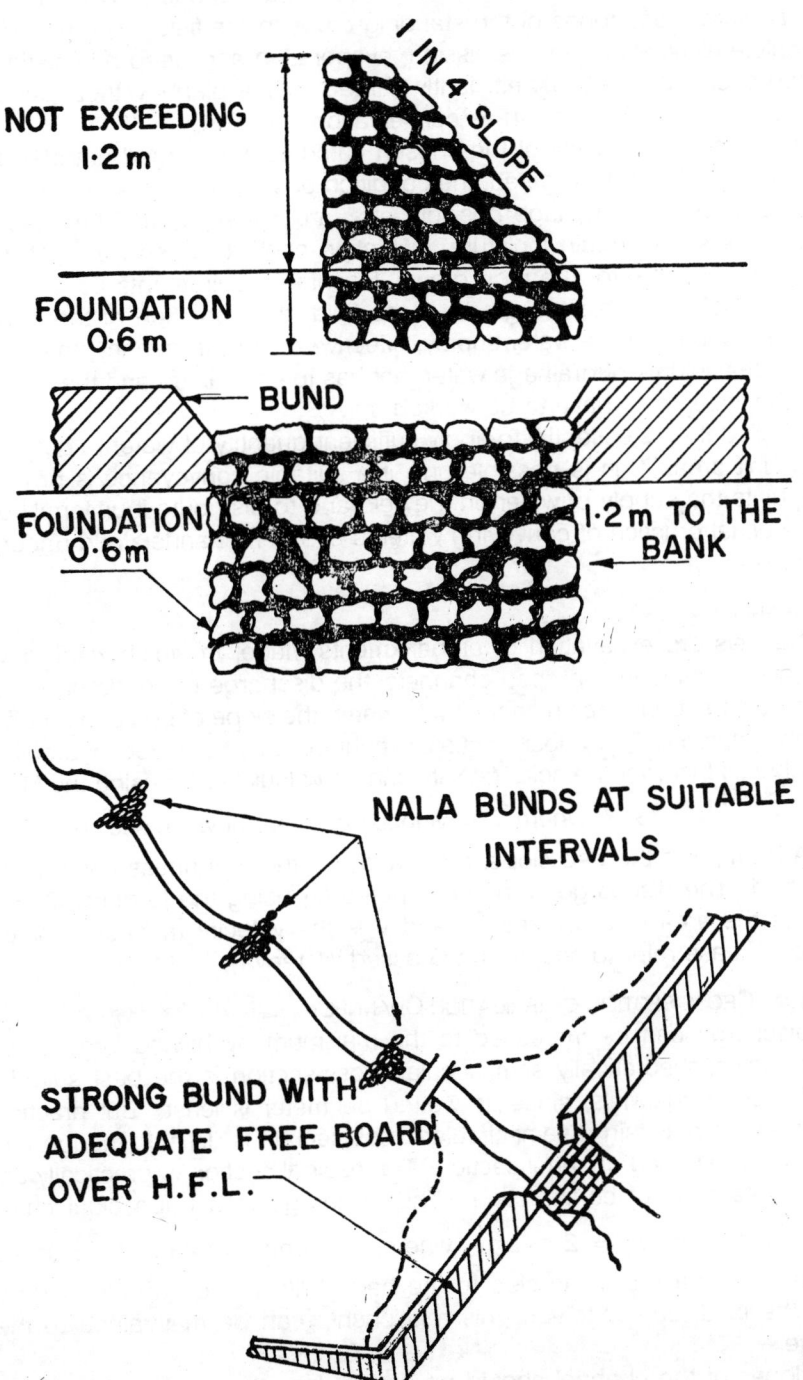

Fig. 4.17 *Nala* bunding

4.4   Conveyance of Irrigation Water

Provision of assured irrigation is a pre-requisite for increased crop production and the maintenance of the national economy at a sustained basis. When the water is applied to fill the root zones of the standing crops in the field, with the minimum if not complete elimination of transmission, evaporation and deep percolation losses and when such water is most efficiently utilized by the plants without causing any damage to the fields, it is known as conservation irrigation.

A detailed contour survey of the chosen catchment is carried out after the preliminary survey. The area irrigated, the condition of supply ditches, distribution, field channels and general drainage position, etc. are investigated. The effective root zone depth of soil to retain moisture, infiltration capacity of soil, the pH, the consumptive use of water for the crop grown, leaching requirements according to the presence of soluble salts, the grade of the field, the condition of the bunds and the field, the source of the water supply, effective rainfall, frequency, the number of irrigations, the volume of drainage water that has to be drained and the time interval to drain the water, etc., have to be worked out.

A controlled flow is essential to apply sufficient quantity of water to get maximum yield per unit area. This is possible only if a suitable conveyance is provided, so as to regulate the supply of water on the field and to distribute it uniformly over the field. The usual practice of conveying water is by open channels and underground pipelines.

OPEN CHANNELS

Open channels are excavation or embankments made, in which water flows due to the gravitational force. In open channels, the discharge depends on the area of cross-section, the perimeter in contact with water, the slope of bed and roughness of the channel material. The velocity of flow is controlled by the slope, hydraulic radius and roughness factor of the soil. Velocity can be calculated by using the Manning's formula, $V = \frac{1}{n} R^{2/3} \cdot S^{1/2}$, where V = velocity of water flow, m/sec; R = hydraulic radius (A/P), m; S is the bed slope, m/m; and n is the roughness coefficient of the channel bed. The discharge is then computed by using the formula, $Q = A \cdot V$, where A is the area of cross-section and V is the velocity (m/sec). For detailed calculation, please refer to chapter on Grassed Waterway.

ECONOMICAL CROSS-SECTION OF IRRIGATION CHANNEL

As the discharge can be increased to the maximum by having largest possible, hydraulic radius, theoretically semi-circular cross-section is the best suited cross-section for open channels, since its wetted perimeter is least. But practically, to construct and to maintain a semi-circular cross-section is difficult, though it can be feasible for similar lined channel section. Trapezoidal section is practically adopted because of its ease of construction. The discharge in a trapezoidal channel is maximum when bed $(b) = 2\, d \tan \frac{\phi}{2}$ where, d is depth of flow of water and ϕ is the angle of inclination of the side to the bed. With a slight modification to suit slope of the land, soil condition, this relationship can be maintained to the best advantage.

Side slopes of the channel should be usually less than angle of repose of the soil adopted. The bed slopes are to be decided based on the type of soil and land slope.

MOST ECONOMICAL CHANNEL SECTIONS

The most economical section of channel is one, which gives the maximum rate of discharge, with a given cost of excavation. Condition for different sections are given below:

(i) Most economical rectangular section (Fig 4.18): $b = 2d$

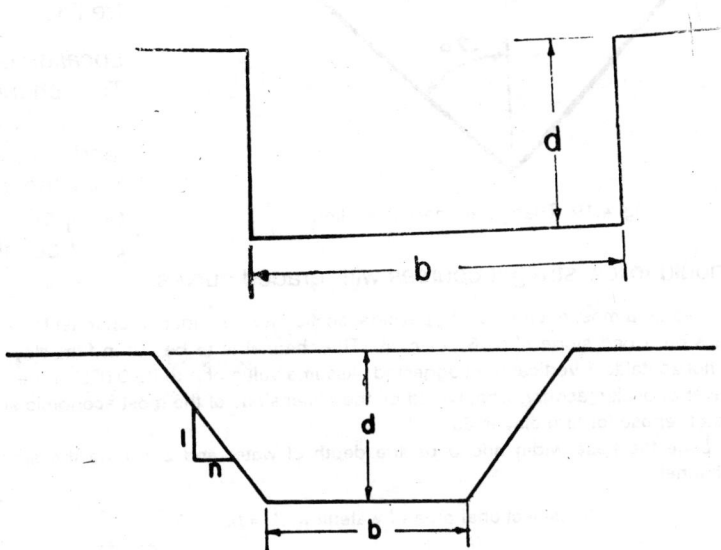

Fig. 4.18 Rectangular and trapezoidal channel section

(ii) Most economical trapezoidal section (Fig. 4.18):

I condition:

$$\frac{h + nd}{2} = d\sqrt{1 + n^2} \qquad \qquad \dots (4.4)$$

Half the top width = sloping side

II condition:

Hydraulic mean depth = half the depth.

III condition:

Perpendiculars drawn from centre of the top width on the bottom and sloping sides are all equal.

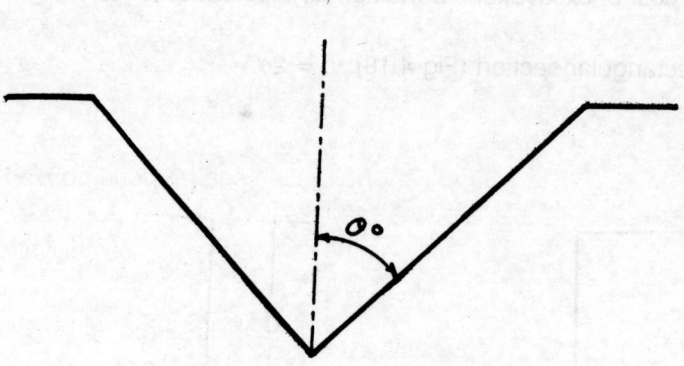

Fig. 4.19 Triangular channel section

(iii) Most economical triangular section (Fig. 4.19):

The most economical triangular section is one having equal sides and making an angle of 45° with centre line.

Location of channels
The channel location should be on high land, so that water from the channel can be applied to the field by free flow. The channel should follow straight courses with graded curves.

Example 30—Design a most economical trapezoidal section for an irrigation channel to carry a discharge of 11.5 cumecs on a bed slope of 0.16 per cent. The channel is to be cut in firm clay, for which side slopes of 1.5 horizontal to 1 vertical are suggested. Assume value of n to be 0.025. If the channel is lined with a thick layer of brick masonry, what would be the dimensions of the most economic section. Assume that the angle of repose for firm clay is 60°.

Solution—Let b be the base width and d be the depth of water and $Z : 1$ be the side slopes of the trapezoidal channel.

$$\text{Cross-sectional area of waterflow, } A = bd + Zd^2 \qquad \dots (1)$$

$$\text{Wetted perimeter, } P = b + 2d\sqrt{Z^2 + 1} \qquad \dots (2)$$

$$\text{Hydraulic radius, } R = \frac{A}{P} = \frac{bd + Zd^2}{b + 2d\sqrt{Z^2 + 1}} \qquad \dots (3)$$

$$\text{For most economical hydraulic section, } R = \frac{d}{2} \qquad \dots (4)$$

where, $R = \dfrac{A}{P}$

$$\frac{d}{2} = \frac{bd + Zd^2}{b + 2d\sqrt{Z^2 + 1}}$$

$$2(bd + Zd^2) = bd + 2d^2\sqrt{Z^2 + 1}$$

$$= bd + 2Zd^2 = 2d^2\sqrt{Z^2 + 1}$$

Substituting value of $Z = 1.5$

$$bd + 3d^2 = 2d^2\sqrt{1.5^2 + 1}$$

$$bd + 3d^2 = 2d^2\sqrt{2.25 + 1} = 3.6d^2$$

$$bd + 3.6d^2 - 3d^2 = 0.6d^2$$

$$b = 0.6d$$

Substituting these values in eq. (1)

$$A = bd + Zd^2$$

$$= 0.6d.d + 1.5d^2 = 0.6d^2 + 1.5d^2$$

$$A = 2.1d^2; \quad R = \frac{d}{2}$$

Hence, $Q = A.V = A \times \dfrac{1}{n}R^{2/3}S^{1/2}$

$$= \frac{2.1d^2}{0.025} \times \left[\frac{d}{2}\right]^{2/3} \times (0.0016)^2$$

But $Q = 11.4$ cumec

Solving for d, $d = 1.88$m
But, $b = 0.6d = 0.6 \times 1.875 = 1.125$m
Providing freeboard of 15% of depth
$D = 1.15 \times 1.875 = 2.15$m

UNDERGROUND PIPELINES IRRIGATION DISTRIBUTION SYSTEM

Underground pipelines offer many advantages over open channels in water conveyance and distribution. A few of them are given below:

— Since the pipelines are placed underground, cultivation can be done above the pipeline; no culverts or other structures are required.

— Open channels often take 2–4 per cent of the land area out of cultivation. Pipelines do not interfere with farming operations.

— They are essentially leak-proof and their placement below ground level prevents damage and water loss by evaporation.

KINDS OF PIPES

The materials used for underground pipelines are concrete asbestos cement, vetrified clay plastic and steel. Concrete pipes are the most common.

Precast non-reinforced concrete irrigation pipes

Precast non-reinforced concrete pipes are commonly used when the pipe is not subject to high pressures. Normally they are suitable for operating heads (pressures) not exceeding 6 m (0.6 kg/cm^2). They are cheaper and are suitable for surface irrigation systems.

Discharge Capacity of Pipelines

The discharge through a pipeline can be determined by applying the Darcy equation:

$$V = \sqrt{\frac{Hdg}{2fl}} \qquad \ldots (4.5)$$

where, V = velocity of flow of water through the pipe, (cm/sec);
H = available head causing flow (difference in elevation between water level in the pump stand and the outlet point) (cm);
d = diameter of pipe (cm);
g = acceleration due to gravity (cm/sec^2);
l = length of pipe (cm); and
f = Darcy's roughness coefficient (Table 4.7)

Table 4.7 presents the values of the Darcy's roughness coefficient f for different kinds of pipes at various values of velocity of flow.

Example 31

Determine the discharge capacity of an underground concrete pipeline from the following data:

Diameter of pipe 15 cm, length of pipeline 150 m, difference in elevation between water levels at pump stand and discharge point 2 m.

Solution—The value of f is assumed to be 0.009 (Table 4.7 with an assumed velocity of flow of 90 cm/sec).

Applying Darcy's equation

$$V = \frac{Hdg}{2fl}$$

$$= \sqrt{\frac{200 \times 15 \times 981}{2 \times 0.009 \times 15000}} = 100 \text{ cm/sec}$$

$$= 1.0 \text{ m/sec}$$

Table 4.7 Values of coefficient 'r' in Darcy equation for pipe flow

Diameter of pipe (cm)	Velocity, per sec														
	Galvanized iron pipe					Caste iron pipe					Concrete pipe				
	30	60	90	120	150	30	60	90	120	150	30	60	90	120	150
15	0.0055	0.0047	0.0043	0.0042	0.0038	0.0061	0.0059	0.0058	0.0057	0.0055	0.0102	0.0094	0.0090	0.0086	0.0084
22	0.0051	0.0044	0.0041	0.0038	0.0036	0.0057	0.0055	0.0054	0.0053	0.0052	0.0080	0.0074	0.0370	0.0067	0.0064
30	0.0047	0.0042	0.0038	0.0035	0.0035	0.0054	0.0052	0.0051	0.0050	0.0048	0.0067	0.0062	0.0059	0.0056	0.0054
45	0.0044	0.0037	0.0035	0.0032	0.0032	0.0052	0.0051	0.0050	0.0048	0.0047	0.0056	0.0051	0.0048	0.0046	0.0044
60	0.0042	0.0035	0.0033	0.0032	0.0030	0.0050	0.0048	0.0045	0.0043	0.0041	0.0050	0.0047	0.0044	0.0042	0.0040
90	0.0037	0.0033	0.0031	0.0029	0.0028	0.0042	0.0040	0.0037	0.0036	0.0034	0.0044	0.0040	0.0038	0.0036	0.0034
120	0.0035	0.0032	0.0029	0.0028	0.0027	0.0036	0.0034	0.0032	0.0032	0.0031	0.0039	0.0037	0.0035	0.0033	0.0030

Area of cross-section of pipe, $a = \dfrac{\pi}{4} \times 0.15^2$

$\qquad\qquad\qquad = 0.0176 \text{ m}^2$

Discharge capacity, $Q = av$

$\qquad\qquad\qquad = 1.0 \times 0.0176$

$\qquad\qquad\qquad = 0.0176 \text{ cu m/sec}$

$\qquad\qquad\qquad = 17.6 \text{ litre/sec}$

Table 4.8 *Discharge capacities of concrete pipes of different diameters at different operating heads and conveyance lengths*

Diameter of pipe (m)	Friction factor, f	Operating head (m)	Discharge, litres/sec — Conveyance length, m						
			50	100	150	200	300	400	500
15	0.00900	2.0	31.8	22.6	18.4	15.9	12.9	11.2	10.0
		2.5	35.5	25.0	20.5	17.7	14.5	12.5	11.0
		3.0	38.9	27.5	22.5	19.4	15.9	13.7	12.3
		4.0	45.0	31.8	26.0	22.4	18.3	15.9	14.2
		5.0	50.0	35.5	29.0	25.1	20.5	17.7	15.9
22.5	0.00710	2.0	99.1	70.1	57.2	49.5	40.5	35.0	31.0
		2.5	110.8	78.3	64.0	55.4	45.2	39.2	35.0
		3.0	121.4	85.8	70.1	60.7	49.5	42.9	38.4
		4.0	140.1	99.1	81.0	70.1	57.2	49.5	44.3
		5.0	156.7	110.8	90.5	78.3	64.0	55.4	49.5
30	0.00595	2.0	222.2	157.1	128.3	111.1	90.7	78.6	70.3
		2.5	248.4	175.1	143.4	124.2	101.4	87.8	78.6
		3.0	272.2	192.4	157.1	136.1	111.1	96.2	86.1
		4.0	314.3	222.2	181.4	157.1	128.3	111.1	99.4
		5.0	351.3	248.4	202.8	175.7	143.6	124.2	111.1

Table 4.8 gives the discharge capacities of concrete pipes at different operating heads and conveyance lengths.

Pipelines are spaced to suit the field layout and soil type. One main line is usually laid along the upper boundary of the field. The closer spacings are suitable for sandy soils and the farther spacings for heavy clay soils.

INSTALLATION OF CONCRETE PIPELINES

Proper installation of the pipes is the key to troublefree services of the underground pipeline irrigation system. The process of laying the pipeline, involves the following steps that follow in succession:

— Selection of depth and grade of laying

— Digging to proper depth and grade

— Lowering the pipe and squeezing

— Sealing the joints and

— Back filling the trench.

To prevent damage of pipelines from loads acting on it, concrete pipes should be laid with their upper surface at a depth of about 60 cm from the ground surface. The minimum recommended depth is 45 cm. The width of the trench should be at least 60 cm, so that it provides sufficient working space. The grade of the pipeline is kept uniform and is usually the same as the average land slope along which the pipes are laid. To obtain uniform depth and grade, the elevations of the trench bottom are fixed with a dumpy level. The trench is dug by manual labour or with a tractor-mounted digger.

Each pipe should be laid on firm, undisturbed soil. The trench should be reasonably straight. The bottom of the trench should be smooth with large stones, clods, or other irregularities removed. When pipelines are to be laid in rocky areas, the trench should be overexcavated and refilled to grade with fine soil or sand. The fill should be properly compacted to produce a firm, uniform foundation. When the pipelines are to be placed in soft, unstable soil, the trench should be overexcavated and backfilled to grade with suitable materials, such as gravel, crushed stones or brick bats to provide a stable bedding for the pipe.

The pipes are first strung along the trench and then tilted into the trench. Heavy RCC pipe may be wrapped at the ends by ropes and then lowered by gradually releasing the ropes till the pipe has rested on the bottom of the trench.

Bell Jointed Pipes

Pipes with bell ends are laid with their sockets (bell ends) facing upstream. The ends of the pipe are cleaned and wetted with a brush. Jute or hemp rope dipped in a cement paste is wrapped round the plain end of each pipe. The rope is just thick enough to be inserted into the socket of the pipe already in position. Before the pipe is inserted in the socket, mortar made of one part cement and two parts and is applied to a thickness of about one cm over the spigot end of the pipe and also inside the socket. The pipe is placed well into the socket and care is taken that the packing is not pressed through the pipe. Steel chisels are used to ram the hemp tight when the pipes are in position. After ramming the hemp tight with a steel tool, the remaining space is the socket is filled with mortar (1:2 mix) and finished with a bead on the outside.

The work of hemp jointing should be kept about six metres ahead of the mortar filling, to ensure ease of working and regular progress. A bag full of straw should be kept inside the pipe and drawn forward by means of a rope, as laying of the pipeline proceeds. This will ensure that no obstruction is left in the pipe. The joints in the pipeline are kept wet for about 24 hours by a covering of wet gunny bag or a layer of fine, moist earth. If a fine soil covering is used, care should be exercised not to disturb the fresh mortar. All openings are similarly sealed at the end of each day's work. The trench is then filled back in 15 cm layers. Water should not be turned into the pipelines unless back filling is completed. The trench should not be flooded before the pipes have been filled with water, because the pipes may tend to float and cracks may develop. The pipeline can be tested about 48 hours after completion of the last section.

Pipes with Tongue and Groove Joints

Pipes with tongue and groove joints are laid with the groove ends facing upstream. The tongue or spigot end of the first section of pipe is cleaned and wetted with a brush. Sufficient mortar to form the lower section of the outside band or collar is placed in a depression at the lower side of the pipe joint. The groove end of the next section is wetted and filled with mortar. This section is then tipped over carefully, so as not to dislodge the mortar and is pushed into place to make a snug, tight joint (Fig. 4.20). Excess mortar will be squeezed out of the joint on both inside and outside of the pipe. Because extruded mortar would reduce flow and increase friction, the inside of the pipe is brushed smooth by a long handled brush, or a bag full of straw drawn by a rope. This is done soon after the pipe is placed true to line and grade, since any movement thereafter might result in leaky joints. The external band of mortar around the pipe is placed by a separate workman working 2 to 5 joints behind the crew laying the pipe. Procedures for curing and back-filling are the same as in bell-jointed pipes.

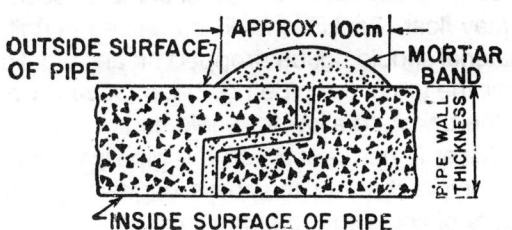

Reinforced Concrete Pipes with Collar Joints

Reinforced concrete pipes are usually available in lengths of 2.5–3 m. The pipes are lowered

Fig. 4.20 Details of mortar joint for concrete pipes in the tongue and groove joint (The outside mortar band is approx. 10 cm wide)

into the trench with the help of ropes by two men standing of the trench bank on either side of the pipe. Before an adjacent pipe is laid, a collar is slipped to its end. The pipes are laid with their ends placed about one cm apart. The gap is left for fixing a rope dipped in bitumen, in the recession of the pipe ends. The rope is dipped in hot bitumen, and placed in the recessed end of the pipe. Squeezing of individual pipes in the line is done when at least four or five pipes have been laid. After having placed the rope, the leading pipe out of the for or five pipes already laid, is forced towards the tail end to such an extent that there exists no gap between the facing ends and the rope threads are forced out to the periphery. A 5-tonne capacity jack can be used to press the pipes. The back of the digger bucket attached to a tractor can also be used to perform this operation. After the squeezing operation is over, the collars are slipped over the squeezed joints, so that half of the collar width covers each side of the joint. In order to maintain a uniform clearance between the pipe joint and the collar, wooden battens of uniform thickness are plugged in on both sides of the collar. The gap between the collar and pipe is then filled with a dry mixture of cement and sand mixed in the ratio of 1:1. The mortar is placed after cleaning the pipe and collar with a wet brush. Immediately prior to placing mortar and jointing the sections, the ends should be thoroughly wetted. The outer edges of the gap between the collar and the pipe are sealed with jute rope or hemp dipped in a 1:1 wet cement-sand mixture. To ensure satisfactory results, the rope is pressed between the gap with the help of a blunt chisel, so that no air gap exists. Once the gap is sealed satisfactorily, the collar is lined with 1 to 1.5 cm thick plaster (1:2 ratio) and bevelled off at an angle of 45° with the outside edge of the collar. The finishing of the joint should be at least five sections behind the laying operation.

Openings in all concrete pipelines should be covered to prevent air circulation, except when work is actually in progress. Such openings should be kept closed until the pipeline is to be filled with water.

There should be initial backfill of soil around the pipe, covering the pipe to a depth of at least 15 cm for the full width of the trench and not more than seven sections behind the laying. Care is taken in placing such earth around the pipe, to avoid injury to the freshly applied mortar bands.

Mortar joints should be protected from drying out. If the soil used in the initial backfill is not thoroughly moist, the mortar is covered with wet gunny bags. Curing is continued for three to five days. It is desirable to backfill the lines with moist soil as soon as practical, to avoid shrinkage of the joints and mortar bands. In placing the backfill the earth should be placed simultaneously on either side of the line, to avoid displacement or injury to the mortar joints and bands. Where the backfill is to be flooded to expedite consolidation, it is essential to fill the pipe with water, otherwise it may float. Backfill should be placed in uniform layers. Large quantities of backfill material should not be dropped on any pipeline, until an initial cover of at least 60 cm over the top of the pipe has been placed. Uncompacted fill is mounted over the top of the trench to allow for settlement.

Water is not turned into the pipeline until all back-filling is completed, preferably not before three or four days of finishing the pipe joints, and in no case within 24 hours of finishing the pipe joints.

STRUCTURES FOR UNDERGROUND PIPELINES

Specialized structures are used with underground pipeline systems to control the water and protect the pipeline from damage. These include the structures at the inlet, water control and diversion structures, air release vents and end plugs.

Inlet Structures

Water may enter a pipeline by gravity from an open channel or it may be pumped from a well, farm pond or other sources. An inlet structure is required to develop the full flow capacity of the pipeline to maintain water surface elevations sufficient to distribute water to the different cause damage, and keep trash from entering the pipe.

Pump Stands

A vertical pipe extending above ground and connected to the underground pipeline system is known as a stand. Pump stands are located at the inlet of the underground pipeline system. It is the larger capacity of the stand that permits dissipation of the high velocity system and release of entrapped air before the water enters the pipeline. To enable the mason to make mortar joints from inside the stand, the minimum diameter of the stand is 60 cm. Any air entrained by the high-velocity stream coming from the pump will have an opportunity to escape at the pump stand. If the entrained air is carried into the pipeline, it will tend to collect in pockets that reduce the amount of water the pipe can carry. Entry of air into the pipeline can also cause a surging flow condition and may contribute to the development of excessive pressures.

Pump stands must extend upward to a point where it will not overflow, except when unusual pressure occur. This sometimes happens when a pump is started, and the pipeline could be broken if the stand did not overflow. The elevation of the water surface is the stand must be sufficient to permit the discharge of water through the outlets at any point on the farm. This should also include the pressure head required to overcome friction in the pipe and valves.

When the stand is very high, it can be capped and vented with a smaller-diameter pie pipe (Fig. 4.21). It is desirable to provide a flexible coupling between the pump and the stand, to prevent damage of the stand due to pump vibration.

Gravity Inlets

When water enters the pipeline from an open channel, a gravity inlet is used (Fig. 4.22). A screen is fixed to the inlet to keep trash out of the pipeline. The top of the structure should be provided with a cover to prevent accidents and to keep trash from blowing in.

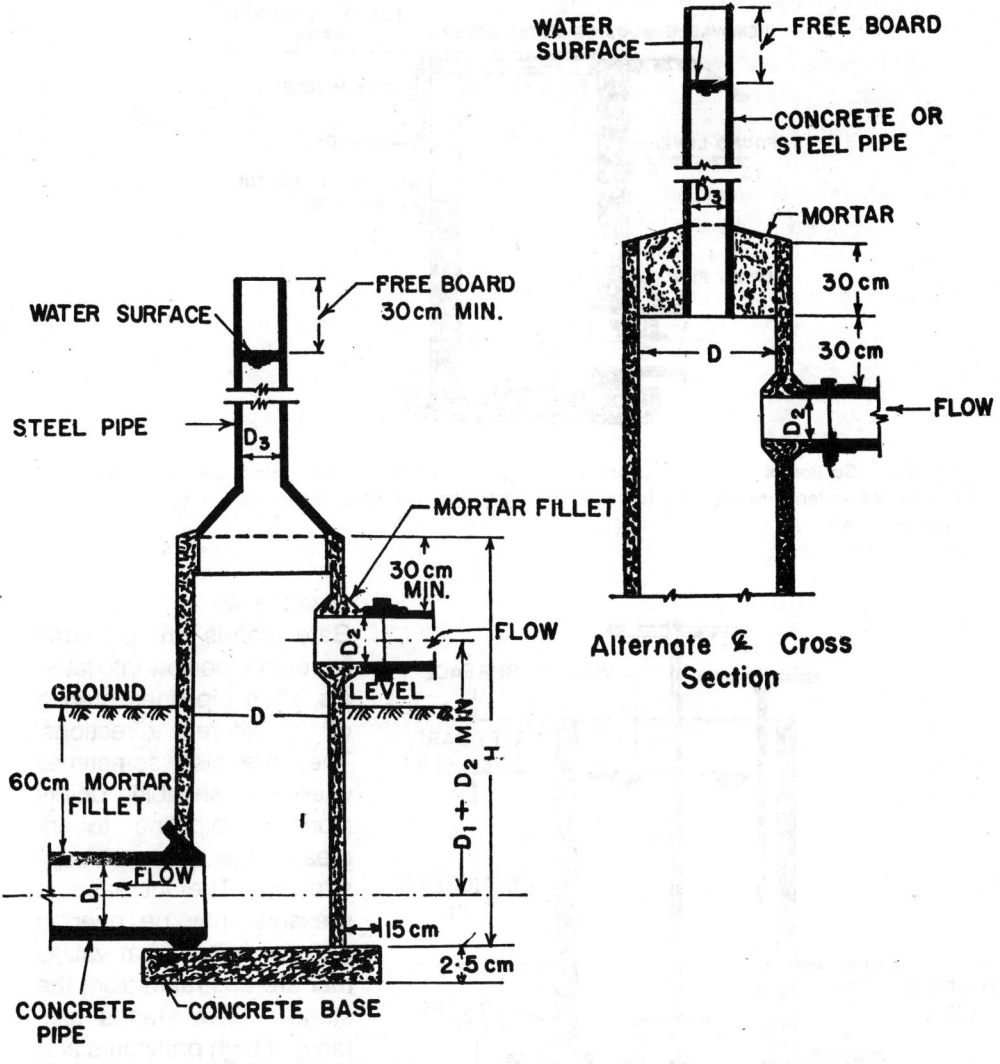

Fig. 4.21 Detailed section of high head tapered pump stand

If the irrigation water contains appreciable quantities of sand, a trap can be built into the inlet structure to remove most of the suspended material. When the stand functions as a sand trap also, it has an extra-large diameter to ensure low velocity of water and its bottom is set some distance (about 60 cm) below the bottom of the pipeline. Stands used as sand traps should be at least 75 cm in diameter for easy access for cleaning.

When the channel water contains considerable quantities of debris and weed seed, a debris screen is provided at the inlet to clean the water before it enters the pipeline. Commonly, the stream is allowed to fall through a fine screen into a gravity inlet. The screen will need frequent cleaning.

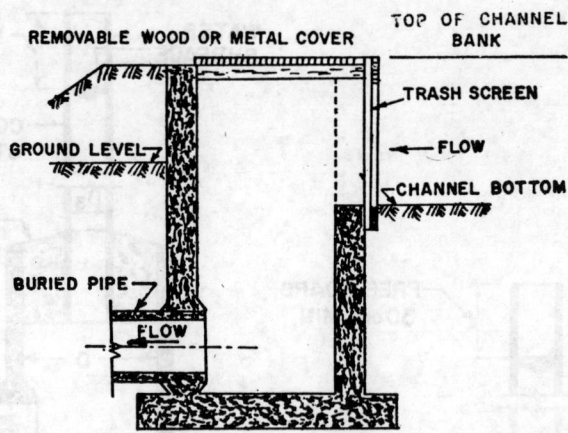

Fig. 4.22 Section of an inlet structure for taking water from a channel into a buried pipeline. A separate water desalting box is necessary when the incoming stream carries appreciable amounts of silt

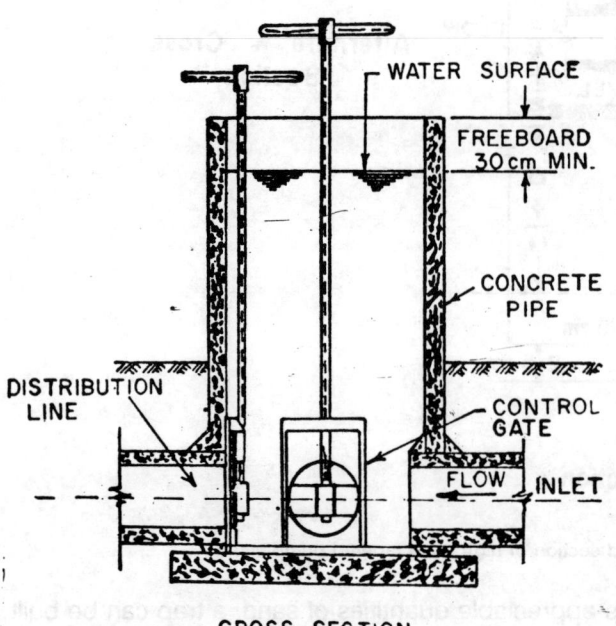

CROSS SECTION

Fig. 4.23 Details of a concrete gate stand used to control the flow into several laterals

Gate Stands

Gate stands are provided to control the flow into laterals when pipelines branch off in different directions. They are also sometimes used at suitable points along a pipeline to increase the pressure upstream. The increase in pressure may be needed to force water from valves that are upstream from the stand. Gate stands also prevent high pressures and act as surge chambers.

Gate stands are made in the same way as pump stands, but are provided with slide or sluice valves to control flow into laterals (Fig. 4.23). Lateral pipelines may take off in any desired direction. The gates are provided with handles, which permit their operations from the top of the structure. The gate may be opened or closed to divert water as desired. It can be partially closed to create upstream water pressure, to make water flow from outlets at upstream points. When sluice valves are used to control the flow into laterals, short pieces of steel pipes may be fixed at the inlet and outlet ends as extensions of the valve. The steel pipe at the inlet end may be fixed directly to the vertical pipe of the gate stand. The extension at the outlet is inserted into the concrete pipe and the joint made with cement mortar. The gate stand must be large enough to accommodate the gates to be used and to permit access for maintenance and repair.

Overflow stands

Overflow stands should be installed in pipelines down steep slopes to prevent excessive pressure in the lower reaches of the pipe. This will limit the pressure developed and still permit the water to be withdrawn from outlets near the upper end of the line. The details of an overflow stand are illustrated in Fig. 4.24. A gate stand serves as both a check and a drop structure. A gate may be provided between the two chambers, so that, when upstream pressure is not necessary, the gate can be opened and the water will pass directly downstream without falling over the check wall.

The falling water may entrain air and can set up surges in the pipeline. It is frequently necessary to install an air release vent directly below an overflow stand, to remove the air entrained by the falling water.

Float Valve Stands

When pipelines are installed on steep slopes, a somewhat automatic control of pressures in the line can be obtained by installing stands equipped with float valves. If pressure is increased downstream, the float closes the valve to prevent the passage of water and thus eliminate the danger of excessive pressures downstream in the pipeline. The valve opens when the pressure downstream falls to some predetermined level, allowing more water to pass to meet the needs. When the lower outlets are closed, the float valve will close automatically and prevent the development of excessive pressures at the lower end.

Float stands are located at intervals of about 3 m, or drop in the pipeline. They are especially good when a pipeline is served directly from storage, in which case full control of water can be maintained from the lower end of the line. They eliminate the need for many high stands of the overflow type, when a line serves steep slopes.

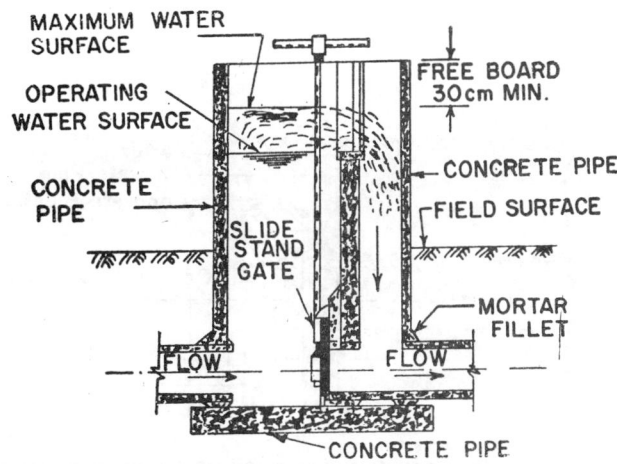

Fig. 4.24 Overflow gate stand for concrete pipelines

Air Vents

Air vents are vertical pipe structures to release air entrapped in the pipeline and to prevent vacuum. Entrapped air must be removed to permit even flow and avoid danger of water hammer (Water hammer is a result of a sudden change in the rate of flow causing excessive momentary pressure build-up). Gates and valves should be opened and closed slowly, to avoid water hammer and damage to the pipeline. They are normally installed at all high points in the line, at sharp turns, at any abrupt change in grade directly downstream from any structure that may entrap air, and at the end of the pipeline. It is also required immediately upstream from gates, where closure of gate would make this the downstream end of the lateral or line. Vents are generally installed at points about 200 m apart on straight pipelines with uniform slope. Any stand (pump stand, gate stand, etc.) may substitute for a vent.

The area of the vent pipe in contact with the pipeline should not be less than half the area of the line. This can be further reduced, until the area of the small pipe is not less than 1/60 of the area of the main line. In no case should diameter of the small pipe be less than 5 cm. The vents should be high enough to provide a freeboard of at least 60 cm above the maximum height, that water will rise at that point under normal operation.

Pipelines designed to operate under higher pressures that an be conveniently served by open air vents, should have air relief valves placed at the critical points along the line. Air relief valves are fixed to the vertical vent pipe at some convenient height above the ground surface. These are usually spring operated valves, which are set to open whenever excess pressures develop in the pipeline. Such a valve will permit air to escape or enter, but will not allow water to pass. Air relief valves should not be used in any location where it may be necessary, to relieve momentary high pressure surges.

End plugs

End plug is provided where the line terminates. The function of an end plug is to close a line and to absorb the pressures developed at the end of the line on account of water hammer. The plug is backed by a concrete block, which provides sufficient strength to meet unexpected high pressures developed due to sudden opening or closing of valves. Figure 4.25 gives constructional details of an end plug and the supporting concrete block.

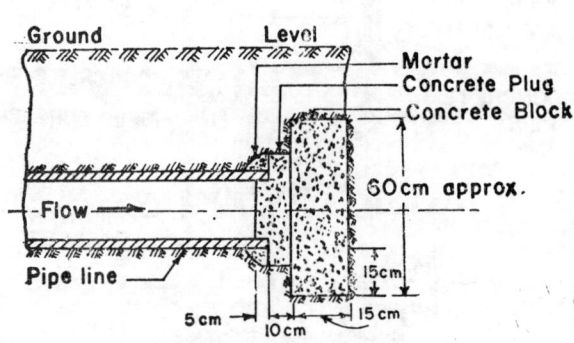

Fig. 4.25   Concrete end plug and block support at the end of a pipeline

Outlets

Outlet structures are necessary to provide controlled delivery of water on to the fields at any desired location. These should be easy to open and close, be of proper size to provide the flow required, and be so constructed that the water released will not cause soil erosion. The most common outlets consists of a concrete riser to bring the water from the buried pipeline to the ground surface, and an attached valve to control the flow of water. The diameter of the riser pipe is usually the same as the main pipe. This will permit the entire flow of the pipeline to be released through the valve. In large sized pipelines, when a number of outlets are to discharge water simultaneously, the size of the riser pipe is smaller than the main pipe. Common sizes of the riser pipe are 15, 20, 25 and 30 cm, depending on the size of the main pipe.

DESIGN OF UNDERGROUND PIPELINE IRRIGATION SYSTEM

An underground irrigation system should be properly designed to handle efficiently, the required flow through the system. If pipelines are too small in diameter pumping costs are increased and the capacity of the system may be seriously limited. On the other hand, pipelines larger than necessary add to the cost of the system and may cause uneven flow.

In designing an underground pipeline system, the head loss due to friction in the pipeline and other factors must be taken into account. Friction between the flowing water and the walls of the pipeline resists flow and cause a loss of head. Loss of head due to friction in the pipe between two points in a pipe at a distance l apart is given by formula:

$$h_f = \frac{flv^2}{2gR} \qquad \qquad \ldots (4.6)$$

where, f = coefficient of friction for pipe;

l = length of pipe (m);

v = velocity of water in pipe (m/sec);

g = acceleration due to gravity (m/sec/sec) (9.81 m/sec^2); and

R = hydraulic radius (m).

$R = \dfrac{a}{p}$, where a = area of cross-section of pipe in square meters.

$a = \dfrac{d^2}{4}$ and $p = d$,

where d = diameter of pipe in metres. Therefore

$R = \dfrac{d}{4}$ and $h_f \dfrac{2flv^2}{gd}$

Table 4.7 presents the values of f for common types of irrigation pipes. Table 4.9 gives the values of friction loss in concrete pipes at varying discharge rates.

In some types of problems, especially those involving short pipes, the head loss at the entrance to pipes is significant. Entrance losses in pipelines may be calculated from the following formulas:

— Pipe and flush with the wall of pump stand

$$h_e = 0.5\frac{v^2}{2g}$$

— Pipe and protruding from wall

$$h_e = 1.0\frac{v^2}{2g}$$

— Pipe with bell entrance

$$h_e = 0.1\frac{v^2}{2g}$$

where, h_e = head lost at pipe entrance in metres, and v and g are the same as defined earlier.

The other losses which may be significant are the velocity head in the pipe and the head loss through riser valves. The velocity head due to flow in pipes is obtained

Table 4.9 *Friction loss in concrete pipe in meters per 100 metres*

Flow rate litre/sec	Diameter of pipe, cm					
	20	25	30	35	40	45
2.8	0.01					
5.7	0.03					
8.5	0.07					
11.3	0.12	0.04				
14.2	0.19	0.06				
17.2	0.26	0.09	0.04			
22.7	0.45	0.15	0.06			
28.3	0.68	0.23	0.09	0.04		
34.0	0.95	0.32	0.13	0.06		
39.6	1.23	0.43	0.18	0.08	0.04	
45.3	1.62	0.55	0.22	0.11	0.06	
51	2.02	0.68	0.28	0.13	0.07	
57	2.45	0.83	0.34	0.16	0.08	0.05
68	3.43	1.16	0.48	0.22	0.12	0.07
79	4.57	1.54	0.63	0.30	0.16	0.09
91	5.85	1.97	0.81	0.38	0.20	0.11
102	7.27	2.46	1.01	0.48	0.25	0.14
113	8.84	2.98	1.03	0.58	0.30	0.17
127		3.71	1.53	0.72	0.38	0.21
142		4.51	1.86	0.88	0.46	0.26
156		5.38	2.21	1.05	0.55	0.31

from the formula:

$$h_v = \frac{v^2}{2g}$$

where, h_v = velocity head, metres and v and g are the same as defined earlier. Head loss through riser valves is given in Table 4.10.

The designer should plan the system, so that the pipeline flows full and the hydraulic gradient remains above the pipeline to prevent surges and trouble due to entrapped air.

Example 32—It is desired to install a concrete pipeline to carry a discharge of 100 litre/sec, so that the friction loss will be equal to the slope of the land. The land slope along the line the pipeline is to be laid, is 1%. What size pipe should be selected?

Solution—From Table 4.9 it will be seen that a 30 cm pipeline carrying 102 litre/sec will have a friction loss of 1.01 m/100 m. Hence a 30 cm size pipe would meet the requirement.

Example 33—A concrete pipeline is to be used to deliver 90 litre/sec of water for a distance of 500 metre. The land has an upward slope of 0.3 per cent. It is desired to limit the pressure in the pipeline to 6 metre of water pressure. Select a suitable size of pipe.

Solution—The difference in elevation for which water is to be lifted is 0.003 x 500 = 1.5 metre. The additional pressure which may be used in overcoming friction is 6−1.5 = 4.5 m for 500 m or 0.9 m per 100 m. From Table 4.9, the friction loss for a 30 cm pipe with a discharge of 91 litre/sec is 0.81 m per 100 m. Therefore, a 30 cm pipe is suitable. The maximum pressure in the pipeline will be 5 x 0.81 + 1.5 = 5.55 metre.

Example 34—A concrete pipeline is to carry water across a distance of 650 m from a pump which discharges 100 litre/sec. The land has a downfield slope of 0.1% along the line the pipes are laid. It is desired that the maximum pressure in the pipeline should not exceed 5 m of water. What size pipe is to be used? How high should be the pump stand?

Solution—Pressure available in overcoming friction = permissible pressure in pipeline + gain in pressure head due to downfield.

Table 4.10 *Head loss through Riser Valves Pressure loss in cm of water*

Flow rate litre/sec	Diameter (cm) of opening					
	15	20	25	30	35	40
10	2	1				
20	10	3	1			
30	26	7	3	1		
40	50	13	5	2	1	
50	83	22	8	4	2	1
60	126	34	12	6	3	2
80	250	64	24	11	5	3
100		105	40	18	9	5
125		165	65	29	15	7
150		250	97	44	22	12
175			136	65	30	17
200			185	83	41	22
225			245	100	55	30
225				137	69	37
250				170	83	45
300				210	100	56
350				300	145	77
400					195	103
450					250	135
500						170
550						210

Gradient $= 5 + 0.001 \times 6.5 = 5.0065$ m

$= 5.0065 + 6.5$

0.77 m/100 m.

Table 4.14 shows that a 35 cm diameter pipe will deliver a discharge of 102 litre/sec and the friction loss will be 0.48 m/100 m. Hence, a 35 cm diameter pipe is selected.

The water will rise to a height of $6.5 \times 0.48 - 0.0065 = 3.1135$ m. Allowing a freeboard of 50 cm, the height of stand pipe will be 3.6135 m or say 3.6 m.

COMMON TROUBLES OF UNDERGROUND PIPELINES

When properly designed and correctly installed, the underground pipeline should operate without giving any trouble. Inadequate procedures in design and installation and unforeseen situations may give rise to the following troubles:

— Development of longitudinal cracks in the pipe, usually at the top or both top and bottom

— Pushing of the pipe into the stands

— Development of circumferential cracks

— Surging or intermittent flow of water

The first three troubles are caused mainly by the expansion and contraction of concrete pipes by wetting and drying. Concrete is also affected by temperature; it expands when heated and contracts when cooled. Circumferential cracks are caused by a drop in water or soil temperature, or by drying out of the pipe. Well waters seldom give this trouble. When pipelines are fed from canal supply in winter, low water temperature may sometimes give rise to circumferential cracks. Such cracks may be partially prevented by prestressing factory made pipes. Prestressing may take place automatically when the pipe, which is laid dry, expands on becoming wet.

Failure of underground pipelines can be avoided by adopting proper procedures in pipe laying. Using moist soil for the initial backfill after laying the pipe, minimizes the circumferential stresses and also reduces excessive longitudinal stress. Another precaution is to minimize air circulation through a line when laying pipe and when the line is not in use. On flat land, this is automatically accomplished because water stands in the lines. On steep grades, it can be accomplished by providing flap covers on stands and keeping the hydrants closed. It may also be done by having overflow stands, so that the pipe is always submerged for a short distance above such stands. As an added precaution against failure, pipelines are not laid in extremely hot, extremely cold or in wet weather.

Pushing of pipes into stands is not a serious trouble, as the joint can be remade with cement mortar.

Surges in Pipelines

Surging is a common disadvantage in pipelines, when overflow stands are used. Air gets entrained in water as it overpours to the downstream side of the stand. The entrained air is carried in the pipeline. Because of the turbulence of the flow, the tendency for the air to separate out is minimized. After a short interval, the upstream portion of this reach of water becomes lighter than the downstream portion. This may cause a reversal of hydraulic gradient, until the water with entrained air flows back to the stand and the air is dissipated. This forward flow is only in cycles.

Surging may be minimized by providing gate valves in the baffle walls (or between the upstream and downstream portions) of overflow stands, and closing these gates only enough to create the pressure necessary for the operation of upstream hydrants or laterals. Use of overflow stands having a relatively large cross-sectional area of the downpour sections, may also minimize the trouble. The large stand will facilitate the release of most of the air before the water gets into the pipeline. Providing an air vent close to the overflow stand on its downstream side will also facilitate the release of the entrained air and minimize surging.

4.5   Drainage of Agricultural Lands

In order to maintain sustained production from irrigated agriculture, removal of excess water and salts from agricultural lands is essential. If lands are not properly drained, it is difficult to maintain agricultural production on a sustained basis at high level. Besides, water logging may occur and environmental hazards would increase. In areas having moderate to high rainfall, the major portion of excess water comes from precipitation which percolates into the soil to become ground water. Where surface drainage is poor on flat land, temporary flooding occurs and a large percentage of the water infiltrates into the soils.

SOURCES OF EXCESS WATER

— Uncontrolled irrigation
— Seepage losses from unlined irrigation canals/field channels
— Ground water moving from shallow aquifers
— Non-maintenance of natural drainage
— Seepage water emerging in the form of springs on ground water under artesian pressure.

In arid regions, drainage follows irrigation while in humid regions it may have to precede agricultural development.

In the report of the working group on soil and water conservation (Anonymous, 1989) the area of water logging in the country has been estimated as 8.53 m ha (updated 1984-85) as compared to 6.00 m ha up to 1980-81. The extent of water logged area in the country (statewise) has been given in Table 1.4. This increase may be due to extension of canal irrigation as well as development of flood plains and deltas. It has been observed by Bhumla (1983) that continued emphasis on having major and medium irrigation works in high rainfall areas during the rainy season is likely to prove disastrous.

As an alternative he has laid stress on provision of minor irrigation through tube-wells and wells and construction of reservoirs.

CLASSIFICATION OF DRAINAGE METHODS

The methods used for drainage may be grouped in two categories. Surface drainage and sub-surface drainage, depending upon the way of removal of water.

Surface Drainage

Land surface is reshaped as necessary to eliminate ponding and establish slopes sufficient to induce gravitational flow overland and through channels to an outlet using land smoothing, land grading, bedding and ditching, as well as using dykes and flood ways.

Sub-surface Drainage

Ditches and buried drains are installed within the soil profile to collect and convey excess ground water to a gravity or pumped outlet, using interceptor and relief drains.

TYPES OF DRAINS

Field Drains

These are graded channel which collect excess water from a field or a holding and is a link between the farm and the carrier drain.

Seepage Drains

These drains are located along earthen/lined canals to intercept surface/sub-surface flow and help in removing excess discharge from fill reaches to the adjoining fields.

Carrier Drains

These are a link between the various field drains and sub-main drain or main drains.

Main Drains

Main/branch/sub-main drains are principal excavated or natural drains collecting water from link drains or directly from field drains.

The drainage investigations for an area require basic information on topography, rainfall intensity, soil characteristics, methods of water application and natural drainage conditions. (Anonymous, 1985).

DESIGN OF SURFACE DRAINAGE SYSTEM DATA NEEDED

1. Maximum 1-day, 2-day and 3-day rainfall occurring with a certain frequency (5 years or 10 years)

2. Infiltration rate of soils

3. Evaporation rate
4. Crops grown and the stage of root growth at the time of heavy rainfall
5. Land slope
6. Gradient that can be given to the drainage channels
7. Outfall conditions

DESIGN DETAILS

Drainage discharge

The following formulae are generally used for calculating the rate of runoff for drainage design.

1.
$$Q = CM^{5/6} \qquad \qquad \dots(4.7)$$

where Q = The rate of runoff at any point in the system from the drainage area above the point in m³/sec or ft³/sec.

C = The appropriate drainage coefficient for a unit area such as one sq km or sq mile.

M = The size of the drainage area in the proper units of area, i.e. km² or mile².

The constant C varies between 35 and 40 for Q in cubic feet per second and A in square mile. The C value is given by

$$C = 16.39 + 14.75 \ Re. \qquad \dots(4.8)$$

Where Re is the rainfall excess which can be obtained using rainfall runoff equation (Hydrologic soil cover complex method). The constant C should be determined by experience with many installed drainage systems, for the degree of protection desired.

2.
$$Q = \frac{ARF}{T} \text{ (in metric units)} \qquad \dots(4.9)$$

where, Q = Discharge (cumec)
   A = Area (km²)
   R = Rainfall (mm)
   F = Runoff coefficient (value of F ranges between 0.4 and 0.6).
For peak runoff, value of F ranges from 0.8 to 0.9
   T = Time of removal in seconds
      For 500 ha = 1 day
         1000 ha = 2 day
         >1000 ha = 3 day

3. *Hydrologic Cover Complex Method*—This method has already been discussed in Chapter 2 and is the best and complete method of finding direct runoff from the rainfall. It takes into account the antecedent soil moisture condition, soil characteristics like infiltration and permeability, land use as well as the land treatment (soil conservation measures). The following relationship is used for computation purposes.

$$Q = \frac{(P - I_a)^2}{(P - I_a) + S} \qquad \dots(4.10)$$

where, Q = Actual runoff, mm
   P = Rainfall, mm

S = Potential maximum retention of water by soil in equivalent depth over the catchment, mm

I_a = Initial abstraction in mm for average antecedent moisture condition in, which

I_a = 0.35 (except for hydrologic) soil group D and paddy cultivation, where I_a = 0.15

Side slopes—In general the side slopes are:

Cut in firm soil 1:1

Cut in loam 1:1.5

Cut in sandy soils 1:2.5

Permissible velocities (m/sec)

Sandy loam   0.60

Loam   0.75

Clay   1.00

Cross-section—The drain is designed as an open channel with uniform flow using Manning's Formula (Refer Chapter 4.4 conveyance of irrigation water).

$$V = \frac{1}{n}R^{2/3}S^{1/2} \text{ (in metric units)}$$
$$\text{and } Q = A \times V$$

where, n = Roughness coefficient

R = Hydraulic mean radius

S = Gradient

The value of n in the above formula should be 0.04, taking into consideration the expected weed growth and the irregular shape it is likely to attain in due course.

The least width at bottom shall not be less than 0.5 m and the minimum depth 0.6 m below ground level. It must be ensured that the drain keeps the water-table normally below root zone depth of the crops grown in the area, i.e. about 1.5 m below the ground level.

Gradient—The gradient should normally follow the natural slope of the area. It should however, be checked that the designed section gives the non-silting and non-scouring velocities.

Surface Drainage Structures

1. *Drop structures*—To keep the bed gradient of the drains within the prescribed limits and dissipate energy and avoid erosion.

2. *Crossings*—To cross an existing road or cart track using R.C.C. pipes of not less than 0.3 m diameter.

3. *Outfalls*—At the junction of subsidiary drain and bigger drain.

DESIGN FACTORS FOR OPEN DRAINS

1. Bed to be low enough to drain the land.

2. Suitable depth to have sufficient capacity at all points to carry the water brought into it. Laterals should be provided at suitable intervals, depending upon the soil permeability and the rate of drainage described.

3. Side slopes to be such as to remain stable ranging from 1/2 : 1 in very stiff compact clays, to flat slopes of 3:1 in loose upon sandy formations.

4. The velocity of flow to be non-scouring and non-silting (optimum velocity 0.6 to 1.2 m/sec).

5. Bed slopes 1:200 to 1:700 should be large, as surface slope may permit. Drains will have to cater to varying discharges.

6. The value of rugosity coefficient in Manning's formula varying from 0.25 to 0.45, depending upon the condition of channel.

7. The usual rate of drainage to be such as to drain the root zone of excess water resulting from a severe storm rainfall within 24 to 48 hours.

8. Spoil to be spread to 0.9 m height or berm provided.

Design Coefficient or Modulus
Suitable drainage coefficient has to be adopted. It is generally expressed as centimetres of water that is drained off from a given area in 24 hours or cumecs/km^2.

Capacity
The design capacity should be sufficient to carry flow from runoff, ground water and flow from irrigation waste water.

Depth and Spacing
The depth and spacing of sub-surface drains are roughly proportional, depending upon the permeability of sub-surface materials. Generally the greater the depth of the drains, the wider the spacing between the drains. The choice of a depth and spacing is often an economic consideration.

SUB-SURFACE DRAINAGE
In planning a sub-surface drainage system, the designer must evaluate the various site conditions and decide whether to use relief or interception drainage. After completing the reconnaissance survey, all feasible detailed survey studies and investigations must be made and sub-soil as well as ground water condition must be established.

Steps
1. Preparation of topographic map with appropriate contour interval
2. Tabulation of ground water information from observation wells in the area to plot observation well hydrographs
3. Preparation of water-table contour maps
4. Preparation of map of depth of water-table
5. Preparation of working map.
6. Preparation of a cross-sectional profile in the direction of ground water flow;

DESIGN OF SUB-SURFACE DRAINS

Drainage Coefficient
The concept of drainage coefficient is used in the design of drainage systems for agricultural lands. It is defined as the rate of water removal, used in drainage design to obtain the desired protection for crops for excess surface or sub-surface water expressed as an amount of water to be removed in 24 hours from the entire drainage area. It may also be expressed as the flow rate per unit area (cumec/km^2). The drainage coefficient is decided such that no appreciable damage is caused to the crops grown in the area. The intensity of rain and its duration are inversely

proportional to the time allowed for removal of water (depending upon the kind of crops grown) with wide variations in drainage Coefficients must be based upon good investigations and local experience within a given area (Table 4.11).

In arid irrigated areas, due to insufficient experience to establish acceptable drainage coefficient for general use, the following formula may be used

$$q = \frac{\frac{(P+C)I}{100}}{24F} \qquad \qquad \ldots (4.11)$$

where, q = Drainage coefficient, cm/hr
P = Deep percolation (based on consumptive use studies)
C = field losses, per cent
I = irrigation application, cm
F = frequency of irrigation, days

Example 35:

1. Deep percolation from irrigation from consumptive use studies is 25 per cent.
2. Field losses estimated to be 12 per cent of the water applied.
3. 10 cm water is applied at an interval of 20 days.

$$q = \frac{\frac{(25+12)}{100} \times 10}{24 \times (20)}$$
$$= \frac{3.7}{480} = 0.007 \text{ cm/hr}$$

Design Capacity

In case of parallel relief drains, the discharge can be expressed by the following relationship:

$$Q = \frac{qS(L+S/2)}{3,60,000}$$

where, Q = drain discharge, cumec
q = drainage coefficient cm/hr
S = drain spacing, m
L = drain length, m

The capacity of interception drain must be equal to the ground water flow intercepted and the flow is governed by the Daney's law.

$$V = Ki \qquad \qquad \ldots (4.12)$$

where, V = velocity of flow through the porous medium
K = hydraulic conductivity
i = hydraulic gradient (undisturbed state)

The flow through a porous material is given by

$$Q = KiA \qquad \qquad \ldots (4.13)$$

Applying this to an interception drain, the cross-sectional area intersected may be mathematically expressed as

$$A = d_e L \qquad \qquad \ldots (4.14)$$

where, A = cross-sectional area intersected (m²)
d_e = average effective depth of the drain, m
L = length of the drain, m

Hence by combining the above two equations, the design discharge of an interception drain is given by

$$Q = \frac{K_i d_e L}{3,60,000} \qquad \ldots (4.15)$$

where, Q = Design discharge of an interception drain, cumec
K = hydraulic conductivity, cm/hr
i = hydraulic gradient of the undisturbed water table, m/m
d_e = average effective depth of the drain, m
L = length of the drain, m.

Assumptions

1. Homogeneous soil profile
2. Uniform hydraulic conductivity throughout the soil profile
3. Accurate determination of cross-sectional area

Example 36: The average hydraulic conductivity along an interception drain is 20 cm/hr; the hydraulic gradient (slope of the original water-table surface) is 0.08 m/m. The effective depth of the drain is 1.5 m and the length of the drain is 1.2 km. Calculate the design discharge.

$$Q_i = \frac{20 \times (0.08) \times (1.5) \times (1200)}{3,60,000}$$
$$= 0.008 \text{ cumec}$$

Desirable depth of water-table below ground level (m) for various crops

Crop	Desirable depth of water-table (m) for		
	Sandy soil	Loam soil	Clay soil
Cereals	0.6	0.7	0.8
Fodders	0.7	0.8	0.9
Tuber, roots fibre, oilseed, sugarcane and vegetable	0.8	0.9	1.0
Orchard, trees	1.0	1.2	1.4

Depth and Spacing of Drains

The depth and spacing of sub-surface drains are roughly proportional. Generally the greater the depth of the drains, wider is the spacing between them (Table 4.12). The choice of the depth and spacing is often an economic consideration.

Equations given by Hooghoudt and Glover can be applied to compute the drain spacing, depending on whether steady state or unsteady state drainage conditions exist. When water-table is steady with respect to input rainfall and drains are discharging at a constant rate, a steady state is said to exist, and this condition is obtained under low and uniform intensity rainfall over long duration. The Hooghoudth's equation is given by

$$R = \frac{8Kd_e m + 4Km^2}{L^2} \qquad \ldots (4.16)$$

where, R = design drainage rate (m/day)
K = hydraulic conductivity (m/day)
d_e = equivalent depth, m

m = maximum depth of water-table above the plane of drain centre, m.
L = spacing between drains, m

Unsteady state drainage condition is said to exist when there is fluctuation of water-table depth. This condition exists in irrigated areas and the areas with uneven distribution of annual rainfall. The flow equation proposed by Glover for this condition is

$$L = \pi \left[KDt/fl_n \left(\frac{4Y_0}{\pi Y_{L/2}} \right) \right]^{1/2} \qquad \ldots (4.17)$$

where, L = spacing between drains, m
$\quad K$ = hydraulic conductivity, m/day
$\quad t$ = time in days for bringing down water-table from
$\qquad Y_0$ to $Y_{L/2}$ in between the two drains.
$\quad D = d + Y_0/2$, m
$\quad d$ = depth of impermeable layer below drains, m
$\quad f$ = effective drainable porosity to indicate
$\qquad$ measure of change in water-table under given
$\qquad$ conditions of recharge or discharge.

Diameter and Gradient of Drains
The depth and spacing having been decided, the next step is to establish the diameter and the gradient of the drains. For pipes flowing full, the discharge can be expressed as

$$Q = \frac{\pi}{4} d^2 v \qquad \ldots (4.18)$$

where, v = velocity of flow, m/sec
$\quad d$ = diameter of pipe, m

Manning's equation can be applied to determine the velocity of flow with a roughness coefficient of 0.014 for corrugated plastic pipes. The discharge is given by

$$Q = 0.312 \ km \ d^{2.67} S^{0.5}$$

For smooth pipes (clay tiles and smooth plastic piles), the discharge is given by

$$Q = 30a^{-0.57} d^{2.71} S^{0.57}$$

where, Q = discharge, cumec
$\quad K_m = \dfrac{1}{n} = 70$ (inverse of Manning's roughness coefficient)
$\quad S$ = Hydraulic gradient, m/m
$\quad a = 0.40$

For non-uniform flow conditions, the flow rate in a pipe increase gradually from $Q = 0$ at the upstream to $Q = qBL$ at the outflow.
where, q = specific discharge, m/sec
$\quad B$ = width of area drained by the pipeline as a rule coinciding
$\qquad$ with drain spacing, m
$\quad L$ = length of drain line, m.

In practical design problems, the pipes are assumed to be flowing full, over their entire length and that it is their maximum capacity that is taken into account. Generally 10 cm diameter is the minimum recommended tile size and mostly maximum permissible grade is provided.

LAYOUT OF DRAINS

Each pipeline has its own outlet into an open ditch. In a composite system the lateral pipelines discharge into a collector pipeline and sometimes several collector drains discharge into a larger collector pipeline (Fig. 4.26 and 4.27)

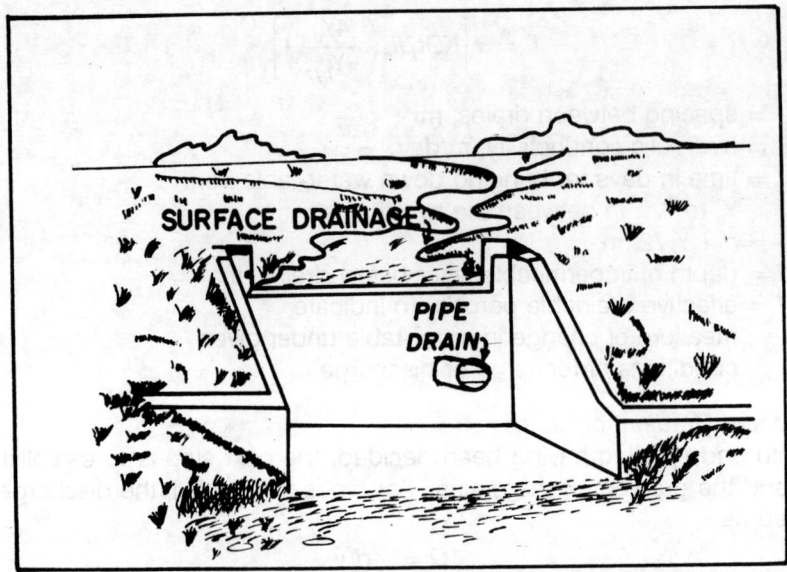

Fig. 4.26 Concrete or masonry headwall for outlet protection

Type of tile drainage systems
There are four types of tile drainage system (Fig. 4.28)

Example 37—Find the drainage coefficient of watershed of 3600 ha, if discharge from this area through a ditch is 3.2 cumec

Total discharge in 24 hr

$$= 3.2 \times 60 \times 60 \times 24$$

$$= 2,76,480 \text{ cum}$$

Area of watershed $= 3600$ ha

$$\text{Drainage coefficient} = \frac{276,480}{3600 \times 10,000}$$

$$= 0.00768 \text{ m}$$

$$= 8 \text{ mm}$$

Example 38—The drainage coefficient of an area of 0.5 km² is 0.5 m. Calculate the capacity of the ditch draining this area.

Drainage coefficient $= 0.5$ m

Total quantity of water drained in 24 hr

$$= 0.5 \times 0.5 \times 1000 \times 1000$$

$$= 2,50,000 \text{ cum}$$

$$\text{Rate of flow or capacity} = \frac{2,50,000}{24 \times 60 \times 60}$$

$$= 2.893 \text{ or } 2.9 \text{ cumec}$$

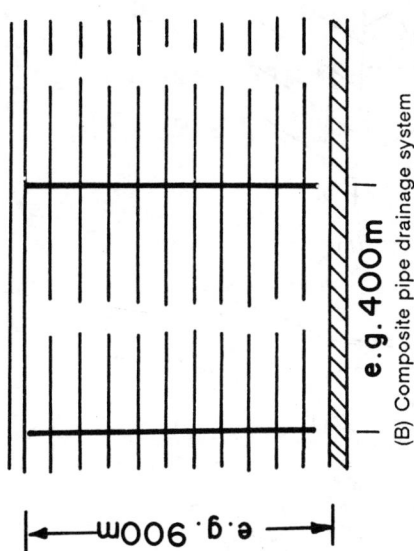

(B) Composite pipe drainage system

— Pipe lateral drain

— Pipe collector drain

▨ Road

‖ Open lateral drain

‖ Open collector drain

‖ Main drainage channel

(A) Singular pipe drainage system

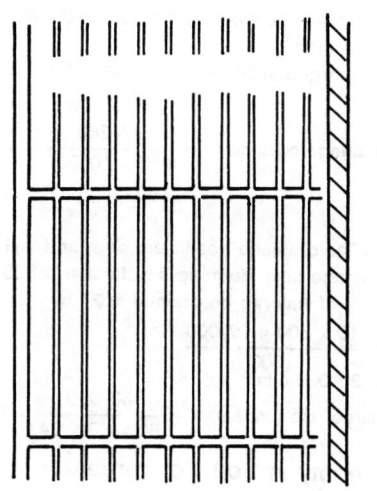

(C) Composite open drainage system

Fig. 4.27 Some arrangements of open and pipe field drains

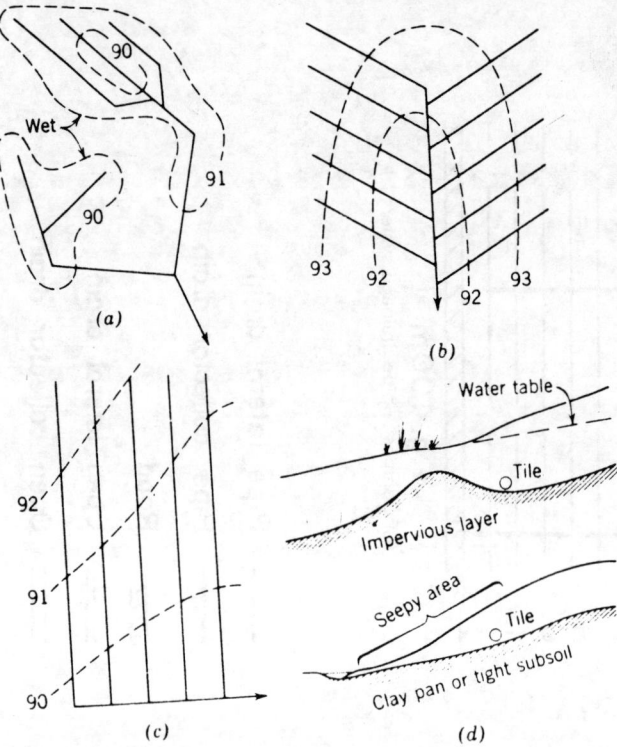

Fig. 4.28 Common types of pipe drainage systems. (a) Natural or random. (b) Herringbone. (c) Gridiron. (d) Cutoff or interceptor.

Example 39—A drainage channel discharges 0.2 cumec of water and drains 250 ha. What is the drainage coefficient of this land?

Total water discharged in 24 hr = 0.2 × 60 × 60 × 24

$$= 17,280 \text{ cum}$$

$$\therefore \text{ Drainage coefficient} = \frac{17,280}{250 \times 10,000} = 0.0069 \text{ m}$$

$$= 0.69 \text{ cum or } 7 \text{ mm}$$

Example 40—The drainage coefficient of a land is 10 mm. Calculate the capacity required at the outlet end of the drainage ditch draining a watershed of 300 ha.

Total volume of water to be drained in 24 hr

$$= \frac{10 \times 300 \times 10,000}{1000}$$

$$= 30,000 \text{ cum}$$

$$\therefore \text{ Discharge rate (capacity)} = \frac{30,000}{60 \times 60 \times 24} = 0.347 \text{ cumec}$$

4.6   Agronomy in Soil Conservation

The aim of soil and water conservation measures is not only to control erosion and conserve moisture, but also to use land according to its capability and get sustained yield of crops per unit area per unit time. To achieve this, engineering measures such as bunding, terracing, etc., are to be executed, depending upon agro-climatic and other characteristics of the region. Unless suitable agronomical measures are adopted, supplementing the above engineering measures in the treated land, the

Table 4.11 *Drainage coefficient for tiles based on average rainfall (annual)*

Average rainfall (cm)	Drainage coefficient for Tiles (cm)
< 75	0.60
75–100	0.80–0.90
100–125	0.90–1.25
125–150	1.25–1.90
>150	2.00–2.25

Table 4.12 *Average depth and spacing of tile drains in different soils*

Soil	Spacing (m)	Depth(m)
Sandy loam	30–60	1.20–1.50
Loam	18–30	1.05–1.20
Clay loam	12–21	0.90–1.05
Clay	9–15	0.90–1.05

process of soil detachability and transportability will continue, resulting in erosion and fluctuating crop yields. To stabilize the crop yields, it is therefore, imperative that suitable agronomical measures such as contour farming, mulching, dense growing crops, strip cropping, mixed cropping/inter cropping, tillage practices, use of adequate fertilizers and organic manures, plant protection measures, crop geometry, runoff farming, suitable high yielding varieties, control of weeds and mid-term correction, etc., are followed.

The above agronomical measures help to intercept rain drops and reduce the splash effect; help in improving infiltration rate by improving soil structure, help in retarding and reducing overland flow.

Contour farming—Carrying out farming operation, namely ploughing, planting and cultivating along contour lines (level lines) marked on the field is known as contour farming. By doing so, every furrow acts as a miniature reservoir to hold the excess runoff and gives increased time and opportunity to the soil to absorb as much water as possible for storage and supply back to the crop.

Prevention of soil erosion and increased supply of moisture to the plant are thus the ready results of the above method which is reflected in increased crop production.

The method of contour cultivation (Plate 18) alone will be effective only on lands with very wild slopes but for lands with greater slopes, it should always be supplemented with other engineering measures of erosion control. Establishment of key lines comprising of species such as subabul is recommended. This facilitates undertaking agricultural operations on the contour.

Mulching—Surface mulches are used to prevent soil from blowing away washing away, to reduce evaporation, to increase infiltration capacity of soil, to keep down weeds, to improve soil structures and eventually increase crop yields. Mulching has to be used with discretion and understanding of soil climatic condition.

Dense growing crops—Crops with maximum canopy cover like cultivated legumes, give better protection to cultivated lands against erosion than clean cultivated crops.

Strip cropping—It is a system of growing different crops in alternating strips, such that they serve as vegetative barriers in controlling erosion and runoff, and thereby maintaining fertility of soil. Suitable width of erosion permitting and erosion resisting crops have to be adopted on different slopes.

Mixed cropping—Important objectives of mixed cropping are better and continued cover on land, good protection from beating action of rains, almost complete protection from soil erosion, assurance of one or more crops to the farm. The roots of various species in a mixed crop feed at different depths in a soil.

Tillage—Proper tillage provides soil condition suited to the growth of crops, control of weeds, maintenance of infiltration and aeration, prevention of erosion and improvement of structure. Tillage operations are to be carried out at the right time and with proper implement, if they are to be economical and efficient.

Fertilizers and organic manures—It is necessary to know the fertility status of soil by testing soil and applying required quantity of inorganic fertilizers at proper time for higher crop production. Judicious use of organic manures are to be practiced to maintain and improve the structure of soil. This is more true in the case of sub-soils exposed during bench terracing, land levelling, etc.

Plant protection measures—Plant protection measures at the right time, are essential to keep the crops free from diseases.

Crop geometry: The geometry of the crops can be suitably selected to offer more resistance to the overland flow, by taking more number of plants in the row across the slope.

Runoff farming: To utilise the runoff from an area which otherwise would go waste by harvesting, storing in a farm pond and recycling is called runoff farming. Recycling is done by way of supplemental irrigation at the earliest opportunity, considering the necessity of irrigation to the crop.

High Yielding Varieties: Suitable high yielding varieties of selected crops should be introduced depending upon the agro-climatic conditions for maximum production.

Weed control: For efficient utilization of moisture and nutrients by the main crop, it is necessary that weeds are eliminated at appropriate time.

Mid-term correction: During years of aberrant weather conditions, mid-term correction such as thinning, etc., have to be practised for getting reasonable crop production and averting crop failures.

RECOMMENDED PRACTICES IN RAINFED AREAS UNDER DIFFERENT AGRO-CLIMATIC REGIONS OF INDIA

The following crop production strategy (Venkateswarlu, 1986) in rainfed areas under different weather conditions have emerged, due to research investigation conducted in Agricultural Universities, Research Institutes and Dryland Research Centres and Research Centres of Central Soil and Water Conservation Research and Training Institutes, Dehradun.

The growing season was identified for different regions in the country (Table 4.13).

The improved but simple practices developed for increased production are efficient management (timely seeding, ideal plant population, timely weeding) use of hybrid or high yielding varieties (HYB/HYV) of crops and moderate level of fertilizers.

IMPROVED FARM MACHINERY

To achieve ideal plant population with better seeding vigour, several bullock drawn seed-cum-fertilizer drills were developed like FESPO plough, 2-bowl seed drill, ragi seed-cum-fertilizer drill "Eenati" *gorru* (multi seed- cum-fertilizer dirll) deep furrow seeder and ridge seeder. These are cheap and can be easily had by the poor dryland farmers.

Table 4.13   *Length of effective cropping season at Dryland Research Centre*

Category	Regional Centres and effective cropping seasons			Cropping intensity
Less than 20 weeks	Bellary (8)*	Jodhpur (11)	Anantapur (13)	Sole cropping
	Hissar (17)	Rajkot (17)	Bijapur (17)	
20–30 weeks	Jhansi (21)	Kovilpatti (21)	Hyderbad (22)	Intercropping
	Udaipur (22)	Sholapur (23)	Agra (24)	
More than 30 weeks	Bhubaneswar (31)	Varanasi (32)	Hebbal (32)	Double cropping
	Hoshiarpur (35)	Indore (36)	Rewa Sambha (36) (44)	
	Ranchi (45)	Dehradun (51)		

* Figures in parenthesis indicate the duration of cropping season in weeks

Table 4.14   *Some suitable intercrops for different regions*

Region	System	Yield (q/ha)	
		Base crop	Inter crop
Bijapur	Pearlmillet	14.1	
	Pearlmillet + pigeonpea	11.6	8.0
Sholapur	Pearlmillet	18.0	
	Pearlmillet + pigeonpea	18.3	17.0
Ranchi	Maize	28.6	
	Maize + pigeonpea	28.2	6.2
Akola	Sorghum	33.5	
	Sorghum + greengram	30.8	7.3
Hyderabad	Sorghum	34.4	
	Sorghum + pigeonpea	33.5	5.5
Rewa	Sorghum	25.4	
	Sorghum + pigeonpea	22.3	4.7
Indore	Sorghum	32.7	
	Sorghum + peanut	28.3	7.6

Optimized intercropping systems were developed (Table 4.14) for the region receiving 625–800 mm rainfall with excess moisture available during the growing season.

The system provides a greater opportunity for producing much needed pulses and oilseeds.

Double cropping systems were developed for regions with 800 mm rainfall and in deep soils that can hold 300 mm rain water in the root profile. (Table 4.15).

WEATHER ABERRATIONS AND CROPPING

There may be aberrations in the weather, like rainfall may be delayed, there may be break in monsoon, or it may withdraw ahead of normal time of receding. Alternate crop strategies were worked out to meet such aberrations. (Table 4.16).

Table 4.15   *Suitable double cropping systems for different regions*

Region	Crop sequence	Yield (q/ha)	
		First crop	Second crop
Samba	Pearlmillet—wheat	21.5	24.0
	Fallow—wheat	–	33.3
Dehradun	Maize—wheat	38.5	31.8
	Rice—wheat	43.1	29.9
	Fallow—wheat	–	16.2
	Maize—chickpea	30.3	25.4
Varanasi	Rice—chickpea	30.2	25.4
	Fallow—chickpea	–	35.7
Hoshiarpur	Maize—wheat	27.3	27.2
	Fallow—wheat	–	23.2
	Maize—chickpea	27.3	15.3
	Fallow—chickpea	–	17.0
Bangalore	Cowpea—finger millet	8.6	27.6
	Finger millet (alone)	26.9	–
Akola	Sorghum—safflower	45.4	14.1
Anand	Cowpea—tobacco	8.2	9.7
Bijapur	Greengram—safflower	7.5	10.6
Indore	Maize—safflower	29.5	10.8
	Sorghum—chickpea	32.1	13.9
	Maize—chickpea	35.5	14.3

The use of fertilizer coupled with efficient management was found to insulate dry-land crops against moisture stress. Short periods of stress could easily be overcome by working the inter-row soil with blade harrows for creating soil mulch.

Table 4.16 *Alternative crop planning to meet weather aberrations*

Region	Alternative crop strategy	
	Normal	Delayed
Chhotanagpur	1) Rice 2) Finger millet + pigeonpea 3) Peanut	1) Transplanted millet 2) Maize + pigeonpea 3) *Kharif* potato
Deccan *Rabi*	1) Sorghum	1) Sorghum (fodder) 2) Safflower 3) Chickpea
Alluvial	1) Rice 2) Maize 3) Pearlmillet ⎫ To be 4) Blackgram ⎬ followed 5) Greengram ⎭ by chickpea 6) Sesamum	1) Rice (short duration) ⎫ To be 2) Pearlmillet ⎬ followed 3) Blackgram ⎭ by 4) Greengram chickpea
Kharif Black soils	1) Sorghum 2) Pearlmillet 3) Peanut 4) Cotton 5) Castor	1) Cotton 2) Castor 3) Sesamum
	Sequence cropping/intercropping	
	Normal	Delayed
Kharif & Rabi Black soils	Sorghum or maize or soyabean to be followed by safflower or chickpea	Shorgum+chickpea Shorgum+soyabean Safflower alone in early *Rabi* if monsoon is further delayed
Seirozem	1) Pearlmillet 2) Greengram 3) Clusterbean	1) Transplanted millet 2) Greengram 3) Clusterbean 4) Cowpea
Submontane	Short duration rice or maize (hybrid), to be followed by wheat or chickpea	Transplanted rice or "Sathi" maize followed by chickpea, rapeseed in September

5

Erosion Control Structures for Non-agricultural, Denuded and Wastelands

Land capability classes, V, VI, VII and VIII have one or more limitations of slope, erosion, stoniness, rockiness, shallow soils, wetness, flooding, climate, etc., which make them generally unsuited to cultivation for agricultural crops and limit their use largely to pasture, forest, wildlife and recreation. Out of a total area of 74.85 m ha of forest land, it is estimated that about 26% area are subject to soil erosion. Further a total area of about 56.5 m ha (17% of total geographical area) classed as "wastelands" do not contribute anything to the Gross National Product (GNP) of India, on the contrary these lands are the source of maximum sediment, run-off and floods. These above denuded forest lands and wastelands (Plate 19) are in fact "wastedlands", as they have a great potential for producing fodder, fuel, fibre, minor fruits and low quantity timber. To achieve this, it is necessary to adapt following suitable soil and water conservation engineering measures supplemented with proper afforestation techniques, horticultural practices, grassland development, etc. (Plate 20).

— Contour and staggered trenches for hill slopes and wasted lands
— Gully control structures for arresting gully erosion
— Permanent drop structures for narrow and deep ravines
— Contour stone walls on steep slopes of hilly areas, especially for tea plantations, etc.; and
— Retaining walls for stabilizing precipitous hilly slopes

5.1 Contour and Staggered Trenching

CONTOUR TRENCHING
Contour trenching is excavated trenches along a uniform level across of the slope of the land in the top portion of catchment. Bunds are formed downstream along the trenches with material taken out of them. The main idea is to create more favourable moisture conditions and thus accelerate the growth of planted trees.

Functions
Contour trenches break the velocity of runoff. The rainwater percolates through the soil slowly and travels down, and benefits the better types of land in the middle and lower sections of the catchment. Where the lower fields are bunded, these trenches also protect the bunds from the runoff from the upper portion of the catchment.

Design—Plants are put out on the trench side of the bunds along the berms. (Fig. 5.1)

Trenches are not more than 15 m long and are generally staggered. In the cross-section they rarely exceed 0.3 m × 0.3 m, the object being merely to fix sufficient moisture in the soil to enable the berms to be revegetated. Trenches must run perfectly level, to use their capacity to the best advantage. As such, a system

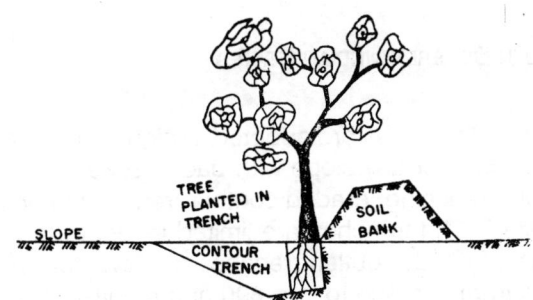

Fig. 5.1 Typical section of a trench

cannot completely check runoff, it is necessary also to take steps to control gullies by one or the other method.

Contour trenches are excavated at suitable intervals (depending upon the slope of the land) and their cross-sections are designed to collect and convey the runoff expected from the inter-space between the successive trenches and this determines the size of the trench. Side slopes of the trenches are 1:1 or 0.5:1, according to the nature of soil. These trenches are meant to intercept the runoff and convey it to a vertical disposal drain excavated at suitable intervals along natural folds of hillocks or valley without causing erosion. The same formula explained earlier, as for the height or contour bunds will apply to the bunds to be put up at the trenches constructed along dead contour.

Graded Trenches

Graded trenches are identical to contour trenches in all respects, excepting in that they are excavated with a longitudinal bed grade, designed by Manning's formula. These trenches are suited to areas receiving high annual rainfall.

Staggered Trenches

Staggered trenching (Fig. 5.2) is excavating trenching of shorter lengths in a row along the contour with interspace between them.

Suitable vertical intervals between the rows are restricted to impound the runoff expected from above, without overflow. In the alternate row, the trenches will be located directly below one another. The

STAGGERED TRENCHES

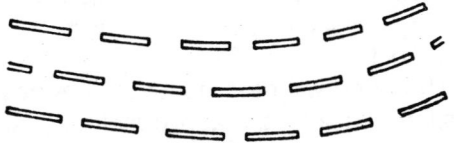

CONTOUR TRENCHES

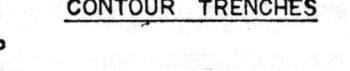

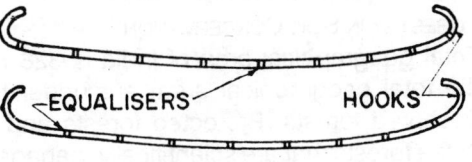

EQUALISERS   HOOKS

Fig. 5.2 Trenching

trenches in successive rows will be staggered, with the trenches in the upper row and the interspace in the lower row being directly below each other. The length of the trench and the interspace between the trenches in the same row may be suitably arrived at, so that there will be no long unprotected or uninterrupted slope to cause unexpected runoff and erosion. As the trenches are not continuous, no vertical disposal drain is excavated. The cross-sectional area of these trenches will be designed to collect the runoff expected from intense storms at recurrence intervals of 5–10 years.

PRACTICES ADAPTED IN DIFFERENT INDIAN STATES

Tamil Nadu

Contour and staggered trenches are adopted in high rainfall hilly areas of lands with slopes steeper than 33%, or any slope with badly eroded soil.

Instead of contour trenching, graded contour trenches (modified American types) have been suggested. The trenches are limited in length to about 450 m, starting from the end farthest from the outlet, trenches run level for 90 to 120 m, than on a gradient increasing from 1 in 500 to 1 in 300 at the outlet. The bunds or equalisers in the trenches are left closer at about 3 to 4.5 m apart. The trenches are located as below according to slopes:

	Slope (%)	V.I (m)
Gentle slopes	5–10	13.5–19.5
Medium slopes	10–25	6–13.5
Steep slopes	Greater than 25	1.25 m

Height of the bund to be put on the downstream
$= 0.3 (1 + 1.81\sqrt{D})$, where D is the vertical drop of the contour trench.

Example 41—If the slope is 10% and the vertical drop is 1.8 m then the trench spacing will be 18 m apart and the height of the bund at trench must be for 152 mm/hr intensity of rainfall.

$$\text{Height of bund} = 0.3 (1 + 1.81\sqrt{D}) \qquad \qquad \dots(5.1)$$
$$= 0.3 (1 + 1.81\sqrt{1.8})$$
$$= 0.3 + (1 + 2.42)$$
$$= 1.02 \text{ m} \quad \text{Ans.}$$

The length of staggered contour trench will be 3 m to 3.65 m while the interspace between the trenches in the same row will be only 2.4 m to 3 m. The trenches will be trapezoidal in cross-section with 0.3 m to 0.45 m bottom width, side slopes of 0.5:1 to 1:1.

The bund will have about 0.15 m freeboard out of 1.02 m. In addition to stabilization of soil by the above methods, steps are to be taken to plant the area with fast growing tree and grass species. Fire protection measures may be achieved by a system of five lines. Area may be closed for grazing.

5.2   Forestry, Agrostology and Horticulture in Soil Conservation

FORESTRY IN SOIL CONSERVATION

Total geographical area of India is 328 m ha, out of which, 74.85 m ha (22.8% of the total geographical area) are under forests. Forest lands are classified under Reserved forests, Protected forests and Unclassed forests. Reserved forests are those forests that are scientifically managed and being well-stocked, provide effective cover to the soil. Due to topographic and climatic factors, some erosion does take place at certain locations, even within these forests. An area of 3.9 m ha (being 10% of the total area of 39.0 m ha) has been estimated to be affected by erosion. Protected forests are those forests that are notified as such under the Indian Forest Act or any Forest Act promulgated by the states whose, unless otherwise prohibited, rights of users are admitted in respect of forest produce, grazing, break-up of land for cultivation, etc. These forests are over-exploited and hence subject to erosion. An area of about 9.28 m ha being 40% of total area of 23.21 m ha, has been estimated to be affected by erosion. Unclassed forests comprise village forests, panchayat forests, civil and soyam forests. Owing to unscientific management and unregulatec. and over-exploitation, these forests are subject to severe erosion. An estimated area of 6.31 m ha, being 50% of the total unclassed forest area of 12.63 m ha is affected by erosion. Thus, out of a total area of 74.85 m ha of forest land, 19.49 m ha are subject to soil erosion.

Vegetation (perennial or annual trees, or shrubs or climbers or grasses) on the site is one of the four main factors that govern the runoff water which affects erosion. It follows that vegetative control would be one of the essential anti-erosion measures, since it can be manipulated and improved upon as required unlike rainfall. Hence one of the main function of forestry would be to counteract the biological factors and calls for organised maintenance of all perennial vegetation on the site.

Effects of Forests
Forests, in general, bring about a long chain of advantages, moderating the local climate, increasing precipitation, preventing floods, regulating stream flow and sustaining off-season discharge and protecting the soil and enriching it.

CORRECT FORESTRY PRACTICES

Method or System of Forest Working
The maintenance of forest vegetations on sites to be set apart for the purpose, is essentially a measure of land and soil conservation. By proper measures based on scientific principles of silviculture and forest management, forests could be availed of in perpetuity, without soil deterioration. Various methods of forest management have been developed taking into account the type of forests, the requirements of the species, particularly with reference to conditions (of soil, water and light) favourable to their growth and the local or industrial needs for produce from the forests. Adoption of one or the other of these methods is obligatory, if the soil is to be conserved and at the same time use the forest to advantage in perpetuity.

From the point of view of soil conservation, among several methods or systems of forest working, the ideal method would be the selection system of fellings. Individual trees as they reach maturity or utilizable dimensions, are selected and removed annually. No area of the forest is cut as such and species without utilization value are not felled at all, except in the interests of securing regeneration of the value species. This method approximates very close to nature's own ways and is practised in all protected forests in the high hills on steep slopes and on erodible soils. Besides correct method of removing the old crop and replacing it, the method of felling conversion at site of timber and extraction from the forests have all to be so carried out, that no exposure of permanent damage to soil ensues. Improper layout of paths or roads, use of heavy machinery, and dragging or rolling of logs directly downhill may all lead to formation of channels for swift flow of water. This will ultimately result in gully development and soil erosion. Unless safeguards are employed, in the end the evil effects of forest denudation will be inescapable.

Control of Shifting Cultivation
Firstly the indiscriminate cleaning of sloping land should be prohibited and no land generally steeper than 1 in 5 (20%) may be cleared for the purpose. In milder slopes, clearing and temporary cultivation may take place, but only in conjunction with the

raising of forest tree crops. The farmer should raise suitable agricultural crops. At the same time, fast growing tree species should be raised at optimum spacing all over the area, suited to the locality. The work should be so regulated that every year, a regenerated area is absorbed back into the forest and an equivalent area made available from clearing and further cultivation.

Thus, the harmful process of shifting cultivation can be effectively and advantageously harnessed to raise very valuable plantations. In any case, shifting cultivation should not return to the same site again, till a forest complex has taken possession of the land and organically improved and restored the soil to its original condition and fertility.

In open or eroded areas (anti-erosion and soil conservation measures trenching and planting)—In sloping lands, steeper than 1 in 10 or with shallow depth of soil, particularly in arid or dry regions, excessive grazing or other misuse, would result in a very open degraded type of vegetation, or even in bare slopes liable to serious losses by erosion.

Such areas are treated by digging trenches strictly along the contours spaced suitably. Tree seedlings suitable to the locality and fast-growing are introduced or seeds of tree species sown on the berms formed of the excavated material, on the down slope edge of the trench.

ARTIFICIAL REGENERATION

As a rule, the artificial regeneration is supplement to the natural regeneration and therefore, all management practices should aim to assist nature's never ending effort to reclothe the soil.

Sowing—Where due to high pressure on the land or successive disturbance to the site, natural means are not sufficient, the site can be vegetated with either sowing or planting. The sowing in strips, trenches or patches do not need elaborate nursery techniques. However, the germinated seedlings in the large area are prone to competition from aggressive weeds, pest, diseases, wild animals and rodents, etc. It therefore, require intensive management.

To keep the seed safe from the rodents and birds, it should be mixed with red lead in 1:10 ratio. The sowing be done at first shower in already prepared trenches, patches and strips. Especially, in areas subject to erosion, it is profitable to plant the seed either in prepared patches or on the berm of trenches. Dibbling is done normally for bolder seeds.

Seed treatment—The seed may not germinate due to seed dormancy, which is, either related to seed coat, embryo or growth inhibiting material.

Mechanical method—Filling, rubbing, puncturing or boiling.

Chemical method—Treatment of the seed with dilute acids and washing it with water.

Stratification—This means to weaken the seed coat by putting it on low and high temperature and moisture conditions. In teak, the seeds are soaked in water for 12 hours and dried in sun for 24–48 hrs. This is continued for 2–3 weeks. Alternatively, the seeds are spread in the nursery with alternate lay of cowdung. These are then watered and dried for 12 hr and 24 hr, respectively. In *Acacia nilotica*, the seeds received from the excreta of the animals come-off well-treated.

Seedling establishment—This depends upon seed size; root system; and moisture and nutrient condition. A well-aerated soil with sufficient essential nutrients favours early establishment of the seedling.

SOWING METHODS

Strip sowing—Several adjoining lines are limited to form a strip of 60–150 cm wide. The strips are spaced at 3–4 m, depending upon the species to be established and its silvicultural requirement. The strips are either continuous or broken, depending upon the configuration or topography. The broken strips are practised in undulating topography, where these are staggered. The main advantage of strip sowing is that, it involves comparatively less soil working, smaller quantity of seed and lesser cost in weeding operations. Seeds are either dibbled or drilled in the prepared strips.

Patch sowing—Square or circular patches of 20 cm or 30 cm diameter are prepared, the soil is worked and the seeds are sown. This can be practised only in sites where weed intensity is low. After seedlings are established, one dominant seedling is retained and the rest removed. The weeding operations are confined around the patch. The common spacement between patches is 3 m× 3 m. This, however, involves skilled personnel in laying out and stacking.

Pit sowing—In localities with low rainfall, pits of 45 cm × 45 cm× 45 cm are dug and sowing done on the filled-up pits. It provides good worked up soil for roots penetration and moisture conservation. The cost of soil working is high, but the ultimate success compensates it. The weeding cost is identical to patch sowing. The extra healthy seedlings for such pits can be used for breaking up the failures.

Trench/ridge sowing—In arid areas, trenches of 1.5 m× 45 cm × 45 cm are dug at 3 m spacement staggered on contour. The excavated soil is piled on the down-hill slope along the trench length. The seeds are either sown on berm of the trenches or in diagonally half-filled trenches. In high rainfall areas, this process runs the risk of inducing sedimentation in the reservoirs.

Mound sowing—At sites subject to waterlogging or areas subject to water accumulation, mounds are prepared by scrapping the soil and raising it to 60 cm height. The top of the mound should, however, be above the main water level. Sowing or planting is carried out on such mounds. The waterlogged areas are often prone to salinity. For successful planting, Seth (1960) advocates that the central core of the mound should be filled with good soil mixed with well-rotten farmyard manure, or mixed to 2 kg of gypsum.

Time of sowing—In all regeneration processes, it is imperative to complete the soil working before the onset of rains. The best sowing time is the first shower of rain.

Depth of sowing—The seed should be covered with soil. In case of smaller seeds, light soil cover may suffice. As a thumb rule, the cover should not exceed the diameter of the seed.

SOIL WORKING TECHNIQUES

The soil working technique vary according to the amount and distribution of rainfall. Soil working technique in the dry zone in relation to rainfall for the country has been worked out (Seth, 1960) in detail. Accordingly, fifteen (0–14) annual rainfall classes (ARC) have been distinguished, depending upon summer (June-September) and winter (October-December) rainfalls. Table 5.1 gives the annual rainfall classes in relation to different summer and winter rainfall and rainy days.

Based on the annual rainfall classes (ARC), some of the common soil working methods for dry zones of our country are given below.

PIT

Ordinary pit—For all rainfall classes in clayey, alkaline and saline soils. It has highest

Table 5.1 *Annual rainfall classes (ARC)*

ARC		Summer		Winter	
		Rainfall (cm)	Rainy days	Rainfall (cm)	Rainy days
Summer high	1	50–75	40–50	up to 37.5	up to 15
Winter low	2	50–75	30–40	up to 37.5	up to 15
	3	37.5–50	30–40	up to 37.5	up to 15
	4	37.5–50	20–30	up to 37.5	up to 15
	5	25–37.5	20–30	up to 37.7	up to 15
	6	25–37.5	15–20	up to 37.5	up to 15
Summer and winter low	7	up to 25	up to 5	up to 37.5	up to 15
Summer low	8	up to 25	up to 15	25–37.5	15–20
Winter high	9	up to 25	up to 15	37.5–50	15–20
	10	up to 25	up to 15	37.5–50	20–30
	11	up to 25	up to 15	50–75	20–30
Summer and	12	25–50	15–30	37.5–75	20–30
winter high	13	25–50	15–30	25–50	15–20
	14	37.5–75	30–50	25–50	10–20

crest with deepest part of the water storage ring away from highest point of mound, Also suited for sandy soils (Fig. 5.3 A).

Saucer pit—Suited for all ARC loamy type of soils. Cresent berm is necessary for slope lands (Fig. 5.3 B).

Ring pit—Suited for dry areas (ARC 5–11). Crest need not be very high. Deep planting to place root mass 30 cm below surface. Ring will infiltrate water (Fig. 5.3 C).

Ridge Ditch (a) Vertical sides

Small ridge ditch—Suited for moist dry zone with large number of rainy days (ARC 1, 2, 13, 14) and loamy soils (Fig. 5.3 D).

Large ridge ditch—For low and ill-distributed rainfall areas (ARC 3, 4, 12, 13) with deep soils (Fig. 5.3 E).

Shallow ridge ditch—For slopes from where real soil is washed away leaving loose gravel or *murrum*. Add better soil if possible (Fig. 5.3 F).

Slope ridge ditch—Preferred in localities with large number of rainy days (ARC 1 to 4, 12 to 14). Shallow surface soil and sub-soil gritty but fine clay with bed crusting properties. It will store enough moisture in plugs of washed up soil and will not cause waterlogging near the ridge (Fig. 5.3 G).

Ring Ditch (b) Slanting sides

For clayey profiles where water will remain standing for a relatively longer period. This device will keep the main water mass away from the sowing or planting line; hence, damage due to waterlogging is reduced. There will be a greater seepage of moisture in a vertical direction and roots will lie in comparatively dry zone.

Half slanting ridge ditch—For ill-distributed rainfall but soils friable; suited for ARC 5–11 (Fig. 5.3 H).

Small slanting ridge ditch—For high and well-distributed rainfall (ARC 1, 2, 13 and 14). Prevent waterlogging (Fig. 5.3 I).

Shallow slanting ridge ditch—For clayey soil with good rainfall ARC 1, 2, 13 and 14 (Fig. 5.3 J).

Deep slanting ridge ditch—For low ill-distributed rainfall ARC 5–11 (Fig. 5.3 K).

Double slanting ridge ditch—For good well-distributed rainfall ARC 1, 2, 13 and 14 (Fig. 5.3 L).

Shelfed trench—For peninsular region where clay and *murrum* form impermeable crust, which on wetting and drying binds granular *murrum* in hard clod. In shelved device, planting is done at ground level or little above it.

Shallow shelfed trench—Water contains mainly in deeper part of trench ARC 8–14 (Fig. 5.3 M).

Deep filled shelfed trench—Suitable for area with high rainfall, which is received in small number of rainy days as torrential showers ARC 4 to 8 and 8 to 10. Suited for saline and alkaline soil and gravelly soils of peninsular region (Fig. 5.3 N).

Double trench—For badly stony and detrital slope with small amount of soil in the interspaces of small and large pieces of stones. Impound water in the filled portion. Sowing or planting done at the top of the ridge.

(i) Double trench (ii) Trench pit—For all annual rainfall classes, especially for ARC 5–11 (Fig. 5.3 O & P).

Trench Ridge—Suited for salt impregnated soils. Provide sufficient leaching of salt and impounded water not in contact with worked-up soil.

Shallow trench ridge—Alkaline/saline and defloculated clay soils in area with more rainy days (ARC 1 to 4; 12 to 14). Deepest part is well away from the ridge to avoid waterlogging and facilitate desalinisation (Fig. 5.3 Q).

Deep trench ridge—In high salt area and scanty rainfall (ARC 5–11), received in few violent storms (Fig. 5.3 R).

Trench mound—It is just like double trench and the trench pit. Useful in low erratic rainfall pattern. It is more suited for flat and slopy land.

Inclined trench mound—In gentle slope, the trench are kept little off-contour to allow water to accumulate near the mound. Suited to ARC 5–12 (Fig. 5.3 S).

Straight trench mound—If slope is constant and gentle, straight trench mound may be made, ARC 5–12 (Fig. 5.3 T).

Wurli—A kind of trench ridge for gentle slope with loamy or granular soils in area with high and well-distributed rainfall, ARC 1–4 and 12–14 (Fig. 5.3 U).

Sowing versus planting—Direct sowing is easy, quick and cheap, but the seed requirement per unit area is more. The ultimate establishment during young age of the seedlings depend upon climate, biotic factors and weed competition. Planting on the other hand, is more sure way, especially on difficult sites. Nursery raised seedlings enjoy congenial planting. The nursery plants are always healthy with well-developed root system, but are expensive. The following should therefore, be considered before deciding either of the method.

Spices—Certain species can be raised from sowing, e.g. *Acacia nilotica, Shorea robusta, Pinus,* spp., etc., but species like *Eucalyptus,* spp. can only be raised by planting.

Site condition—On different sites like steep slopes, landslides, sowing may be necessary in micro-topography, but for immediate clothing in remaining area, and on the degraded lands and sand dunes, planting will give more success.

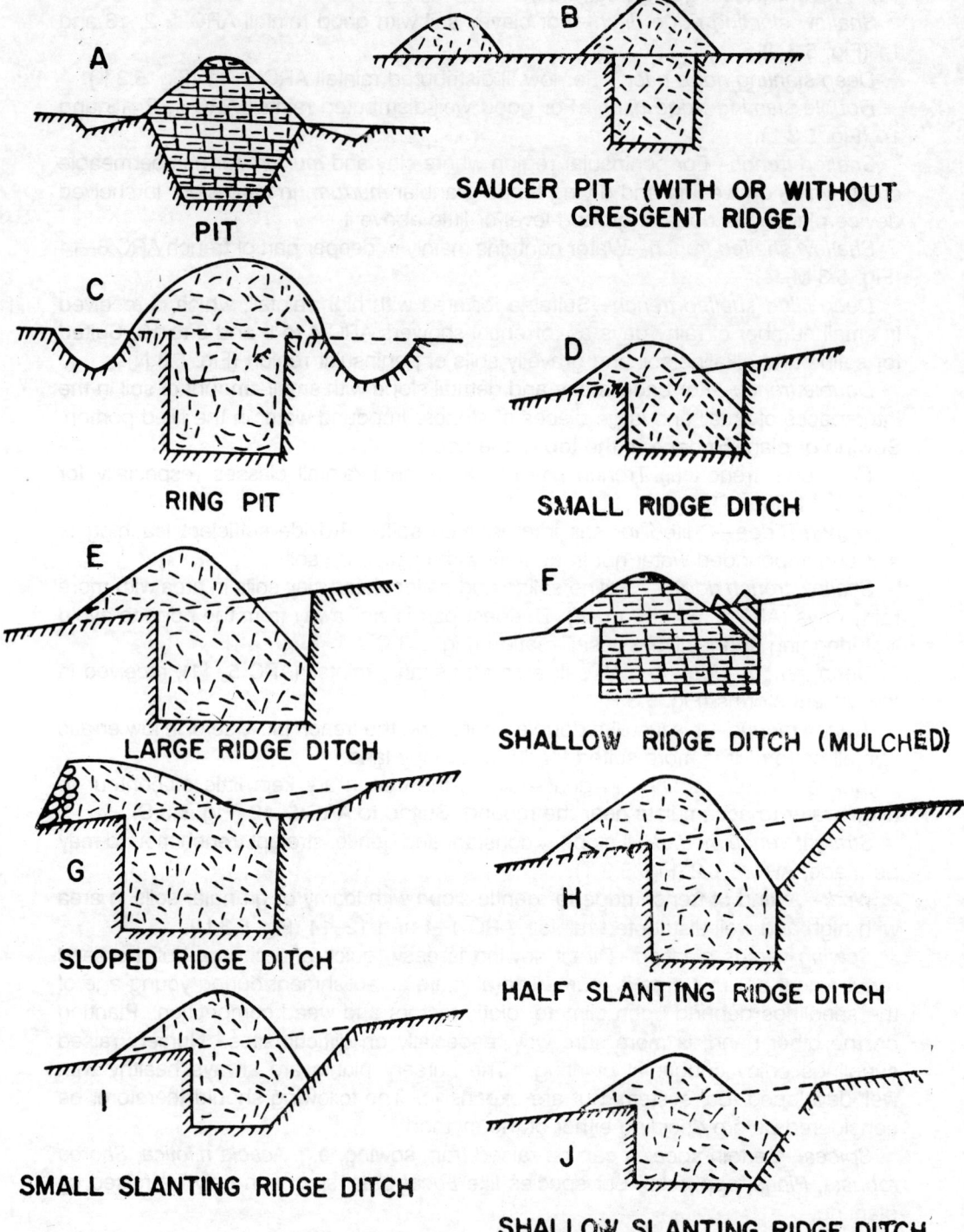

A PIT

B SAUCER PIT (WITH OR WITHOUT CRESGENT RIDGE)

C RING PIT

D SMALL RIDGE DITCH

E LARGE RIDGE DITCH

F SHALLOW RIDGE DITCH (MULCHED)

G SLOPED RIDGE DITCH

H HALF SLANTING RIDGE DITCH

I SMALL SLANTING RIDGE DITCH

J SHALLOW SLANTING RIDGE DITCH

Fig. 5.3 Soil working techniques

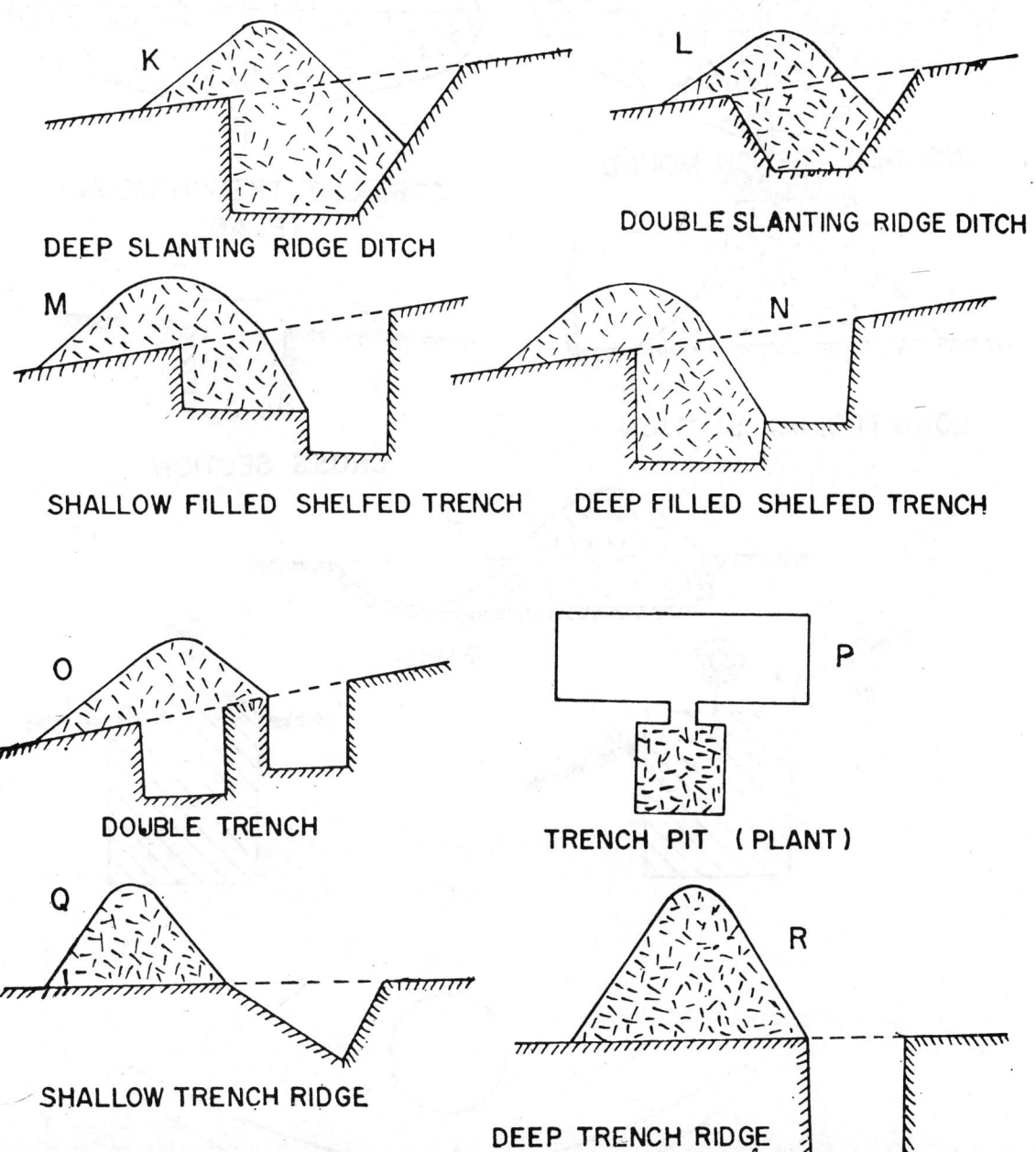

Fig. 5.3 Soil working techniques

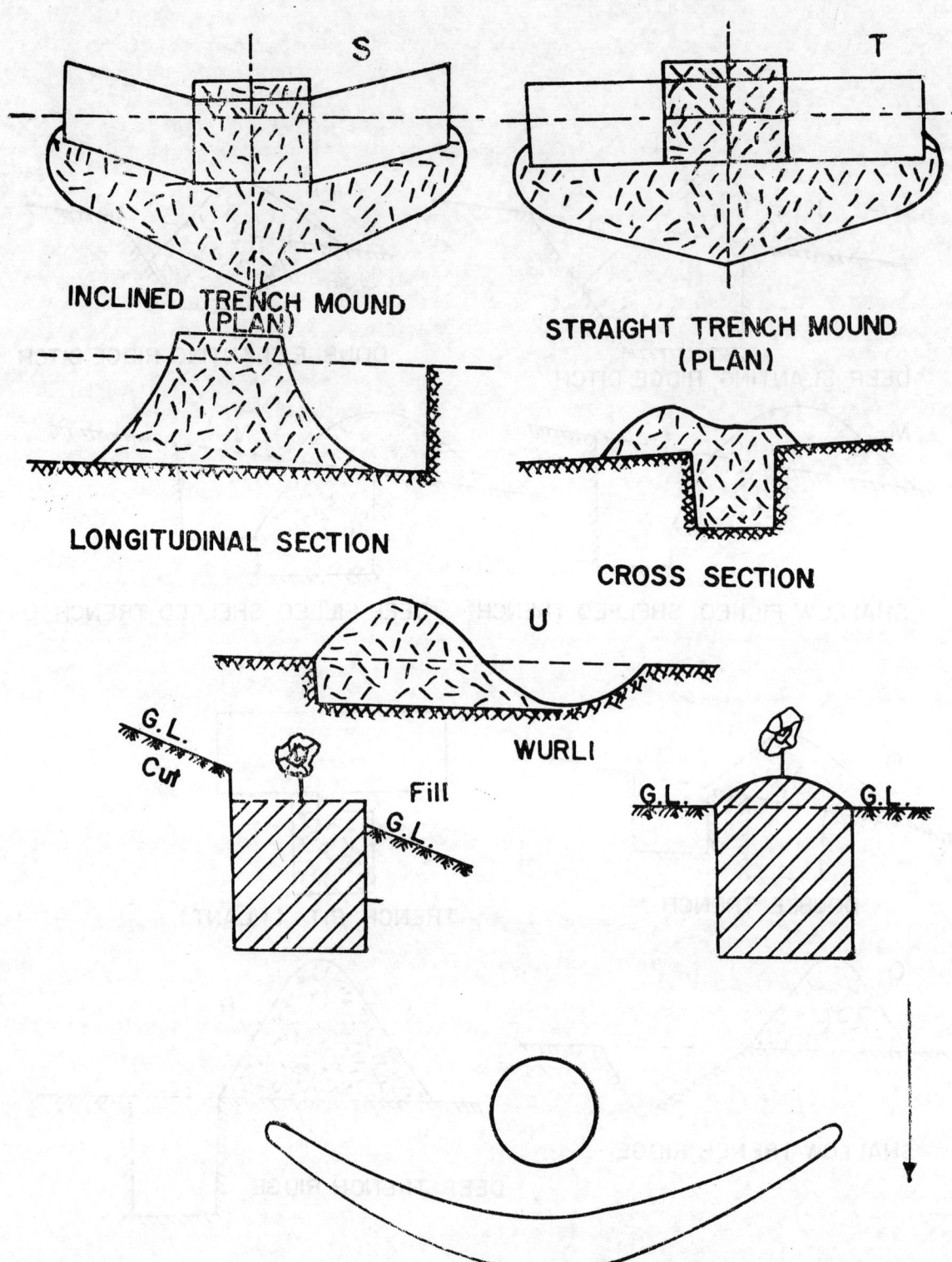

INCLINED TRENCH MOUND
(PLAN)

STRAIGHT TRENCH MOUND
(PLAN)

LONGITUDINAL SECTION

CROSS SECTION

WURLI

G.L.
Cut

Fill

G.L.

G.L.

G.L.

Fig. 5.3 Soil working techniques

Seed availability—The species whose seeds are in short supply, or whose viability is usually low or require pressed treatment, planting may be better than sowing.

Finances availability—Final cost up to establishment will determine the method of regeneration. Sowing is definitely cheaper than planting if funds are constraints and can cover more areas. The first three factors play a major role in its decision. However, in the long run, planting may prove more beneficial than sowing, especially in Watershed Management Programme.

PLANTING

Certain species may give perfect results only by planting with ball of earth, e.g. *Eucalyptus* spp. Certain seeds may take more than one year to germinate, during which period they remain exposed to various adverse agencies if directly sown at site. On difficult sites, viz. poor exposed soils, hot dry localities, landslips, waterlogged and wind or water eroded areas, planting in the long run may prove better than sowing. Similarly, the species whose seeds are not available in adequate quantity, transplanting should be preferred to get good healthy planting stock. Seedlings for planting are, therefore, raised in nurseries.

Nursery Techniques

Nursery sites—The nurseries should be located at a central place. The site for the permanent nursery should be such, where there is a constant supervision for timely operations and adequate water and labour supply is available. Locating nursery at the headquarters of a responsible officer and connected with means of communications will be an ideal site.

Light sandy loam or loamy sand soil should be preferred to clayey soils. There should be no waterlogging, but if it is unescapable, adequate drainage should be provided. On heavier soils, gentler slope would prove beneficial. In soils with more than 5% slope, the beds should be terraced. In higher elevation of Western Himalaya, northernly aspect and south-westerly or westerly slopes would prove better. Aspect matters little in plains. Narrow valleys and frost holes should be avoided. A permanent live hedge around the blocks saves the seedlings from hot and cold winds.

Development of nursery—A plan for selected nursery site should show the permanent features like topography, water supply, soil, climate, etc. The nursery should be divided into convenient blocks separated by one metre wide paths, which are sub-divided into sub-plots separated by 45 to 60 cm wide footpaths. Each sub-plot is further divided into nursery beds. The size of the nursery beds should not exceed 12 m in length and 120 cm in width, separated by 30 cm wide footpath. The width restriction has its importance for, it helps in the easy nursery operation, viz. weeding, watering, hoeing, etc. A normal nursery bed is 2–3 m long and 1.2 to 1.5 m wide. In arid zones, sunken beds are preferred to reduce the evaporation and save the seedlings from hot winds.

In case of very small size seeds, broadcast or line sowing is adopted, and seeds covered with fine earth or sand. Medium seeds are drilled in lines 15 cm apart and 8 to 10 cm from seed to seed. Root and shoot cuttings, or stem cuttings should be planted at a distance of 20–30 cm in lines 30 cm apart. Drill and line sowing help in avoiding root injury, while uprooting seedlings and also facilitate weeding. If entire transplants are to be used, sowings should be done 8 to 10 cm in lines 15 cm apart. In dry localities with sandy soils, seed may be covered four times the diameter of the seed and soil consolidated with light roller. Watering should invariably be done with fine rose watering cane. If soils are dry at the time of sowing, it should be brought to the optimum moisture condition. Raised beds are adapted in high rainfall areas and sunken in arid and semi-arid regions.

In case of potted plants, the sunken nursery beds should be preferred. As the seedling grow, the plants should be spread out to provide adequate sun and air to the developing plants.

Permanent water storage arrangement is necessary for perennial flow of water and invariably a water storage tank should be provided. An implement-cum-store hut should be planted at some convenient commanding place. A small green house should also find a place in the permanent nursery.

The nursery should be fenced with angle Iron barbed wire-cum-chicken wire fence. This may be supplemented with a live hedge all along the fencing.

Protection of the beds—In frosty localities, the seedlings should be protected from frost at night and from the early morning sun, but too much of shading should be avoided. For birds and rodents damage, the nursery should be covered with thorns or with chicken wire frames during early stage of seedling establishment.

In tender species as *Eucalyptus*, and frosty localities, some shade may be necessary during very hot period of the day. The most common shading material is thatch, chicks, *Sirkis*, bamboo matting and batten shades, which can be easily rolled. The shading material should however, be locally available. The seedlings should be hardened as it approaches planting time, by gradually removing the shade and subjecting the seedlings to hardy condition for making it fit for their ultimate success in the field. For guard against sun, it is advisable to keep the shades at least 90 cm higher on the north side.

Soil working—The soil in a nursery should be dug to a depth of about 30–45 cm, which may be increased in case of poor soils. All stones should be removed, big lumps broken and earth sieved. In case of raised beds, it may be raised 20–25 cm, slight camber given for good drainage and top-dressed with washed sand. The beds should be manured with well-rotten farmyard manure, compost and leaf manure, etc. In case of sheep manures, the nodules should be well-broken. Chemical fertilizer, insecticide and fungicide should be used for fast growth and hygiene of seedlings.

Sowing of seed—The quantity of seed required may be calculated from the following formula (approximately):

$$W^* = \frac{A \times D}{P \times N} \times 100 \left.\right\} \quad \text{* Twice } W \text{ for drill and four times } W \text{ for broadcast sowings.}$$

where, W = weight of the seed required in gm
    A = area of the bed in m²;
    P = plant per cent (the % of plants ultimately obtained);
    D = number of plants required per m²; and
    N = number of seed per gm.

Germination tests should be conducted to test the viability of the seed. It helps in getting a fairly accurate idea of seed requirement for required planting stock.

Watering—In general, nurseries should be watered with a fine rose watering cane or by percolation or lawn sprinkler. Sunken bedded nurseries are normally irrigated by furrow irrigation or by flooding. The main advantage of furrow irrigation is that, it does not form crust at the top of the bed, but it does cut the edge. As a rule the nurseries should be irrigated during early part of the morning hours. Excess irrigation should be avoided.

Transplanting—The seedings are ready for transplanting in about a year's time, but some species like deodar takes 1.5–2.5 years to get fit for transplanting. The seedlings are pricked in the nursery bed for better root development. As a rule, the seedlings should not be smaller than 60 cm in height for transplanting in the field.

In case of species with tender root system, or for planting up in difficult sites, the seedlings should be raised in containers and pots. Various types of containers in use are—polythene bags, galvanised iron sheet tubes, baked earthen tubes and pots, bamboo baskets and tubes and leaf *dona*. The most common containers now in use are polythene tubes/bags made up of black or white perforated polythene sheets. It has been observed that the plants raised in flower pots develop coiled root system and their success in the field is affected, if proper care is not taken to straighten the coil before planting in the field.

Grading—The seedlings should be graded in the nursery and weaklings weeded out before they are taken out for field planting. The best plants can be judged on the basis of height, collar diameter and vigour in growth. Best healthy plants will give more survival than weak unhealthy seedlings.

Temporary nursery—These nurseries are created when a large area is to be taken up for planting, for which transportation of seedlings from the permanent nurseries is either not feasible or expensive. The transportation of seedlings over a long distance, especially when the areas are not covered by the normal means of communication, deteriorates the quality of the nursery stock. Temporary nurseries are, therefore, created in the centre of the proposed plantation area, provided adequate water, labour and supervision facilities are available. Such nurseries are closed after the area is fully stocked.

Field Plantation

Time of plantating—Normally most of the planting is done during the monsoon after a good soaking rain, but pre-monsoon and winter plantings can be taken up provided irrigation facilities are available. As a rule, all plantings should be carried out within a period of 3 to 4 days time, after a good soaking rain. In case of pre-monsoon planting, additional advantage of the full rainy season is available. In area which get winter rain or snow, winter plantings meet with success. In case of deodar, acer, prunus, etc., winter plantings are normally carried out. Casuality, if any, should be beaten up during current and succeeding year.

Spacement in plantation—For all species, there is an optimum initial spacing which may vary considerably, depending upon the following factors:

— Wider spacings are indicated for fast-growing species

— Species with branching habit are closely spaced to induce natural pruning

— Close spacing is indicated for producing close grained timber for greater mechanical strength

— Closer spacings are indicated in the denuded areas for side protection

— Closer spacings are advocated in the areas prone to heavy weed infestation

— Taller and light demanders are spaced wider

— In arid areas, where there is a competition for moisture between the plant and weed, weeding becomes necessary for the first three years. The spacing should be adjusted for easy operation of farm equipment to remove weeds, provide rough surface and absorb more moisture during rains; and

— Wider spacing may be practised when the aim is to get fuel, fodder and grass.

General Guidelines for Planting

— The seedlings should have long and well-developed root system
— Collar of the seedlings at planting should be at the ground level
— The root system should be given its natural position and coiling if any, should be straightened before planting
— The depth of the pit should be slightly more than the seedling root
— Mound or ridge planting should be done in wet or waterlogged soils and furrows or trench planting in the arid areas
— The soii must be thoroughly firmed after planting around the plant, so that root hairs come in intimate contact with the mineral soil and
— Seedlings should be partially pruned in locality with more sunshine and drier climate to reduce evapotranspiration

Plan of work for artificial regeneration—Before an area is taken up for regeneration, a plan should be drawn well in advance for sowing or planting, which should include amongst other things the following information:

— Description of the tract; location and other allied features
— Climate of the area, viz. mean annual, maximum and minimum temperature, mean annual rainfall and its distribution, wind velocity and its direction, etc.
— Soil characteristics
— Stock map of the area in a suitable scale
— Purpose of sowing and planting
— Suitable species for the locality and its silvicultural requirement
— Seed of seedlings requirement and its source
— Location of temporary or permanent nursery
— Source of labour and water supply for the nursery and plantation and
— Estimate of financial implications

A stock map should be prepared showing vegetation, blanks, and undergrowth. It should be accompanied with a brief description of the locality factors. Soil characteristics will be indicated by the vegetation growing in the locality, supplemented with actual soil test at places. The growing flora will also indicate the edaphic and climatic conditions of the locality, e.g. *Balsam* and *Strobilanthus*, indicate difficult conditions for *Deodar*, and *Taxus*, *Iris* and *Arundinaria*, for fir regeneration. The purpose of regeneration, i.e. protective or productive, will guide the necessary soil working treatment, system of management and rotation to be observed. The silvicultural performance of the selected species with reference to the soil and climate of the locality will give a hand in success of the plantation.

In denuded areas, soil conservation measures for site protection should have a first place in implementation of the programme.

Choice of species—The following are guiding principles:

— In hilly catchments where the aim is to get maximum yield of usable water in the stream flow, species with low transpiration rate should be selected; and the forest should be worked on short rotation

— In arid and dry areas, non-exacting and xerophytic species should be selected

— In localities under uncontrollable retrogression, species with dense foliage and leguminous should be preferred

— Conifers like fir should be mixed with broad-leaved species to avoid accumulation of under-composed humus

— Avoid mixture of species whose leaves contain growth inhibiting substances and

— Aim at mixture in plantations to provide natural resistance to insect and fungus attack.

List of the tree species suitable for different agro-climatic regions are given in Appendix-E-1.

Choice of Exotics

Sometimes exotics prove better than indigenous, if selected from the homo-climates of the locality, e.g. *Acacia tortilis*, (Forsk) introduced from Israel has suited to the arid climate of India. The following points should be born in mind before introduction of exotics on a large scale.

— It must be tested for better in growth and utility than indigenous

— It must be tested to suit the soil and climatic conditions of the locality

— It must be more valuable than indigenous and

— It should be easy to grow, reproduce and yield good viable seeds for further propagation.

Afforestation of Catchment Areas

As different from the denuded hillocks and bare slopes of local or small catchments, the higher slopes and hills at the heads of large catchment areas are to be afforested. There will be need for regular forestry undertakings and forest management in such areas. Existing poor forests should be improved. Shifting, cultivation, if locally in vogue, could be harnessed and systematic forest operations adopted to the lasting benefit of the valley and the project.

Farm Forestry

Raising tree crops and practising forestry methods on farm lands as an adjunct to other farm operations, has been termed Farm Forestry. The aim is to make the farm or group of farms self-supporting in fodder, green manure, fuel, grazing and small timber. Apart from parts of the farm not wholly fit for cultivation being set apart for raising forest crops, trees and shrubs could be raised as live-hedges for wind breaks on field bunds and along margins of roads, paths. These would also serve indirectly to protect the farm lands from intruding cattle, from dessicating hot or cold winds, and from the soil being blown away during the fallow season.

Live hedges raised around farm lands or farm holdings or tree crops could be more effective and cheaper to maintain than other farms of fencing. Thorny and goat hardy species serve for the purpose. They should be fast-growing, spreading in habit and forming inpenetrable thickets, at least in mass.

Wind breaks are commonly three or more rows of small trees and shrubs planted suitably on a farm to break the force of wind and thus protect the soil as well as the crop. Planting should be at right angles to the general wind direction.

Farm Woodlots

These are areas in the farm set apart for wood production for fuel and other farm needs.

AGROFORESTRY

When trees are grown on agricultural lands alongwith agricultural crops, the term farm forestry has been used. The term agroforestry has recently been defined as a sustainable land management system, which increases the overall yield of the land, combines the production of crops (including tree crops) and forest plants and/or animals simultaneously or sequentially, on the same unit of land and applies management practices that are compatible with the cultural practices of the local population (King and Chandler, 1978). This definition obviously includes farm forestry, silvo-pastoral, horti-pastoral and fodder-fuel plantation systems. With emphasis only on fodder and forage production, in which grasses and fodder shrubs/trees are combined, the studies have been referred to as silvo-pastoral studies.

Agroforestry, as applicable to lands not suited for agriculture, is a sustainable management of lands (that are not suited to agriculture) for increasing production of tree crops, including horticultural trees, grasses, agricultural crops (for very short durations whenever practical) and/or animals simultaneously or sequentially on the same unit of land, and one that applies management practices compatible with the cultural practices of the local population.

The unit of management of land under these conditions can be a watershed, or part of a watershed, provided the emphasis is on trees/grasses that will protect the land as well as produce fodder, fuel, fruit, etc.

In prospect, it will be necessary to focus greater attention on agroforestry for the utilization of wasted lands in developing countries, where pressure of human and cattle populations is very high on the land-water-plant systems. It will be necessary to identify multi-purpose trees with two or more uses as fuel, fodder, food, fruit, fibre, industrial raw material or timber. Since there is a shortage of fuel and fodder in India, the emphasis may continue to be laid on fuel and fodder production. As more than one crop (i.e. trees, grasses, agricultural crops) will be grown together, it will be necessary to study their compatibility, their effect on soil-building/deteriorating processes, the techniques of propagation, fertilization, harvesting and use and the economic evaluation of the promising systems of agroforestry so identified.

Growing of field crops like pearlmillet, legumes and oilseed crops in a field staggeredly predominated by khairi, (Prosopis cineraria), and bordi, (Zizyphus spp.) is an example of traditional agroforestry followed by farmers of Rajasthan, Punjab, Haryana and Gujarat, since ages past. By reasonable combination of tree plantations with agricultural crops and, where possible with cattle farming, impairment of the ecosystem can be avoided, yields increased and crops diversified.

SILVO-PASTORAL SYSTEM

The fuel and fodder plantations or the silvo-pastoral system of grassland development is probably the best system for overcoming the shortage of fuel and fodder in the country today. This system is applicable to vast areas of culturable wasteland and marginal forest land spread over nearly 47 m ha in the country, comprising of undulating degraded terraces. The leaf fodder obtained from the trees is exceptionally rich in some of the essential elements, like nitrogen, crude protein, phosphorus, calcium, etc., and reduce cost on concentrates fed to animals during lean periods of fodder availability. A number of fodder trees such as *Leucaena latisiliqua, Bauhinia variegata, Albizzia lebbek, A, Amara Grewia oppositifolia, Celtis caucasica, Moringa oleifera, Milletia aureculata, Sesbania sesban, S. grandiflora, Hardwickia binata* are fed to the animals depending on the region. Some of the species recommended for various soil regions are given in Table 5.2.

SILVI-PASTORAL SUITABLE MULTI-TIER PLANT COMBINATIONS FOR DIFFERENT AGROCLIMATIC REGIONS (AFTER PATIL AND PATHAK, 1977)

Temperate and Humid Western Himalayan Region

Trees
Populus ciliata, Quercus dilatata, Q. incana, Q. semicarpi folia, Salix alba, Robinia pseudoacacia, Morus nigra, Celtis australis, Grewia oppositifolia, Robus sp., Albizzia amara, A. procera, A. lebbek, Acacia catechu, Ficus carica.

Shrubs
Grewia oppositifolia, Leucaena latisiliqua, Dichrostachys nutens, Bauhinia sp., Sesbania sesban.

Grasses and Legumes
Themeda anathera, Chrysopogon fulvus, Arundinella nepalensis, Heteropogon contortus, Cenhrus ciliaris, Setaria anaps, Phaseolus atropurpureus, Stylosanthes hamata, Phleum pratens, Muhlenbergia duthieana, Poa pratensis, Dactylis glomerata, Medicago sp., Trifolium subterraneum.

Humid Bengal-Assam Region

Trees
Azadirachta indica, Dalbergia sissoo, Emblica officinalis, Peltophorum pterocarpum, Pithecellobium dulce, Pongamia pinnata, Albizzia lebbek, A. stipulata, Artocarpus heterophyllus, Bauhinia sp., Leucaena latisiliqua, Moringa oleifera, Morus alba, Syzygium cumini, Tamarindus indica, Eucalyptus sp.

Shrubs
Leucaena latisiliqua, Sesbania grandiflora, S. sesban, S. microcarpa, Bauhinia sp., Desmanthes virgatus, Desmodium uncinatum, Morus alba, Moringa oleifera.

Grasses and Legumes
Setaria anceps, Pennisetum pedicellatum, Panicum antidotale, Chrysopogon aciculatus, Marenga porphyrocoma, Panicum notatum, Arundinella bengalensis, Atylosia scaraboides, Desmodium uncinatum, Puereria thunbergiana, Clitoria terneata, Vicia sp., Glycine javanica, Stylosanthes hamata.

Humid Eastern Himalayan Region and Islands

Trees
Eucalyptus globulus, Pongamia pinnata, Querous semicarpifolia Salix tetrasperma, Albizzia chinensis, Artocarpus heterophyllus; Bauhina sp., Moringa oleifera, Morus serrata, Syzygium aqueum, Mesua ferrea, Populus ciliata.

Shrubs
Desmodium cephalotus, Leucaena latisiliqua, Sesbania grandiflora, S. sesbanl, Moringa oleifera, Morus alba, Desmanthes virgatus.

Table 5.2 *Leguminous tree species and associated grasses recommended for various regions of the country*

Plant species	Soil type	Associated grass(es)
1	2	3
Acacia catechu	Poor stony soils of Siwaliks and outer Himalaya.	Eulaliopsis binata
A.cupressiformis	Loam to sandy loam soils of semi-arid regions on field boundaries and roadsides.	Eulaliopsis binata
A.cupressiformis	Loam to sandy loam, soils of semi-arid regions on field boundaries and roadsides.	Cenchrus ciliaris, C. setigerus
A.jacquemontii	Sandy soils of riverbed and sand dune	Cenchrus ciliaris, Lasiurus sindicus
A.nilotica spp indica	Black soils of peninsular India, loamy to sandy loam	Dichanthium annulatum Sehima nervosum
A.leucophloea	Gravelly soils on pedimont regions	Dichanthium annulatum Sehima nervosum
A.senegal	Hills of arid and semi-arid regions and sand dunes	Dichanthium annulatum Cenchrus ciliaris and Lasiurus sindicus
A.tortilis	Sandy soils of arid regions	Cenchrus ciliaris, C. setigerus
Albizzia spp.	Sandy to sandy loam soils (Calcareous)	Dichanthium annulatum
Bauhinia retusa	Lime rich soils of outer Himalaya	Bothriochloa spp. Dichanthium annulatum, Pennisetum orientale, Chrysopogon fulvus.
B.variegata	Loamy to loamy sand	Cenchrus ciliaris, C.setigerus
Butea frondosa	Loamy to gravelly soils of hill regions	Dichanthium annulatum
Cassia siamea	Loamy to sandy loam	Dichanthium annulatum, Cenchrus ciliaris.
Dalbergia sissoo	Riverbed soils loamy sand, plains and outer Himalaya at low altitudes	Dichanthium annulatum, Cenchrus ciliaris.
Erythrina suberosa	Outer hills	Bothriochloa spp., Panicum spp.
Glyricidia maculata	Peninsular India	Cenchrus ciliaris.
Hardwickia binata	Peninsular India	Dichanthium annulatum
Leucaena leucocephala	Loamy to sandy loam	Cenchrus ciliaris
Ougenia dalbergioides	Outer Himalaya and low hills	Dichanthium annulatum, Sehima nervosum and Chrysopogon fulvus.
Parkinsonia aculeata	Sandy to sandy loam	Canal banks
Pithecolobium dulce	Sandy to sandy loam	Dichanthium annulatum, Cenchrus ciliaris.
Pongamia glabra	Sandy loam	D.annulatum, C. ciliaris.
Prosopis cineraria	Sandy loam to loamy sand,	Lasiurus sindicus, Cenchrus ciliaris. C.setigerus
P.juliflora	Saline areas, gravelley loamy to clay loam	D.annulatum, Sporobolus spp.
Sesbania grandiflora	Clay loam to loamy soils	Dichanthium annulatum.
Robinia pseudoacacia	Brown hill soils	Chrysopogon spp.

Grasses and Legumes
Setaria anceps.

Sub-Humid Sutlej-Ganga Alluvial Plains

Trees
Acacia nilotica, A. tortilis, Anogeissus latifolia, A. pendula, Azadiracuta indica, Dalbergia sissoo, Kydia calycina, Morus alba, Pithecellobium dulce, Pongamia pinnata, Zizyphus mauritiana, Ailanthus excelsa, Albizzia lebbek, A. pocera, A. amara, Bauhinia variegata, Cordia dichotoma, Hardwickia binata, Leucaena latisiliqua, Cordia dichotoma, Moringa oleifera, Adina cordifolia, Bridelia retusa, Schleichera trifuga, Gmelina arborea.

Shrubs
Leucaena latisiliqua, Sesbania grandiflora, S. sesban, Morus alba, Dichrostachys nutens, Desmanthes virgatus, Desmodium diffusum, D. cephalotus.

Grasses and Legumes
Cenchrus ciliaris, C. setigerus, Chrysopogon fulvus, Setaria anceps, Dichanthium annulatum, Isilema laxum, Sehima nervosum, Panicum antidotale, Clitoria terneata, Macroptelium atropurpureum, Stylosanthes hamata, Phaseolus calcaratus, Desmodium uncinatum.

Sub-Humid/Humid Eastern and South-Eastern up and Regions

Trees
Acacia nilotica, Anogeissus latifolia, Azadirachta indica, Cordia dichotoma, Dalbergia sissoo, Delonix elata, Emblica officinalis, Grevillea robusta, Hardwickia binata, Kydia calycina, Pithecellobium dulce, Pongamia pinnata, Zizyphus mauritiana, Alianthus excelsa, Albizzia chinensis, A. lebbek, A. amara, Artocarpus heterophyllus, Bauhinia purpurea, B. variegata, Moringa oleifera, Morus alba, Leucaena latisiliqua, Mimusops hexandra, Glyricida maculata.

Shrubs
Morus alba, Leucaena latisiliqua, Desmanthes virgatus, Sesbania grandiflora, S. sesban, Desmodium sp.

Grasses and Legumes
Dichanthium annulatum, Iscilema laxum, I. anthephoroides, Setaria anceps, Panicum antidotale, Chloris gyana, Chrysopogon fulvus, Eremopogon faveolatus, Atylosia scaraboides, Macroptelium atropurpureum, Stylosanthes hamata, S. graiclis, Clitoria terneata, cenhrus ciliari, sehina nervosum.

Arid Western Plains

Trees
Acacia tortilis, Azadirachta indica, Cordia rothi, Hardwickia binata, Morus alba, Parkinsonia aculeata, Pithecellobium dulce, P. seman, Salvadora oleoides, Tamarix sp., Zizyphus mauritiana, Alianthus excelsa, Albizzia lebbek, Moringa oleifera, Tecomella undulata, Eucalyptus sp., Prosopis cineraria, P. juliflora.

Shrubs
Dichrostachys nutens, Leucaena latisiliqua, Capparis decidua, Sesbania sesban.

Grasses and Legumes

Cenchrus ciliaris, C. setigerus, Lasirus sindicus, Dichanthium annulatum, Cymbopogon jwaraneusa, Panicum antidotale, Macroptelium atropurpureum, Desmodium triflorum.

Semi-Arid/Lava Plateaux and Central Highlands

Trees

Acacia auriculiformis, A. nilotica, Cusuarina equisetifolia, Cordia rothi, Emblica officinalis, Kydia calycina, Morus alba, Pithecellobium dulce, Pongamia pinnata Tamarindus indica, Tamarix sp., Zizyphus mauritiana, Ailanthus excelsa, Albizzia amara, A. lebbek, Bauhinia variegata, Hardwickia binata, Leucaena latisiliqua, Moringa oliefera, Tecomelia undulata, Eucalyptus sp., Glyricida maculata, Thespesia populnea.

Shrubs

Leucaena latisiliqua, Sesbania grandiflora, S. sesban, Glyricida maculata, Desmanthes virgatus.

Grasses and Legumes

Sehima nervosum, Dichanthium annulatum, Cenhrus ciliaris, Chrysopogon fulvus, Panium antidotale, Heteropogon contortus, Atylosia scaraboides, Stylosanthes hamata, S. gracilis, Macroptelium atropurpureum, Desmodium sp.

Humid and Semi-Arid Western Ghats

Trees

Acacia auriculiformis, A. melanoxylon, A. nilotica, A. planifrous, Albizzia amara, A. procera, Anogeissus latifolia, Cassia auriculata, Casuarinia equisetifolia, Eucalyptus sp., Grevillea robusta, Kydia calycina, Morus alba, Peltophrum pterocarpum, Pithecellobium dulce, Pongamia pinnata, Zizyphus mauritiana, Aegle marmelos, Ailanthus excelsa, Cordia dichotoma, Hardiwckia binata, Leucaena latisiliqua, Moringa oleifera, Tamarindus indica, Glyricida moculata, Mesua ferrea, Thespehia populnea.

Shrubs

Leucaena latisiliqua, Sesbania grandiflora, S. sesban, Glyricida maculate, Desmanthes virgatus.

Grasses and Legumes

Chrsopogon vulvus, Pennisetum clandestinum, Ischaemum indicum Setaria anceps, Panicum antidotale, Glycine javanica, Paspalum dilatatum, Stylosanthes hamata, S. gracilis, Macroptelium atropurpureum.

AGROSTOLOGY IN SOIL AND WATER CONSERVATION

Introduction

In India out of a total geographical area of 329m ha, an area of 12.01m ha has been classified under permanent pasture and other grazing lands (Fig. 5.8). These are cultivable lands but are being used as permanent pastures and meadows in hill slopes and village common lands in the plains. While high altitude pastures and meadows are relatively less affected by erosion, the lower slopes, foothills and village grazing lands in the plains are severely eroded. Hence, on an average, 40%, i.e. 4.16m ha of the total area of 12.01m ha has been estimated (Das, 1985) as affected by erosion.

From 1951 to 1971, human population in India increased by 52% from 361 to 541 millions. It will be 931 millions by 2000 A.D. Animal wealth in India is vast. The per capita availability of land for production of food, fibre, and other needs shrank from 0.33 ha to 0.292 ha and this will be further decreased to 0.175 ha by the year 2000 A.D. Thus the great pressure of human beings and animals on land, specially grassland, results in over-grazing causing soil erosion and shortage practically of all the feeds, fodder requirements, animal products like milk (shortage more than 200%), meat (600%), egg, wool, etc. This deficit is likely to increase, because animal population is increasing annually by 2% (Swaminathan, 1976).

Grasses in Soil and Water Conservation

The role of grass plants in protecting the soil is based on their ability to prolong the hydrologic cycle from its inception as falling precipitation to its final disposal as runoff in streams. The grasses control water erosion through a three-tier action. The first tier is offered above the ground through the dense thatched roof action of the leaves and stems of grasses exposing innumerable little surfaces aggregating an area several times greater than that of the ground beneath. The action comprises of direct dispersion, interception, energy dissipation and evaporation of falling rain drops.

The second tier is offered at the ground floor, where the grass bulwarks against erosion and runoff comprising of mechanical resistance by plant clump, stolons or runners and the protective blanket of littermass of leaves and fragments of stems in various shape stages of disintegration, performing double function of increased surface friction, which reduces volume and velocity of runoff and of absorbing a good part of water for deeper percolation.

The third tier is offered direct in soil mass. The knitting and binding effect of grass root and rhizome system protect the soil from detachment and washing. The ramifying, close and elaborate network in all direction of grass roots, literally hold the soil particles together and provide a mesh of reinforcement that both anchors the soil and resists the scouring action of water flowing over it.

The sum effect of soil conserving/protecting values of grasses are ultimately reflected in the runoff and soil loss.

With a rich variety of characters like ease in establishment, perennial nature, bunch, mat, sod, sward and turf formation, adaptability to a variety of edaphic and climatic conditions and amenability to various management practices like sowing, cutting, etc., the grasses offer a lot to choose from, for protection or production or for both. For stabilisation, consolidation and protection of and production from the soil conservation earthen structures, like terrace faces, bunds, checkdams, waterways, diversion channels outlets, wasteweirs, spillways, etc., the grasses are the only choice.

Grassland and Rangeland

In popular sense the word grass includes all true grasses, grass-like plants and plants grazed by livestock. The natural grasslands are termed Rangelands also, when the areas are large, naturally vegetated, mostly unfenced and located in low rainfall regions. Areas spoken of as pastures are usually fenced and developed by seeding, fertilising or irrigation for grazing domestic livestock. Pastures receive abundant rainfall. They are called permanent when seeded to perennial grasses. Grassland or rangeland management is the science and art of planning and directing range use, so as to obtain maximum livestock production consistent with conservation of the range resources. In the present context, a grassland means the area raised normally with perennial grasses primarily and specifically to save the soil from erosion and permit only safe and conservative use of the forage crop to ensure improvement and build up the soil component of the habitat.

Grass Covers of India
Five types of grass covers have been recognized in the country which are as follows:

Sehima-Dichanthium Type
This cover type spreads over the whole of peninsular India, comprising the states of Gujarat, Maharashtra, Madhya Pradesh, Orissa, Andhra Pradesh, Karnataka, Tamil-nadu, Kerala, south-west Bengal, southern Bihar and the southern hilly portions of Uttar Pradesh and Rajasthan and also the coastal regions. Kota and Vasad are within this type of grass cover. In this grass cover there are about 24 predominant grass communities, of which *Themeda* and *Iseilemia* are most wide spread. These grasslands hold high potentiality to produce up to 6,300 kg/ha of hay. When sub-jected to grazing, the dominant perennial communities are degenerated to annual ones in the order of *Dichanthium-Bothriochloa-Hetoropogon-Eremopogon-Aristida-Eragrostis-Melanocenchris.*

Dichanthium-Cenchrus-Lasiurus Type
This type is associated with sub-tropical arid and semi-arid regions, comprising the northern portions of Gujarat, the whole of Rajasthan excluding the Aravalli ranges in the south, western Uttar Pradesh, Delhi and the Punjab and Haryana. In this type there are 11 predominant grass communities. Under best developed conditions, the potential production of air dry forage ranges from 1,000 kg/ha (*Sporobolus* com-munity) to 6,000 kg/ha (*Dichanthium* community). When subjected to grazing, the dominant communities are degenerated to *Aristida* (loose soils) and *Chloris* (com-pact soils) communities.

Phragmites-Saccharum-Imperata Type
This cover type occurs throughout the Gangetic plain, the Brahmaputra valley and extends westwards into the plains of Punjab. These areas are characterised by low-lying, ill-drained lands with high water-table. When subjected to burning, cutting, grazing, etc., the dominant communities are succeeded by those of *Chrysopogon* and *Paspalum*, indicating that biotic interference is beneficial if these grasslands are to be used for production of palatable forages.

Themeda-Arundinella Type
This cover type occurs in the entire northern and north-western mountain tract in the states of Manipur, Assam, West Bengal, Uttar Pradesh, Punjab, Himachal Pradesh and Jammu & Kashmir. *Themeda* community in its best developed stage produces 2,200 kg/ha of hay. When subjected to grazing, *Themeda-Arundinella* communities are replaced by *Chrysopogon, Bothriochloa* and finally by *Cynodon* community.

Temperate-Alpine Type
This cover type occurs on the high hills of the northern montane belt comprising Jammu & Kashmir, Himachal Pradesh, Punjab, Uttar Pradesh, West Bengal and Assam above 2,100 m in the north and west and 1,500 m in the east. Snow during winter is quite a common feature.

    In order that grasslands play their due role in conserving soil and water and in the animal production drive of the country, the deteriorated and overgrazed grassland including the forest grasslands have to be developed to their potential value.

For the development of any grassland, it is important to know the production potential of that grassland, in relation to the present status and also the techniques to achieve the potential production. Most of the grasslands in India may be classified as poor to very poor.

Grassland Improvement
The first step for the improvement of any deteriorated grassland/pasture is to protect it from biotic factors. Angle iron post with barbed wire fencing is one of the most efficient and economic methods. Also other methods of fencing suggested by different scientists include ditch-cum-wall with planting of thorny vegetation, or sowing of useful trees like Vilayati Babool (*Prosopis juliflora*) and Israeli Babool (*Acacia tortilis*) along the border.

Land Preparation
The soil is ploughed with light discing or harrowing and Pata is used finally before monsoon in the semi-arid conditions, so that all roots of weeds and shrubs are exposed. Land during rains at the time of sowing will require only the minimum tillage which is accomplished with a Desi plough or even by the use of pick-axe. Complete soil working followed by reseeding with appropriate grasses result in increased establishment and forage yield.

Choice of Species
Selection of suitable grass and legume species for reseeding the rangelands is generally accomplished from analogous bio-climates depending upon peculiar soil conditions prevailing, e.g. *Iseilema laxum* is suitable for low-lying areas with heavy soils while *Dichanthium annulatum* prefers medium heavy soils and can also bear salinity to some extent. Similarly, *Cenchrus ciliaris* and *C. setigerus* are most suitable species for sandy loam to loamy sand type of soils. *Chloris gayana* though has a high moisture requirement, but does not tolerate water stagnation. Therefore, choice of species varies greatly with climato-edaphic features. Some of the grasses and legumes recommended for various regions of the country are recorded in Table 5.3.

Method of Sowing
Broadcasting seeds of grasses is economical and quick, while line sowing has the advantage of mechanised sowing, intercultural operations, fertilization, etc.

Depth of Sowing
Since grass seeds are small, if sown deep, they fail to germinate or germination is delayed. The optimum depth of sowing is 1–2 cm, by covering the seed with soil either by a light broomstick or by dragging a small twig with foliage over the land. Depth of 0.5–1 cm has been considered optimum for very small seeds.

Seed Rate and Spacing
Availability of certified grass seeds and their cost are the major constraints for grassland development programmes. Though high seed rates are reported to give rapid ground cover, competition result in ultimate production levels. Results show optimum forage yield from *Cenchrus ciliaris* and *Chrysopogon fulvus* with 50 cm spacing from row-to-row and 30 cm from plant-to-plant, while optimum seed yield of these grasses was obtained under 75 cm × 30 cm spacing.

Soil and Water Conservation Measures
Unless a rangeland is flat or very mildly sloping, it should be improved and man-

Table 5.3   *Grasses and legumes adapted to different soil climatic regions in India*

High hills of J&K, HP and UP	Dactylis glomerata, Festuca, Lolium	Trifolium pratense, T.repens, Lupinus hirsutus.
Eastern high hills	Dactylis glomerata Festuca spp., Lolium.	Trifolium pratense, T.repens, Lupinus hirsutus.
Low hills of W.Himalaya	Dichanthium annulatum, Chrysopogon fulvus, Cenchrus ciliaris, Pennisetum pedicellatum.	Pueraria hirsuta, Phaseolus atropurpureus, Stylosanthes humilis.
Low hills of Eastern Himalaya	Dichanthium annulatum, Panicum maximum, Pennisetum pedicellatum.	Medicago sativa, Stylosanthes gracilis, Dolichos lablab, D.axillaris, Glycine javanica, Vigna sinensis, Desmodium intortum.
Southern plateau	Dichanthium annulatum Panicum antidotale, Sehima nervosum, Cenchrus ciliaris, Csetigerous and Chrysopogon fulvus.	Dolichos lab lab, D.axillaris, Stylosanthes humilis, Phaseolus atropurpureus.
Southern hills	Dichanthium annulatum, Pennisetum purpureus, Panicum maximum, Sehima nervosum, Pennisetum pedicellatum.	Stylosanthes gracilis, S.humilis, Desmodium intortum.
Eastern plains	Brachiaria mutica, Setaria sphacelata, Dichanthium annulathum, Pennisetum polystachyon, P.pedicellatum.	Medicago sativa, Phaseolus calcaratus, Dolichos lab lab, Glycine javanica.
Dry regions of Rajasthan, Gujarat, Haryana and UP.	Dichanthium annulatum, Panicum antidotale, Cenchrus ciliaris, C.setigerus and Lasiurus sindicus.	Phaseolus atropurpureus, Stylosanthes humilis.
Coastal regions	Setaria sphacelata, Panicum maximum, P.antidotale, Brachiaria mutica, Sporobalus helvolus.	Dolichos lab lab, Medicago sativa, Vigna sinensis, Glycine javanica.
Waterlogged area	Brachiaria mutica, Iseilema laxum, Dichanthium spp.	Sesbania aegyptiaca
User soils	Sporobolus spp., Chloris spp., Dichanthium annulatum, Cynodon dactylon.	Rhynchosia minima, Alysicarpus regosus, Desmodium spp.

aged on a watershed basis. The measures for soil and water conservation depend upon the rainfall, topography, soil and condition class of the range. Light harrowing, contour furrowing at appropriate vertical intervals are very effective for soil and moisture conservation in the arid and semi-arid regions. Small brushwood check-dams have to be constructed for gully plugging, stabilization and improvement of the gullied rangeland. Efficient utilization of water from the natural water courses by water spreading increases the productivity of the range. It should not be assumed that water erosion hazard is insignificant in the drought prone areas. Even rare high intensity storms in one year or in a period of two or three years are sufficient to cause serious erosion for two reasons: (a) generally the soil is loose and vegetation less dense in the development stages; (b) interception of precipitation by grasses is not very high, because of the structural habit of the plants, water hitting the blades of grass runs readily down towards the main stem and thence the ground. Hence, soil and water conservation measures and erosion control structures are a must in projects for range improvement and management.

Weed Control

In good and excellent rangelands, weeds are not many, for the simple reason that the desirable forage plants grow vigorously. However, in poor and fair rangelands, weeds may be common. Even so, what may be weeds for one category of livestock (say, cattle) may be forage for another category (say, sheep, goats, camels, etc.). Goats browse on shrubs and bushes. It is, therefore, advisable to study the forage value of all species, their seasonal palatability for the various livestocks, and arrange the grazing practices in such a way that the best utilization of the range in all the seasons by the different livestock would be possible. As soil fertility increases naturally, or is increased by the use of organic manures and chemical fertilizers, high-yielding perennial grasses grow vigorously and also the weeds. Troublesome weeds should be grubbed out. Weedicides though efficient are costly and may have harmful effects of the grazing livestock.

Eradication of Noxious Plants

Poisonous herbs and shrubs cannot be eradicated or controlled by any grazing system, as the livestock graze selectively leaving these to multiply rapidly and infest the range. These are very injurious to the livestock, which eat such plants accidentally or out of intense hunger. Some noxious plants cause rash, irritation and skin diseases to the livestock.

The cause for the invasion of such plants have to be investigated into, before deciding on the measures for their eradication. Hand grubbing is feasible only when such plants are a few in number. Carefully controlled burning of the heavily infested rangeland will destroy such plants and increase forage production. Specially designed power machinery (like bulldozers with special equipment for the purpose) cover large areas within a short time for a uniform operation. Chemicals like 2-4-D, 2, 4, 5–T, Weedone 64, Bladex-H, Picloram, etc., are effective.

Use of Fertilizers

Application of fertilizers not only increase the forage yield but also increase the quality of forages. 20 or 40 kg N per ha would boost the growth of the perennial grasses. The cost of fertilizers required for vast areas is very high and so the use of fertilizers has to be restricted to selected sites, where returns are assured.

An example of a plan, adopted for developing rangelands in Saurashtra 20 years ago, may give an idea of how it can work:

This is a three-area regulated plan to improve poor rangelands during six years, say from 1977 to 1982. It may be schematically represented as shown below:

Area A	Area B	Area C
1977, 1978—Closed-Ungrazed Contour furrows, sowing seeds grasses or sodding if required	1977, 1978-Grazed continuous controlled grazing, (Controlled Stocking rate only 1/3 of the usual)	1977, 1978, 1979, 1980 Grazed as in B during 1977, 1978
1979, 1980-Closed. Ungrazed (June -Oct.) Cut for stall-feeding or hay if growth is good. No winter grazing	1979, 1980-Closed. Ungrazed. Contour furrows, seeding, sodding—using the best method as found out from experience in A during 1977, 1978	1981, 1982-Closed. Ungrazed Contour furrows, seeding and sodding
1981, 1982-Light grazing. Leave 40 to 50% growth on the ground to improve soil, check erosion and increase water infiltration	1981, 1982–Cut for stall-feeding and hay if growth is good	

This process will go on till all the three areas are fully developed. This practice of rotational grazing has to be modified and adjusted every year to suit the local conditions and rainfall.

Contour furrows at 10–15 cm vertical interval or 5 m horizontal interval arrest water in rains. Planting of sods of desirable grasses in the wet place along the furrows gives good success. Sods must be dug-up, handled, transported (only over short distances) and planted carefully and properly; and all these operations must be done very quickly at the right time during the monsoon, just before rains.

Forage production on the reserved areas (closed for grazing) average from three to six times than that on heavily grazed areas. In quality vegetation on the reserved areas is greatly superior to that on those badly damaged by heavy grazing.

All the improvement measures will be futile if the rangelands are not managed scientifically; and sound management is not possible without improvement measures. Such is the intimate relationship between the two.

Balancing numbers of animals with grazing capacity (Carrying capacity)
"Balancing numbers of animals with grazing capacity is probably the biggest and most serious problem of grassland management in the Asia-Pacific region, as well as many other parts of the world. The scant forage production, the poor development and low production of animals, the catastrophic periodic starvation losses of livestock, particularly during periods of drought and the serious erosion of soil by both wind and water, all join in stark testimony of this lack of balance. In addition, many countries do not produce sufficient cropland forage to offset the grassland, and that which is produced is often considered too valuable to feed to range livestock" (Holscher).

Carrying capacity (grazing capacity) is defined as the ability of a grassland unit to give adequate support to a constant number of livestock for a stated period each year, without deterioration with respect to this and/or other proper land use.

This definition implies a harmonious balance among the land, range resources and the livestock for maximum sustained production. Moreover, all the three should progress towards betterment in course of time for progressively increased production, both of the range and the livestock. The one is measured by the criteria enumerated earlier and the other by the good health and increasing body weights and yields of milk, etc. In the case of draught animals, their working power and efficiency as also the duration in their lifetime for work would increase. As the utilization of the vegetation for grazing should not exceed 60–75%, soil and water conservation is ensured.

At present, on an average, taking the range-condition class as poor, the yield of air-dry range forage per year is 750 kg/ha at best, which is sufficient for only 75 days for a cattle unit—CU (equal to a cow of 300 kg body weight). The minimum requirement for a cattle unit is estimated at 10 kg of air-dry range forage per day, apart from necessary supplemental feeds to the productive cattle during the dry months (say 8) when the nutrient content of the range vegetation is low. At this rate, one cattle unit requires 5 ha for year-long grazing and without supplements. The livestock population in our country is so large, that, even if we succeed with the best improvement and management practices to raise the carrying capacity to 1 CU/ha, it would not be possible to balance the numbers of the livestock with carrying capacity.

It is imperative, therefore, that the livestock population be regulated by removing the unproductive animals from competition with the better livestock. The breed of the useful animals should be improved and their good health ensured at all times.

Reduction of livestock population may be achieved by preventing promiscuous breeding, fixing limits to the numbers of livestock owned by villagers, by heavy grazing fees and by restriction of grazing rights.

Controlled grazing—Regulation of grazing on the basis of carrying capacity for year-long grazing (*Continuous controlled grazing*) or *seasonal grazing* or for *deferred grazing* or for *rational grazing* or for *deferred-cum-rational* grazing. In a sound management practice, grazing always means controlled grazing.

Early versus Deferred Grazing—The nutritive value of the range vegetation is the highest during period of active growth from July to September and hence the livestock production is the highest in this period. But grazing in this period is harmful to the poor and fair ranges, because the grasses are grazed before flowering, fruiting and seed production, which is so essential for regeneration in the range.

Deferred grazing is postponing or delaying grazing, either completely for the entire growing season (complete deferment) or for the beginning of the growing season (early deferment) or for the later part of the growing season (late deferment) to enable the vegetation to grow well, maintain its vigour and produce abundant seed for regeneration of the rangeland. Grazing is allowed after seeding (usually from the middle of October) but may have to be withdrawn to prevent overgrazing and exposure of soil after a few months.

Rotational Grazing—Year-long grazing in blocks or compartments in rotation. The objective is to give rest to the land and hence full opportunity for the vegetation to grow and develop well.

The simplest method is to divide entire grazing land into two blocks and to allow grazing in alternate years in each block, while in the closed block range improvement would be done. However, one year rest may not be sufficient. It is advisable to divide the entire grazing land into three blocks to give rest for two years to each block. But the block open for grazing would be overgrazed. This situation has to be tolerated for 2 years. Later on there will be improvement in all the three blocks. Supplemental feeds and concentrates may be arranged in greater bulk during the first two years.

Deferred-Rotational Grazing—As already said, deferment of grazing to the growing season in the poor and fair rangelands is a must for effective recuperation of the vegetation.

Deferred-cum-rotational grazing aims at achieving both the objectives in one operation. Here all the three blocks are used each year, changing the sequence of grazing in such a way that each block is grazed for 1/3 year and protected for 2/3 year. Thus each block gets deferment once in three years with equal grazing stress in all the three blocks during the period of three years.

Year	A	B	C
1977	Grazing in rains	Grazing in winter	Grazing in summer
1978	Grazing in summer	Grazing in rains	Grazing in winter
1979	Grazing in winter	Grazing in summer	Grazing in rains

This is the time-bound deferred-rotational grazing. However, it is far better to have this system of grazing on the basis of the development of the range vegetation, rather than a fixed period of time.

Plan for Grazing Where Grassland is Divided into Four Areas and Grazed in Rotation

A	B	C	D
x	x	x	x
Begin grazing on 15th July and continue until the height of grass is reduced to 10 cm.			
Then remove live stock to B	Graze as in → A and remove to C	Same. Then → to D	When area D is → grazed to desired height, livestock are returned to A to begin the cycle again.

The second year of grazing should start on area having longest period of growth from previous season. The number of divisions would depend upon size and topography of the total area, number of livestock and availability of water. The number of livestock used in any rotational scheme should be such that satisfactory regeneration occurs between periods of grazing. The value of rotational grazing is that, it compels livestock to utilize grazing with approximately equal intensity, developing several watering places distributed in the range uniformly, placing salt-licks and other mineral nutrients at scattered points uniformly distributed to attract the livestock, herding the livestock in the areas which are ungrazed or less grazed, avoiding concentrated movement of the livestock in the range, construction of shelters and dividing the range into units by fences, ensure uniform grazing in the rangeland. These practices should particularly be done in remote rangelands, so that the pressure on the ranges near habitations will be reduced. Adequate water and mineral nutrient supplies should be ensured for the livestock.

Top Feeds
Besides grasses and legumes, good top-feed tree species should be planted in the range for green and nutritious fodder during winter. Some of the useful species are:

Arid Region
Prosopis cineraria, Prosopis juliflora, Acacia tortilis, Moringa pterygosperma, Albizzia lebbek, Ailanthus excelsa.

Semi-Arid Region
All the above 6 species, *Acacia nilotica, Dalbergia sissoo, Azadirachta indica, Morus alba, Sizygium cuminii.*

Silage
It is a matter of common observation that forage production is quite high in good rain years and low in drought years. Good quantities of forage produced in good rain years may be suitably treated for preservation and use for the livestock in drought years.

RECOMMENDATIONS OF CENTRAL SOIL & WATER CONSERVATION RESEARCH & TRAINING INSTITUTE AND ITS RESEARCH CENTRES

Central Soil & Water Conservation Research and Training Institute, Dehradun
The tropical deciduous forest cover the outer hills in the south of the District near Dehradun on the foothills of Himalayas. Shorea robusta Gaertn. is the important species of these forests. Extensive forests of Chir pine occur in outer Himalayas and Shiwaliks. There are evergreen Oak and coniferous forests extending over most

part in the temperate zone of the Himalayas. Cedrus deodara is common in the Tons region.

Pinus caribaea, a quick growing tropical pine tree spp. considered to be promising for denuded areas and useful as fuel and pulp, was introduced at Dehradun in 1970. It has been found to be very promising and has maintained an average increment of 96.8 cm and basal diameter increment of 2 cm/annum for the last 7 years. *Eucalyptus camaldulensis*, *E.hybrid*, and *E.citriodora* have been found to be successful.

It has been observed at Dehradun that if class V and VI wastelands in Doon Valley are planted with *Chrysopogon fulvus* grass (0.75 m× 0.75 m) and *Dalbergia sissoo* trees (9.14 m× 9.14 m), not only high yield of grass (10.55 tonnes/ha/annum) is obtained but about 97 trees per ha will also be available for exploitation for fuel after 15 years. From the benefit: cost ratios, it was inferred that *Dalbergia sissoo* at 9.15 m× 9.15 m + *Chrysopogon fulvus* for fodder and *Acacia catechu* + *Eulaliopsis binata* for fuel and fibre requirements are economically justified to be grown in the wastelands of Doon Valley.

At Dehradun, bouldry VII river bed lands can be economically utilised to grow *Eulaliopsis binata* (Bharbar grass). 40,000 plants/ha population for giving the maximum air-dry grass yield of about 56 q/ha/annum (average of seven cuttings taken in 4 years) of *bhabar* grass. The grass is used in making country ropes and serves as a source of income for landless labourers.

Torrentbeds and old riverbeds which are unfit for cultivation of agricultural crops and lie waste, can be profitably used to produce hybrid napier (var. NB-5 and NB-21) green forage at the rate of 34 and 31 tonnes/ha/cut (average of seven cuttings taken in 4 years). The hybrid napier will need application of nitrogen at 120 kg/ha in two equal doses during the second and third years of its establishment.

Stabilizing Road Cuts and Torrent Beds
Kudze vine (*Peuraria hirsuta*) gave 217–231 q/ha/annum of good quality green forage and left behind 45 to 47 q/ha/annum leaf litter to enrich the degraded sites like torrent beds and roadside cuts with boulders. Kudzeu vine yields valuable fodder of high protein value and raw material for paper.

Checking Gullies
For small gullies and check dams, *Arundo donax*, *Agave americana*, *Ipomea carnea* and *Vitex negundo* are the most successful.

CS & WCR & TI, Research Centre, Chandigarh
With the help of staggered contour trenches (2.5 m × 0.45 m × 0.45 m) spaced 2 m apart, both in the same line and row-to-row planting, it has been possible to control the runoff completely from the hilly area.

Tie-Ridge Technique for Raising Trees and Grasses
Tie-ridge technique has been developed at the centre for increasing the growth of trees and grasses. In this technique, pits are dug-out at a spacing of 2 m × 2 m, where tall plants (2.5 m and above) of *Eucalyptus* hybrid are planted. Twentyfive cm high ridges are made joining the pits from all sides. Thus the entire area is converted into small quadrates of 2 m × 2 m with ridge from all sides to arrest most of the rainfall in it. *Eulaliopsis binata* (Bhabhar) was planted at a spacing of 75 cm × 75 cm in the quadrates under *Eucalyptus*. The average yield of *Eucalyptus* (air dry)

works out to 15 tonnes and that of *Eulaliopsis binata* to 5 tonnes making a total of 20 tonnes/ha/year.

Production Technology for Raising Bharbhar
With the same tie-ridge technique it has been possible to obtain 15 tonnes/ha/year of air-dry bhabhar. The present price of bhabhar is Rs. 400/tonne which means gross income of Rs. 6000/ha/year.

A Simple and Cheap Technique for Erosion Control on Sloping Agricultural Fields
Up to 4% slope, it has been possible to reduce soil erosion and increase production through a simple technique. The fields are laid in such a fashion as to leave 1 m space after every 33 m. In this strip of 1 m space, *Eulaliopsis binata* was planted. It has been possible to get an average yield of 2.6 tonnes/ha of maize (Ganga-5) and 1.5 tonnes/ha of taramira (Selection-A). It has been possible to get 0.78 tonnes of Bhabhar/ha of cropped area. With the introduction of grass species in strips, the slope has reduced from 4 to 2.7 per cent in 5 years.

Reducing Rotation of Eucalyptus Hybrid
By planting 3 m high seedlings of *Eucalyptus* hybrid on ridge of trenches (1 m × 0.45 m × 0.45 m), the volume growth can be increased by 50% over the plants of normal initial height of 1 m raised in pits (60 cm × 60 cm × 60 cm). Thus it is possible to cut down rotation of eucalyptus with improved techniques.

CS & WCR & TI, Research Centre, Kota
Studies on introduction of suitable tree species for marginal and ravine lands have been made. Following species have been found suitable:

— By sowing: *Acacia nilotica, Acacia catechu, Prosopis juliflora*
— By transplanting: *Acacia catechu, Acacia tortilis, A. farnensiana, Albizzia lebbek, Dalbergia sissoo, Eucalyptus camaldulensis, E. tereticornis, Morus alba, Pongamia pinnata, Salvadora oleoides.*

Among the grasses, *Dichanthium annulatum* (strain no. 490) and *Cenchrus ciliaris* (strain no. 303) were found promising (Plate 21).

Para grass (*Bracheria mutica*) was successfully established on water logged saline riverbeds.

CS & WCR & TI, Research Centre, Vasad
Studies on soil working technique indicated that contour staggered trenches 3 m (*l*) × 0.3 m (*w*) × 0.60 m (*h*) with raised mounds were more effective for the growth of *Acacia nilotica.*

Among the tree species, *Acacia tortilis, Acacia benthamii,* and *Eucalyptus camaldulensis* in ravine humps. *Eucalyptus camaldulensis* (Jodhpur), *Eucalyptus hybrid* (Jodhpur) in slope, *Dendrocalamus strictus* in gully beds were found suitable for planting in the ravines after closure to biotic interference. Teak plantation is recommended at 2 m × 2 m spacing. *Dalbergia sissoo* at the age of 15 years about 1750 plants are available in one ha area.

Among the grass species suitable for fodder, *Dichanthium annulatum, Cenchrus ciliaris* and *Andropogon ischemum* were found promising.

Sodding of grasses like *Panicum antidotale, Dichanthium annulatum* and *Cynodon dactylon* with and without application of fertilizers stabilized bunds and terraces.

CS & WCR & TI, Research Centre, Ootacamund
Mixed plantations of bluegum and black wattle at a spacing of 3.65 m × 3.65 m

gave maximum height, growth and yield of bark for black wattle, at a spacing of 3.65 m × 3.65 m gave maximum height growth and yield of bark for black wattle (*Acacia mearnsii*) and 3.65 m× 4.97 m for Bluegum (*Eucalyptus globulus*). Growth studies on different eucalyptus species indicated that maximum height was observed in *Eucalyptus saligna*, *E. tereticornis* and *Eucalyptus globulus*.

The important fodder grasses and clovers with their yields are given below:

Name	Yield (tonnes/ha)	Remarks	Name	Yield (tonnes/ha)	Remarks
Cynodon swannae	50 –210	SC & F	Natural grasses of Chrysopogon		
Agropyron semi-costatum	20 –40	SC & F	zeylanicus and its		
Lolium perenii	7.5 –42	F	associates	2.5 –20	SC & F
Digitaria creeping	50 –210	SC & F	Clovers (Trifolium		
Eragrostis curvula	50 –100	SC	repens, Ladino		
Tripsacum laxum	60 –150	SC	cover)	10 –14	SC & F
Hybrid Napier, NB			Trifolium subter-		
21 NB 17, Napier	80 –200	SC & F	raneum (clare		
Digitaria bunch			strain)	20 –30	SC & F
type	45 –112	SC & F	Trifolium subter-		
Phalaris tuberosa,			raneum (Bachhus		
Choloris gayana			marsh)	6 –10	SC & F
and Paspalum			Trifolium hirtum	10 –24	SC & F
dilatatum	50 –150	SC & F			

Yield data of Bluegum and Black wattle felled after 1st rotation of 10 years

Treatment	Wood (m³/ha/rotation)	Bark (kg/ha)	Leaves (kg/ha)
A. Shola	–	–	–
B. Bluegum	456	–	13789
C. Black wattle	322	12722	–
D. Mixture of bluegum and black wattle	600	6852	10944

Note: Clovers contain 2.5 to 3.4% Nitrogen; SC—Useful for soil and water conservation; F—Useful for fodder.

Farm forestry is a must in high hills for erosion control and additional return to farmer. This Centre has demonstrated the same by planting trees of bluegum and cupressus on farm boundary and bluegum, wattle on small patches adjoining culti-vated farm lands and the same provides about Rs. 30,000/- to Rs. 70,000/- per ha for a rotation of 10 to 12 years depending on the site conditions, protection and care during the rotation.

CS & WCR & TI, Research Centre, Bellary

Marginal lands and degraded woodlands can be stocked with trees, grass and legumes by closure. Artificial regeneration has proved to be a failure or too costly. Eucalyptus hybrid, *Acacia nilotica*, *A. nubica*, *Prosopis cineraria* and *Azadirachta indica* have shown promise in the tract. However, their yield potential appears to be low. A ten-year plantation of Eucalyptus hybrid yielded 21.7 m³ of fuel/ha/rotation. Prosopis juliflora live hedge interfered seriously with agricultural crops and drastically reduced *jowar* yields up to a distance of 28 m from the hedge. *Acacia nilotica* and *Cenchrus ciliaris* have been found to be a good tree-cum-fodder combination for rainfed black soils of the tract.

Native grasslands fall under the category *Sehima Dichanthium* type. Sehima is totally absent with a high proportion of fodder legumes like Alysicarpus and Desmodium species. Strains No. 214 of *Cenchrus ciliaris*, 412 of *C. setigerus* and 499 of *Dichanthium annulatum* among grasses and *Alysicarpus longifolias, A. rugoses, Indigofera, Phaseolus trilobus, Phaseolus autropurpureus* and *Dolichos lab lab* among legumes show promise for the tract. Maximum yields are obtained in *Cenchrus ciliaris* and *Dichanthium annulatum* has not responded to nitrogen application, 20 kg N/ha is observed to be optimum for *Cenchrus ciliaris* under rainfed conditions. Rangelands showed response to phosphorous application. Foliar application failed to show any superiority over soil application.

Among the various grasses tried, *Cenchrus ciliaris* on bunds and *C. ciliaris* and *Dichanthium annulatum* in channels and waterways are found to be the best for stabilization of these structures.

HORTICULTURE IN SOIL AND WATER CONSERVATION

Horticultural species can be cultivated in degraded and denuded wastelands, which help in controlling the soil erosion and conserving the water. Land capability Classes V to VII are put to perennial vegetation like forests or grasses or horticultural crops including plantation crops depending upon the situability, adaptability and other facilities such as marketability, transportation, etc. In the case of the above lands, specially if it is a very much denuded and wasteland, it is imperative that on sloping lands, raising of horticultural plants would be more profitable and economical per unit area per unit time as compared to that of trees or grasses. Where soil and climatic conditions are favourable, either multi-storeyed cultivation of horticulture plants (ex. coconuts with cocoa, pepper, etc.) or agronomical crops with fruit trees (ex. peaches and ginger in outer Himalayas; cashewnuts and *ragi* in semi-arid red soils of peninsular India) can be raised successfully and thus increase the productivity per unit area per unit time. Cultivation of fruits is a highly remunerative enterprise. An apple orchard can give an annual income of Rs. 25,000 to 30,000 per ha (1969 rates). There are examples of a family subsisting on as little as 0.1 ha. The necessity and scope for expanding the fruit cultivation in India and its profitability are evident.

The total area under fruits in India is about 1.47 m ha, which represents about 0.9% of the total cropped area.

The area under fruit crops in different States of India is given in Table 5.4.

India, is the second largest producer of fruits (24, 767 m tonnes) next only to Brazil (25, 529 m tonnes). The estimates of principal fruits in India is given in Table 5.5.

Horticulture has been, is now and will continue to be of great economic, political and social importance to mankind. Present day horticulture may be defined as the science and technology involved in the production, processing and merchandising of fruits, vegetables, flowers, etc.

Importance of Fruits

Cultivation of fruits is a very important factor contributing to the prosperity of a nation. In fact, the per capita production and consumption of fruits is often taken as an index of the standard of living of the people in a country. The nutritive value of fruits in human diet is universally recognized. Fruits are the chief source of vitamins and certain minerals, which are necessary to maintain proper health and are resistant to diseases.

Table 5.4 *Area (Thousand ha) under total fruits as* per landuse statistics 1984–85 (Provisional)

State	Area	State	Area
Andhra Pradesh	276	Mizoram (b)	1
Arunachal Pradesh(b)	3	Nagaland	8
Assam(b)	58	Orissa	220
Bihar	130	Punjab	26
Gujarat (b)	71	Rajasthan	15
Haryana	13	Sikkim	4
Himachal Pradesh	32	Tamil Nadu	176
Jammu & Kashmir	37	Tripura (b)	25
Karnataka	117	Uttar Pradesh (b)	251
Kerala	322	West Bengal (b)	53
Madhya Pradesh	54	Others	52
Maharashtra (b)	121		____
Manipur (b)	2	Total	2081
Meghalaya (b)	4		____

Note: (b) relates to area under forecast crops.

Source: Indian Agriculture in brief, 22nd edition. Directorate of Economics and Statistics, Department of Agriculture and Cooperation, Ministry of Agriculture, Government of India.

Table 5.5 *Adhoc estimates of fruits (1986–87)*

Fruit	Area (m ha)	Production (m tonnes)
Mango	1.22	10.11
Apple	0.18	1.31
Citrus	0.26	2.53
Guava	0.18	1.16
Grapes	0.61	0.32
Pine-apple	0.95	1.41

Source: Horticulture Division Department of Agriculture and Cooperation, Govt. of India, New Delhi.

Scope of Fruit Cultivation in India

India is a vast country with a variety of climates, where all types of fruits can be grown. In the Himalayas, the temperate fruits can be grown most successfully from Kashmir to the hills of Uttar Pradesh. The eastern region of the Himalayas above Assam, Bengal and Bihar is too wet. Heavy rainfall and high humidity in this area are conducive to the occurrence of diseases of fruit trees. In the western Himalayas fruit cultivation is limited to hail-free areas. Apples, walnuts, and cherries are cultivated at elevations above about 1800 m, except in the Kashmir Valley, the altitude of which is about 1500 m. Pears and persimmons grow at slightly lower altitudes. Plums, apricots and peaches are cultivated at elevations of from 1200 m to 1500 m. Some temperate fruits are grown on the hills in south India. Varieties of plums and peaches with low chilling requirements are also grown in the sub-montane areas. Mango is found growing all over India, up to an altitude of 1200 m, but it does not fruit well above 600 m. Banana is grown principally in the south and the east. Citrus fruits grow in most parts of the country, except at high elevations. Guava is common in Uttar Pradesh and Bihar and papaya in all frost-free areas. Grapes can be grown in most places, except at very high altitudes and in wet and humid areas. Litchi and loquot can be grown in the sub-tropical sub-montane areas. At the foot of the Nilgiri Hills in south India, several exotic fruits have been grown successfully. These include mangosteen, durian, avocado and *ranbutam*. *Ber* can be grown anywhere in the plains and the date-palm can be cultivated in the dry desert areas. Other fruits successful in India include *phalsa* (*Grewia subinaequalis*), pomegranate, fig, pineapple, custard-apple, *jaman* (*Syzygium cuminii*), jackfruit, *sapota* (*Acharas zapota*), cape gooseberry, mulberry, passion fruit, *aonla* (*Emblica officinalis*) and tree tomato (*Cyphomandra betacea*).

Fruits are available in India almost all through the year. An almost unlimited number of varieties with different flavours is available. Mango starts ripening in Cape Comorin in January. As we go north, the ripening becomes later. Some varieties in Uttar Pradesh and the Punjab ripen in August. Citrus fruits ripen from August to April in different parts of India. In central and south India in the same locality there are two or three crops of citrus. Banana ripens from September to April. Loquat comes to the market in April and litchi and mulberry in May. Cherries, peaches, plums and apricots ripen from May to July. Pears come to the market from August to September and apples up to November. A variety of fresh fruits is, therefore, available all through the year. The scope for growing a variety of luscious fruits of different types is, thus, unlimited.

Groups of Fruits

The horticulturist recognizes two large groups of fruits: tree fruits and small fruits. Tree fruits are produced on trees while small fruits, in general, are produced on shrubs or vines. Both tree fruits and small fruits, are produced on deciduous and non-deciduous, or evergreen plants. Fruit plants are grouped as follows:

1) *Tree Fruits*

    a) Deciduous

        i) Pome (false fruits)
            Apple, pear, quince, medlar, etc.

        ii) Drupe (simple fruits)
            Peach, cherry, plum, apricot, etc.

    b) Evergreen

        i) Citrus (simple fruit)
            Orange, grapefruit, lemon, lime, etc.

        ii) Avocado (simple fruit)

        iii) Mango (simple fruit)

2) *Small Fruits (Including Vine Fruits)*

        Grape (simple fruit—a true berry)
        Strawberry (false fruit)
        Current (simple fruit)
        Gooseberry (simple fruit)
        Red raspberry (aggregate fruit)
        Black raspberry (aggregate fruit)

Factors related to cultivation of fruits are proper selection of site, soil condition, water supply and other factors. The factors which should be taken into account for selecting a site for large-scale fruit growing are many, such as location or the distance of the nearest market, natural flora in vegetation with particular reference to the fruit trees to be planted in the orchard, soil condition, water supply, labour availability, and transport facilities, etc. The soil condition, i.e. all the physical, chemical and biological properties should be ideal for the best performance of fruit trees. Of course most of the fruit trees, however, are not very specific in soil requirement and can grow under a varied soil and climatic condition; for example mangoes are found to grow in the Gangetic alluvium soil, sandy soil, lateritic soils and in red soils or in other words from sea level to 1500 m above the sea level in the Himalayas. The presence of large varieties of rootstocks for different fruit species provides opportunity to extend fruit cultivation even in comparatively poor lands. Judicious choice of rootstocks–scion combination may dilute the negative reaction of fruit trees to adverse soil conditions. A rootstock having good surface concentration of fibrous feeding roots and with well-developed deep tap root branching is ideal for poor wastelands. The selection of rootstocks which can tolerate adverse soil reaction like acidity or alkalinity, soil-borne diseases or insect infested lands, low soil temperature lands, makes it possible to grow many fruit crops even in unfavourable soils. Before taking up the cultivation of fruits, a number of points like what to grow, when to plant, how to plant and what are the cultural practices, etc., are to be considered.

What to grow

Do not attempt the larger fruit trees unless you are prepared to wait for four to six years. Pomelo, limes, etc., bear fruits in three to four years, litchi and mango take six to eight years before a bumper crop can be gathered. Of course the plants raised by vegetative propagation will come to flowering and fruiting much earlier than the one obtained from seed. They might bear at the very first year after planting, but precocious bearing should not be encouraged. It will hamper the vigour of the fruit tree. Where seedlings are planted, the fruiting period is protracted and one is never certain of obtaining a good type from a seedling, unless careful selection has been practised. Plants propagated by vegetative means retain the good qualities of their mother without any deterioration. For instance, a seedling *Kaghzi* lime of a think skinned mother, may have a thick rind and little juice, while one propagated by gooties will perpetuate the thin skin character. Always buy from a reliable source as foliage differences cannot be depended on for judging the quality and type of the plant.

When to plant

The rainy season is the safest period of the year for planting the fruit trees. Of course if irrigation facilities are available, the planting can be done at any time of the year.

How to plant

As a general rule, shrubs should be planted 3 to 4 m apart, dwarf trees 4 to 6 m tall trees from 10 to 13 m. There must be at maturity a clearance of a few metres between plants. Planting may be done in various ways, such as square, rectangular, quincunxial, triangular, and hexagonal method.

For planting trees, pits should be dug up to a depth of 1 to 1.5 m and about 1 m in diameter. The pit should be refilled with the excavated earth, to which a basket of leafmould, same quantity of decayed cow manure and sufficient sand may be added to counteract any sticky clay tendencies that may exist and to make the compost porous. If possible, irrigate the pit so that the soil settles down with proper compactness.

Before planting, selection of proper plants should be made. Choose plants where grafts and buddings are made low down on the stock. The graft union should be firm and care should be taken to see that the stock is stouter than the scion. A flexuose scion should be avoided. While planting grafts, see that point of union is half below ground. All other plants should have the ball of earth covering the roots buried a couple of cm below the soil. Staking and fencing may be done, if required. No further manure is necessary till the plant has started fruiting. An annual dose of bone-meal, oilcake, decayed cow or horse dung should be applied.

A catch crop like vegetables or papaya may be cultivated in the open space between the trees during the first few years, till the fruit trees occupy the whole area. It should always be noted that the catch crop must not choke the permanent plants.

To guard against collar rot, white ants and also to prevent sunburn of the base of stem, use half circles of earthen wire pipes placed three to four inches above the ground. When fruit trees are much exposed to the fierce sunshine and the stem burns, it should be white-washed with a thing coat of lime.

Watering
Fruit trees should have an adequate and steady supply of water. The presence of too much or absence of sufficient water in the soil will result in injury to the plants. An excess of water suddenly following a prolonged dry period often results in the cracking of fruits, which is often found in the case of citrus fruits. Shortage of water also on the other hand has many adverse effects. Never let a plant show signs of flagging leaves during the hot months. Stop watering altogether at the end of November, allow it to winter naturally, or artificially according to variety and wait for the flowers to appear. As soon as the petals fall and the fruits have started to set, commence watering and also give liquid manure in small doses. This applies particularly to the bush and dwarf tree types. During watering do not allow the water to come nearer than 50–90 cm of the collar of the plant.

Pruning
Pruning means the removal of unwanted shoots and is usually done with an aim to maintain a balance between the vegetative and reproductive growth. Unlike the ornamental plants, pruning in fruit trees is not done for beautification. Fruit trees are usually pruned to secure good crop yields. Of course in our country for the evergreen fruit trees very little pruning is required. It is mainly restricted to the removal of dead old branches or branches infested with insects and pests. All unhealthy stems must be removed.

Root pruning or any injury to the root will result to temporary increase in fruit bud formation. Root pruning of fruit trees is better done half at a time carrying the operation to a second year. This permits the tree to partially recover from the shock. A regular practice of root pruning to induce fruit bud formation, however, had adverse effect on the plants and should not be practised every year.

While a tree is bearing well, do not prune; simply clean out the dead branches.

Ringing, notching, etc., are some of the special orchard practices that usually result in increased fruit bud formation due to the carbohydrate accumulation around the operated region, provided the tree has attained the bearing age.

In case of root pruning of fruit trees, do not excavate the earth very close to the trunk. Digging of soil should be done at least 1 to 2 m away from the main trunk. Only the thin weak roots should be pruned leaving intact the main anchor roots.

Fruit Ripening
Fruits are often forced to ripe by being wrapped in straw, damp grass, using ethylene, etc. Though the fruits become soft and show colouration, yet they remain astringent or acid. The fruits which ripe naturally on the tree will have much better flavour

and taste than the artificially ripened fruits. Certain pests, however, necessitate the removal of half ripened fruits, if we wish to enjoy any return from the fruit garden.

Bananas should be cut as the deep green colouration of the fruit commences to change to a paler shade. Hang the bunch keeping stem downwards to obtain slow ripening. Other varieties of fruits should also be harvested with a portion of the stem, if possible. Never harvest the fruits until they show a definite alteration in tint.

Classification of Fruit Crops

The ability of a region to produce a fruit crop is limited by climate and soil. Fruit crops may be classified geographically as follows, those of temperate region, those of sub-tropical regions and those of tropical regions.

Temperate Fruits

Fruits which do best under severe winter conditions usually experienced at elevations above 1500 m in the Himalayas and other hills. The apple, the pear, the europian plum, the cherry and the walnut. Fruits which can thrive in comparatively warmer situations at elevation of 1050–1500 m–the peach, the Japanese plum, the apricot, the almond, the *Vinifera* grape and the persimmon.

Subtropical Fruit

The orange, grape fruit and citrus fruits are the most common ones. Dates, figs and olives are also important.

Tropical Fruits

The cashewnuts, the mango, the banana, the pineapple, the coconut, avocado, papaya, guava, supodilla, *ber* (*Zizyphus*), pomegranate, litchi, custard apple, *phalsa*. Important fruit crops in wastelands like cashew, etc., which have successfully been raised as a soil conservation measure in India and fruits like citrus, etc., are discussed below:

FRUIT CROPS IN WASTELANDS

Cashew (Anacardium Occidentale L.)

Cashew is generally grown as a wasteland crop. Well-cared-for plantations of cashew do not exist. Its cultivation up to 5000 m is possible. It grows in areas with a rainfall ranging from 50 to over 400 cm. The cashew is a hardy tree and survives the attack of animals, birds, diseases like die-back and mildew and insect pests like thrips, caterpillars and boarers. The plant provides a very good canopy to land and is a dollar earning crop. Once established, cashewnut trees keep on producing fruits for about a period of 30–40 years. Thus it is imperative that it is one of the most important fruit crops and a plant for soil conservation in India.

In India, cashew is grown mainly in Kerala, Tamil Nadu and Goa and also in Maharashtra, Orissa and Assam. Cashew is grown in coastal areas or on rough hilly lands with no irrigation, manuring or pruning. It is grown with almost no care but it is not planted in heavy black cotton soils. Cashew does not tolerate severe summer or winter conditions as in north India.

Cashew is grown both for its fruit (cashew apple) as well as nuts mainly the latter.
Varieties—There are no distinct varieties of cashew.
Propagation and planting—Sowing *in situ* is a usual practice but it is possible to transplant month old seedlings after cutting down them back by one third. It can also be propagated by layering, inarching, side grafting and shield budding. The

distance for planting varies from 6 m in lateritic and rocky soils to 12 m in deep loamy soils.

Bearing—The trees may start bearing after 2 years but regular cropping starts after 5 years. It gives a good yield after 10 years.

Harvesting—The fruits ripen from March-May and is harvested.

Curing and processing—The nuts are separated for cashew apples immediately after harvest. The dried nuts are roasted in either open pans over a furnace or by other means. The shelling is done by hand soon after roasting. The Kernels so obtained are dried in the sun. They are then kept in sweating chambers for a time. The nuts are then ready for grading and packing. Major diseases of Cashew in India resulting in shoot and inflorescence drying can be controlled by removal of affected parts and application of crude carbolic acid followed by bordeaux paste.

Use of Cashewnuts—Cashewnut is sweet and delightful in taste. It is enriched with proteins (21%) and fats (47%). Its proteins are claimed even better than that of meat.

Zizyphus (Ber)

Ber is a hardy fruit tree and in some places it grows wild. The Indian jujube is *Zizyphus mauritiana* and belongs to the family Rhamnaceae.

This fruit can be of importance in localities where other fruits do not thrive well. It can be grown in dry land and also even in slightly alkaline soils.

The improved varieties require a spacing of 6–9 m. Budded plants are planted at a required distance and there is no necessity of digging any pit for accommodating them, provided the soil is not very poor.

Varieties—Some local varieties which are propagated by budding are of outstanding merit. The varieties Peondi, Kala ponda, Thin skinned, Umran, Gola, etc., are popular in northern India.

Propagation—In most places, *ber* is propagated by seed. Naturally, variation found is wide. However, improved types are vegetatively propagated either by shield-budding or ring-budding. In the former case, stock-plants are headed back to about one foot from the ground level in February or March. On the new shoots, budding is done in June approximately 1.2 m above the ground level. The stock mainly used is the *ber* seedlings. *Zizyphus rotundifolia* or *Z. nummularia (jharberi)* can also be used as a rootstock. Inferior wild plants can be top-worked with improved varieties.

Irrigation—Ber does not require much irrigation. It is better to provide one or two irrigations while the fruits are developing. It helps in checking the falling of the berries.

Pruning—A *ber* tree develops many slender branches and becomes overcrowded. Regular pruning is, therefore, essential. Irregular branches should be cut away in order to ensure a strong frame-work. A heavy pruning may be done just after fruiting and then superfluous growth is thinned before flowering.

The fruit is mostly consumed fresh, but also makes an excellent candy. It also forms a component of certain types of jellies. Dried fruits powder is used in several ways.

Guava

(Psidium guava L.)—The total area under guava in the country is about 30,000 ha of which Uttar Pradesh has the largest area (9,840 ha) followed closely by Bihar (4,800 ha). It is a very hardy tree, withstands heat and prolonged droughts, but is susceptible to frost. A cool winter induces heavy fruiting. It grows in all types of soils

having pH ranging from 4.5 to 8.2. Its fruits is rich in Vitamin C (35 to 100 mg per 100 gm) content.

Varieties—Lucknow-49, Allahabad Safeda and Seedless are white-flesh varieties. Several types having pink flesh and white flesh with bright red skin are also known.

Propagation and planting—Propagated by seeds as well as vegetatively. Inarching, layering and air-layering are commonly practised. Root suckers, root cuttings and budding are sometimes successful. The fruit is generally propagated in the rainy season; the plants are ready to be set out after a year. The usual distance for planting is 5.5 to 6 m.

Culture—Growing a green manure crop during the rainy season and clean cultivation during the rest of the year is recommended. One or two irrigations between the end of monsoon and harvest time (winter) are given in northern India. In south India, irrigation throughout the year is necessary. In addition to bulky organic manures, supply of 45 to 60 kg N, 77.5 to 90 kg P and 100 kg to 110 kg K per ha is recommended.

Pruning—Young trees require pruning several times a year to avoid long slender branches. As the fruit is borne on new growth, heavy pruning of bearing trees helps fruiting. All flowers should be removed until the framework is strong enough.

Harvesting—Fruits must be plucked as they ripen. This extends over several weeks. For long distance marketing, it is necessary to harvest somewhat sooner.

Indian Gooseberry (Aonla)

The *aonla* fruits is well known as a rich source of Vitamin C and is eaten in several ways such as in pickles and preserves.

Aonla is botanically called (*Phyllanthus emblica*) and thrives on a variety of soils and can do well even in slightly alkaline ones. It can be safely recommended for planting wastelands.

It is commonly raised from seed but the improved varieties are propagated by grafting and budding. Budding has given higher percentage of success. The trees, which are to be top-worked, are headed back in March and the cut surface painted with coal-tar. No shoots emerge by May-June and are budded with the desired improved variety.

Aonla varieties are classified according to their colour as green, reddish-tinged and white-streaked. The Banarasi *aonla* is superior to all for the big size of its fruit.

The fruit trees are planted at a distance of 7.5 m to 9 m apart. It is always better if the pits of the size 0.9 m × 0.9 m × 0.9 m are dug sometime before planting and filled with a mixture of soil and manure. They are mostly dug before the commencement of rains. Planting should be done in the rainy season when the soil of the pits has finally settled. The plants require frequent irrigation till they are fully established.

The trees start fruiting at the age of eight years. If there is any decline in the yield, each tree should be manured with three baskets of organic manure and 4 kg of superphosphate early in the spring.

The fruit is used in various forms, like *aonla morabba* and pickles. Sometimes fruits are dried and chips are prepared. Every part of *aonla* trees are utilized, one way or other, in medicine. Large-scale plantation of this fruit is bound to prove everpaying. The fruits are not generally eaten by birds and when properly packed can also withstand long journey.

Citrus Fruits

Among the major fruits in India, citrus stands next to mango and banana. Citrus fruits comprise all types of oranges, limes and lemons. Citrus fruits are fondled for their refreshing and delicious juices which are rich in vitamins. Citrus are found to grow in almost all kinds of soil and climate though a dry climate with a rainfall between 60–120 cm is preferable.

Oranges

Oranges in India can be mainly divided into two groups—Sweet oranges (*Citrus sinensis*) and Mandarine oranges (*C.retuculata*). The typical examples of sweet oranges in our country are Malta, Mosambi and Washington Navel, etc., and of Mandarine group or all types of loose skinned oranges commonly known as Nagpur Santra, Assam Santra, Coorg Santra and Sikkim Orange, etc. Unlike the Mandarine oranges, sweet oranges are tiger skinned and heavy.

Sweet Oranges

Sweet oranges thrive under both subtropical and tropical conditions. Low rainfall tracts with pronounced summer and winter season are very suitable for the cultivation of sweet oranges. It can grow on a wide range of soils, from light sandy to heavy clays having good drainage system. Sweet oranges are usually propagated by budding. The trees should be planted 6–8 m apart in July-September. The ground for oranges should be well-ploughed. As this plant requires much nitrogen, use a green manure crop. For a plant two years old, 10 kg of FYM, 1 kg bone meal and 250 gm of superphosphate should be used. From the fourth year, this annual application should be double. All branches starting from a few cm of the bud union should be pruned, leaving about 60 cm of clean straight stem with a few well-selected branches. Before three years no crops should be taken. In case of bearing trees very little pruning is required. During harvesting, a few cm piece of stem should be taken along with the fruit, which will serve the purpose of pruning. Root exposure and withholding of water in proper time bring the plants into good bloom. After the first heavy application of water at the time of planting, a second light irrigation should be given within a week. Thereafter, the interval of irrigation will depend upon the climatic and soil condition. Grafted, budded or gootied plants should bear in 3 to 4 year, but seedlings take 8 to 10 years and are seldom true to type.

Mandarine Oranges

The soil and climactic requirements of Santra oranges are almost equal to that of Sweet oranges. Only the difference is that it stands more humidity than the Sweet oranges. Budding on rough lemon and seed propagation are better prevalent in Santra oranges. The spacing, planting time and method, pruning, manuring and irrigation methods are similar to that of Sweet orange. In Santra oranges also the budded trees come to fruiting much earlier than the seedling trees and start to bear the crop from fourth year onwards, while the seedling trees take at least seven years to bear the first crop.

Lime (C. aurantifolia)

Limes are of two types—sweet and sour. Limes are small, round or slightly oval in shape and are only 3–4 cm in diameter. Its skin is very thin and the juice is highly acidic. This dwarf tree thrives well in all parts of India where frosting is absent. Seed propagation and budding are usually practised in sour lime. Sweet lime is propagated both by stem cutting and seed. Planting method, pruning and manuring, etc., of limes are same as that of Sweet orange. It bears twice a year, once in August and again in February.

Lemon (C. limonia)

This struggling tree bears large heavy fruits with prominently long nipples. Unlike the lime, the lemons have thick rind and the juice is less acidic. The lemon can be cultivated up to an elevation of 900 m but is susceptible to frost. Tahiti, Lisbon, Eureka, Villafranca and Italian lemon are some of the notable varieties of lemons.

Grape Fruit (C. paradisi)

It is very similar to the Pummelos. Its climatic and soil requirements are similar to those of Oranges. The multiplication of plants is usually done by budding or grafting and the tree bears in 4 years. Planting, irrigation, manuring and other intercultural practices are similar to that of Oranges, except lesser pruning is required. Harvesting season is November to January. The popular varieties are Duncan, McCarthy, Marsh seedless and Triumph, etc.

Shaddock (C.decumana)

The Pummelo or Shaddock is a small tree which can be grown up to an elevation of 1,500 m. The same soil as recommended for other citrus fruits suits the Pummelo. Plants should be grown from gooties or buddings. A basket-full of well decomposed cow manure and a mixture containing equal proportions of bone meal, super-phosphate and muriate of potash at the rate of 250gm/plant should be applied in the first year. Increase 250 gm of this mixture for every subsequent year with a maximum quantity of 2.0 kg per plant. Pummelo bears the fruit in 3 years. Do not allow the plants to flower earlier, as this will weaken the plant. Reduce the number of fruits borne and thin out interlaced twigs. The fruit ripens from July to November. Stalkarts, Society's No. 1 and Society's No. 3 are some of the good varieties of Pummelo.

Intercrops

It is always beneficial to take some intercrop in a citrus orchard till the trees start bearing. The intercrops should be such as may not compete unduly with the citrus plants for nutrients and moisture. Vegetables like carrot, tomato, radish, brinjal and chilly can profitably be grown as intercrops. Groundnut can also be successfully grown, depending upon the soil and climatic conditions of a place. Papaya can also be grown in the beginning.

Cover Crops

In a bearing orchard, leguminous crops, such as berseem, pea and methi are ideal as cover cops. During *Kharif*, guar or some dwarf variety of mung can be grown profitably. Care should be taken not to irrigate the orchard too frequently, as it may prove detrimental to the growth of the trees. The orchard should be kept clean and ploughed. This will automatically be affected if the intercrops and cover crops are taken regularly. Ploughing should be shallow, as deep ploughing is likely to injure the feeder roots.

Pruning

Pruning is done with a view to giving a desired shape to the trees and getting rid of the diseased twigs. Branches inside the tree should also be removed to allow sufficient light for the whole tree. All dead and diseased branches or shoots should be regularly removed.

Recommendations of Different Indian States

Maharashtra

The mango plantation can be raised on the varkas, hilly areas which are at present lying barren. This will help in converting barren slopy lands into mango. The mango plantation is expected to change the economy of the hilly tract and bring, about an upliftment and economic development of the farmers.

5.3 Gully Control Structures (Temporary)

Structure in Soil and Water Conservation Programmes for non-agricultural lands are used for one or more of the purposes, such as grade and gully control; sediment storage; surface water disposal; water level control, etc.

Gully erosion is an advanced stage of rill erosion, while the latter is an advanced stage of sheet erosion. Stabilization of gullies through vegetation is a difficult task when the gullies have to be used for conveying runoff during the time plantations are started. In such cases, mechanical measures have to be adopted to prevent washing away of the plantations by large volume of runoff. Such protective measures need be only temporary, vegetation when once established, will be able to take care of the gully.

Where mechanical measures are necessary in gully control, then permanent structures such as masonry check dams, flumes or earth dams supplemented by vegetation, should be provided to convey the runoff over critical portions of the gully.

CHECK DAMS

Principles

In control of gullies, the erosive velocities are reduced by flattening out the steep uniform gradient of the gully, by constructing a series of checks which transform the longitudinal gradient into a series of steps with low risers and long flat treads. Where temporary structures are used, they are intended only to function until the vegetation becomes well established, to provide necessary protection. Check dams of this type are usually made of brush, wire, poles or loose rock. Substantial checks of masonry, concrete or earth are built where it is necessary to rely upon these alone for permanent control. Temporary check dams thrown across the bed of a gully serve two purposes:

— to collect sufficient soil and water to enable the proper growth of vegetative cover; and

— to check channel erosion until sufficient stabilizing vegetation can be established at that critical point.

Design details regarding check dams are given in the succeeding pages under Drop Spillways.

Flumes or Chutes

Another way of protecting waterfall erosion is to cut back the earth to a slope of 30° or 40° and sides smoothened and channel lined with turf, sod or paved with rubble masonry or concrete reinforced with wire netting. Such structures are called flumes or chutes.

Design details regarding flumes or chutes were given in the previous chapters under Weirs. Turfed or sodded chutes may be used for small catchments and masonry chutes for bigger catchments.

Temporary Check Dams

These are adopted for controlling runoff in small and medium sized gullies, where permanent protection is sought by stabilized vegetative cover. Temporary dams do hold a certain amount of soil for the vegetation to take a foothold and to that extent they are called Soil Savers. Gullies stabilized with vegetation should be closed to livestock.

Brush Dams

In Small gullies, 1.2 to 2.1 m in depth, check dams are usually constructed with brush and hay. Construction of such dams does not require any skilled labour and the farmer can make use of materials that are available in his farm. They are inexpensive and can be repaired with available materials at site.

One Row Post or Single Row Post Brush Dam

This method consists of a singlerow of country wood stakes, to which are tied long branches of trees laid lengthwise, of the gully with their bull-ends facing upstream. The longest branches are laid first and progressively shorter length on top till the required height is obtained.

Construction—Before the dam is begun, the sides of the gully at the dam site and sloped to 1:1 and the gully bottom for the whole length of the dam lowered by about 15 cm. The 15 cm excavation is carried up into the bank as high as required, to give the necessary notch capacity for discharging the runoff. Then countrywood stakes about 7.5 m in diameter, are driven 0.6 m apart along the dam line. The stakes should go not less than 0.9 m into gully bed and their tops are kept at such heights as to form a distinct depression in the middle, to form a notch of the required waterway to enable the maximum runoff being discharged without undermining the dam at the ends. First a layer of straw is placed at the bottom and over it, longest branches are specially selected and laid lengthwise of the gully and well-pressed. Over this, another layer of straw is spread and shorter branches laid. This process is repeated till a dam of required height at the gully bed is obtained. The brush is anchored on to the stakes by means of galvanised iron wire, so that it may not be washed away. Intermediate stakes of shorter lengths are driven and the brush anchored on to them to prevent its being lifted from the bed by water. The longer branches act as an apron for the dam and prevent overfall erosion scour. As the green leaves rot, the branches get loose and the dam cannot be kept rigid. This is overcome by the use of additional rows of stakes. These stakes can be driven down to take up the slack, wherever it is found necessary.

Two-row or Double-row Post Brush Dam

This method is used in the control of medium deep gully (about 2 to 2.5 m deep) and about 6 m wide, which have a contributory watershed of 40 ha and more.

Construction—The construction of the dam is very much same as the single-row post, excepting that in the case of two-row post type, the straw and brushwood is laid across the gully between two rows of country wood posts, the distance between the rows being not more than 0.9 m. The stakes are 10 to 13 cm in diameter and are driven 0.9 m apart to go at least 0.9 to 1.2 m into the hard bed of the gully. A brushwood apron held by galvanized iron wire is necessary to prevent to prevent scour. The double-post type is more efficient and stable (Fig. 5.4)

Semi-permanent Dams

These have a longer life and usually do not require any maintenance. They do not

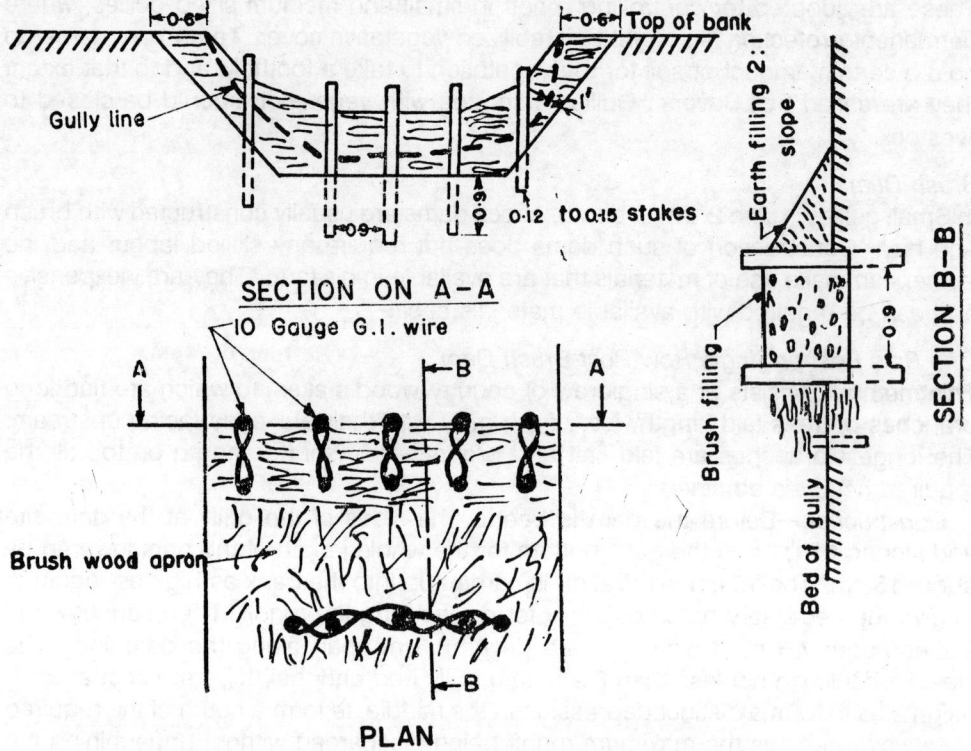

PLAN

Fig. 5.4 A double-row post brush dam

require the assistance of vegetative growth for controlling the gully. They can be constructed in places where materials are available in large quantity.

These dams are very effective in steep gullies traversing hilly and mountainous regions. They are also useful in ravines where passage for livestock has to be provided for.

Loose Rock Dam

If loose stones of fairly good size are available in large quantities, they can be used for farming check dams.

Construction—The site where the dam is to be erected is cleared and the sides sloped to 1:1. The bed of the gully is excavated to a uniform depth of about 0.3 m and dry stones packed from that level as shown in Fig. 5.5. In the centre of the dam portion, sufficient water-way is allowed to discharge the maximum runoff from the catchment. The stone filling should go up to 0.3–0.6 m into the stable portion of the gully side to prevent end cutting. In the rear, sufficient length and width of apron has to be provides to prevent scour. The thickness of the apron packing should not be less than 0.45 m and the gully sides above the apron have to be protected with stone pitching to a height of at least 0.3 m above the anticipated maximum water level to prevent side scours being formed by the falling water. Care should be taken to place bigger sized stones on top to prevent their being dislodged or carried away by the current. The American practice is to hold down this dry stone fill with woven wire netting. In this country, it is not usual to do so, but stability is secured by using stones as large as can be procured and careful packing, bedding and wedging.

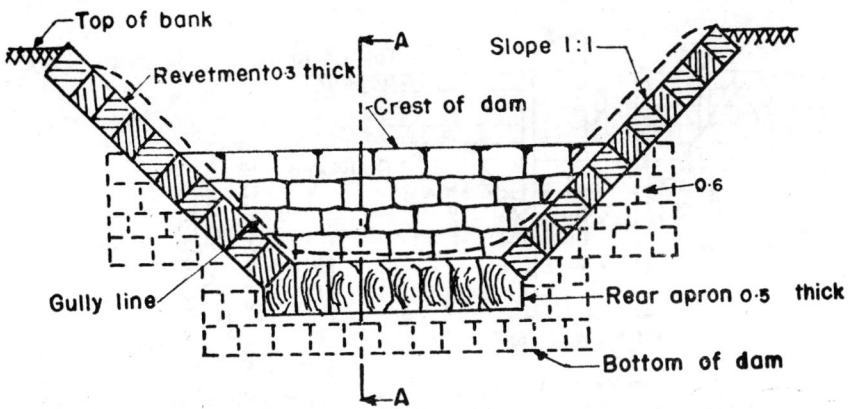

SECTIONAL ELEVTION LOOKING UP GULLY

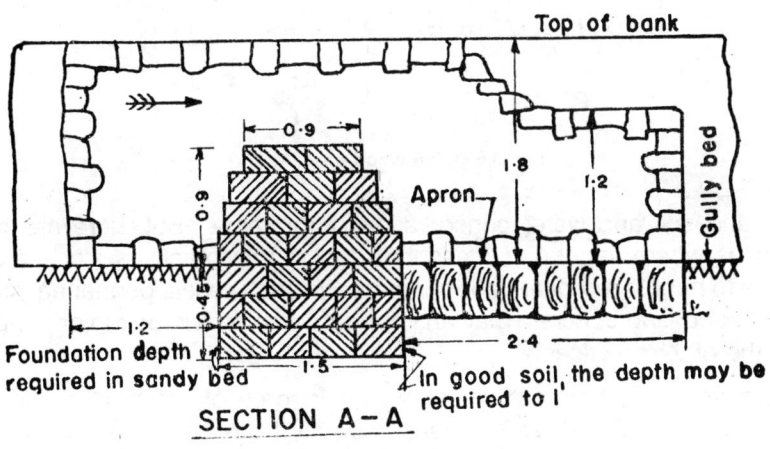

SECTION A—A

Fig. 5.5 A dry stone dam

Log Dams
When timber is plentiful and semi-skilled labour is available, long dams may be erected. Figure 5.6 gives the details of construction. In the regions where attack of termites is anticipated, necessary care should be taken.

Rough Stone Dry Packed Dams
When good building stones of durable quality can be quarried in sufficient large quantities, *pucca* dams of random rubble (dry and packed) can be constructed. The stones should however, be dressed and properly set in with wedges and chips. The bottom of dam should be taken to firm earth at least 0.6 m below the bed of the gully. Design particulars are given in Fig. 5.8.

5.4   Gully Control Structures (Permanent)

GENERAL FUNCTIONS OF CONCRETE AND MASONRY STRUCTURES

— Concrete and masonry structures are efficient supplemental control measures. Good vegetative practices together with proper land use are indispensable in

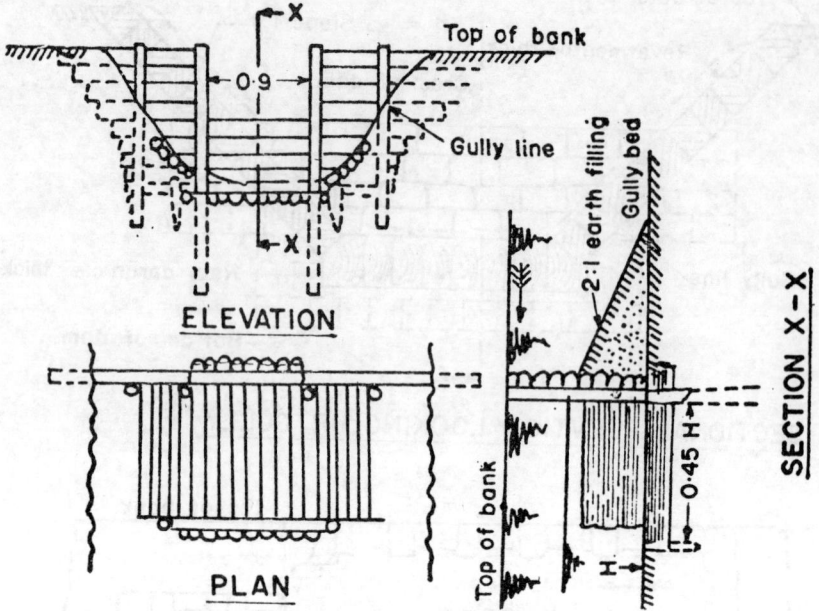

Fig. 5.6 A log wood check dam

a sound soil and water conservation programme. But there are many in-stances where vegetative measures and simple practices alone are inade-quate to handle a concentration of water. In such cases, permanent structures of masonry and concrete play an important part, in reinforcing or supplement-ing the other practices.

— There are also instances where a high degree of safety and permanence are desirable. Conservation measures may be required which will be good insurance against loss of life or destruction of property. Vegetative control measures are subjected to the influences of such uncertain factors as climate, insects, etc., and therefore, are not too dependable. On the other hand, properly designed and installed structures are of longer life and dependability.

— The structure has a main function to safely dispose peak rate of runoff for a given frequency, from higher elevation to a lower elevation. It should have arrangements to dissipate the kinetic energy of discharge within the structure, in a manner and degree that will protect both, the structure and downstream channel from damage.

TYPE OF STRUCTURES

There are three principal types of spillways, viz. Drop spillway; Drop inlet spillway; and Chute spillway. These are further described with respect to their inlet, conduit and outlet example straight box inlet pipe spillway with cantilever outlet. Profile of a gully showing the application of several types of permanent structures is shown in Fig. 5.7.

COMPONENT PARTS OF STRUCTURES

Most of the commonly used structures consist of four major components—the earthen

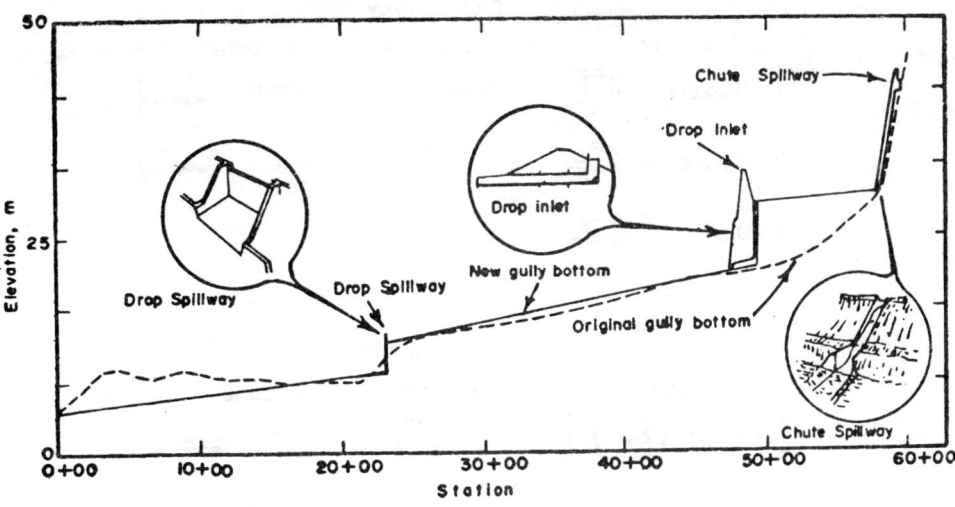

Fig. 5.7 Application of several types of permanent structures in a gully

embankment, spillway inlet, conduit and the spillway outlet. Various types of inlets, conduits and outlets and their nomenclature of these components are shown in Fig. 5.8.

Embankment—The embankment checks and diverts the flow of water and directs it through the spillway. The embankment for a drop spillway or chute, generally extends from the spillway to high ground or to a vegetative spillway. In the case of an earth dam constructed for a farm pond, the embankment details and impounds water as well as discharges storm flow through the spillway.

Spillway inlet—Water enters the spillway through the inlet, which may be in the form of a box, a weir in a wall, or a culvert-type entrance. The box may be straight or flared while the wall may be straight, flared or curved. The culvert-type entrance may be round, square edge, hood, or flared entrance.

Vertical walls extending into the soil foundations under the inlet are known as cutoff walls. Their main purpose is to prevent water seepage under the structure. Similar walls, extending laterally from the inlet to prevent seepage and erosion around the ends of the structure, are called headwall extensions. These walls also protect against burrowing animals.

Spillway Conduit—The Conduit receives the water from the inlet and conducts it through the structure. The conduit may be closed in the form of a box or pipe, or it may be open as in a rectangular channel. Cutoff walls or antiseep collars usually are constructed as a part of the conduit to prevent seepage along its length and possible failure from this source.

Spillway outlet—The water leaves the structure through the outlet. Its function is to discharge the water into the channel below at a safe velocity. The outlet may be of the cantilever (propped) type, a plain apron outlet, or an apron with any type of energy dissipator to minimize the erosive effect of the water. Cantilever outlets are necessary in locations where the channel grade below the structure is unstable.

Vertical walls, known as toe walls, are extended below the front of the apron to prevent undercutting. Wingwalls are vertical walls, extending from the outlet into the

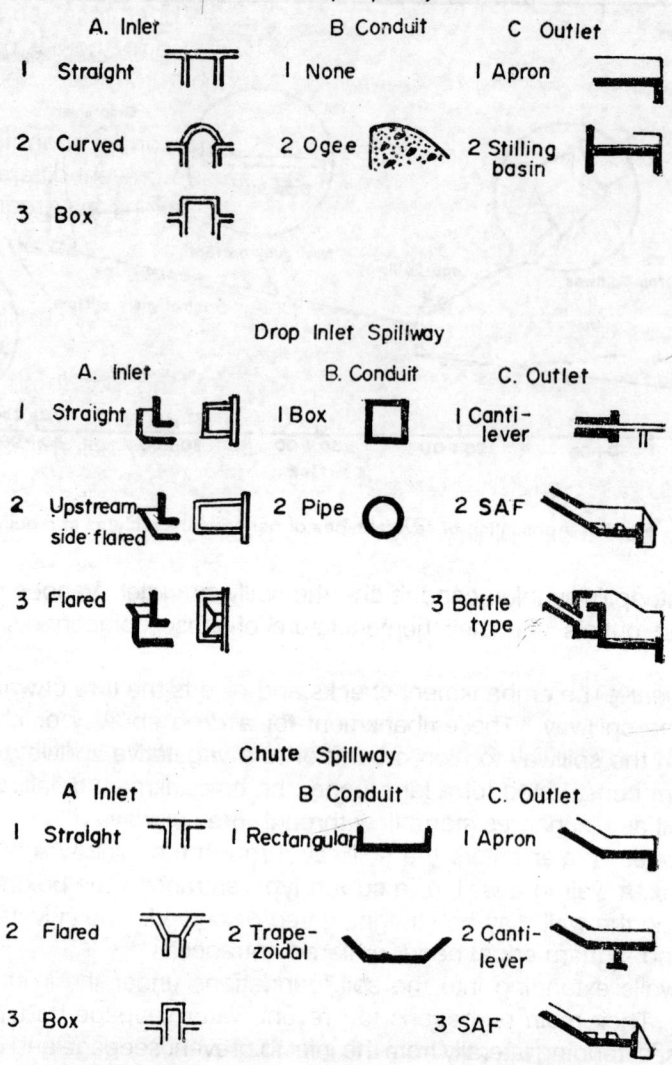

Fig. 5.8 Classification of component of hydraulic structure

channel banks to protect against the swirling effect of the water, as it leaves the structure.

STRUCTURE SELECTION

Selecting the proper structure for a given location and function is the key to successful and economical control of erosion or runoff. Each type of structure has its own range of use for a given set of conditions. Some sites will permit the use of more than one type of structure; however, there is generally one type that will provide the most economical control.

Layout

For proper selection of site, enough field survey and foundation data of all practical alternative sites should be collected. In case of costly installations, comparative cost estimates of alternative sites probably will be useful to determine the best site layout. In case of gradient control drops with definite approach channels as far as possible, the spillway should be located on a straight section of channel, so that at least for 25 to 50 m from the structure (upstream and downstream), there is no curve. Where the velocity of approach to the weir will be less than 0.6 m/sec., the effect of poor approach channel may be ignored.

The foundation material should have required supporting strength, resistance to sliding or piping and be reasonably homogeneous to prevent differential or uneven settlement of the structure. The foundation investigations may require one or two test holes for determining the various types of soils.

Structural Treatment of Gullies
Treatment of gullies generally falls into two classes: control by shaping and seeding or sodding; or structural control plus vegetation.

If slopes cannot be controlled by seeding or sodding, due to an overall or steep portion of channel, or the width of the gully or draw, into which water is being discharged is materially less than the width of waterway being treated, permanent structures will be required.

Structure Selection
Generally, the degree of control or protection and the size of the watershed are the primary considerations in structure selection.

To ensure long life and stability, structures are designed to handle 50 years peak discharge. To determine the expected peak discharge, the area (the catchment or watershed), the water draining from which shall pass through the structure, shall be demarcated on a map and information on watershed characteristics influencing the runoff, such as rainfall, land slope, vegetative cover and soil infiltration be obtained. Area of the watershed shall be determined with a planimeter. The design peak discharge can be determined using the rational formula as described earlier. Spillway with adequate dimensions has to be provided in the structure for safe conveyance of the design discharge, otherwise water will flow over the sides and undermine the structure.

With the design discharge and the drop determined from the site conditions, the structure selection diagram, Fig. 5.9 can be used for determining the type of structure needed.

This diagram is for average field conditions and is based on the most economical structure for the given head and discharge, provided the site will permit installation of the structure. Site and foundation conditions, therefore, are important factors in selecting the type of structure.

Stability of Grades below Spillways
The outlet of a spillway should be so designed that its function or stability will not be reduced by scour or deposition in the exit channel. The channel grade below the spillway should be stable to prevent undercutting of the outlet toe wall or cantilever support. The possibility of sediment deposition in the channel below the spillway should be investigated. When sediment is a problem, the outlet of the spillway should be designed, so that deposition will not interfere with the spillway discharge during the expected life of the structure.

Channel Alignment
For gradient control drops with definite approach channels, the site should be se-

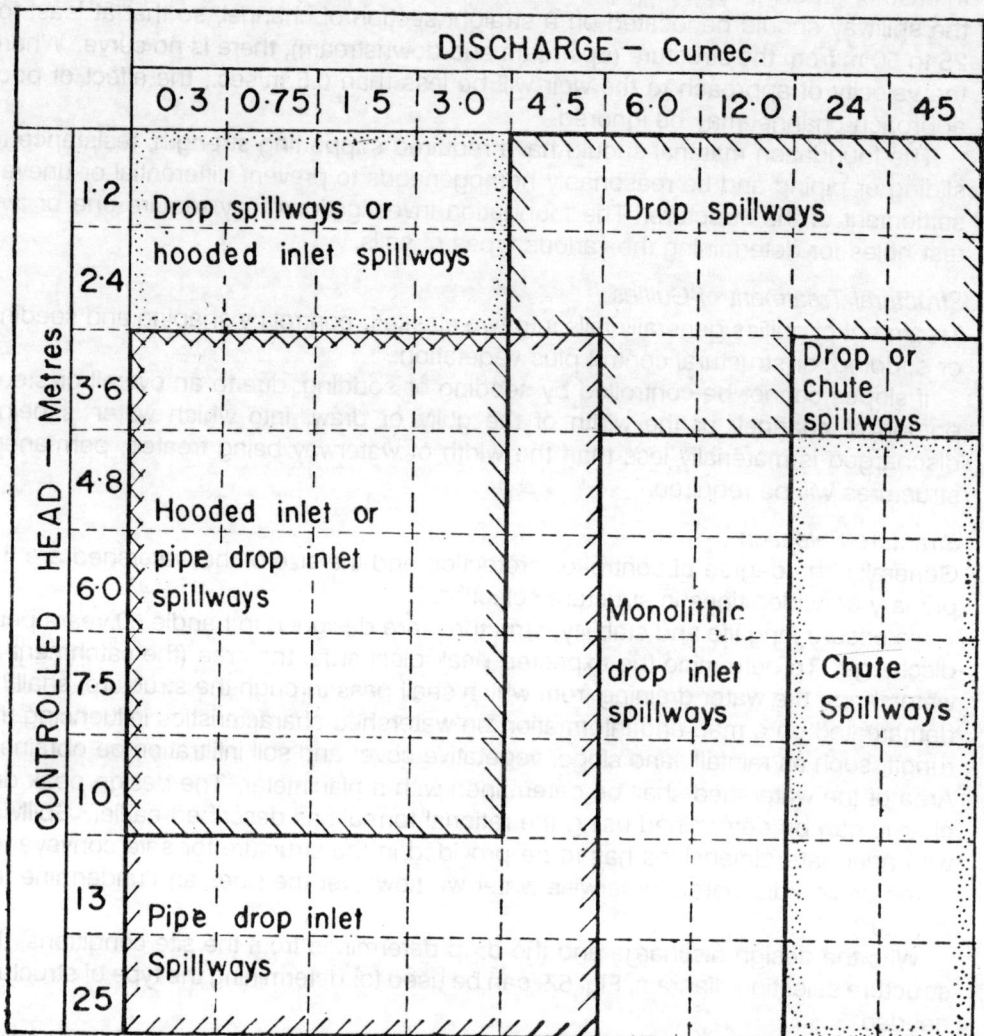

Fig. 5.9 General guide to selection structure

lected so that the spillway is located on reasonably straight section of channel (on tangent) with neither upstream nor downstream curves within 30 to 60 m of the structure. If often will be desirable to obtain straight alignment above and below the spillway by channel changes, that merge smoothly with the existing channel.

Poor upstream alignment results in uneven distribution of velocity and discharge over the weir will be less than 0.6 m/sec throughout the anticipated life of spillway, the effect of poor approach channel alignment may be ignored. Where the approach velocity is apt to be higher, the approach channel must be straight.

DROP SPILLWAY

Description—The drop spillway (Plate 22) is a weir structure. Flow passes through the weir opening, drops to an approximately level apron or stilling basin and then passes into the downstream channel. Nomenclature for the various parts of drop spillways are shown in Fig. 5.10

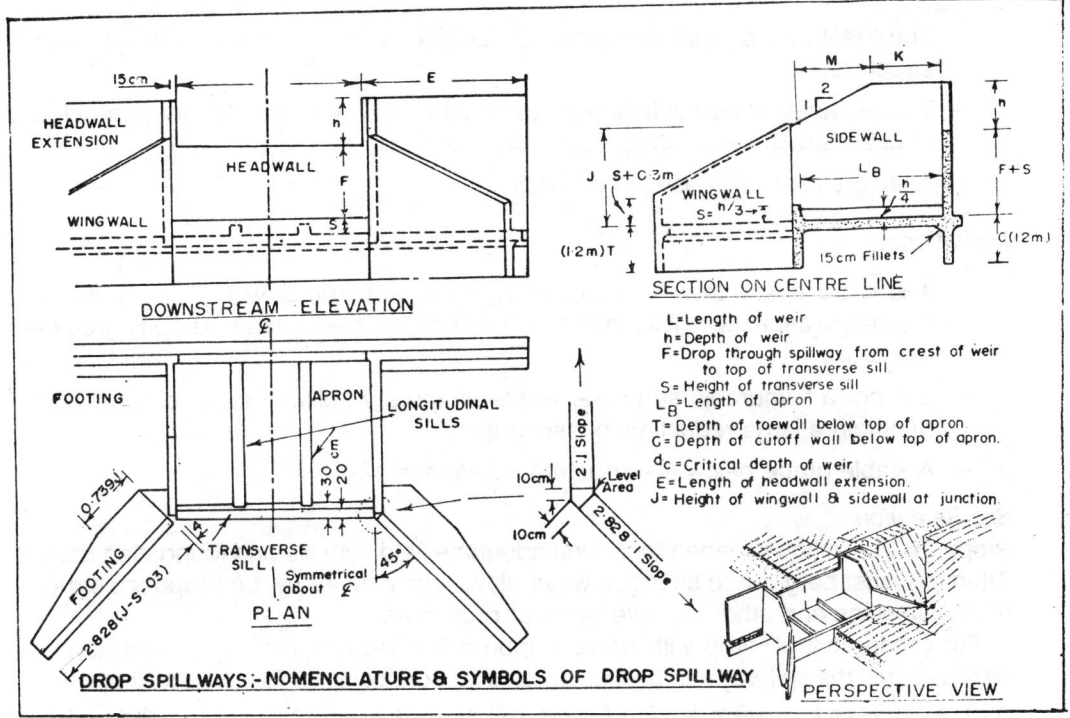

Fig. 5.10 Nomenclature and symbols of drop spillways

Materials

Drop spillways may be constructed of reinforced concrete, plain concrete, rock masonry, concrete blocks with or without reinforcing, or gabions.

Functional Use

-- Grade stabilization in lower reaches of waterways and outlets.

— Erosion control for protection of fields, roads, buildings and other improvements from gullies

— Grade control stabilizing channels

— Outlets for tile and surface water at the upper and along drainage ditches. Where the channel width below the proposed structure site is limited, the box inlet drop spillway is more effective

— Reservoir spillway where the total drop is relatively low

— Control of tail water at the outlet of a spillway or conduit

— Protection of the outlet and of grassed water-ways and sod chutes; and

— Control of irrigation water.

Adaptability

The drop spillway is an efficient structure for controlling relatively low heads, normally up to 3 metres.

Advantages

— The likelihood of serious structural damage is less than for other types of structures;

— The rectangular weir is less likely to be clogged by debris than the openings of outer structures of comparative discharge capacities; and

— They are relatively easy to construct.

Limitations

— It is more costly than some other types of structures, where the required discharge capacity is less than 3 cumec and the total head or drop is greater than 3 m;

— It is not a favourable structure, where temporary spillway storage is needed to obtain a large reduction in discharge;

— A stable grade below the structure is essential.

Site Selection

Proper site selection is dependent upon adequate field surveys and foundation data. Attention must be given to changed water elevations caused by the proposed structures, pipelines and other improvements or properties.

For grade control, drop with definite approach channels, the site should be selected so that the spillway can be located on a reasonably straight section of channel, with no upstream or downstream curves within at least 30 m of the structure. It is often desirable to straighten the channel alignment upstream and downstream of the spillway, so that it merges smoothly with the existing channel. Poor alignment may result in a reduction in discharge capacity and excessive scour of the embankment and channel banks. There should be no channel restrictions or obstacles in the approach channel, that would interfere with the design flow entering the spillway inlet.

The site selected should provide an adequate foundation for the spillway. The foundation material must have the required supporting strength, resistance to sliding and piping, and be reasonably homogeneous, so as to prevent uneven settlement of the structure.

Design

The design of a drop spillway proceeds from the hydraulic design of the capacity of spillway opening (weir), which should be more than the design discharge determined earlier.

Freeboard

Freeboard is the vertical distance, from the maximum water surface elevation on the upstream side of the headwall extension to the top of headwall extension for peak design discharge over the weir. It is a safety factor to provide against occurrence of conditions not anticipated during the design, that would decrease the capacity of the spillway or increase the discharge requirements and to provide protection against overtopping by wave action where it can take place.

As wave action does not generally occur upstream of the structures, except in case of long water bodies (large ponds and reservoirs), it is convenient and logical to consider freeboard in terms of increased weir discharge capacity. It also seems logical to assume that the required freeboard should be some function of the overall through the spillway, F, since the possible damage due to failure increase with an increase in F. The capacity requirement is modified to take care of freeboard of equation:

$Q = 1.711 Lh^{3/2}$ for flow through rectangular weirs is modified to:

$$Q = \frac{1.711Lh^{3/2}}{(1.1 + 0.01F)} \qquad \ldots (5.2)$$

where, Q = maximum discharge capacity of the weir (cumec)
(with provision for freeboard);
L = length of weir (m);
h = total depth of weir (including freeboard) (m); and
F = net drop from top of transverse sill to crest (m).

In case of reservoir outlet, where the wave freeboard F_w is to be included, it is given by:

$$0.000095 \; D \times F_w = \frac{(F)^{1/2}}{2} + 0.27$$
for D = 2000 m; and F = 6 m

where, F_w = wave freeboard (m); and
D = length of fetch (m).

Graphic solution of this equation is given in Fig. 5.11 for weir length L, ranging from 1 to 10 m and depth of weir, h ranging from 0.25 to 1.5 m, for an overfall, F of 2 m. For other drops up to 3 m, the capacity is only marginally different (within ± 1 per cent). The discharge capacities for the common range of dimensions for an overfall of 2 m with correction factors of other values of overfall are in Table 5.6. Generally L or h is given (fixed) by the site or functional requirements and a suitable combination for L, h and F to provide the design capacity can be obtained from the table. However, an important consideration is that, as the ratio h/F increases, for this reason, and because the most economical spillways for a given discharge tend towards low values of the h/F ratio, it is recommended that this ratio be kept lower than 0.50 with an absolute maximum of 0.75.

The ratio of L/h should always be equal to or greater than 2 for all rectangular weirs.

Structural Design (For Type B)
After L, h and F have been decided by the hydraulic requirements, the dimensions of the components of the structure can be obtained from the proportions shown in Fig. 5.10 and are as follows:

E = Minimum length of headwall extension (m) (3+0.6) or (1.5 F) whichever is
greater (5.3)

$$L_B = \text{Length of basin (m)} = F\left(2.28\frac{h}{F} + 0.52\right) \qquad (5.4)$$

J = Height of wingwall and sidewall at junction (m)

$$(2h) \text{ or } \left[F + h + s - \frac{(L_B + 0.10)}{2}\right] \qquad (5.5)$$

Table 5.6   Discharge capacities for straight drop spillways with net drop. F = 2 m. Multiply by correction factors for other drops

$$Q = 1.711Lh^{3/2}(1.1 + 0.01F)$$
(Discharge Capacity Q in cumec)

h (metre)	Length of weir, L, in metres										
	1.0	1.5	2.0	2.5	3.0	3.5	4.0	4.5	5.0	5.5	6.0
0.40	0.39	0.58	0.77	0.97	1.16	1.35	1.55	1.74	1.93	2.13	2.32
0.50	0.54	0.81	1.08	1.35	1.62	1.89	2.16	2.43	2.70	2.97	3.24
0.60	0.71	1.07	1.42	1.78	2.13	2.49	2.84	3.20	3.55	3.91	4.26
0.70	0.89	1.34	1.79	2.24	2.68	3.13	3.58	4.03	4.47	4.92	5.37
0.80	1.09	1.64	2.19	2.73	3.28	3.83	4.37	4.92	5.47	6.01	6.56
0.90	1.30	1.96	2.61	3.26	3.91	4.57	5.22	5.87	6.52	7.17	7.83
1.00	1.53	2.29	3.06	3.82	4.58	5.35	6.11	6.87	7.64	8.40	9.17
1.10	1.76	2.64	3.52	4.41	5.29	6.17	7.05	7.93	8.81	9.69	10.57
1.20	2.01	3.01	4.02	5.02	6.02	7.03	8.03	9.04	10.04	11.05	12.05
1.30	2.26	3.40	4.53	5.66	6.79	7.93	9.06	10.19	11.32	12.45	13.59
1.40	2.53	3.80	5.06	6.33	7.59	8.86	10.12	11.39	12.65	13.92	15.18
1.50	2.81	4.21	5.61	7.02	8.42	9.82	11.23	12.63	14.03	15.44	16.84

Correction factors for the other drops from 0.5 m up to 3.0 m

Net drop, F (meter)	0.5	0.75	1.0	1.25	1.50	1.75	2.0	2.25	2.5	2.75	3.00
Correction Factor	1.114	1.112	1.009	1.007	1.004	1.002	1.000	0.998	0.996	0.993	0.991

Total depth of weir (including freeboard)

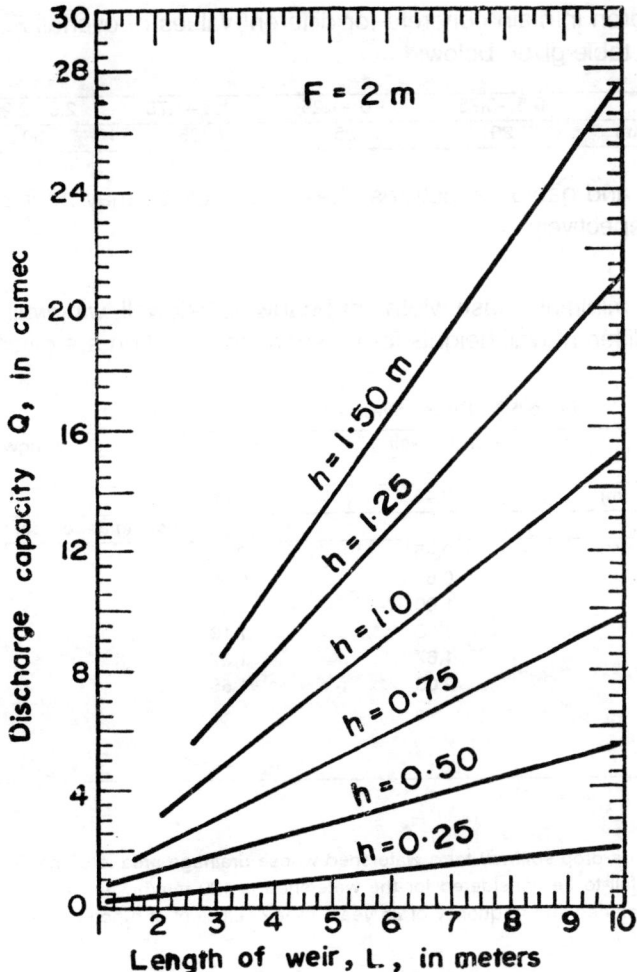

Fig. 5.11   Graphic solution of the equation $Q = \dfrac{1.711 L h^{1/2}}{(1.1 + 0.01F)}$

whichever is greater

$$M = 2 (F + 1.33 h - J) \qquad (5.6)$$

$$K = (L_B + 0.1) - M \qquad (5.7)$$

$$S_h = \text{Height of longitudinal sill} = \frac{h}{4} \qquad (5.8)$$

$$S_t = \text{Height of transverse sill} = \frac{h}{3} \qquad (5.9)$$

The direction of the headwall extensions and the wingwalls with respect to the headwall and the sidewalls need not be strictly according to the drawing. It can be changed to suit local conditions for economical anchorage and maximum stability determined by the natural channel banks.

Apron Thickness

Thickness of apron in plain concrete for different values of overfall F, can be determined from the table given below:

Overfall, F (m)	0.5 –0.75	1.0 –1.25	1.5 –1.75	2.0 –2.25	2.5 –3.0
Apron thickness (cm)	20	25	25	30	30

For masonry and gabion structures, these thicknesses may be increased by 1.5 and 2 times, respectively.

Wall Thickness

Top widths and minimum base widths of headwall, sidewall, wingwall and headwall extensions for different wall heights for masonry construction are given in Table 5.7.

Table 5.7   *Drop spillways in stone or brick masonry*

Description	Headwall	Sidewall	Wingwall and headwall extension
Minimum top width (m)	0.45	0.30	0.30
H		Recommended base widths	
0.5	0.45	0.30	0.30
1.0	0.67	0.55	0.40
1.5	1.00	0.82	0.60
2.0	1.33	1.10	0.80
2.5	1.67	1.37	1.00
3.0	2.00	1.65	1.20
3.5	–	–	1.40
4.0	–	–	1.60
4.5	–	–	1.80

Example 42: Design a drop spillway for a watershed whose drainage area is 58 ha. The drop is 2.0 m. The intensity of rainfall to be considered for the watershed is 120 mm/hr. In duration equal to time of concentration of watershed and frequency of 25 years. The coefficient of runoff is 0.3.
Solution:

$$Q = \frac{CIA}{360} \text{ (rational formula)}$$

$$= \frac{0.3 \times 120 \times 58}{360} = 5.8 \text{ cumec}$$

Obtain values of crest length and height of crest from Table 5.6 and tabulate.

	1	2	3	4	5
L	3.0	3.5	4.0	4.5	5.5
h	1.1	0.20	1.0	0.9	0.80

A number of combination values for L and h for disposing the peak runoff rate and the first adaptability test, have been presented below:

$\dfrac{L}{h}$	4	5	6.87	3.18	2.5
$\dfrac{h}{f}$	$\dfrac{1}{2}$	0.45	0.4	0.55	0.6

The value h/f is 0.55 and 0.6 for crest lengths 3.5 and 3.0 m, respectively, showing that they are not adoptable, since h/f values are greater than 0.50. Therefore, crest lengths 4, 4.5 or 5.5 can be adopted depending upon the site conditions. Say, $L = 4$ m and $h = 1.0$ m are suitable.

Structural Design

After L, h and F have been decided by the hydraulic requirements, the dimensions of the components of the structure are presented in Fig. 5.10.

Minimum headwall extension, $E = 3h + 0.6$
or $= 1.5f$ whichever is greater

$$E = 3 \times 1 + 0.6 = 3.6 \text{ m}$$
or $\quad 1.5 \times 2.0 = 3.0 \text{ m}$
$\therefore \quad$ Adopt $E = 3.6 \text{ m}$

Length of apron or basin, $L_B = F_B(2.28\dfrac{h}{F} + 0.54)$
$$= 2(2.28\tfrac{1}{2} + 0.52) = 3.32 \text{ m}$$

Height of wingwall and sidewall at junction

$$J = 2h \text{ or } (F + h - s\frac{L_B + 0.1}{2})$$

whichever is greater.

$\therefore \quad J = 2 \times 1.0 = 2.0 \text{ m}$
or $\quad (2 + 1.0 = 0.25 - \dfrac{3.42}{2}$
$= 2.75 - 1.7 = 1.0 \text{ m}$
Therefore, adopt $J = 2.0 \text{ m}$

$M = 2(F + 1.33h - J)$
$= 2(2 + 1.33 - 2) = 2.66 \text{ m.}$

Apron Thickness

The apron thickness is a direct function of overall and therefore, apron thickness for an overall of 2.0 m is equal to 30 cm. If the structure is intended to be masonry or gabion, the thickness may be increased by 1.5 and 2.0 times, respectively.

Wall Thickness

From Table 5.7, it may be seen that the thickness of walls in metres is given in Table 5.8 and may be adopted:

Table 5.8 *Thickness of walls (m)*

Description	Top width	Bottom width
Headwall	0.45	1.33
Sidewall	0.30	1.10
Wingwall and Headwall extension	0.30	0.80

Earthfill against Headwall and Drainage

Details of earthfill and type of drain are shown in Fig. 5.12. Type A drain is recommended where filter materials are not readily available at a conservative cost and type B is recommended where filter materials are readily available at a conservative cost.

For releasing pore water pressure built-up in the backfill weepholes of 5 cm diameter may be provided.

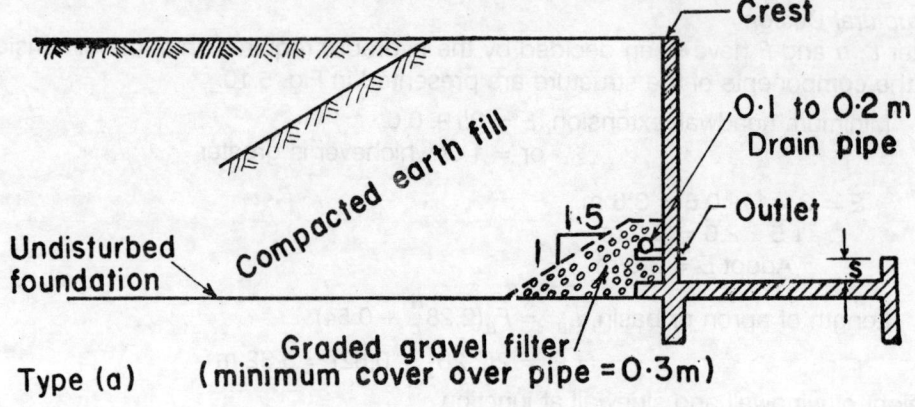

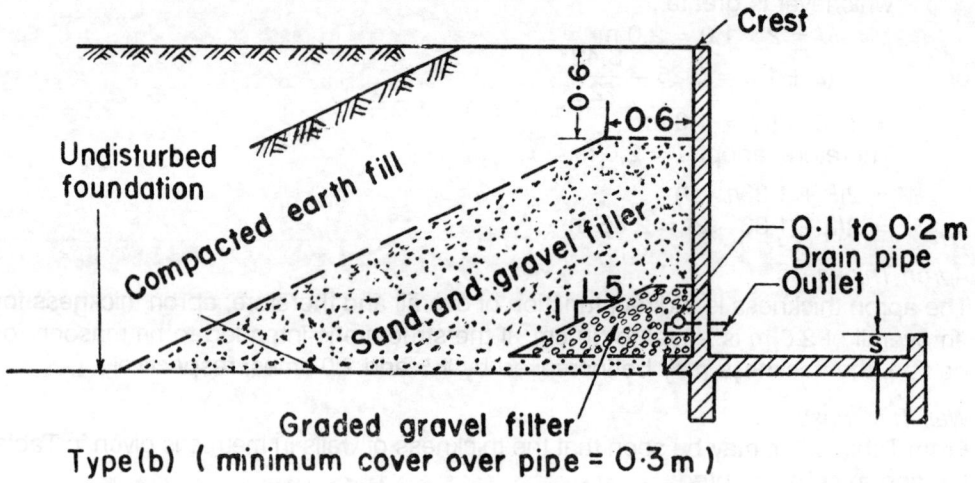

Fig. 5.12 Earthfill against headwall & drainage (Anonymous, 1953).

Riprap Approach Channel

Field experience has shown that earth backfill, just above the crest of a weir and at the end of embankments adjacent to the ends of the weir opening, is scoured out and carried away by discharge, unless it is protected by adequate riprap or vegetation. The magnitude of discharge and its duration, erodibility of backfill, alignment of approach channel, construction at the ends of the weir, sediment being transported and density, vigour and type of vegetation on the backfill and other factors necessitate riprap. Recommendations on the layout and requirements of riprap are presented in Fig. 5.13.

Notes: The riprap material should be of hard, durable stone or broken concrete with a unit weight equal to or greater than 2.5 tonnes/m^3

Angular, fragmented rock is preferable to rounded stone.

At least 75% of the riprap, by weight, should consist of pieces of rock or concrete, which equal or exceed the weight given in the table opposite the required depth of weir.

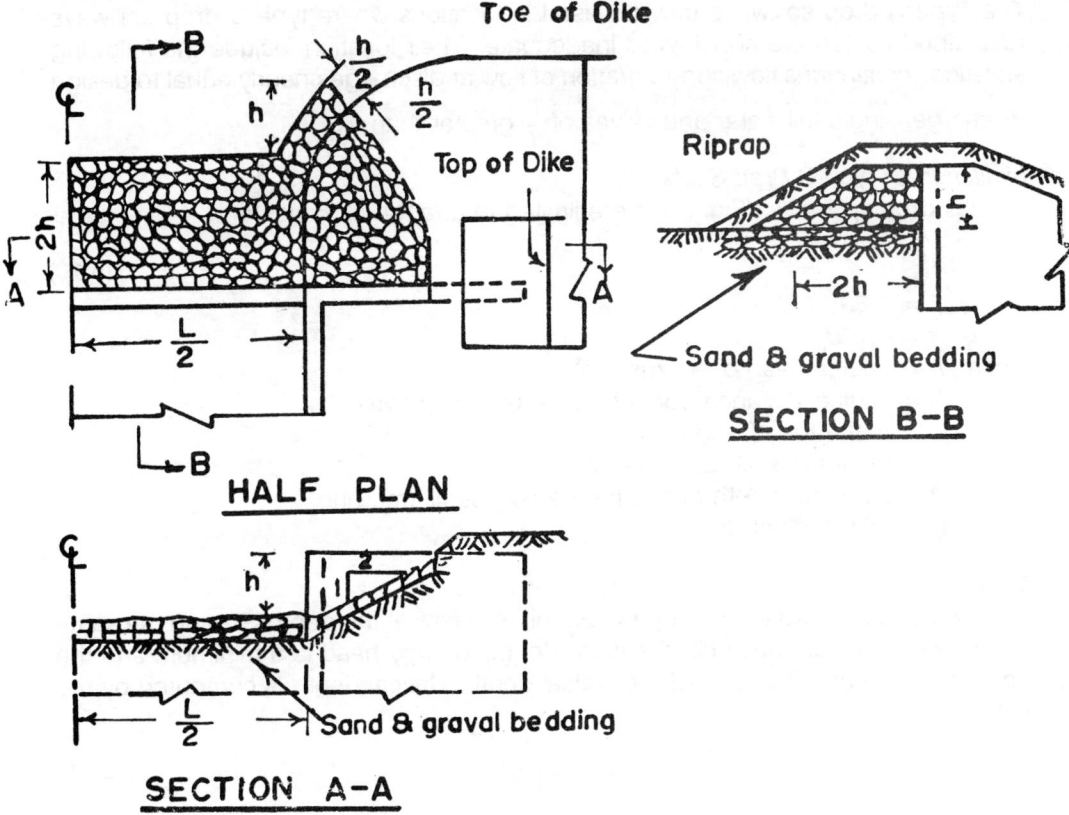

Fig. 5.13 Drop Spillways; riprap of approach channel; layout and requirements, Anonymous, 1953).

The thickness of the layer of riprap should be at least equal to the average diameter of rock D, indicated in the table.

Depth of weir, h, in metres.	Average diameter of rock, D, in cm.	Weight of rock in kg.	Minimum thickness of bedding in cm
0.25	7.5	1.0	7.5
0.50	7.5	1.0	7.5
0.75	12.5	3.0	7.5
1.00	15.0	5.0	7.5
1.25	20.0	10.0	10.0
1.50	25.0	20.0	12.5

The average diameter, D, is defined as the diameter of a spherical rock of equal weight and density.

The riprap should be placed on a bed of coarse pit-run sand and gravel. The minimum thickness of the bedding is indicated in the table.

The spaces between the large rock of the riprap should be filled with spalls, smaller rock, and pit-run material.

The dimensions of the area of riprap shown in the above sketches are minimum dimensions.

The surface of the riprap should be as smooth as possible.

HYDRAULIC DESIGN OF TYPE-C DROP SPILLWAYS

The Type C drop spillways may be used in locations where type B drop spillways (described earlier) are considered inadequate. Their location include the following situation: continuous flow, long duration of flow at discharges nearly equal to design discharge, single tail water and valves of $\frac{h}{f}$ greater than 0.5.

Limitation of Type C Drop Spillways

Type C drop spillways, (Fig. 5.14) are limited to a range of values of:

$$0.1 \leq \frac{h}{f} < 1.43;$$ ... (5.10)

$$L = 1.5d_c$$

$$t = 1.75d_c$$

where, h = design head over crust (m);

f = vertical distance from the crest of the spillway to the top of end fill (m);

L = length of spillway crest (m);

t = tail water depth above the transverse fill (m); and

d_c = critical depth (m).

Critical Depth (d_c)

A given quantity of water in an open conduit may flow at the depths having the same energy head. When these depths coincide, the energy head is a minimum and the corresponding depth is termed the critical depth. Critical depth is computed by the formula:

$$d_c = \left[\frac{Q^2}{l^2 g}\right]^{1/3}$$ ... (5.11)

where, Q = peak rate of runoff (cumecs); and

l = length of spillway (m).

The parameter d_c is used in the determination of various dimensions of drop spillway, which are set by the hydraulic design. The critical depth, d_c is that critical depth corresponding to the capacity without freeboard in the weir notch of the drop spillway.

Design Discharge

The design discharge, Q is that discharge which the structure is required to convey with a freeboard. It is determined from hydrologic data using rational formula, $Q = \frac{CIA}{360}$.

The required capacity without freeboard is that discharge the structure must convey without freeboard.

$$Q_s = (1.10 + 0.01F)Q$$ ... (5.12)

where, Q = discharge with freeboard and Q_s = discharge without freeboard.

Tail Water Depth, $t = 1.75d_c$

Tail water depths over the transverse sill are determined by computing water surface profiles.

The tail water depths over the transverse sill, t must be greater than or equal to 1.75 d_c, to prevent excess scour in the downstream bed and banks. Sufficient tail

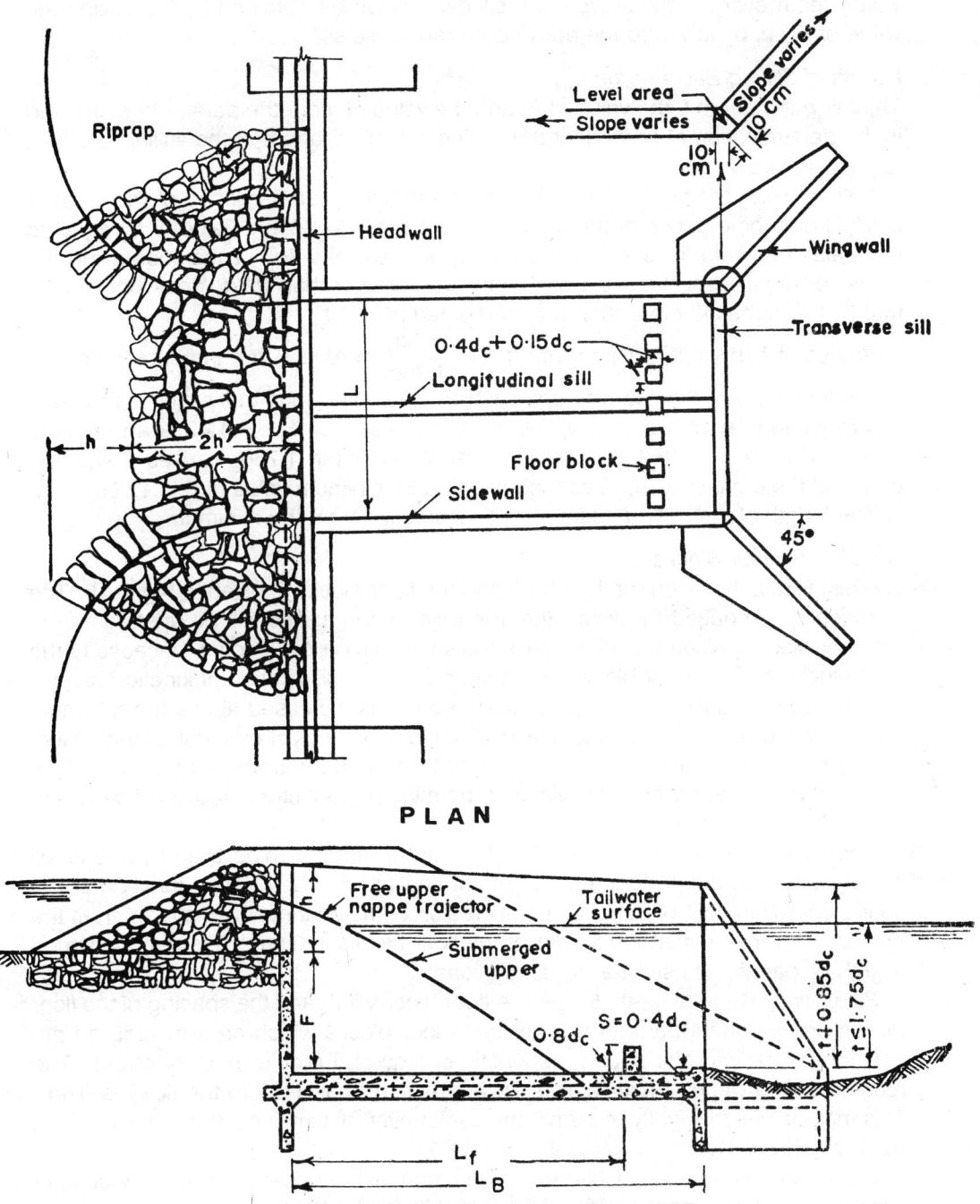

PLAN

SECTION ON CENTERLINE

Fig. 5.14 Type C Drop spillway (Anonymous, 1953)
Symbols-d_c = Critical depth for the weir section of the spillway; F = Vertical distance from top of transverse sill to spillway crest; h = Depth of weir; L = Crest length = stilling basin width; L_B = Minimum stilling basin length; L_f = Distance from downstream face of headwall to upstream face of floor blocks; S = Height of transverse sill; t = Vertical distance from tail water surface to top of transverse sill.

water depth over the transverse end sill can always be obtained by increasing the value of F; i.e. by lowering the apron and transverse sill.

Length of Stilling Basin Apron L_B

The tail water depth t, the value of F, and the value of h are the parameters required in the determination of apron length L_B. The minimum length of the stilling basin L_B is given in Fig. 5.15.

Values along the right side of the graph represent submergence of the crest of $0.7d_c$. For submergence of the crest greater than $0.7d_c$, use a value of L_B equal to that value obtained for a submergence of the crest of $0.7d_c$. Thus, increasing the tail water depth over the crest of the spillway greater than $0.7d_c$ does not require that L_B be increased more than that computed for $0.7d_c$.

Values of $h/t > 0.857$ (Note that $h/t = \dfrac{1.5d_c}{1.75d_c} = 0.857$) are impermissible, because they represent tail water depths which are smaller than that which is required. It is required that the value of $h/F < 1.43$. The value of $h/F = 1.43$ is a maximum value. When $h/F = 1.43$, the minimum tail water depth $1.75d_c$ causes a submergence of the crest of $0.7d_c$. Because of this, the minimum value of F is $1.05d_c$.

The length of the stilling basin may be increased from the minimum.

Location of Floor Blocks L_f

The distance L_f between the headwall and the floor blocks is given in Fig. 5.16. The distance L_f is required to assure that the trajet of the nappe will be upstream from the floor blocks. When this distance is too small, a high boil occurs, because of the floor blocks and the floor blocks are ineffective in the dissipation of kinetic energy,

If, for some reason, the length of the apron L_B is increased above the minimum amount, the distance L_f from the headwall to the floor block should not be increased.

The minimum distance between the floor block and the transverse sill, $L_B - L_f = 1.75d_c$, may be increased. The distance permits the reduction of turbulence downstream from the floor blocks.

Height of Floor Blocks $0.8\ d_c$—The heights of the floor blocks and the end sill are significant in the performance of the stilling basin. The primary function of the floor blocks is to control bank or lateral erosion of the channel downstream from the spillway. The recommended height of the floor blocks is $0.8d_c$. This may be varied slightly to permit the use of even dimensions.

Floor Block Width $(0.4 \pm 0.15)d_c$—The floor block width and the spacing of the floor blocks are important parts of the design. Floor blocks which are too wide do not function properly in dissipating the kinetic energy and require high sidewalls. The recommended width of floor blocks (in a direction transverse to the flow) is $0.4d_c$. This may be varied slightly to permit the use of even dimensions, but the floor block width should be within the interval $(0.4 \pm 0.15)d_c$.

Floor Block Length $(0.4 \pm 0.15)d_c$—The recommended length (in the direction of flow) of floor blocks is $0.4d_c$. This dimension affects the required dimension between the floor blocks and the end sill. This distance is required for energy dissipation of the flow, which has been divided by the floor blocks. The length may be varied slightly to permit the use of even dimensions.

Floor block spacing—Floor blocks which occupy over 60% of the transverse length of the stilling basin tend to function like a solid sill. If they occupy less than 50% of the transverse length of the stilling basin, they function less efficiently. A half space

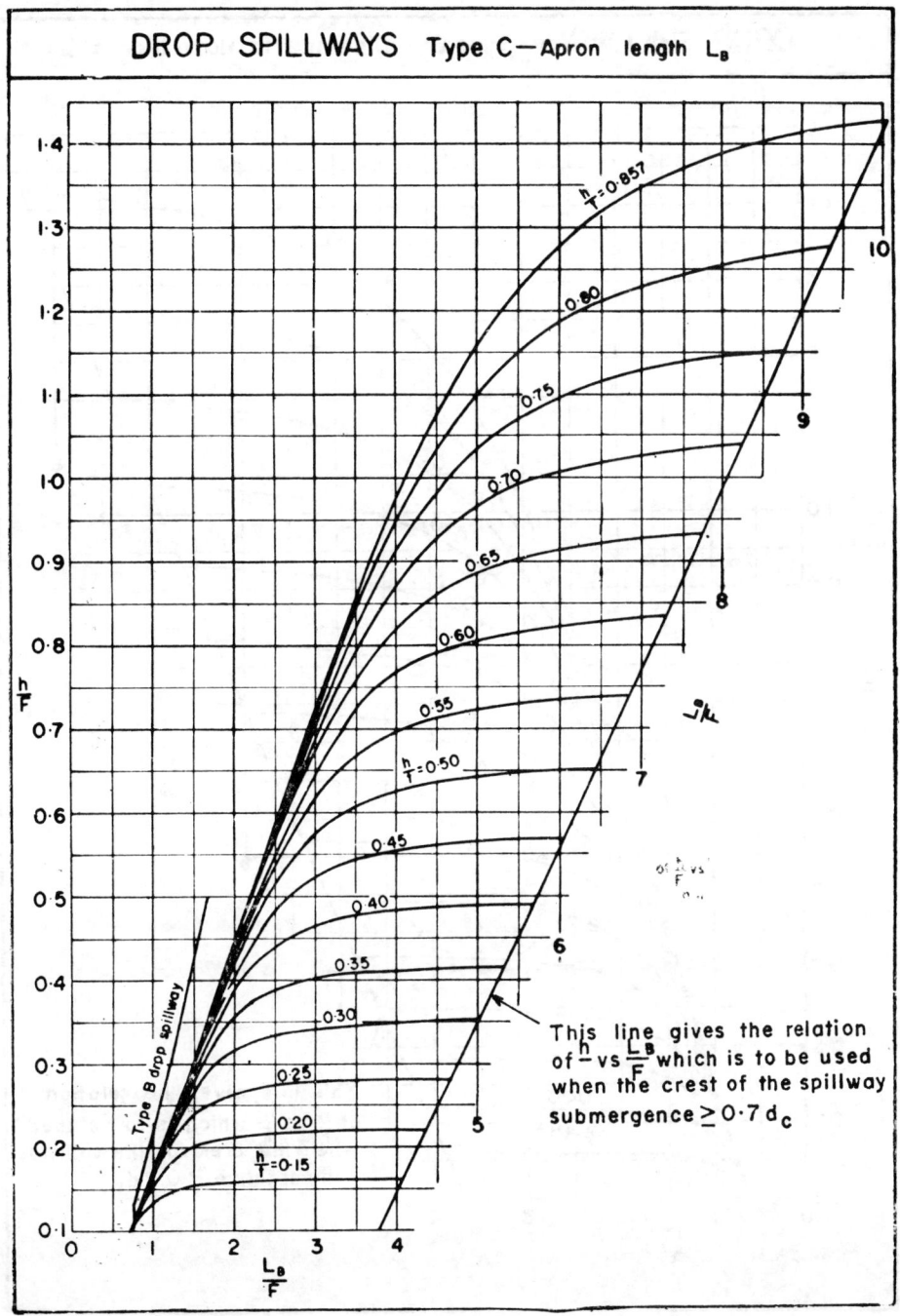

Fig. 5.15 Nomograph for solving L_f (Anonymous, 1953)

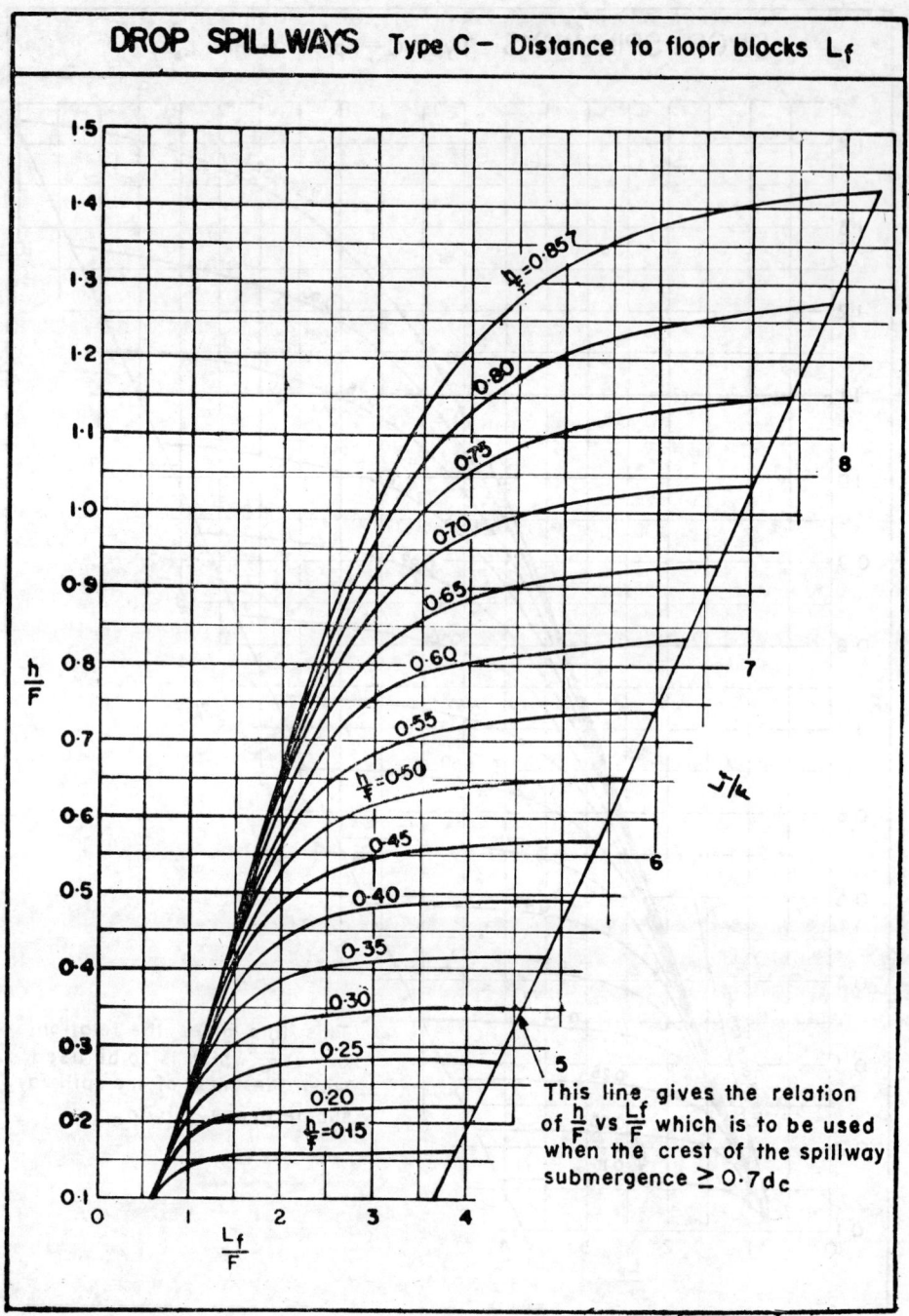

Fig. 5.16 Nomograph for solving L_f (Anonymous, 1953)

$(0.2d_c)$ shall be allowed adjacent to the sidewall and first floor block. Thus, no floor block will be placed adjacent to the sidewalls.

Longitudinal Sills—Longitudinal sills may be used for structural purposes. Their width will be equal to or less than the floor block width, and their height is determined from structural requirements. They are not to be spaced between the floor blocks. Longitudinal sills are neither beneficial nor harmful hydraulically.

Transverse Sill Height $0.4d_c$—The transverse sill prevents erosion in the channel bed immediately downstream from the drop spillway. The lowest height of the transverse sill was selected from model study to reduce the tail water requirement. The recommended height of the transverse sill is $0.4d_c$. This height may be increased slightly to permit the use of even dimensions.

Sidewall Height $(t + 0.85d_c)$—The sidewall must extend above the tail water to prevent overtopping of the sidewalls. The water surface in the stilling fluctuates considerably. The floor blocks and end sills cause boils and standing waves. The height boils are $0.60d_c$ above the tail water. The recommended minimum height of the sidewall at the end sill is $t + 0.85d_c$. From the stand point of hydraulics, the top of the sidewalls may be level and have the recommended height.

Wingwalls—Wingwalls are set at an angle of 45° with the centreline of the basin. The top of the wingwall should have a slope not steeper than 1:1. The length of the wingwall is usually controlled by the backfill slope and should be sufficient to intersect the backfill slope in the horizontal plane at the top of the transverse sill.

Approach Channel—Certain approach channel conditions are necessary for this type of drop spillway to function properly. These conditions are:

— The bottom of the approach channel must be level and have the same elevation as the crest of the drop spillway for a minimum distance of $6d_c$ upstream from the crest.

— The dikes covering the upstream face of the headwalls are essential for the proper functioning of this structure. It is preferable hydraulically, that the slope of the dike along the face of the headwall be steeper than a 2:1 slope. When this slope is flatter than 2:1, the discharge over the weir is concentrated in the central portion of the stilling basin.

When dikes are omitted in wide channels, or when the toe of dike at the upstream face of the headwall is not at the weir notch corner, a significant contraction of flow occurs in the weir section. This causes an unfavourable distribution of discharge in the stilling basin and poor stilling basin performance.

If, for some reason, the bottom width or the approach channel is equal to the length of the weir notch, no dikes will be required, provide the side slope of the channel at the structure is not flatter than 2:1.

— The channel bottom and the dikes covering the upstream face of the headwall require riprap to prevent their erosion. The recommended use of riprap and the specifications for riprap size and weight were given in the earlier designs. Of course, concrete paving may be used in place of riprap.

Design Example 43—The design discharge, $Q = 20$ cumecs. The approach channel is flat and has a bottom width of 13 m. The maximum total energy head in the approach channel of the weir notch is limited to $H = 1.2\,m$. A drop to be controlled in the channel is 2.5 m. The depth of flow in the downstream channel is 1.2 m. Two buttresses and longitudinal sills are used in the design. Determine weir notch depth; vertical distance, t from the top of the transverse sill to the tail water surface; the vertical distance F from the top of the transverse sill to the crest; the required capacity without freeboard Q_{fr}, the crest length L, and the capacity without freeboard Q_s; approach channel hydraulic requirements; minimum transverse sill height s; stilling length L_B; location, width, spacing, and height of floor blocks; minimum sidewall height; and wingwall length.

Solution

Weir notch depth—Set the weir notch depth equal to the minimum available total energy head in the approach channel, $h = 1.2$ m. (Minimum specific energy $= \dfrac{3}{2} \times$ critical depth).

$$\text{then, } d_c = \frac{2}{3} \times h = \frac{2}{3} \times 1.2 = 0.8 \text{ m.}$$

Vertical distance, t from the top of the transverse sill to the tail water surface

$$t = 1.75 d_c = 1.75 \times 0.80 = 1.4 \text{ m}$$

Vertical distance, F from the top of the transverse sill to the crest

If the controlled drop is 2.5 m and the tail water depth is 1.2 m, then $F = 1.2 + t = 1.2 + 1.4 = 2.6$ m. The required tail water depth places the top of the transverse sill 0.1 below the downstream channel grade.

Required capacity without freeboard

$$Q_y = (1.10 + 0.01F)Q$$
$$= (1.10 + 0.01 \times 2.5)20$$
$$= 1.125 \times 20 = 22.5 \text{ cumec.}$$

Since the weir is submerged less than $\dfrac{1}{3}d_c$, the value of $\dfrac{q}{h^{3/2}} = 1.71$.

$$q = 1.71 \times 1(1.2)^{3/2}$$
$$= 2.24 \text{ cumec/m.}$$

where, $q =$ capacity without freeboard per metre length of crest.

Crest length, $L = \dfrac{22.5}{2.24} = 10$ m

The capacity without freeboard

$Q_{sr} = 10 \times 2.24 = 22.4$ cumec.

Approach Channel Hydraulic Requirement

The bottom width of the approach channel must be reduced to 10 m at the spillway crest. The channel side slopes at the head-wall must be 2:1. This is accomplished by the addition of a conical shaped fill between the upstream face of the headwall and the side slope of the 13 m approach channel. The approach channel is then riprapped as already dealt.

Minimum Transverse Sill Height (s)

$$s = 0.4 d_c = 0.4 \times 0.8$$
$$= 0.32 \text{ m.}$$

Stilling basin L_B is determined as shown below:

$$\frac{h}{F} = \frac{1.2}{2.5} = 0.48, \qquad \frac{h}{t} = \frac{1.2}{1.4} = 0.85 \qquad \frac{L_B}{F} \text{ (from Fig. 5.28)} = 2.04$$

$$\text{Hence, } L_B = 2.04 \times F$$
$$= 2.04 \times 2.5$$
$$= 5.1 \text{ m} \qquad \text{Use 5.15 m.}$$

Location, Width, Spacing and Height of Floor Blocks

The distance from downstream face of the headwall to the upstream face of the floor block, L_f determined from Fig. 5.16.

$$\frac{h}{F} = 0.48 \qquad \frac{h}{t} = 0.85 \qquad \frac{L}{F} = 1.50$$
$$\therefore L_f = F \times 1.50 = 2.5 \times 1.5$$
$$= 3.75 \text{ m}$$

The block are square in plan. The width, $W = 0.4d_c = 0.4 \times -0.8 = 0.32$ m, Crest length = 10 m. Taking 55% of crest length (10 m) and width of each block equal to $0.4d_c$ (0.32 m).

$$\text{Number of blocks} = \frac{0.55 \times 10}{0.32} = \frac{5.5}{0.32}$$
$$= 17.1 \quad \text{Say 17 numbers}$$

The block are spaced at $0.4d_c = 0.32$ m

The extra end blocks are spaced $0.2d_c$ from the sidewall.

Height of blocks = $0.8d_c = 0.8 \times 0.8 = 0.64$ m.

Minimum Sidewall Height

The sidewall height above the top of transverse sill is $t + 0.85\ d_c$.
$$= 1.4 + 0.85 \times 0.8 = 1.4 + 0.68 = 2.08 \text{ or Say 2.0 m.}$$

Wingwall Length

The 2:1 sill slope of the dyke works out to 1.23 m above the top of the transverse sill (and elevation of the top of the wingwall) at the junction of wingwall and sidewall.

$$\text{Wingwall length} = \frac{2.45}{\cos 45°}$$
$$= \frac{2.45}{0.707} = 3.45 \text{ m.}$$

Suitable aeration may be provided. The details of designed structure is given in Fig. 5.17.

CHUTE SPILLWAY

Description

A chute spillway (Plate 23) is an open channel with a steep slope, in which flow is carried at supercritical velocities. It usually consists of an inlet, vertical curve section, steep-sloped channel, and outlet. The major part of the drop in water surface takes place in a channel. Flow passes through the inlet and down the paved channel to the floor of the outlet. Nomenclature for various parts of chute spillway are shown in Fig. 5.18.

Material

Reinforced concrete is the most widely used and safest material for large chutes. Plain concrete and masonry, though not as suitable as reinforced concrete, can also be used.

Functional Uses

— To control the gradient in either natural or constructed channels.

— To serve as a spillway for flood prevention, water conservation, and sediment collecting structures.

Adaptability

The chutes, specifically the concrete chute, is particularly adapted to high overfall, where a full flow structure is required and where site conditions do not permit the use of a detention-type structure. It also may be used with detention dams, taking advantage of the temporary storage to reduce the required capacity and the cost of the chute.

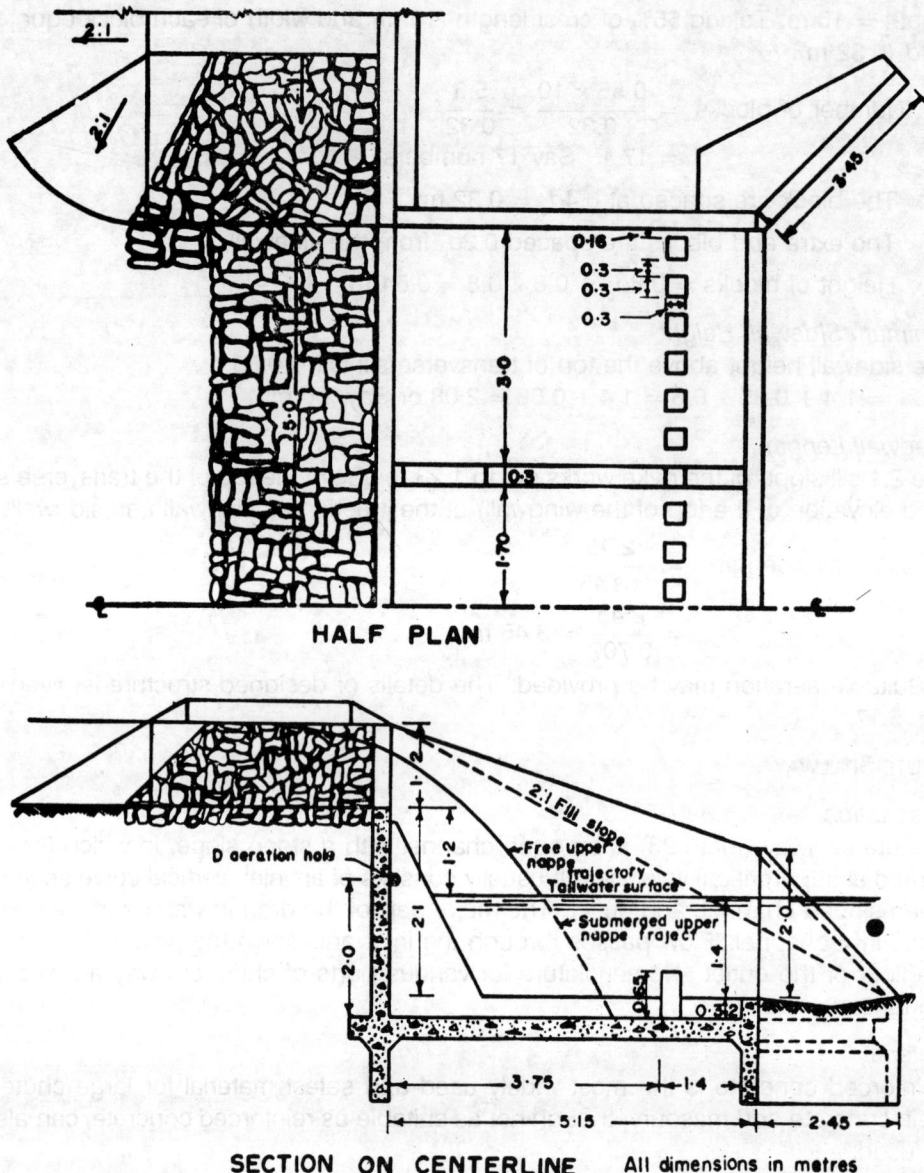

HALF PLAN

SECTION ON CENTERLINE   All dimensions in metres

Fig. 5.17 Design example of straight Drop Spillway-Type C (Anonymous, 1953)

Advantages

It usually is more economical than a drop-inlet structure, when large capacities are required.

Limitations

There is a considerable danger of undermining of the structure by rodents. In poor drain locations, seepage may weaken the foundation. It must be placed on compacted fill or on undisturbed soil in an abutment.

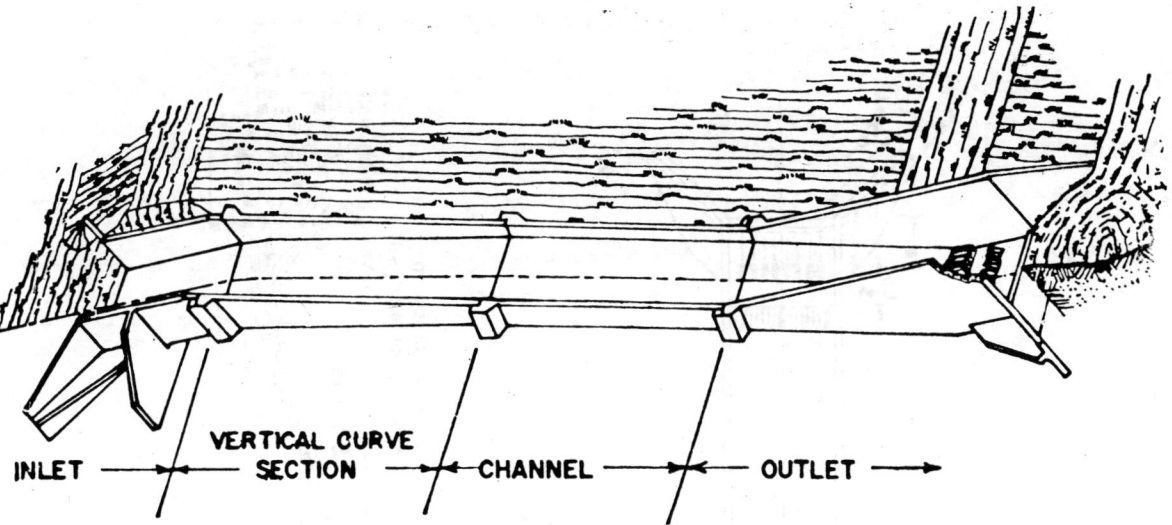

INLET ⟶ |← VERTICAL CURVE SECTION ⟶|← CHANNEL ⟶|← OUTLET ⟶

Fig. 5.18 Nomenclature of various parts of chute spillway

Design

Hydraulic design for a straight inlet drop spillway is similar to that for the straight inlet drop spillway described earlier. For other types of inlet, the design requires assistance of an experienced engineer.

Structural details for a straight inlet, straight channel and SAF type outlet, in plain concrete, are shown in Fig. 5.19 to 5.22. The channel is generally constructed at an inclination of 3:1, 4:1 or 10:1. The material thickness for masonry construction may be increased to 1.5 times of those shown in the drawing. Weep holes must be provided in the pressure built up in the back-fill.

DROP INLET SPILLWAYS

Description

A drop inlet spillway is a closed conduit generally designed to carry water under pressure from above an embankment to a lower elevation. An earthen embankment is required to direct the discharge through the spillway. Thus, the usual function of a drop inlet spillway is to convey a portion of the runoff through or under an embankment without erosion. Vegetated or earth spillways around one or both ends of the embankment should always be used in conjunction with drop inlet spillways. Nomenclature for various parts of drop inlet spillway are shown in Fig. 5.23.

Materials

The riser of a drop inlet spillway may be of plain concrete, reinforced concrete blocks, masonry or pipe. The barrel may be of reinforced concrete, concrete or clay tile, or corrugated or smooth metal pipe having watertight joints. In India, R.C.C. pipes are generally used.

Functional Uses

— Principal spillways for farm ponds or reservoirs.

— Grade stabilization

— At lower end of disposal system

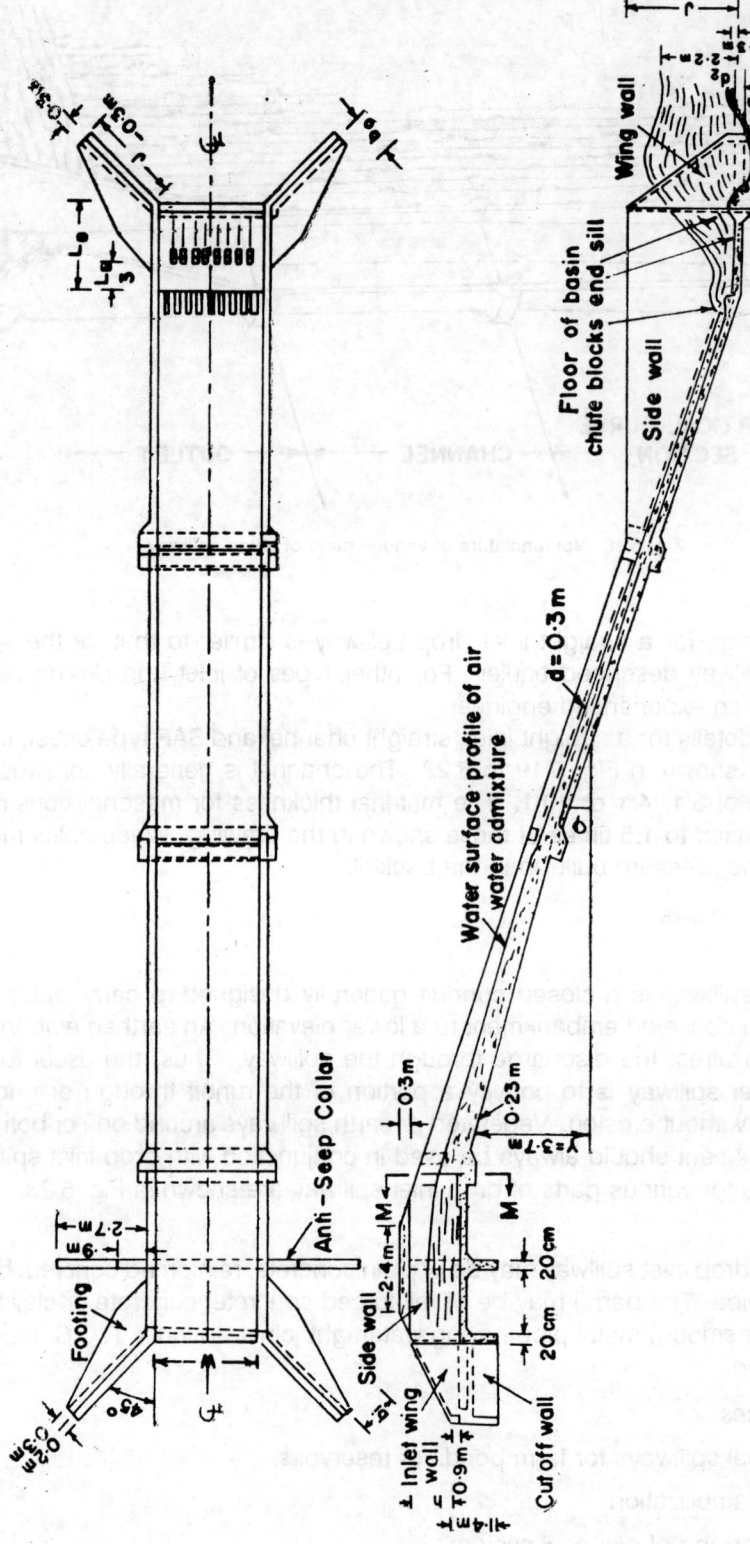

Fig. 5.19 Structural details of a chute spillway (Anonymous, 1965)

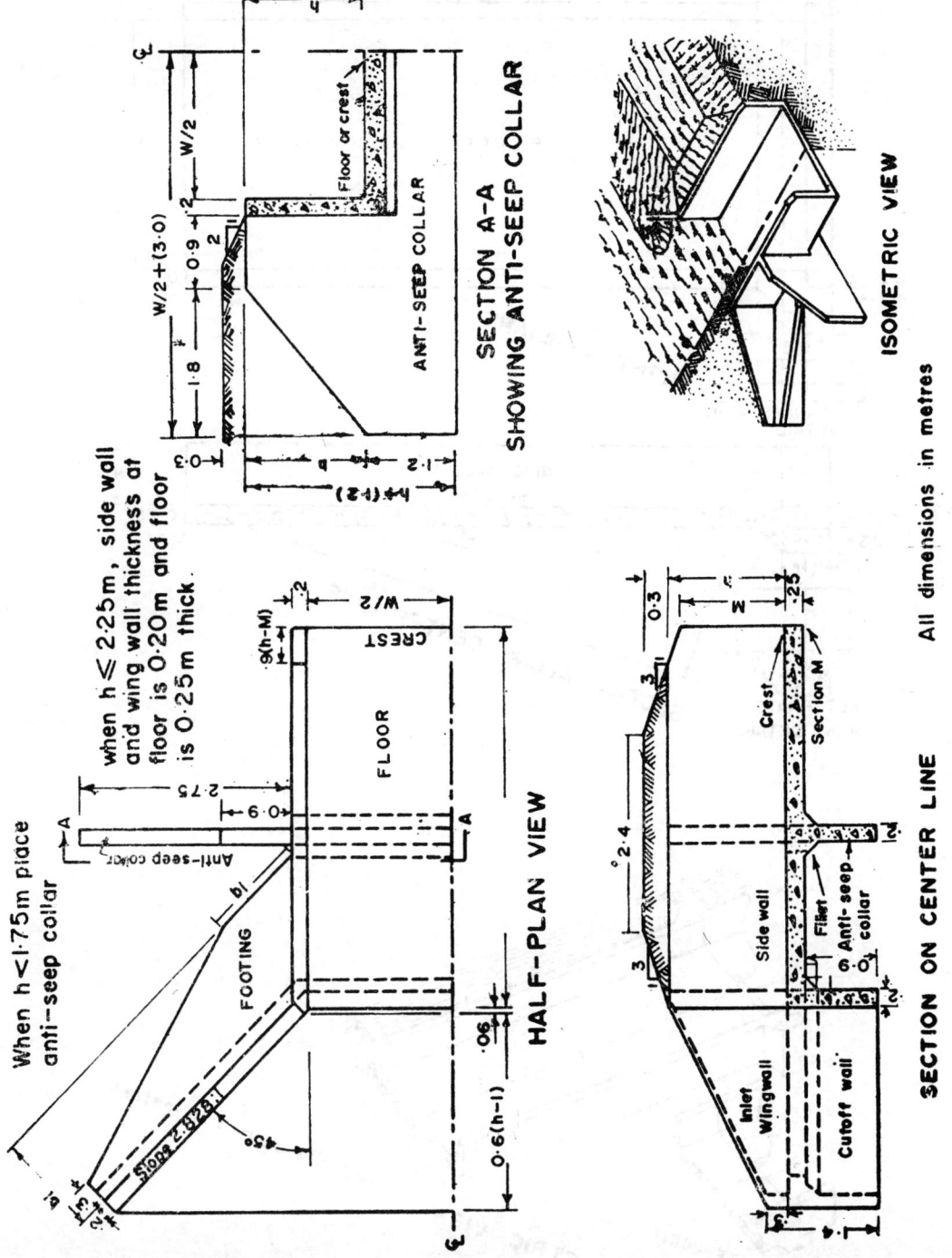

Fig. 5.20 Chute spillway—Inlet details (Anonymous, 1965)

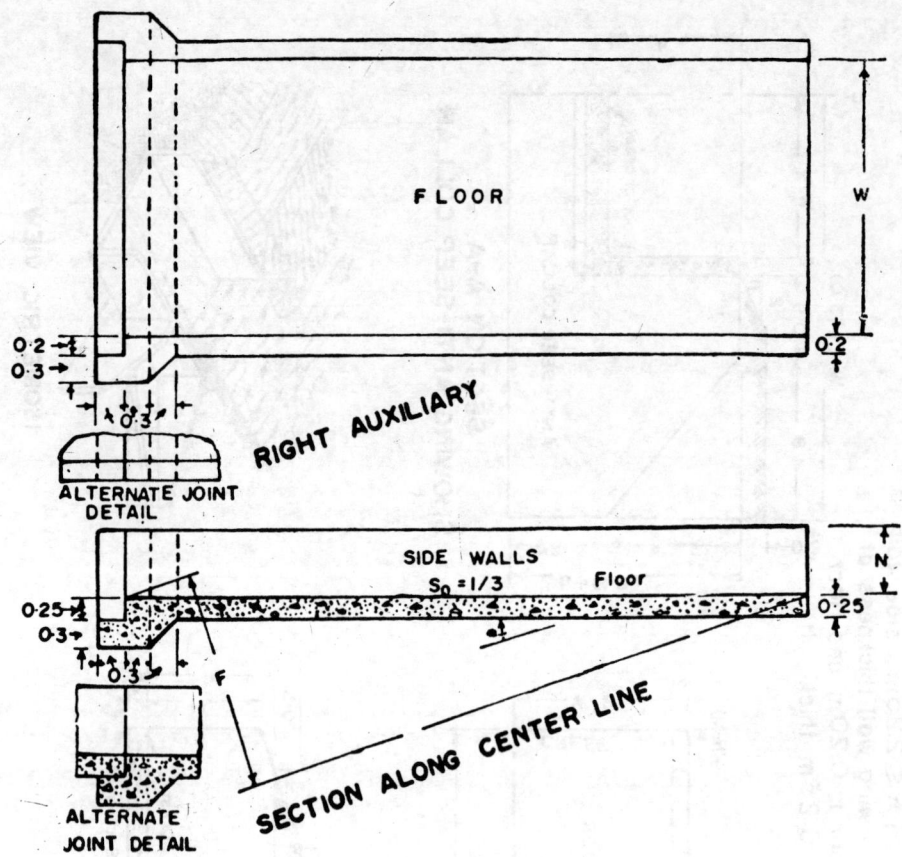

FLOOR

W

RIGHT AUXILIARY

0·2
0·3

0·3

ALTERNATE JOINT
DETAIL

SIDE WALLS
$S_0 = 1/3$ Floor

N

0·25
0·3

0·3

F

SECTION ALONG CENTER LINE

ALTERNATE
JOINT DETAIL

0·25

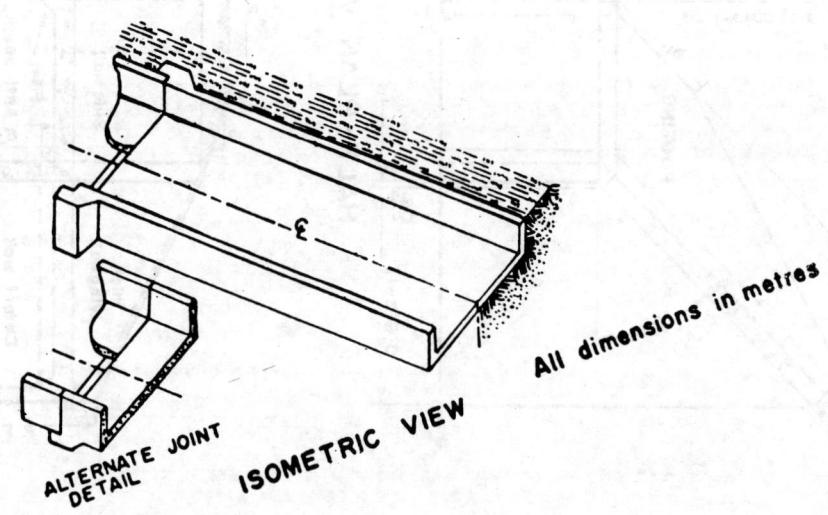

ALTERNATE JOINT
DETAIL

ISOMETRIC VIEW

All dimensions in metres

Fig. 5.21 Chute spillway—channel details (Anonymous, 1965)

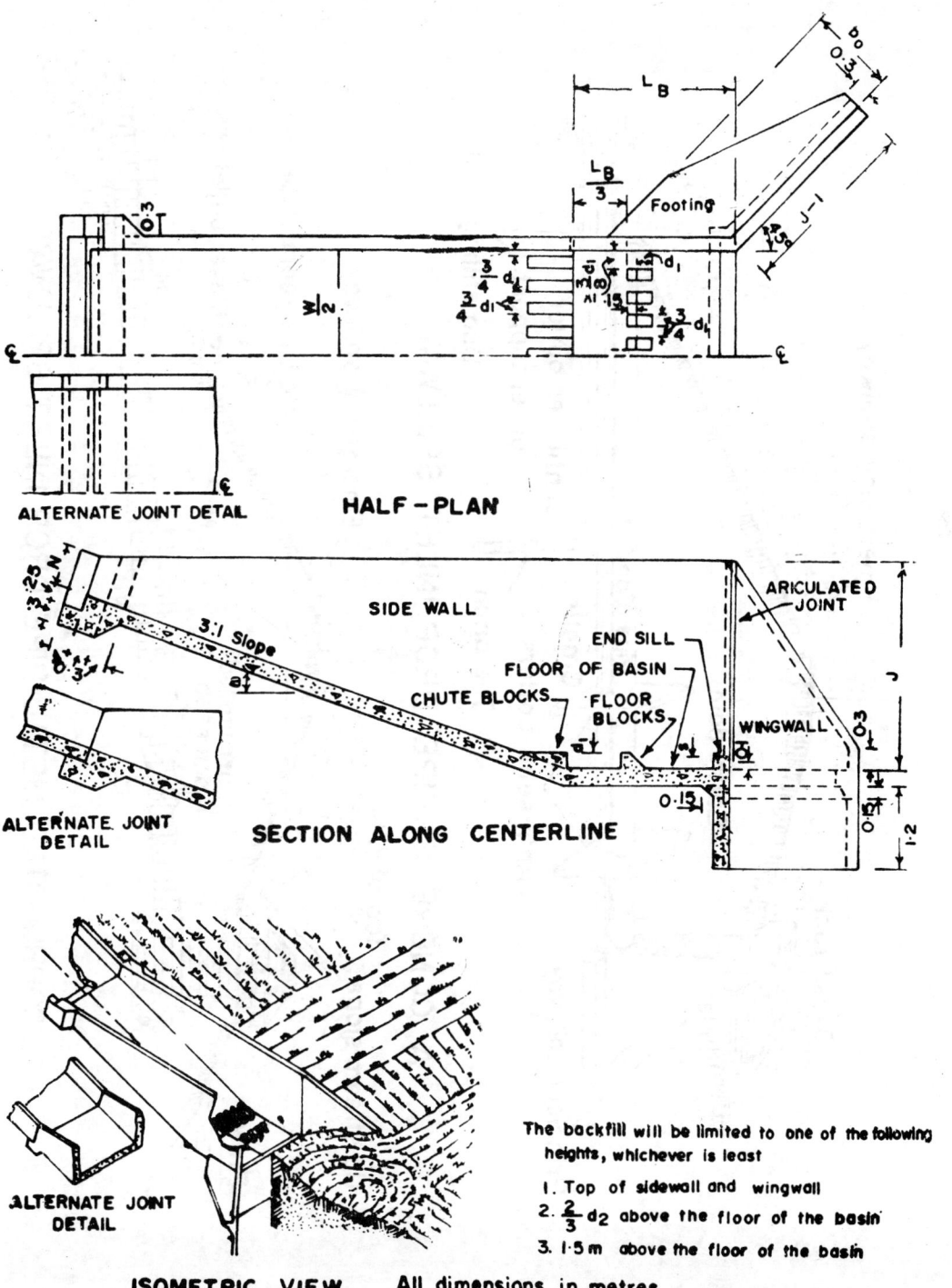

ALTERNATE JOINT DETAIL

HALF - PLAN

SIDE WALL

ARICULATED JOINT

END SILL

FLOOR OF BASIN

CHUTE BLOCKS

FLOOR BLOCKS

WINGWALL

3:1 Slope

ALTERNATE JOINT DETAIL

SECTION ALONG CENTERLINE

ALTERNATE JOINT DETAIL

The backfill will be limited to one of the following heights, whichever is least

1. Top of sidewall and wingwall
2. $\frac{2}{3} d_2$ above the floor of the basin
3. 1·5 m above the floor of the basin

ISOMETRIC VIEW   All dimensions in metres

Fig. 5.22 Chute spillway—outlet details (Anonymous, 1965)

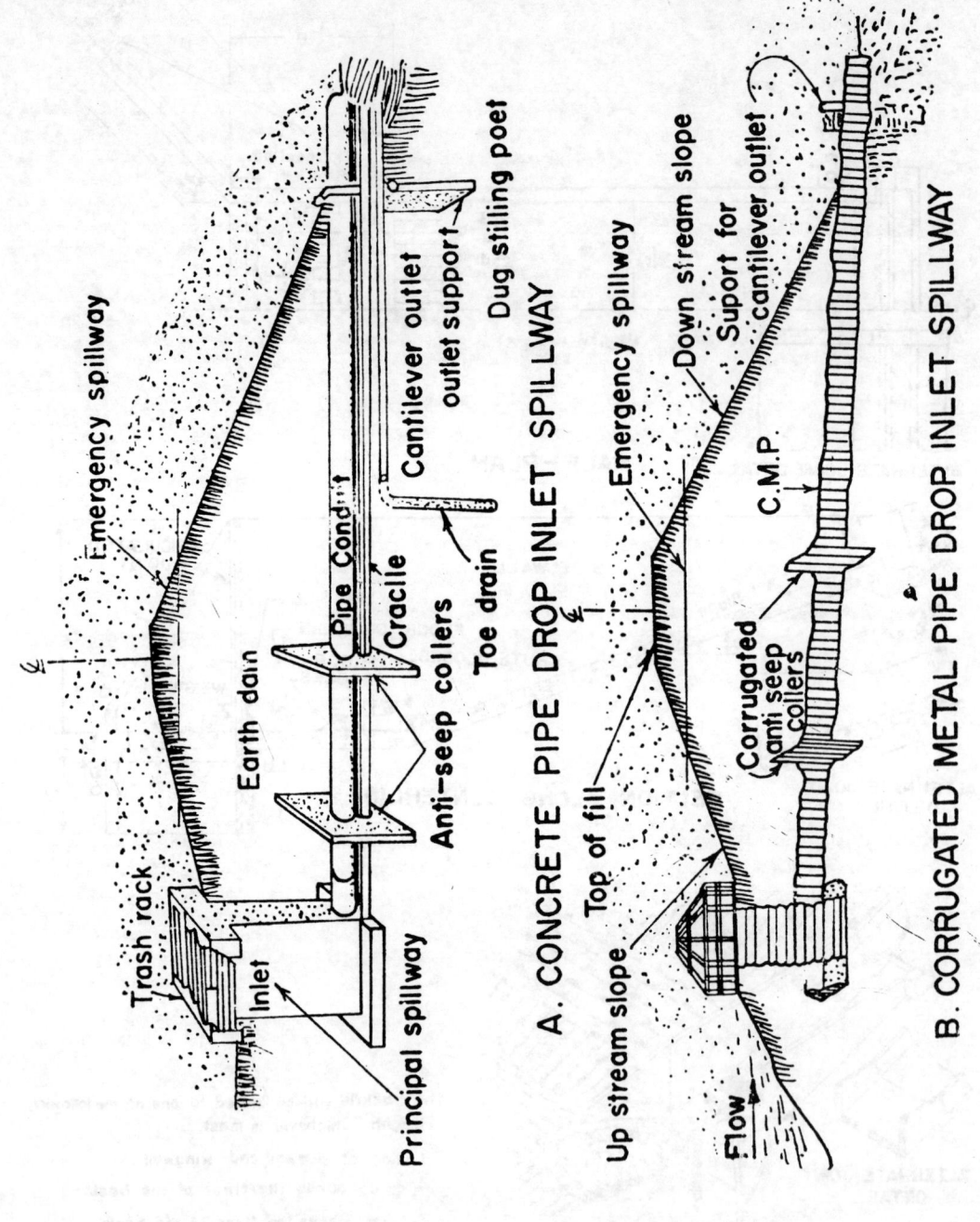

A. CONCRETE PIPE DROP INLET SPILLWAY

Emergency spillway

Cantilever outlet
outlet support
Dug stilling poet

Earth dam
Pipe Conduit
Cracile
Anti-seep collers
Toe drain

Trash rack
Inlet
Principal spillway

B. CORRUGATED METAL PIPE DROP INLET SPILLWAY

Emergency spillway
Down stream slope
Suport for
cantilever outlet
C.M.P.
Corrugated
anti seep collers

Up stream slope
Top of fill
Flow

Fig. 5.23 Nomenclature for various parts of drop inlet spillways

— Principal spillways for debris basins
— Roadway structures
—- Flood prevention structures
— Surface water inlet for drainage or irrigation

Adaptability
It is a very efficient structure for controlling relatively high gully heads, usually above 3 m. It is well-adapted to sites providing an appreciable amount of temporary storage above the inlet. It may also be used in connection with relatively low heads, as in the case of a drop inlet on a road culvert, or in passing surface water through a spoil bank along a drainage ditch.

Advantages
For high heads, it requires less material than a drop spillway. Where an appreciable amount of temporary storage is available, the capacity of the spillway can be materially reduced. Besides effecting a reduction in cost, this reduction of discharge results in a lower peak channel flow below, and can be a favourable factor in downstream channel grade stabilization and flood prevention.

Limitations
Small drop inlets are subject to stoppage by debris. It is limited to locations where satisfactory earth embankments can be constructed.

Classification
Pipe drop inlets usually are confined to smaller jobs, where

— the value of the improvement may not justify the use and cost of monolithic reinforced concrete;
— where considerable storage is available in proportion to the size of the watersheds; and
— where the useful life of the project is limited.

Large size pipe drop inlets required the services of an engineer. When corrugated or helical metal pipe is planned, only the heavier ones should be used. A coating of bituminous material will extend the effective life of this type of pipe. All joints should be provided with watertight metal bands caulked or otherwise, sealed against leakage, and antiseep collars used to prevent seepage along the pipe. Sheet metal antiseep collars, or diaphragms with a watertight connection to the outside of the pipe are superior to concrete collars for metal pipe, because distortion of the pipe from loading may crack the concrete collar or rupture the pipe; whereas a metal antiseep collar will adjust and remain intact. When pipe drop inlets are used as spillways for storage reservoirs, where the water must be released downstream, such as irrigation reservoirs, some type of release facility must be provided.

The design of a drop inlet spillway cannot be made independently of the design of the earth embankment, emergency spillway, and other elements of the total structure.

The design should provide for sufficient temporary storages between the crest of the inlet and the emergency spillway to permit a drop inlet spillway of reasonable size and cost. The size of the drop inlet spillway depends largely on the amount of this temporary storage. Tail w. r will influence the layout of the spillway and the amount of hydraulic head available to produce discharge through the spillway. Therefore, it must be determined accurately for each location. Taking temporary storage into account, design discharge for drop inlet spillway can be determined by the relationship.

$$\frac{V_s}{V_r} = 1 - 2\frac{Q_o}{Q_i} + 1.8\frac{Q_o^2}{Q_i} - 0.8\frac{Q_o^3}{Q_i} \qquad \ldots (5.13)$$

where, V_s = volume of temporary storage (ha-m);

V_r = volume of runoff (ha-m);

Q_o = required principal spillway discharge (cumec); and

Q_i = peak flow from design storm (cumec).

Solution of the equation to provide Q_o/Q_i ratio against V_s/V_r ratio is presented in Table 5.9.

Table 5.9   *Estimate of principal spillway discharge allowing for temporary storage (For watersheds of less than 100 ha)*

$\frac{V_s}{V_r}$	$\frac{Q_o}{Q_i}$									
	0.00	0.01	0.02	0.02	0.04	0.05	0.06	0.07	0.08	0.09
0.0	1.00	0.99	0.98	0.96	0.95	0.94	0.92	0.91	0.90	0.88
0.1	0.87	0.85	0.84	0.82	0.81	0.79	0.78	0.76	0.74	0.73
0.2	0.72	0.70	0.68	0.67	0.65	0.64	0.62	0.61	0.60	0.58
0.3	0.57	0.55	0.54	0.52	0.51	0.50	0.49	0.47	0.46	0.45
0.4	0.44	0.43	0.42	0.41	0.40	0.39	0.38	0.37	0.36	0.35
0.5	0.34	0.33	0.32	0.31	0.30	0.29	0.28	0.27	0.27	0.26
0.6	0.25	0.24	0.23	0.23	0.22	0.21	0.20	0.20	0.19	0.18
0.7	0.18	0.17	0.16	0.15	0.15	0.14	0.14	0.13	0.12	0.12
0.8	0.11	0.11	0.10	0.09	0.09	0.08	0.08	0.07	0.07	0.06
0.9	0.05	0.05	0.04	0.04	0.03	0.03	0.02	0.02	0.01	0.01

Example 44

Given V_s = 2.0 ha-m; V_r = 3.0 ha-m;

         Q_o = 5 cumec;   Find Q_i

Solution

$$\frac{V_s}{V_r} = \frac{2.0}{3.0} = 0.67; \qquad \frac{Q_o}{Q_i} = 0.20 \text{ (from Table 5.9)}$$

Q_o = 0.20 × Q_i = 0.20 x 5.0 = 1.0 cumec.

Fig. 5.24 along with Table 5.10A and 5.10B can be used to determine the capacity of 20 cm and 30 cm corrugated metal (C.M.) pipe drop inlets, as well as the height of riser required to provide the capacities for larger concrete pipes of 20 m length with correction factors for other lengths are given in Table 5.11.

Reinforced concrete culvert pipe or water pipe will make a more satisfactory pipe drop inlet than corrugated metal, particularly for embankment heights greater than 6 m, or where long service life is desired. Concrete pipe must be properly cradled and bedded. All joints must be watertight. Size of riser pipe in relation to pipe conduit can be determined as follows:

Inlet Proportions

Pipe conduit D (cm)	20–30	45	60	75	90
Pipe riser D (cm)	45	60	75	90	120

Height of Riser

— Enter Table 5.10A with the planned conduit slope (see view above and use next largest whole number for entering table).

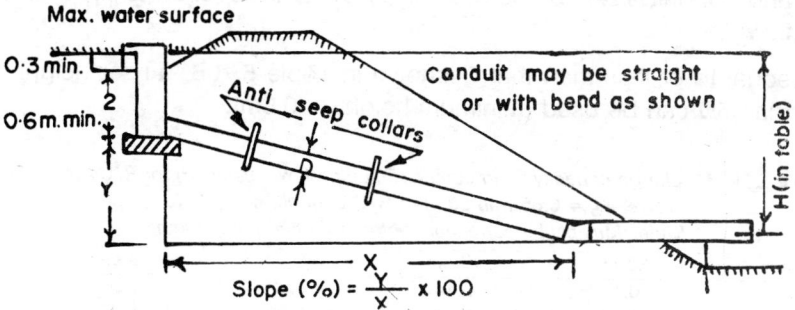

Fig. 5.24 Cross-section of a dam and of a pipe spillway

Table 5.10A

Table 5.10B *Capacity table for pipe inlet*

Slope %	Discharge (cumec)		Head (H)		20 cm conduit – 45 cm riser for pipe length of			30 cm conduit – 45 cm riser for pipe length of		
	20 cm pipe	30 cm pipe	Ft.	m.	50' or 15.24 m	70' or 21.34 m	90' or 27.43 m	50' or 15.24 m	70' or 21.34 m	90' or 27.43 m
5	0.040	0.116								
6	0.042	0.127								
7	0.048	0.139	5	1.52	0.051	0.045	0.040	0.14	0.12	0.11
8	0.051	0.147	6	1.83	0.057	0.048	0.042	0.16	0.14	0.12
9	0.054	0.156	7	2.13	0.059	0.054	0.048	0.17	0.15	0.13
10	0.057	0.164	8	2.44	0.065	0.057	0.051	0.18	0.16	0.14
11	0.059	0.173	9	2.74	0.068	0.059	0.054	0.19	0.17	0.15
12	0.062	0.181	10	3.05	0.074	0.062	0.057	0.20	0.18	0.16
13	0.065	0.187	11	3.35	0.076	0.065	0.059	0.21	0.19	0.17
14	0.068	0.195	12	3.66	0.079	0.068	0.062	0.22	0.20	0.18
15	0.068	0.201	13	3.96	0.082	0.071	0.065	0.23	0.20	0.18
16	0.071	0.207	14	4.27	0.085	0.074	0.065	0.24	0.21	0.19
17	0.074	0.215	15	4.57	0.088	0.076	0.068	0.25	0.22	0.20
18	0.076	0.221	16	4.88	0.091	0.077	0.071	0.25	0.22	0.20
19	0.076	0.227	17	5.18	0.093	0.082	0.072	0.26	0.23	0.21
20	0.079	0.232	18	5.49	0.096	0.085	0.076	0.27	0.24	0.22
21	0.082	0.238	19	5.79	0.099	0.088	0.076	0.28	0.25	0.22
22	0.082	0.244	20	6.10	0.102	0.088	0.079	0.29	0.25	0.23
23	0.085	0.249								
24	0.088	0.255								
25	0.088	0.260								
26	0.091	0.263								
27	0.093	0.269								
28	0.093	0.275								
29	0.096	0.280								
30	0.096	0.286								

— From Table 5.10A obtain value for discharge (Q) for planned conduit size.

— If Q obtained from Table 5.10A is:

(a) greater than Q shown in Table 5.10B (for the design head, conduit length and conduit size): a riser height (z) of $5D$ is required to provide full pipe flow;

(b) equal to or less than that Q shown in Table 5.10B, a riser height (z) less than $5D$ can be used (minimum height = 0.6m).

Table 5.11 *Discharge capacity Q, in cumec (Full pipe flow assumed) for R/C drop inlet, $K_e + K_b = 0.65$ with 20 m of R/C conduit; n = 0.013.*
(Note: Multiply by correction factors for other pipe lengths)

Head Dia. (m)	30 cm	45 cm	60 cm	75 cm	90 cm
1.0	0.17	0.44	0.83	1.36	1.93
1.5	0.20	0.54	1.02	1.65	2.47
2.0	0.24	0.61	1.18	1.92	2.85
2.5	0.26	0.68	1.30	2.16	3.18
3.0	0.28	0.75	1.44	2.36	3.50
3.5	0.33	0.81	1.55	2.54	3.79
4.0	0.34	0.86	1.66	2.71	3.83
4.5	0.35	0.92	1.77	2.87	4.27
5.0	0.37	0.97	1.85	3.03	4.51
5.5	0.40	1.02	1.95	3.18	4.74
6.0	0.41	1.06	2.04	3.36	4.97
6.5	0.44	1.12	2.12	3.46	5.13
7.0	0.45	1.16	2.19	3.58	5.32
7.5	0.47	1.19	2.27	3.70	5.50
L (m)	Correction factors for other pipe lengths				
15	1.076	1.055	1.034	1.024	1.014
20	1.000	1.000	1.000	1.000	1.000
25	0.938	0.947	0.957	0.959	0.961
30	0.889	0.905	0.917	0.935	0.937

The outlet of the drop inlet spillway should be in line with the downstream channel. The layout providing the shortest conduit will exist when the conduit is straight and at a 90-degree angle with the centreline of the embankment.

Emergency Earth Spillways

An emergency earth spillway is an earth or a vegetated earth channel, usually designed to discharge flow in excess of the principal spillway design discharge. Where watersheds are small and long duration flows are not a problem, it may be feasible to handle the runoff safely with only a vegetated spillway.

Earth spillways, as discussed here, apply to both the vegetated and non-vegetated spillways, the latter being used where climatic or soil conditions make it impossible to grow or maintain a suitable grass cover. Earth spillways are usually excavated, but may exist as a natural spillway, such as well-vegetated natural draw, saddle or drainage way. In either case, the spillway must discharge the design peak flow at a non-erosive velocity to a safe point of release. Ordinarily, earth spillways whether vegetated or non-vegetated, should not be built on fill material.

Limitations

Earth spillways have certain limitations. They should be used only where the soils and topography will permit safe discharge of the peak flow at a point well away from the dam and at a velocity which will not cause appreciable erosion. Temporary flood storage provided in the reservoir may be used to reduce the design flow or frequency of use of the spillway.

Design Spillway Capacity

Emergency earth spillways should have the capacity to discharge the peak flow from the watershed, resulting from a storm expected to occur once in 25 years, where the flow in the principal spillway is appreciable, the design capacity of the emergency spillway may be reduce by that amount.

Elements of Excavated Spillways

Excavated earth spillways consist of the three elements shown in Fig. 5.25. These are the approach channel control section and exist channel. Each element has a special function. The flow enters the spillway through the approach channel. The flow is controlled in the level portion and passes through critical depth at the control section, which is the downstream edge of the level portion. The flow is then discharged through the exit section. Designed flow condition will occur only where the exit section slope is equal to or greater than the critical slope.

Excavation of the approach section or the exit section or both, may be omitted where the natural slope meet the minimum slope requirements. The direction of slope of the exit section may be such that outflow will not flow against any part of the dam. Wing dikes, sometimes called kicker levees or training levees, may be used to direct the outflow to a safe point of release.

The spillway should be excavated into original earth for the full design depth. Where this is not practical, the end of the dam and any earth fill constructed to confine the flow should be protected by vegetation of riprap. It is desirable that the entrance to the approach channel be widened, so that it is at least 50% greater than the designed bottom width at the control section. The approach channel should be reasonably short and should be planned with smooth, easy curves for alignment. It should have a slope towards the reservoir of not less than 2.0 per cent, except in rock, to insure drainage and low inlet losses.

The control section should be located near the intersection of the extended centreline of the dam with the centreline of the spillway. A level section at least 6 m in length, should be provided just upstream from the control section.

The exit section must have a slope that is adequate to discharge the peak flow within the channel. The slope, however, must be no greater than that which will result in maximum permissible velocities for the soil type or the planned grass cover. Permissible velocities usually do not exceed 1.5 m/sec and seldom should exceed 2 m/sec. The exit channel should be straight and should confine the outflow to a point where the water may be released without damage to the fill.

PRACTICES USED IN DIFFERENT INDIAN STATES

Tamil Nadu

Semi-Permanent Structures

In Tamil Nadu, extensive areas of wet lands are being irrigated from water stored in tanks or reservoirs. These tanks have their independent catchments. In addition, many of them are in groups, such that, each tank in the group either receives the surplus water from tanks situated above it or it discharges its surplus into lower tanks or does both. The runoff from the independent catchment is collected and led into the tanks through supply or feeder channels. These feeder channels are uncontrolled and during rainy season, they get a substantial quantity of bed and rolling silt from the catchment into the tank.

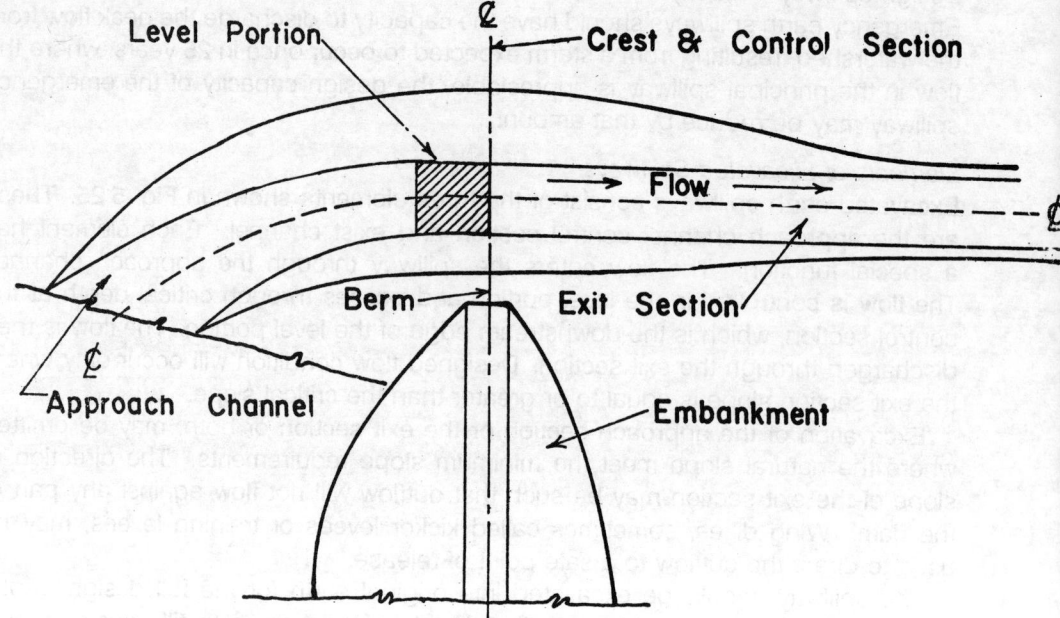

PLAN VIEW OF EXCAVATED EARTH SPILLWAY

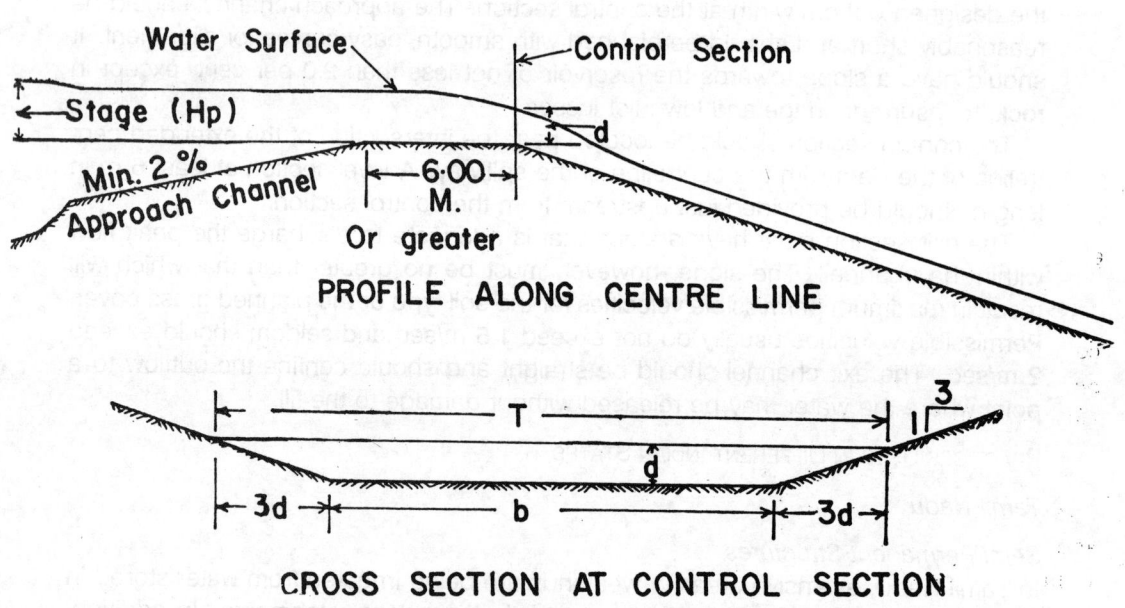

PROFILE ALONG CENTRE LINE

CROSS SECTION AT CONTROL SECTION

Fig. 5.25 Profile of the cross-section of excavated earth spillway

Check dams can be effectively used in preventing silting up of irrigation tanks and eventually jeopardizing the irrigation requirements of the ayacut under the tanks.

In principle, these check dams are a little different from those adopted in gully control. These dams are expected to prevent bed silt from getting into the tank and are porous in construction. They are not expected to hold water and aid in establishing vegetative growth.

Rough stone dry packed dams are the best for the purpose. If a series of such check dams are installed at proper places along the whole length of a feeder channel and its tributaries, practically no bed and rolling silt will get into tank bed. As in the upper reaches in the first instance and gradually worked down the channels.

It is reported that the Tamil Nadu Public Works Department have constructed a series of rough stone check dams in the Arni river upper basin in the Ponneri Taluk of the Chenglepet district, along various feeder channels draining into Nagalapuram red tank. The length of these dams vary from 4.5 m to 12.6 m depending upon the width of the channel across which they have been constructed. These dams are 0.9 m in height and project 0.45 m above the beds of the channels. The top widths of the dam is 1.2 m and the bottom 2.4 m. These are reported to be functioning very satisfactorily.

Permanent Structures: (a) Check dams

Considering the economy of construction as well as the stabilized bed of the gully, check dams at an interval of 150 m were adopted. No provision of check dams is made where the depth of flow is less than 0.3 m.

Rubble masonry dams are constructed in places where stones or rock is available in plenty. Cement-mortar is preferred to lime-mortar.

The empirical formula adopted for design of irrigation canal drops were found to be useful in the erosion control dam designs. The base width (B) of the weir is calculated using the formula $B = \dfrac{H}{\sqrt{P}} + d$ where H is the height of the dam to notch crest, d is the maximum depth of water passing over the crest and P is the specific gravity of masonry which is taken as 2.25.

The width, T of the stone crest of the dam is $T = \frac{3d}{2B}$. The minimum of notch should not be less than 7/8 of the average bed width of the gully.

The width A of the main apron downstream of the dam should be equal to the width of the notch (L) + $\frac{1}{2}$ the maximum depth (d) of water passing over the crest, $A = L + \dfrac{1}{2}d$.

The length of horizontal floor of the drop is $2d + \sqrt{dh}$, where d is the maximum depth of water passing over the weir and h is the difference of depth of water level above and below weir. If the floor level of the drop is kept at the bed level of the gully, then h may be taken as the height of weir crest from the floor level. The formula used for calculating the depth of water cushion $= \frac{d}{2}\sqrt{h-2}$, where d is the depth of water, h is the difference in water level above and below dam.

In addition to the solid apron, side revetment is provided to protect the sides of gully for erosion due to eddies downstream of the dam. Its length $= 4(d+h)$ subject to a minimum of 6 m from the edge of the solid apron. For at least half of this length, the bed of the channel should also be protected with pitching. Before building the revetment, the sides should be sloped to 1:1 or 1.5:1. The thickness of the revetment may be 0.3 m, built of stone.

Where good building stones are available in large quantities, reinforced concrete dams are recommended.

Check Dams with Pipe Outlets

For conveying lower peak discharge with lower heads of flow from a small and medium gullies, check dams with pipe outlets are adopted.

Glazed earthware pipe of 10 to 30 cm diameter are adopted.

Uttar Pradesh

Drop spillways for drops ranging for 1.5 to 2 m drop, dealing with discharge up to 1.75 cumecs are adopted.

In alluvial soils, the slope of the hydraulic gradient line adopted is 1:4, while in heavier soils like *mar* and *kabar*, the slope may be taken as 1:3. Based on the above criteria, the length of floor is determined.

While adopting drop inlet spillways, the following design has been used in determining the size of the pipe after selecting appropriate peak rate of runoff (Q) and the head (h)

$$Q = AV = A \sqrt{\frac{2gh}{1 + C + f_1\dfrac{l}{D} + f_2}}$$

where, A is the area of pipe or box (m²); V = velocity (m/sec), h = total static head (m) from surface of water to the centre of the pipe at the outlet, l is the length of pipe (m), d is the diameter of the pipe (m), C is the entrance loss coefficient, f_1 = coefficient of loss of head due to friction in pipe, f_2 = coefficient of loss of head due to friction in pipe at bend, values of C are taken as below:

Sharp cornered entry = 0.5
Bell mouth = 0.05

Values of f_1 for smooth pipes can be taken up to a diameter of 45 cm = 0.02; 45 to 105 cm = 0.015; 105 to 210 cm = 0.011.

Values of f_2, for bend of 90° may be taken as 1.25–1.50. The size of the riser is usually kept 25 to 50% more than the size of the pipe, depending upon the head of water over the lip of the riser available. Discharge through RCC Hume pipes for pipe drop spillway are given in Table 5.12.

Table 5.12(a) *Discharge through RCC Hume pipes for pipe drop spillway*

Pipe length (m)	1.8288			2.4384			3.6576			4.8768		
Head (m)	0.3048	0.6096	0.9144	0.3048	0.6096	0.9144	0.3048	0.6096	0.9144	0.3048	0.6096	0.9144
Diameter of pipe (cm)												
12.70	0.0269	0.0382	0.0467	0.0260	0.0368	0.0450	0.0244	0.0345	0.0422	0.0229	0.0326	0.0399
15.24	0.0339	0.0566	0.0694	0.0385	0.0547	0.0668	0.0362	0.0513	0.0629	0.0346	0.0487	0.0598
20.32	0.0728	0.1028	0.1257	0.0708	0.1003	0.1226	0.0677	0.0957	0.1172	0.0645	0.0914	0.1121
22.86	0.0926	0.1311	0.1606	0.0906	0.1280	0.1566	0.0867	0.1226	0.1501	0.0832	0.1177	0.1432
25.40	0.1153	0.1628	0.1994	0.1127	0.1594	0.1951	0.1082	0.1532	0.1875	0.1041	0.1474	0.1806
30.48	0.1679	0.2376	0.2908	0.1648	0.2331	0.2855	0.1592	0.2251	0.2756	0.1540	0.2179	0.2669
38.10	0.2642	0.3738	0.4577	0.2605	0.3684	0.4511	0.2520	0.3563	0.4358	0.2462	0.3481	0.4262
45.72	0.3846	0.5440	0.6661	0.3795	0.5367	0.6570	0.3704	0.5239	0.6410	0.3608	0.5102	0.6249
53.34	0.5259	0.7440	0.9111	0.5197	0.7352	0.9003	0.5089	0.7199	0.8810	0.4981	0.7047	0.8629
60.96	0.6913	0.9773	1.1971	0.6845	0.9683	1.1858	0.6720	0.9501	1.1626	0.6591	0.9322	1.1413

Table 5.12(b)   *Discharge through RCC Hume pipes for pipe drop spillway*

Pipe length (m)	5.4864			7.3152			9.1440		
Head (m)	0.3048	0.6096	0.9144	0.3048	0.6096	0.9144	0.3048	0.6096	0.9144
Diameter of pipe (cm)									
12.70	0.0224	0.0317	0.0388	0.0210	0.0295	0.0360	0.0195	0.0275	0.0337
15.24	0.0334	3.0473	0.0578	0.0314	0.0445	0.0544	0.0297	0.0419	0.0513
20.32	0.0631	0.0894	0.1095	0.0597	0.0846	0.1036	0.0569	0.0804	0.0985
22.86	0.0815	0.1155	0.1415	0.0775	0.1095	0.1341	0.0739	0.1044	0.1279
25.40	0.1022	0.1446	0.1772	0.0974	0.1378	0.1687	0.0931	0.1319	0.1616
30.48	0.1520	0.2148	0.2629	0.1452	0.2052	0.2513	0.1395	0.1973	0.2414
38.10	0.2428	0.3436	0.4208	0.2338	0.3508	0.4050	0.2312	0.3269	0.4002
45.72	0.3574	0.5057	0.6192	0.3461	0.4896	0.5994	0.3562	0.4749	0.5816
53.34	0.4933	0.6976	0.8541	0.4791	0.6778	0.8300	0.4668	0.6600	0.8082
60.96	0.6534	0.9243	1.1320	0.6365	0.9002	1.1023	0.6209	0.8498	1.0754

5.5   Ravine Reclamation

Extent of Problem

It is estimated that about 4.0 m ha of land are subject to gully and ravine erosion and another 4 to 6 m ha of productive cultivated lands are seriously threatened by encroachment of gullies and ravines (Plate 24). Further, it has also been estimated that by developing and managing the gullied and ravine areas, the country could prevent annual loss of production of food grains, fodder and firewood to the tune of Rs.157 crores. Details regarding the extent of ravines and gullies, achievements by treating the lands in different states of the country, have been given in Chapter 1.

Location

These ravines and gullies are generally found along the rivers of Chambal, Mahi and Sabarmati, Yamuna, etc., and foothills of the Himalayas and Shiwaliks as well as in the plateau area of eastern India.

Causes

The gently sloping nature of the sand, loamy sand, sandy loam, silty loam textural soil (except in Chambal, where soil is clay loam), intense rains in the monsoon, improper land use by way of overgrazing, biotic interference with natural vegetative cover and faulty agricultural practices are the chief causes of gully erosion all over the country.

Gully Development

There are three stages of gully development:

— The first is of rill erosion

— Development of the gully (most serious and harmful stage of gully formation). Stage of gully development is characterized by vertical and caving gully heads and

— The third stage is stabilization of gully (the gully readjusts itself to a stable horizon with a relative flat head and side slope).

Even though vegetation appears to get established in most of the cases, the gully pass through a second cycle of erosion. Thus the gully grows bigger and bigger in all directions with the passing of each cycle.

Planning

It is important to have a large-scale map of the area for classification and detailed planning of various works. Topographical survey, preferably by a plane table is carried out and the configuration of the topography such as gully rims, field boundaries, gully beds, water courses, conspicuous changes in the profiles of gully faces, vertical faces of gullies are plotted.

Before gully classification is adopted/developed, it is necessary to study the drainage systems in the upper, middle and lower parts, especially with respect to width, depth and side slopes of gully.

The interpretation in relation to slope classes of the land and the susceptibility to erosion hazard by active had to be modified to suit the condition in ravine lands and then a tentative capability classification has to be developed.

Steps for control and reclamation of gullies and ravines are as below:

Step 1. Closure to grazing and other biotic interference.

Step 2. Checking the growth of gullies—This is done by adopting contour, graded and peripheral bunds following usual norms in the design of bunds, etc. (Please refer for details, chapter under bunding.

Step 3. Gully plugging—The details of designing and construction of suitable gully plugs (temporary), semi-permanent structures, may kindly be referred under the chapter erosion control structures.

Step 4. Stabilization of active gully heads—Adopt suitable economical, immediate steps to stop further progress of the gully head, depending upon seriousness of the situation. For example, filling the cave and face of the gully head to top up to a suitable height from the bottom, then easing the gully for the remaining top position of the vertical face. The newly formed slope is stabilized.

Step 5. Reclamation of gullies for cultivation—Small gullies are reclaimed by cleaning, minor levelling and constructing diversion bunds (with suitable cross-sections) at appropriate horizontal intervals. Grassed ramps are provided for disposal of excess runoff at the end of bunds near the gully sides. At the end of the small gully, a composite check dam of earth and brick masonry spillway portion needs to be constructed.

A medium gully is reclaimed by clearing and levelling the bed and constructing a series of composite earth and brick masonry check dams, at suitable vertical intervals and terracing the side slopes (Plate 25). For detailed designing of composite check dams, refer to the chapter under erosion control structures.

The uneven side slopes of the medium gully having moderately steep slopes are bench terraced into level terraces at suitable vertical intervals and also with appropriate inwards and longitudinal gradient. A ring bund of suitable cross-section may be provided after edge of each terrace. The terrace spaces, grassed outlets and earthen check dams are stabilized by sodding or growing with suitable grass.

Runoff water from the cultivable area may be harvested and stored in suitable storage structures, such as farm ponds, etc., for further recycling of the stored water by way of the supplemental irrigation to the crops for maximising production per unit area.

Step 6. Reclamation of deep (Plate 26) and narrow gullies—The best land use of the type of above ravine land is to retire them to permanent vegetation. Suitable fast growing, protective and productive species of trees, grasses, etc., are to be raised (Plate 27).

PRACTICES ADOPTED IN DIFFERENT INDIAN STATES

Rajasthan
In semi-arid tracts of the state, with a mean annual rainfall of about 750 mm, having alluvial deposits of Chambal and its distributions, ravine reclamation projects are undertaken.

— In flat and gently sloping lands, where major portion of the area is rainfed, is brought under irrigation by a lift system. Land levelling operations are planned to suit soil, climate, crops to be grown, methods of irrigation and desire of the farmer. Proper water disposal arrangements are provided.

— Marginal cultivated lands with small gullies are found between gullies and gently sloping cultivated lands and have slopes of 1 to 5%. Intensive soil conservation measures like bench terracing, contour bunding and other soil conservation measures are done. With the help of heavy earth moving machines, shallow and medium ravine lands are bench terraced for agriculture and for horticulture. Irrigation facilities are provided to lift irrigation.

— Deep ravines are closed to grazing and other biotic interferences. Plantation of suitable species such as *Acacia nilotica, Dalbergia sissoo, Dendrocalamus strictus*, are done in staggered trenches, pits and also on terraces. Besides other engineering works, live hedges of *Ipomea carnea, Arundo donax, Vitex negundo, Euphorbia* are put in gully bottoms at suitable location. A peripheral bund also is constructed along the periphery, maintained and stabilized. Suitable outlets for excess water are provided.

— Fencing of the area: Besides soil conservation measure, engineering structures, and other afforestation works in the ravine, fencing of the entire project area is also done.

RECOMMENDATIONS OF THE CENTRAL SOIL & WATER CONSERVATION RESEARCH AND TRAINING INSTITUTE, DEHRADUN

Research Centre, Vasad
The Central Soil & Water Conservation Research and Training Institute, Research Centre, Vasad, has for the last 25 years carried out research investigations on the control of gullies and reclamation of ravines, especially on the banks of river Mahi in Gujarat state. The following specifications (Tables 5.13 and 5.14) have been worked out for the ravine lands of Gujarat, (Fig. 5.26) (Tejwani, 1968).

Land capability classes (Fig. 5.27) II, III, IV, VI and VII are to be annexed by symbol 'e' indicating damage by past erosion, present hazard and future susceptibility to gully erosion.

Checking the Growth of Gullies
After closure of ravine lands, contour and peripheral bunds are constructed. As a result of research investigation, it was recommended that in Gujarat, ravine lands average c.s. of 0.9, 1.3 m² spaced at 0.90 to 1.20 m vertical interval will effectively serve the purpose of contour and peripheral bunds up to 6% only. As an alternative to the borrow pits in the case of bunds a shallow or elliptical channel with 6 m top width and 0.3 m depth has been found to be useful in cultivation and early filling up of the depression.

For lands with 6–12% slope, bunds of 1.3 m² in cross-section at vertical interval of 1.8 to 3.6 m is recommended. Grass ramps were provided in the bunds for easy flow of runoff water and also to serve as passage for implements and bullocks. Ramps

Table 5.13 *Classification of gullies*

Symbol	Description	Specification
G$_1$	Very small gullies	Up to 3 m deep. Bed width not greater than 18 m. Side slopes vary.
G$_2$	Small gullies	Up to 3 m deep. Bed width greater than 18 m. Side slopes vary.
G$_3$	Medium gullies	Depth between 3 and 9 m. Bed width not less than 18 m. Side slopes uniformly sloping between 8 and 15 per cent.
G$_4$	Deep and narrow gullies	(a) 3 to 9 m deep. Bed width not less than 18 m. Side slopes vary. (b) Depth greater than 9 m. Bed width varies. Side slopes vary, mostly steep or even vertical; with intricate and active branch gullies.

Table 5.14 *Land capability classification in ravine lands, Vasad*

Land form	Slope(%)	Distance from gully rim (m)	Land capability class
Table lands	0–1	Beyond 60	I
Table lands	1–3	Beyond 60	II
Table lands and wide humps in between gullies	0–3	Beyond 6 to 60	III
Table lands	3–5	Beyond 6	III
	5–10	Beyond 6	
Table lands	10–15	Beyond 6	IV
Marginal land between the gully rim and the table lands	0–15	Within 6m of the gully rim	VI
Table lands	15–25	—	VI
Very small, small and medium gullysides and beds (G$_1$, G$_2$, G$_3$)	—	—	VI
Table lands	25	—	VII
Deep and narrow gullies	—	—	VII

were so located that runoff will pass over flatter slopes without causing erosion. Research Centre's recommendation regarding the suitability of grasses on the bunds were presented earlier under the chapter on bunding.

Gully plugging—Different types of gully plugs suitable for ravines of Gujarat (Tejwani et al., 1960 a) are given in Table 5.15.

Brick masonry gully plugs are constructed at the confluence of all gully branches of a compound gully. For gullies where no runoff is expected from the top, earthen gully plugs of 1.1 m^2 cross-section with a grassed ramp of 22.5 cm below the top level and spaced at 45–60 m horizontal interval are suitable; for gullies in which excess runoff from the top is expected, an earthern gully plug of 2.2 m^2 cross-section with a pipe outlet is to be provided. The diameter of the pipe shall be determined by the catchment area [15 cm diameter R.C.C. spun pipe up to 2 to 3 cusec (0.03 to 0.09 cumec) discharge from an effective catchment of 1.6 ha is suitable]. A composite check dam of earth and brick masonry (spillway portion) is necessary for larger catchments (more than 1.6 ha). This is located at the confluence of a big compound gully with the main drainage system, or in the bed of the main drainage system at 1.2 m vertical interval or 120 m horizontal interval.

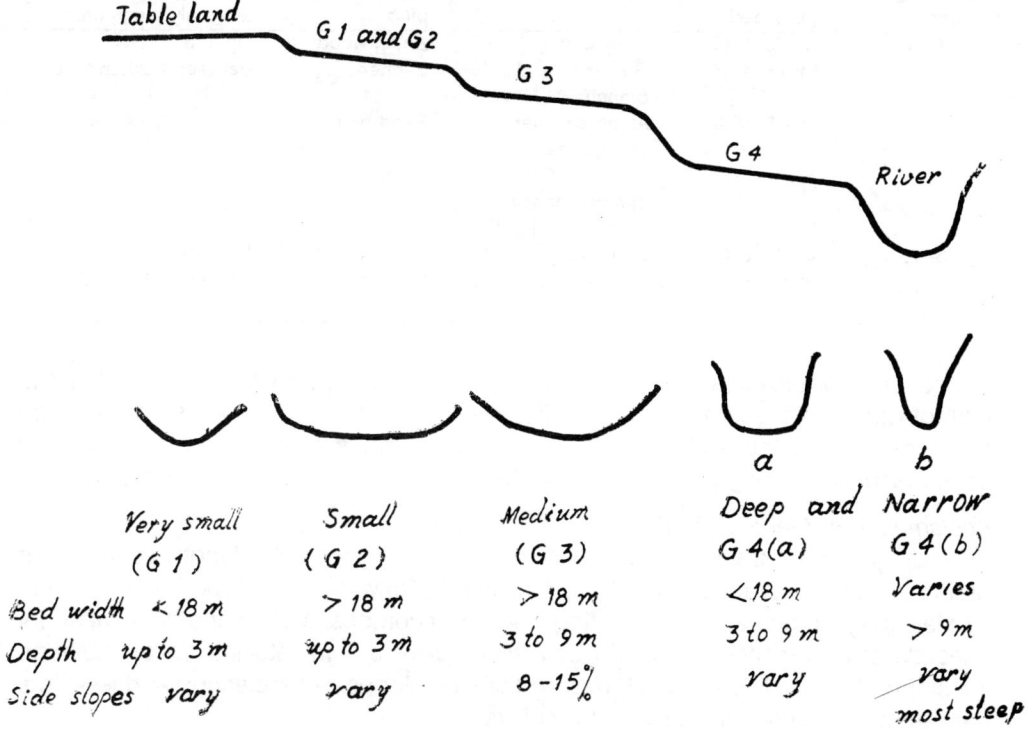

Fig. 5.26 Classification of gullies

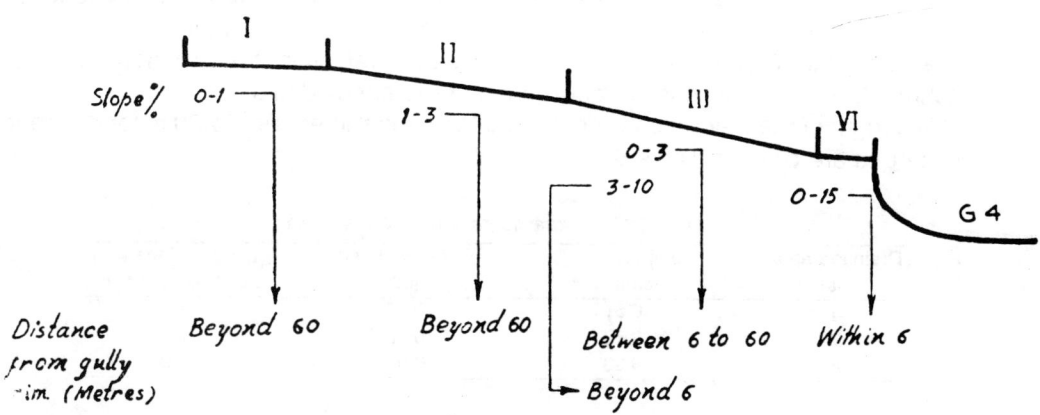

Fig. 5.27 Land capability classification in ravine lands

Reclamation of Gullies for Various Land Uses

Reclamation of Small Gullies

Small gullies were reclaimed (Tejwani et al., 1960 b) by clearing, minor levelling with bulldozer and putting up diversion-cum-check bunds of 1.5 m² cross-section spaced at a horizontal interval of 30–45 m. Grassed ramps were provided for overflow of runoff in excess of 30 cm ponding at the ends of bunds near the gully sides.

Table 5.15 *Specifications for materials and location of gully plugs tried for ravines (Vasad)*

Slope of gully bed (%)	Width of gully bed (m)	Location	Type of gully plug	Vertical interval between two gully plugs (m)
0–5	a) Up to 4.5	Gully bed	Brush wood	Up to 3
	b) 4.5–10.5	Gully bed and side branch	Earthen	Between 2.25 and 3.0
	c) 7.5–15.0	At the confluence of 2 gullies	Sand bag	–
	d) 7.5–15.0	At the confluence of all branches of a compound gully.	Brick masonry	–
5–10	a) Up to 4.5	Gully bed	Brush wood	Up to 3
	b) 4.5–6.0	Gully bed and side branch	Earthen	Between 1.5 and 3.0

Consecutive grassed ramps were diagonally opposite to each other, so that the path of runoff was lengthened and its flow velocity was reduced, so as not to cause any scouring. At the end of the small gully, a composite checkdam of earth and brick masonry spillway portion was constructed.

Reclamation of Medium Gullies

A small gully gets transformed into a medium gully along the length of the main drainage system. A medium gully is reclaimed (Tejwani et al., 1960 b) by clearing and levelling the bed and constructing a series of composite earth and brick masonry checkdams at vertical intervals of 1.2 m (which gives a horizontal interval of 120 m on 1% slope of the gully bed) and terracing the side slopes. After clearing and levelling, the bed of medium gully is ready for cultivation.

Design of Composite Check Dam

In Gujarat, where the watershed characteristics of ravine lands are 50% cultivated rolling and 50% pasture hilly, an average value of $C = 0.5$ was adopted in the rational formula, $Q = \frac{CIA}{360}$. In Gujarat ravine lands, maximum intensity of rainfall is observed to be 75 mm/hr. These assumptions were used in evaluating the peak flow from the catchment, expected to pass through each of the check dams.

The length of the weir notches computed for vertical intervals of 1.20 m for different discharges are given in Table 5.16.

Table 5.16 *Hydraulic design of check dams*

Drainage area (ha)	Total discharge (cumec)	Overflow head (m)	Length of the weir notch adopted (m)
5	0.51	0.30	1.8
2	0.72	0.30	2.4
2	0.93	0.30	3.0

Structural Design

With a view to keeping the cost of each check dam as low as possible, the non-overflow portion is made of earth and the overflow portion in brick masonry. The brick masonry portion was designed (Dhruva Narayana et al., 1962) as solid gravity dam. The forces considered in the design were: (i) horizontal water pressure, (ii) weight of the dam, and (iii) uplift pressure (reaction of the foundation). The design was checked for safety against sliding, turning over the toe and the resultant force was made to pass through the middle third portion. The masonry wall was taken to a minimum depth of 105 cm below the bed, so as to avoid the danger due to scouring and to give a firm foundation. The joints between the earthen dam and brick masonry portion were made secure by providing wing walls, both on upstream and downstream sides and providing 150 cm anchor of body wall on either side into the earthen portion. The earth dam was designed to withstand the force of water collected on the upstream side. The top width of 120 cm and side slopes of 2 horizontal to 1 vertical were provided. The principal dimensions of the check dams were as under:

Earthern Portion

Top width = 120 cm;   Side slope = 2:1
Height above ground level varies (135 cm, adjacent to the spillway portion).

Brick Masonry Spillway Portion

Length L = as calculated above.

Anchorage on either side	= 150 cm;	Depth of water notch	= 45cm
Height above ground level	= 90 cm;	Height below ground level	= 105 cm
width at ground level	= 105 cm;	Width at spillway level	= 45 cm
Width of top	= 45 cm;		
Length of downstream side		Length of upstream side	
wingwalls	= 240 cm	wingwalls	= 270 cm

	Length	Width	Depth
Dimensions of water cushion	240 cm	Varies	30 cm
Dimensions of curtain walls	Varies	23 cm	68 cm
	(L+61)		all below ground level

No battering was given to the upstream face and was kept vertical. Instead an earth fill was formed on the upstream side to reduce the wave action, if any.

To avoid intricacies of construction and form of work for placing concrete, a very simple trapezoidal section with stepping on the downstream side in brick masonry was adopted.

The water cushion of 30 cm depth was adopted on the downstream side with curtain walls, the top of which is in flush with ground level.

Instead of the dry rubble pitching downstream of the water cushion a sodded strip of about 6 m was provided (Fig. 5.28)

Construction Features of Check Dams

The object of constructing a series of check dams was to flatten out bed slopes which would minimize the scour and erosion during peak flow. The point of vital importance is the vertical spacing of check dams in the stream bed. As discussed earlier, the check dams must be only so far apart that the top of each is practically on a level with the base of one upstream from it. This ensures that a check dam makes flat terrace behind it, in which the water moves down without gaining momentum. On 1% slope the horizontal spacing was 122 m, so that the top of one check dam was practically at the same level with the base at one on its upstream side. At every 120 cm vertical interval (i.e, 122 m horizontal interval) along the gully bed, cross-sections were taken with offsets at every 3 m and plotted. The top of the checkdams were fixed in such a way that one was 135 cm below the previous one. In this cross-section, where the top of the checkdam was 135 cm above the ground level, the spillways were located in that portion, so as to keep a constant height

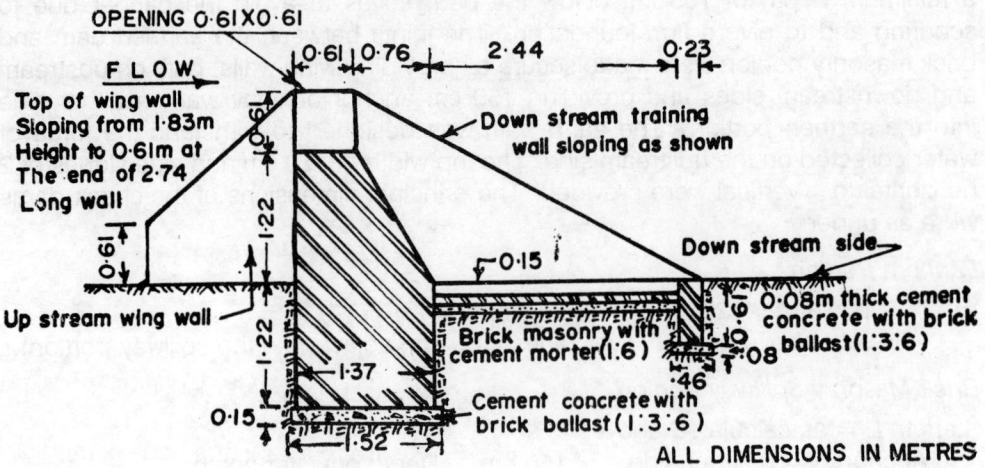

Fig. 5.28 Brick check dam for Mahi ravines

of the spillway above the ground level and to adopt the same cross-section of the spillway portion.

Wingwalls were constructed on the upstream side to give the shape of a diverging mouthpiece, with (a) the wingwalls splayed and (b) the wingwalls in a shape of an arc of a circle. The later shape provided ideal conditions for maximum discharge during the peak flow, as the flow of water was trained with the least resistance. The top of these wingwalls were sloping from the top of the check dam to 60 cm above ground level at the end of 270 cm long wingwall. The radius of the arc was 180 cm and the angle made by the arc at the centre was 90°. The downstream wingwalls were also of diverging shape, to reduce the energy of flowing water. If L is the length of the spillway, $L + 61$ cm shall be the enlarged width of water cushion. The top of these wingwalls were also sloping from the top of the body wall to the ground level at the end of the water cushion. The top the curtain wall shall be in flush with the ground level. The water cushion must be least 30 cm deep from the top of the curtain wall.

Medium Gully Reclamation

The uneven side slopes of the medium gullies having 8 to 15% slope were bench terraced into level terraced at 0.9–1.2 m vertical interval. The terraces were given a back slope of 1 in 50 and a longitudinal grade of 1 in 200 towards the grassed outlet. A ridge bunds of 0.3 m² cross-section was provided at the edge of each terrace. Terrace faces were given a slope of 1.5:1. To make the terrace construction economical, terracing was done only in cases where a minimum uniform sloping length of 120 m was available.

During the process of terracing, the top soil on the surface is covered with the poor sub-soil. This requires a planned programme to raise the fertility level of soil, involving good crop rotations and heavy manuring. The terraces require careful maintenance for the first two years, in view of the unsettled conditions of the soil. The ridge bunds terrace faces, graded outlets and earthen checkdams were stabilized by sodding or growing with suitable grasses like *Dichanthium annulatum* and *Cenchrus ciliaris*.

Medium gullies may thus be reclaimed economically for cultivation, if it is possible to grow a cash crop of orchards under rainfed conditions or irrigation facilities are available.

Reclamation of Deep and Narrow Gullies
Deep and narrow gullies may be retired to permanent vegetation and cover of grasses and trees. Among the many tree species tried at Vasad are *Acacia nilotica*, *Acacia benthamii*, *Ailanthus excelsa*, *Albizzia lebbeck*, *Azadirachta indica*, *Dalbergia sissoo*, *Dendrocalamus strictus*, *Eucalyptus camaldulensis* (Bangalore), *E. citriodora*, *E. hybrid*, *Pongamia glabra*, *Emblica officinalis*, *Salmalia malabaricum* and *Tectonia grandis* are quite promising species for Gujarat ravines.

Research Centre, Agra
As a result of research investigations carried out at the Research Centre, Agra in Uttar Pradesh, the following are the recommendations:

Terracing has been one of the most effective erosion control measures in ravine lands. In the coarse soil of Yamuna ravines, table-top or level bench terraces have been successfully constructed on very small and small gullies in the beds of medium and deep gullies and on the hump tops. Of the three kind of power, viz, bullock-cum-man power, machine-cum-man power and hydraulic-cum-man power used for terrace construction, the machine-cum-man power proved to be the most suitable. Grass outlets for drops up to 1.5 m with 6:1 slopes served well as ramp-cum-waste weir. Amongst the masonry outlets, the chute spillway with the conduit capable of gently conducting the excess water to the outlet proved to be most suitable for drops up to 4.0 m *Cynodon dactylon* grass provided efficient protection to all types of earthen structures.

Research Centre, Kota
Studies were undertaken at the Kota Centre for reclamation of medium and deep ravines and their economic utilization. Methods adopted and found suitable for reclamation were:

Fencing
The area was fenced for protection against biotic interference.

Provision of Diversion Bund
Diversion bund 700 m long was provided at a distance twice the depth of ravine head. Bund dimensions: bottom width 5 m, top width 1 m, side slope 1:2, cross-sectional area 2.7 m². This completely diverted the runoff going into the ravines.

Provision of Spillway
Runoff so diverted was safely disposed of into the ravines by means of two spillways made in coarse rubble masonry with lime-mortar. These were designed for safe delivery of peak discharge of 30 cusecs. These are having head falls of 4.5 and 5.5 m. Each spillway takes care of 4 ha of catchment area and is functioning satisfactorily.

Stabilisation of Steep Ravine Heads
Rough sloping of 1:1 of ravine heads is sufficient to establish a good cover. *Dichanthium annulatum* was found very suitable for sodding the eased slope. This type of work is expensive, and is recommended where protection of costly construction, like roads, buildings, etc is required. This stabilisation of gully heads can also be achieved slowly, if the area is protected against grazing. In that case the heads develop a natural angle of repose in due course of time.

Stabilization of Gully Beds

Boulder, brushwood and live-hedge check dams were tried in the ravine beds. Out of these, live-hedge check dams have proved most effective and economical. Species such a *Ipomea carnea*, *Agave americana*, *Arundo donax* and *Vitex negundo* were found suitable.

Plantation

The top and side slopes of the ravine and marginal lands were planted with different tree and grass species. Following species were found suitable.

Trees

Prosopis juliflora (Hump and side slopes); *Acacia nilotica* (side slopes); and *Dendrocalamus strictus* (beds). *Acacia tortilis* and *Acacia catechu* also do well in ravine areas.

Grasses

Dichanthium annulatum (by sowing) and *Cenchrus ciliaris* (by sowing).

By giving the treatments listed above, ravines were stabilised and good forage species like *Dichanthium annulatum* and *Cenchrus ciliaris* increased in vegetal composition. Yield of grasses obtained was 4 tonne/ha.

Shallow ravines can be reclaimed after clearing and minor levelling for agriculture or Horticulture, if facilities for irrigation are available.

5.6 Sediment Retention Structures

Use of vegetation reduce soil erosion from exposed areas, and structural measures carry runoff in a non-erosive manner to suitable outlets. Despite the best efforts to reduce the quantity of eroded soil, however, some erosion is inevitable. This chapter deals with ways to capture and retain sediment once soil has been eroded.

Sediment retention structures do not stop erosion; they trap eroded soil before it can reach a water body. Sediment retention devices should be used only as back-up systems, if preferred measures, such as vegetation and mulches fail, or if no other measures are feasible. Sediment retention structures are usually temporary solution until permanent measures are in place.

The sediment retention structures work by slowing the velocity of runoff and letting suspended soil particles settle by gravity. Typical structures include straw bale dykes, filter fabric fences, sediment traps and sediment basins.

The sediment retention structures have several weaknesses. The efficiency of the system is dependent upon clay and silt fraction, which do not settle easily. Watersheds that contain soils high in clay and silt require large basins to capture the soil that has been eroded. A retention structure is typically designed with a removal efficiency of 50 to 75 per cent. If such a structure performs as designed, as much as half the eroded soil will pass through the basin and be deposited in a water body such as lake, bay or stream.

Sediment retention structures need maintenance and cleaning at regular intervals. If too much sediment is allowed to accumulate in them, they will cease to function. Little or no settling will occur and trapped sediment will be resuspended and wash away.

Design Concepts for Temporary Sediment Basins and Traps

The most commonly used sediment retention structures are sediment basins and traps. Sediment basins are larger than sediment traps and they are more precisely designed.

DESIGN THEORY FOR SURFACE AREA FORMULA

The soil particles settle through water under the influence of gravity and follow one of three modes of settling as below:

— Particles settle as separate elements with little or no interaction among them. This type of settling is usually found in waters with relatively low solids concentration and is called free or ideal settling.

— Independent particles coalesce or clump together during sedimentation. The larger resulting particles settle at a faster rate. This type of settling is often aided by the addition of chemicals, which pull particles together.

— At some concentration higher than in free settling, particles will start to interact and hinder settling. Instead of falling freely, the particles will settle as a group. This is called zone settling.

SEDIMENT BASIN DESIGN

A simple model (Goldman et al., 1966) of an ideal sediment basin illustrates the fundamentals of basin design. For simplicity, the soil particles are assumed to have uniform density. In Fig. 5.29, a flow Q (cum/sec) enters a basin of settling depth D, width W and length, L. It is assumed that there exists uniform flow in one direction.

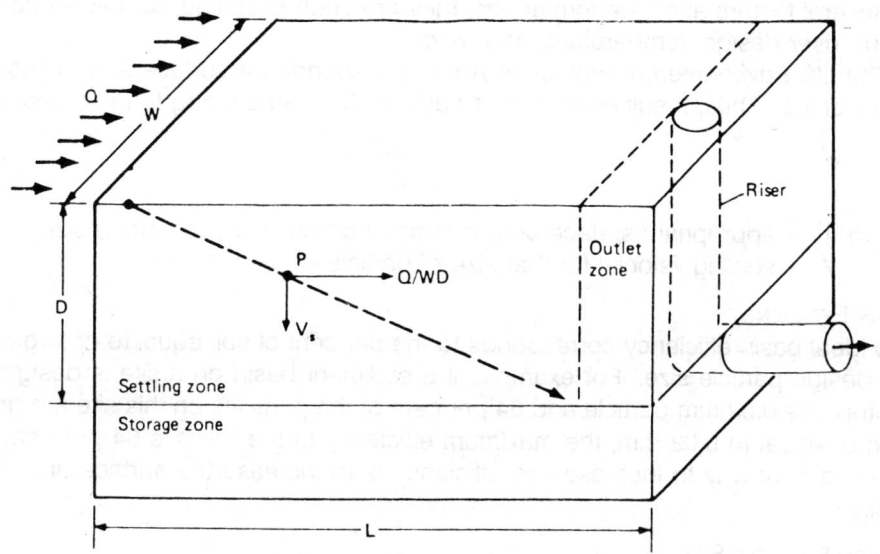

Fig. 5.29 Idealized sediment basin

A particle will travel horizontally with the water through the basin at velocity of Q/WD. The particle will fall at a vertical velocity of V_s (specific for each particle size). The time T_Q for the particle to traverse the length of the basin will be

$$T_Q = \frac{L}{(Q/WD)} \qquad \ldots (5.14)$$

The time for the particle to fall to the storage zone T_v will be

$$T_v = \frac{D}{V_s} \qquad \ldots (5.15)$$

In a properly designed basin, the smallest particle to be captured will fall to the storage zone just before, or as it reaches the outlet zone. Thus $T_Q = T_v$. Settling the transit and falling times to be equal, gives us:

$$T_Q = T_v = \frac{D}{V_s} = \frac{L}{(Q/WD)}$$

By simplifying the equation, we get

$$V_s L = \frac{DQ}{WD}$$

or

$$V_s = \frac{Q}{WL} \qquad \ldots (5.16)$$

Note that WL is the surface area of the basin. Thus, by rearranging terms, we have

$$WL = \text{basin surface area} = \frac{Q}{V_s} \qquad \ldots (5.17)$$

The basin surface area has been established as a function of inflow Q and particle settling velocity. Note that basin depth and volume are not yet design parameters.

Several factors affect performances; they are short circuiting, turbulence, bottom scour, riser design, temperature, and wind.

The US Environmental Protection Agency responded a surface area adjustment factor of 1.2. Thus, resulting sediment basin surface area sizing formula becomes:

$$A_s = \frac{1.2Q}{V_s} \qquad \ldots (5.18)$$

where A_s = appropriate surface area for trapping particles of a certain size.
       V_s = settling velocity for that size of particle.

BASIN EFFICIENCY
The ideal basin efficiency corresponds to the per cent of soil equal to or larger than the design particle size. For example, if a sediment basin on a site is designed to capture the 0.02 mm particle and 64 per cent of the particles on this site are greater than or equal to 0.02 mm, the maximum efficiency of the basic is 64 per cent. The only practical way to increase this efficiency is to increase the surface area of the basin.

DESIGN PARTICLE SIZE
The equation $A_s = 1.2Q/V_s$ defines the relation between size of particle to be captured and the surface area required for the basin. From Table 5.17 it can be seen that the surface area required increases very rapidly as the particle size decreases. To capture the 0.02 mm particle, the area must be 6.5 times larger than the area required to capture the 0.05 mm particle. To capture the 0.01 mm particle, the basin area must be four times larger than the 0.02 mm particle and 25 times larger than for the 0.05 mm particle.

Example 45—*Calculation of required surface area and storage volume*

Table 5.17 *Surface area requirements of sediment traps and basins*

	Settling velocity		Surface area requirements	
	ft/sec	m/sec	ft² per ft³/sec	m² per m³/sec
0.5 (coarse sand)	0.19	0.058	6.3	20.7
0.2 (medium sand)	0.067	0.020	17.9	58.7
0.1 (fine sand)	0.023	0.0070	52.2	171.0
0.05 (coarse silt)	0.0062	0.0019	193.6	635.0
0.02 (medium silt)	0.00096	0.00029	1250.0	4101.0
0.01 (fine silt)	0.00024	0.000073	5000.0	16404.0
0.005 (clay)	0.00006	0.000018	20000.0	65617.0

Given A construction site has a drainage area of 12 acres (4.8 ha). The original plans call for a smooth graded surface, without seeding or mulching. The site is on a hill side. House pads will be terraced up the slope with the following final gradients and slope lengths.

3 acres (1.2 ha): Cut and fill embankments, 3:1 slopes, 35 ft (11 m) long

9 acres (3.6 ha): 10:1 slopes, 150 ft (46 m) long

Diversions will channel runoff away from the steep slopes and convey all site runoff to a single sediment basin. The particles of 79 per cent of the soil, by weight, are equal to or larger than 0.02 mm. Average annual rainfall is 32 in (813 mm), and the 10-year, 6-year rainfall is 2.62 in (67 mm). The rainfall erosion index (*R*-factor) is 34 and *K*-factor is 0.32.

Find: (1) The required surface area to capture the 0.02 mm and larger particles

(2) The storage volume required to retain 1 year's soil loss and

(3) The basin depth required for once per year cleaning.

Solution

1. Calculate average runoff by using the 10-year, 6-hr rainfall, using the rational method

$$Q = CIA$$

Coefficient of runoff (C) Factor: Choose a value of 0.5 for bare, smooth earth and moderate slopes.
i-factor: Average intensity of rainfall is 2.62 in (67 mm) in 6 hr, or 0.44 in (11 mm) in 1 hr.
A-factor: The area is 12 acres (4.8 ha)

$$Q = 0.5 \times 0.44 \times 12 \left[\frac{0.5 \times 11 (mm/hr) \times 4.8 (ha)}{360} \right]$$

$$= 2.64 \text{ ft}^3/\text{sec} = 0.073 \text{ m}^3/\text{sec}$$

2. Sieve analysis indicates that 79 per cent by weight of the soil is equal to or larger than 0.02 mm.
3. The settling velocity of the 0.02 mm particle V_s is 0.00096 ft/sec (0.00029 m/sec)
4. The minimum required surface area A_s is

$$A_s = \frac{1.2Q}{V_s}$$

$$= \frac{1.2 \times 2.64 \text{ ft}^3/\text{sec}}{0.00096 \text{ ft/sec}} \left[\frac{1.2 \times 0.073 \text{ m}^3/\text{sec}}{0.00029} \right]$$

$$= 3300 \text{ ft}^2 \qquad = 302 \text{ m}^2$$

5. Settling depth must be at least 2 ft (0.6 m). The settling zone of any sediment basin be maintained free of accumulated sediment for a rest of at least 2 ft (0.6 m).
6. The storage depth is estimated by using the USLE. Apply the USLE to each of the two length-slope categories on the site.

$$A = RKLSCP$$

R - factor : 34 (given)
K - factor : 0.32 (given)
C - factor : Since no vegetation or mulch is planned, $C = 1.0$
P - factor : For smooth, compacted soil, $P = 1.3$
LS - factors : By interpolation
3:1, 35 ft (11 m) : $LS = 5.57$
10:1, 150 ft (46 m) : $LS = 0.81$

　　Estimate soil loss for 1 year. On 3 acres (1.2 ha) $A = 34 \times 0.32 \times 5.57 \times 1.0 \times 1.3 = 79$ tons/acre (177 tonnes/ha)

Assuming 1 ton of soil = 1 yd³ (1 tonne = 0.843 m³), multiplying by 3 acres (1.2 ha) = 237 yd³ (179 m³). >

　　On 9 acres (3.6 ha), $A = 34 \times 0.32 \times 0.81 \times 1.0 \times 1.3 \times 9 = 11$ tonnes/acre (25 tonnes/ha). Again assuming 1 ton of soil = 1 yd³ (1 tonne = 0.843 m³), multiplying by 9 acres (3.6 ha) = 99 yd³ ¦76 m³). Add the two together, multiply by 0.79 (the fraction of soil larger than 0.02 mm) and convert to cubic feet:

237 + 99 = 336 yd³ (179 m³ + 76 m³ = 255 m³) total soil loss.

336 × 0.79 × 27 ft³/yd³ = 7167 ft³ [225 m³ × 0.79 = 201 m³] retained in basin (assuming ideal basin performance).

Now divide by minimum surface area

Storage depth = $\dfrac{7167 \text{ ft}^3}{3300 \text{ ft}^2} = 2.2$ ft $\left(\dfrac{201}{302} = 0.67 \text{ m}\right)$

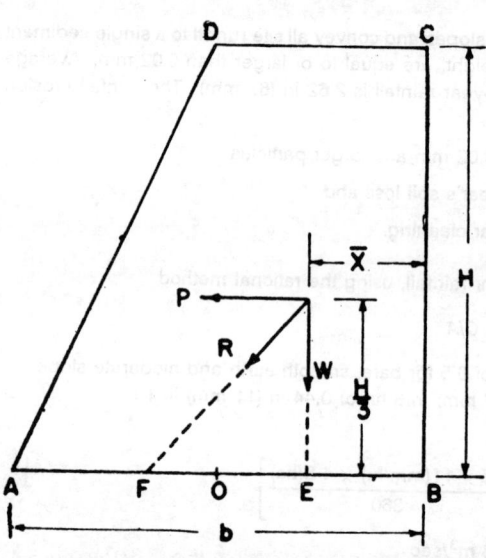

Fig. 5.30 Analysis of forces acting on dam

5.7　Retaining walls and their design

The stability of a gravity retaining wall is due to the self-weight of the wall, perhaps aided by passive resistance developed in front of the wall. The walls of reinforced concrete are more economical. These structures can be classified as (i) structures subjected to water pressure and (ii) structures subjected to the earth pressure.

STRUCTURES SUBJECTED TO WATER PRESSURE

These are mainly dams and weirs. Considering per metre length of retaining wall, the forces acting on it are, (i) weight of dam or retaining wall acting vertically downwards W, and (ii) horizontal water pressure p (Fig. 5.30).

　　The weight of dam per unit length (of m) is given by

$$W = \frac{(a + b)}{2} \times H \times p \qquad \ldots (5.19)$$

and this acts at a distance

$$\bar{x} = \frac{a^2 + ab + b^2}{3(a + b)} \qquad \ldots (5.20)$$

　　The horizontal water pressure p is computed by using the formula for intensity of pressure of water at any depth.

$$P = wx$$

where, w = density of water,

　　　x = depth below surface of water where pressure is measured.

The pressure intensity at water surface is zero, since $x = 0$ and the pressure intensity at the base is wH as $x = H$. In between, $x = 0$ and $x = H$, it observes a straight line law.

The total horizontal water pressure is given by the area of the pressure intensity diagram

$$P = \frac{1}{2} \times H \times wH = \frac{wH^2}{2}$$ and this pressure acts at a distance $\frac{H}{3}$ above the base

When water is impounded, the resultant force on the dam is given by $R = \sqrt{P^2 + W^2}$, and let it act at base AB at F.

Where there is no water, the value of horizontal water pressure, P, is zero. Hence the resultant is given by $R = W$ and let it cut the base AB at E. The distance EF is called shift of reaction.

For the structure to be in equilibrium, the following conditions must be satisfied.

— The algebraic sum of all the vertical forces must be zero, i.e. $\Sigma V = 0$

— The algebraic sum of all the horizontal forces must be zero, i.e. $\Sigma H = 0$

— The moment of all forces acting on the wall about the point B must be zero to check its overturning, i.e. $\Sigma M = 0$.

From statement (i), $W = R_v$
From statement (ii), $P = R_H$
Taking moments about B,

$$P \times \frac{H}{3} + W\bar{x} = R_v(\bar{x} + Z)$$

where, Z = shift of reaction, i.e. EF.

Since $R_v = W$

$$P \times \frac{H}{3} + W\bar{x} = W(\bar{x} + Z)$$

On simplification, $Z = \frac{P}{W} \times \frac{H}{3}$

If O is the middle point of base AB, then $e = OF = BF - BO$

$$= \bar{x} + Z - \frac{b}{2}, \qquad \qquad \dots (5.21)$$

and is called eccentricity.

Example 46—A masonry dam is 5 m high, 1.0 m wide at top and 4.0 m at bottom (Fig. 5.31) and has a vertical water face. The dam impounds water to a height of 4.0 m. Calculate the magnitude of the resultant force and its point of application with the base, when the reservoir is full and when it is empty. Given the density of masonry as 2.2 gm/cc and of water 1.0 gm/cc.

Solution

Weight of dam per m length

$$= \frac{(a + b)}{2} \times H \times P$$

$$= \frac{1 + 4}{2} \times 5 \times 2.2 \times 1000$$

$$= 27500 \text{ kg}$$

The horizontal water pressure, P

$$P = \frac{wh^2}{2}, \text{ where } h = \text{ depth of water}$$

$$= 1.0 \times 1000 \times \frac{4 \times 4}{2} = 8000 \text{ kg/m}$$

When the reservoir is full

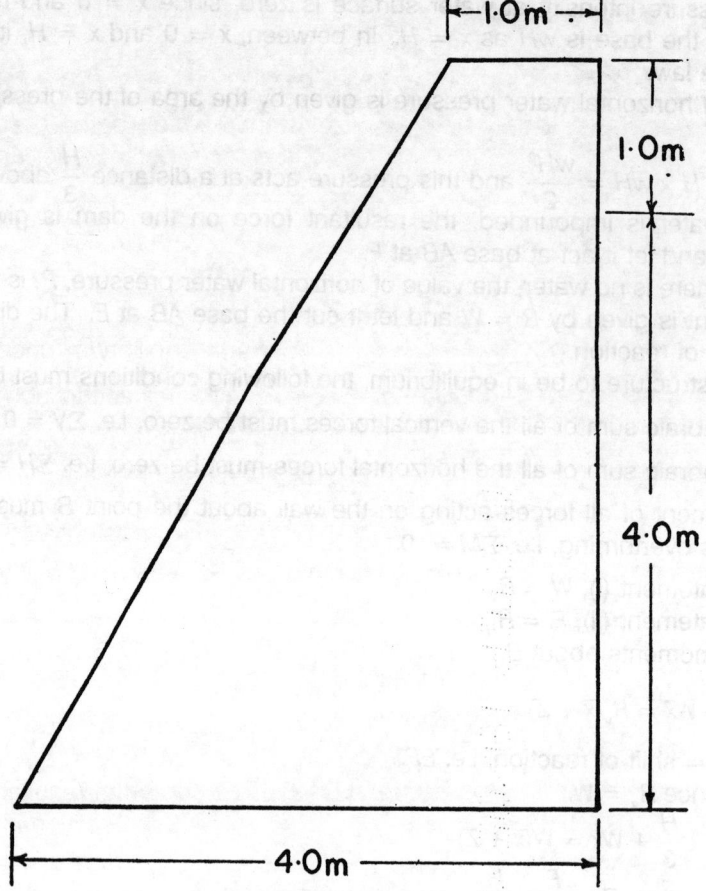

Fig. 5.31 Cross-section of masonry

Resultant, $R = \sqrt{P^2 + W^2} = \sqrt{8000^2 + 27500^2}$

$= 1000 \times \sqrt{64 + 756.25} = 1000 \times 28.6 = 28600$ kg

$\bar{x} = \dfrac{a^2 + b^2 + ab}{3(a + b)} = \dfrac{1 + 16 + 4}{3(4 + 1)}$

$= \dfrac{21}{15} = 1.4$ m

$Z = \dfrac{8000}{27500} \times \dfrac{4}{3} = 0.38$ m

The point of application of Resultant $(\bar{x} + Z) = 1.4 + 0.38 = 1.78$ m. When the reservoir is empty,

Resultant = Weight of dam = 27500 Kg/m

Point of application = $\bar{x} = 1.4$ m

Condition of Stability

A masonry structure can fail in the following ways:

— it may slide forward

— it may overturn

— the material may get crushed due to the maximum compressive stress acting normal to the section, and

— the tensile stress set up in the section, which may open the joints of the masonry and cause its failure. Therefore, the tension should be avoided

and for that, the resultant must be within the middle third of the base.
[Refer to Fig. 5.30]

(a) *Safety against sliding*—The horizontal pressure, P causes the section to slide but it is resisted by the frictional resistance set up at the base. If μ is the coefficient of friction, the maximum frictional resistance set up is equal to μW.

Hence, for stability against sliding, P must never exceed μW. $P = \mu W$

$$\text{Factor of safety} = \frac{\mu W}{P} \qquad \ldots (5.22)$$

(b) *Safety against overturning*—The section is in equilibrium under the action of four forces—(i) horizontal pressure, P of water acting at $\frac{h}{3}$ from base; (ii) the weight, W of the section acting at $\bar{x}$ from face, BC; (iii) the vertical component $R_v = W$ at F and (iv) horizontal component, $R_H = P$, due to frictional resistance.

The horizontal pressure, P of water and the frictional resistance, P at the base form a couple of magnitude $P \times \frac{h}{3}$ and it tends to overturn the retaining wall, hence this is called overturning moment. For the stability of the section against overturning, the balancing moment must be equal to overturning moment.

$$\therefore W \times Z = P \times \frac{h}{3}$$
$$Z = \frac{P}{W} \times \frac{h}{3}$$

The section can overturn about the point, A. So long as the resultant, R hits the base, the section cannot overturn. If R hits the base at A, the section is on the point of overturning and if it fails outside the base, the section will overturn. Hence the limiting value is when F coincides with A, i.e. $EF = EA$ and the balancing moment will have a value $W \times EA$.

Factor of safety against overturning

$$= \frac{\text{Limiting balancing moment}}{\text{Overturning moment}}$$

$$= \frac{W \times EA}{P \times \frac{h}{3}} \qquad \ldots (5.23)$$

(c) In order to avoid crushing of the masonry at the base, f_{max} the maximum compressive stress acting normal to the base must be less than the permissible compressive stress for the masonry.

i.e. $f_{max} \leq$ Permissible compressive stress

or $\quad \dfrac{W}{b}\left(1 + \dfrac{6e}{b}\right) \leq$ Permissible compressive stress $\qquad \ldots (5.24)$

(d) To avoid tension within the structure, the eccentricity, e should not be more than $\frac{b}{6}$ on either side of middle of base, i.e. about point O. Thus the resultant, R will have to be within the middle third, i.e. the extreme limit for F will be $BF = \frac{2}{3}b$.

Hence, for no tension at the base, $BF = \frac{2}{3}b$

or $\qquad BE + EF = \frac{2}{3}b$, or $\bar{x} + Z = \frac{2}{3}b$ ... (5.25)

Example 47—A dam of trapezoidal section with a vertical waterfall has top width of 1.5 m, base width 3.0 m, height 6.0 m. It impounds water to a height of 5.5 m. Test the structure for stability. Assume the following:

Density of masonry = 2.2 gm/cc; Density of water = 1.0 gm/cc
Coefficient of friction (μ) = 0.50; Bearing capacity of soil = 25,000 kg/m²

Solution

Weight of dam per m,

$$W = \frac{a+b}{2} \times H \times P$$
$$= \frac{1.5 + 3.0}{2} \times 6 \times 2.2 \times 1000$$
$$= \frac{4.5}{2} \times 6 \times 2200 = 29700 \text{ kg/m.}$$

The horizontal pressure

$$P = \frac{Wh^2}{2} = \frac{1000 \times 5.5 \times 5.5}{2} = 15125 \text{ kg}$$
$$\bar{x} = \frac{a^2 + b^2 + ab}{3(a+b)} = \frac{1.5^2 + 3^2 + 1.5 \times 3}{3(1.5 + 3)}$$
$$= \frac{2.25 + 9 + 4.5}{3 \times 4.5} = \frac{15.75}{13.5} = 1.16 \text{ m}$$
$$Z = \frac{P}{W} \times \frac{h}{3} = \frac{15125}{29700} \times \frac{5.5}{3} = 0.93 \text{ m}$$

Testing the Stability

For tensile stress:

$x + Z = \frac{2}{3}b$ for no tension condition, $\bar{x} = 1.16$ m; $Z = 0.93$ m and $\frac{2}{3}b = 2$ m

As $\bar{x} + Z$ is greater than $\frac{2}{3}b$, tensile stress is likely to develop and failure of structure by tension is possible.

Crushing:

$$f_{max} = \frac{W}{b}\left(1 + \frac{6 \times e}{b}\right)$$
$$e = \bar{X} + Z - \frac{b}{2} = 1.16 + 0.93 - 1.5 = 0.59 \text{ m}$$
$$f_{max} = \frac{29700}{3}\left(1 + \frac{6 \times 0.59}{0.30}\right) = 9900(1 + 1.18)$$
$$= 9900(2.18) = 21582 \text{ kg/sq m}$$

As f_{max} is less than the bearing capacity of soil (permissible compressive stress), it is safe against crushing.

Overturning:

Overturning moment $= P \times \frac{h}{3}$
$$= 15125 \times \frac{5.5}{3} = 27730 \text{ kg-m}$$
Balancing moment $= W(b-x) = 29700(3 - 1.16)$
$$= 29700 \times 1.84 = 54648 \text{ kg-m}$$

As the balancing moment is greater than overturning moment, the structure is safe. The factor of safety against overturning, $\dfrac{54648}{27730} = 1.97$.

Sliding:

Frictional resistance set up at base

$$\mu W = 0.5 \times 29700 = 14850 \ kg$$
$$P = 15125 \ kg.$$

As μW is less than P, the structure has a tendency to slide forward.

Factor of safety against sliding $= \dfrac{14850}{15125} = 0.98$

Example 48—Calculate the minimum bottom width required for a dam of height 7.0 m. Maximum depth of water to be impounded is 6.0 m and the face in contact with water is vertical. Top width of section is to be 1.5 m. The density of masonry is 2.2 gm/cc, density of water is 1.0 gm/cc, coefficient of friction between masonry and earth is 0.50.

Solution

Let b, be the bottom width in m.

$$W = \frac{a + b}{2} H \times p = \frac{1.5 + b}{2} \times 7 \times 2200 = 7700(1.5 + b) \ kg$$

$$P = \frac{Wh^2}{2} = \frac{1000 \times 6 \times 6}{2} = 18000 \ kg$$

$$x = \frac{a^2 + b^2 + ab}{3(a + b)} = \frac{1.5^2 + b^2 + 1.56}{3(1.5 + b)}$$

$$Z = \frac{P}{W} \times \frac{h}{3} = \frac{18000}{7700(1.5 + b)} \times \frac{h}{3} = \frac{360}{77(1.5 + b)}$$

But for no tension condition $\bar{x} + Z = \dfrac{2}{3}b$

or $\quad \dfrac{2.25 + 1.5 + b^2}{3(1.5 + b)} + \dfrac{360}{77(1.5 + b)} = \dfrac{2}{3}b.$

Solving for b, it is 3.35 m.

Therefore, the bottom width should be at least 3.35 m, so that no tensile stress is developed.

— Minimum bottom width for safety against sliding $\mu W \geq P$

$$0.50 + 7700(1.5 + b) \geq 18000 = 3850(1.5 + b) \geq 18000$$

$$(1.5 + b) \geq \frac{18000}{3850} \geq 4.74$$

$$b \geq (4.74 - 1.5) \geq 3.24 \ m$$

Since 3.35 m is minimum bottom width needed for no tension condition, we can adopt $b = 3.35$ m, as it satisfies both the conditions.

Example 49—A trapezoidal dam 4.0 m high is 1.5 m wide at top and 2.5 m at the bottom with its water face vertical. To what height water can be impounded in the reservoir, so that there is no tension at the base section. Take density of masonry and water as 2200 kg/m³ and 1000 kg/m³.

Solution

$$W = \frac{a + b}{2} . H \times p$$

$$= \frac{1.5 + 2.5}{2} \times 4 \times 2200$$

$$= 2 \times 4 \times 2200 \times 17600 \ kg$$

$$P = \frac{WH^2}{2} = \frac{1000h^2}{2} = 500h^2$$

$$\bar{X} = \frac{a^2 + b^2 + ab}{3(a + b)} = \frac{1.5^2 \times 2.5^2 \times 1.52 \times 5}{3(1.5 + 2.5)}$$

$$= \frac{2.25 + 6.25 + 3.75}{12} = \frac{12.25}{12} = 1.02 \ m$$

$$Z = \frac{P}{W} \times \frac{h}{2} = \frac{5\phi\phi h^2}{176\phi\phi} \times \frac{h}{3}$$

$$= \frac{5}{528}h^3$$

For no tension, $\bar{X} + Z = \frac{2}{3}b$

$$= 1.02 + \frac{5}{528}h^3 = \frac{2}{3}b = \frac{2}{3}2.5$$

$$= \frac{5}{3} = 1.66$$

$$\frac{5}{528}h^3 = 1.66 - 1.02 = 0.64$$

$$h^3 = \frac{0.64 \times 528}{5} = \frac{337.9}{5} = 67.5$$

$$h = 4.075 \text{ m}$$

Or, say the water can be impounded up to the top without causing tension in the structure.

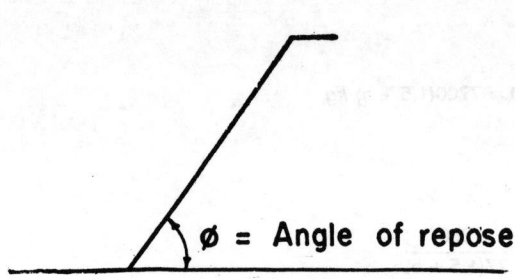

Fig. 5.32 Slope of equilibrium

STRUCTURES SUBJECTED TO EARTH PRESSURE

The slope of a mass of loose dug earth thrown upon a horizontal plane will gradually slip until it finally attains a slope of equilibrium as shown in Fig. 5.32. The greatest inclination of the slope to the horizontal at which the earth will stand permanently is called angle of repose or angle of internal friction. Its value depends on the nature of the earth and on its wetness (Table 5.18)

Table 5.18   *Angle of repose and unit weights*

Substance	Angle of repose	Unit weight (gm/cc)
Sand, dry	30°–37°	1.45–1.90
Sand, wet	26°	1.45–1.90
Earth, dry	29°	1.60–1.92
Earth, moist	45°–49°	1.60–1.92
Clay, dry	29°	1.92–2.20
Clay, damp	45°	1.92–2.20
Gravel, clean	48°	1.45–1.75
Gravel with sand	26°	1.45–1.75

Let H = height of wall (m); W_e = Density of earth (kg/cu-m):

P = Density of masonry (kg/cum); ϕ = Angle of repose of earth, degrees

a & b = top and bottom width, m

$$\text{Considering metre length of wall, } P = \frac{W_e H^2}{2}\left[\frac{1 - \sin\phi}{1 + \sin\phi}\right] \qquad \dots (5.26)$$

which acts at $\frac{H}{3}$ above base

W = weight of wall per metre length $= \frac{(a + b)}{2}.H.P$

which acts at $\bar{X}$ for the vertical face BD and is given by

$$\bar{X} = \frac{a^2 + b^2 + ab}{3(a + b)}$$

$$\text{Eccentricity, } e = \bar{X} + Z - \frac{b}{2} \qquad \qquad \ldots (5.27)$$

The maximum and minimum stress intensities acting normal to the base can be found by applying the equation

$$f_{max} = \frac{W}{b}\left(1 + \frac{6e}{b}\right) \qquad \qquad \ldots (5.28)$$

$$f_{min} = \frac{W}{b}\left(1 - \frac{6e}{b}\right) \qquad \qquad \ldots (5.29)$$

Example 50—Design a retaining wall for height of 5.0 m. The face in contact with the earth is to be vertical and earth level is to be vertical and earth level is with the top. Given density of masonry and earth is 2.1 gm/cc and 1.8 gm/cc, respectively. Angle of repose of earth is 30°. Coefficient of friction, $\mu = 0.5$. Maximum compressive stress for the masonry is 20000 kg/m².
Solution

$$W = \frac{a + b}{2}.H \times p$$

Assume $a = 1.0$ m and base width be b m.

$$W = \frac{1 + b}{2} \times 5 \times 2.1 \times 1000 = 5250(1 + b) \ kg$$

$$P = \frac{W_e H^2}{2} \times \left[\frac{1 - \sin\phi}{1 + \sin\phi}\right]$$

$$= \frac{1.8 \times 1000 \times 5 \times 5}{2}\left[\frac{1 - \sin\ 30°}{1 + \sin\ 30°}\right]$$

$$= \frac{1.8 \times 1000 \times 25}{2} = \frac{1 - 0.5}{1 + 0.5} = 7500 \ kg$$

$$\bar{X} = \frac{a^2 + b^2 + ab}{3(a + b)}$$

$$= \frac{1 + b^2 + b}{3(1 + b)}$$

$$Z = \frac{P}{W}.\frac{H}{3} = \frac{7500}{5250(1 + b)} \times \frac{5}{3} = \frac{2.38}{1 + b}$$

Now for no tension condition, $\bar{X} + Z = \frac{2}{3}b$

or $1 + b + b^2 + 7.14 = 2b(1 + b)$

On simplification, $b^2 + b = 8.14$ or $b = 2.4$ m

Checking the Section for Stability

Against Sliding:

$$\mu W = 0.5$$

Frictional resistance $= \mu W = 0.5 \times 5250(1 + 2.4)$
$$= 0.5 \times 5250 \times 3.4 = 8925 \ kg$$

$P = 7500$ kg

As μW is greater than P, the wall is safe against sliding.

$$\text{Safety factor} = \frac{\mu W}{P} = \frac{8925}{7500} = 1.19$$

Against Crushing
Maximum compressive stress for the masonry is given as 20000 kg/m².

$$e = \frac{b}{6} = \frac{2.4}{6} = 0.4$$

$$W = 5250 \times (1 + 2.4) = 5250 \times 3.4 = 17850 \text{ km/m}$$

$$f_{max} = \frac{W}{b}\left(1 + \frac{6e}{b}\right) = \frac{17850}{2.4}\left(1 + \frac{6 \times 0.4}{2.4}\right) = 14875 \text{ kg/m}^2$$

As f_{max} is less than the permissible compressive stress for masonry, it is safe against crushing.

$$\text{Safety factor for crushing} = \frac{20000}{14875} = 1.34$$

Safety Against Overturning:

$$\text{The overturning moment} = P \times \frac{H}{3} = 7500 \times \frac{5}{3} = 12500 \text{ kg-m}$$

$$\text{Limiting balancing moment} = W(b - \bar{x}) = 17850 \times (2.4 - \bar{x})$$

$$\bar{x} = \frac{1 + b + b^2}{3(1 + b)} = \frac{1 + 2.4 + 2.4^2}{3(3.4)}$$

$$= \frac{1 + 2.4 + 5.76}{3 \times 3.4} = 0.89 \text{ m.}$$

Substituting

$$\text{Limiting balancing moment} = 17850 \times (2.4 - 0.89)$$
$$= 17850 \times 1.51 = 26953 \text{ kg-m}$$

As the limiting balance is greater than overturning moment, the section is safe against overturning.

$$\text{Factor of safety against overturning} = \frac{26953}{12500} = 2.15$$

Since *b* value has been obtained for no tension condition, the structure is safe against tensile stress.

Plate 16.   Grassed waterway.

Plate 17.   Earthen dam in Sukhomajiri village in India.

Plate 18.   Contour cultivation.

Plate 19.   Bouldery riverbed land (wasteland).

Plate 20.   Fodder trees and fibre grass *(Eulaliopsi binata)* have been grown successfully in the bouldery river bed lands of Dehradun in India.

Plate 21.   Fodder bank.

Plate 22.   Drop spillway.

Plate 23.   Chute spillway in Vasad ravine region in India.

Plate 24.   Ravine land along Mahi river in India.

Plate 25.   Reclaimed shallow and medium ravines in
Yamuna river in India showing terrace land
and grassed waterway.

Plate 26.   Reclaimed deep ravine for Permanent
vegetation in India.

6

Special Problems

6.1 Wind Erosion

A total estimated area (NCA, 1976) of 32 m ha is subject to wind erosion, which includes 23.49 m ha of desert and about 6.5 m ha of coastal sandy lands. The remaining area has been included under other land uses subject to soil erosion. The desert area is spread over the states of Rajasthan (9.692 m ha), Gujarat (0.704 m ha) and Haryana (1.4 m ha). Even within the desert areas, there are pockets of agricultural activity and, therefore, only 50% of the total area (11.77 m ha) has been taken as subject to soil erosion by wind. Coastal sandy lands fall mostly in the states of West Bengal, Orissa, Andhra Pradesh, Tamil Nadu, Karnataka, Kerala, Maharashtra and Gujarat. In the case of such areas, the problem of erosion is encountered at a number of places. Therefore, only 25% of such lands (1.47 m ha) is estimated to be affected by erosion (Das, 1985).

Due to action of high velocity of wind, the soil material on the surface of the land is loosened, lifted, slid or bounced along the surface of the ground caused by the turbulence and irregularity of the movement of wind. The soil thus lifted from one place gets deposited in another. Such process of soil movement is called wind erosion.

Wind erosion is most common in arid and semi-arid regions, where the rains are scanty and erratic, thereby leaving the land surface dry with more or less no vegetation. Wind erosion varies only in degree and hence there are no types as in the case of water erosion.

Important factors affecting wind erosion are climate, soil and vegetation. The climatic factors constitute precipitation, temperature, humidity, wind and density of air. Evaporation and transpiration influenced by temperature, humidity and wind deplete soil moisture, causing soil more susceptible to wind erosion. The principal characteristics of wind leading to erosion are direction, duration, velocity and turbulence.

Texture, structure, density of particles and soil mass moisture, organic matter and surface roughness are the important soil factors affecting wind erosion. Drier the soil, more is the susceptibility for wind erosion. Surface roughness or crust has a retarding influence on the movement of soil by wind. Type of vegetation, its height and density as well as seasonal distribution are some of the factors which influence the soil erosion by wind.

The three types of soil movement leading to wind erosion are saltation, suspension and surface creep. Soil moved by saltation process is chiefly composed of fine particles ranging in diameter from 0.1 to 0.5 mm. In the movement of particles through suspension, very fine dust particles of less than 0.1 mm in diameter are only lifted. The difference in the suspension process and saltation lies in that, in the former case the fine dust raised to great heights and long distances from its original location may result in total loss to the eroding area, whereas in latter case and surface creep, the particles raised from the ground drop down within the eroded area or its immediate vicinity. Movement of coarse grained particles varying between

0.5 mm and 1.0 mm is called surface creep. Movement through surface creep is the outcome of the kinetic energy derived from the impact of particles moved in saltation. These three types of movement occur simultaneously at heights not more than 1 m. Above this height, movement can take place only through suspension.

The process of wind erosion involves three phases, namely initiation of the movement of soil particles, their transport and deposition. Particles having 0.1–0.15 mm diameter require a wind velocity of 12–14 km/hr at 15 cm height above the ground for initiation of movement. The amount of soil moved is governed by the size of the particles and their gradation, velocity of the wind and distance across the eroding area. The rate of soil movement varies with the distance from the windward edge of the field or eroded area. The ability of the wind to carry or transport soil is enormous. Assuming an average wind velocity in the atmosphere to be 48 km/hr, the carrying capacity of the storms would be equivalent to about 956 m tonnes of dust carried over about 2300 km. The capacity of the atmosphere for transporting soil particles smaller than 0.1 mm diameter is very great. Whatever helps to decrease the velocity of wind will favour retention and deposition.

The wind erosion process is better understood by recognizing the close interdependence of five main ways the soil particles are loosened and transported. These ways are destruction, effluxion and abrasion. In the case of effluxion, the wind initiates the removal of soil particles having 0.05 to 0.5 mm diameter. Saltation plays the major role on the removal of these particles with surface creep. Thus effluxion is a pre-requisite for other forms of wind erosion. Hence the prevention and control of wind erosion would have to be based on reduction in the amount of particles having 0.05 mm to 0.5 mm diameter, or in slowing down the movement of wind at the ground surface.

Control of Wind Erosion
The three principal methods of reducing surface velocity of wind are vegetal measures, tillage practices and mechanical means.

VEGETATIVE METHOD

Trees and Shrubs
Shelterbelts and wind-breaks are important soil conservation practices improving the micro-climate for the production of crops, and the protection of crop and rangelands, against destructive wind erosion. A wind-break is a narrow belt of trees planted in one or a few rows in a field or in one or more sides of a farmstead to provide protection from the wind. A shelterbelt comprises of a wide belt of trees planted in several rows at right angles to the prevailing wind direction. The factors influencing the effectiveness of wind-breaks are density, height and length. The three systems of wind-breaks recognized usually are permanent wind-breaks, intermediate wind-breaks and temporary wind-breaks. The spacing of wind-break depends upon the density and angle of wind-break to the direction or directions of the hazardous wind. The species suitable for a site much depends upon the soil type, climate including rainfall, elevation, moisture supply, etc. The selection of species should be so made that the tallest may be in the middle rows and low trees or shrubs are planted along the end rows of the wind-break. A more or less conical cross-section of the wind-break will provide about the best protection from wind effects and also increase the zone of protection. The tall growing and shrub-like species should therefore, be intermingled to obtain such a cross-section of the wind-break.

Protection of shelterbelts are carried out by effectively fencing the area, filling-up of casualties so that there are no gaps, measures to protect from fires, and carrying out cleanings and thinnings of shelterbelts according to needs of the belts.

In India, the following species may be recommended, specially for dry localities; although actual species will depend on the locality.

For a 5-row Belt

Central Row
Acacia Arabica (Babul), *Albizzia lebbek* (Siris), *Azadirachta indica* (Neem), *Dalbergia sissoo* (Shisham), *Eucalyptus rostrata*, *Ficus* (Species), *Holoptelia integrifolia. kigelia pinnata* (Sausage tree), *Prosopis specigera* (Khejri), *Tamarindus indica* (Imli).

Flank Rows
Acacia senegal, *Acacia leucophloea*, *Anacardium occidentale*, *Casuarina equiseti-folia*, *Cassiasiamea*, *Inga dulcis* (Madras thorn), *Moringa pterygosperma* (Sainjna), *Prosopis juliflora*, *Tamarix articulata* (Frash).

Side Outer Rows
Acucia jacquemontii, *Agave* Species, *Capparis aphyila*, *Calligonum polygonoides* (Phog). *Cassia auriculata*, *Dodonea viscosa*, *Glyricida maculata*, *Parkinsonia ac-uleata*, *Prosopis juliflora*, *Saccharum munja* (Sarkanda), *Savladora persica*, *S. oloides*, *Vitex negundo*, *Zizyphus* Species.

For a Three-row Belt
Central row—Same species as in Central Row Flank row for a 5-row belt.

Outer row—Same species as for side or outer rows for a 5-row belt.

For a single-row 'Belt'—*Tamarix articulata*, *Acacia* species, *Albizia amara*, *Casuarina equisetifolia*, *Cypresses*, *Inga dulcis*, *Parkinsonia aculeata* (Jerusalem Thorn), *Prosopis juliflora*.

Tamarix articulata (Frash) is ideally suited as a single-row wind-break or buffer-strip species, as it starts branching from the ground-level, and presents a partially penetrable belt throughout its height. It can be raised by putting in branch-cuttings. It has a quick growth and grows on saline and sandy soils, having little precipitation.

Casuarina equisetifolia, where it can be grown, is also a very good break-wind species.

Parkinsonia aculeata (Jerusalem thorn) is also a very good plant for wind-break and live-hedges, and can be grown from sowings, although root-shoot-cuttings or transplants give best results.

The mesquite (*Prosopis juliflora*) also forms a good wind-break due to its habit of low branching and bushy form in early stages of growth. Best grown sowings or from root-shoot-cuttings.

In places where they can be grown, various species of Cypresses are very useful (especially *Cupressus macrocarpa*).

A single-row belt may be made more thick and thus more effective by periodic cutting of the growing branches. This is also the secret of successful live-hedges.

TILLAGE PRACTICES

— The cropping programme should be so devised that some vegetal cover is continuously maintained and sufficient canopy is developed and maintained, particularly during the period of critical wind erosion.

— While harvesting crops, the stubble should be retained at least up to a height of 0.3 m. If possible, the straw should also be left on the land.

— Adopting measures of wind strip-cropping by which strips of crops like pulses or grams or tall-growing *sorghums* or *Jowar* are alternated with low growing crops like groundnut or *ragi*, etc. These strips are laid across the direction of wind.

— During summer fallows, it is advantageous to adopt sub-surface tillage or chemicals for controlling weeds. Implements which do not pulverise soil and do only rough tillage, leaving clods on the land should only be used.

— Wherever possible and practicable, retain grasses on the land or even more and then take up cultivation. Particularly areas that are too sandy to be put under agriculture crops can be put under grasses or shrubs or trees.

MECHANICAL MEASURES

Erosion control structures like contour bunds or terraces along contour provide beneficial support to the cropping practices to control wind erosion. These measures help to conserve moisture and successful crop growth.

As a result of constant wind erosion, coarser particles removed are deposited in hummocks drift. These hummocks may be lowered and levelled to permit better conservation of moisture, easy and quick establishment of vegetation. In case the sand could be removed economically, the removal of sand and levelling could be done and the land brought under agriculture. Gullies or ravines, if any, existing in the area should be reclaimed.

CONTROL OF COASTAL WIND EROSION

During the high tides in sea, huge quantity of sand is brought and deposited in dunes along the seashore. As the height of the fore-dunes increases, the high velocity wind blows the sand materials interior and engulf large extent of agricultural lands and damage even roads, wells, buildings, villages, etc.

In order to control coastal wind erosion, it is necessary to establish vegetative cover on the entire surface of dune in the active part of seashore, and stabilize the same. Then the rest of the area interior should be protected by establishing windbreaks at regular intervals. The initial step in controlling coastal wind erosion is to plant grasses, shrubs and trees, commencing from the windward side of the shore and proceeding towards the leeward side. When once the fore-dunes are stabilized, wind erosion control interior will be easy and successful.

RECOMMENDATIONS OF PRACTICES ADOPTED IN DIFFERENT STATES

Tamil Nadu

Wind erosion is a problem over limited areas in Tirunelveli and Madurai districts of Tamil Nadu. The adverse effects of sand drift are observed from the dry areas of Kangayam, Dharapuram in Coimbatore district and Bodinaickanur in Madurai district in the inland regions. The wind erosion is severely felt in a 30 km stretch between Bodinaickanur and Kombai and to a lesser extent in the area between Chinnamanur and Elumalai on a stretch of 70 km from the west to the east. This malady is the result of deforestation of the ridges and slopes of the Western Ghats. Due to the whirly action of the winds which blows at a velocity of over 65 km/hr, the lands at Sambalmedu get drilled and the soil is scooped out, leaving mounds resembling dead-men. The soil so lifted, is deposited as sand dunes and these sand dunes go on moving year after year affecting large-areas and ultimately invading the agricultural lands.

Control measures

-- Afforestation successfully with *Acacia Planifrons* in the sand dune areas of Jambalmedu and reducing the mobility of sand particles.

-- Raising of shelterbelts, wind-breaks, grasses and orchards.

Recommended number of rows and tree species

For permanent wind-breaks, three rows each comprising shrubs (low or tall), deciduous trees and evergreen trees planted from the windward side, are found to be satisfactory for ordinary situation.

If the area exposed is open and experiences high wind velocity, five or more rows are recommended.

In dryland system, it is recommended that five rows may be adopted for ordinary circumstances and six to seven rows will be necessary for very exposed sites experiencing high wind velocities. The following order of planting is recommended five or more rows of wind-break.

Five-row wind-break

First row   — Low shrubs (commencing from windward side)
Second row   — Tall shrubs
Third row   — Deciduous trees
Fourth row   — Deciduous or evergreen trees
Fifth row   — Evergreen trees.

Six-row wind-break

Insert deciduous trees between fourth and fifth row in the five-row wind-break.

Seven-row wind-break

Insert deciduous trees between fourth and fifth row and add evergreen trees as the seventh row.

Planting along Highways

The planting of rows of trees as wind-break along the highways, should be done on the leeward side of the road.

In pure sandy soils, Casuarina, Screwpine, Kali-manda, Babul and cashew trees are found very efficient in arresting sand drift. *Casuarina* plants are planted during the latter part of the monsoon period. If planting is done as soon as the monsoon starts, the plants will not survive on account of excessive rain. Usually seedlings two-to-three years old are planted at two-to-three plants in each hole (0.9 to 1.2 m) apart. They require watering during two consecutive summers after planting, after which they do not require any attention. Cashew trees are grown by sowing good cashew seeds during rainy season in pits (0.22 to 0.3 m) deep. No watering is done. Kali-manda is grown from cuttings planted during rainy season. This forms a good hedge. Palmyras are grown from seeds which are pre-sprouted by heaping ripe palmyra fruits and covering the heap with some rubbish kept wet. Palmyrahs grow very slowly and in their early stages if planted closely in rows prevent sand drift. They do not require any watering and attention. Castor plants grow very well in sandy soil and protect the area from sand drift.

Species Suitable for Shelterbelts and Wind-breaks

First Row

Agave americana and Agave sisalana, Aruudo donax, Balanites roxburghii, bamboos, Calotropis gigantea, Casuarina equeistifolia, Euphorbia royleana and Euphorbia neripholia, Gliricidia maculata, Ipomoea carnea, Lawsonia alba, Leucaena glauca, Ricinus communis, Saccharum munja, Sesbania aegyptica, Tamarix articulata, Tecoma stans, Tephrosia candida, Thevetia neriifolio, Vitex negundo Zizyphus nummularia.

Second Row

Acacia catechu, A. mollisima, Anacardium occidental, Acacia arabica, Borrasus flabellifer, Boswellia serrata, Cassia siamea, Casuarine spp., coconut palms, Melia azadirachta, Parkinsonia aculeata, Pionciana alata, Pongamia glabra, Prosopsis juliflora or P. spicigera, Zizyphus jujuba.

Third Row

Acacia arabica, Albizzia lebbeck, Anacardium occidentale, Artocarpus integerifolia, and other palms, bamboos, Casuarina spp., Cedrelatoona, Dalbergia sisoo, D. Latifolia, Eucalyptus spp., Eugenia jambolana, Grevillea robusta, Hardwickia binata, Mangifera indica, Tamarindus indica, Tectona grandis.

Recommendation of CAZRI, Jodhpur

Indian arid zone comprise a vast area of about 3.2 lakh km², which is about 12% of geographical area. Out of this about 1.96 lakh km² falls in the state of Rajasthan. Shelterbelts are essential to protect vast agricultural fields, orchards, highways, railway lines, canals, etc., from hot winds and moving sands and these may be of five to seven rows of trees. Trees are planted staggered in rows at 5 m apart row-to-row and at 3 to 5 m apart plant-to-plant within the row.

Species Recommended

Centre Row

Acacia tortilis, Prosopis juliflora, Cassia siamea

Flanked Row

Dichrostachys glomerata, Acacia senegal, Colophos-permum mopane.

Outer Row

Zizyphus nummularia, Cassia auriculata, Saccharum bengalense, Agave spp., etc.

Roadside, Canal Bank and Railway Line Plantations

These are very essential in arid areas, as trees provide adequate shade, aesthetic beauty and protection from accumulation of sand particles. Specially spots which are vulnerable to moving sand hazards should be tackled on priority basis. Three rows of staggered planting of tree species are recommended for planting at 50 m away from the centre of the road, canal and railway line on the windward side and no planting to be done on the leeward side, as this would help to check the moving sand on the windward side.

Species Recommended

Prosopis juliflora, Acacia tortilis, Dalbergia sissoo, Azadirachta indica, Tamarix articulata, Cassia siamea, Eucalyptus spp., Parkinsonia aculeata, etc.

Fixation of Shifting Sands

Western Rajasthan has about 59% of the area under moving and semi-stabilized sand dunes (Plate 28) of different degree and extent. The main factors involved for stabilization process are:

— Protection of dunes against biotic factors by fencing. This should be completed before the onset of monsoons. If strict watch and ward is enforced, then fencing need not be insisted upon.

— Treating the affected dunes by fixing barriers in parallel strips or in chess board designs using the locally available shrubs, etc., to act as micro-wind-breaks. This operation should be completed before the onset of monsoons. Wherever wind velocity is not intensive and rainfall is over 300 mm per year, the erection of micro-wind-breaks need not be done.

— Revegetating by direct seeding or transplanting seedlings immediately after receipt of a good shower with indigenous and exotic nursery raised tree species. Simultaneously planting of grass slips, cuttings of *Calligonum polygonoides* and sowing seeds of grasses on the leeward sides of the micro-wind-breaks should be undertaken.

— Continuous and proper management of afforested dunes till the cost of input is recovered, say for about 10 to 15 years.

Plantation on sand dunes may be done in strips 20 m wide across the wind direction leaving gaps of 40 m wide strips for raising grasses and shrubs, as this would facilitate both trees, shrubs and grasses to grow free from moisture competition and also serves as shelterbelts.

The ultimate success is also based on choosing the right tree species, planting sturdy stocks, planting deep and in time, timely replacement of casualties and its after-care.

Species Recommended

Acacia tortilis, Prosopis juliflora, P. cineraria, Ailanthus excelsa, Dalbergia sissoo, Acacia senegal, Albizzia lebbek, Colophosphermum mopane, Dichrostachys glomerata, Zizyphus rotundifolia, Calligonum polygonoides, Saccharum bengalensis, Lasiurus sindicus, Cenchrus ciliaris, C. setigerus.

Sand Dune Afforestation

1½ to 6 months old nursery seedlings are planted in pits of 45^3 cm or 63^3 cm at 5 x 5 m or 5 x 10 m spacing for fuel and silvi-pastoral plantations respectively. Plantation programme should commence with the onset of monsoon. Weeding and soil working is necessary for at least 3 years in the early stage of the plantation. After planting, if there happens to be a well-distributed rainfall, no watering is needed for the plants, otherwise, watering at 9 lit/plant fortnightly is desirable, till next monsoon for proper establishment of the seedings. Wherever sand dunes afforestation is undertaken, watering is not feasible, but the seedlings are planted during rains. They develop deeper root system and invariably reach the moisture zone or barren dunes.

Soil working techniques recommended for different soil types are detailed below:

Type of soil	Soil working technique	Man days per ha
Deep sandy soil	Pits of 60^3 cm are dug at required spacing and filled with weathered soil prior to the commencement of monsoon. After planting saucer shaped depressions (1 m diameter) are made around the plants to harvest rain water.	160
Shallow soil, sandy loam soils overlying hard calcareous pan beneath	Pits of 90 cm depth and 60 cm diameter are dug at required spacing and filled with a mixture of weathered soil and farmyard manure on equal proportion, prior to the commencement of monsoon and seedlings planted on receipt of a good shower.	200
Rocky terrain with scattered soil pockets. Semi-rocky terrain with accumulation of transported soil	Wherever soil pockets of accumulation of soil exist, pits of 45^3 cm or 60^3 cm are dugout and half-filled with the dug out weathered soil and the remaining soil is made into crescent-shaped ridge 15 cm high, across the local slope to harvest rain water.	160

Species Recommended for Different Types of Soil with Average Rainfall of over 250 mm to 400 mm

Deep Sandy Soils

Acacia tortilis
Prosopis juliflora
Propsopis cineraria
Azadirachta indica
Albizzia lebbek
Cassia siamea
Acacia senegal
Dichrostachys glomerata
Colophospermum mopane
Tamarix articulata.

Acacia aneura
Brasilettia mollis
Hardwickia binata
Eucalyptus camaldulensis
Holoptelia integrifolia
Zizyphus nummularia
Zizyphus mauritiana
Z.rotundifolia
Euphorbia antisyphilifica

Shallow Sandy Loam Soils Overlying Hard Calcareous Pan

Acacia tortilis
Prosopis juliflora
Azadirachta indica
Albizzia lebbek
Dalbergia sissoo
Cassia siamea

Holoptelia integrifolia
Dichrostachys glomerata
Acacia aneura
Zizyphus nummularia
Euphorbia antisyphilitica

Rocky and Semi-rocky Refractory Sites

Acacia tortilis
Prosopis juliflora
Acacia senegal
Cassia siamea
Albizia lebbek

Butea monosperma
Euphorbia antisyphilitica
Agave americana
Commiphora wightii
Dichrostachys glomerata

Saline Areas

Prosopis juliflora	Prosopis tamarugo
Tamarix spp.	Acacia catechu
Salvadora persica	Acacia nilotica spp. indica
Salvadora oleoides	Atriplex nummularia

Silvipastoral Systems

This system is a combination of growing mainly fodder trees with grasses as ground cover. This would meet the local demand for fuelwood, small timber for agricultural implements, top-feed and fodder, marginal lands, wastelands, and areas unfit for agricultural purposes may be profitably utilised under this system. Instead of raising trees with grasses as under cover, it would be advantageous to raise trees in strips 20 m wide across the wind direction, alternated with strips of 40 m width for grasses and legumes. This also provides ample scope for protecting the tree strips by fencing and allowing grazing of livestock within the grass strips till the trees attain considerable height from being browsed for at least a period of 5 years.

Species Recommended

Trees
Prosopis cineraria, Ailanthus excelsa, Acacia aneura, Colophospermum mopane, Brasilettia mollis, Hardwickia binata, Acacia tortilis, Acacia nilotica spp. indica.
   Dichrostachys glomerata, Zizyphus mauritiana, Prosopis juliflora (pods only), etc.

Grasses
Cenchrus ciliaris, C.setigerus, Lasiurus sindicus and Dichanthium annulatum (in heavy soils)

Promising Fuelwood Species
The cycle for the main fuel wood species, viz. Acacia tortilis and Prosopis juliflora may be fixed at 10 years under coppice, system. At the end of the rotation, a tree would normally yield about 1 q fuel wood in addition to top-feed for livestock and thorns, etc., for fencing. These trees also provide shade, leaves as fodder from A tortilis and pods of both the species as concentrates for the livestock in addition to small timber for agricultural implements.

Results of Works to Arrest Wind Erosion Carried out in Haryana State (formerly Punjab)
Out of a total of area of 43.22 lakh ha, about 14 lakhs ha is affected by wind erosion in the Haryana state. Extremes of climate, low rainfall, low water-table, fires and dry summer winds, clearing of vegetation for colonization, defective cultivation, over-grazing by cattle, unrestricted felling of trees from field, etc., are the climatic and biotic factors causing total wind erosion.

   The work carried out during first two Five-Year Plans in combating wind erosion are raising of shelterbelts, formation of wind-breaks, afforestation of hills, raising of shelterbelts along border on roads, canals and in gaps, plantation and fixation of sand dunes, etc.

   Mohindergarh town, which was once endangered by shifting sands has been saved, as active sand dunes are fixed and the danger spot now bears a thick cover of trees and bushes. In other places, sand dunes have been stabilized by *Kana* planting done at 0.6 m × 0.6 m against wind direction.

Results of work carried out indicated that grasses like *Cenchrus* spp. and *Hetero-pogon contortus* extend gradually in the area. *Leptadenia spartium* and *Calligonum polygonoides, Citrullus colocynthis* (a trailer), *Cyperus arenarius, Calotropis procera, Saccharum munja, Agave sisalana, Ricinus communis. Arnebia hispidissima, Aristida depressa, Aerua javanica, Tephrosia purpurea* and *Cenchrus* ciliaris are species best suited to fix up active sand dunes. When sand dunes were fixed, they were treated like flat bits or hollows between dunes. The species which succeeded on such areas are *Acacia senegal, A.modesta, Prosopis spicigera, P. juliflora (Arid form), Acacia arabica, Zizyphus jujuba, Z.jujuba* var. *Fruticosa, Cercidium terryanum, Balanites roxburghii, Dalbergia sissoo, Albizzia lebbek, Teccomella undulata* and *Azadirachta indica*. Planting of plants raised in tubes, pots and presprouted stumps is preferable to sowing due to adverse factors.

6.2 Shifting Cultivation

In India, shifting cultivation is practiced by many tribal communities in different forms in a total area of 4.36 m ha (1.36 in NE Hill region and 3.0 m ha in A.P., Orissa, Bihar and Madhya Pradesh, etc.). Shifting cultivation comprises of a wasteful cycle, cutting and burning the natural vegetation of a rich forest soil followed by growing crops for short periods (1–3 years) followed by long periods (10–40 years) of fallow to allow regeneration of natural vegetation and replenishment of soil fertility. At the end of the fallow period, the cycle may be repeated or the cultivators may move to entirely new land and start a new cycle there.

The intensity of shifting cultivation varies with the changing conditions of rainfall, topography, density of population and accessibility. The people who practice shifting cultivation can be grouped into three categories, viz. (i) primarily dependent; (ii) partially dependent and (iii) marginally dependent. By and large, the seven stages of N.E. India can be categorised as people primarily dependent on shifting cultivation. They live in high rainfall zone (above 2,500 mm per year) with low density of population and low accessibility.

Orissa and Andhra Pradesh may be categorised as those partially dependent on shifting cultivation. These people live in medium rainfall zone (1500 to 2000 mm per year), with medium to high density of population and better facilities of communication.

In the states of Bihar, Madhya Pradesh, Sikkim, Kerala, Karnataka and Maharashtra, it is seen that people are marginally dependent on shifting cultivation. This zone receives less than 1,500 mm rainfall per year.

The states, the number of districts and blocks and the minimum and maximum density of population per sq km, where the shifting cultivation is being practised are given below:

State	No. of districts	No. of blocks	Density of population per km² at Block level	
			Minimum	Maximum
Andhra Pradesh	3	10	16	73
Arunachal Pradesh	5	33	3	40
Assam	2	9	10	34
Bihar	1	9	90	233
Karnataka	1	1	100	
Kerala	3	3	54	177
Madhya Pradesh	6	10	4	192
Maharashtra	1	1	9	
Manipur	5	20	7	61
Meghalaya (All over the state)			15	80
Mizoram (All over the state)			10	60
Nagaland (All over the state)			12	100
Orissa	8	43	18	300
Sikkim	1	1	52	
Tripura	3	10	26	364
All India picture				
No. of States	: 15			
No. of Districts	: 54			
No. of Blocks	: 220			
Density of population per km² at block level			3	364

Shifting cultivation is restricted mostly below 1,300 m contour level throughout the country. It is also observed that in most of the N.E. states, where rainfall is high and density is low, people hold the land for cultivation for only one or two years, as due to heavy rain, there is risk of soil erosion. On the other hand, the fallow period is also less, and mostly 5–6 years. But in the low rainfall zone with higher density of population, the people hold the land for more than three years as risk of soil erosion is less in comparison to the heavy rainfall zone. Population pressure is also one of the reasons for holding the land for longer period. Similarly, fallow period is extended up to 10 to 12 years.

The methods adopted by the people in shifting cultivation vary from place to place, depending on their social customs and beliefs. Since these people mainly depend on shifting cultivation for their livelihood, the entire scheme of operations from the clearing of forests to the harvest is closely interwoven with their beliefs, rituals, customs, manners and festivals. Shifting cultivation forms an integral part of the life of the people who are primarily dependent on it. In the partially dependent and marginally dependent categories, the impact of developmental activities in the area has changed the methods of practice of shifting cultivation.

The cycle of shifting cultivation varies from three years to 15 years depending on the availability of land. In certain places in Nagaland, the cycle has come down to two years. When the people move from one area to another for shifting cultivation, some people in N.E. region like Noctes sow seeds of *Macaranga denticulata* to enable them to have sufficient material for their use as poles, etc., and for burning, when they return to the same area after some years. Some others like the Wanchoos, leave scattered trees like *Sehima wallichii* in the area to provide fodder, firewood and timber during the fallow period. In Nagaland, pollareded stools of *Alnus nepalensis* are left for the same purpose. In Andhra Pradesh, trees like tamarind and mango are left in the area to obtain the usufructus to supplement their diet. Such practices have been evolved by the people according to their needs and requirements.

With increase in population densities, small farm sizes, and the need to produce more food, the fallow period in the cycle becomes shorter. Thus the shorter fallow period is insufficient to even partly restore the fertility of the land. This leads to rapid soil degradation and decreases in crop yields. The only possible way to stop this process is to develop these lands for permanent agriculture.

To convert such lands to permanent agricultural use, the first and most difficult task is to clear it of its existing vegetation, to remove tree stumps and roots, followed by the introduction of adequate soil conservation practices.

This not only provides the stepping stone for higher and sustained yields and provides better land for more people, but also prevents accelerated forest destruction, siltation, floods and damage to the lowlands and the infrastructure.

The existing density of population on the land to be cleared depends on the climate, the length of the shifting cultivation cycle and on the frequency of the cycle. Lands nearest to existing villages are in most cases used more intensively than areas far from the villages. The former should be developed first. Generally, the forest regrowth is poorer there than in the less used and distant plots.

Unless the shifting cultivators can be weaned from the practice by a profitable alternative vocation suiting their sociocultural background and adopting an integrated approach of involving agriculture, forestry, horticulture and animal husbandry supplemented by soil conservation measures, the problems of shifting cultivation may not be solved. Though it may not be possible to stop shifting cultivation totally, with above measures it would be possible to control, regulate and contain shifting cultivation and bring it within reasonable limits. In these programmes, it is necessary to win the confidence of people and get them involved.

RECOMMENDATIONS ADOPTED IN DIFFERENT INDIAN STATES

Tripura
The experience gained in controlling shifting cultivation in Tripura indicated that an integrated multidisciplinary approach involving agriculture, forestry, animal husbandry, fisheries, horticulture, health and education programmes was successful.

Arunachal Pradesh
The Forest Department, (Thangam, 1980) Arunachal Pradesh has suggested the following programme for controlling shifting cultivation. Land with slopes up to 20% (say 1/3 of the lower slope areas) would be brought under terraced cultivation facilities for irrigated paddy crop by constructing low level bunds across the nullahs in the area and constructing irrigation channels. In the area between 20% and 40% slope (say middle 1/3) cash crops like coffee, big cardamom, black pepper, tea and silver oak and other trees, etc., would be grown as shade trees to provide necessary

small wood and timber for the people. For the area above 40° slope, mainly multiple use trees like *Eucalyptus* species, Subabul, Gamari and other varieties would be grown with fodder grass under them. These tree crops will provide timber for house construction, firewood and also material for small cottage industries. People will be encouraged to have poultry and rear cattle where necessary. They could also breed fish in the water stored by bunds that will be built for irrigation purposes. Arrangement will have to be made to market the agricultural and other produces grown by the people at competitive prices. For this purpose, a Fair Price Shop will be opened, which could collect the local produce for marketing and provide the people with necessities of life. The main object should be to place the land under each village to the best use, so that the people could derive the maximum benefit from the land. It is expected that in the course of 4 to 5 years, it will be possible to cover the entire village. The programme has to be organised in such a manner, as to provide the employment to all able-bodied persons in the village throughout the year. Towards this end, minimum mechanical equipment like tractors etc., will be purchased under the scheme. In this way, it is expected that it would be possible to take up development of the land under shifting cultivation. It is also expected that this multi-disciplined approach will provide the best results and will help us to achieve the object the object of controlling shifting cultivation.

N.E. Hill Region

The ICAR Research Complex for N.E.Hill region has identified model land use, as an alternative to *jhum* in which the lower 1/3 portion of a slope may be put under agriculture after bench terracing, the middle 1/3 portion under hortipastoral system with half moon terracing and the upper 1/3 portion under silvipastoral or forestry. Similarly, several alternatives have to be worked out which are acceptable to *jhum* farmers. Mixed farming involving crop production to meet their food requirement and other subsidiary occupation of animal husbandry and horticulture may offer a possible substitute to *jhuming*. There is need to develop mixed crop production techniques involving low input and low risk of agricultural technology.

ICAR Pilot Project

In order to wean away the *Jumias* from the traditional practice of shifted cultivation, a package of treatments comprising permanent cultivation, forest and cash crop plantation, was launched in the states/union territories of north-eastern region and Andhra Pradesh and Orissa during the Fifth Plan. Till the end of the Seventh Plan, about 2500 families have been settled over 5000 ha at a cost of about Rs.2.17 crores.

6.3 Landslides[*]

A landslide is defined as the downward and outward movement of slope forming material, composed of natural rocks, soils, artificial fills or combination of these materials. Landslides, in a strict sense, do not include creep phenomena or subsidence,

---

[*] The subject matter in this Manual deals with man-induced landslides/landslips and not with mass movements which are very complex in nature.

but usually these are considered along with land slides, because of their relation to instability of slope.

FACTORS CAUSING LANDSLIDES

Factors causing landslides have been broadly classified as geological, hydrological and seismic (Deb et al., 1969) land use. Almost all the landslides involve the failure of earth material under shear stress.

Geological Factors

Landslides are dependent completely on the nature of materials involved and on their structure. This, therefore, calls for a careful study of the local geology. It will certainly bring out the weak spots/formations susceptible to sliding. Thin beds of clayey limestones, shales, highly jointed sedimentary beds, ash beds and schist varieties are all pointers to weak zones (Deb et al., 1969). If along with these, structural deformities like steep dips, folds, faults accompany, the likely danger increases. Landslides hazard is indicated if a stronger formation overlies a weaker one. The landslides at Nalota Nala, Kalagarh Nala on Dehradun-Mussoorie road are some of the examples. The Himalayas and Shiwaliks have interacted and Shiwalik formations have intruded into the Himalayan formations, thus contributing to instability of the area.

Hydrological Factors

Water seeping through disturbed slopes, toe cutting by rivers and torrents and pore water pressure in the soil zone are major agents responsible for landslides. Torrents, especially in their early stages, because of excessive velocities of flow and turbulence carry out quick removal of debris and cutting of sides. The landslides mostly take place after heavy rainfall. The rain water has mainly three effects namely, (a) it increase the effective weight of the material due to saturation, (b) lubricates any sliding places, especially of shales and (c) causes weakening of strata, e.g., if this is a clayey stratum it will swell because of moisture intake. One or all these effects in combination may bring about a landslide in the rainy season. Whenever these factors are causing slope failure, improving the drainage of the area is called for.

Seismic Factors

The intensity and frequency with which earthquakes are felt in a particular region, will also influence the occurrence of landslides. Sometimes landslides are so great that they themselves initiate earthquakes (Deb et al., 1969). In this way, both are complementary to each other. It is also a common observation that generally in mountainous areas of Tertiary age group, rocks are relatively younger where seismic activity is common. In case of fine sand, silt and loess deposits, shocks due to earthquake or blasting reduce the shear strength due to liquification and initiate sand and mud follows. In the Himalayan region, blasting for limestone, quarrying and road making is common and mild seismic activities are reported.

Land Use

Landslides may also be caused by a single or a combination of activities such as (a) indiscriminate felling of trees, overgrazing, unscientific removal of land cover and fire, (b) adoption of improper agriculture on steep-slopes, (c) blasting for mining and road making, etc., (d) unscientific mine spoil disposal, (e) undercutting of the base of existing slope by torrents or for road making, and (f) improper alignment of roads on weaker and unstable rock formation. Also initiation of sliding may be caused by gradual disintegration of the soil starting with hair width cracks, which subdivide the soil into angular fragments.

The commonly accepted geomorphic divisions of India into the Peninsula, the Indo-Gangetic plain and the Extra-Peninsula, could be adopted as the basis for evaluating the relative incidence of landslides. The different geological history, the varying character of the geological formations and the contrasted physiographic make-up of the three geomorphic divisions also define the pattern and the quantum of incidence of landslides therein.

The Peninsular Area

The triangular-shaped peninsula, pointing southwards with the base to the north, encompasses some of the most ancient crystalline rock formations of the Earth's crust, that have not been disturbed by young, mountain-building movements; these constitute terrains of generally subdued relief and are hence generally devoid of landslides, except locally, as exemplified by the Baripeda subsidence of Orissa, caused by slump-slides in montmorillonite clay-bearing beds of Tertiary age; or in engineering excavations involving deep rock cuts into Archaean joined gneisses and schists as in the Nagarjunasagar canals, Andhra Pradesh. Sporadic development of landslides has been recorded in the mountain ranges that bound the Peninsular shield to the west and the east, viz., the Western and Eastern Ghats and, more pronounced landslides in the hill ranges close to their junction, as in the Nilgiri and other nearby hill areas of Tamil Nadu and Kerala states. The Aravali ranges to the north-west of the shield, as well as the Vindhyan and Satpura ranges to the north, both by virtue of the nature of the slopes bounding them, do not show any significant development of landslides, except locally, illustrated by the slump-slides in the Rewa shales of Upper Proterozoic age that constitute the upper portions of the left abutment hill of Ranapratapsagar Dam across the Chambal Valley in Rajasthan.

In the horizontally disposed lava flows constituting a greater part of the Western Ghats, slump-slides have been generated only in the overburden of trap-derived debris, set in a clayey matrix, and these slope failures have often been guided by the gently-inclined interface of overburden and bedrock. These slides in Maharashtra state are not as large in volume, nor as damaging in their impact on environment as the Himalayan slides. In come cases, saturation of the toe of slope made up of such clayey overburden, induced by man-made reservoir as at Mula in Ahmednagar district, has triggered off mass-movement.

Other then the state of Maharashtra, Kerala is the state encompassed by the Western Ghats, which have been subjected to sporadic landslides. The formations affected by these landslides rarely include the bedrock and, generally, involve scree and rock debris with clay, resting on the steep, western hill slopes. The failure of such slope-forming materials are common after intense saturation by the monsoon rainfall.

A great majority of the recent landslides in the Nilgiri hills (Krishnaswamy, 1980) relate to the cover of debris on slopes, the debris being made up of boulders of gneisses set in a high percentage of clayey matrix, and to beds of lithomargic clay developed in the lateritic weathering profile on the bedrock—both types of slope-forming materials being mobilised by the lowered shear strength of the clays, upon intense saturation by rainfall. Some of the failures take the shape of even debris—avalanches hurtling down from a height of 100–150 m. In fact, a valley in the Nilgiris is also known by the name of Avalanche Valley, due presumably to the past incidence of such types of landslides here.

The Indo-Gangetic Plain

Although this geomorphic division is made up of soft, unconsolidated Quaternary sediments, the nature of the terrain, with no relief, makes it a landslides free area, except where bank erosion of steep alluvial bluffs permits slope failures. Slides in the Quaternary sediments also arise in deep, man-made cuts for the location of engineering structures, if these cuts are not adequately designed in terms of the shear strength properties of the materials, and if the water-table is not lowered by pumping.

The Extra Peninsula \

A combination of adverse factors of high relief topography, complexly folded and faulted and highly jointed rock formations and high rainfall, besides the activity erod-ing hydraulic regime of the river systems, make the Extra-Peninsular terrain most vul-nerable to large-scale landslides. Furthermore, the inherently landslide prone slopes in the geo-topographic and hydrologic-climatic set-up of the terrain, are rendered into active landslide areas by Man's developmental activities by way of road and building construction, or by the execution of flood control, irrigation and power projects for deriving the maximum benefit of the resource-potential of the Extra-Peninsula.

REGIONAL SIGNIFICANCE

Bansal and Mathur (1976) have estimated that on an average the major landslides in the Himalayas result in an annual loss of more than 50,000 man hours and 5000 vehicle hours per km of road per year due to disruption of communication and communication alone. Assuming Rs.2 per man-hour and Rs.50 per vehicle hour, annual loss works out to be Rs.350 million. With the completion of a network of more than 10,000 km of hill roads in the Himalayas, the frequency of landslides has increased considerably—in fact more than half of landslides are due to the road construction. Thus, the need to reduce damage by these landslides by proper maintenance of road and also treatment of the slides has assumed great importance and urgency.

In the Nilgiri hills, however, the slide-incidence has been unusual and rather severe, being as high as 1 slide per 2–3 km² and extending over an area of 250 km². More than 100 slides have been recognised through the study of air photographs and verification by ground reconnaissance. In 1978 and 1979 such intense sliding caused severe damage to communication routes, tea-gardens and potato-plantations. In 1979 alone, the damage of roads cost 1 crore of rupees; of public property 3 crores; and of tea estates 2 crores.

Landslides and slips increase non-point pollution, which goes up to 8000 pm recorded during November and December floods of 1978 rains in Nilgiri rivers.

In August, 1978, widespread mass movements, of saturated glacial morainal de-posits, transported as debris flows by the Kanauldhia Ghad, a tributary joining the Bhagirathi river upstream of Uttarkashi in the Uttar Pradesh. Himalaya, spread a debris-cone fully across the main river, and impounded the river course up to a height of 30 m. Subsequently, the top 25 m of this barricade was partly breached, leading to flash floods in the valley downstream. A 1.5 km long lake, 20 m deep, was left behind by the landslide dam, which of course, will silt up in course of time.

Similar landslide dams are known to have been formed in the Nepal Himalaya. Some years ago, the apprehended failure of one such landslides dam was expected to cause high flood flows at the site of the Trisulli Hydel Project. Consequently, the entire layout of the second stage extension of this project had to be modified, so that the planned engineering structures would lie far above the flood leaves that are likely to be reached by the breath of landslide-dams higher up in the valley.

EFFECT OF LANDSLIDES ON THE REGION

The landslides adversely affect utility services like roads, power generation units, dams, reservoirs, human settlements, agriculture, forests, pastures, orchards, trade, tourism and all other developmental, cultural and economic activities.

Stabilization of Landslides/Landslips

The stabilization of landslides and landslips can be achieved by the following methods.

— Project formulation for any landslide control including reconnaissance survey.

— *Protective measures from biotic factors*—Four band barbed wire fencing or to similar fencing to prevent cattle, sheep and other animals from grazing in the area; protection measures which can be achieved by an Act of Law, educating the general public through different publicity media describing the need for protecting the hills from the landslides and in extreme cases fencing the area.

— Structural measures to stabilize the torrent to prevent cutting and control the bed slope of torrent bed, for example, drop structures with shallow foundations and aprons in the main torrent; retaining wall and gabion deflecting type of spurs in the lower reaches; series of drop structures in the middle reach; and series of drop structures and stone check dams in the upper reaches.

— Landslide slope provided with contour wattling, which may·include mulching, etc.

— Slip area to be permanently stabilized with immediare cover with quick establishing species of trees and shrubs and permanent cover to restore the original conditions.

— Transfer of technology to the farmers, foresters, engineers of roadways, public works departments, electricity board is an important aspect of the Project. This can be achieved by training farmers and other personnel by giving short courses regarding the control of landslides, demonstration of landslide control in farmer's fields and highways to be executed by the Government, and providing plant materials for stabilization (free or with subsidy) to the farmers and other agencies. Village level workers, other Government officials must be given first hand knowledge of the problem and ways of tackling the same. In case of emergency caused by landslides, Home Guards, School and College students, members of different associations and missionaries to be kept educated and informed to tackle the situation.

— Suitable maintenance of structures is necessary. Minor damages to the structures such as failure of gabion wire or settlement of structure should be attended to immediately.

RECOMMENDATIONS OF CENTRAL SOIL & WATER CONSERVATION RESEARCH & TRAINING INSTITUTE, DEHRADUN

A 4 ha Nalota Nala landslide (located at about 18 km from Dehradun on Dehradun-Mussoorie Road at an elevation of 1100 to 1500 m above m.s.l.) has been successfully stabilized by mechanical (gabion, checkdams with wide-aprons, inward sloping and projecting masonry spillways) and biological (contour wattling, mulching and planting of *Ipomea carnea, Vitex negundo*, Napier for quick covers and *Erythrina suberosa, Dalbergia sissoo* and *Acacia catechu* for permanent cover control measures (Plate 29 and 30). The technology is available for transfer (Sastry et al., 1981).

CS & WCR & TI, Research Centre, Ootacamund

Landslides and landslips in Peninsular India have been classified (Chinnamani et al., 1980) into landslides of pure soil, soil and boulders, and boulders and landslips on terrace embankments, urban lands and roads and torrents perennial streams and rivers.

Stabilization of the above landslides and landslips included the following steps:

— project formulation; protection measures; soil and water conservation measures which include graded bunds/graded trenches or bench terraces or contour stonewalls or gully control measures, etc., suitable to the area; planning good disposal system for rain water which includes longitudinal drains and vertical drains with drops pits; planting of suitable grasses/trees or a mixture of grasses and trees or castor and agave in between the contour trenches; transfer for technology; and maintenance after completion of the project.

6.4 Torrent and Stream Bank Protection

Torrents

The problem of torrent erosion in both the foothills of the northern Himalayan region known as *chos* and the north-eastern Himalayan region, has been increasing. The National Commission on Agriculture observed that the devastation by *chos* in the Punjab alone is over 2.5 m ha. Similar information for the north-eastern Himalayan region is not available.

Cause of Torrents

The main cause of the problem is the high runoff down the hill slopes with heavy silt loads that fill up the channel beds thereby reducing their capacity to carry the runoff and sediment. In consequence, the flow shifts from the original course. The process is repeated many times until vast stretches of fertile land are criss-crossed by courses swamped with coarse sediments and detritus. The *chos* break up habitation, affect communications, agriculture, recharge of shallow wells and other social amenities.

Approach for Treating Torrents

The solution lies in regulating the quantum of runoff coming down the hill slopes and the accompanying silt load. Treatments must therefore, cover measures in the catchment to moderate the runoff peak and volume, and to reduce the soil erosion and consequent silt load. The main package of ameliorative practices include afforestation and grassland development with trenching across the land slope and growing agriculture crops on terraced lands. As for as the main torrent is concerned, remedies are:

— Control of grazing and deforestation

— protection of banks from erosion by providing marginal *bunds* at a reasonable distance from the edge; for sections subject to serious erosion, riprap or loose retaining walls can be used

— Construction of revetments, spurs and jetties (retards) to confine the flow and protect the bank from scouring. Training walls, made of flexible semi-permanent materials, can also be used in double line, parallel to the banks, to facilitate setting of silt and growth of vegetation; and

— construction of temporary or permanent structures in sections where the gradient is steep, to facilitate siltation and thereby stabilize the grades. Fig. 6.1 illustrates some control measures.

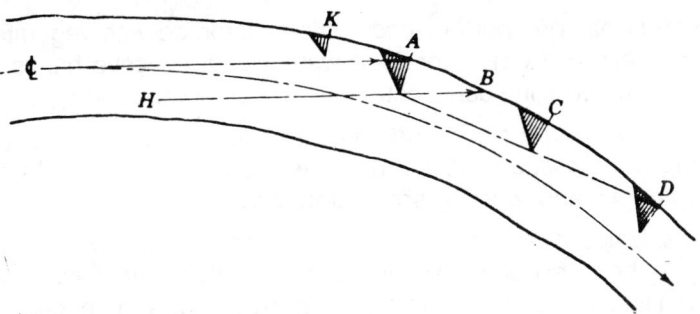

Fig. 6.1 Design and location of retards (Redrawn from Saveson and Overholt, 1937)

METHOD OF LOCATING RETARDS

Stream Bank Protection

A method of locating retards is shown in Fig. 6.1. The first major retard at A is located by the intersection of the projected centre line of flow with the concave bank. In locating the second major retard C and a line HB is drawn parallel to the above projected centreline and through the end of the retard A. The intersection of this line with the concave bank locates, point B. AC is then made equal to twice AB. Additional retards are located by the intersection of a line connecting the end points of the two previous retards with the concave bank (see D). An auxiliary retard at K is located a distance AB upstream from A and is extended into the stream about one-half the length of the other retards. The retards should extend into the stream at an angle of 45 degrees for a distance of about 30 per cent of the channel width. On small streams the spacing of the retards may be made equal to the stream width, and the length, 0.25 times the spacing. On 30 degree curves or larger, continuous bank protection on should be provided rather than retards.

Certain plants are suited to torrent control schemes, particularly the outsprouting types, which, grow profusely near stream beds, e.g. *Salix species, vitex negundo, Populus* species *Arundo donax, Ipomea carnea, Tatropha curcas, Pennisetum purpureum* (Napier, etc.). A series of checkdams made of tree longs, buttressed by permanent checkdams at wide spacing, can be used to control torrents rushing down steep slopes. The torrent banks can be protected by planting water-loving vegetation.

RECOMMENDATIONS OF THE CENTRAL SOIL & WATER CONSERVATION RESEARCH & TRAINING INSTITUTE DEHRADUN

Study conducted in the Bainkhala torrent flowing along the western boundary of the Soil Conservation Research Farm, Selakui (Dehradun), which crosses the Dehradun-Chakrata road (about 18 km) in the Doon Valley, (average width of the torrent varying from 100 to 300 m and bank erosion was quite active specially at the concave banks) resulted in the recommendation of following scheme of operation for treatment of such torrents (in their reaches below the hills):

— Planting of live hedges of *Vitex negundo* of *Arundo donax* mixed with *Ipomoea carnea* along the banks needing production or the areas to be reclaimed.

— Erection of 2 to 3 m long (depending on torrent width) deflecting type of spurs alongwith live hedges at intervals of 6 to 10 m, depending upon the bank curvature to check scouring along the banks. Wire cages of one metre cube filled with boulders (gabion) should be buried at the nose of these spurs to prevent nose scouring.

— Erection of gabion spurs or post jetties reinforced with vegetation at crucial points receiving direct hit of flood waters, e.g. concave banks and channel bunds. The spurs in such location should be of repelling type.

— Sloping back of the steep and vertical banks to a grade of about 1.5:1 and planting with *Aristida cynantha* and *Vitex negundo* and side-by-side planting of live hedges and erecting spurs at their toe.

— The freshly deposited silt near the spurs and behind the live hedges should immediately be stabilized by planting cuttings of *Pennisetum purpureum* (Napier) in rows laid normal to the general direction of flow and spaced 1 to 2 m from row to row. The sites having excessive proportion of shingle and boulders should preferably be planted with *Aristida cynantha, Saccharum bengalensis* and *S.Spontaneum.* The areas behind the bank should be afforested with suitable tree species like *Dalbergia sissoo, Acacia catechu, Albizza stipulata* and *Eucalyptus* spp.

— The torrent training and reclamation works should be started from both the banks, taking care that the channel width is not much restricted and sufficient section is left for safe discharge of the expected peak runoff.

— Any obstruction in the channel bed (e.g. uprooted trees) should immediately be removed to avoid further aggregation.

6.5 Roadside Erosion Control and Erosion along Railway Lines

ROADSIDE EROSION CONTROL ALONG MOUNTAIN ROADS

Roadside erosion (Plate 31) in many of the new mountain roads constructed in recent times is one of the main causes of high sediment yield to the reservoirs and severe damage to the roads. Though the Border Roads Organization has connected many places in the Himalayan region in short time, it is facing a serious problem of erosion along the roads. Roadside erosion is thus a problem, which is of concern to both the road engineer and the soil conservationist. Just as a road construction is a specialised job, stabilization of mountain slopes, torrent control, landslide stabilization are also specialized works. For the best results, there is a great need for collaboration of road and soil conservation departments.

Roadside erosion control works may involve control of landslides and landslips; control of torrent and stream bank erosion; stabilization of cut and fill slopes; and stabilization of roadside drains.

Control of landslips, torrent and stream bank erosion have been discussed earlier. No systematic work on the stabilization of cut-and-fill slopes and road drains has been undertaken at the Central Soil and Water Conservation Research and Training Institute and its Research Centres.

STABILIZATION OF CUT-AND-FILL SLOPES OF MOUNTAIN ROADS

During the construction of mountain roads, hill slopes are disturbed and if stabilization measures are not simultaneously undertaken, this may lead to development of landslips and slides, which causes disruption of traffic and high maintenance cost. It has been observed that even extensively over-grazed bare mountain slopes are normally in natural balance. But slight disturbance due to excavation or undercutting leads to complete failure of mountain slopes. This is evident from the fact that landslips and landslides are generally found along the newly constructed roads. The various steps in stabilization of cut-and-fill slopes of mountain roads are as under (Gupta, Tejwani and Mathur, 1969).

Control of Runoff above Cut Face

In mountains, there is a considerable area above the cut face of the newly constructed road and the runoff from the upper slopes causes development of rills and gullies. The first measure needed in such cases is the elimination of runoff from flowing over the bare cut slopes. For the same, interception drains are required to be constructed. These drains should be a minimum of 35 m away on the upstream side from the top of the cut face. The water diverted across the slope may be disposed of in natural, well vegetated water course or safely conducted through drop structures, lined channel or pipes.

If the length of slope above the cut face is too much, it may be desirable to divert the water at every 100 to 300 m instead of one interception.

Control of Runoff from Cut Face

In small cuts, runoff may not be of sufficient peak and volume to cause serious erosion. But large cut surfaces (usually developed due to erosion) need provision of safe disposal of excess water. For the same, catchment water drain, gutters or narrow inwardly sloping bench terraces along with well protected outlet will be required. The main outlet will need a series of structures or paved channel to carry safely the water along the slope.

Control of Runoff on Fill Slopes

No runoff from the top catchment or road shoulders may be allowed to flow over loose fill slopes. This can be conveniently done by providing a roadside drain of adequate capacity to handle peak rate of runoff. If the length of fill slopes is more than 10 m or so, construction of cross slope gutters at 10 to 15 m along the slope may be desirable in initial stages, if compaction of fill slopes as described latter has not been done.

Stabilization of Cut Slopes by Vegetation

If the road bank is not very high (as in valley) it is advisable to dress to 1:1 preferably 1.5:1. In case the rills and gullies have developed, these need to be smoothened before planting. Use of checkdams, wattling etc., may be required in gullies to assist in retention of the loose soil in place.

After levelling, wattling at 3–4 m distance along the slope may be done which will assist in prevention of rill formation, till vegetative cover is established.

Wattling is needed when the cut slopes are long, while on short slopes vegetation can be directly planted.

It is seen that natural vegetation from the adjacent vegetated areas will invade and colonise the cut surfaces along the highways. Invariably the process is slow one and would take considerably long time. To provide immediate cover, planting is to be resorted. The first need of the area is protective cover, which should be established quickly, this may be of a temporary nature. This should be supplemented by planting up of woody shrubs and trees, so as to provide a permanent cover.

It is seen that natural vegetation from the adjacent vegetated areas will invade and colonise the cut surface.

The selection of planting material will be guided by a number of factors such as climate, altitude, aspect and biotic factors. The species should be easy to propagate and establish fast growing deep roots with spreading foliage.

STABILIZATION OF FILL SLOPES

Toe of steep fill slopes may need protection by masonry, concrete, gabion or even loose boulder retaining walls.

Vegetation offers the most economical and effective means of control. Results of planting or sowing of raw fill slope, before the soil had been consolidated by rain, are generally very encouraging during the first year itself, except on very infertile material. In old fill slopes, compacted by rains, loosening and roughing, application of straw mulch or some type of organic material is found to be very useful. Mulch protects the fill from impact of rain drops, erosion by surface runoff, conserves moisture, and when straw is used with seeds, it disperses these seeds and assists in germination. In case of infertile soil, application of fertilizer has been found useful for establishment of thick cover.

In places where excessive absorption of water is found to encourage sloughing, after spreading of straw mulch (about 10 tonne/ha, exact quantity depends upon the number of roller trips) on 1.5:1 slope, use of sheep for roller by drag line, dozer power unit have been tried. It has been observed that by this method about 10 cm top soil uncompacted (forming excellent seed bed) and lower layer of soil was compacted to about 90 per cent a disintegrated granite fill slope after 6 round trips by standard sheep foot roller (Bowers, 1950). This compaction reduces water holding capacity of soil and the tendency of soil to liquify.

On deep fills, mechanical anchoring by use of wire reinforced brush mat may be useful. These mats and layers act as second line of defence and are usually used when surface protection alone is in inadequate. The outer edge of mesh is left flush.

It is essential to keep proper watch during first year and repair any damage which may be found. The fill slopes should be thickly vegetated by locally suited vegetation.

STABILIZATION OF ROADSIDE DRAINS

Eroded drainage channels are generally found in rolling topography. In many cases it has been observed that these eroded drains are not attended to till they are transformed into gullies and endangers the roadside shoulders. At this stage also, a spillwall is constructed without any adequate provision of the head wall extension, apron and side wall. Due to these reasons, these spill walls are flanked on sides, resulting in secondary alignment of the gully. This can be prevented by providing safe grade in the channel at the time of construction. If the existing slope along the road drain alignment is high, it is far more economical to construct grade stabilization structures in the initial stages rather than installing them after gully formation has taken place. In some places, there may be need of constructing paved channels due to excessive grade.

USE OF GRADE STABILIZATION STRUCTURES

It may be noticed that with increase in runoff and slope, the top width of road drain required will increase. If due to nonavailability of land, the same is not possible, the bed slope may be reduced by construction of grade stabilization structures. These structures can be either constructed at site or use of prefabricated structures may be more economical and feasible under certain conditions. In high gradient, the paved channel may be the only possible means of safely conducting water.

In gentle bed slopes (less than 0.5 per cent) usually natural vegetation gets established naturally. In steep gradient, seeding or planting with permanent grasses at once may be essential. For the same, use of mulch, seeding of some annual grain crops may be useful.

EROSION ALONG RAILWAY LINES

Erosion along railway lines is also considerable. It differs from place to place depending upon the amount of rainfall and type of soil. Common measures to check such erosion are turfing, pitching, retaining walls and even terracing the slopes of the fill section. To check erosion by meandering rivers, which threaten the railway lines, protection is provided in the form of guide bunds with pitched slopes, toe guards of sausage structure or concrete blocks, spurs and revetments. Among the local items, bamboo screens, bamboo bundles and triangular permeable screens of bamboo are used with great success. To prevent erosion along out faces of catch-water drains and deep boulder drains, cross bunds, etc., are used.

7

Prediction Models for Runoff and Soil Loss

Reliable runoff and soil loss estimation is valuable for design of soil erosion control structures to reduce soil losses to specified acceptable levels and thereby ensure maximum safe economic use of each piece of land. Attempts have been made by several workers to quantify the effect of cropping practices on runoff and soil loss in numerical form, which would allow erosion to be predicted for a given set of conditions.

7.1 Runoff Prediction Models

PEAK DISCHARGE AREA RELATIONSHIP (STOCHASTIC)
Based on the data collected, annual peak discharge for the period ranging from 11 to 24 hours from five Doon Valley watersheds (areas ranging from 4.4 to 83.4 ha), a relationship for peak discharge was developed (Ram Babu and Dhruva Narayana, 1984), as follows:

$$Q_P = 0.07 F^{0.406} A^{0.742} \qquad \qquad \dots (7.1)$$

where Q_p = predicted peak discharge, cumec
F = return period, years
A = area of the watershed, ha.

Also runoff peak (Q_P) and volume (Q_T) were related to rainfall and watershed characteristics by expressions of the form (Ram Babu and Dhruva Narayana, 1983).
Model A

$$Y = b_o + \sum_{i=1}^{n} b_i x_i \qquad \qquad \dots (7.2)$$

Model B

$$Y = b_o \sum_{i=1}^{n} [X_i]^{b_i} \qquad \qquad \dots (7.3)$$

where Y is the dependent variable, Q_p or Q_T. X_i, X_2, are independent variables; and $b_o, b_i \dots, b_n$ are regression coefficients.
While eq. (7.2) for a given data is solved in the usual manner, eq. (7.3) is solved by linearization to the form:

$$\ln Y = \ln b_o + \sum_{i=1}^{n} b_i \ln X_i \qquad \qquad \dots (7.3.1)$$

The storm and watershed characteristics (independent variables) considered in the analysis were:

X_1 = watershed area (A), ha,
X_2 = main channel length (L), km,
X_3 = duration of the storm (D), hr
X_4 = total rainfall (P), mm

$X_5 =$ maximum rainfall occurring in any interval of 30 min during storm, P_{30} mm, and

$X_6 =$ antecedent precipitation index (API) based on the previous 7 days values.

7.2 Results and Discussion

The pooled rainfall and runoff data from the four watersheds W_2A, W_2B, W_2C and W_2D were utilized for developing the regression equations of the form given by equations (7.4 to 7.7). The relationships developed on the basis of 180 data events are:

Model A

$$Q_T = 2.15 + 0.172A - 4.705L + 0.779D + 0.163P$$
$$- 0.025P_{30} - 0.010API (R^2 = 0.52) \qquad \ldots (7.4)$$

$$Q_P = 0.02 + 0.053A - 0.989L + 0.034D + 0.008P$$
$$+ 0.007P_{30} - 0.006API (R^2 = 0.91) \qquad \ldots (7.5)$$

Model B

$$Q_T = 0.852A^{-0.303}L^{0.486}D^{0.164}P^{1.002}P_{30}^{0.312}$$
$$API^{-0.039} (R^2 = 0.32) \qquad \ldots (7.6)$$
$$Q_P = 0.33A^{-0.003}L^{1.155}D^{0.136}P^{0.153}P_{30}^{0.545}$$
$$API^{0.096} (R^2 = 0.40) \qquad \ldots (7.7)$$

PROCESS BASED MODEL FOR RUNOFF PREDICTION

A computer model to predict runoff from bench terraced watershed with suitable outlets is presented. The continuing equation in the differential form is given as:

$$\frac{\partial y}{\partial t} + \frac{\partial q}{\partial x} = i \qquad \ldots (7.8)$$

Where $y =$ depth of water
$q =$ unit discharge
$x, t =$ distance and time respectively
and, $i =$ rainfall excess.

The bench terraces are assumed to be level fields with shoulder bunds. In these fields initially the rainfall meet the demands of detention storage and infiltration. The bench terraces can be treated as a series of rectangular storage tanks, in which the water level rises vertically as there is more and more rainfall (Fig. 7.1). When the water level reaches the level of outlet sill in the terrace, overflow begins. The model predicts the overflow at a pre-specified outlet.

NUMERICAL SOLUTION

Considering a part of the $x - t$ plane, the terms $(\partial y / \partial t)$ and $(\partial q / \partial x)$ in eq. (1) of any station P (Fig.7.1) are substituted and rising and recession limbs of hydrograph are obtained as:

$$Y_p = Y_m + \left[i_{LM} + \frac{q_N}{x} \right] * K * \Delta t \qquad \ldots (7.9)$$

$$Y_p = Y_m + Y_m \left[+ \frac{q_L - q_M}{n} \right] * \Delta t \qquad \ldots (7.10)$$

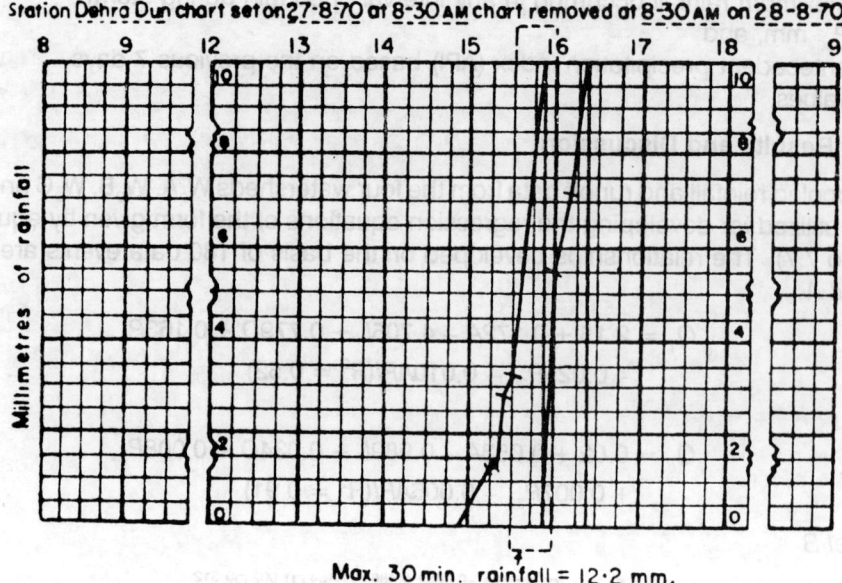

Fig. 7.1 Sample chart of Syphon type (I.M.D.) automatic recording rainguage

respectively. The weir flow is obtained from equation $Q = CL\, H^{3/2}$ for a set of initial and boundary conditions.

7.3   Soil Loss Prediction Model

UNIVERSAL SOIL LOSS EQUATION

The USLE (Universal Soil Loss Equation) is an erosion prediction model, for estimating the long-time averages of soil losses from a specified land in a specified cropping and management system. The equation predicts only the losses from sheet and rill erosion under specified conditions. It computes the soil loss for a given site, as a product of six major factors, whose most likely values at a particular location can be expressed numerically (Wischmeier and Smith, 1978) as

$$A = RKLSCP \qquad \qquad \dots (7.11)$$

where

A = The computed soil loss per unit area, expressed in the units selected for K and for the period selected for R. In practice, these are usually so selected that they compute A in metre-tonne per ha per year, but other units can be selected.

R = The rainfall erosivity factor, is the number of rainfall erosion index units for a particular location.

K = The soil erodibility factor, is the soil loss rate per erosion index unit for a specified soil as measured on a unit plot, which is defined as 21.13 m (72.6 ft), length of uniform 9 per cent slope continuously in clean tilled fallow.

L = The slope length factor is the ratio of soil loss from the field slopes length, to that from a 21.13 m (72.6 ft) length, under identical conditions.

S = The slope-steepness factor, is the ratio soil loss from the field slope gradient to that from a 9 per cent slope under otherwise identical conditions.

C = The cover and management factor, is the ratio of soil loss from an area with specified cover and management, to that from an identical area in tilled continuous fallow.

P = The support practice factor, is the ratio of soil loss with a support practice like contouring, strip-cropping, or terracing to that with straight-row farming up and down the slope.

RAINFALL EROSIVITY FACTOR (R)

The rainfall factor (R) in the USLE is the number of rainfall erosion index units (EI_{30}) for a particular location. It is defined (Wischmeier, 1959) as one hundredth of the product of the kinetic energy of the storm(KE) and the 30 min intensity (I_{30}) as the most reliable single estimate of rainfall erosion potential and was termed as EI_{30}. Annual total of storm EI_{30} value is referred to as the rainfall erosion index. The location value of this index is the rainfall factor, R in the USLE. The EI_{30} can be expressed as:

$$EI_{30} = \frac{KE \times I_{30}}{100} \qquad \ldots (7.12)$$

where EI_{30} = erosion index.
   KE = kinetic energy of storm and
   I_{30} = maximum 30 min rainfall intensity of the storm.

The KE (metric units) is expressed as:
(Wischmeier and Mannering, 1969)

$$KE = 210.3 + 89 \log I \qquad \ldots (7.13)$$

where KE = kinetic energy in metric tonnes per ha-cm
   I = rainfall intensity, cm/hr.

Example 51—Compute erosion index (EI_{30}) value for the raingauge chart provided below:
Solution: The section of the rainfall line which have differing slopes are separated and tabulated (Table 7.1).

In order to obtain weekly, monthly, seasonal and yearly values, the storm EI values for that length of period are summed up.

7.4   Soil Erodibility Factor (K)

This factor relates the rate at which different soils erode, due to inherent soil properties. Methods to determine the soil erodibility factor are based on (a) runoff plots and (b) soil properties.

RUNOFF PLOTS

The runoff for the runoff plots (varying sizes) is collected in a tank and measured gravimetrically, using multislot divisor, if necessary.

For estimating the soil loss, the water in the bank is churned thoroughly and a small runoff sample of 500–1000 cc is drawn. This sample is then evaporated in the laboratory and the amount of soil is measured gravimetrically to give soil loss in g/litre. This quantity is further multiplied by the total runoff volume and divided by 10^6 to give total soil loss in tonne per plot. This is further multiplied by the size of the plot to get the soil loss in tonne/ha, for that particular storm. The soil loss from all the storms during the year are added to get the annual soil loss in tonne/ha/year.

Table 7.1   Rainfall record from recording raingauge and computation of EI_{30} values—Dehradun

Date	Starting time (hr. min)	Shifting time (hr. min)	Time interval (min)	Reading at the start (mm)	Reading at the shifting (mm)	Rainfall (cm) (Col. 6 – Col. 5)	Rainfall intensity (l) (cm/hr)	KE* (m-tonnes/ ha-cm)	K.E of the rain (Col.9 × Col.7)	Maximum 30 min. intensity (l_{30}) (cm/hr)	EI_{30} (Total of Col.10 × Col.11)/100
1	2	3	4	5	6	7	8	9	10	11	12
27-8-1970	1455	1515	20	0.0	0.13	0.13	0.39	173.9	22.61		
	1520	1525	5	1.3	2.8	0.15	1.80	233.0	34.95		
	1525	1530	5	2.8	3.3	0.05	0.60	190.6	9.53		
	1530	1552	22	3.3	10.0	0.67	1.83	233.7	156.58	2.44	11.42
	1552	1600	8	10.0	15.5	0.55	4.13	265.1	145.81		
	1600	1610	10	15.5	17.1	0.16	0.96	208.7	33.39		
	1610	1622	12	17.1	20.0	0.29	1.45	254.7	65.16		
									468.03		

*$KE = 210.3 + 89 \log l$

The K value is obtained as given below:

$$K = \frac{\text{Adjusted soil loss}}{\text{Total } EI} \qquad \ldots (7.14)$$

where adjusted soil loss (tonne/ha) =

$$\frac{\text{Observed soil loss for plot length, } L \text{ and slope, } S}{LS \text{ factor}} \qquad \ldots (7.15)$$

The LS factor is obtained from Fig. 7.2.

By referring to Fig. 7.2 we get LS factor for a plot of 30 m length on 5 per cent as 0.54. Adjusted soil loss (tonne/ha)

$$= \frac{\text{Observed soil-loss (tonne/ha)}}{LS \text{ factor}}$$

$$= \frac{50}{0.54} = 92.6$$

$$K = \frac{\text{Adjusted soil loss (tonne/ha)}}{R}$$

$$= \frac{92.6}{800} = 0.116$$

ERODIBILITY BASED ON SOIL PROPERTIES

Direct measurement of erodibility factor is time consuming and costly and is feasible for only for a few major soil type. Many studies were carried out to correlate the soil erodibility factor with various soil properties such as per cent sand, silt, clay, organic matter, aggregation index, antecedent soil moisture, structure, etc. and consequently several empirical erodibility equations were developed (Barnett and Rogers, 1966; Wischmeier and Mannering, 1969).

The equation involving 24 parameters is so cumbersome and require the determination of so many properties, that it remained an equation good for academic purposes only:

Example 52—Workout the soil erodibility factor K for the plots given below:

Length of runoff plot = 30 m
slope gradient   = 5 per cent
R factor   = 800
Soil loss from the plot = 50 tonne/ha

Solution: Adjust the data to plot size of 22.13 m long on 9 per cent slope. For this obtain LS factor from Table 7.2.

Table 7.2 *Computed value of soil erodibility factor, K from various research stations in India*

Station	Soil	Computed K
Agra	Loamy sand alluvial	0.17
Dehradun	Dhulkot silt loam	0.15
Hyderabad	Red *chalka* sandy loam	0 08
Kharagpur	Soils from lateritic rock	0.04
Kota	Kota-clay loam	0.11
Ootacamund	Laterite	0.04
Rehmankhera	Loam, alluvial	0.17
Vasad	Sandy loam, alluvial	0.06

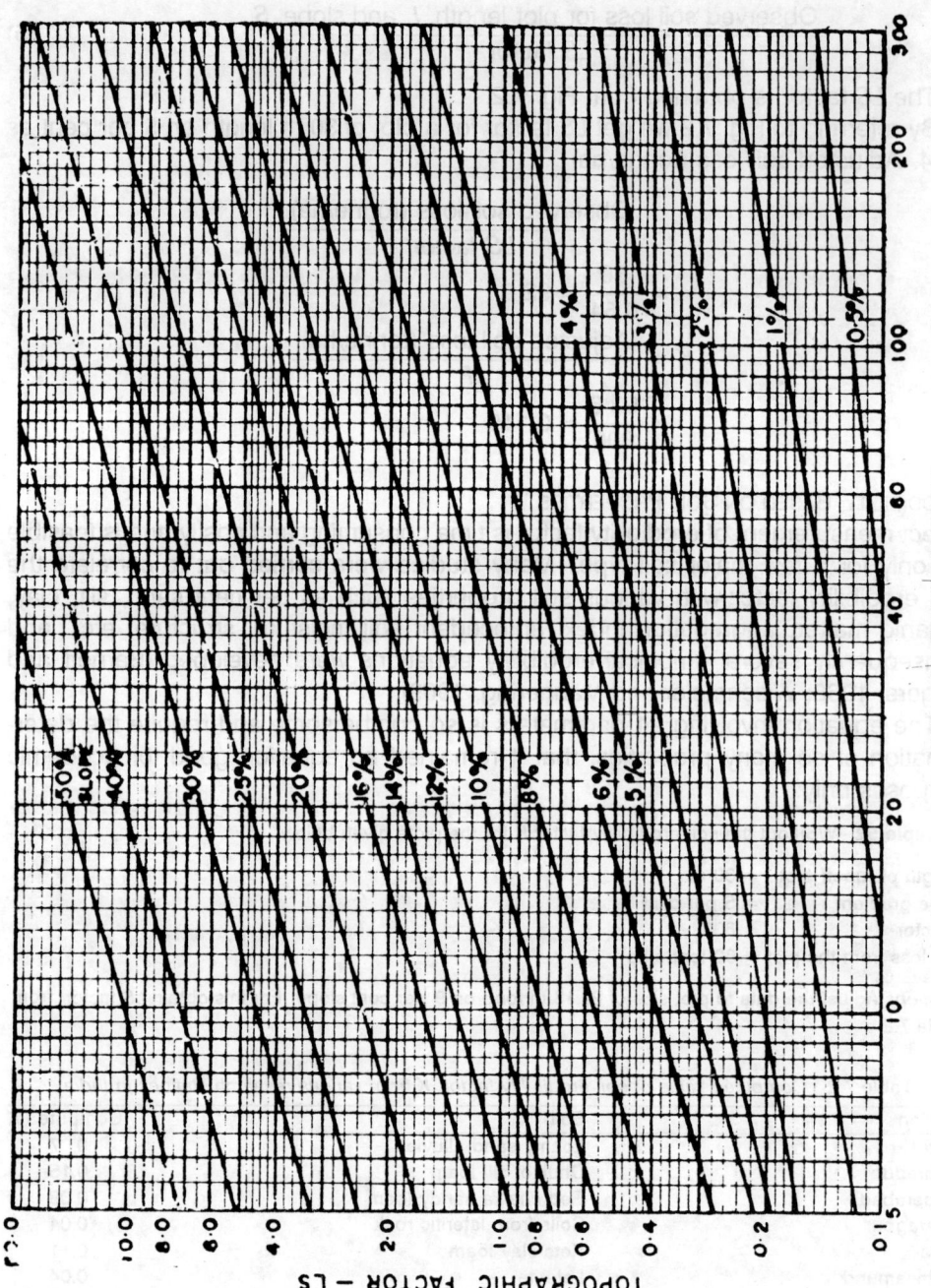

Fig. 7.2 Slope—effect chart—Topographic factor, LS, (after Wischmeier et al., 1978)

TOPOGRAPHIC FACTOR (LS)

Although L and S factors can be determined separately, the problem has been simplified by causing the L and S factor and considering the two as a single topographic factor. The equation considering the effect of L and S factors is as follows:

$$L = \left(\frac{\lambda}{22.13}\right)^m [65.4 \sin^2 Q + 4.56 \sin Q + 0.065] \qquad \ldots (7.16)$$

where λ = field slope length, m

m = exponent factor varying from 0.2 to 0.5

Q = angle of slope.

Based on above equation, a nomograph (Fig. 7.2) for determining the LS factor was developed. The LS factor can be obtained from Fig. 7.2.

CROP MANAGEMENT FACTOR (C)

This item reflects the combined effect of cover crop sequence, productivity level, length of growing season, tillage practices, residue management and the expected time distribution of erosive rain storm with respect to seedling and harvesting date. This factor is most complicated, because there is an almost infinite number of ways of managing the growing crops. Values c factor for different regions given Table 7.3.

Table 7.3 Value of C factor for different regions

Station	Crop	Soil loss (tonne/ha)	Value of c
Agra	Cultivated fallow	3.80	1.00
	Bajra	2.34	0.61
	Dichanthium annulatum	0.53	0.13
Dehradun	Cultivated fallow	33.42	1.00
	Cymbopogon grass	4.51	0.13
	Strawberry	8.89	0.27
Hyderabad	Cultivated fallow	5.00	1.00
(Av. of	Grass	0.59	0.12
4 years)	Bajra follwed by cowpea	1.91	0.38
	Bajra	2.00	0.40
Rehmankhera	Cultivated fallow	9.95	1.00
(Av. of	Jowar-Arhar	2.73	0.28
4 years)	Til-gram	4.50	0.45

SUPPORTING CONSERVATION PRACTICE FACTOR (P)

It is the ratio of soil loss with a specific supporting practice to the corresponding loss with up-and-down cultivation. Table 7.4 presents the P factors for various practices followed at different places.

Table 7.4 *Values of P factors*

Station	Practice	P Factor
Dehradun	Contour cultivation on maize	0.74
Ootacamund	a) Potato up-and-down	1.00
	b) Potato on contour	0.51
Hazaribagh	a) Up-and-down utilization of maize	1.00
	b) Cultivation of maize along contour	0.31
Kanpur	a) Up-and-down cultivation of *jowar*	1.00
	b) Contour utilization of *jowar*	0.39
Chandigarh	Contour bunding	0.28
Dehradun	(a) Up-and-down cultivation	1.00
	(b) Contour farming	0.68
	(c) Channel terraces with contour farming	0.38
	(d) Channel terraces (at 1.5 times VI) with graded furrows	0.35
	(e) Strip cropping 3:1 (maize-cowpea)	0.51
	(f) Terracing and bunding in agricultural watershed	0.03
	(g) Brushwood checkdams in forest (Shorea robusta) watersheds.	0.52

8

Soil & Water Conservation Technology

Central Soil & Water Conservation Research & Training Institute, Dehradun, and its Research Centres and allied ICAR Institutes have evolved soil and water conservation technology for hilly, ravine and semi-arid black and red soil regions. Brief summary of each of the regions is given below, so that the technology can be applicable elsewhere under similar situations.

8.1   Hill Regions

About 93 m ha out of 328 m ha area of India is mountainous. The break-up of area in different regions is as given below:

Region	Area(m/ha)
Himalayan Region	51.43
Vindhya Region	9.27
Western Ghats	7.74
Eastern Ghats	18.02
Satpura Ranges	6.60
Total	93.06

(Ref.: Report of the Committee of experts on draft outline of National Landuse Policy (1988), National Landuse and Conservation Board, Ministry of Agriculture, New Delhi)

(a) WESTERN, NORTH-WESTERN AND CENTRAL HIMALAYA

The hill region of 31.13 m ha comprises of the state of Jammu and Kashmir, Himachal Pradesh, and 8 hill districts of Uttar Pradesh. It extends from towering snow-capped peaks in the north to flat plains in the south. The region supports a variety of forest eco-systems. Below 1200 m lie tropical and sub-tropical broadleaf forests. Between 1200 and 2200 m pine forests predominate. Moist temperate evergreen broadleaf forests and mixed coniferous forests occur around 3500 m with the timberline (upper limit of forests) situated at about 4000 m.

Skeletal soils of cold regions, podsolic soils, mountain meadow soils and hill loam soils occur in the region.

The area is prone to erosion hazards due to weak geology, deforestation, faulty landuse practices and hill road construction.

(b) EASTERN HIMALAYAN REGION

The hill region (17.7 m ha) comprises of the states of Arunachal Pradesh, Assam, Mizoram, Nagaland, Meghalaya, Manipur, Tripura, Sikkim and West Bengal. The average annual rainfall in this region varies from 2100 to 4100 mm. Alluvial, laterite, sub-montane red and yellow soils are found in this region. The region bears high forest cover, comprising of tropical moist deciduous, tropical evergreen, sub-tropical wet hill forest, sub-tropical pine forest, wet temperate and sub-alpine and alpine forests.

Shifting cultivation (Jhum) is practised in nearly one-third of the cultivated area and has caused denudation and degradation of soils with the resultant heavy runoff and massive soil erosion and floods in the lower reaches and basins.

(c) Shiwalik Region

The hill region (1.6 m ha) comprising of the states of Punjab, Haryana, Himachal Pradesh and union territory of Chandigarh. The average annual rainfall in the region is 1100 mm. Shiwaliks are made up of sand stone, grits, conglomerate and clays. The soils in the hilly areas of Haryana are silty clay and silty clay loam, while in the case of Punjab and Himachal Pradesh, the soils are mostly sandy loam. *Acacia catechu, A.modesta* and *A.nilotica* are the dominant species coming up naturally in the area. *Eulaliopsis binata* (Bhabbar) is the promising grass of these hills.

The region is prone to heavy soil erosion due to deforestation, faulty landuse practices and overgrazing.

(d) Western Ghats

The hill region (7.74 m ha) lies in the states of Tamil Nadu, Kerala, Karnataka and Maharashtra. The average annual rainfall in this region varies from 1300 to 6000 mm. Laterite and lateritic soils, red, black and coastal alluvium are found in these hills. The natural vegetation comprises of tropical, sub-tropical, montane and temperate flora having evergreen, deciduous and bamboo forests.

The hill region is prone to severe soil erosion due to deforestation, faulty landuse practices and overgrazing.

8.2   Ravine Region

Total area of gullied land in India is estimated to be 3.67 m ha spread over in the states of Uttar Pradesh (1.2 m ha), Madhya Pradesh (1.7 m ha), Bihar (0.6 m ha), Rajasthan (0.45 m ha), Gujarat (0.4 m ha) and also in parts of Punjab, West Bengal, Tamil Nadu and Maharashtra. The region has arid to semi-arid climate and supports dry deciduous forest type vegetation. Sandy loam, loamy sand clay loam and clay soils are found in this region.

Back water effects, faulty landuse practices, biotic interference with the natural vegetation cover, overgrazing, etc., are the chief causes of soil erosion in the region.

8.3   Semi-arid, Black and Red Soil Region

About 97 m ha (Maharashtra—19.0, Karnataka—13.9, Andhra Pradesh—13.9, Rajasthan—12.1, Tamil Nadu—0.5, Gujarat—9.1, Uttar Pradesh—6.4, Madhya Pradesh—5.9, Punjab—3.2, Haryana—2.7 and Jammu and Kashmir—1.3 mm) of geographical area in the country is in the semi-arid tropical region.

These areas receive annual rainfall ranging from 500 to 2000 mm. About 80–90 per cent of annual rainfall is received in a total time of 30 to 70 hours period, interspersed with dry periods. The vegetation in the region consists of tropical deciduous and thorn forest vertisols (64 m ha) (shallow, medium and deep-black soils) and inceptisols (72 m ha) are predominant in this region. Coarse cereals, oilseeds, pulses, commercial crops like cotton and tobacco are primarily grown in the area.

Sheet erosion caused by short duration high intensity rainfall events, moisture stress due to low and erratic rainfall, and low soil fertility are some of the major problems of the region (Plate 32).

8.4   Technology for Hill Regions

HIMALAYAN REGIONS (WESTERN AND NORTH WESTERN HIMALAYAS)

(a) Land up to 33 per cent slope may be cultivated with agricultural crops.

Lands with soil depth of 90 cm can be bench terraced. Existing terraces may be improved by providing shoulder bunds, levelling and inter-terrace drains.

Agricultural crops can be cultivated (rainfed or irrigated farming) using good agronomical practices like contour farming, mulching, inter-cropping with legumes, high yielding improved seeds, fertilizers, manures, pesticides, etc., and also other improved technology.

Development of water resource by constructing tanks (mini ponds lined with low density polyethylene (LDPE) sheets of 1000 gauge thickness) and water reservoirs at suitable sites, having preferably perennial sources should be given priority for harvesting, storing and recycling runoff water, existing *ghuls* (water channels) (Plate 33) may also be lined with LDPE films to reduce seepage losses. Construction of new lined *ghuls* may be explored to increase irrigation potential.

(b) Land from 33 to 50 per cent slopes may be utilized for suitable horticultural plantations. Land shaping, such as orchard terraces may be used.

(c) Lands with slopes more than 50 per cent should be brought under permanent vegetation of suitable fuel-fodder tree species of grasslands, with soil conservation measures like contour trenching/staggered trenching/contour furrows.

Civil and soyam lands (common village grazing lands) should be used for raising fuel-fodder species.

Southern slopes, which have shallower soil are not suitable for tree growth, may be developed into grasslands.

(d) All gullied lands should be treated with engineering measures, viz. gully plugs, checkdams, spurs, etc. and rehabilitated by proper vegetative measures.

(e) Terrace risers may be protected by growing fodder tree species/horticulture plants/grasses.

(f) Animal husbandry should be improved and milch cattle developed. Improved breeds of goats, sheep, poultry, pig and angora rabbit may also be taken up in the hill regions.

(g) Stall feeding should be practised/rotational grazing adopted to reduce grazing pressure on hill slopes.

EASTERN HIMALAYAN REGION

[Ref.: Prasad, R.N., Singh, A. and Arun Varma (1987). *Application of Research findings for management of land and water resources in Eastern Himalayas*, ICAR, Research Complex for NEH Hill Region, Shillong.]

1. Bench terraces may be constructed across the hill slopes with a vertical interval of not more than 1.0 m and where soil depth is not less than 1.0 m. Agricultural crops may be grown on the terraces.

For taking agricultural crops on steep slopes, i.e., greater than 33%, construct parabolic channels (0.03 m top and 0.2 m deep) on contours and keeping the dug-out soil in the form of a bund at the lower edge of the channel. The vertical interval of these bunds may vary from 0.5 m to 5.0 m depending on the landuse and soil depth. With slow process of silt deposition near the bunds, the inter bunded area gets levelled up and form the shape of a terrace in the course of 4 to 8 years. NEH Hill Region Complex mention that vegetative barriers alone will not be able to form such terraces on steep slopes. The cost of formation of the above technique is about one-third of that of the cost of bench terracing. Excess runoff can be safely drained from one terrace to another, by placing the outlets diagonally.

2. For raising horticulture/fodder species on hill slopes, half-moon terraces are recommended. These are level circular beds 1.0 to 1.5 m diameter cut into half-moon shape on the hill slopes.

3. Very steep slopes may be afforested with suitable tree species.

4. Grassed waterways may be laid, preferably on natural drainage lines in the watershed and runoff may be collected in dug-out-farm ponds at a suitable location.

SHIWALIK REGION

1. For undulating region, minor land levelling along with good cultural practices like improved seeds, fertilizer and manures, weed control, etc., are found to increase crop yields by two or three times.

2. For denuded Shiwalik hill region, the following measures may be adopted:

— Digging of contour trenches (200 nos./ha)—trench size 2.5 m × 0.45 m × 0.45 m at 2 m apart, both in the same line and from row-to-row. In heavily eroded areas, the cross-section may be increased suitably.

— Bhabbar grass (*Eulaliopsis binata*) may be planted on slopy areas, where contour trenches were not possible to be dug out, in view of prohibitive slope.

Construction of sediment retention structure/sediment basins at suitable places (one structure for a watershed of 30 to 40 ha, with a storage capacity of 1.2 to 1.5 ha-m). In areas having drainage density 6.5 km or more per sq.km² of catchment, the storage capacity of the structure should be one-and-half times that of the above.

Construction of earthen embankments across the horse-shoe type catchments for harvesting, storing and recycling runoff water. About 50 per cent of rainfall as runoff may be assumed for design purposes.

3. *Acacia Catechu (Khair)* is promising on slopy areas and *Dalbergia sissoo (Shisham)* in gully bottom (*cho* beds).

WESTERN GHATS REGION

1. Lands up to 10% slope may be cultivated with agricultural crops by following contour farming, improved farming including crop rotation and other good agronomical practices.

2. Lands from 10 to 15% slope may be treated with graded trenches at 2.5 m vertical interval and can be cultivated with agricultural crops by following good agronomical practices.

3. Lands from 16 to 33% slope may be treated with inward sloping bench terraces (vertical interval ranging from 1 to 2 m) with water disposal system and can be cultivated with agricultural crops by following good agronomical practices.

4. Lands above 33% slope may be treated with staggered contour trenches and afforested with bluegum and black wattle, or raised with tea plantation, in which case trenches are filled with mulch material.

Eroded lands can be protected with grass species such as *Eragrostis curvula* for stabilization.

8.5 Technology for Ravine (Gully System) Region

The technology for ravine regions comprise of treating (a) table and marginal lands and (b) gully system itself.

TABLE AND MARGINAL LAND

1. Diversion bund/peripheral bunds may be constructed at a distance from the gully rim equal to twice the depth of the gully and the head cross-section of the bund may be kept as 2.75 m².
2. Lands up to 4% contour/graded *bunds* (1.0 m² cross-sectional area) can be provided at 0.5 to 1.0 m vertical interval. Drainage may be effected where drainage problems are anticipated. Wasteweirs of suitable capacity may be provided for safe disposal of excess runoff water.

GULLY SYSTEM

1. Small gullies (3.0 m deep) can be reclaimed by clearing, minor levelling and construction of a series of contour bunds at a vertical interval of 1.0 m. Pipe outlets are to be provided to drain excess runoff water, if any, from the treated area. At the end of small gully system, small earthen dam with a masonry spillway (composite checkdam) is provided, as a protective measure to check soil loss.
2. Medium gullies (3 to 9 m deep) can also be reclaimed by clearing, levelling the gully and construction of a series of composite earthen and brick masonry check dams, at a vertical interval of 1.2 m with an outward slope of 0.5 to 0.75% between two consecutive structures and bench terracing the side slopes (8–15 per cent).
3. Deep gullies (> 9 m) are reclaimed by afforestation techniques with suitable tree species like *Prosopis juliflora* (hump, side slopes), *Acacia nilotica* (side slopes), *Dendrocalamus strictus* (gully beds) and constructing gully plugs in the bed of the main and branch gullies. Gully beds and sides are stabilized by planting grass species like *Dicanthium annulatum*. Gully plugging is done with small earthen check dams and live hedges. Horticultural species (papaya, citrus, etc.) can be raised in the gully beds and terraces, where irrigation water is available.

8.6 Technology for Semi-arid Red and Black Soils

[Ref.: Task force on "semi-arid Tropical region" for the working group on soil and water conservation including watershed development for Eighth Five Year Plan, held on 7th January 1989 at CRIDA, Hyderabad.]

(a) RED SOILS [SHALLOW/LOW RAINFALL (LESS THAN 750 mm)]

Arable Lands

(i) Open and contour bunds or graded bunds (0.5 m² section/0.35 m² section) with outlets.

(ii) Development of waterways preferably on the existing water courses or at the boundaries.

(iii) Inter-terrace smoothing.

(iv) Establishing a live bund of suitable vegetation. The live barrier should be established in the trench, combined with a small bund on the down-stream side.

(v) Adoption of cultivation practices, like contour cultivation, dead furrows, deep tillage, ridge and furrow method.

Non-Arable Areas

(i) Contour trenches planted with forest species and pasture crops like stylosenthes in between tree rows (Plate 34). Horticultural species like *ber* can also be planted.

(ii) *Nala* bunds in gullied areas.

(b) DEEP RED SOILS (MORE THAN 750 MM AVERAGE ANNUAL RAINFALL)

Arable Lands

(i) Graded bunds (0.32 m²) with outlets.

(ii) Graded border strips with 0.2 to 0.4 % gradient.

(iii) Waterways with drop structures.

(iv) Internal smoothing to provide the required gradient, if it is already not provided at the time of construction.

(v) Farm ponds, Approximate capacity 250–300 m³ for every ha of catchment.

(vi) Vegetative bunds at an interval of about 15m (horizontal).

(vii) Planting of agro-forestry species like casuarina and silver oak in the upstream side of the bund at a distance of 2m.

Non-Arable Lands

(i) Trenching and planting of forest species and horticultural plants like jack, mango, sapota, etc.

(ii) *Nala* bunds in gullied area.

(iii) Gully protection through vegetative means, like brush wood dams, bamboo, etc.

(c) BLACK SOILS: SHALLOW AND MEDIUM DEEP SOILS (LESS THAN 750 MM AVERAGE RAINFALL)

Arable Lands

(i) Contour bunds (0.6 m²) with surplussing arrangement.

(ii) Graded bunds with waterways.

(iii) Land smoothing in the inter-bund area.

(iv) Bund stabilization by grasses.

(v) Vegetative bunds (15–20 m) on the contour as an inter-terrace management.

(vi) Farm ponds wherever feasible.

(vii) Compartment bunds for soils with 45 cm and above depth.

Non-Arable Lands

(i) Contour trenching and planting forest and pasture species in the inter-trench area.

(ii) Dryland horticulture with species like *ber*, custard apple, *amla*, drumstick, etc.

(iii) *Nala* bunds and gully control.

(d) SHALLOW BLACK SOILS (MORE THAN 750 MM AVERAGE ANNUAL RAINFALL)

Arable Lands

(i) Graded bunds (0.6 m²) with surplussing arrangement.

(ii) Land smoothing.

Plate 27. Successful bamboo plantation in the deep ravines along Mahi river in India.

Plate 28. Sand dunes of Rajasthan in India.

Plate 29.   Landslide before stabilization.

Plate 30.   Landslide area stabilised by mechanical
and vegetative soil conservation measures.

Plate 31.   Road side erosion in the Himalayas in India.

Plate 32.   *Ghuls* (Water channels) and water storage
tanks in the Himalayas in India.

Plate 33.   Denuded hills in red soil region of Karnataka
State in India.

Plate 34.   Denuded hills afforested after treating with
soil and water conservation measures has
resulted in the greenary of hills.

Plate 35.   A watershed boundary which includes sloping
areas as well as plain land

(iii) Vegetative bunds.

(iv) Farm ponds.

(v) Horticultural crops like mango, guava, tamarind.

Non-Arable Lands

(i) Pastures and natural vegetation.

(ii) *Nala* bund and gully control.

(e) DEEP-BLACK SOILS (LESS THAN 750 mm ANNUAL RAINFALL)

Arable Lands

(i) Graded bunds with surplussing arrangements (grassed waterways).

(ii) Internal smoothing in the inter-bund area.

(iii) Vegetative bunds at an interval of 15–20 m (horizontal).

(iv) Compartment bunds.

(v) Farm ponds.

(vi) Dryland horticulture—mango, guava.

(vii) Gully stabilization structures like checkdams, gabion structures.

(f) DEEP-BLACK SOILS (MORE THAN 750 mm ANNUAL RAINFALL)

Arable Lands

(i) Graded bunds with surplussing arrangement (grassed waterways).

(ii) Farm ponds.

(iii) Vegetative bunds at an interval of 15–20 m (horizontal).

(iv) Management practices like broad bed and furrow (BBF), raised and sunken bed are to be adopted as permanent systems.

(v) Gabion structures for gully stabilization.

(vi) Horticultural programme involving mango, *amla*, guava.

9

Watershed Management

Watershed (Plate 35) or a drainage basin is a natural unit draining runoff water to a common point. It can be demarcated based on ridge and gully lines. The size of the watershed can be selected depending upon the possibilities of developing it completely within a reasonable period of 3–5 years. Mini-watersheds and sub-catchment could be the basis for planning and execution.

AIMS AND OBJECTIVES

— Protect, conserve and improve the land resources for efficient and sustained production.

— Protect and enhance water resource, moderate floods and reduce silting up of tanks, increase irrigation and conserving rainwater for crops and thus mitigate droughts.

— To utilize the natural local resources for improving agriculture and allied occupation or industries (small and cottage industries), so as to improve socio-economic conditions of the local residents.

CRITERIA FOR PRIORITY WATERSHEDS

The basis for identification of the priorities will be governed by the objectives, contents and operational details of each development programme. In most of the cases, basic data which includes physical data, present land use, socio-economic condition and economics of development activities, as well as information needed on some of the specific cases are as follows:

— Areas yielding maximum silt load per unit need to be identified in the catchment areas, costly dams and reservoirs.

— For flood control, areas contributing maximum runoff need to be determined.

— Potentiality of different areas for maximum water harvesting possibility, coupled with nature and type of cultivable soils would be important criteria, in drought prone area programme, dryland and rainfed farming programmes. There is also a need to demarcate watersheds/areas having different potentialities for development of forest, grasslands and agriculture.

— The command areas will have to be categorized into land irrigability and soil irrigable classes. Differential water requirements and a set of cropping patterns have also to be considered. The need for development and its quantum, type of water conveyance system and magnitude of requirement of drainage would be additional useful criteria.

— Areas having excessive problems of alkalinity with ownership pattern may have to be selected for the reclamation programme.

— Reclamation of ravines for agriculture and permanent vegetation will need ravine areas with maximum area under shallow and medium as well as deep and narrow ravines, respectively.

— For the control of shifting cultivation, availability of easily terraceable land and irrigation facilities could be important criteria for permanent programme of Jhumias and

— In hill area development, the suitability classification for afforestation, grassland development, horticulture and agriculture have to be developed. Criteria and parameters that affect erodibility and excessive runoff also need to be considered.

COLLECTION OF DATA

Toposheets which give details of contours, streams, rivers, etc., of the watershed under consideration, have to be obtained. The watershed boundary is demarcated on the toposheet. With the toposheet plan as a guide, delineation on the land is done. While this is done, the villages and survey number through which watershed boundary line passes, are noted and the line is fixed on the respective village map by measurements with reference to fixed points, such as survey number, boundary stones, etc.

After collecting all the necessary information as illustrated in the format, prepare a map showing generalized future proposed land, based on land capability. Prepare a master plan of the watershed management, which will include needed land treatment measures both, vegetative and structural (namely engineering measures required for arable lands and non-arable lands; agronomical practices for maximizing crop production per unit area; forestry and grassland management in non-arable lands; treatment of special problems like landslides, stream bank erosion, gully control, roadside erosion, etc., met in the watershed).

The plan should also indicate benefits accruing from implementation of the proposed soil conservation and land reclamation programmes, as ecological (protection of soil against erosion), economic (increase in the productivity of agricultural and non-agricultural lands) and employment, generation.

Ecological benefits comprise (i) prevention of on site erosion; (ii) direct protection of land from getting out of production through gullying, stream bank erosion, landslide etc., and (iii) protection of existing production from land getting lost, as a result of restoration/reclamation, etc. Economic benefits include additional production as a result of (i) land treatment; (ii) increased irrigation potential and (iii) restoration/reclamation of land. Employment generation benefits should include categories preferably under casual, regular, technical and allied employment.

Execution

The treatment being multi-disciplinary, different departments will be involved in the execution of works. A systematic execution of the programme from the highest ridge to the lowest valley line has to be drawn up and implemented.

Follow-Up Practices

After the plans are implemented, an improved production plan is superimposed to get the maximum benefit. The farmers concerned in the watershed should be made aware of the different follow-up practices. Conservation education by laying out relevant demonstration, bringing out technical bulletins and hand outs are also necessary.

Maintenance

Maintenance of the works after implementation is of the utmost importance. This is more true about engineering structures.

Monitoring and Evaluation

After implementation of the programme, it is necessary to continuously monitor and evaluate, in order to assess the effect of treatment on the watershed.

9.1   The Format

N.B. 1. To be prepared for each watershed. The watershed Management Project (or some may prefer to use the more dynamic term of watershed Development Project) should provide for the following essential features:

   (a) A description and analysis of each watershed

   (b) The specific changes proposed and the investment required

   (c) A specific plan to implement these changes and

   (d) A recurrent evaluation of the steps undertaken.

2. Some of the information contained in this format will be common to other watershed—especially if they are contiguous. In such cases there would be no need to repeat the information in each format. It would be sufficient to refer to the first watershed project prepared.

3. The project prepared under the format will be fit for appraisal and later allotment of funds. Annual parts of the Project details will be required to be prepared at the implementation stage. Detailed plans and designs will be prepared by the field staff themselves during implementation, for individual major conservation structure, pond or any other such item. Type designs and specifications will be given with this format for other smaller structures.

1. Introduction

Name of the watershed (the word watershed was preferred to micro-watershed) and brief explanation of what the planning format sets out to achieve have to be delineated. Relate the watershed (notional size 1000–5000 ha) to the Implementation Area/macro catchment and the general problem area as a whole. (It would be desirable that a Master Plan for the Implementation Area/macro-catchment be also prepared, so that each individual watershed plan can then be related to the general framework). The Master Plan of an Implementation Area/catchment will describe the maladies and the remedies in a general way, and will set out the strategy and approach clearly.

2. Criteria for Selection of the Implementation Area/Catchment and the Watershed

(a) *Implementation Area*

Rainfed farming areas of rainfall above 750 mm and suitable soils will be selected. For the other project, the Himalayan area below the permanent snow line will be the implementation area. Other states can also join the programme later, if they meet the necessary conditions. In a general way, the criteria for selection of the watershed will also apply to the selection of the implementation area/catchment. However, certain organization and administrative factors might also come into play in the selection of the implementation area. Regional coverage of development activity and funds will also perhaps be a factor in area. However, the land and water resources problem and potential and the human needs should be the over-riding guiding principles in selection of both the implementation area/catchment as well as the small watersheds.

(b) *Criteria for Selection of Watersheds*
Seven point criteria for guidance: (i) Problem intensity, (ii) Development potential, (iii) Technology availability, (iv) Catalytic effect, (v) Accessibility, (vi) Investment aspects, (vii) Infrastructure availability.

Other criteria would be existence (or proposal) of major dams downstream, people's willingness to participate (as shown by past self-help achievements), prospects of extending minor irrigation, etc. This chapter does not have to be descriptive; criteria can be presented in telegraphic style. People's co-operation is emphasised so as to make the projects self-replicating and self-regenerating.

3. **General Description (Watershed Resource Data)** (See details in Enclosure-1)

In most preparation reports, this chapter accounts for 80% or more of the completed documents. There is a tendency to present too much background information, resource data, etc., and not enough on the following essential elements: what watershed and how, and by whom, the project is to be implemented? It is, therefore, suggested that watershed resource data be compiled on the lines indicated in Enclosure-1. This chapter of the report should focus on the analysis of the data provided in Enclosure-1 (climate, land, water, crops and vegetation, human resources, livestock, resources, existing cottage industries, socio-economic survey, existing government structure and institution, etc.).

Source of Data may be given
Data relevant to the project problems should only be given.

4. **Major Problem Needs and Potential of the Area**

What are the major problems, needs and potentials of the area as conceived by (a) the farmers and (b) the preparation team? What is the technical assessment of soil and water conservation production problems on, (a) agricultural land, (b) horticulture land, (c) grazing land, (d) forest land, (e) wasteland, (f) special problem area (like landslides, stream bank erosion, etc.). The needs do not imply only to erosion control, flood moderation, sediment reduction, etc., but also to the needs of the people in quantitative terms of food, fodder, fuel, fruit, fibre, timber and water. In rainfed farming projects, the focus will be optimum production, while in the Himalayan project, the focus will be protection of the resource base.

5. **Future Land Use Plan**

This chapter would, (a) indicate potential of area for various land uses; (b) review the type and scales of aerial photographs and maps required for project planning and implementation; (c) provide a brief review of the approach taken to soil and capability classification and results obtained; (d) describe the present land use classes, identify special problem lands, e.g. gullies, land slides, mine spoils, etc. No land use capability system should be universalized. Adopt what is practical (but not irrational). The Indian Soil Survey Manual prescribes one system; the World Bank Expert —N.W.Hudson presented another. No standard system is proposed yet; (e) give proposed land use changes; prepare contingency (i.e. alternative land use maps) plans; (f) include the economic analysis of alternative farming systems for different land capability classes using farm budgets; and (g) present the optimal land use plan (description should be reduced to the minimum, make use of maps).

6. Proposed Management Plan

This is the most important part of the planning format. It explains not only what physically needs to be done to rehabilitate and develop the micro-watershed but how to do it. It deals with all the physical components to be financed under the project, how they would be implemented. Enclosure-2 contains a check list of all the items that might be included.

(a) *Agricultural lands*: Whether rainfed or irrigated

   (i) Engineering measures on agricultural lands like diversion bunds, bench terraces, grassed waterways, etc., so as to prevent erosion, promote soil and moisture conservation and help secure the foundation of land and water resource in the area. Water harvesting may be given high priority.

   (ii) Agronomic practices to extend the results of research to obtain higher yields and income.

(b) *Forest lands:* Give classification; propose forestry land use as an integral part of the project for both protection and production. Tree growing should be incorporated not only for definite forest lands, but also interwoven into the whole project structure—on bunds, in corners, in farmsteads, along roads and streams and in all shallow areas, where cultivation means only uneconomic agricultural venture. Fuel is as much necessary as food. Biomass may soon become an important source of energy. Vegetation both for protection and production is, therefore, of vital importance.

— Management of the forest: Vegetation, silvicultural system proposed, rotation and yields and management practices

— Management of degraded forests

— Management of scrub areas with potential of development

— Farm forestry and

— Engineering measures to be adopted in forest lands (guidelines as given in agricultural lands). Measures to improve soil moisture conditions for better and quicker growth may be given preference.

(c) *Grasslands*: For present grazing lands and those which should be put under this land use. This is a crucial part on which hopes of controlling the livestock number and improvement of quality depend:

(i) Pastures, (ii) Grasslands management and improved practices including grazing system to be indicated.

(d) *Special problems*: Landslides; torrents; mineral exploitation in the area, if any; roadside erosion; brick kiln areas and their rehabilitation after use and other special problems.

(e) *Gully control*: Checking further spread; utilization of the gullied land; water development possibilities in the gullied land.

(f) Water harvesting and silt retention structures including restoration of degraded land and recycling of harvested water. Ponds should be given a high priority. The social problems of water distribution need equal attention, however, if the developed water is to be used efficiently and equitably.

    (g) *Animal Husbandry*: Curtailing numbers, upgrading, increasing production, etc.

    (h) Maintenance of Works

7. Project Costs

This should include cost of bench mark survey, project planning, project implementation (works), staff, training, research (if any), monitoring appraisal and evaluation, building, vehicles, stores, etc., also specifically provide for maintenance of works.

    Provide a summary year-wise and project component-wise in detailed 5-year cost tables.

8. Financial Plan

This section would indicate how total project costs are to be financed; who is to pay for what? It would specify the major sources of finance by project components and indicate what are to be budget financed items and credit financed items. It would indicate what provision is to be made for project cost recovery and discuss the question of farmers' acceptance (how to deal with defaulters and individuals who reject the management plan). It should also indicate the financing proposals for private lands, that should be taken out of foodgrain production.

    This chapter will deal with financial resources, need, their source, the mode of their spending, rates of subsidies, recoveries, etc. Also provide for consultancy funds, if any needed, for surveys, investigations, studies project preparation, evaluation, etc. Use of consultancy services could open up a new vista for watershed project preparation and implementation.

9. Organization

A vitally important chapter which spells out clearly the proposed management structure and states by whom the project will be planned and implemented. It would cover the role of the Project Officer for one or more watersheds and other items as follows:

    (a) General

    (b) GOI Central Committee and Secretariat

    (c) State Watershed Management Directorate's role (Watershed management Special Groups)

    (d) Role of Line Departments

    (e) Watershed Management Committees/Cooperatives

    (f) Extension—T.V.System

    (g) Research

    (h) Monitoring

    (i) Evaluation, and

    (j) Other aspects

    This chapter deals with organization aspects of watershed management. However, while preparing the project proposal, the project formulation team should provide for organization chart of staff needed for bench mark surveys, project preparation, project implementation, project monitoring, research component (if any) and evaluation. Also, mention the role of consultancy agencies and services, as well as the role of the people and Voluntary Agencies. Inter-disciplinary and multi-agency approval is suggested for the organization. The National Seminar has spelt out the following organisational requirements:

(I) NATIONAL LEVEL

A National Land and Water Use Board with a Secretariat to process not only the overall policies, but also the appraisal and sanction of individual projects of Watershed Management to be nationally and internationally financed.

(II) STATE LEVEL

(a) Multi-disciplinary Watershed Management Directorate is proposed, which can be developed around the nucleus of the present soil conservation organisations in the states. This will deal with project identification, priority determination, planning, monitoring, evaluation and other overall inter-disciplinary issues. To begin with a State Land Multidisciplinary and Multi-agency Watershed Group is to be set up in each of the concerned states.

(b) Implementation should be done by the existing like departments of Agriculture, Animal Husbandry, Forestry, etc., under system of time and money tagged sub-projects.

(c) Watershed Planning Groups for individual projects.

(d) Project Officer to manage the implementation coordination for one or more watershed projects.

(III) LOCAL LEVEL

A Watershed Management Committee or Cooperative should be organized at the watershed level.

10. Marketing and Co-operatives

This chapter deals with the proposed marketing of all products generated from the micro-watershed.

11. Benefit-Cost Analysis

(a) Short term, Phase 1 (5 years)

(b) 25 years projection with and without project Estimated (b):(c) ratio may be provided.

12. Phasing

Phasing will be for five years for all inputs (e.g. staff, training, planning, implementation, material requirements, etc.) and outputs. Use bar charts, etc. Phasing of costs and benefits will be done in detail.

13. Built-in Monitoring and Evaluation System

A built-in system of multi-point monitoring and evaluation is necessary. Gauging stations for hydrology and sedimentation should be part of this built-in system. As many items of costs and benefits will be quantified as possible and systems set up for their periodic monitoring and evaluation. Information and data systems of other organisations relevant for the project should also be used.

14. Any other items

The format should be considered a guide and not an iron-frame. Flexibility is stressed. Each watershed has individuality, and needs its own format to best analyse and plan for its development. The guiding points given in the format would themselves remain under review for effecting continuous improvement.

ENCLOSURE-1

General Description (Watershed Resource Data)
Details of Chapter 6

NB. 1. In general assess the climate, land, water, plant, human, livestock and other resources;

2. Give source of data (outside source; original etc.)

1. Location, climate, soils and vegetation

(a) *Location*: Available maps, landsat and aerial photo coverage, type, scale, data and availability. Describe the villages, blocks, tehsil, district, state, longitude and latitude, etc. Relate the watershed to the sub-catchment, the catchment, river basin and the general hydraulic region.

(b) *Area*: Relation to state and region; access and communications; locations of research centres; seed farms; training institutes; etc. (a good map will provide most of this information and thereby do away with the need for lengthy description). Maps for project planning will be on the scale of 1:25000 (preferably), or 1:50000 (or any other suitable scale).

(c) *Physiography*: Elevations, topography, drainage pattern, channel morphology, (again most of this information can be shown on a good map), shape of watershed, length-width ratio aspect.

(d) *Climate*: Including characteristics of major meteorological parameters (other than those listed in (f) below). Relate the data to the project problems and needs. Give data relevant to upstream engineering measures and their design, crop production, vegetation growth, droughts and floods, etc.

(e) *Geology and soils*: Standard detailed soil survey should be done for all micro-watersheds, include erodibility characteristics also. Refer to the work of All India Soil and Land Use Survey Organization; National Bureau of Soil Surveys and Landuse Planning, National Remote Sensing Agency (Indian Photo Interpretation Institute, Dehradun), State Soil Survey Organisations and other agencies. Consultancy services can also be used in this field.

(f) *Hydrology*: Main elements of hydrologic cycle, including precipitation, evapotranspiration, and stream flow characteristics (Rainfall intensity will be an important element in this section). Iso-erodent maps of India (Dehradun Institute) and Intensity-duration-frequency nomographs; nomographs for calculating peak rate of discharge are available from Central Soil & Water Conservation Research and Training Institute, Dehradun. Hydrology Hand Book and Sedimentation Hand Book of Government of India are also available with the states for use.

(g) *Major Vegetation*: Cover, types, extent and condition. (A map again would be preferable to lengthy descriptions).

(h) *Existing engineering structures* and their efficiency (e.g. tanks, wells, roads, bridges, etc.)

2. **Present Land Use**
   It is best presented in tabular form (Job Sheet No. 1) with supporting map

(a) *Agriculture*

Rainfed: Crop types; cropping intensities; rotations; fallow; input usage; yields; prevalent diseases; problems encountered, etc.

Irrigated: Crop types; cropping intensities; rotations; fallow; input usage; yields; problems, etc.

Extent of cultivated land terraced land on very steep slopes that might be converted to orchards, tree farms, etc. (Relate the development of agricultural practices to the physical and socio-economic factors and bring out the capabilities, needs and the potential).

(b) *Horticulture*: Describe the species, growth potential, period, investment, benefits, as compared to agriculture and other uses, need for packing cases, etc.

(c) *Grasslands*: Hay fields and other grazing areas. Assess their present conditions, degraded or otherwise.

(d) *Forest lands*: Type, legal status, reserved forest, Panchayat forest, Civil Soyam forest, protected forest, etc., pure and mixed; forest density, etc. Describe the forest resource condition and trace the trend from the past, especially since independence to the present and project to the future indicating the need for urgent investments and development. Describe how the biotic factors are affecting the forests and disturbing the ecology.

(e) *Wastelands*: Bringing out the scope for utilisation and reclamation from the description of the problem affecting the wastelands:

   (a) Culturable
   (b) Unculturable

(f) *Miscellaneous habitations*: Roads, rail lines, bridges, gullies, buildings, water bodies and other landuses etc.

3. **Water Resources**

(Assess all surface water and ground water resources).

(a) Inventory of all perennial streams, and spot gauging of low flow and sediment (V-notch or other methods).

(b) Determination of water requirements in terms of crop calendar and crop growth factors, potential evapo-transpiration, and effective rainfall

(c) Inventory and priority rating of potential headwater dam sites

(d) Inventory of existing water supply schemes, details of ongoing programmes

(e) Inventory and gauging of available perennial spring. Determination of water quality

(f) Determination of present and projected human and animal water requirements

(g) Spring development sites

(h) Pond sites and sediment storage dams

Job Sheet No. 1

Details under present Land use

Agriculture: Rainfed/Irrigated

Rotation

Duration

Cropping intensity

Name of crop	Area	Variety	Preparatory tillage practices		Sowing				Manures & Fertilizers			Intercultural practices	
			Time	Method	Seed	Spacing	Time	Method	Time	Doses	Method	Time	Method
1	2	3	4	5	6	7	8	9	10	11	12	13	14

Plant Protection Measures			Irrigation				Harvest		Yield (q/ha)	
Time	Chemicals	Method	Time	Amount	Method	Source	Time	Method	Grain	Straw
15	16	17	18	19	20	21	22	23	24	25

Note: Present cost or cultivation for each crop may be found out. All the above information must be collected by gathering details from cultivators in different villages in the watershed.

(i) Attempt water budgeting for the watershed, so as to bring out the potential for water development and utilization in an overall manner (Mapping indices should be uniform, can be taken from CS & WCR & TI, Dehra Dun)

4. Human Resources

(Population; characteristics, professions, socio-economic conditions, land ownership, tenure, etc., also give employment status, outside jobs, etc.).

(a) *Population* with age and sex distribution.

(b) *Land holdings*: Total, distribution, average size, for different types of land, landless persons, tenancies, extent of fragmentation and consolidations (if any), etc.

(c) Area of different types of lands not individually owned but used by the village including shamlat areas and shamlat to be retained for distribution to landless families or available for development, common lands, forest area. Relationship between total requirements of villages included in the watershed for food, fibre, fodder, fuel, timber and other products from land and available resources.

(d) *Employment Migration Patterns*: Total employment season-wise, numbers of individuals working outside as season and permanent migrants. (This information would permit estimates of labour availability and time of availability).

(e) *Community activities*: Undertaken by panchayat within the micro-watershed in the last 3 years.

5. Livestock Resources

Population characteristics, type, numbers, quality; distribution, feeding habits, etc. Bring out the problem, posed by the livestock to the ecology of watershed.

(a) *Herd Projections:* To obtain herd projections obtain livestock numbers of various categories of both cattle and buffalos and break-down into the following classes (this classification varies with season, specify for December).

Breeding bulls; bullocks—3 years; cows—3 years
(i) in milk ; (ii) dry; young female cattle—3 years; young male cattle—3 years
Sheep: Goats: Others:

(b) Indicate reasons for any recent changes (if any) in bovine numbers, as this may give useful clue to controlling cattle numbers, and outline the possibility of disposing of surplus animals. Attempt the same for other major types of livestock.

(c) Check market outlet for milk and investigate possible development of cottage industries for milk sweets and cheese making.

(d) Prepare inventory of available fodder resources.

(e) Check on attitudes in upgrading local cattle with jerseys.

(f) Investigate economic status of farmers who have introduced Jersey cross-bred cows and provide a summary of comparative performance of the cross-breeds and local cows in the following situations; large farms, small farms, marginal farms, landless people.

(g) Investigate relative merits of keeping buffaloes instead of upgrading Jersey cross cows.

(h) Check practical feasibility of exchanging two local non-descript cattle for one Jersey cross cow and determine mechanisms by which it may be accomplished, particularly in respect of the following:

(i) Procurement and availability of Jersey; (ii) disposal of non-descript cattle;

(iii) transport of both groups; (iv) need for cattle sheds and holding yards;

(v) provision for feeding; and (vi) provision for milk sales.

6. Government Departments and Institutions

(a) *General*: Existing Government Organisational structure at the state, district and micro-watershed levels (best shown by organisation charts) for the relevant departments.

(b) *Staffing Pattern*: Proposed Watershed Management Directorate Staff Watershed Project Officer, present staffing patterns of line departments at the micro-watershed level, etc.

(c) *Development Programmes*: Brief tabular presentation of on-going government programmes in the micro-watershed. This must include health, education, energy, market outlet, roads, communications and other needed infrastructure (include all the activities which are relevant to the watershed project).

(d) *Panchayat system*: Their number, effectiveness and brief resume of their ongoing self-help schemes.

(e) *Extension*: Activities and effectiveness. Whether T.V. system introduced.

(f) *Co-operatives*: Existence, effectiveness, etc., and other special purpose co-operatives.

(g) *Credit facilities*: Existence, uptake by farmers, repayment record, etc.

(h) *Private voluntary organisations*: Existence, role, effectiveness, etc.

(i) *Inputs*: Availability, inventory of stores covering fertilisers, HYV seeds, pesticides, fungicides, implements, etc. System of distribution. Distance of input stocks.

(j) Voluntary agencies

(k) Watershed Management Committees/Co-operatives or other watershed bodies.

7. Industries

Inventory of forest industries, major, minor and cottage industries, their location, type, raw material inputs, outputs and numbers employed, energy availability.

ENCLOSURE-2

Project Components

N.B. The Project components would generally belong to two major categories:

(a) Foundation Practices to provide protection to the resource base

(b) Super-structure of production

Practices—to develop and exploit the optimum production potential of the resources of climate, land, water, plant, man and livestock, so as to produce abundance in a sustained manner without deteriorating the resource base.

Job Sheet No.2
Graded Bund or Channel Terraces. Cross Sectional Area

Block	Sub-block	Area in ha	Slope %	Vertical interval m	Horizontal distance m	Length in m/ ha.m³	Earth work in m³	Rate per 1000 cu.m³	Cost per hectare	Total cost on the block Rs.

Job Sheet No. 3
Bench Terraces

Block No.	Sub-block No.	Area in ha	Slope %	V.T. in m	Width in m	Earth work in cu.m³	Earth work rate	Cost per ha	Total	Cost

Shoulder Bund

Length of bund per ha	Total length	Earth work in m³	Rate	Cost	Total cost

Cost of terrace
Cost of shoulder bund

Job Sheet No. 4
Grassed Waterway

Block No.	Sub-block No.	Drainage area in ha	Slope %	Length of grassed waterway in m	Total discharge expected in m³	Design discharge capacity in m³	Cross section area in m²	Top width	Total depth earth (flow work depth m³ F.B.)	Rate	Cost

Cost of earth work ... m³ @ Rs. per m³ Rs.

Cost of sodding ... m² @ Rs. per m² Rs.

Total

Job Sheet No. 5
Diversion Ditch

Block No.	Sub-block No.	Drainage area in ha	Expected discharge (cumec)	Slope %	Length of ditch (m)	Cross section area (m²)	Earth work (m³)	Rate	Cost	Total

(a) Cost of Earth work _____ m³   Rs.
(b) Cost of sodding m²   Rs.
(c) Cost of structure   Rs.

Total   Rs.

Job Sheet No. 6
Peripheral Bund

Block No.	Sub-block No.	Length of bund in m	Cross sections in m²	Earth work in m³	Rate per 1000 m³	Total	Cost	Remarks

Job Sheet No. 7
Farm Pond

Block No.	Sub-block No.	Chainage	Cross sectional interval, m	Cross sectional area, m²	Average sectional area, m²	Earth work	Total E.W. m³	Cumulative earth work	Remarks

1. Foundation Practices of Engineering and Biological Measures for Soil and Water Conservation

(a) *Agricultural lands*: Water and sediment control using contour cultivation, graded channel terraces, bench terraces, orchard terraces, waterways (construction and maintenance), ponds, water harvesting, etc. (Job Sheet No. 2 to 7)

(b) *Grazing lands*: Gully control, check dams, retention dams, roads, ground cover etc.

(c) *Forest lands*: (as for 1.02)

(d) Special problem lands

(e) Fuel fodder and timber supply depots

2. Agricultural Practices

(a) Water Resource Development and utilisation

    (i) Water collection, storage and recycling; ponds

    (ii) Ground water development

    (iii) Water use and maintenance

    (iv) Drinking water supply

(b) Agronomic Practices

    (i) Rainfed

    (ii) Irrigated or with supplemental and life saving

3. Grazing Land Practices

(a) Pasture and fodder development

(b) Grazing land improvement

(c) Stall feeding and fodder supplies

4. Animal Husbandry Practices

(a) Reduction of grazing pressure

    (i) Cattle exchange

    (ii) Bullock sharing

    (iii) Reduction of numbers

(b) Improved Milk production

    (i) Use of Jersey cross breed

    (ii) Use of artificial insemination

    (iii) Use of Murrah bulls.

(c) Other livestock development

    (i) Sheep

    (ii) Goats

    (iii) Pigs and poultry

    (iv) Other livestock

5. Forestry practices

(a) Establishment of plantations, bush or grass cover for soil conservation and water retention

(b) Plantations for fuel, fodder and timber (agricultural implements and house construction)

(c) Plantations for commercial and industrial use

(d) Farm forestry on private lands including commercial grass (bhabar, lemon, etc.) production

(e) Supporting services—nurseries, fire protection, etc.

(f) Management of protected, reserve forests

(g) Management of commercial, reserve forests

(h) Establishment of Forest Labourers Cooperative Societies

(i) Establishment of wood-based industries (cottage or larger) including minor forest products

6. Special Problems and Proposed Solutions

(roads, landslides, torrents, gullies, etc.)

7. Research

This section would identify the research needs and priorities by disciplines and indicate whether they should be central (ICAR) or state (Agricultural Universities) responsibility—Results obtained by the Central Soil and Water Conservation Research and Training Institute, Dehra Dun and its Centres may be fully utilised. Facilities need to be strengthened at the Dehra Dun Institute and at Hyderabad and Bangalore K.V.K. among others.

(a) *Hydrology and Sedimentation*

Watershed approach, watershed model studies, time replication studies, benchmark watersheds, water budgeting, siltation of reservoirs (big and small), instrumentation.

(b) *Agricultural and Horticultural*

    (i) Crop selection and rotations

    (ii) Plant populations

    (iii) Pesticides, fungicides, etc.

(c) *Pastures and Fodders Crops*

    (i) Selection of pasture, grass and legumes

    (ii) Evaluation of pasture species under grazing and haycutting conditions

    (iii) Fertilizer requirements of legume based pastures

    (iv) Legume seed inoculation requirements

    (v) Pasture establishment methods including oversowing techniques

    (vi) Cropping systems involving fodder crops and inter-row planting of legumes.

(d) *Forestry*

    (i) Land use, runoff, sediment relations

(ii) Fuelwood and fodder species trials

(iii) Preparation of growth and yield tables

(iv) Effect of burning

(v) Agro-forestry.

8. Training

This section would deal with training requirements at all levels for both farmers (man and woman) and Government employees at Central and State departments and institutions. Special provision will have to be made for training in integrated watershed management. This section would start with a list of existing facilities, number trained, duration of courses, etc. Personnel already trained at the Central Soil and Water Conservation Research & Training Institute, Dehra Dun should be fully utilized. They would also need watershed orientation training.

9. Credit Facilities

This section would indicate what provision needs to be made for strengthening the credit mechanisms. It would also give ways of improving repayment terms and providing for crop insurance of the credit taken to raise crops.

10. Other Components

9.2   A Case Study

A Project Report on Watershed Planning and Management (Belan-Jharia Sub-Watershed) (Anonymous, 1977)

INTRODUCTION

The Belan-Jharia Sub-Watershed comprising of 51 villages and having a geographical area of 7,752 ha was considered an ideal site for planning and execution of different conservation as well as utilisation activities in an integrated manner, which is expected to have the demonstration value as the area is connected by *pucca* roads and also showing distinct physiographic features. The rainfall of the area is about 102 cm annually, but most of it gets wasted in the form of runoff, which carried the valuable top soil also along with it, continuously making the area poorer in terms of cultivable soil and its productivity. The strategy following in planning this sub watershed would therefore, be to conserve the soil by checking the runoff. This would increase the infiltration of harvested water for better utilisation and thus increase the productivity of the area. The utilisation of land has been planned or the basis of land capability. Conservation of water is also expected to increase the recharge of the ground water, position of which is otherwise very difficult in this hard rock area. The conservation measures proposed under the project plan are construction of water harvesting bundhies and contours bunding in order to check soil erosion and conserve valuable soil from being washed away. Through these measures, more area under crops will get irrigation and thus productivity per unit of land will increase.

Introduction of new technology on dryland farming will also help the farmers to harvest more per unit of area. Apart from this, the improvement of village pond would make it possible to culture fishes and thus increase the income of the people of the areas. Pasture development and afforestation is expected to provide fodder and fuel to the area and after the activities are implemented, subsidiary occupation will reach a stage, where a planned development may be felt necessary.

Under the sub-watershed, it is proposed to increase the utilisation of runoff from very little to 59% of the average total precipitation. Water harvesting bundhies are proposed to be constructed, which would provide protective irrigation to 1814 ha of land. *Nala* bunding measures will provide protection to 469 ha. Dug-out ponds (28) and 24 dug wells will be constructed. Afforestation in 1788 ha and pasture development in 316 ha will be undertaken. After the development is effected, the cropping intensity in the area is expected to range between 165 to 225%, as against the existing intensity of 100–157%.

More striking feature is that, under the proposed programme, crop productivity is expected to register an increase of about 400%. Bankable schemes in respect of minor irrigation, Bundhies command Development and contour bunding have been proposed. Total capital investment (Tables 9.1 & Tables 9.2) is worked out Rs.91.46 lakhs in 3 years (excluding cost of infrastructure development).

Detailed planning could be made only for 19 contiguous villages out of 51, because of paucity of time and this has been termed as a pilot area, wherein the activities would be implemented first based on the details of the pilot area, the projection has been made for the entire sub-watershed and during the period the activities are implemented in the pilot area, the details for the remaining area will be worked out.

Apart from watershed planning and management, the feasibility studies were conducted to formulate special schemes based on existing potential, primarily with a view to strengthen the traditional activities providing employment and income generating opportunities to the weaker section of the society, as a part of the strategy for providing them employment and income to the poor people in the area.

The sub-watershed area is very poor in the general infrastructure, therefore, for proper communication, construction of roads have been suggested in the Plan. This would be necessary for the supply of inputs and marketing of the produce of the area at a reasonable price.

Selection of Watershed

Belan-Jharia Sub-watershed selected represents largely the drought prone area in the Mirzapur district, in terms of its various characters, viz., soil type and depth, irrigation potential, cropping pattern, climate and rainfall, geology and ground water drainage, socio-economic features and conservation needs, etc. It was also considered that the area should be approachable, as it has to serve as a model and visitors would have to be taken to the site at different stages of its management. Based on above considerations and detailed examinations of the Belan river basin through field visits, the Belan-Jharia sub-watershed was selected. The entire area fell in Ghorwal block of Robertsganj Tehsil. Since a perennial *nala* named Jharia is the main tributary to the Belan in the area, the sub-watershed was named as Belan-Jharia sub-watershed.

DESCRIPTION

The Belan-Jharia sub-watershed is comprised of 51 villages, out of which two villages are only partly involved. Total geographical area is 7752.0 ha. The sub-watershed lies between latitudes 24°38' to 24°45' (S-N) and longitudes 82°49' to 82°55' (W-E).

The area is bounded by Kaimur hills on its upper ridge (south) and Belan river down below (north) as the common drain of the area. Towards north-east side there is a metalled road running between Ghorwal and Robertsganj. On south-eas

Table 9.1   *Project Area—Belan–Jharia Sub-watershed*

(Physical—ha)
(Financial—Rs. in lakhs)

Phasing	Contour bunding		Water harvesting Bundhi		Land levelling		Nala Bunding		Gully Control		Dug-out ponds	
	Physical	Financial	Physical	Financial	Physical	Financial	Physical	Financial	Physical	Financial	Physical	Financial
1st year	1149.43	2.60	12	16.605	113.0	1.13	234	1.17	165.75	0.35	12	4.24
2nd year	1270.33	2.26	20	13.560	351.0	3.5	137	0.88	87.75	0.33	10	4.25
3rd year	936.00	1.46	12	4.020	429.0	4.29	98	0.29	–	–	6	2.37
Total	3355.66	6.32	44	34.185	893.8	8.93	469	2.34	253.5	0.68	28	10.86

Phasing	Water courses		Large dia. met. open wells		Pasture development		Forestry		Total income (Rs. in lakh)
	Physical	Financial	Physical	Financial	Physical	Financial	Physical	Financial	
1st year	752.7	1.02	–	–	195	1.95	975	3.90	32.965
2nd year	1320.15	1.720	12	1.98	121	1.21	975* 813**	6.18	35.88
3rd year	436.8	0.41	12	1.98	–	–	1788* 813*	5.36 2.44	20.18
Total	2509.65	3.15	24	3.96	316	316	1788 813*	17.83	91.465

* Maintenance

** New plantation

Table 9.2 *Project Area—Belan-Jharia Sub-watershed*
Resource Development in the Pilot Area Showing physical and financial targets otherwise
(Physical—ha)
(Financial—Rs. in lakh)

Phasing	Contour bunding		Water harvesting Bundhi		Land levelling		Nala Bunding		Gully Control	
	Physical	Financial	Physical	Financial	Physical	Financial	Physical	Financial	Physical	Financial
1st year	589.45	1.33	6	8.52	58	0.58	120	0.60	86	0.18
2nd year	651.49	1.16	10	6.95	180	1.80	70	0.45	45	0.17
3rd year	480.00	0.75	6	2.06	220	2.20	50	0.15	–	–
Total	1720.94	3.24	22	17.53	458	4.58	250	1.20	130	0.35

Dug-out ponds		Water Courses		Large dia. open wells		Pasture development		Afforestation		Total finances involved
Physical	Financial	Physical	Financial	Physical	Financial	Physical	Financial	Physical	Financial	
6	2.17	386	0.52	–	–	100	1.00	500*	2.00	16.90
5	2.18	677	0.88	6	0.99	62	0.62	500*	3.17	18.37
								417**		
3	1.22	224	0.21	6	0.99	–	–	917*	2.75	10.33
								417*	1.25	1.25
14	5.57	1287	1.61	12	1.98	162	1.62	917	9.17	46.85

* Maintenance
** New plantation

side Jharia *nala* forms the boundary whereas on the west, there is a *kacha* road connecting Ghorwal and Gurwal which forms the boundary of the selected sub-watershed. It is considered to be an ideal sub-watershed selected for planning and management on a pilot basis.

Physiography

The area is composed of undulating tracts of high ridges and low valleys. The level difference between the ridges and valleys is 3 to 10 m. The general slope of the area is from south to north, varying from 1 to 3.5%. There are five main *nalas* in the area, viz. Rehia, Dhobi, Ghatwa, Khirihata-Gadma *nala*, Dumkhari-Khirihata *nala* and Jharia *nala*. All these *nalas* join the Belan river. All the *nalas* are seasonal, carrying the runoff at a very high velocity and subside after a few hours of stoppage of the rains. The area as a whole is well-drained, rather excessively drained, in most of the parts. Some villages on upper side like Karaundia suffer from highly undulating topography, others on down side like Kushma and Rajin are comparatively flat and more productive.

Rainfall

The average rainfall of the area is about 1000 mm (approximately). Main rainy months are July, August and September. Although the quantity of precipitation is not less, the distribution is very uneven. This is characterised by long dry spells, early stoppage of rain and also late setting of rains, due to which every 2nd or 3rd year is a drought year.

Climate

The project area (sub-watershed) falls under semi-arid to sub-humid climate. Maximum temperature ranges between 24 to 40° C, while the minimum temperature is between 4.5 to 25° C. The climate is of extreme type and during May and June, the temperature sometimes goes as high as 45° C. The winters are also severe.

Geology

The geological formations encountered in the area are Kaimur sandstone, laterite and a thin cover of alluvium. The sandstone is quartizitic in nature and is also known as Dhandraul quartzite.

GROUNDWATER CONDITION

Source

Precipitation is the main source of groundwater in the area. A considerable part of the rainwater is lost as surface runoff and by way of evaporation and transpiration; and only a small portion seeps below land surface to be conserved as groundwater.

Occurrence

In the area under reference, groundwater occurs both, in the consolidated and unconsolidated formations. In the hard rock area (Dhanraul quartzite), it occurs in planes of weakness, such as joints, bedding planes, fissures and fractures. In the alluvium and laterite the groundwater occurs under water-table conditions in the zone of saturation.

SOCIO-ECONOMIC CONDITIONS

Population

Total number of villages falling in the Belan-Jharia sub-watershed are 51. As per 1971 census, the total population of these villages is 10604, out of which the male and female population is 5421 and 5183, respectively. On the basis of random sampling, the detailed socio-economic investigations were carried out in 24 villages of the sub-watershed in the selected villages. All the families were covered under the study. On the basis of this study, it has been worked out that 43.6% population falls in the age group up to 15 years, whereas only 0.37% of the population falls above the age of 59. The population falling in the age group between 15 and 59 years is 56.02%, which constitute the work force. It is therefore, imperative that 56% of the population in the sub-watershed area needs employment.

Occupation
Main occupation of the area is agricultural activity. A very small percentage, i.e. 3.29 is engaged in other occupations like shop-keeping, services in school and other business. 76.17% of the total population are land-holders, whereas 19.21% are landless agricultural labourers. New land allottes constitute 4.26%. Among the land owners, small and marginal farmers constitute 56.09% of the population and 24.70% are big farmers. The growth rate of the population is worked out at 8.15% and the average size of the family in the project area in terms of number is 4.74.

58% of the total households belong to the schedule-caste and 3% of them are schedule-tribes. The area is very backward from literacy point of views, as only 9.93% of the population is literate.

Land Holding Pattern
The total geographical area of 51 villages falling in the Belan-Jharia sub-watershed is 8628.27 ha, out of which 7752 ha is within the sub-watershed. The area under cultivation is 5771.53 ha. Sub-marginal and marginal farmers own 3.2% and 5.5% of the total operational area, respectively. 64.6% of the total operational area belongs to large farmers. It can be observed that small farmers who comprise 55.7% of the total households, have only 21.4% of the total operational area and big farmers who comprise 19.1% of the total households have 78.5% of the total operational area under their command.

SOILS
Detailed soil survey conducted in the area indicated that there were 16 soil series, 91 soil types and general soil survey map was prepared and used as a base for detailed watershed management plan. Description of one of the above series namely Karaundia-2 series is given below:

Karaundia-2 Series (Kr2)
Karaundia-2 series is identified along the Ghorawal to Gurwal road starting from foot hill. It consists of shallow to very deep soils. Soils are invariably slowly permeable and intense mottling in B horizon is common. Surface texture varies from sandy clay to clay loam, whereas sub-soil is sandy loam to clay. Wide variation in B horizon with varying depth is due to deposition of transported materials through *nalas*. But below the surface soil, clay loam and alluvial clay is the main characteristics of this series. Profiles are imperfectly drained. But surface drainage is rapid to very rapid, as soils are located in between *nalas* and at foot hills, which occupy high terraces with undulating topography. In general, soils are very gentle sloping, except small landscape near *nala* having moderate slope. Owing to slope gradient, soils are left open for erosion hazards, which varies from moderate in small patch to severe in large tract. At places soils are in rocky and stony phases.

TYPIFYING PEDON

Depth (cm)	Description
Apx Cn	Light brownish gray (2.5 Y 6/2) clay loam; prismatic strong, structure; very hard, firm, slightly sticky and plastic under different conditions of moisture; few, fine, faint mottles with sharp boundary; iron concretions commons; abundant roots; small pore space; thick clay films on peds. pH 7.6; non-calcareous; gradual and smooth boundary.
ABx Cn	Yellowish brown (2.5 Y 6/4) clay loam; strong, prismatic structure; very hard, extremely firm, slightly sticky and plastic consistency under varying condition of moisture; iron concentration pea grain size are common; few, fine, faint with sharp boundaries mottle; small pores; clay films around peds, mildly alkaline (pH 7.6) ; non-calcareous; smooth and gradual boundary of horizon.
Bl 48-72	Brown (10 YR 5/3), sandy loam, granular, indistinct peds; soft, very friable, non-sticky and non-plastic when wet; large pores, mildly alkaline reaction (pH 7.7); non-calcareous, smooth and diffused boundary.

DRAINAGE AND PERMEABILITY

Soils of this series are defectively drained and prone; rapid surfacing runoff underlying layer is least permeable.

MAPPING UNITS IDENTIFIED WITHIN THE SERIES

— Karaundia-2 sandy clay, shallow and rocky soil $\dfrac{Kr2\ id\ 2R}{C - e4}$. About 50% of the landscape is covered with rock out crops. Slope gradient varies from 50% and soil is under very severe erosion.

— Karaundia-2 sandy clay, very deep and severely eroded $\dfrac{Kr2\ i\ d5}{B - e3}$—slope varies from 1 to 3% and terrace is poorly bunded. Paddy crop is cultivated during *Kharif.*

— Karaundia-2 sandy clay loam, severely eroded soil $\dfrac{Kr2\ hd5}{B - e3}$ Poorly bunded land is susceptible to severe erosion. Slope varies from 1 to 3%.

— Karaundia-2 sandy clay, very gentle sloping $\dfrac{Kr2\ id5}{B - e2}$—Landscape is located in between *nalas.* Poorly bunded soil is moderately eroded. Slope gradient is slightly above 1%.

— Karaundia-2 clay loam, slightly rocky, moderately alkaline $\dfrac{Kr2\ Hd\ 5\ stl\ s2\ R1}{D - e3}$ —Severely eroded. Located adjacent to Wala soils are severely eroded. Slope varies from 5 to 6 per cent.

Crops of the Area

Principal crops of the area are paddy and *sawan* in *Kharif* and wheat and barely in *Rabi.* These crops cover 72% of the area under 'gross cropped area,' paddy accounts for 33%, wheat 18.95%, barley 11.88% and *sawan* 9.19%. The other crops of the area are maize, *kodo, karvi khesari* and *alsi,* etc. The area also produces a small quantity of vegetables and sugarcane. Betelvine is cultivated as a special cash crop in village Murahi on a limited scale.

Topographical Survey

The entire Belan-Jharia sub-watershed was selected for detailed topographic survey at 30 m grid. Standard permanent bench mark was taken as base for the calculation of all the temporary bench marks and ground levels. Contours at 0.3 m interval were drawn on contour map. Size of grid was reduced wherever there were significant changes in the topography. Detailed contour map at 1:1980 scale was prepared, in order to obtain maximum possible information of topography and land features. Detailed planning was done for 19 contiguous villages designating it as a pilot area.

Soil Survey

A variety of soils occur in the watershed. They are either formed on or derived from a wide range of parent material. In order to manage land, water resources for optimum crop production, a detailed soil survey to examine its physical, chemical characteristics and profile studies is considered necessary.

The procedure laid down in "Soil Survey Manual (1970)" published by All India Soil and Land Use Organization was adopted for Soil Survey of the watershed. Reconnaissance of whole of the Belan-Jharia Sub-watershed, which included 7752 ha geographical area and 51 villages was done. It was followed up by detailed reconnaissance survey of 19 villages (pilot area), for which investigation report was prepared. It resulted into sketching of soil boundary, soil type and phrases on a broad basis. Revenue maps at 1:3960 scale were used as base for demarcating soil boundaries. Land capability and irrigability maps were worked out, depending upon detailed study of soil texture, structure contour consistency, soil phase, intensity of surface salt deposits, free $CaCO_3$, soil reaction mottling, infiltration and erosion. Soils have been classified into different taxonomic classes based on their chemical, physical and morphological characteristics.

The information collected and generated through the study of prepared land capability, irrigability maps for the pilot areas, set the guidelines for suggesting and recommending the soil reclamation and management measures. Total area under different soil series was worked out to understand its implication in relation to crop management.

Hydrogeological Survey

A report on ground water in Mirzapur district prepared by Central Ground Water Board in 1973, and a short note on ground water availability in Mirzapur district prepared by the Ground Water Investigation Organization, U.P. (1975) were referred and taken as the base information in assuming the ground water potential of the project area.

Water Resources Survey

The objective of such a survey was to explore the available water resources, which could be exploited for the conservation and optimum utilisation for increased productivity.

SOIL AND WATER CONSERVATION MEASURES PROPOSED

Engineering Measures

The following measures were considered to be useful considering topography and land capability classes met within the area.

Contour Bunding

Contour bunding in 1720.94 ha will be carried out in order to intercept the runoff to hold water for moisture conservation and to check soil erosion. Total area where contour bunding will be done, has been divided into 47 sub-segments based on the topography, soil type and depth. Slope of the contour bunding segment varies from 0.31% to 3.42%. Out of the total 1720.94 ha area, maximum area (1036.06 ha) falls under 0.51% to 1% slope group.

As far as possible, contour bunding has been proposed in the area, where the soils are medium to deep. In very shallow soils having a depth of less than 7.5 cm, contour bunding has not been proposed.

Planning of contour bunding has been done from higher elevation to lower elevation. The cross-sectional area of the bund adopted is 0.815 m² with 0.45 m top width, 2.25 m bottom width, 0.6 m height and side slopes of 1.75:1 in case of sandy soils and 1.50:1 in case of soils other than sandy. In case the bund has to be deviated by any unavoidable reasons, backfilling or back-cutting has been recommended to bring the bund exactly on contour.

When the bund has to pass a gully or depression, additional earthwork in the form of buttress has been provided to ensure safety against breach.

An adequate system of outlets has been proposed. Through the pipes, water after attaining an average depth of 0.3 m will be disposed into the drain, natural depression/stabilized gully. Reinforced cement concrete pipe of 0.15 m is recommended to take care of water for 3 ha catchment area.

At suitable places, wherever possible, ramps are constructed.

Detailed Design

An area of 82.5 ha has been selected for detailed design and layout of contour bunding including peak rate of runoff computation. Average slope of the area has been calculated as 0.685% (highest RL of segment is 309 m, the lowest point is 303 m and total span is 875 m).

Most of the soils are sandy clay to sandy loam texture and crumbly type structure. Infiltration of the least permeable layer varies from 0.12 to 2.5 cm/hour. Depth of soil varies from 0.45 m to 1.2 m and more.

The soil is moderately to severely eroded. Sheet and rill erosion is prominent. Most of the land is under land capability class II, few patches are of class III and class IV.

One hour rainfall intensity for 25 years recurrence interval is taken as 95 mm.

Spacing and Length of Bund

The *VI* has been worked out to be 0.44 m by using the formal $VI = \dfrac{S+2}{6}$. Horizontal interval and length of bund works out to be 64.7 m and 12,751.1 m respectively.

Storage Area and Height of Bund

Considering the average slope of the area as 0.68%, maximum expected rainfall during 3 years recurrence interval is 140 mm, that the soil absorbs 40% of rainfall and slope of the seepage line is 4:1, the maximum runoff to be stored is rainfall minus infiltration $= 140 - \dfrac{14 \times 40}{100} = 8.4$ cm.

$$\text{Storage area required} = \frac{\text{Runoff (cm)} \times HI}{100}$$

$$= \frac{8.4 \times 64.7}{100} = 5.4348 \text{ sq.m.}$$

Height of bund works out to be about 30 cm. Taking provision for freeboard for 15 cm, total height of bund will be 45 cm. Since RCC pipe for disposal is provided, conventional provision of (HFL—FSL) does not add up to the height of the bund. The top width and base width works out to be 0.15 and 1.725 m respectively, with side slopes of 1.75:1. The cross-sectional area will be therefore 0.422 m². Considering soil loss in initial rains and also soil compaction and siltation, a cross-sectional area of 0.81 m² has been suggested.

Length of side and hooking bund works out to be 45 m. Hence bund should be hooked 30–50 m upward. Wherever the contour bunds are longer than 300 m, lateral bunds are provided.

A standard size of borrow pit of 3 m × 1.5 m × 0.3 m or 3 m × 3 m × 0.3 m is recommended downstream.

Water Harvesting Bundhies

As a measurement of conserving soil and utilizing the runoff for moisture conservation and irrigation, construction of water harvesting bundhies are proposed. Most of the bundhies will be put across the natural *nallahs,* which would serve dual purpose of water harvesting and *nala* bunding.

In the pilot area of about 4000 ha, 22 water harvesting bundhies have been proposed. It will harvest 403.6 ha-m, out of which 333.02 ha-m can be utilized for irrigation. From all the 22 bundhies, 6 acre-inch water would be available to 851.6 ha area in *Kharif* and the same quantity of water would provide irrigation for 981 ha area in *Rabi.* Total area under the command of all these 22 bundhies works out to be 1400 ha, out of which 1287 ha is culturable.

Whatever water is available in both the seasons, a cropping intensity of 200% has been proposed and where the water is available only in *Kharif* season, cropping intensity of 165% has been proposed and in such cases, the residual moisture will be available for wheat crop in *Rabi.* In areas having good soils, even with the provision of protective irrigation, 70% land is proposed to be put under paddy considering the farmers' preference.

Details of calculation of Bundhi No. 1 are given below as an example:

Location

Water harvesting bundhi No. 1 has been proposed across Gadma-Khirihata *nala* of about 1.5 km (reduced distance).

Hydraulic details

Top bank level	= 318.2 m	Catchment area	= 125 ha
Highest flood level	= 316.7 m	Dead storage level	= 313.5 m
Highest water level	= 316.2 m		

Type of catchment and hydrology

Cultivated with shallow soils above impervious layer	= 25 ha
Area under forest with shallow soils above impervious layer	= 100 ha
Weighted value of runoff co-efficient	= 0.42
Length of the catchment	= 1000 m
Drop in elevation	= 9.10
Intensity of rainfall of the 25 years recurrence interval	= 9.5 cm/hr
Time of concentration	= 24.27
Intensity of rainfall for the duration equal to time of concentration	= 15.60 cm/hr

Peak rate of runoff   = 22.604 cumec
Reservoir capacity   = 15.7 ha m
Minimum rainfall in 75% of the years   = 93.8 cm
Average yearly rainfall adopted for the area   = 100 cm
Minimum runoff available for the irrigation purposes
for the rainfall 95 cm and an average catchment   = 0.2460 ha m/ha
Minimum runoff adopted   = 0.2187 ha m/ha
         = 27.34 ha m
Area under submergency   = 7.91 ha
Area available for *Rabi* cultivation from the
submergence area   = Nil

Proposed irrigation

Gross command area	= 63.0 ha	*Kharif*	= 26 ha
Cultivated command area	= 52.0 ha	*Rabi*	= 38.9 ha

Storage requirement

Reservoir capacity	= 15.7 ha m	Evaporation losses	
Requirement for *Kharif*	= 4.72 ha m	assuming 15 cm per	
Requirement for *Rabi*	= 7.08 ha m	month during 5 months	
		of rainy season	= 1.57 ha m
		Dead storage	= 2.33 ha m

Sectional design details of the water harvesting Bandhi

Maximum height	= 6.1 m	Length of the	
Top width	= 6 m	Bandhi	= 250 m
Maximum base width	= 70.80 m	Maximum cross-	
Average base width	= 26.09 m	sectional area	= 311.04 m²
Free-board	= 1.5 m	Average cross-	
Side slope of the		sectional area	= 56.20 m
upstream side	= 4:1	Area of sloping side	= 1675.12 m²
		Land used for	
		the construction	= 0.6522 ha

Emergency Escape

Type of escape	= Rectangular weir type open spillway		
Crest level	= 316.2 m	Height of crest	= 0.50 m
Peak rate of runoff for the	= 25.99	Length of crest	= 43.12 m
design of emergency escape	cumec		

Irrigation outlets

Type	= Pipe outlet having silting boxes on upstream		
	and on stream sides		
Type of pipe	= Circular,	Length of the pipe	= 35 m
	RCC;	Velocity of flow	= 212 cm/sec
Dia. of pipe	= 0.15 m;	Discharge	= 37.8 lit/sec

Irrigation channel

Type and shape	= Trapezoidal earthen channel		
Discharge	= 38.0	Side slope	= 1.5:1
	lit/sec	Grade	= 1:1000

Bed width	= 0.30 m	Length of the	
Full supply depth	= 0.25 m	main channel	= 620 m
Freeboard	= 0.15 m	Total earth work	= 14050 m³

Calculation Area of Sides of the Bandhi

Area of pitching if pitching is to be provided on the complete upstream side of the water harvesting bandhi up to the Highest Flood Level = 1300.12 m².

Area of sloping side of downstream side of the bandhi = area of pitching + area where pitching has not been provided. Area of sloping side of the bandhi where pitching has not been provided.

= (Top bund level–High flood level) × Length of bandhi
= (318.2 – 316.70) × 250 Total area of sloping side off the bandhi
= 1.5 × 250   = 1300.12 + 375.0 = 1675.12 m²
= 375.0 m²

Availability of Water for Irrigation (Water Budgeting)

In water harvesting, Bandhi No. 1, water up to the 316.2 m (HWL) would be available. It conserves water 15.70 ha-m (Table 9.3). An irrigation outlet from the bandhi has been provided at 313.5 m R.L. It is expected that water up to the level 313.5 m would not be utilised for irrigation. It would remain in the bandhi as a dead storage. Quantity of dead storage would be 2.33 ha-m. Evaporation losses would be according to the water surface area. It is expected that the maximum water spread at 316.2 m R.L. would be 7.91 ha. Water losses for five months has been considered as 10%. Therefore, the total quantity of water losses would be 1.52 ha-m. Amount of water which would be available for irrigation is 11.8 ha-m. Areas within the command of Bandhi No. 1 is sloping and has comparatively shallow soils, therefore, the land is recommended for *Bajra* and Sorghum in the *Kharif* season.

Table 9.3 *Reservoir capacity of water harvesting bundhi*

Water level (m)	Depth of water (m)	Area of water spread (m)	Average area (ha)	Volume of water (ha-m)
316.2	–	7.91	–	–
315.9	0.30	7.06	7.49	2.2470
315.6	0.30	6.31	6.69	2.007
315.3	0.30	5.88	6.09	1.827
315.0	0.30	5.62	5.75	1.725
314.7	0.30	5.25	5.44	1.632
314.4	0.30	3.94	4.57	1.377
314.1	0.30	3.06	3.5	1.050
313.8	0.30	2.75	2.94	0.873
313.5	0.30	2.06	2.40	0.720
313.2	0.30	1.06	1.16	0.348
312.9	0.30	1.06	1.16	0.348
310.1	2.8	–	0.53	1.484
				15.632 or 15."

It is proposed that 0.15 m water could be provided to the *Kharif* crop within 2-3 irrigations. Use 40% of water in the *Kharif*. Water used in *Kharif* would be 4.72 ha-m.

Therefore, water available for *Rabi* would be 7.08 ha-m. It is proposed that this water would provide irrigation to the *Rabi* crop. It is expected that 1.22 ha submerged area would be available for *Rabi* cultivation.

Peak rate of runoff

Use rational formula for computing peak rate of runoff:

$$Q = \frac{CIA}{360}$$

where, Q = peak rate of runoff in cumecs

C = runoff coefficient depending on the watershed characteristics(0.42);

I = Intensity of rainfall for the duration equal to time of concentration for the · selected catchment (156 mm/hr); and

A = Catchment area (125 ha).

Hence, $Q = \dfrac{0.42 \times 156 \times 125}{360}$ cumec

= 22.604 cumec.

DESIGN OF EMERGENCY SPILLWAY

It is assumed that after filling of Bundhi No.1 up to the maximum capacity and up to its H.W.L. 316.20 m, all the runoff is to be disposed safely. For this, emergency spillway has been designed.

Watershed area   = 125 ha

Peak rate of runoff as calculated here = 22.604 cumec

Design the spillway to take care of 15% more rate of runoff.

Final $Q = Q + 0.15 \pm Q$

= 25.99 cumec

Height of the crest of the emergency spillway = 0.50 m

$Q = CLM^m$

= $1.705LH^{3/2}$

Length of the crest of the emergency spillway = 43.12 m

According to the topography, emergency spillway can be provided towards Gadma village having following specifications:

Length of the crest = 43.12 m

Height of the crest = 0.50 m

Q = 23.99 cumec

Area operation should be carefully seen during rainy days. According to nature of flow of water beyond the capacity of the captioned bandhi, a masonry drop spillway is recommended. Detailed investigations are needed before the construction of the spillway. Provision of the construction of masonry earthen spillway is made.

Catchment Area

Catchment area of the bandhies ranges from 25 to 200 ha.

Area Submerged

Study reveals that 302.22 ha area is under submergence in the optimum conditions, when the proposed reservoirs are filled up to the highest water level. Out of the total submerged area, about 20% (60.451 ha) which would have a very shallow depth of water could be utilised for *Kharif* cultivation. It is suggested that a submergence resistant variety of paddy (floating paddy) could be grown there. Therefore, the area which would remain under submergence during *Kharif* is 242.78 ha. In *Rabi*, another 50% area would be available for the wheat cultivation. Various bandhies just as Bandhi No.II is proposed only for *Kharif* irrigation and all the submerged area would be free in *Rabi* for cultivation. Such area would be about 121.89 ha. Therefore, the submerged area in all the 22 bandhies, which would not be available for cultivation would be about 120.89 ha only.

CATCHMENT AREA V/S SUBMERGENCE AREA

On an average, the catchment area is about 8.5 times of the total submerged area. If submerged area is 1 ha, the catchment would be 8.5 ha area. This ratio suits the norms and conditions of the bandhi construction.

Reservoir Capacity

The total reservoir capacity (in all the proposed bandhies) is 403.06 ha-m. Total runoff volume available from the catchment is 503.76 ha-m. It shows that about 72% of the runoff would be stored in the proposed bandhies. Though the actual quantity available for irrigation would be only 333.25 ha-m after considering evaporation and storage losses. Thus 59% of the total runoff would be available for irrigation purposes through the proposed water harvesting techniques.

Irrigation Outlet from the Water Harvesting Bandhi

A pipe drop outlet has been proposed to release water for irrigation. Sometimes construction of an open drop structure is not possible without disturbing an existing bund or dam. In such cases, water could be safely discharged from a higher elevation to a lower one by providing a pipe drop.

A silting basin (0.75 m × 0.75 m size) made of stone masonry has been provided at the outlet of the pipe conduit to dissipate the turbulent energy of the stream. A masonry apron-cum-silting pit has also been provided around the inlet end of the pipe to prevent seepage and erosion around it.

Velocity of Flow of Water

The velocity of flow of water in pipe spillways using different size pipes may be calculated from the following relationship obtained by the application of Bernauli's theorem:

| Available head | = | Frictional losses in the pipe line | + | Velocity head | + | Head at the entrance of pipe | + | Head loss at bend |

$$H = \frac{4flv^2}{2gd} + \frac{v^2}{2g} + K_1\frac{v^2}{2g} + K_2\frac{v^2}{2g}$$

In design, a silting pit of size 0.75 m × 0.75 m has been used, therefore, consider head loss at the entrance of the pipe as well as at the bend as negligible. Resolving the Bernoulli equation

$$H = \frac{4flv^2}{2gd} + \frac{v^2}{2g}$$

$$= \frac{v^2}{2g}\left[\frac{4fl}{d} + 1\right] = \frac{v^2}{2g}\left[\frac{4fl + d}{d}\right] \qquad v^2 = \frac{2gdH}{4fl + d} \text{ or } V = \sqrt{\frac{2gdH}{4fl + d}}$$

where, V = velocity of flow in the pipe, m/sec;
      g = acceleration due to gravity, m/sec (9.81 m/sec²);
      d = diameter of the pipe, m;

f = coefficient of friction for the pipe usually assumed to be about 0.01;

H = difference in elevation between the water level at the upstream and downstream ends of the structure, m; and

l = length of pipe in m.

Design of Irrigation Outlet from Bandhi No. 1

An outlet to irrigate the command of Bandhi No. 1 has been proposed at 170 m. The hydraulic details of bandhi at this particular point are as follows:

Top bank level = 318.20 m	Side slope of earthen embankment
Highest water level = 316.20 m	Upstream side =: 4 : 1
Highest flood level = 316.70 m	Downstream side = 4 : 1
Freeboard = 1.5 m	Normal ground level= 313.5 m

Height of the crest of emergency escape = 0.50 m

Base width of the earthen dam at this point = 39.60 m

Static head of water available at this point = 2.70 m

Length of the RCC hume pipe required = 35 m

Diameter of the RCC hume pipe to be used = 0.15 m

Velocity of flow of water could be calculated as follows:

$$V= \sqrt{\frac{gdH}{4fl + d}}; \qquad g= 0.81 \text{ m/sec/sec}; \qquad d= 0.15 \text{ m}$$

H= 2.70 m; l= 35 m; and f= 0.01

Substituting the values and solving the equation, the velocity of flow V can be found as 2.27 m/sec.

Now the discharge capacity of the pipe drop outlet would be calculated as follows:

$$Q= A \times V$$

where, Q= discharge in m³/sec; A = area of cross-section in m²;

V= Velocity of flow in m/sec;

$$A= \frac{\pi d^2}{4} \qquad Q = \frac{\pi d^2}{4} \cdot V$$

Substituting the values and solving the equation, A is 0.0177 m² and Q is 0.0402 m³/sec. Hence the size of the pipe is sufficient to carry the discharge of 0.0401 cumec (40.2 Lps).

Now trapezoidal shaped earthen or cement concrete lined channel has been proposed for construction, in order to irrigate individual farm under the command of this bandhi.

DESIGN OF GRASSED WATERWAYS TO CARRY THE WATER FROM THE EMERGENCY ESCAPE OF WATER HARVESTING BANDHI NO. 1

Peak rate of runoff as calculated in case of Bandhi No. 1 is 22.06 cumec. It is assumed that 50% of the water will have to be disposed off through the proposed grass waterway immediately after rains. Remaining water will pass through this grassed waterway within 24 hours after the rains. It is suggested that the submerged period would be under the tolerance limit of crops grown in the area. The channel should be designed to drain the water from the land at a rate that will ensure the removal of the water before it causes damage to the crop sown in. Hence, peak rate of runoff for which the grassed waterway is to be designed would be 11.03 cumec.

Assume following section:

Bed width of the grassed waterways = 20 m
Full supply depth = 0.30 m
Side slope = 2:1

Assume maximum permissible velocity of flow of water into the grassed waterway = 1.80 m/sec

$$\text{Area of cross-section of the channel} = (21.20 + 20) \times \frac{0.30}{2}$$

$$= 41.2 \times 15 = 6.180 \text{ m}^2$$

Carrying capacity; $Q = A \times V$ $= 6.18 \times 1.80 = 11.1$ cumec

Hence, the section is suitable.

Add freeboard = 15 cm

Adopt section having 20 m bottom width, 0.45 m depth and 2:1 side slopes and sodded with dub grass.

COST ESTIMATION

Total quantity of earthwork involved in the construction of the one metre length of the proposed vegetated waterway has been worked out as 9.4 cm. Considering the cost of the earthwork as Rs.1.10 per cm, the cost of earthwork for the construction of waterway amounts to Rs.10.34 only.

Add 50% more for meeting out the cost of survey, dogbelling and grass turfing.
The total cost works out to be Rs.15.51.
Now add 5% for contingencies and price escalation = 0.78
The total cost per m = 16.50

It is considered that a substantial length of such water from the bandhi to the lower bandhi *nala* flows at the safer velocity. The cost of construction has been taken into account in the estimation of the present bandhi, from which water is to be diverted to the grass waterway. It is also suggested that the artificial grassed waterway may be constructed till it reaches the natural course.

Vegetation Establishment

It is considered that the water in the grassed waterway should be diverted only after the proper establishment of the vegetation. It is advised that the runoff would be diverted into a temporary bye-pass until the vegetation in the waterway is established. A dike may be constructed to keep the water out.

Maintenance

The waterways should be inspected after each heavy rain to avoid major damage. Damages caused in the vegetation cover should be repaired immediately to avoid further soil scouring. Wherever possible, over-grazing of the waterways should be avoided. Gram Panchayat/ESS/beneficiaries should look after the maintenance. Waterway should be protected from cattle trailing and should not be used as roadways. Sod farming may be encouraged.

Command Area Development

A programme of optimum utilisation and better management of the water harvested through bundhies has been proposed. Proper alignment of water courses according to the available ridges and the command under every bundhi has been identified. Most of the channels would be ridge channels, only a few of them would be contour channels.

Out of the total water storage, 154.84 ha-m water will be available for *Kharif* irrigation and 178.41 ha-m for *Rabi* irrigation. Total irrigation intensity will be 142.4 with respect to the cultivation command area. 20% losses in the distribution of system have been considered, which will be minimized after construction of proper irrigation channels. Detailed L-section and X-section map has been prepared to be used for the purpose of construction. In this command, the length of water courses will be 46 m. Total length of water courses proposed in all the commands is 26,860 m. The length/ha works out to be 20.87 m. Field channels will be constructed later on by the cultivators, under the guidance of the executing department.

Land Shaping

About 50% of actual commands of bundhies need land levelling/land shaping—Average cost of levelling works out to be Rs.1000/ha—Construction of water courses for bandhi command.

Nala Bunding

Four *nalas* have been identified and the total number of permanent *nala* bunding structures (drop spillways) proposed are eight and this would directly benefit about 250 ha of land.

A masonry check dam with rectangular water opening has been proposed at 1880 m, which is 1110 m below the location of water harvesting Bundhi No. 1.

Details of Cross-Section of the Nala at 2880 m

Bed level of the *nala* = 305.5 m (R.L.)   Maximum depth of the *nala* = 4.5 m
Right side ground level = 310.01 m (R.L.)   Crest level of the rectangular weir
                                                      = 308.5 m
                                                             (R.L.)
Left side ground level = 309.88 m (R.L.)   Maximum depth of
Maximum width of   water stored   =3.0 m
the nala   = 16 m

Design of Peak Rate of Runoff

Length of flow (L)   = 750 m
Fall in gradient (H)   = 12 m

Constant K $= 3.2\sqrt{\dfrac{750^3}{12}} = 19448$ cumec

Time of concentration $T_c = 0.0078K^{0.77}$
                                   $= 0.0078 \times 19448^{0.77}$
                                   $= 15.65$ min.

Intensity of Rainfall

Rainfall intensity considered for 25 years frequency, for the area-95 mm/hr.
Intensity of rainfall for the duration equal to time of concentration = 175 mm/hr.

Runoff Coefficient

For cultivated land with low infiltration rates, we may adopt coefficient = 0.5
Peak rate of runoff $= \dfrac{0.5 \times 175 \times 20}{360} = 4.86$ cumec

Design of Rectangular Weir Notch

Designed peak rate of runoff $= 0.15 \times Q + Q$

$$= 0.73 + 4.86 = 5.59 \text{ cumec}$$

$$\text{Design } Q = 1.705 \times LH^{3/2}$$

$$\text{Assume } H = 0.75 \text{ m}$$

$$5.59 = 1.705 \times L \times 0.75^{3/2}$$

$$L = \frac{5.59}{1.705 \times 0.65} = 5.05 \text{ m}$$

Add freeboard 0.15 m

Provide the crest with following specifications:

Length 5.0 m;   Height 0.90 m;

Level of crest 308.50 m;   Top level 309.4 m.

Quantity of water impounded

Cross-sectional area of *nala* at 2880 m

for which water will be impounded $= 13.5 \text{ m}^2$

Volume of water $= 0.75 \text{ ha m}$

Design of masonry spillway

Top width of the wall $= 0.45 \text{ m}$

The drop at the structure $= 3 \text{ m}$

Depth (height) of the Weir (D) $= 0.9 \text{ m}$

Headwall

Length of the headwall (L) $= 5.6 \text{ m}$

Height of the headwall (H) $= 3.0 \text{ m}$

Bottom width of headwall $= 2.1 \text{ m}$

Headwall extension

Length $= 1.5(H-0.5D) + 1.2$

$$= 1.5(3.0-0.5 \times 0.9) + 1.2$$

$$= 5.025$$

$$= \text{or } 5.0 \text{ m}$$

Height $= H + D = 3.0 + 0.9 = 3.9 \text{ m}$

Bottom width $= 1.2 \text{ m}$

Side wall and Wing Wall

Height of side wall and wing wall, $T = 1.5D = 1.5 \times 0.9 = 1.35 \text{ m}$

But no less than H/2 $= \dfrac{3}{2} = 1.5 \text{ m}$

Provide side wall 1.5 m

Length of wing wall $= 1.5T = 1.5 \times 1.5 = 2.25 \text{ m}$

Bottom width of wing wall

and side-wall $= 0.70 \text{ m}.$

Apron

Total length $= 0.45 + \dfrac{1.5(H + D) + 2H}{2}$

$$= 0.45 + \frac{1.5(3 + 0.9) + 2 \times 3}{2}$$

$$= 0.45 + 5.925$$
$$= 6.375 \quad \text{Say } 6.4 \text{ m.}$$

Thickness of apron $= 0.40$ m.

Gully Control

The selected sub-watershed comprised of 19 villages, have four main *nalas*. Gullies have been classified as very small gullies, small gullies and medium gullies according to depth, width and side slopes, which they attain due to action of water. According to stages of growth of development of gully, treatments for their reclamation and stabilization have been proposed.

Name of gully	Treatment
Gully No.1	Afforestation + Pasture + earthen check dams
Gully No.2	Afforestation + Pasture + earthen check dams
Gully No.3	Afforestation + Pasture + earthen check dams
Gully No.4	Masonry check dam with rectangular weir crest constructed 30m above the junction point of the gully and Belan river + earthen checkdam at gully head.
Gully No.5	Earthen drop inlet spillway + masonry rectangular weir crest spillway at 30 cm above the river junction point + filling of the depression up to the length gully head. The depth of the gully up to their length is only 0.40 m and width is 0.2–2.8 m only.
Gully No.6	Random rubble stone check dam + earthen check dams in series.
Gully No.7	The area is proposed for fencing under afforestation. Chain of earthen check dams and loose stone check dams.

All areas have been proposed for fencing and restricted from grazing. It will give growth to the permanent vegetation, which in turn will help in gully-stabilization. An area of 130 ha would be covered under the gully control. The main benefits of the scheme are—loss of productive soil would be checked; silting of reservoir lakes, river and *nalas* would also be checked; reduction of peak rate of runoff, which in turn will help in controlling the floods; the water which will be stored in ponds, would thus be used for life saving irrigation and other domestic purposes; the impounded water will also help keeping the water-table height by way of increasing the ground water; and further fragmentation of the fields because of these gullies would be checked. Cost per ha of gully control works out to Rs.269.29.

Dug-out Ponds

Keeping the urgency of water in mind and thinking of various alternatives for the same, the community ponds seem to be the most reasonable proposition. As a result, construction of 14 number of farm ponds have been proposed for construction in the selected sub-watershed. It includes renovation and deepening of existing ponds. Total water conserving will be 43.25 ha-m, out of which 26 ha-m will be used for cattle and domestic purposes and for fishery development. The balance 17.25 ha-m water will be used for providing life saving irrigation to the nearby areas and for the development of community paddy and *bajra* nursery. In general, following objectives have been kept in mind while proposing the scheme for construction of ponds.

Irrigation

Ponds would provide 17.25 ha-m of water for irrigation purposes, to irrigate the nearby areas, use of water for raising the paddy/*bajra* nursery for community purposes will also be made.

— Ponds would supply water to the livestock population of the area.

— *Domestic purposes*—Water will be utilized for taking bath and other domestic purposes by the villagers, which will be available throughout the year.

— *Recreation and production of food*—A specific scheme for raising the fishery have been proposed in this report. Experience show that in the areas where water runoff is collected through the system of contour bunds, ponds have been proved successful for providing protective irrigation.

Average size of ponds is 1 ha and depth is 2.8 m. It is anticipated that on an average, they will store sufficient water to provide irrigation in August. During rainy season from last week of August to 1st week of September, the ponds would again be filled-up. This will help in providing irrigation in the month of November. An irrigation to maize/*jowar*/*bajra* at this time would coincide with flowering stage, which is a critical period for moisture demand. In some years, water for providing one irrigation in *rabi* would also be available. One bathing ghat for each tank has been proposed. It will provide safety to the human beings as well as to the pond. Farmers have to hire pumping sets.

Selection of Site

Estimation of volume of runoff from the selected watershed have been made and it shows that enough quantity of water will be available for storage. The rate of water runoff has been taken as 0.2187 ha-m/ha. After ascertaining the quantities of runoff water, the site of pond is selected to have maximum water holding capacity at cheaper rate. The ponds have been proposed only where the soils are heavy. Clear site availability for discharging the excess amount of water is also a must.

Maintenance

Maintenance of ponds will be done by the beneficiaries.

Large Diameter Open Wells

Sinking of wide open wells, in order to increase the storage capacity under the extent soil and sub-soil conditions of the area, is the only means of exploiting the available ground water for the purpose of irrigation and domestic utilities.

No open wells are presently used for the purpose of irrigation. The area has a thin soil cover and weathered rock underlaid by impervious formation. Wells, if located properly, may be able to yield considerable quantity of water for irrigation.

The area receives about 1000 mm of rainfall and this is the principal source of recharge. The overburden is thin and is generally semi-pervious, consisting of either alluvium or laterite. The sub-surface formations are well-jointed quartzitic sand stones, which act as a fractured shallow aquifer and is the chief repository of groundwater of the area. Groundwater occurs under water-table condition and the depth to water-table varies from 1.86 to 5.4 m. Mean annual fluctuation of waters-table is 3 to 3.5 m and movement of groundwater follows the topographic gradient approximately. The proposed soil and water conservation measures will be able to contribute considerable quantity of water as artificial increment, development of groundwater can therefore, be best attempted only by sinking wider diameter (5–10 m) and with an average depth of 15 m open wells in the area. The yield of water may vary between 2000 gph and 4200 gph. The cost would include well sinking, retaining wall, pumpset and other accessories. During the first stage, 12 open wells have been proposed to be sunk in the pilot area. The present cropping intensity is 127% and it is expected that following the development, the intensity will be 225%. Wells and pumpsets are to be maintained by beneficiaries themselves. One well would be able to provide protective irrigation to about 2 ha of land. Further it would provide drinking water facilities also.

Farm Engineering and Tillage

Due to the constant use of indigenous *desi* plough since long in the area, the earth crust has become hard. It does not allow the water to infiltrate properly to the complete crop root zone, and thus conserving the moisture sub-soil layer. Therefore, it is proposed that a mole plough/sub-soiler should be used once in three years, so that the existing hard pan of the earth crust could be broken. It would increase the infiltration rate and moisture holding capacity of the soil. It would ensure availability of more moisture to the crop root zone. It has also been considered essential that at the time of seed bed preparation, the practice of minimum tillage would be followed. It will allow pulverization on only top soil, so that the moisture is not lost through evaporation.

Farm Machinery and Equipment

As sowing period is limited in the sub-watershed, similarly harvesting and threshing period is also limited, particularly for *Kharif* crops. The high yielding varieties in general have a more critical time schedule for these operations. Threshing becomes exceedingly difficult on too early a harvest. On the other hand, if there is considerable delay, there is much grain loss during cutting and carriage of harvest.

All these facts and limitations observed in the Belan Jharia sub-watershed in particular and in the drought prone area of Mirzapur in general, need considerable improvement in adoption of efficient and improved agricultural machinery and implements. It is essential to remove yield-reducing handicaps, like poor and delayed land preparation and sowing, lack of proper fertilizer placement and lack of quick and protected harvesting and threshing operations. In view of this, the following farm equipments have been proposed to be introduced and extended in the area.

Name of machinery	Purpose
Dozer (95 HP)	Land levelling and subsoiling
Tractor (65 HP)	Land shaping and levelling
Tractor (35 HP)	For agricultural operations, levelling and transport
Plough (Disk)	Ploughing the land
Tractor drawn or bullock-drawn	
Harrowing (spring type or disk)	Harrowing and pulverization of the land after
Tractor drawn or bullock-drawn	ploughing
Cultivators (7–9 types)	For inter-culture operation
Tractors drawn	
Seeder (Tractor-drawn or bullock-drawn	For sowing the seeds at proper place and depth
Patela bullock-drawn	For final preparation of seed beds before sowing
Leveller (tractor-drawn)	For levelling the land and smoothening the surface
Threshers (power-drawn or hand-operated)	For winnowing and threshing the food grains
Trailer (tipping/non-tipping)	For transporting the inputs of the farm and products to the market
Bullock-cart (improved type)	For transporting the inputs of the farm and products to the market

Infrastructural Development

An anticut-cum-bridge has been proposed for construction on river Belan at 5–7 km south of Ghorwal. About 25 km of unmetalled road is proposed for construction in the pilot area, which would provide means of communications for the seasons. Rural electrification programmes have been proposed in 9 villages to be taken up in the first phase. In the remaining villages, the electrification could be done later on.

Agronomic Measures

Among the soil and water conservation measures proposed for the conservation of natural resources and their rational utilisation, agronomic measures come next to engineering measures discussed earlier. Under this category falls rational utilisation of natural resources in terms of production. Agronomic measures as such would include the types of crops and crop varieties to be grown and the farming practices to be followed. Talking of conservation measures, contour farming, i.e. carrying out all cultural and management practices along the contours and eventually increasing the yield and reducing erosion strip cropping, i.e. planting a strip of erosion resisting crop and mixed or relay cropping to avoid soil for being left bare, particularly during the rains has generally been recommended. In other words, it can be said that the ecology based crop production programme is essential for avoiding frequent crop failures in such areas.

Application of new technology now available in the field of dryland farming, has been considered, while suggesting the agronomical practices to be followed in the project area, on the basis of land capability. The results obtained on the recommendations made by the All India Co-ordinated Research Project on Dryland Agriculture, Varanasi and All-India Co-ordinated Dryland Farming pilot development project, at Robertsganj have been considered for adoption in the project area. The research project at Varanasi feeds the pilot development project at Robertsganj. The technology so recommended is tested on the farmers fields in the project area adjacent to the sub-watershed. It is expected that the extension effect with regard to adoption of new technology in dryland farming would easily spread in the area. The following are the recommendations made on crops and crop planning as a result of the experiments conducted at Varanasi and applied in the fields in the pilot development project area.

Crops and varieties		Seed rate (kg/ha)	Nutrients (kg/ha)
Rice —	Saket-3	100	60:30:20
	Ratna		
	Cauvery		
Bajra —	HB 1	8	60:30:20
	HB 3		
Maize —	Ganga-2	15	50:30:20
	Ganga-5		
Til —	T-4	5	40:30:30
	T-12		
	T-13		
Urd —	T9	15	15:30:20

TECHNOLOGY IN DRYLAND FARMING

Kharif

20 kg/ha of 10% BHC should be used at the time of land preparation for termite control. Direct line sowing of rice and *urd* 30 cm apart, *bajra* and *til* 45 cm apart and

maize 60 cm apart in recommended. 2/3N, all P_2O_5 and K_2O to be placed in furrow 10 cm deep and remaining 1/3N to be top-dressed between 45 and 50 days after sowing, depending upon the moisture condition of the soil. Proper weed control and plant protection measures should be taken. First 30 days of the crop should be weed-free. This can be achieved by hand or mechanical weeding, or by applying 5.0 l/ha (commercial) Lasso or Machate as pre-emergence spray followed by 2.5 l/ha of Stam F 34 as post-emergence.

Rabi

Soon after the harvest of *Kharif* crops, land preparation for *rabi* should begin without loosing much time and soil moisture. BHC as recommended for *Kharif* should be used. Barley (varieties Ratna, DL3, K124 and K112) at the rate of 100 kg/ha, 30 cm apart, safflower (local, HU(s) N62-8, Hungund-2 at 15 kg/ha, at 45 cm, gram T1,T3,BG2 and C130) at 80 kg/ha, 30 cm apart, linseed (Mukta, Neelam and T397) at 15 kg/ha, 30 cm apart and mustard (T59) at 5 kg/ha, 45 cm apart may be sown. Sowing should be done in lines, preferably placing the seeds in moist layer with a drill. The entire dose of fertilizers should be placed at the time of sowing 2–3 cm deeper than the seed. In case of barley, 60:30:20, gram 15:30:15, linseed, mustard and safflower 40:30:20 kg/ha of N, P_2O_5 and K_2O are recommended.

Crop Rotations Recommended

Upland paddy-gram/*barley*/*sarson*/*alsi*; bajra-chana/barley/alsi sarson; urd/alsi/sarson/barleytil/gram/alsi/barley.

Early varieties of paddy, viz. Ratna and Cauveri should be drilled in the furrows in the last week of June or 1st week of July, with the onset of the monsoon. Seeds and the fertilizers should be put in the alternative furrow at the distance of 15 cm, keeping the row-to-row distance of 30 cm. Drilling of seeds can be followed in respect of other *Rabi* and *Kharif* crops also. All the fertilizers should be placed 10 cm below from the ground and 3 cm below the seeds in the form of 'basal dressing'. 20 to 25 kg/ha of BHC 10% dust should be applied to check the termite effect.

Cropping Pattern (Existing)

Proposed for irrigated area (through different sources), for rainfed areas (treated with different soil conservation measures).

Integrated Farming

Approximately 1311 ha of land are supposed to be brought under irrigation through various sources discussed elsewhere in the report.

Depending on the land capability, the following cropping patterns can be followed in the area with advantage:

— Early paddy-wheat/gram
— Hybrid *Bajra*-wheat/barley
— Maize-potato/wheat.

FORESTRY MEASURES

Afforestation

Scope

Mirzapur zone lies in tropical dry deciduous forest zone, which ranges from southern Rajasthan to Bihar. The area on the southern side of Gurwal, Karaundia, Barouli, Banda, Damkhari and Khirihata is surrounded by Vindhyan hills. These hills were, in the past, covered with dense forests. Now due to deforestation and over-exploitation, the density of plants has considerably gone down. The importance of forests is far more in such areas from *ecological-balance* point of view. They are a powerful media for moderating the climate and mitigating its extremes. They reduce soil erosion, sediment production and stream runoff by improving the soil–water relation in the sands. The existing forest area of the captioned pilot project is so depleted, that supply of firewood, timber, minor forest produces, etc., is extremely limited and it is very essential to augment the same.

Techniques
It is proposed that identified area should be brought under barbed wire/live hedges fencing. Programme of soil conservation like gully plugging contour trenching would be carried out in the identified area for plantation purposes. Digging of trenches, viz., double trench, trench and mound, wurly type trench or saucer-type trench would be done (Fig. 9.1). The preference of trench would depend upon the area of operation and the available soil depth. Planting at a density of 170–200 seedlings/ha would be done. Maintenance of these plants would be done till these are well-established. Species recommended for plantation are Shisham, Sal, Semul, Babool, Kher, Bargad, Neem, etc. The following combinations may also be used for the purpose:

— *Acacia nilotica* + *Cenchrus ciliaris*—In case of trees, plant-to-plant distance may be kept as 10 m and row-to-row distance as 5 cm. The rotation period is 10 years.

— *Acacia nilotica* + *Crysopogon fulvus*

— *Eucalyptus* hybrid + *Azadirachta indica*—Plantation may be raised in staggered contour trenches of 4 m × 0.5 m × 0.5 m size spaced at about 10 m.

Cost
The average cost of afforestation work is estimated at Rs.1,000 per ha. The cost includes items like protection of area, planting of seedlings and their maintenance.

Roadside Plantation
About 25 km road would be constructed in the pilot area. It is proposed that roadside plantation would be carried out. It will provide shelter to the travellers as well as would provide fruits and timber and firewood needs of the population of some extent. It is proposed that this programme would be carried out by the village panchayat and villagers themselves on voluntary basis. They should be responsible for the maintenance of trees and their utilisation.

Spacing
The plantation should be done at 0.51–0.64 m from the centre line of the row. Tree-to-tree distance may be kept at 0.13–0.64 m according to the species. In the case of *Eucalyptus*, plant-to-plant distance may be kept as 1.1–1.5 m, whereas in the case of mango, plant-to-plant distance may be kept as 6.1–7.6 m. Recommended species of mahua (*Madhuca latifolia*), mango, shisham, eucalyptus, ornamental trees like gulmohar, kanher and ashok, etc.

Plantation on Ponds
Contour bunding in about 286.25 km length would be carried out. It has been found useful to plant trees like *Eucalyptus* along the bund. It will not come in the way of crop production, since it is a tall tree and does not give much shade. It would

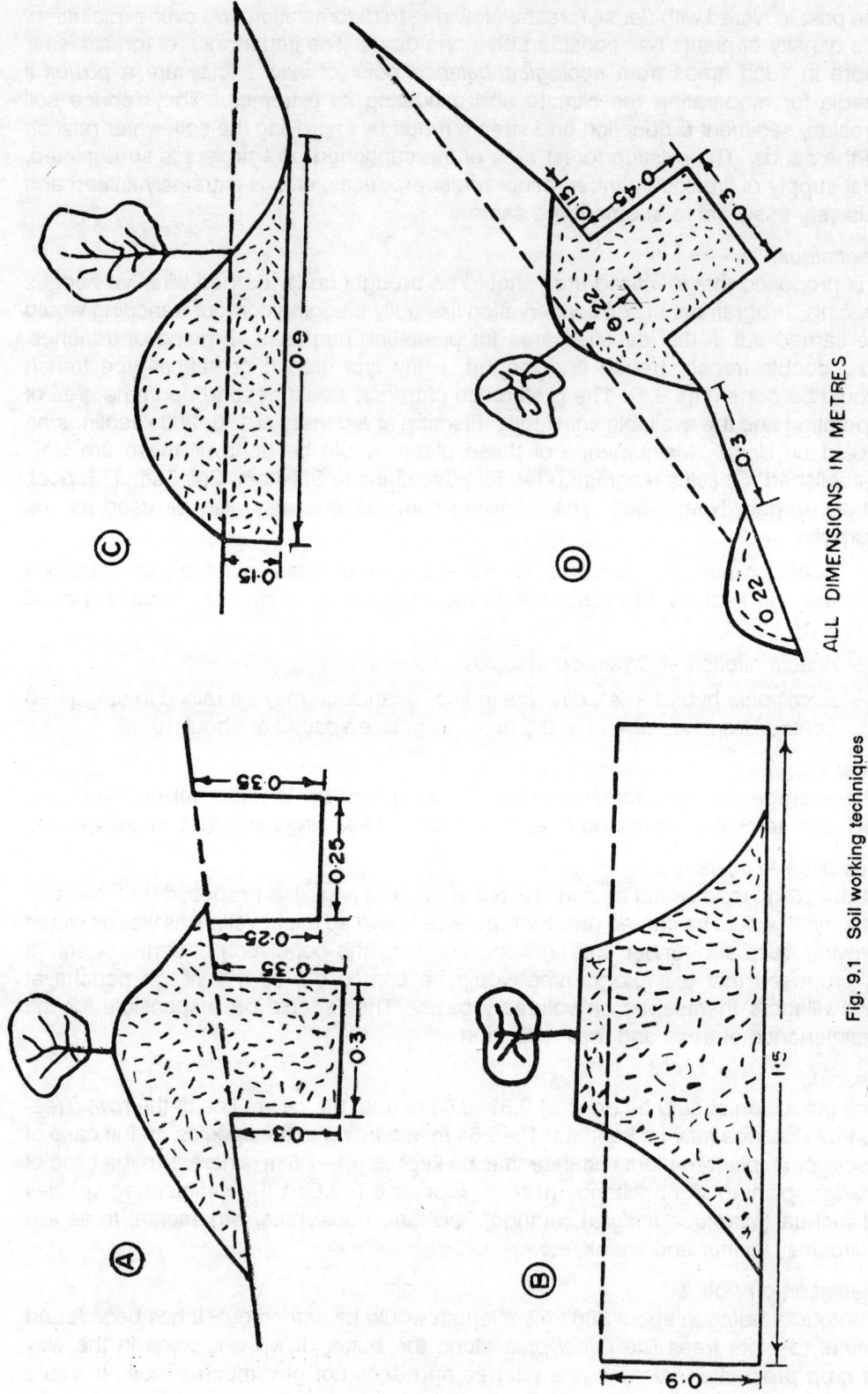

ALL DIMENSIONS IN METRES

Fig. 9.1 Soil working techniques
(A) Double trench (B) Trench and mound (C) Wurli and (D) Saucer type

provide firewood. Cowdung, which at present, is used as fuel would be utilised as farmyard manure. One tree will provide on an average, 1 to 2 q firewood once in five years. Another advantage with this tree is that, after cutting, copping growth is ready within a period of further five years. Castor is also recommended in suitable cases.

Mixed and Farm Forestry

In drought prone areas, emphasis should also be laid on increasing area under permanent vegetation. Farm forestry is more an ecological necessity. Production of foodgrains and commercial crops is a man controlled agro-ecosystem covering major land area. This has reduced the diversity of ecosystem resulting in elimination of natural enemies of insects and other pests and creation of ideal conditions for their multiplication. This can be achieved by creating blocks of tree population. Apart from creating a diverse ecosystem, tree plantation programme would help in checking soil erosion. A few species for fruit plantations are *sitafal, bel, ber, chiraunji,* etc. In between trees, various grasses could be raised.

Pasture Development

Pastures as such, do not exist in the pilot area. The common and wastelands in the village are used as grazing grounds. Such lands are very poor and do not make any significant contribution to fodder resources. It is, therefore, desirable to develop such lands by regenerating them and bringing them under regular management. No work so far has been done in this direction.

It is proposed that in the areas where soil depth is less and soil erosion is prominent, programme of pasture development would be carried out. Apart from providing protection to the eroding lands, a good grass cover would supplement the fodder need of a sizeable cattle improvement programme, which would be carried out in the area later on. The grasslands would generally be used for maintenance of animals other than cross-bred ones, who are generally required to be stall-fed.

Village commonlands, which are available for raising the grass, should be developed through panchayats. Apart from this, 162 ha would be developed as pastureland in the pilot area.

First of all, the area would be fenced with barbed wire fencing on wooden poles and by digging a trench 0.5 m deep and 1 m wide all round the area, to ensure proper safety against stray cattle and illicit grazing. Then the area will be cleared off, bushes and weeds. It will be ploughed with tractor or bullock drawn implement, in order to provide a proper seedbed and have a desirable tilth. A plank will be run over the area before the operation of seeding is carried out. The seed rate of grassing is 5 to 8 kg/ha. The seed will be sown with the break of monsoon and the sowing will be completed by the end of July. The grass seeds will be sown, broadcast after mixing the seed with most earth. Two to three weedings would be done to remove the weeds and other grasses. It is also desirable that a basal dose of 125 kg Super phosphate and 75 kg calcium nitrate/ha would be applied. Deferred grazing by removing stock, when the more desirable species are flowering and seeding, can help greatly to improve the composition and increase the density of native pastures. Dehydration of forest grasses would be carried out to support the cattle and to increase the palatibility. Cutting of grasses after the shedding of natural seeds in the ground would also be done. This would help in natural multiplication of wood grasses. Apart from this, it is suggested that trees like babool, neem, seesam, etc., would be grown, which will serve the purpose of shade to the cattle. It is proposed that 20–30 trees and shrubs/ha would be planted in the pastureland. Recommended varieties of grasses are Anjan grass (*Cenchrus ciliaris*), Churant grass (*Hetropogon contortus*), Dub grass (*Cynodon dactylon*). Recommended varieties of trees and shrubs are babul and ber.

Cost

The costs including digging of trench around the pilot live hedge fence/barbed wire fence on wooden poles, survey and preparation of gardoney, cost of grass seeds planting would be taken as Rs.1000 per ha. It includes the cost of maintenance for subsequent years.

SPECIAL SCHEMES

Scheme for Lac Development

The object of the Scheme would be to introduce and expand the extent of improved method of lac cultivation and bring all suitable host trees under cultivation for increased productivity of the sticklac and thereby more income to the cultivators, and arrange extension support to the cultivators and supply of brood lac to the cultivators, timely and at competitive cost.

Lac cultivation is in vogue in Dudhi Tehsil of Mirzapur district, so the area of operation of the scheme would be different blocks of Dudhi Tehsil, viz. Muirpur, Dudhi and Babhani.

Indian Lac Research Institute, Namkum, Ranchi has given recommendations of improved method of lac cultivation, which consists of technique of an appropriate time and mode of pruning, inoculation, phoonky removal and also effective control of the two major enemy insects of lac.

SCHEME FOR INTEGRATED TASAR SILK DEVELOPMENT

According to a report, 6 lakh people depend for their livelihood on wild sericulture by way of cocoon production, reeling, spinning, weaving, dyeing and manufacturing of finished silk commodities. India is the only country in the world, where all the four varieties of natural silk, viz. mulberry, tasar, eri and muga are available. Out of all the three wild silks, only tasar is exported. While in mulberry, India occupies first position in the world, in tasar, she enjoys second position next only to China, accounting for nearly 10% of the total silk output.

Tasar silk cocoon rearing and tasar silk weaving were one of the important industries of the Mirzapur district. The host trees namely Anjan (*Terminalia arjuna*) and Asan (*Terminalia tomentosa*) were available in Dudhi and Sukrut forest area and also in areas of Chandraprabha in district Varanasi. The industry has declined due to the shortage of host trees and thus disruption in supply of cocoon, lack of organisation and support to the poor cocoon rearers and some difficulties felt in the marketing of tasar at local level, in view of the competitive synthetic silk. This could be achieved under the integrated project, taking care of plantation of suitable forest trees in the area supporting the tasar cocoon rearers and linking the end product with organised markets.

The area of operation of the scheme would be the miscellaneous plantation area of the forest department, where regular plantation of arjan and asan will be taken up under DPAP. The reeling and weaving will be done in Ahraura town, located below the Sukrut area to start with.

Plantation of trees to the extent of 25% of the total population can be undertaken. About 250 trees could be planted/ha. On an average, one adivasi family can maintain

20 to 30 trees. It is estimated that one loom would consume about 72,000 cocoons per year of 300 working days and one loom would produce 3 m of cloth everyday, on an average and thus 900 m/year of 300 days. Thus one family of about 5 persons in all would be employed to produce 900 m of tasar silk cloth.

The scheme is employment-oriented and is worked out for self-employment of tasar cocoon rearers and tasar silk weavers families.

SCHEME FOR PISCICULTURE

Utilization of harnessed water received through ponds are being suggested for fisheries development, with a view to generating more gainful employment opportunities for the rural masses.

These tanks belong to Gram Sabhas of the respective villages and are presently utilised for drinking water and other domestic purposes. Most of these tanks have sufficiently high embankment and retain a good depth of water, which is generally clean without the occurrence of thick acquatic weeds. With the development of soil and water conservation measures, in the area more water can be stored in the tanks.

Total area of the 9 tanks = 7.2 ha   Average area of one tank = 0.8 ha.

It is proposed that a Fish Farmers' Co-operative Society should be organised with its headquarter at Ghorawal, drawing 2–3 members from each of the above villages, where the tanks are located. The society will take the above tanks on lease from the respective Gram Sabhas on long-term basis and its members will start pisciculture in these tanks.

Table 9.4 *Proposed land utilization in the watershed (pilot area)*

Description	Area, ha
Total geographical area of 19 villages	4615.4
Total geographical area in the selected pilot area	3979.8
Inhabitated area	20.83
Area under ponds and khantis	9.49
Area under hills	62.59
Area under *nala* and river	49.70
Area proposed for afforestation	917.0
Area proposed for pasture development	162.0
Area proposed for crop cultivation	2758.19
(Land capability class II = 11.55.81 ha;	
Land capability class III = 1361.23 ha; and	
Land capability class IV = 241.15 ha)	

To start with, mixed culture of Indian major crops, rahu, catla and mrigal will be initiated. Depending on the availability of seeds, composite culture with exotic carps and Indian major carps may also be undertaken in due course. There is no local market for fish in the area, the society has to arrange for sending fish to Calcutta market by arrangement with some private agents or through Central Fishing Corporation. Therefore, sufficient margin on price has to be kept for marketing.

At the rate of 3000 kg of fish per tank, production from 9 tanks is expected to be 27 tonnes/annum. If one tank is assigned to two members for cultivation, 18 families will be directly benefited from the scheme, earning more than about Rs.2000 per member per year for the first five years and double the amount in subsequent years, after the complete repayment of the loan instalment.

Appendix A1   Hydrology Determination peak runoff rates chart for determining for peak rates of runoff based on 50 years frequency and rainfall factor 1.0

Drainage area in ha	Watershed characteristics

Drainage area in ha	25	30	35	40	45	50	55	60	65	70	75	80
1.6188	0.1416	0.1982	0.2032	0.3115	0.3682	0.3965	0.4248	0.5098	0.5947	0.6797	0.7930	0.9629
2.4232	0.1699	0.2266	0.3115	0.3965	0.4248	0.5098	0.6514	0.7080	0.8496	0.9629	1.1328	1.3594
3.2376	0.1982	0.2832	0.3682	0.4814	0.5098	0.6797	0.7930	0.9629	1.1328	1.2744	1.4726	1.7558
4.0470	0.2266	0.3115	0.4248	0.5381	0.6797	0.8213	0.9912	1.2178	1.4160	1.6426	1.8691	2.1240
4.8565	0.2549	0.3398	0.4814	0.6230	0.7930	0.9629	1.1611	1.4160	1.6709	1.9258	2.2090	2.4922
5.6658	0.2832	0.3965	0.5381	0.7080	0.9062	1.1045	1.3310	1.6142	1.9258	2.2090	2.5488	2.8603
6.4752	0.3115	0.4248	0.5947	0.7930	1.0195	1.2461	1.5010	1.8125	2.1523	2.4638	2.8320	2.2285
7.2846	0.3398	0.4814	0.6797	0.8779	1.1328	1.3877	1.6709	2.0107	2.3789	2.7187	3.1152	2.5683
8.0940	0.3882	0.5381	0.7363	0.9346	1.2178	1.5010	1.8125	2.1806	2.6054	2.9736	3.3984	3.9082
10.1175	0.4531	0.6230	0.8779	1.1328	1.4726	1.8125	2.2090	2.6338	3.1152	3.6243	4.1347	4.7578
12.1410	0.5098	0.7080	0.0195	1.3310	1.6992	2.1240	2.5771	3.0869	3.6250	4.2197	4.8710	5.6074
14.1645	0.5664	0.7930	1.1611	1.5010	1.9258	2.4355	2.9453	3.5117	4.1347	4.8144	5.5507	6.4570
16.1880	0.6230	0.8779	1.2744	1.6709	2.1523	2.7470	3.3134	3.9365	4.6445	5.3808	6.2587	7.2782
18.2115	0.6797	0.9629	1.3877	1.8408	2.3789	3.0302	3.6816	4.3613	5.1542	5.9472	6.9384	8.1562
20.2350	0.7363	0.0478	1.5010	2.0107	2.6054	3.3134	4.0214	4.7578	5.6640	6.5136	7.5614	8.9208
24.282	0.8213	1.2178	1.7558	2.3222	3.0586	3.8515	4.6728	5.5790	6.6269	7.6464	8.8925	10.422
28.329	0.9062	1.3877	1.9824	2.6338	3.4834	4.3896	5.3242	6.4003	7.5898	8.7792	10.195	12.035
32.376	1.0195	1.5293	2.2020	2.9453	3.8798	4.8994	5.9755	7.2216	8.7509	9.9120	11.498	13.537
36.423	1.1328	1.6709	2.4072	3.2285	4.2763	5.4658	6.5986	7.9579	9.4589	11.017	12.687	15.010
40.470	1.2178	1.8125	2.6054	3.5117	4.6728	5.9472	7.2216	8.6942	10.337	12.348	13.877	16.709
48.564	1.3877	2.0957	3.0302	4.0781	5.4374	6.9667	8.4960	10.166	12.0936	14.160	16.256	19.541
56.658	1.5576	2.3789	3.4267	4.6445	6.1738	7.9579	9.7704	11.611	13.792	16.142	18.635	22.373
64.752	1.7275	2.6621	4.6445	5.1826	6.8818	8.9208	11.0448	13.027	15.491	18.125	20.957	25.205
72.846	1.8974	2.9170	4.1630	5.7206	7.5898	9.8837	12.1776	14.443	17.190	20.107	23.222	28.037
80.940	2.0674	3.1435	4.5312	6.2304	8.2694	10.8466	13.3104	15.859	18.889	22.090	25.488	30.586
89.034	2.2090	3.3701	4.8994	6.7118	8.9491	11.7811	14.4432	17.275	20.504	23.923	27.754	33.134
97.128	2.3506	3.5966	5.2675	7.1933	9.6288	12.7157	15.5760	18.691	22.118	25.771	30.019	35.683
105.222	2.4922	3.8232	5.6357	7.6747	10.2802	13.6219	16.7088	19.937	23.732	27.470	32.115	38.232
113.316	2.6338	4.0498	5.9755	8.1562	10.9315	14.5282	17.8416	21.183	25.318	29.170	34.182	40.781
121.410	2.7754	4.2763	6.3154	8.6376	11.5829	15.4344	18.9744	22.429	26.904	30.863	36.250	43.330
129.504	2.9170	4.5029	6.6552	9.1190	12.2342	16.0574	19.9656	23.676	28.320	32.568	38.232	45.878
137.598	3.0586	4.7294	6.9950	9.6005	12.8856	17.1053	20.9568	24.922	29.736	34.267	40.214	48.427
145.692	3.2002	4.9277	7.3349	10.0819	13.5370	17.9266	21.9480	26.168	31.152	35.966	42.197	50.976
153.786	3.3418	5.1542	7.6464	10.5634	14.1883	18.7478	22.9392	27.385	32.568	37.666	44.179	53.525
161.800	3.4834	5.3808	7.9579	11.0448	14.8114	19.5691	23.9304	28.603	33.984	39.365	46.162	56.074

Appendix A1 *(Cont'd...)*

| | | | | | | Watershed characteristics | | | | | | |
Drainage area in ha	25	30	35	40	45	50	55	60	65	70	75	80
169.974	3.6250	5.5790	8.2694	11.4696	15.4061	20.3904	24.9216	29.679	35.343	41.007	47.974	58.452
178.068	3.7666	5.7773	8.5810	11.8944	16.0008	21.1834	25.9128	30.756	36.703	42.650	49.787	60.831
186.162	3.8798	5.9795	8.8925	12.3192	16.5955	21.9763	26.9040	31.832	38.062	44.292	51.599	63.210
194.256	3.9930	6.1738	9.2040	12.744	17.190	22.741	27.895	32.908	39.421	45.935	53.412	65.589
202.350	4.1064	6.3720	9.4872	13.169	17.785	23.506	28.886	33.984	40.781	47.578	55.224	67.968
210.444	4.2197	6.5702	9.7704	13.594	18.351	24.497	29.736	35.060	42.084	49.107	56.923	70.120
218.538	4.3330	6.7685	10.054	14.018	18.918	24.978	29.170	36.136	43.386	50.636	58.622	72.723
226.632	4.4462	6.9384	10.337	14.443	19.484	25.715	31.718	37.212	44.689	52.165	60.322	74.425
234.726	4.5595	7.0800	10.620	14.868	20.051	26.451	32.285	38.289	45.992	53.695	62.021	76.577
242.820	4.6728	7.2216	10.903	15.293	20.617	27.187	33.134	39.365	47.294	55.224	63.720	78.730
263.055	4.9977	7.6464	11.555	16.199	21.891	28.886	35.117	41.914	50.410	58.764	67.968	84.252
283.290	5.1826	8.0712	12.206	17.134	23.166	30.526	37.241	44.462	53.525	62.304	72.216	89.491
303.525	5.4091	8.4960	12.857	18.040	24.440	32.285	39.223	47.011	56.640	65.844	76.464	94.730
323.760	5.6640	8.9208	13.509	18.974	25.743	33.984	41.347	49.560	59.755	69.384	80.712	99.970
343.995	5.9189	9.3456	14.160	19.881	27.017	35.683	43.330	52.109	62.870	72.924	84.960	105.21
364.230	6.1737	9.7704	14.811	20.815	28.320	37.382	45.454	54.658	65.986	76.464	89.208	110.45
384.465	6.4285	10.195	15.463	21.721	29.594	39.082	47.436	57.206	69.101	80.004	93.456	115.687
404.700	6.6552	10.620	16.142	22.656	30.869	40.781	49.560	59.472	72.216	83.544	97.704	120.926
445.170	7.0800	11.328	17.275	24.214	33.134	43.754	53.242	64.003	77.597	90.058	104.784	129.564
485.640	7.5048	12.036	18.408	25.771	35.400	46.728	56.923	68.534	82.978	96.571	111.864	138.202
526.110	7.9296	12.744	19.541	27.329	37.666	49.702	60.605	73.066	88.358	103.085	118.944	146.839
566.580	8.3544	13.452	20.674	28.886	39.931	52.675	64.286	77.597	93.739	109.598	126.024	155.477
607.050	8.7792	14.160	21.806	30.464	42.197	52.817	67.968	82.128	99.120	116.112	133.104	164.256
647.520	9.2040	14.868	22.939	31.860	44.179	58.339	71.366	86.093	103.651	121.776	140.184	172.752
687.980	9.6288	15.576	24.072	33.276	46.162	61.171	74.765	90.058	108.182	127.44	147.264	
728.460	10.054	16.284	25.205	34.692	48.144	63.862	78.163	94.022	112.714	133.104	154.344	
768.930	10.478	16.992	26.338	36.108	50.126	66.694	81.562	97.987	117.245	138.768	161.424	
809.400	10.903	17.700	27.470	37.524	52.109	69.384	84.960	101.952	121.776	144.432	168.504	

Conversion Factors—Metric—English

Length

1 metre	= 3.2808 ft
1 metre	= 39.37 inches
1 centimetre	= 0.3937 inches
1 kilometre	= 0.6214 miles

Volume

1 cubic metre	= 35.314 ft
1 cubic metre	= 1.308 cu yds
1 cubic metre	= 1000 litres
1 cubic centimetre	= 0.061 cubic inch

Area

1 sq metre	= 10.764 sq ft
1 sq cm	= 0.155 sq inches
1 sq km	= 0.3861 sq miles
1 hectare	= 10,000 sq m
1 hectare	= 1,07,640 sq ft
1 hectare	= 2.471 acres

Rates of flow

1 cubic metre per second	= 35.314 cusec
1 cubic metre per hour	= 0.278 litres sec
1 cubic metre per hour	= 4.403 US gallons/min
1 cubic metre per hour	= 3.668 Imp. gallons/min
1 litre/second	= 0.0353 cubic ft/sec
1 litre/second	= 3.6 cubic metre/hour

English—Metric

Length

1 ft	= 0.3048 metre
1 inch	= 2.54 centimetre
1 mile	= 5280 ft
1 mile	= 1.609 km

Area

1 sq ft	= 0.0929 sq m
1 sq inch	= 6.452 sq cm
1 acre	= 43560 sq ft
1 acre	= 0.4047
1 sq mile	= 640 acres
1 sq mile	= 258.99 ha
1 sq mile	= 2.59 sq km

Volume

1 cu ft	= 0.0283 cu m
1 cu ft	= 28.32 litres
1 cu ft	= 6.25 Imp.gal.
1 cu ft	= 7.48 US gal.

1 cu. yard	= 0.7645 cu m
1 US gal.	= 3.7854 litre
1 Imp.gal	= 1.201 US gal
1 Imp. gal	= 4.5436 litre
1 acre-ft	= 43560
1 acre-ft	= 1233.5 cm m
1 acre-inch	= 3630 cu ft
1 acre-inch	= 102.8 cu m

Rates of flow

1 cu ft/sec	= 0.0283 cubic = metre/sec
1 cu ft/sec	= 28.32 lit/sec
1 cu ft/sec	= 448.8 US gal per min
1 cu ft/sec	= 373.8 Imp. gal/min
1 cu ft/sec	= 1 acre inch/hour
1 cu ft/sec	= 2 acre ft/day
1 US gal/min	= 0.06309 lit/sec
1 Imp. gal/min	= 0.07573 lit/sec

References

Anonymous, (1953) *Engineering Hand Book Drop Spillways*, Section II, Soil Conservation Service, USDA, Washington DC.

Anonymous, (1960) *Design of small dams*, US Deptt. of Interior, Bureau of Reclamation.

Anonymous, (1961) *National Engineering Hand Book*. Irrigation Section 15 (Chapter 12), Land Levelling, Soil Conservation Service, USDA, Washington DC.

Anonymous, (1965) *Engineering Hand Book*, Chute Spillways, Section 14, Soil Conservation Service, USDA, Washington DC.

Anonymous, (1972) *Ravine Reclamation Programme*, Report of the Working Group on Ravine Reclamation, Govt. of India, Ministry of Home Affairs, New Delhi.

Anonymous, (1975) *USDA Engineering Field Manual for Conservation Practices*. Soil Conservation Service, Washington DC.

Anonymous, (1976) *Report of the National Commission on Agriculture*, Part V, Chapters 17 and 18, Ministry of Agril. & Irrigation, New Delhi.

Anonymous, (1977) *Drought Prone Area Programme*, Mirzapur, U.P. A Project Report on Watershed Planning and Management, Agricultural Finance Corp. Ltd.

Anonymous, (1978) *Soil Conservation Statistics*, Bulletin Progress of Soil Programme (VII Edition), Deptt. of Agril., Ministry of Agril. & Irrigation, Govt. of India.

Anonymous, (1979) *Proceedings of the Regional Workshop on Watershed Management*, organised by the Department of Agri., Govt. of Karnataka, Bangalore.

Anonymous, (1980 a) *25 years Research on Soil and Water Conservation in semi-arid Deep Black Soils*, CSWCRTI, Research Centre, Bellary.

Anonymous, (1980 b) *Brochure*, Central Soil and Water Conservation Research & Training Institute and its Research Centre at Kota, Chandigarh, Vasad & Ootacamund.

Anonymous, (1980 c) *Operation Watershed Management*, Proc. of the National Seminar on Watershed Management—Rainfed Farming and Integrated Himalayan Development, held at New Delhi from January 28 to Feb. 02, Ministry of Agriculture, Govt. of India, New Delhi.

Anonymous, (1980 d) *Notes, News and Views*, by Das, D. C. Indian Journal of Soil Conservation, Indian Association of Soil & Water Conservationists, Vol. 8(1): 67–73.

Anonymous, (1982) *25 years Research on Soil and Water Conservation in Southern Hilly High Rainfall Regions*, CSWCRTI, Research Centre, Ootacamund.

Anonymous, (1984) *Draft Report of the Committee of Experts for preparation of an outline of India's Landuse Policy, Soil & Water Conservation Division*, New Delhi.

Anonymous, (1985) *The Water Management Manual*, Technical Series No. 3(Revised), Govt. of India, Ministry of Water Resources, Water Management Division, New Delhi.

Anonymous, (1988) *Report of the Committee of Experts on Draft outline of National Landuse Policy*, National Landuse & Conservation Board, Deptt. of Agril. & Coop., Ministry of Agriculture, New Delhi.

Anonymous, (1989) *Report of the Working Group* (Chairman—Dr. J. S. Kanwar) *on Soil & Water Cons. including Watershed Management for formulation of 8th Five*

Plan, Deptt. of Agril. & Coop., Ministry of Agriculture, New Delhi.

Bhumla, D. R., (1983) *Small Reservoirs*. A programme for improving rainfed agriculture special lecture to the officer trainees in Soil Conservation, CSWCRTI, Dehradun.

Bowers, H. D., (1950) *Erosion control on California State Highways*, Deptt. of Public Works, Div. of Highways.

Chinnamani, S., Venkataramanan, C. and Tejwani, K. G., (1980) *Landslides and landslips in Peninsular India*, Bull. No. 4, Central Soil & Water Conservation Research & Training Institute, Dehradun.

Das, D. C., (1977) *Soil Conservation Practices and erosion control in India—A case study—Soils Bulletin* FAO of U. N., Rome 33:11.

Das, D. C., (1980) *Surface water development in Arid Zone/Lands*. Paper presented at FAO/DAINDA Training Course on Sand Dune Stabilization, Shelterbelt and Deforestation in the dry Zone, CAZRI, Jodhpur.

Das, D. C., (1981) *Influence of current landuse policies on some watershed problems*. Paper presented at GOI—UNESCO sponsored National Workshop on Watershed Management, Dehradun, April 22–24, 1981.

Das, D. C., (1985) *Problem of Soil erosion and land degradation in India*. National Seminar on Soil Conservation and Watershed Management, September, 17–18, New Delhi, 1–24.

Deb, A. K., Joshi, S. S. and Gholap, S. D. (1969), *Landslides—causes and remedial measures*. Paper presented at National Seminar, Hill Roads Slope Stabilization, Border Roads Organisation, New Delhi.

Deb Roy, R., Patil, B. D. and Pathak, P. S., (1980) *Development of Grassland in India with Special Reference to Silvi-pastoral Research and Development*. Second Indian Forestry Conference, Forest Research Institute & Colleges, Dehradun.

Dhruva Narayana, V. V., Tejwani, K. G. and Satyanarayana, T., (1962) *Ravine reclamation methods in vogue in Gujarat and their possible improvement* J. Soil Water Conservation India 10(3 & 4): 41–52.

Dhruva Narayana, V. V., and Ram Babu, (1983) *Estimation of soil erosion in India* J. of Irrigation and Drainage Engineering, 109 (4):419–434.

Dhruva Narayana, V. V., Singh, R. P., Bhardwaj. S. P., Sharma, N., Sikka, A. K., Vittal, K. P. R. and Das, S. K., (1987) *Watershed Management for Drought mitigation*, Indian Council of Agril. Research, New Delhi.

Dixit, D. V., (1980) *Soil and Water Conservation on Agricultural lands in Maharashtra*, National Symposium on 'Soil Conservation and Water Management in 1980's held at CSWRTI, Dehradun.

Gadkary, D. A., (1954) *Soil Conservation (Engineering Aspect)* in Bombay, J. of Soil and Water Conservation in India, Vol. 2(3):127–146.

Gadkary, D. A., (1966) *A Manual on Soil Conservation*. Department of Agriculture, Poona, Government of Bombay.

Gil, N., (1979) *Watershed Development with Special reference to Soil & Water Conservation* . FAO Soil Bull. No. 44, FAO of the United Nations, Rome, 1979.

Goldman, S. J., Jackson, K. and Bursztynsky, P. E., Taras, A., (1986) *Erosion and sediment control handbook*. McGraw-Hill Book Company, U. S. A.

Gupta, R. K., (1979) *Grassland Development and Management*. Lecture Note, Second Short Course on Watershed Management for Project Managers (5–14th June,), CSWCRTI, Dehradun.

Gupta, S. K., Tejwani, K. G., Mathur, H. N. and Singh, L. B., (1969) *Stabilization of cut and fill slopes of mountain roads*, National Seminar, Hill Road Slope Stabilization, New Delhi.

Gupta, S. K., Tejwani, K. G., Mathur, H. N. and Srivastava, M. N., (1970) *Land resource regions and areas of India.* J. Indian Soc. Soil Sci. 18(2):187–198.

Gurmel Singh, Joshi, B. P. and Singh, P. N., (1981) *Water Management for High Rainfall and Seasonally Dry Regions (in North-Western Hilly Regions)*, Bull. No. R-9/D-7, CSWCRTI, Dehradun.

Gurmel Singh, K. D., Koranne, L. S. Bhushan, Chandra, S. and Ghosh, S., (1981). *Advances in Rainfed Farming.* Bull. No. R-10/D-8, CSWCRTI, Dehradun.

Hatwalne, S. V., (1980) *Water Harvesting and recycling in DPAP, Maharashtra.* Paper presented at 'National Symposium on Soil Conservation and Water Management' in 1980's held at CSWCRTI, Dehradun.

Joshi, P. G., (1976) *Soil and Water Conservation Techniques*, Govt. of Karnataka, Department of Agriculture.

Khanna, S. S., (1989) *Farm Planning*—the agro-climatic approach. *The Hindu*, Survey of Indian Agriculture.

Khybri, M. L., (1973) *Ravine Reclamation in Kota.* Soil Conservation Digest, Vol. 2 (1):57–60.

Kingh, K. F. S. and Chandler, M. T., (1978) *The Wastelands*, ICRAF, Nairobi, Kenya.

Kirpich, P. Z., (1940) *Time of concentration of small agricultural watersheds civil engineering* (New York) 10, page 362.

Koluvek, P. K., (1970) *Design criteria construction guide and materials standards for pipelines.* A report submitted to Govt. of India, United States Agency for International Development.

Krishnaswamy, V. S., (1980) *Geological Aspects of Landslides with particular reference to the Himalayan Region*, Proc. International Symposium on Landslides, New Delhi.

Lakshmipathi, B. M. and S. Narayanaswamy, (1956) Bench *Terracing in the Nilgiris.* J. of Soil and Water Conservation in India, 4(4):161–168.

Michael, A. M. Arora, D. R., Battacharya, A., Mandal, A. K. and Gupta, (1970) *Hand Book of Farm Irrigation Structures*, Division of Agriculture Engg., IARI, New Delhi.

Midwest Plan Service, (1968) *"Private Water Systems".* MPS Iowa State University, Ames, Iowa.

Muthana, K. D., (1980) *Role of Forestry in Desert Reclamation.* 2nd Forestry Conference held at FRI & Colleges, Dehradun.

Ogrosky, H. O. and Mockus, V., (1957) *The Hydrology Guide.* National Engineers Hand Book, Section 4, Hydrology Supplement A., G. C. A., USDA.

Patil, B. D. and Pathak, S., (1977) *Agroforestry* Technical Bulletin, IGFRI, Jhansi.

Prajapati, M. C., (1980) *Grassland Development in gullies—criteria for planning.* Lecture notes. Short Course on ravine reclamation and project formulation, (4th–18th Feb.) CSWCRTI, Research Centre, Vasad.

Prakash, M., (1959) *Importance of 'Shelterbelts' to check wind erosion.* J. of Soil and Water Conservation in India, Vol. 7 (4 & 5):61–66.

Puri, D. N., (1979) *Afforestation Techniques.* Lecture note. Second Short Course on Watershed Management for Project Managers (5th–14th June) CSWCRTI, Dehradun.

Puttanaik, H. V. and Kumar, V. L., (1979) *Integrated Watershed Management Strategy for conserving Soil and water resources for Dryland Farming*, Govt. of Karnataka, Deptt. of Agriculture.

Raghunath Reddy, D., Sitha Pathi Rao, C. and Narayana Reddy, B., (1973) *Bench Terracing in Andhra Pradesh*, Technical Bulletin, Deptt. of Agriculture, Hyderabad.

Raju, C. P., Reddy, G. H. S. and T. V. Seshadri, (1956). *Bunding in Deep Black Soils of Andhra State*. J. of soil and water conservation in India, 4 (4):143–149.

Rama Rao, M. S. V., (1957) *Standardization of Soil Conservation Practices* J. of Soil & Water Conservation in India, 6 (1):34–38.

Rama Rao, M. S. V., (1974) *Soil Conservation in India*, Indian Council of Agril. Research, New Delhi.

Ram Babu, Tejwani, K. G., Agarwal, M. C. and L. S. Bhushan, (1979) *Rainfall Intensity Duration—Return Period equations and Nomographs of India*, Bulletin No. 3, CSWCRTI, Dehradun.

Ram Babu and Dhruva Narayana, V. V., (1983) *Estimation of Runoff from small watersheds of Doon Valley*. 1 E(I), Journal EN 64:1–4.

Rao, D. H., Chittaranjan, S. and Sastry, G., (1980 a) *Bunding/Terracing as a Soil and Water Conservation Measure in Deep Black Soil of India* —a case study. National Symposium on 'Soil Conservation and Water Management in 1980's held at CSWCRTI, Dehradun.

Rao, D. H., Chittaranjan, S. and Sastry, G., (1980 b) *Role of farm ponds in rainfed agriculture in Deep black soils of Bellary region*. National Symposium on 'Soil Conservation and Water Management' in 1980's held at CSWCRTI, Dehradun.

Rege, N. D. (1980) *Soil and Water Conservation*, Agricultural Refinance and Development Corporation, Bombay.

Sankaranarayan Reddy, N., Shanmugam, C. R., Narayanaswamy, S. and Thiruvengataswamy, K. R., (1976). *Soil Erosion*, its prevention and control (revised), Govt. of Tamil Nadu, Deptt. of Agriculture, Madras.

Sastry, G., Mathur, H. N. and Tejwani, K. G., (1981). *Landslide control in North-Western Outer Himalayas—A case study.* Bull. No. R-8/D-6, CSWCRTI, Dehradun.

Sastry, G., Hussenappa, V., Bansal, R. C. and Tejwani, K. G., (1981) *Hydrological aspects of farm ponds in Doon Valley*, Bull. No. 6, CSWCRTI, Dehradun.

Saveson, I.L. and Overholt, V., (1937) *Stream bank protection*, Agricultural Engineering, 13:489–491.

Schwab, G. O., Frevert, R. K., Edminster, T. W. and Barnes, K. K., (1981) *Soil and Water Conservation Engineering*, (Third edition) John Wiley & Sons, Inc., New York.

Seth, G. R., Sukhatme, B. V. and Manwani, A. H., (1971) *Sample surveys of Mangoes and Guava in U. P.*, IARI, New Delhi.

Seth, S. K., (1960) *Soil working techniques in Dry Zone in relation to Rainfall and Soil Types*, Ind. for 86 (5):241–273.

Shanmugam, C. R., (1977) *Technical Hand Book on Soil* Conservation, Deptt. of Agriculture, Govt. of Tamil Nadu.

Sharma, A. K., Pradhan, I. P., Nema, J. P. and Tejwani, K. G., (1981) *25 years research on Soil and Water Conservation in Ravine lands of Gujarat*. Monograph No. 2, CSWCRTI, Research Centre, Vasad.

Singh, G. B. Rai, R. N. and Singh, A., (1980). *Shifting cultivation and its control efforts in the North-Eastern Hill region—A critical review*. Paper presented in National Symposium on 'Soil Conservation and Water Management' in 1980's held at CSWCRTI, Dehradun.

Singh, L. B., (1962) *Horticulture in North-Eastern region*. ICAR, New Delhi.

Swaminathan, M. S., (1976) *Science and integrated rural development*. Presidential Address, 63rd Session, Ind. Sci. Congress.

Thangam, E. S., (1980) *Shifting Cultivation and Rehabilitation of Degraded Forests*. Paper presented at the II Forestry Conference, FRI & Colleges, Dehradun.

Tejwani, K. G., Dhruva Narayana, V. V., and Satyanarayana, T., (1960 a) *Control of gully erosion in the ravine lands of Gujarat*. J. Soil Water Conserv. India, 8:65–74.

Tejwani, K. G. and Dhruva Narayana, V. V., (1960 b) *Reclamation of small and medium size gullies in Gujarat Ravines*, J. Soil Water Cons. in India, 8 (2 & 3):26–39.

Tejwani, K. G., Gupta, S. K., and Mathur, H. N., (1975) *Soil & Water Conservation Research*, (1956–71), ICAR, New Delhi.

Tejwani, K. G., (1979) *Soil fertility status, maintenance and conservation for agro-forestry systems on wasted lands in India*. Soils Research in Agro-forestry, Proc. of an Expert consultation held at the ICRAF, Nairobi.

Tejwani, K. G., (1988) *Classification and reclamation of ravines*. Symposium on a survey and reclamation of wastelands, Indian National Science Academy, New Delhi, Bulletin 44:161.

Vaydande, C. D., (1980) *Raising Mango plantation in Maharashtra State* through soil conservation section under land development-cum-horticulture development scheme. National Symposium on 'Soil Conservation and Water Management' in 1980's held at CSWCRTI, Dehradun.

Venkataramanan, C. Tejwani, K. G., and Deshmukh, G. R., (1980) *An Annotated Bibliography of Scientific contribution of the CSWCRTI*, (1955–79), CSWCRTI, Dehradun.

Venkateswarlu, J., (1986) *Dryland Farming*. An era of self-sufficiency in food production, A tribute to Indira Gandhi, ICAR, Krishi Anusandhan Bhawan, New Delhi.

Viswanatham, M. K., (1977) *Range (Grassland) Management for the Drought Prone Areas Development Programmes*. Lecture note, Drought Prone Area Programme, Short Course in Soil & Water Conservation for Officers from DPAP States, held at CSWCRTI, Dehradun.

Acknowledgement

The assistance rendered by S/Shri. M. S. Nayal, T-5, Ashok Kumar, T-4 and Sunil Kurnar, Jr. Steno, CSWCRTI, Dehradun are acknowledged.

Gurmel Singh
Venkataramanan, C.
Sastry, G.
Joshi, B. P